JOHN MILTON

PARADISE
LOST

The Bayfordbury portrait of John Milton, attributed to William Faithorne (c. 1670). Used with permission of the Department of Rare Books and Special Collections, Princeton University Library.

JOHN MILTON
PARADISE LOST

Edited, with Introduction, by

David Scott Kastan

Based on the classic edition of
Merritt Y. Hughes

Hackett Publishing Company, Inc.
Indianapolis/Cambridge

Copyright © 2005 by Hackett Publishing Company, Inc.

19 18 17 16 15   4 5 6 7 8

For further information, please address:
Hackett Publishing Company, Inc.
P.O. Box 44937
Indianapolis, IN 46244-0937

www.hackettpublishing.com

Cover art: From *Paradise Lost*, 1688, Folio edition. Illustration for Bk. 12: St. Michael expels Adam and Eve from the Garden of Eden, as the Cherubim guard Paradise. One of a set of engravings by Michael Burghers.

Cover design by Abigail Coyle
Interior design by Jennifer Plumley
Composition by Professional Book Compositors, Inc.

Library of Congress Cataloging-in-Publication Data

Milton, John, 1608–1674.
    Paradise lost / John Milton ; edited, with an introduction, by David Scott Kastan.
        p. cm.
    "Based on the classic edition of Merritt Y. Hughes."
    Includes bibliographical references.
    ISBN 0-87220-734-X (cloth) —
    ISBN 0-87220-733-1 (pbk.)
    1. Bible. O.T. Genesis—History of Biblical events—Poetry. 2. Adam (Biblical figure)—Poetry. 3. Eve (Biblical figure)—Poetry. 4. Fall of man—Poetry. I. Kastan, David Scott. II. Hughes, Merritt Yerkes, 1893– III. Title.
    PR3560.A2K37 2005
    821'.4—dc22
                                     2005017552

    ISBN-13: 978-0-87220-734-9 (cloth)
    ISBN-13: 978-0-87220-733-2 (pbk.)

CONTENTS

PREFACE

"Shakespeare and *Paradise Lost* every day become greater wonders to me."
—John Keats

It was in Merritt Hughes' edition that I first read *Paradise Lost*, in my sophomore year in college. I read it again, in the same edition, in graduate school, and I taught the poem twice a year for most of the first fourteen years of my teaching career in that familiar, ever more dog-eared and marked-up, red paperback. At Dartmouth, where I was teaching then, every freshman took English 5, and there was only one required text in the course: *Paradise Lost*. (You also had to assign a Shakespeare play of your own choosing.) I assume Dartmouth was the only place in the world where this was ever the case. Unsurprisingly, it is no longer true, though I have been told that one instructor (a second Abdiel) still assigns *Paradise Lost*. I have continued to teach Milton almost every year since, though admittedly I began to use other editions, but always with unsettling feelings of disloyalty.

When I was asked to undertake a revision of Hughes' edition, I hesitated, not least because it seemed to me that it should always exist exactly as I had known and admired it. It is a monument. But in the strange world of academic publishing, it was available only in an outrageously expensive paperback edition. As a result, it was no longer an affordable course text, and in fact it was in danger of disappearing from everywhere but library shelves and secondhand bookstores. A change of publishers allowed the paperback to be reissued, but only as a prelude to this edition. Some, no doubt, will miss the old version; more, I hope, will find that most of what was there is here too, but in more accessible form, and bolstered by another generation of thought about the poem, necessarily unavailable to Hughes.

Hughes had first published his edition of *Paradise Lost* in 1935. In 1957 a revised edition appeared in his *Complete Poems and Major Prose,* and in 1962 the edition was further revised and published again on its own. For the majority of the 20th century most American students who read *Paradise Lost* did so guided by Merritt Hughes. In recent years, however, much has happened in Milton scholarship, and a number of impressive editions of the poem have joined Hughes' on the bookshelves. For a variety of reasons his edition no longer is unquestioned as the edition of choice, though its scholarship usually underpins the editions that have challenged it. If it is here now thoroughly revised, it is so with the deepest admiration and respect for Hughes' remarkable achievement.

All editions incur enormous unpaid and unrepayable debts to their predecessors, and mine to Hughes are indeed both; but so are they also to all the editors whose editions have become part of what we know as *Paradise Lost*. Editing is a collective activity, not a competitive one. Editions, particularly editions of *Paradise Lost,* do not supplant one another; rather they join together in a community of engagement with the poem, which more than most seems to need their labors. Perhaps unsurprisingly, *Paradise Lost* was the first English poem to receive full scholarly annotation. In 1695, a mere twenty-eight years after the poem first appeared, Patrick Hume (though identified only as P. H.) published his *Annotations . . . Wherein the Texts of Sacred Writ Relating to the Poem are Quoted; The Parallel Places and Imitations of the Most Excellent Homer and Virgil, Cited and Compared; All the Obscure Parts Render'd in Phrases More familiar; The Old and Obsolete Words, with their Originals, Explained and Made Easie to the English Reader.* Editions have sought to provide much the same ever since, building on Hume's insights and learning to expose ever more of the poem's extraordinary density of allusion and to help a reader navigate what Dr. Johnson called the "uniform peculiarity" of its diction and syntax.

I want to register my indebtedness (though I realize it is not thereby settled) to Hume, Jonathan Richardson (father and son), Zachary Pearce, Thomas Newton, and H. J. Todd, even to the often maligned Richard Bentley, those early scholars whose extraordinary achievements, accomplished without benefit of reference tools we take for granted, are usually too little appreciated; to Thomas Keightley and David Masson in the 19th century; to the great editorial work of the 20th century by A. J. Verity and Helen Darbishire, and more recently by John T. Shawcross, Alastair Fowler, Scott Elledge, John Leonard, and of course Merritt Y. Hughes himself. Others, nearer to me, also deserve thanks: certainly the teachers with whom I was fortunate to study Milton, all three sadly no longer alive: Maurice Kelley, George Williamson, and John Wallace; but also the many students with whom I have read and discussed Milton over the years, whose agile, sometimes resistant, readings have continued to teach me, perhaps most unforgettably Thomas Festa, James Fleming, David Hawkes, Steve Hequembourg, Peter Herman, Mary Klages, William Kolbrener, Jesse Lander, Zach Lesser, Claire McEachern, Shannon Miller, Douglas Pfeiffer, and Dan Vitkus; and the many friends and colleagues whose learning, enthusiasm, and generosity lie behind so much of what is here, including Sharon Achinstein, David Armitage, Julie Crawford, Margaret Ferguson, Lori Ferrell, Andrew Hadfield, Peter Lake, Molly Murray, Michael Murrin, David Norbrook, Stephen Orgel, Annabel Patterson, John Rogers, Jim Shapiro, Victoria Silver, Nigel Smith, Peter Stallybrass, Edward Tayler, and Steven Zwicker.

No doubt there are others who will think their names unfairly omitted. They are right to think so, and I apologize. All those mentioned will probably be only marginally happier, finding the bare listing inadequate recompense for their contributions. They are also right. But all, I hope, will not only find something in the edition to make it clear I really was paying attention but also will find something to keep the old arguments alive. In addition, Deborah Wilkes must be thanked, because she believed. She will find this too much acknowledgment. She is wrong.

And always there is love for MK, JK, and AL. They are usually always happy.

INTRODUCTION

"a reader of *Milton* must be Always upon Duty; he is Surrounded with Sense,
it rises in every line, every Word is to the Purpose."
—Jonathan Richardson (1734), and copied by Coleridge into his commonplace book

"Meditating Flight"

One day in the autumn of 1667, according to a member of Parliament, Sir John Denham entered the House of Commons excitedly waving a sheet of *Paradise Lost* still "wet from the Press," and pronounced it "Part of the Noblest Poem that was ever Wrote in any Language or any Age."[1] Denham's reported enthusiasm may well be apocryphal, but from its first appearance the nobility of *Paradise Lost* has rarely been in doubt. In January of 1668, one of its first readers, Sir John Hobart, sent his cousin a copy of the poem with a letter remarking that "Some resemblance it has to Spenser's way, but in the opinion of the impartial learned, not only above all modern attempts in verse, but equal to any of the Ancient Poets."[2]

Hobart does mention Milton's role as an antimonarchical polemicist (indeed he calls Milton a "criminal"), but this does not detract from Hobart's regard for the poem. A few early readers, however, did find their admiration tempered by their reaction to Milton's revolutionary politics. William Winstanley, for example, in 1687 admitted that Milton's poetic achievement should have merited him "a place amongst the principal of our English Poets"; he insists, however, that "his Fame is gone out like a Candle in a Snuff, and his Memory will always stink," because he was "a notorious Traytor," who "impiously and villainously bely'd that blessed Martyr, King Charles the First."[3] But for most *Paradise Lost* unquestionably has merited its place among the greatest works of English literature.

Certainly later generations, when the politics of the English Revolution could be viewed with more dispassion, have readily acknowledged the poem's

---

[1] Jonathan Richardson, *The Life of Milton and A Discourse on "Paradise Lost"* (1734), in Darbishire, *The Early Lives of Milton,* p. 295. Sir George Hungerford was Richardson's informant. Edmund Malone thought the story "wholly unworthy of credit"; see his *Critical and Miscellaneous Prose of John Dryden* (London, 1800), vol. 1, p. i. But Denham indeed spoke in Parliament in November 1667, so the story is at least plausible; see T. W. Baldwin, "Sir John Denham and *Paradise Lost," MLN* 42 (1927); 508–9.

[2] Quoted in Rosenheim, p. 281. I have modernized the idiosyncratic spelling.

[3] Winstanley, p. 195.

greatness; but if they have been characteristically generous in their praise, they have often been less so in their affection. Samuel Johnson's pungent observation that "*Paradise Lost* is one of the books which the reader admires and lays down and forgets to take up again"[4] has too often been borne out in experience. It is not a poem that sits comfortingly by the bedside. It is undeniably difficult, and even more so now when the assumptions on which it rests can no longer be taken for granted. But the poem justifiably remains at the center of the curriculum of English literature, and, as Milton has been returned to the vital intellectual and political life of his times by the work of modern scholars, the poem has again found a generation of enthusiastic readers drawn to the "vast design," as Andrew Marvell called it (see p. 3 below), of this remarkable poem, arguably unrivaled in its intellectual scope and poetic ambition.

Although Milton published *Paradise Lost* when he was almost sixty, he had imagined writing such a poem even as a young man. At nineteen, he was already confident that his poetry would one day "sing of secret things," ("At a Vacation Exercise," line 45) and "soar / Above the wheeling poles, and at Heaven's door / Look in" (lines 33–34).[5] But if he foresaw his own epic achievement, early on he conceived of it solely in the traditional terms of a celebration of "kings and queens and heroes old" (line 47). Only when he was fully engaged with *Paradise Lost* did he understand his task as a radical reformation of epic itself.

Milton's precocious talents were carefully nurtured. Born in December 1608 to a religious, middle-class family, he was meticulously prepared for a career in the Church. He was educated first at home, and probably at twelve he entered Saint Paul's School, very near his home in London and at the time arguably the finest school in England.[6] Even then, additional tutors were provided to satisfy the "instinctive ardor for learning" that led the studious Milton, from the age of twelve, "rarely" to retire "from his lucubrations till midnight."[7] At seventeen, he "went up" to Cambridge, enrolling at Christ's College. He received his B.A. in 1629 and his M.A. *cum laude* in July 1632. Upon graduating, he returned to his family and continued his studies, first in the house in the then London suburb of Ham-

---

[4] "Life of Milton" (1779), in Shawcross (ed.), *Milton 1732–1801*, p. 305.

[5] *Works* 1, part 1, 20; further references to Milton's poetry will be cited parenthetically by title and line number.

[6] The St. Paul's records were destroyed, along with the school buildings, in the Great Fire of 1666. Milton says in the *Defensio Secunda* that "from the age of 12" he studied until midnight, hence the assumption that he began school then; in fact it might have been as early as 1615 or as late as 1622.

[7] *Defensio Secunda*, in *Works* 8, 119; further references to Milton's prose will be cited parenthetically.

mersmith to which the family had moved sometime in 1631, and then, after the family moved again in 1635, in their new home in the village of Horton in present-day Berkshire (until 1974, in Buckinghamshire). Yet in these years after leaving Cambridge there were few tangible accomplishments, at least by his lights. In a letter of 1633 he acknowledges his "tardie moving," and laments his life "as yet obscure, & unserviceable to mankind." In a sonnet included with the letter, Milton frankly admits that he had as yet achieved nothing worthy of his abilities ("no bud or blossome shew'th"), but he is confident that there is a goal "toward which Tyme leads me, & the will of heaven" (*Works* 12, 322–24).

But it was not to be as a clergyman that he would fulfill God's will. Finding the Church that he had planned to serve both theologically conservative and socially corrupt, he was, as he would later say, "Church-outed by the Prelats" (*Of Reformation* [*Works* 3, part 1, 242]). The English Church under the influence of William Laud, Archbishop of Canterbury, seemed to have betrayed the principles of the Reformation. For Milton, it was now a church that only found "in outward rites and specious forms / Religion satisfied" (*PL* 12.534–35). The career for which he had been trained was abandoned to the career for which he was born. "It was my lot to have been born a poet," he wrote in "Ad Patrem," and he tried to reassure his disappointed father that poetry too was "holy work"(line 61), reminding us of "our heavenly birth" (lines 17–20).

Early on, then, Milton saw poetry as a calling from God, a true vocation, and he shaped his career with an unusual sense of purpose to clarify his ambitions, which were considerable. In late 1637, he wrote to his friend Charles Diodati: "You ask me what I am thinking of? So may the good Deity help me, of immortality! And what am I doing? Growing my wings and meditating flight; but as yet our Pegasus is still himself on very tender pinions" (*Works* 12, 27). In fact Milton had written most of the poems that would appear in print only in 1645. He was already an accomplished poet if not a public one. Still, he clearly thought the "wings of his Pegasus" still "tender" and looked to the time when they would allow his imagination to soar. Already by 1642, he understood the "power" of the poet

> to inbreed and cherish in a great people the seeds of virtu and publick civility, to allay the perturbations of the mind, and set the affections in right tune, to celebrate in glorious and lofty Hymns the throne and equipage of Gods Almightiness, and what he works, and what he suffers to be wrought with high providence in his Church, to sing the victorious agonies of Martyrs and Saints, the deeds and triumphs of just and pious Nations doing valiantly through faith against the enemies of Christ, to deplore the general relapse of Kingdoms and States from justice and Gods true worship. (*The Reason of Church Government* [*Works* 3, part 1, 238]).

For Milton, the poet was polemicist, patriot, pastor, and priest. His audience was the nation, and his muse nothing less than almighty God. If he knew he must prepare for his calling by "industrious and select reading, steddy observation, insight into all seemly and generous arts and affaires," he knew also that such preparation could not in itself be enough. The complex role demanded something more: "devout prayer to that eternall Spirit who can enrich with all utterance and knowledge, and sends out his Seraphim with the hallow'd fire of his Altar to touch and purify the lips of whom he pleases" (ibid., 241).

His plea for divine assistance is not, however, a conventional poetic appeal for inspiration. Its unmistakable echo of Isaiah 6 betrays his decidedly unconventional understanding of what it means to be a poet. There the Hebrew prophet is purified for his chosen task, as a seraph touches his lips with a live coal taken from God's altar. Milton's allusion signals his ambition. It is to be prepared for a place among God's prophets, those prophets of the Hebrew Bible who spoke for God against the corruption of worldly power. It is necessarily an uncomfortable role, almost always unsought and unwanted by those who are called. Isaiah initially shrank from his election; Milton enthusiastically claimed his own.[8]

"This Subject for Heroic Song"

Once Milton abandoned the Church for poetry, it was almost inevitable he would eventually write an epic. His was an imagination certain to be drawn to what he called the genre "of highest hope, and hardest attempting" (*Works* 3, part 1, 237). Even as he was inhabiting "the cool element of prose" as he engaged in his early polemical writing, he was imagining himself "soaring in the high region of his fancies with his garland and singing robes about him," already thinking that he "might perhaps leave something so written to aftertimes, as they should not willingly let it die" (ibid., 235–36). But if early the ambition was clear, to write an epic "doctrinal and exemplary to a Nation" (ibid., 237), the precise subject that would prove worthy of the genre remained in doubt. Initially his plan was to write an epic about ancient Britain, and he wondered "what king or knight before the conquest might be chosen in whom to lay the pattern of a Christian hero." In two early Latin poems, Milton identified the exploits of his "native kings" as his likely focus, possibly the heroism of the Arthurian court ("Mansus," lines 80–81), or the eventful reigns of Brennus, Arviragus, or Belinus ("Epitaphium Damonis," lines 163–66).

[8] See Kerrigan, *The Prophetic Milton;* Wittreich, *Visionary Poetics,* esp. pp. 73–86; see also Helgerson, esp. pp. 268–78.

Yet it was not to be a "British theme" ("Epitaphium," line 171) that would provide the argument for his epic. The history of preconquest Britain was shrouded in unreliable legend. In Milton's *History of Britain* he would say of this material that he would "neither oblige the belief of other person, nor over-hastily subscribe my own" (*Works* 10, 30–31). But no doubt as telling for Milton was the fact that "the matter of Britain" regularly served English monarchs as a powerful source of imagery to legitimize their authority. As his revolutionary fervor grew, it became clear that Milton's epic would have to find a different subject for his poem.

The biblical story of the fall had long interested him as a possible topic. In the 1640s he had drawn up four drafts of an outline of "Paradise lost" or, in another version, "Adam unparadiz'd," with accompanying casts of characters. But it was not as epic that the story was first conceived. Milton's cousin, Edward Phillips, recalls that "This subject was first designed a tragedy, and in the fourth book of the poem there are six verses, which several years before the poem was begun, were shown to me and some others, as designed for the very beginning of the said tragedy" (pp. 420–21 below). The lines intended to begin a five-act tragedy eventually found their way into a ten-, then twelve-book epic as 4.32–41, and although the intended tragedy still exerts itself upon the structure of Milton's poem, it is as epic that the story of "Paradise lost" is told.

The subject, then, was indeed of "long choosing," although its form was decided "late" (*PL* 9.26). Epic held undeniable appeal for the ambitious poet, but it was a genre not unproblematic. Milton admits that he was "not sedulous by nature to indite / Wars" (*PL* 9.27–28), but it was not merely that warfare, epic's traditional subject, did not suit his temperament. Especially in the romance mode, developed in Renaissance Europe in the hands of Tasso, Ariosto, Boiardo, Camoens, even Spenser, it could too easily be dismissed as the "long and tedious havoc" of "fabled knights / In battles feigned" (*PL* 9.30–31) and disliked for the royalist associations that had accrued to the genre.

For the Protestant Milton the problems were, however, more fundamental. Epic is not just a compilation of heroic acts, but it makes those acts expressive of the communal values of a culture. But for a religion that holds with Paul that "by grace are ye saved through faith; and that not of yourselves" (Ephesians 2:8), heroic action can never be as fully articulate of its values as the form presumes. The generic implications of this can be clearly heard in Book 1 of *The Faerie Queene*. There Spenser sounds the Pauline note, warning against the "boasts of fleshly might," since "If any strength we have it is to ill, / But all the good is Gods, both power and eke will" (1.10.1). It is much the same for Milton. Though Satan declares to Abdiel that "our puissance is our own" (*PL* 5.864), Gabriel has earlier reminded him of the true nature of creatural power: "Satan, I know thy strength, and thou know'st mine, / Neither our own but given; what folly then / To boast what arms can do" (*PL* 4.1006–8).

What then is an epic to be when "to boast what arms can do" is mere "folly" and when celebrating "kings and queens and heroes old" is impossible? What, that is, is a Protestant and a republican epic? *Paradise Lost* is, of course, the answer. Milton insists on his poem's both fulfilling the formal demands of epic and transcending epic's traditional logic. Epic is not repudiated; it is, we might say, reformed. However unconventional, the argument of *Paradise Lost* is intended to be "Not less but more heroic than the wrath / Of stern Achilles" (*PL* 9.14–15).

Carefully Milton establishes his relationship to the traditional epic. Joseph Addison's eighteen essays on the poem written in *The Spectator* in 1712 patiently trace its debts to its classical models, with the aim to show "that there is in the *Paradise Lost* all the Greatness of Plan, Regularity of Design, and Masterly Beauties which we discover in *Homer* and *Virgil*."[9] Addison's critical effort reflects his desire to depoliticize Milton's poem as much as to claim the poem for the neoclassicism of his own age, but it indeed shows that Milton has self-consciously followed "the Rules of Epic Poetry" (*Spectator,* 2, 539), enabling, in Addison's judgment, "a Work which does Honour to the *English* nation" (ibid., 3, 312). But even when one notices that Milton begins *in medias res*, includes the expected catalogues of commanders, uses the extended similes that mark the classical epic, and even, in Book 6, recounts scenes of epic warfare, one feels that too much of the poem still is unexplained. Editions (and this one too) point out the echoes of Homer, Virgil, Tasso, and Spenser, but Milton invokes recognizable epic scenes and conventions not to claim his place in the tradition but to proclaim his superiority over it. "The precursors return in Milton," as Harold Bloom nicely observes, "but only at his will, and they return to be corrected."[10]

As many have observed, it is the early scenes of Satan that most comfortably satisfy the expectations of epic. The action opens on the burning lake on which the fallen angels are chained (see Fig. 1), a result whose cause is found in Book 6, when "headlong themselves they threw / Down from the verge of Heaven" (lines 864–65). The first six books lead us back in time to the point at which the narrative begins. The poem thus starts precisely in the middle of things, as epic convention demanded, but that

---

[9] *The Spectator* 297 (February 9, 1712), Joseph Addison and Richard Steele, *The Spectator*, ed. Donald Bond (Oxford: Clarendon Press, 1965), vol. 3, p. 173; see also Blessington, Martindale, and Porter.

[10] Bloom, *A Map of Misreading* (New York: Oxford University Press, 1975), p. 142.

Fig. 1. Engraving, by Michael Burghers from an illustration probably by John Baptist Medina, accompanying Book 1 in the 1668 fourth edition of the poem. It shows a heroic Satan prodding the fallen angels on the burning lake, with Pandemonium visible mid-left.

middle is Satan (with God, we could say, as the alpha and the omega). The fall of the rebel angels, which took "Nine times the space that measures day and night" (1.50), echoes the fall of the Titans in Hesiod's *Theogony* (664–735), which also took nine days. Satan and the other fallen angels are the focus, too, of many of the striking epic similes (e.g., the rebellious angels lying "thick as autumnal leaves that strew the brooks / In Vallombrosa" (1.302–3), itself an echo of *Aeneid* 6.309–10). The fallen angels transformed into pagan gods are presented in a parody of the Homeric catalogue of ships and commanders (1.376–521). The council in hell in Book 2 of *Paradise Lost* parallels the debate in the second book of the *Iliad,* where what seems open discussion is in fact manipulated to ensure the decision to attack Troy. The war in Heaven, of course, offers the most obvious epic parallel, and here the point is clearest in its comic deflation of epic warfare. If the war in Heaven is not mock heroic, certainly it is, in William Riggs' witty turn of phrase, "mock*ed* heroic,"[11] as self-sealing angels (6.433–36), pointlessly armed and arrayed in armor, fight to no purpose beyond their own effort, where all is "foreseen" and "permitted" by God (6.673–74), and where victory comes as the rebel angels flee before Christ's chariot and throw themselves from Heaven's "verge" (6.864–65), an outcome known as early as lines 44–45 of Book 1. "War wearied hath performed what war can do" (6.695), says Milton's God before the third day of battle, and Milton too insists on the limitations of war as a significant arena of excellence.[12]

Epic is thus fully reimagined in Protestant terms. The traditional forms of heroic action are here but are largely displaced onto Satan and the fallen angels. They enact the familiar heroic roles, display the familiar resilience and defiance, are defined by the familiar devices (one measure: there are over thirty epic similes in Books 1 and 2; none in Books 11 and 12), and are located in the familiar structures, in part producing the Romantic misreading that Milton was "of the Devil's party without knowing it."[13] But epic's traditional celebration of the virtues of warfare, "hitherto the only argument / Heroic deemed" (9.28–29), has been supplanted by something new: "the better fortitude / Of patience and heroic martyrdom" (9.31–32), a heroism of courage and commitment, but a heroism of faith rather than action.

---

[11] Riggs, p. 120.

[12] Cf. Milton's sonnet "On the Lord General Fairfax": "For what can war, but endless war still breed." On the war in Heaven, see Arnold Stein, pp. 17–37; and Revard.

[13] The phrase is William Blake's, from *The Marriage of Heaven and Hell,* in *Complete Poetry and Prose,* ed. David V. Erdman (New York: Doubleday, 1988), p. 35.

"With Dangers Compassed Round"

The shift from the values of the traditional epic has been seen by some as the evidence that *Paradise Lost* is an epic born in defeat, a conscious turn from history to theology, from contingent values to "eternal verities," in the wake of the failed revolution.[14] If this can now be seen to overstate Milton's retreat from politics and indeed to misunderstand the connection between his political and religious commitments (see pp. xxvii–xxxiii below), there can be little doubt that *Paradise Lost* registers Milton's experience of the turbulent years between 1658 and 1665, while the poem was being written. Deeply disappointed that the revolutionary fervor of the Commonwealth had faded, Milton, in *The Readie and Easie Way* (1660), upbraided his countrymen for welcoming the restoration of the "once abjour'd and detested thraldom of Kingship" (*Works* 6, 117). "All this light among us" (ibid., 147), which earlier had illuminated the path of the godly, was now eclipsed as England called "a captain back for *Egypt*" (ibid., 149). Yet *Paradise Lost* pointedly announces itself as a poem of restoration as well as of loss. It begins by looking to the time when "one greater man" will "restore us" (1.4–5) and its last spoken word is also "restore" (12.623); but clearly this restoration looks well past the return to England of Charles II.

Though many did, of course, welcome the restoration of the monarchy in 1660, for Milton it was an event that could only be greeted with dismay. However much he recognized that following the death of Oliver Cromwell in September 1658 the hopes for what Milton in *The Readie and Easie Way* called a "free Commonwealth" had become increasingly desperate, he supported a series of shaky compromises in a passionate effort to counter the "noxious humour of returning to bondage" (*Works* 6, 111) and the inevitable attack on Puritan religious liberty that would follow the return of the King. In the first edition of *The Readie and Easie Way*, published in March 1660, he could still express confidence that "God hath yet his remnant, and hath not yet quenched the spirit of liberty among us" (ibid., 361), but by the time of the revision of the tract in late April, he could only hope that "God may raise of these stones to become children of a reviving libertie," as England, driven by "the deluge of this epidemic madness" to restore the monarchy, stood at "a precipice of destruction" (ibid., 148–49).

The tide indeed proved irresistible, and on May 25, 1660, Charles II landed at Dover; he entered London four days later. Certainly Milton, notorious as a defender of the trial and execution of Charles I, felt himself in

---

[14] The phrase and the sentiment are Blair Worden's in his "Milton's Republicanism and the Tyranny of Heaven," in *Machiavelli and Republicanism*, ed. Gisela Bock, Quentin Skinner, and Maurizio Viroli (Cambridge: Cambridge University Press, 1990), p. 244.

mortal danger, and for three months he hid in "a friend's house in Bartholomew Close." According to Edward Phillips, Andrew Marvell "acted vigorously in his behalf," and, with others of influence, succeeded in keeping Milton from the executioner (see pp. 421–22 below). On August 13 the Convention Parliament passed a resolution, perhaps as a compromise to ensure his personal safety. The proclamation called for the arrest of Milton and John Goodwin, another prominent supporter of the regicide, but ordered, that as both had "fled" and could not "be brought to Legal Tryal," two of Milton's prose tracts (*Eikonoklastes* and the *Defense of the English People*) and one of Goodwin's (*The Obstructors of Justice*) should be confiscated and "publickly burnt by the hand of the Common hangman" (see Fig. 2).

Milton came out of hiding soon after the Act of Oblivion was passed in late August, and in September he took up residence in Holborn in what is now central London. His sense of safety was short lived, however. Sometime in the fall he was arrested according to the warrant of the August 13 decree. Milton's application for pardon under the Act of Oblivion had not yet been acted upon, but on December 15 the Commons ordered "That Mr. *Milton,* now in custody of the Serjeant at arms attending this House, be forthwith released, paying his Fees."[15] Although he was freed, the costs were not insubstantial. Marvell complained, according to a contemporary, "that the Serjeant had exacted £150 of Mr. Milton," though others said the heavy fees were appropriate, indeed merciful, as in fact he "deserved hanging."[16]

With the Restoration, Milton's fervent political hopes were dashed, his financial situation was dire, and his safety was in jeopardy. He was the object of vitriolic polemical attacks, and, even after the Act of Oblivion was passed, he continued to fear for his life. As Jonathan Richardson reported, he "kept Himself as Private as he could," because he was "in Perpetual Terror of being Assassinated, though he had Escap'd the Talons of the Law."[17] The rage of royalist mobs was regularly visited upon the supporters of the now repudiated revolution. Even the dead were not safe from their fury. On January 30, 1661, the anniversary of the execution of Charles I, the bodies of Cromwell, Bradshaw (who had presided at the King's trial), and Henry Ireton (a signer of the King's death warrant) were exhumed and taken to Tyburn, where they were hanged on the gibbets until sundown. The corpses were then decapitated, the bodies thrown into a pit, and the heads set out on Westminster Hall (where they stayed until 1684!). In such an environment, the sightless Milton (totally blind since 1652) must have more

---

[15] *Commons Journal,* 8.208.

[16] See Lewalski, *Life,* p. 404.

[17] Quoted in Darbishire, *Early Lives,* p. 276.

By the King.

A PROCLAMATION

For calling in, and suppressing of two Books written by *John Milton* ; the one Intituled, *Johannis Miltoni Angli pro Populo Anglicano Defensio, contra Claudii Anonymi alias Salmasii, Defensionem Regiam* ; and the other in answer to a Book Intituled, *The Pourtraiture of his Sacred Majesty in his Solitude and Sufferings.* And also a third Book Intituled, *The Obstructors of Justice,* written by *John Goodwin.*

CHARLES R.

Hereas John Milton, late of Westminster, in the County of Middlesex, hath published in Print two several Books. The one Intituled, Johannis Miltoni Angli pro Populo Anglicano Defensio, contra Claudii Anonymi, alias Salmasii, Defensionem Regiam, And the other in Answer to a Book Intituled, The Pourtraiture of his Sacred Majesty in his Solitude and Sufferings. In both which are contained sundry Treasonable passages against Us and Our Government, and most Impious endeavors to justifie the horrid and unmatchable Murther of Our late Dear Father, of Glorious Memory. And whereas John Goodwin, late of Coleman-Street, London, Clerk, hath also published in Print, a Book Intituled, The Obstructors of Justice, written in defence of his said late Majesty. And whereas the said John Milton, and John Goodwin, are both fled, or so obscure themselves, that no endeavors used for their apprehension can take effect, whereby they might be brought to Legal Tryal, and deservedly receive condigne punishment for their Treasons and Offences.

Now to the end that Our good Subjects may not be corrupted in their Judgments, with such wicked and Traitrous principles, as are dispersed and scattered throughout the beforementioned Books, We, upon the motion of the Commons in Parliament now assembled, doe hereby streightly charge and Command, all and every Person and Persons whatsoever, who live in any City, Burrough, or Town Incorporate, within this our Kingdom of England, the Dominion of Wales, and Town of Berwick upon Tweed, in whose hands any of those Books are, or hereafter shall be, That they, upon pain of Our high Displeasure, and the consequence thereof, do forthwith, upon publication of this Our Command, or within Ten days immediately following, deliver, or cause the same to be delivered to the Mayor, Bayliffs, or other chief Officer or Magistrate, in any of the said Cities, Burroughs, or Towns Incorporate, where such person or persons so live; or, if living out of any City, Burrough, or Town Incorporate, then to the next Justice of Peace adjoyning to his or their dwelling, or place of abode; or if living in either of Our Universities, then to the Vice-Chancellor of that University where he or they do reside.

And in default of such voluntary delivery, which We do expect in ob서bance of Our said Command, That then and after the time before limited, expired, the said Chief Magistrate of all and every the said Cities, Burroughs, or Towns Incorporate, the Justices of the Peace in their several Counties, and the Vice-Chancellors of Our said Universities respectively, are hereby Commanded to Seize and Take, all and every the Books aforesaid, in whose hands or possession soever they shall be found, and certifie the names of the Offenders unto Our Privy Council.

And we do hereby also give special Charge and Command to the said Chief Magistrates, Justices of the Peace, and Vice-Chancellors respectively, That they cause the said Books which shall be so brought unto any of their hands, or seized or taken as aforesaid, by vertue of this Our Proclamation, to be delivered to the respective Sheriffs of those Counties where they respectively live, the first and next Assizes that shall after happen. And the said Sheriffs are hereby also required, in time of holding such Assizes, to cause the same to be publickly burnt by the hand of the Common Hangman.

And we do further streightly Charge and Command, That no man hereafter presume to Print, Vend, Sell, or Disperse any the aforesaid Books, upon pain of Our heavy Displeasure, and of such further punishment, as for their presumption in that behalf, may any way be inflicted upon them by the Laws of this Realm.

Given at Our Court at *Whitehall* the 13th day of *August*, in the Twelfth year of Our Reign, 1660.

LONDON, Printed by *John Bill* and *Christopher Barker*, Printers to the Kings most Excellent Majesty, 1660.

Fig. 2. The third issue of the proclamation (August 13, 1660; first ordered on June 27), calling in and ordering a public burning of copies of Milton's *Eikonoklastes* and the *Defensio* for "sundry Treasonable passages."

than occasionally felt abandoned by his God in a world "Whence heavy persecution shall arise / On all who in the worship persevere / Of spirit and truth" (12.531–33).

"This Great Argument"

Though "argument" in the poem usually, as in 1.24, means "subject," it is also clear that Milton was aware of his poem as an extended proposition set forth and defended. No other epic as explicitly offers itself as a theological *argument,* not just didactic but polemical. The poem is written to "assert eternal providence / And justify the ways of God to men" (1.25–26), a task rendered urgent by the personal and political events of the years of its composition. A poem more orthodox would eschew both acts: "providence" and "God's ways" would be axiomatic and trusted rather than asserted and justified. And a poet more orthodox would in the first place never presume to take on such a task.

But neither Milton nor his poem is orthodox. From the Book of Job to Calvin, it was held that God's ways will not endure the presumptuous scrutiny of human reason,[18] but *Paradise Lost* subjects them to precisely that review and begins by allowing, perhaps even encouraging, the thought that God's ways are indeed in need of justification. It is Satan who voices the aphoristic claim "Not just, not God" (9.701), and Milton rises to the challenge he has placed in Satan's mouth—but not until the weight of the implication is fully felt, as it must often have been felt by Milton himself in the years surrounding the Restoration.

What needs justification is God's relation to the evil that is so manifestly present in the world, a world that too often proves "To good malignant, to bad men benign" (12.538). Milton traces the problem to its source: the fall, the originating act that "Brought death into the world and all our woe" (1.3). The particular political question raised by the undeniable failure of the bright hopes of the Commonwealth becomes a more general moral one, but does not thereby repudiate politics. Who is ultimately responsible for that "woe," felt in various ways throughout human history? *Unde malum,* "whence evil?" was the famous question of the early third-century Church father, Tertullian.[19] Where does evil come from? If it is part of God's creation, God becomes responsible for evil and its effects. If it is not, God is not

---

[18] John Stachniewski, in *The Persecutory Imagination: English Puritanism and the Literature of Religious Despair* (Oxford: Clarendon, 1991), says that Milton's theodicy was a direct response to the vehemence of Calvinist insistence that "God should not be brought before the bar of human justice" (p. 333).

[19] Tertullian, *Adversus Marcionem* 1.2.2.

supreme, but only one half of a dualistic principle in the universe. Put differently, if God creates evil, he is not good; if he doesn't, he is not God.

Milton's way out of the conundrum is to insist that evil is not of the same order of being as good. God does not create evil, but evil comes into being when free creatures turn away from the good. For Milton, creatures are created free and rational, "sufficient to have stood, though free to fall," as God insists (3.99). Evil is a function of free choice, thus acquitting God of responsibility for its existence, which is always and only ontologically secondary, though its effects are all too real.

But the demonstration is not so straightforward. God insists that man is responsible for his own fall: "Whose fault? / Whose but his own" (3.96–97). But if Milton allows God the firm assertion, he also allows the reader the opportunity to resist God's self-defense. It is not self-evident that it is man's "fault." Only if Adam and Eve are truly "sufficient" to withstand the temptation and completely "free" to stand or fall can it possibly be their own fault. But the poem makes us wonder about both.

Their sufficiency is called into question before the end of Book 3. Uriel, "the sharpest-sighted spirit of all in Heaven" (3.691), is deceived by Satan, unable to see through Satan's disguise and dissimulation. The narrator explains that "neither man nor angel can discern / Hypocrisy," which is seen only by God and, "by his permissive will," is allowed to exist in "Heaven and earth" (3.682–85). In the very book, then, in which Adam and Eve's sufficiency to resist the temptation is asserted, we see an archangel fooled by Satan's wiles, and we are told that it is by "God's permissive will" that such hypocrisy cannot be detected. Is man then sufficient? Is God not somehow implicated in his fall?

Ultimately we may have to bow before God's "permissive will," but not until after we have wondered why "the will / And high permission of all-ruling Heaven" has left Satan "to his own dark designs" (1.211–13) instead of keeping him safely chained to the burning lake; or why it was the "will of Heaven" that Sin and Death pave "a broad and beaten way" to enable "spirits perverse / With easy intercourse . . . To tempt or punish mortals" (2.1024–32); or why a God, "in all things wise and just, / Hindered not Satan to attempt the mind / Of man" (10.7–9); or why the fallen angels, turned to serpents after the fall of Adam and Eve, are "permitted" to resume "their lost shape" (10.574); or why hypocrisy is allowed to walk invisible to all but God. These cannot be questions that merely prove us fallen, but questions that prove us alert to the complexities of the poem we read and the world we inhabit. Why isn't God responsible for evil, if he created Satan, could have kept him chained, allowed his hypocrisy to be undetectable, and, even after Adam and Eve's fall, allowed him to resume his shape-shifting form?

The poem, then, does not allow us simply to acquiesce to the assertion of Adam and Eve's sufficiency, any more than it does to the assertion of their freedom. God asserts that man is free, but we must wonder if he is only "free to fall." God's very certainty that Satan "shall pervert, / For man will hearken to his glozing lies / And easily transgress the sole command" (3.92–94) calls that freedom into question. If God is omniscient—if, that is, this is not prediction but a statement of fact—in what sense are Adam and Eve free not to fall? Can God be wrong? "If I foreknew," says God, "foreknowledge had no influence upon their fault" (3.117–18). But the claim must sound defensive and may well seem disingenuous, since there is apparently no way, given that foreknowledge, that they could stand faithful.

And even if we can convince ourselves that Adam and Eve were indeed both sufficient and free and that God is not responsible for their fall, it still may seem as if Satan achieves his goal "to confound the race / Of mankind in one root, and earth with hell / To mingle and involve" (2.382–84). Hasn't Satan succeeded in his plan? The simple answer—that the fall is a "fortunate fall"—raises as many unsettling questions as it satisfies. The idea of the fortunate fall is that it enables the Incarnation and the Redemption, allowing God to show his magnificent love by sacrificing his only Son and allowing mankind the possibility of an eternity of bliss, not only robbing Satan of his victory but decisively showing God's ability to bring good out of evil.[20] If, however, the fortunate fall is not an afterthought (and it is hard to see, in a providential universe, how it could be or even what "afterthought" might mean), then it does seem as if God must have both wanted and contrived the fall, as William Empson notoriously insisted.[21] Even if the fall is the means to bring about the greater happiness of mankind, does not this make God responsible for sin and render his efforts "to render man inexcusable" (5, Argument) something close to bad faith?

These are the difficult questions asked by someone "whose spirit," in Arthur Sewell's phrase, "has been unsettled in his faith in God and trust in man."[22] Milton has set out to justify God's ways, not least to himself. There are precise theological answers to the questions Milton poses. First, Adam and Eve are sufficient because, regardless of the guise in which the temptation comes, the interdiction not to taste of the tree is straightforward and binding: "they knew, and ought to have still remembered / The high injunction not to taste that fruit" (10.12–13). Second, they are free in spite of

[20] See Lovejoy, who traces the "Paradox of the Fortunate Fall" as it finds "recurrent expression in the history of Christian religious thought" (p. 163).

[21] Empson, esp. pp. 189–92.

[22] Sewell, p. 80.

God's foreknowledge, because divine foreknowledge is possible, as Milton understands it, without predetermination. Foreknowledge works exactly like human memory. God exists outside of time, and "past, present, future he beholds" at once (3.78). If he knows, his knowledge is no more influential on the acts he foresees than is human memory upon the acts it remembers. And the fall does not prove either Satan victorious or God hypocritical, because good does come out of evil, but man would have been still "Happier, had it sufficed him to have known / Good by itself, and not evil at all" (11.88–89).

At the level of doctrine, then, Adam and Eve are indeed "sufficient to have stood, though free to fall," and God's goodness is shown victorious. But it is not at the level of doctrine that we either formulate or satisfy our doubts. They come to us insistently provoked by the poem. And it is that provocation that demands explanation every bit as much as the doctrinal strain itself. If Milton ultimately offers answers to the awkward questions, it is undeniable that he makes us ask them, proving us alert to and engaged with both the poem and the world. The goal of criticism of *Paradise Lost* surely cannot be to "prevent the reader from asking certain questions,"[23] as C. S. Lewis stated, nor can it be, as Stanley Fish has argued (and what is virtually the same thing), to authorize our questions but only by showing how they prove us, again and again, fallen.

In Fish's view, to question is always and only to reveal our fallen nature, and what we mainly learn is "distrust of our own abilities and perceptions." Thus for him the poem's putative theodicy is a feint: "'that thou may'st believe and be confirm'd' would be a more honest—literal is the better word—*propositio* than 'justify the ways of God to men.'"[24] But Milton's poem is a genuine theodicy—an "honest" effort to "justify the ways of God to men" rather than a mere pretence for convincing (convicting?) humanity of its fallenness—precisely because it recognizes that our "abilities and perceptions" allow and lead us to ask such questions, even as the poem admits that its own answers may be neither self-evident nor immediately satisfying.

For example, it is hard to understand why God's foreknowledge does not establish the necessity of Adam and Eve's fall, especially as God says it "had no less proved certain unforeseen" (3.119). Where then is their freedom not to fall? There are potential philosophical escapes from the seeming contradiction in the difference between "certainty" and "necessity" (though 3.119 seems dangerously to blur it) and between timeless and time-bound

[23] Lewis, p. 70.

[24] Fish, *Surprised By Sin* (1967; 2nd ed. Cambridge, MA: Harvard University Press, 1997), pp. 22 and 289.

understandings,[25] but the crucial point is that we need these escapes. Milton's poem makes us struggle for ways to respond to its unsettling suggestions. If we are told that God sees the world from beyond time, we are unable to share the vantage point. We are time bound, as are our narratives. If Milton succeeds, as I think he does, in his project to "justify the ways of God to men," he does so not by merely declaring God's ways just and showing us that our questions are inappropriate but unavoidable. It cannot be that we ask our questions, voice our doubts, only to be imperiously told: "you have made a mistake, just as I knew you would" (Fish, p. 9).

Fish's Milton is a poetic Calvinist, if not a theological one, whose poem, in Fish's influential version, formally enacts the predestination that doctrinally it would repudiate. But *Paradise Lost* both theologically and poetically insists on the radical (in both senses) possibility of freedom. Milton in this sense is a consistent Arminian.[26] His angels and humans are endowed with free will, and his God in no way impinges upon it: "God decreed nothing absolutely which he left in the power of free agents" (*Works* 14, 65). But this freedom is not limited to the characters of Milton's epic; it extends also to its readers. The poem does not trap us in its orthodoxies but releases us to our questions. The "fit audience" (7.31) Milton imagines for his poem is not one that bows passively before its assertions but one that exercises its reason upon them, doubting, challenging, criticizing, just as Milton did with the orthodoxies of his time. If we are alert to the need and to the difficulty of justifying God's ways to men, our alertness has been honed by the poem itself; and if the poem finally succeeds in its theodicy, it is not least because it has, in its unflinching honesty, dared possibly to fail.

"My Adventurous Song"

In many ways the most audacious voice in *Paradise Lost* is that of its narrator. Though it is convenient to call this voice "Milton," the narrator, as

---

[25] See for example Dennis Danielson's "The Fall and Milton's Theodicy," in Danielson, ed., pp. 144–59.

[26] Arminianism (taking its name from the Dutch theologian Jacobus Arminius, 1560–1609) has been used to label a doctrine distinguished from Calvinism in its recognition of conditional election and resistible grace. Though some recent historians, like Julian Davies, in *The Caroline Captivity of the Church* (Oxford: Clarendon Press, 1992), have objected to the sharp distinction usually made between Arminianism and Calvinism—at least in England—it is undeniable that Arminius himself did object to strict Calvinist ideas of predestination on the grounds that it made "God the author of sin" ("*Deum peccati auctorem*," Arminius, *Opera Theologia* [Frankfurt, 1631], p. 536); see Stephen M. Fallon, "'Elect above the Rest': Theology as Self-representation in Milton," in Dobranski and Rumrich, eds., pp. 93–116.

Anne Ferry was perhaps the first to insist,[27] is analytically distinguishable from the poet. Although the narrator often sounds like the historical Milton, expressing emotions, attitudes, values, and ideas recognizable as the poet's own, he is created as a character no less (and no more) than any of the others who populate the poem. Indeed his relation to Milton is surprisingly like the heterodox relation of Milton's Christ to Milton's God: he is "begotten" and cannot therefore be identical with his creator,[28] and yet he has a no less privileged role in the realization of the "author's" design. Indeed, what God says to Christ could almost exactly articulate the relation of Milton to his narrator: "All hast thou spoken as my thoughts are, all / As my eternal purpose hath decreed" (3.171–72).

But in spite of the unsettling parallel with Christ here, there is a further, and arguably even more unsettling, parallel established with Satan. As critics have regularly noted, the narrator voices Milton's own literary aspirations in terms that troublingly but unmistakably identify them with Satan's perverse ambitions. The narrator sees himself "Escaped the Stygian pool" (3.14) as his focus changes from hell to Heaven, but the language exactly echoes the description of Satan and Beelzebub rising from the burning lake, "Both glorying to have scaped the Stygian flood" (1.239). Both Satan and the narrator aspire to glory in similar terms: Satan, who "Thus high uplifted beyond hope, aspires / Beyond thus high" (2.7–8), is seen to be not unlike the narrator, who aspires "with no middle flight . . . to soar above the Aonian mount" (1.14–15). In the invocation in Book 1, the narrator can criticize Satan for "Aspiring / To set himself in glory above his peers" (1.38–39), while only a few lines earlier he had declared his own desire to pursue "Things unattempted yet in prose or rhyme" (1.16), claiming, through the ironic quotation of Ariosto (see 1.16n.), his own radical originality and announcing his aspirations to outdo his literary peers. The narrator's "flight / Through utter and through middle darkness" (3.15–16) exactly parallels Satan's course as he leaves hell and crosses chaos on his "obscure sojourn" (3.15) to earth. Both have "thoughts inflamed of highest design" (2.630), and the narrator's acknowledgment of his "adventurous song" (1.13) finds an ominous echo in Sin and Death's "adventurous work" (10.255).

Perhaps the differing scale of aspiration allows the parallels between the narrator and Satan to do little more than voice Milton's anxiety about the

---

[27] Ferry, esp. pp. 20–66; ; see also Riggs, pp. 1–45. C. S. Lewis had earlier written, "Even the poet, when he appears in the first person within his own poem, is not to be taken as the private individual John Milton" (*A Preface to "Paradise Lost,"* p. 50).

[28] This is the heretical Arianism that has worried many commentators on Milton—the anti-Trinitarian insistence that God alone, unlike Christ or the Holy Spirit, is unbegotten; see *PL* 3.384 and note. For a compelling account of the issues, see Rumrich, *Milton Unbound,* pp. 40–49.

magnitude of his undertaking, but the transgressive potential is written deep into the texture of the poem. Raphael tells Adam that "Heaven is for thee too high / To know what passes there" and warns him to "be lowly wise" (8.172–73). This is not advice that Milton takes to heart, for his poem indeed presumes to know "what passes" in Heaven: "Into the Heaven of Heaven's I have presumed, / An earthly guest, and drawn empyreal air" (7.13–14).

What might differentiate the poem's presumption from Satan's is that Satan undertakes his journey "Alone, and without guide" (2.975), while the narrator is well aware of his need for help. If he has "presumed" to enter into Heaven, it has done so only "led by" Urania and hoping to be "with like safety guided down" by her to his "native element" (7.12–16). But even his invocations confirm the audacity of his undertaking. If he submits his imagination to his muse, he does so without even the conventional humility of the gesture. "Sing heavenly muse," he asks (1.6), but his muse dwells well above "the Olympian hill" (7.3) of the classical muses. The muse he invokes in Book 1, by whatever named called, is that being "that on the secret top / Of Oreb, or of Sinai, didst inspire / That shepherd, who first taught the chosen seed" (1.6–8). On Sinai, God himself spoke directly to Moses, and Milton's apparent gesture of submission thus identifies him with the privilege of the patriarch, and his muse, not with the classical muses on Helicon but with God himself, who sits "high throned above all height" (3.57).

We are meant finally to distinguish the narrator's ambition from Satan's pride. If this seems in any doubt, think of the difference between the narrator's invocation to light in Book 3 (1–55) and Satan's invocation to the sun in Book 4 (32–41). But Milton makes us see the parallel between the ambition of Satan and the presumption of his narrator, not neatly as "emulation opposite" (2.298) but as an unnerving sign of both how much is at stake in Milton's poetic undertaking and how difficult it is.

"The Points of Liberty"

It was to justify the ways of God, rather than the ways of the godly Commonwealth, that Milton wrote his epic; nonetheless it is clear that *Paradise Lost* is saturated with language familiar from his earlier political tracts. What is surprising is that Heaven, with its absolute monarch, is organized exactly as the form of government Milton had consistently opposed in his political writings, and Hell, with its council, debate, and election, more like what Milton had hoped would prove the pattern of a reformed English nation.

One might decide that this is evidence of the radical divorce of Milton's religious belief from his political ideology or, alternatively, argue that this proves Milton indeed of the Devil's party; but in fact Milton is guilty of neither inconsistency nor sacrilege. What produces the appearance of contradiction is that Milton's God, in spite of being called "all-powerful king" (2.851), "matchless king" (4.41), "all bounteous king" (5.640), is not a king in the same sense as an earthly monarch.

Milton's view of earthly kings came from a political philosophy that consistently held, as in *Tenure of Kings and Magistrates* (see Fig. 3), that kings "have been exalted to that dignitie above thir Brethren" (*Works* 5, 7) only by "a human ordinance" (ibid., 16) rather than by divine decree. Milton's politics are underwritten by the belief that "all men were naturally borne free," but that civil government is a response to the "wrong and violence" that followed the fall, an agreement "by common league to bind each other from mutual injury." But "because no faith in all was found sufficiently binding," they established "authoritie, that might restrain by force and punishment what was violated against peace and common right" (ibid., 8). Since the king is thus created by and for the people, it follows that "the people [may], as oft as they shall judge it for the best, either choose him or reject him, retaine or depose him . . . meerly by the liberty and right of free born Men to be govern'd as seems to them best" (ibid., 14).

But although this is the precise logic that was used to justify the trial and subsequent execution of the King (see Fig. 4), it is not the logic that determines the relation to God. Milton's Heaven is (literally) ruled by divine right. It is not, however, that Milton's politics have changed. The poem confirms what Milton has always held. Kings are not due absolute obedience, but God is. Milton's politics, as Nigel Smith has said, are consistently "monarchist in heaven, republican on earth."[29] In fact the monarchist politics of Milton's Heaven are exactly what underpin his own republican commitments. The poem establishes the crucial difference between an earthly king and Heaven's "Immutable, immortal, infinite, / Eternal king" (3.373–74). Earthly kings are not different in kind from those they rule. God, however, differs radically in kind from beings, earthly or celestial, who are his creatures. On this fundamental distinction rests the claim for obedience.

And it is this distinction that Satan must deny. The putative justification for Satan's rebellion against God is that God is a tyrant, unreasonably assuming "Monarchy over such as live by right / His equals" (5.795–96). If it were true that the rebel angels and God were equal, it would indeed be heroic to refuse "to bow and sue for grace / With suppliant knee, and deify his power" (1.111–12). Surely Milton would do no less, and, even as the Restoration was upon him, he was still hoping his nation might refrain from "deifying and adoring" the returning King. But that is the point:

[29] *"Paradise Lost* from Civil War to Restoration," p. 263.

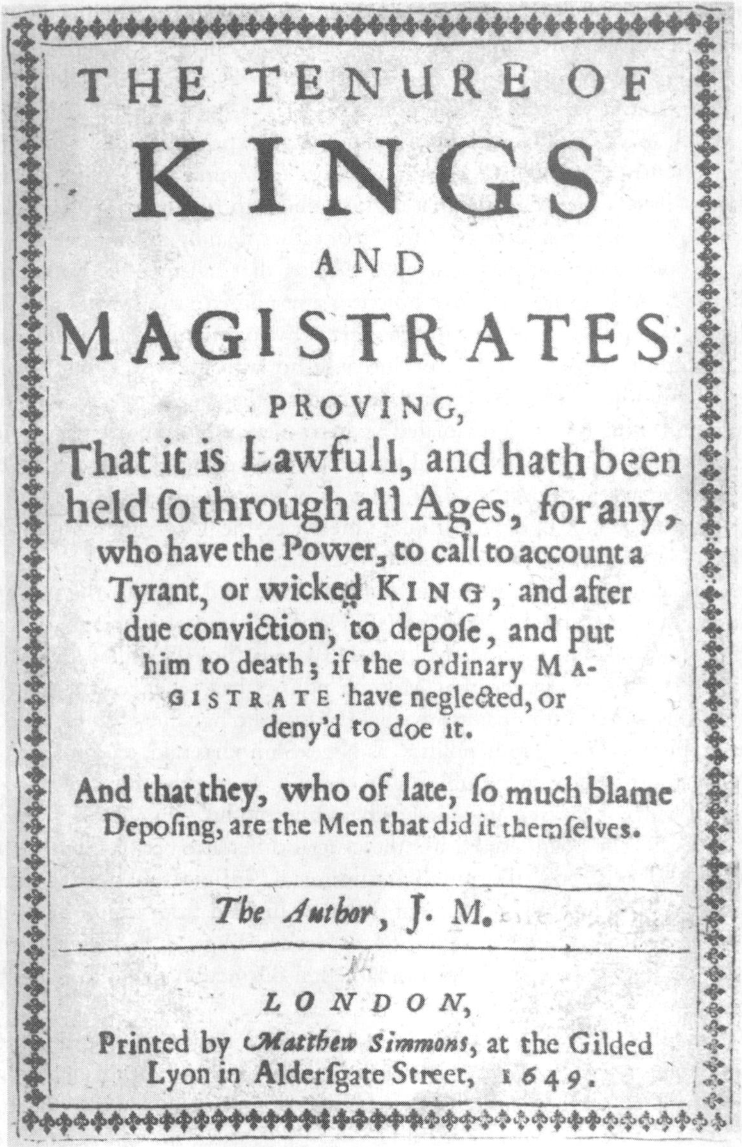

THE TENURE OF
KINGS
AND
MAGISTRATES:
PROVING,

That it is Lawfull, and hath been
held so through all Ages, for any,
who have the Power, to call to account a
Tyrant, or wicked KING, and after
due conviction, to depose, and put
him to death; if the ordinary MA-
GISTRATE have neglected, or
deny'd to doe it.

And that they, who of late, so much blame
Deposing, are the Men that did it themselves.

The Author, J. M.

LONDON,
Printed by *Matthew Simmons,* at the Gilded
Lyon in Aldersgate Street, 1649.

Fig. 3. Title page of Milton's *Tenure of Kings and Magistrates* published on February 13, 1649, fifteen days after the execution of King Charles I.

Fig. 4. German engraving of the execution of Charles I (1649), with portraits of General Fairfax and Oliver Cromwell flanking one of King Charles. Used by permission of the British Library, Crach.1.Tab.4.c.1(18).

deifying the English king is the base action "of an abject people" (*The Readie and Easie Way* [*Works* 6, 121]), but adoring the king of kings is appropriate, not least because God alone does not need to be deified.

This is exactly the thinking that determines Abdiel's defiance of Satan. He repeats the Satanic charge before he devastates its contention: "Unjust, thou say'st, / Flatly unjust, to bind with laws the free, / And equal over equals to let reign," and then scathingly asking, "Shalt thou give law to God? Shalt thou dispute / With him the points of liberty, who made / Thee what thou art . . . ?" (5.818–24). This is not, as it might seem, an echo of the mystifying voice from the whirlwind that answered Job, but a reasoned and irrefutable argument. What invalidates Satan's position is not its political logic. Abdiel willingly grants that it is "unjust, / That equal over equals monarch reigns" (5.831–32). That principle is crucial to Milton's politics. Adam sees that Nimrod is "execrable" to "aspire / Above his brethren, to himself assuming / Authority usurped from God, not given" (12.64–66). But Abdiel takes exception to Satan's ontological presumption. The legitimacy of Satan's resistance depends on an assertion of equality that is unsustainable, radically undercut by an ontological distinction: "by his word the mighty Father made / All things, even thee" (5.836–37). Satan and God are not equals if Satan and the rebel angels are God's creatures. Satan, of course, cannot agree that they were "made," for with that admission the legitimacy of the rebellion collapses. In sight of Eden he admits to himself that God "created" him (4.43), but publicly he must insist the angels were "self-begot, self-raised / By our own quickening power" (5.860–61).

Neither Heaven nor hell represents a political ideal for Milton.[30] Satan's revolutionary principles are both insincere and unstable, and hell's institutions too easily manipulated. For all his republican rhetoric, Satan, of course, is the one who most aspires "To set himself in glory 'bove his peers" (1.39), and who rebels, not to free God's angels from the tyranny of Heaven but because he thinks that "one step higher / Would set [him] highest" (4.50–51). And, if in Heaven, God's absolute rule is ontologically justified, it also fails, precisely for that reason, to provide a model for earthly polities. Announcing Christ's exaltation, he tells the angels, "him who disobeys / Me disobeys, breaks union, and that day, / Cast out from God and blessèd vision, falls / Into utter darkness" (5.611–14). God demands total and unquestioning obedience. If this is joyfully given to the creator, it does not suggest a pattern of civic governance among his creatures that Milton could have embraced.

---

[30] Among many fine account of the politics of Milton's poem see Loewenstein, "The Radical Religious Politics of *Paradise Lost*," pp. 448–62; Knoppers, esp. pp. 87–91; Norbrook, esp. pp. 433–91; and Christopher Hill's still-interesting *Milton and the English Revolution*.

Neither Heaven nor hell points the way to the "free Commonwealth" that even in 1660 Milton still imagined might be possible. By the time *Paradise Lost* was finished, however, Milton knew those hopes were gone. In the final two books of the poem we see the grim effects of the fall upon human history. Since Adam's "original lapse, true liberty / Is lost" (12.83–84); the faithful are persecuted, and "tyranny must be" (12.95). Yet if in these dispiriting times "works of faith / Rarely be found" (12.536–37), still there are those solitary voices, who, like Abdiel, maintain "the cause / Of truth" (6.31–32), not least Milton's own revolutionary voice, which remained "unchanged / To hoarse or mute, though fallen on evil days" (7.24–25).

"Their Sex Not Equal Seemed"

Although to many modern readers Milton's civic imagination seems progressive, his gender politics usually seem at best conformist, at worst offensive. The poem too easily seems to reproduce the assumptions of a patriarchal age. Adam and Eve, who together "seemed lords of all, / And worthy seemed" to Satan as he first views them, are quickly distinguished: "though both / Not equal, as their sex not equal seemed: / For contemplation he and valor formed, / For softness she and sweet attractive grace; / He for God only, she for God in him" (4.295–99). One might hear the reiterated "seemed" as evidence that this may not be intended as an unqualified truth, but it is hard to avoid the distinction of the final line. It might be said that it improves upon an earlier, more invidious formulation. In *Tetrachordon*, Milton had more sharply expressed the difference: "he not for her, but she for him" (*Works* 4, 76); but even in its emended form in *Paradise Lost* the contrast "seems" clearly to establish Adam's superiority.

Today many readers find in the poem dismaying evidence of how thoroughly Milton has internalized a Pauline view of the inequality of the sexes (e.g., 1 Cor. 11:7–8), or strive with admirable ingenuity to deny it.[31] Closer to Milton's own time, however, Richard Bentley could confidently say that "Our Author, through the whole Poem, had certainly that in his View, to make the Female Sex favour it" (*PL*, 1732, gloss 4.634). Bentley is wrong about many things, and perhaps this is but one more; nonetheless, it is at very least a useful reminder that history is a record of change.

Still it would be foolish to deny how deeply the poem is marked by patriarchal, sometimes even misogynist, sentiments, though it is important also to remember that statements made by characters need not represent Milton's own views, or even honestly their own. One might well observe

---

[31] There are many fine and provocative studies of the gender relations in the poem. See, among others, Froula; Lewalski, "Milton on Women"; Kelsey; Turner; Walker (ed.); Wittreich; and Martin (ed.).

that Adam sees Eve as "the inferior . . . resembling less / His image who made both" (8.541–44), and that Raphael offers quick confirmation that she is indeed "less excellent" (8.566). After the fall, Christ seems unmistakably to insist upon the gender hierarchy that has proven so troublesome to modern readers: "Thou didst resign thy manhood and the place / Wherein God set thee above her, made of thee, / And for thee, whose perfection far excelled / Hers in all real dignity" (10.148–51).

Yet there are other aspects of the poem that might well have made "the Female Sex favour it." Adam's praise of Eve as he first contemplates her fallen—"O fairest of creation, last and best / Of all God's works" (9.896–97)—at once recognizes her excellence and suggests, like the familiar feminist joke, that her belated creation enabled God to improve upon the prototype. But if Adam's praise merely inverts their hierarchical relation, his request to God for a mate articulates an attractive ideal of companionate marriage that repudiates the gender hierarchy altogether. When God suggests that the earth is filled "With various living creatures" with whom Adam might "find pastime" (8.370–75), Adam observes that all these are "inferior," and he tellingly asks: "Among unequals what society / Can sort, what harmony or true delight?" (8.383–84). God commends him for his vision of "A nice and subtle happiness" (8.399), and with that approbation any justification of gender inequality seems impossible. Adam's vision of "Collateral love and dearest amity" (8.426) depends upon a fundamental equality to which God has assented—and which Milton subtly reinforces. If Genesis gives Adam the privilege of naming the animals, *Paradise Lost* matches it with Eve's nonscriptural naming of the plants (11.273–77).[32]

The poem gives us incompatible views of the relation between the sexes; Adam and Eve are at once unequal and equal, an ambiguity evidenced in various ways but not least in the syntax concerning Adam's view of Eve as "superior, or but equal" (10.147). Seemingly Adam is charged with abdicating his natural superiority in viewing her either as a "superior" or as "but equal." But the syntax might as easily mean that he has abdicated his responsibility in seeing her as his superior instead of seeing her appropriately as "but equal." Perhaps the ambiguity reflects an ambiguity in Milton's own mind, both conditioned by and suspicious of the orthodoxies of his time. Or perhaps it reflects something more deliberate and systematic. Adam is obviously sincere in his desire for a mate that is his equal, and God seems

---

[32] Mary Nyquist, however, sees this as merely another hierarchical gesture: "Eve's 'naming' becomes associated not with rational insight and dominion but rather with the act of lyrical utterance, and therefore with the affective responsibilities of the domestic sphere into which her subjectivity has fallen"; see Nyquist, "The Genesis of Gendered Subjectivity in the Divorce Tracts and in *Paradise Lost*," in Nyquist and Ferguson, p. 100.

pleased with his request; yet Raphael and Christ, just as obviously, assume the rightness of gender inequality, with Eve, in Christ's words, "Unseemly to bear rule, which was [Adam's] part" (10.155). One could accept the inequality, ceding authority to the celestial viewpoint and the conventional thought of Milton's age, but that would make God's assent to Adam's request for a mate who is his equal (8.379–97) at best patronizing, at worst hypocritical. But arguably the ambiguity is deliberate, pointing to a distinction between heavenly and earthly hierarchies.

From the point of view of God, all is arranged hierarchically on a graduated "scale of nature" (5.509), with those things "more refined, more spirituous, and pure . . . nearer to him placed or nearer tending" (5.475–76). Human society, however, does not develop on the analogy of God's creation (though that analogy—naturalizing kingship—is central to the royalism Milton rejects). Although God has given mankind "dominion absolute" over "beast, fish, fowl" (12.67–68), establishing a hierarchy of kind, he does not establish an analogically parallel social hierarchy within the rank of the human. A social structure that permits some individuals to assume superiority over others grants them, according to Milton, "dominion undeserved" (12.27): "man over men / He made not lord, such title to himself / Reserving, human left from human free" (12.69–71). In a human polity, one might argue that "inferior, who is free" (9.825), though it is literally a fallen understanding in the poem, uttered by Eve only after she has tasted the fruit of the forbidden tree. On the "scale of nature," however, one finds one's freedom in recognizing one's own place in God's dynamic hierarchy.

This double focus may account for some of the contradictions that have exercised critics. An unfallen Adam can at once "understand" that Eve is "inferior in the mind / And inward faculties" and yet several lines later admit that "Authority and reason on her wait / As one intended first, not after made," sensing her "Greatness of mind" (8.540–57). What he experiences is different from what he understands. Critics, however, inevitably focus on his excessive love, assuming his understanding, rather than the experience, is right. But we might wonder on what his understanding rests. Adam doesn't experience Eve as intellectually inferior—and neither do we. Although Raphael immediately warns Adam not to attribute "overmuch to things / Less excellent" (8.565–66), Adam insists that he and Eve share "Union of mind" (8.604), as is appropriate for a relationship born of the confidence that true society cannot exist "among unequals" and that "in disparity" no true "fellowship" can flourish (8.384–89). Adam internalizes both the hierarchical logic of Heaven and the egalitarian hopes of mankind.

In the fullness of time, these are not in conflict, since distinction in God's hierarchy is temporary and inessential. All things "proceed" from God "and up to him return / If not depraved from good" (5.470–71). Even gender distinctions will disappear, since gendered "bodies may at last turn all to spirit" (5.497), and "spirits when they please / Can either sex assume or both" (1.423–24). For God the only real hierarchy is the moral binary of good and evil. In our fallen world it is different. Although we may imagine an ideal of "fair equality, fraternal state" (12.26), fallen humanity can never fully achieve it. Inequality is part of our fallen condition.

Some critics, however, see inequality in the poem inscribed into the very nature of creation. If Eve unfallen is meant to "acknowledge" Adam "her head" (8.574), in what sense does her punishment for their transgression— "to thy husband's will / Thine shall submit, he over thee shall rule" (10.195–96)—change the essential relationship? The difference, if there is one, is certainly subtle. It is hard not to see this as evidence that gender inequality is established with the creation and reinforced after the fall.

The poem, however, refuses simply to reflect and reproduce a patriarchal ideology. Eve is far too active and intelligent for her inferiority to be in any sense axiomatic, if it is the fact at all. If the biblical account insists that she be the focus of the temptation, Milton has framed it so her intellectual and spiritual activity is emphasized. She begins the conversation that leads to their separation (9.205) and argues her case compellingly; after their fall, she faces up to their guilt before Adam does, and she is the one who breaks the futile cycle of "mutual accusation" (9.1187) by her Christ-like willingness to allow God's wrath to fall on her alone, with reiterated *me*'s: "On me, sole cause to thee of all this woe, / Me, me only, just object of his ire" (10.935–36; cf. 3.236–38). It is untrue that she is "sole cause . . . of all this woe," but her willingness to accept the guilt as her own anticipates the "heroic martyrdom" (9.32) that will prove the pattern of human excellence. Hers are the last human words spoken in Eden, and they humbly articulate her understanding of her own agency in the redemptive action of providential history: "This further consolation yet secure / I carry hence: though all by me is lost, / Such favor I unworthy am vouchsafed, / By me the promised seed shall all restore" (12.620–23).

The poem, then, affectively challenges its own ideological underpinning, so we are led to see Eve as Adam's emotional, intellectual, and spiritual equal, and to see their relationship as offering, as Adam sought, the "harmony and true delight, / Which must be mutual" (8.384–85). Fittingly, the final image of our first parents is identical to the first (4.321), affirming their fundamental equality measured in the mutual need and mutual comfort that joins them. Once again they walk "hand in hand" (12.648), now bravely walking out of Eden into history.[33]

---

[33] Note, however, that the cover illustration of this book, which was taken from the 1688 edition of the poem, pointedly does not show the two of them "hand in hand"; the angel has a

"The World's Material Mold"

One way in which Milton neutralizes the charge of gender inequality is through the poem's philosophical materialism, which modern readers may overlook or think a mere philosophical curiosity.[34] For him all creation is equally endowed with God's virtue and equally has the capacity to be refined. Social distinctions are thus, at worst, inessential and temporary in what Barbara Lewalski aptly identifies as Milton's "curiously fluid conception of hierarchy."[35]

This materialism, a form of monism,[36] is most evident in the richly imagined cosmos of Milton's poem. The physical universe is created from matter pre-existent in "the vast immeasurable abyss" (7.211). With "golden compasses," God circumscribes that which he wants to act upon, which he then infuses with "vital virtue" and "vital warmth" (7.225–36). Matter thus precedes creation, existing as a "passive principle, dependent upon the Deity and subservient to him" (*Christian Doctrine* [*Works* 15, 19]).[37] But this begs the question of the origin of matter. Milton recognizes that it must come from God, "or God will not have been the perfect and absolute cause of every thing" (ibid., 21). But if matter exists prior to the creation, of what does it consist? Milton answers that since not even God could "produce bodies out of nothing," there must be "some bodily power in the substance of God" (ibid., 25) that can be "diffused and propagated and extended as far and in such a manner as he himself shall will" (ibid., 23). Milton holds, then, "that God did not produce everything out of nothing, but of himself" (ibid., 27), thus generating two radically heterodox notions: 1) that creation is not *ex*

---

hand on Adam's shoulder, and Eve's hands are occupied covering her body; she looks up; he covers his eyes in shame. The illustrator, probably Henry Aldrich, bases his image on Raphael's famous painting rather than the poem.

[34] On Milton's materialism, see Curry; Hunter, "Milton's Power of Matter"; Stephen, Fallon, and Rogers, esp. pp. 112–22.

[35] Lewalski, "Milton on Women," p. 6.

[36] See Kerrigan, pp. 193–262.

[37] I assume, with most scholars, that Milton is indeed the author of *Christian Doctrine*. Though William Hunter has argued that Milton was not its author, the evidence seems unmistakable that the treatise, found in 1823 and translated two years later, is the work of Milton, who called it his "dearest and best possession" (*Works* 14, 6). See Hunter, "The Provenance of the *Christian Doctrine*," and responses to Hunter by Barbara Lewalski and John T. Shawcross, plus a rebuttal by Hunter, all in *SEL* 32 (1992): 129–66; Hunter continued the argument in "The Provenance of the *Christian Doctrine*: Addenda from the Bishop of Salisbury" in *SEL* 33 (1993): 191–207, which provoked responses from Maurice Kelley and Christopher Hill in *SEL* 34 (1994): 153–63 and 165–93, and a further response from Hunter on pp. 195–203. See also Gordon Campbell et al., "The Provenance of *De Doctrina Christiana*," *Milton Quarterly* 31 (1997): 67–121.

nihilo but *ex Deo;* and 2) that God is in some sense corporeal, manifesting a "diversified and substantial virtue" (ibid., 23).

The philosophical subtleties are, for the reader, perhaps not as important as their unmistakable implication: that Milton, as William Kolbrener says, undoes the "conventional distinctions between soul and body, matter and spirit,"[38] even, we might add, between Heaven and earth, angel and human. All these pairs exist not as binaries but as points on an ontological continuum of "various degrees / Of substance" (5.473–74) that all reflect their common origin and end in God. Milton's cosmology is thus more than cosmic geography; it becomes a mode of metaphysics.

Nonetheless readers inevitably seek to visualize Milton's cosmos, and it is easy to do so. Heaven, though "undetermined square or round" (2.1048), is above. The sphere of the universe, which contains the earth, hangs by "a golden chain" from the side of Heaven from which the angels fell (2.1005–6). A retractable staircase can be "let down" from Heaven to provide angels "A passage to the earth" (3.510–28). After the fall, the earth is also linked by "a stupendous bridge" (10.351) to hell, which lies "As far removed from God and the light of heaven / As from the center thrice to the utmost pole" (1.73–74). Between Heaven and hell is the "wild abyss" of chaos, the "womb of nature" that is the repository of unformed matter that God has not yet endowed with spirit and purpose (2.910–11).

The different environments are all material, though each reveals, in the particular nature of its materiality, its closeness to God. Even the regions of Heaven, those "happy realms of light" (1.85), are thoroughly material. Heaven is three dimensional: it has length—Abdiel travels "All night . . . Through Heaven's wide champaign" as he returns from the rebel angels to God (6.1–2)—and depth, for the rebel angels dig up "the celestial soil" and find "beneath" the surface raw materials for their arms (6.509–20). It has walls "With opal towers and battlements adorned / Of living sapphire" (2.1049–50). The angels are themselves corporeal and are endowed with "every lower faculty / Of sense whereby they hear, see, smell, touch, taste." Embodied, they "require" food and drink no less than humans (5.407–11) and enjoy sex, though innocently blush to discuss it (8.618–29).

These all might be thought mere narrative conveniences, "likening spiritual to corporal forms" (5.573) for the benefit of fallen readers. But Raphael himself suggests that perhaps things on earth and Heaven are "Each to other like, more than on earth is thought" (5.576), and Milton's radical materialism insists it is so. Matter in heaven is, however, closer to spirit, more powerfully charged with God's virtue, than elsewhere; thus the sapphire of Heaven's battlements is "living," meaning "indigenous" but also

[38] Kolbrener, p. 87.

perfectly suggesting the superior animation of heavenly matter. The chariots that accompany Christ "came forth / Spontaneous, for within them spirit lived" (7.203–4); and at their meals the angels "Quaff immortality and joy" (5.638).

Further from God, the material world is necessarily still infused with spirit, for that is the very condition of being, but matter is less refined. In the unfallen Eden (see Fig. 5), the natural world is good, but not self-regulating. Trees may wave their tops "in sign of worship" (5.193–94), not least to show that "the debt immense of endless gratitude. / So burdensome" in Satan's view (4.52–53), is satisfied merely by created substances doing what they naturally do; but the unusual animation stops short of reproducing the order of Heaven. Unfallen earthly nature is "Wild above rule or art" (5.297) and demands the labor of Adam and Eve to "reform" it (4.625). In chaos, on the other hand, reform is not enough. It is a "wild expanse" (2.1014), a "wild abyss" (2.910, 2.917), which only God's goodness can order. Its wildness, however, is not the "enormous bliss" (5.297) of Eden, however excessive in its profusion, but a "universal hubbub wild / Of stunning sounds and voices all confused" (2.951–52). It is not hostile to God—indeed it is of God—but it is matter that God has not yet chosen to inspire with his virtue.[39]

Hell is, in every sense, farthest from God. Satan may believe that "farthest from him is best" (1.247) as he contemplates his own defeat, but materially, farthest from God is clearly worst. Although hell is itself a creation of God, a place, unlike chaos, where God's intentionality has been fully active, it is a place of punishment "prepared / For those rebellious" (1.70–71). It is "A dungeon horrible, on all sides round / As one great furnace flamed, yet from those flames / No light, but rather darkness visible" (1.61–63). Hell too is called an abyss, but, unlike the abyss that is chaos, the abyss of hell is "hollow" (2.518) and its inhabitants conform to the nature of their prison. Thus Satan can say "myself am hell / And in the lowest deep a lower deep / Still threatening to devour me opens wide" (4.75–77), but always hell remains external to the mind that experiences it, revealing the monism of all of Milton's cosmos. It does not consist of matter empty of spirit, but of matter that God's spirit has emptied of everything but his own will to justice.

Milton's cosmology is thus at once metaphoric and material, and, indeed, it is his radical monism that allows these two modes to reinforce rather than contradict one another. Monism turns metaphor into metonymy, as the similarities sensed turn out to be not products of active

---

[39] Some have seen chaos as an almost autonomous source of evil; see, for example, Regina Schwartz, esp. p. 35. But also see John P. Rumrich, *Milton Unbound,* esp. pp. 140–46.

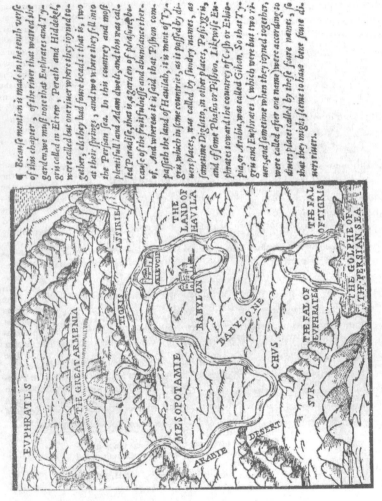

¶ Becau∫e mention is made in the tenth ver∫e of this chapter, of the riuer that watred the garden, we mu∫t note that Euphrates and Tygris called in Ebrew, Perath and Hiddekel, were called but one riuer where they ioyned together, els they had fowre heads: that is, two at their springs, and two where they fel into the Per∫ian ∫ea. In this countrey and mo∫t plentifull land Adam dwelt, and this was called Paradi∫e, that is, a garden of plea∫ure, becau∫e of the fruitfulne∫∫e and abundance thereof. And whereas it is ∫aid that Pi∫hon compa∫∫eth the land of Hauilah, it is ment of Tygris, which in ∫ome countries, as is pa∫∫ed by diuers places, was called by ∫undry names, as ∫ometime Diglato, in other places, Pa∫itygris, and of ∫ome Pha∫is or Pi∫hon. Likewi∫e Euphrates toward the countrey of Cu∫h or Ethiopia, or Arabia, was called Gihon. So that Tygris and Euphrates (which were but two riuers, and ∫ometime when they ioyned together, were called after one name) were according to diuers places called by the∫e fowre names, ∫o that they might ∫eeme to haue bene fowre diuers riuers.

Fig. 5. Map of Eden and its description from the "Geneva Bible," first published in 1560, here from the London edition of 1602.

minds searching for analogies between unlike things but evidence of a shared, substantial reality in their common origin in God. The anonymous letter in *Gentleman's Magazine* in 1739 accusing Milton of "corrupting our Notions of spiritual things, and sensualizing our Ideas of heaven," an early example of the unsettling recognition of Milton's monist materialism, at once completely misses and fully gets the point. For the letter writer this can only produce "ill Effects on Religion in General,"[40] but for Milton such "corrupting" and "sensualizing" were merely the poetic acknowledgment of a world in which God, "Author and end of all things" (7.591), was fully active and alive.

"To Model Heaven and Calculate the Stars"

Copernicus' *De Revolutionibus* was published in 1543, and over the next hundred years scientists like Galileo, Kepler, and Brahe confirmed and extended his insights. Nonetheless the older, Ptolemaic view of the universe with the earth at its center continued to be accepted by many in Milton's time, even among the well educated. Seven "planets"—Mercury, Mars, Venus, Jupiter, Saturn, the moon, and the sun—and beyond them the "fixed" stars (*PL* 10.651–64), circled around the earth in transparent spheres moved by a primum mobile, "the "utmost orb / Of this frail world" (2.1029–30), which imparted movement to everything except the motionless earth (see Fig. 6). "New philosophy," as Donne called it in "The First Anniversary" (1611), did, however, call all of this "in doubt." The observations of the astronomers, especially Galileo, "the Tuscan artist" with his "optic glass" (*PL* 1.288), exposed the failings of almost all of the central assumptions of the geocentric Ptolemaic system, most fundamentally by locating the sun at the still point of our solar system and recognizing it as potentially only one of many in the immeasurable heavens.

Milton's poem is strikingly agnostic about the nature of the heavens (not, however, about the nature of Heaven). In Book 8, Adam asks Raphael why nature imposes upon the stars and planets "Such restless revolution day by day / Repeated, while the sedentary earth, / That better might with far less compass move, / . . . attains / Her end without least motion" (8.31–35). He assumes the Ptolemaic system, but recognizes an alternative that is more economical. Raphael does not settle the matter, though he counters Adam's empirical geocentricism by hypothetically asking "What if the sun / Be center to the world?" (8.122–23). Indeed, even as Raphael authorizes Adam's question, he refuses a definitive answer and denies that an answer could have any real importance: "whether heaven move or earth, /

---

[40] Quoted in Shawcross (ed.), *Milton 1732–1801*, p. 101.

Schema prædictæ diuisionis.

Fig. 6. View of the "Ptolemaic" universe published in 1524 in Peter Apian's *Cosmographia;* this taken from the edition of 1584. It shows the familiar understanding of the "seven planets"—the moon, Mercury, Venus, the sun, Mars, Jupiter, and Saturn—and beyond them the "fixed stars" revolving around the earth.

Imports not" (8.66–71). God, according to Raphael, has, however, left the "fabric of the heavens" to the "disputes" of men, "perhaps to move / His laughter at their quaint opinions wide / Hereafter, when they come to model heaven / And calculate the stars" (8.76–80).

Milton is no more decisive. He describes the sun "fallen / Beneath the Azores"—perhaps merely a familiar metaphor, but he then literalizes it, wondering if the sun "hath thither rolled" or "this less voluble earth" (4.593–94). In the account of the change of seasons that comes about as a result of the fall, Milton inscribes the same uncertainty. Before the fall the sun is always exactly aligned with earth's equator, the "ecliptic" (3.740) plane of the sun's course parallels the equatorial plane, so the world, except at the poles, experiences "spring / Perpetual" (10.678–79). With the fall comes the seasonal variation that brings "pinching cold and scorching heat" (10.691), but this demands the disarticulation of the ecliptic and equatorial planes. Milton provides two tentative accounts of how this might happen, each corresponding to one of the dominant hypotheses about the universe. "Some say [God] bid his angels turn askance / The poles of earth twice ten degrees and more / From the sun's axle" (10.668–70). The tilt of the earth on its axis $23^1/2$ degrees from perpendicular is indeed what produces the variation of the seasons. But in case the heavens correspond to the Ptolemaic system, Milton provides an alternative explanation: "some say the sun / Was bid turn reins from the equinoctial road / . . . to bring in change / Of seasons to each clime" (10.672–78).

Perhaps this merely shows Milton's own indecision about the structure of the universe or an unwillingness to commit to a view that could possibly be experimentally invalidated. But the precision with which he imagines the alternatives suggests that more is at stake than either doubt or diffidence. The fact that Galileo is the only contemporary of Milton identified by name (5.262 and see also 1.288–91; 3.588–90) indicates Milton's interest in the scientific revolution.[41] He is aware of newly discovered phenomena like the phases of Venus (7.366), and certainly aware of speculation that, if the earth is not at the center of the universe—indeed merely "a spot, a grain, / An atom" (8.17–18) in the vastness of the universe—there well may be other inhabited worlds. Even Raphael will allow the thought that if the "spots" on the moon are actually clouds, then "clouds may rain, and rain produce / Fruits in her softened soil, for some to eat / Allotted there" (8.145–48).

---

[41] In *Areopagitica,* Milton says he met "the famous Galileo . . . a prisoner to the Inquisition for thinking in astronomy otherwise than the Franciscan and Dominican authorities thought" (*Works* 4, 330). For opposed readings of the role of Galileo in the poem, see Flannagan; and Walker, "Milton and Galileo." See also Boesky.

For Raphael this is mere, if (just barely) permitted, speculation. It is indeed allowed to wonder "What if . . . " (8.122, 140), although "[H]eaven is . . . too high / To *know* what passes there" (8.172–73; emphasis mine). Yet for Milton the work of the astronomers scanning the heavens does seem to push the boundaries of permissible curiosity. Adam and Eve are told to "think only what concerns thee and thy being; / Dream not of other worlds, what creatures there / Live" (8.174–76). They are, however, urged not think of "things remote / From use" (8.191–92), not because such thought is forbidden but because it "renders us in things that most concern / Unpracticed, unprepared, and still to seek" (8.196–97). Astronomy is not in itself an "unlawful or unprofitable" inquiry, as Milton admits in *Christian Doctrine*. But the proof of its usefulness is revealing: "as appears from the journey of the wise men and still more from the star itself, divinely appointed to announce the birth of Christ" (*Works* 17, 151). The evidence of its usefulness, taken, of course, not from the work of the contemporary scientists who were remapping the heavens but from the bible, clearly shows that Milton thinks the study of the heavens is not important as an end in itself. Astronomy is lawful and profitable, one of those things that "most concern," only when its study, as is literally the case in Milton's example, leads to God.

"Desire of Knowledge"

Yet knowledge can hardly be an unproblematic concept in a poem where "death . . . and all our woe" (1.3) are the consequences of eating fruit from the Tree of Knowledge. The particular form of Satan's assault on Adam and Eve is decided after overhearing them discussing their situation in Eden: "One fatal tree there stands, of Knowledge called, / Forbidden them to taste. Knowledge forbidden? / Suspicious, reasonless. Why should their Lord envy them that?" (4.514–17). It is not an unreasonable question. Why should God "envy them that"? "Can it be a sin to know" (4.517)? Could Satan be right when he says to Eve that the interdiction was "but to keep ye low and ignorant" (9.704)?

One might escape the disturbing implications of these questions by insisting that God *doesn't* envy them knowledge. Satan is guilty of a category error produced by his own envious mind. The fruit of the Tree of Knowledge does not contain knowledge in the same way that fruit contains vitamins and minerals. Raphael warns them about "the tree / Which tasted works knowledge of good and evil" (7.542–43), but it is clear that the tree "works" that knowledge not by imparting something present in the interdicted fruit but through the change in the relation to God that results from violating the interdiction. It is the tasting that matters, not the fruit. If, after the fall, Adam and Eve "know both good and evil" (11.85), this means only, as Adam sadly confesses, that they have learned of "good lost and evil got" (9.1072).

Certainly Satan misunderstands and misrepresents the interdiction. He assumes that the prohibition is "invented with design / To keep them low whom knowledge might exalt / Equal with gods" (4.524–26). He believes that there is something inherent in the apple that is being denied Adam and Eve because, if tasted, it would make them like the "gods." And his temptation of Eve follows those assumptions exactly. "Constrained" (9.164) in the serpent, Satan uses his ability to talk and reason to demonstrate to Eve that some actual benefit inheres in the apple: "O sacred, wise, and wisdom-giving plant, / Mother of science, now I feel thy power / Within me clear not only to discern / Things in their causes but to trace the ways / Of highest agents, deemed however wise" (9.679–83); and then arguing that the only reason that God might have to deny her that benefit is that "in the day / Ye eat thereof . . . ye shall be as gods" (9.705–8).

Moral critics, like Dennis Burden or Michael Lieb, are of course right in insisting that Satan's argument is nonsense. Both see correctly that the tree functions only as an arbitrary "sign of . . . obedience" (4.428) rather than as a potential source of knowledge.[42] But if intellectually this is clear, imaginatively it is more confusing. If no knowledge is at stake in its fruit, why is the interdicted tree not called the Tree of Obedience or the Tree of Trial? Indeed at one point it is called "the tree / Of prohibition" (9.644–45), but in the poem it is again and again "the Tree of Knowledge" and once, more explicitly, "the tree / Of interdicted knowledge" (5.51–52). Milton is well aware that the name of the tree seems at best to mislead and at worst actually to tempt, as Eve reveals addressing it immediately before she eats: "thy praise he also who forbids thy use / Conceals not from us, naming thee the Tree / Of Knowledge" (9.750–52).

As certain as is the fact that there is no "knowledge" in the tree, then, is the fact that the poem (like the bible; see Genesis 3:6: "And when the woman saw that the tree . . . was a tree to be desired to make one wise") sometimes makes it seem as if there is. There is a constant confusion of moral and epistemological issues, evident not least in Satan's phrasing for his plan to corrupt Adam and Eve: "I will excite their minds / With more desire to know" (4.522–23). How can this be bad, especially in a poem almost half of which is devoted to explicit scenes of education? Yet clearly in the poem the "desire to know" often does seem dangerous, something not to be excited but to be controlled—and not just from Satan's perverse perspective on the prohibition. The exact phrase appears later when Adam is described as "Led on, yet sinless, with *desire to know*" (7.61, emphasis mine).

---

[42] Burden, p. 103; Lieb, *The Poetics of the Holy*, pp. 89–99.

The need to specify that he is "yet sinless" suggests the anxiety surrounding knowledge, and Raphael is explicit that knowledge must be limited: "knowledge is as food, and needs no less / Her temperance over appetite; to know / In measure what the mind may well contain" (7.126–28). Why should there be limits to knowledge? What is it that the mind may *well* contain—and what not?

Of course Satan's plan to "excite their minds with more desire to know" is but one half of his strategy; the other is to get Adam and Eve "to reject / Envious commands, invented with design / To keep them low" (4.523–25). His goal is not really to excite the "desire to know" but to lead them, so excited, to "reject" God's sole command (Satan's pluralizing of what is singular—see 9.652–53—a characteristic strategy of his temptation). But that he knows the way to achieve the latter is through the former suggests how deeply the confusion between moral and cognitive understandings of knowledge is written into the logic of *Paradise Lost*. Adam and Eve are not to eat of the Tree of Knowledge, but they are explicitly given knowledge, so they cannot "pretend / Surprisal, unadmonished, unforewarned" (5.244–45) if (or rather, when) they do eat.

Though Satan wonders if Adam and Eve only "stand / By Ignorance" (4.518–19), it is clear that the poem is determined to show the opposite. For four books Raphael patiently instructs Adam, both advising "him of his happy state" (5.234) and warning "him to beware" (5.237). What the angelic narration offers Adam and Eve is explicitly "knowledge," and knowledge unavailable immediately to human intelligence (unlike the intuitive knowledge that allows Adam to name the animals, and Eve, the plants). Adam understands the angel as a "Divine interpreter, by favor sent / Down from the empyrean to forewarn / Us timely of what might else have been our loss, / Unknown, which human knowledge could not reach" (7.72–75). This is, one might say, "bidden" rather than forbidden knowledge; God bids Raphael to "Converse with Adam" and "tell him withal / His danger, and from whom" (5.230–39) that he and Eve might recognize and resist the temptation.

Some critics have seen this only as the cynical maneuvering of a self-protective God,[43] but it is difficult to see what God might do that would better render man sufficient to stand and yet keep him "free to fall." What may, however, be more troubling is that Raphael must know his efforts will fail. In Book 3, lines 213–15, we are told that all the "heavenly powers," not just Christ, know of "man's mortal crime," raising unsettling questions

---

[43] See, for example, Thomas Greene's claim that "When it is scrutinized, God's generosity in dispatching Raphael turns out to be not at all true magnanimity but a petty legalistic self-righteousness," p. 409.

about Raphael's seeming disingenuousness in saying "I in thy persevering shall rejoice, / And all the blessed" (8.639–40). But this is no more than the inevitable rhetorical awkwardness accompanying foreknowledge that is not predetermining, i.e., the celestial awareness of a future that is freely made by those unknowing. Raphael's embassy, if in some ways like other examples of unnecessary and unsuccessful angelic effort in the poem that are mainly designed, as the angel says, "to inure / Our prompt obedience" (8.239–40), is at least potentially efficacious and clearly intended primarily for Adam and Eve's benefit: "for thy good / This is dispensed" (5.570–71).

Intended for his "good," the narration excites Adam "with more desire to know," and he presses the angel for more information: "But since thou hast vouchsafed / Gently for our instruction to impart / Things above earthly thought which yet concerned / Our knowing, as to highest wisdom seemed, / Deign to descend now lower and relate / What may no less per haps avail us known" (7.80–85). The angel does not deny the request, and admits that "such commission from above / I have received to answer thy desire / Of knowledge within bounds" (7.118–20).

Oddly, however, there is little marking of the permissible boundaries of human knowledge. Adam is told only not to "let thine own inventions hope / Things not revealed which the invisible king, / Only omniscient, hath suppressed in night, / To none communicable in earth or Heaven" (7.121–24), a strangely obscurantist prohibition that does not make it at all clear what is being disallowed. If the limit is only "things not revealed," then seemingly nothing in the created world is out of bounds. Even "heaven," as Raphael says, "is as the book of God before thee set," though the book is presented and opened to allow us to "read" God's "wondrous works" rather than to have them "scanned by them who ought / Rather admire" (8.66–75). Adam had earlier begun his questioning of Raphael by suggesting that his curiosity was motivated not by any desire to pry into God's "secrets" but by the wish to glorify God, insisting on the ability "the more / To magnify his works, the more we know" (7.95–97). The syntax here is revealingly and reassuringly recursive: the more we know the more able we are to magnify God's works, but also the more we magnify his works the more we know. Love and knowledge are at least imaginable as mutually constituting.

"Sense Variously Drawn Out"

Criticism of *Paradise Lost* has tended to concentrate more upon the political and theological issues it engages rather than directly focusing on its stylistic achievement. The "great argument" of the poem has more exercised critics rather than the formal resources by which it is advanced, although

Milton himself was well aware of his need for a style "answerable" (9.20) to his extraordinary ambitions. Nonetheless, no reader is unaware of the poem's grandeur of expression. Milton's "natural port is gigantick loftiness,"[44] Dr. Johnson claimed, and perhaps the seeming inevitability of the style for both the subject of the poem and the temperament of the poet is what accounts for its relative critical neglect.

It is easy to point to characteristic aspects of what has been called the "grand style."[45] The diction is often elevated, abstract, and surprising. Words are sometimes used in unusual senses, shifting grammatical functions—as in "the vast abrupt" (2.409) where an adjective becomes a noun—or exploiting unfamiliar etymological meanings buried in the word, like "reluctant" (used to describe Satan turned to a "monstrous serpent" [10.514–15]), which not only means "unwilling," as in modern usage, but also retains its Latin sense of "struggling"; or in sonorous blends of complex Latinate and simple Saxon words: hell described as a "dark opprobrious den" (2.58) or the "scential sap" (9.837) of the interdicted tree. The syntax is similarly stylized and unconventional, often treating English as if it were an inflected language like Latin, allowing Milton a freedom of word order that permits remarkable expressive effects even as it frustrates syntactic norms—"Him the almighty power / Hurled headlong flaming from the ethereal sky / With hideous ruin and combustion down / To bottomless perdition" (1.44–47)— or that allows syntactic ambiguities, impossible in conventional English, that condense complex ideas like the relationship of God the Father and the Son into memorable language: "him who disobeys / Me disobeys" (5.611–12).

In these ways, Milton's language achieves an extraordinary density of meaning, but at the cost of familiarity and ease of comprehension. Words are often obscure or made to seem so, and the syntax often refuses conventional word order (e.g., "But that thou shouldst my firmness therefore doubt / To God or thee because we have a foe / May tempt it I expected not to hear," 9.279–81). Dr. Johnson recognized the distortions as the very essence of Milton's style: "there prevails a uniform peculiarity of Diction, a mode and cast of expression which bears little resemblance to that of any former writer; and which is so far removed from common use, that an unlearned reader, when he first opens the book, finds himself surprised by a new language." But if Johnson finds his style founded on "a perverse and pedantick principle," he concludes that "such is the power of his poetry,

---

[44] Johnson, in *Milton 1732–1801*, p. 301.

[45] The term is Matthew Arnold's from his essay "A French Critic on Milton" (1877); but see Ricks, *Milton's Grand Style*.

that his call is obeyed without resistance, the reader finds himself in captivity to a higher and nobler mind, and criticism sinks in admiration."[46]

Yet it is important also to note the moving simplicity that Milton can attain. In the invocation to light, he poignantly, but without self-pity, calculates what has been lost with his blindness: "Thus with the year / Seasons return, but not to me returns / Day, or the sweet approach of ev'n or morn, / Or sight of vernal bloom or summer's rose, / Or flocks, or herds, or human face divine" (3.40–44). There is little here of the "gigantick loftiness" Dr. Johnson remarks; the syntax for the most part is straightforward, the diction simple, the frame of reference comfortingly domestic. The calculus begins with light and moves through time ("Day," dusk, dawn; spring flowers, "summer's rose") and up the scale of nature from the vegetative to the animal ("flocks," "herds," "human face divine"). The generalizing cliché "vernal bloom" gets reanimated through its position next to the specific and individual "summer's rose." Though obviously carefully patterned, the lines are neither artificial nor grandiose; the language neither abstract nor remote. The simplicity permits an expression of emotion that is recognizable and affecting, as it does again, for example, when Adam comforts Eve after her dream: "So cheered he his fair spouse, and she was cheered, / But silently a gentle tear let fall / From either eye and wiped them with her hair" (5.129–31). Clearly Milton's style is more flexible and various than is often admitted, and eloquent in whatever mode is demanded of it.

The same might be said of his prosody. Milton writes in blank verse, a ten-syllable line (there are very few eleven-syllable lines ending with an extra unstressed measure, a so-called "feminine ending"), mainly unrhymed, and written with a recognizable but by no means regular iambic pattern. The conventional iambic rhythm, with every other syllable stressed, can be heard in lines like "Of that forbidden tree, whose mortal taste" (1.2). But there are so many variations of the pattern—adding, omitting, or shifting stresses—that there is no firmly established norm against which variation is to be measured. Of the first twelve lines of the poem, line 2, the one quoted just above, is the only one that is unquestionably "regular."

Of course readers may hear lines differently. Tempo and stress are not mandated, and sensitive readers may disagree about how they may be heard in any individual line. Also, we know too little about 17th-century pronunciations in general, and Milton's in particular, for assertions to be other than circular about how they might affect versification. What is clear is that Milton's metrical practice allows for a far more various set of rhythmical possibility than a strict understanding of blank verse might suggest. His

[46] Johnson, in *Milton 1732–1801*, pp. 308–9.

versification is based less on metrical regularity than upon a fluid arrange-
ment of stresses within an understood temporal norm capable of various ex-
pressive effects. Raphael's warning to Adam provides a dramatic example: "I
in thy persevering shall rejoice, / And all the blessed. Stand fast; to stand or
fall / Free in thine own arbitrament it lies" (8.639–41). In the second line
"stand fast" is a spondee bracketed by two iambic feet on either side, the
unusual stress emphasizing the (literally) central imperative of the line and
the poem. The characteristic enjambment also is used expressively, not
merely to free the sense from metrical restraint, but sometimes almost
mimetically. The extension of sense across the line break is given verbal em-
phasis (or is it that the thought gets visual reinforcement?) as in the de-
scription of "airy flight / Upborne with indefatigable wings / *Over* the vast
abrupt" (2.407–9; emphasis mine), or, alternatively, "And light from dark-
ness by the hemisphere / *Divided*" (7.250–51; emphasis mine).

The freedom of Milton's poetics finds its most notorious expression in
his ostentatious rejection of rhyme for his epic. His prefatory note on the
verse immediately announces "the measure is English heroic verse without
rhyme" (p. 4 below). Critics have been quick to take Milton at his word, es-
pecially as Milton himself sharply politicized his prosody, giving it more
than mere formal force: "This neglect then of rhyme so little is to be taken
for a defect, though it may seem so perhaps to vulgar readers, than it rather
is to be esteemed an example set, the first in English, of ancient liberty re-
covered to heroic poem from the troublesome and modern bondage of
rhyming." Still, it is worth observing two things: first, that Milton's eluci-
dation of his poetic principles was decidedly an afterthought. The prefatory
note on the verse makes a belated appearance, not included until 1668 in
the fourth issue of the poem, and then only after the publisher, Samuel
Simmons, was prompted to solicit "a reason . . . why the Poem Rimes not,"
which practice, he said, playfully echoing 6.624, has "stumbled many"
readers (*PL*, 1668, sig., A2ᵛ; p. 2 below). And second, although Samuel
Butler would reinforce Milton's own understanding of the declared abjura-
tion of rhyme with the pointed joke that the poet "is noncomformable in
point of rhyme,"[47] the fact is, as a number of scholars have observed, that
the poem is not "without rhyme."

Not infrequently rhyme erupts out of Milton's blank verse; one scholar
has identified over two hundred lines of the poem that contain rhymes.[48]
When Eve reports her dream and her mistaking of Satan's voice for Adam's,

[47] *The Transproser Rehears'd* (Oxford, 1673), line 1020; the identification of Samuel Butler as
the author is made by Nicholas von Maltzahn in his "Samuel Butler's Milton," *SP* 92 (1995):
492–95.

[48] See Diekhoff, p. 539.

she creates a rhyme with his word: hearing that "nature's desire" is "attracted by thy beauty still to *gaze*," Eve says that she followed the voice until "alone I passed through *ways* / that brought me on a sudden to the Tree" (5.45–51; emphasis mine). When Eve later suggests to Adam that they might in the name of efficiency divide their labor, she and the narrator collaborate in a couplet that looks to the very outcome her proposal makes possible: "'the hour of supper comes unearned.'/ To whom mild answer Adam thus returned" (9.225–26). Satan will later seduce Eve in rhyme: "But all that fair and good in thy divine / Semblance, and in thy beauties heavenly ray / United I beheld; no fair to thine / Equivalent or second" (9.606–9). Satan suggests that what is "divine" should be "thine," and his pairing betrays his own ambitions. And having transgressed, Eve on her own falls into rhyme, hoping to play upon Adam's sympathies: "This happy trial of thy love, which else / So eminently never had been known. / Were it I thought death menaced would ensue / This my attempt, I would sustain alone / The worst and not persuade thee" (9.975–79), the rhyme of "known" and "alone" brilliantly condensing the effects of the fall.

But rhyme is not merely identified with transgression. For example, God's elevation of the Son in Book 6 also generates a rhyme, acknowledging Christ "to be heir and to be king / By sacred unction, thy deservèd right," and ordering him to "Go then, thou mightiest in thy Father's might" (6.709–11). Christ's "right" merits God's "might," and God's "might" is justified by Christ's "right." The familiar rhyme here reinforces an orthodox theology, and is oddly similar to the absolutist poetics Milton rejects in his prefatory paragraph on "The Verse."

The rhyme of Heaven, like the rhymes of the fall, might equally be seen as correlative of a hierarchical imagination. The poem has consistently recognized hierarchy as appropriate, even necessary, in Heaven, but it has no less consistently rejected it as an appropriate form of human social imagining, evidence of a tyranny that must be resisted. Even the appearances of rhyme less obviously meaningful than those discussed become, then, evidence of a susceptibility to what Ben Jonson called "tyrant rhyme,"[49] just as the poem's dominant blank verse declares its resistance to the forms of "modern bondage." Milton's robust blank verse expresses his unwavering commitment to the principles of "ancient liberty" here "recovered to heroic poem" (p. 4 below), not as a dispirited admission that stylistic freedom is the only kind of freedom possible in Restoration England but as a defiant assertion that poetry is politics by other means.

[49] Jonson, "A Fit of Rhyme Against Rhyme," l. 46.

"Proud Imaginations Thus Displayed"

Paradise Lost was first published in 1667 by Samuel Simmons, although apparently it had been finished at least two years earlier. Thomas Ellwood, a young Quaker friend of Milton, reports that in August 1665 he had visited the aging poet and, "After some common Discourses had passed between us, he called for a manuscript of his; which being brought he delivered to me, bidding me take it home with me and read at my Leisure."[50] Events, however, conspired to delay publication. The second Dutch war of 1665–1667 severely restricted the supply of paper, in addition to raising the general level of fear and confusion in a London in which plague in 1665 had claimed over 50,000 lives, about one-fifth of the population, and the Great Fire in September of 1666 had destroyed two-thirds of the city, including the center of the book trade.

But by early 1667 it was possible again to think about publishing the poem. Indeed in one sense the terrible events may even have helped it reach print by sufficiently occupying the authorities that a poem by the notorious Milton, which might have been expected to provoke governmental opposition, would raise only minor concerns and be licensed.[51] Thomas Tomkins, the licenser and chaplain to the Archbishop of Canterbury, seems to have objected to six lines in particular—the account of the eclipse that, "with fear of change, / Perplexes monarchs" (1.594–99). The report of Tomkins' sensitivity belatedly comes from John Toland, scornfully writing in 1698 that "we had like to be eternally depriv'd of this Treasure by the Ignorance or Malice of the Licenser, who, among other frivolous Exceptions would need suppress the whole Poem for imaginary Treason" in these lines.[52] Tomkins' sensitivity to the political interpretation of astronomical phenomena in truth would have been unsurprising in the anxious environment of the moment, but in the event he did license the poem, no doubt because its biblical subject and grand style clearly differentiated it from the provocative sectarian tracts that were the immediate concern of official censorship.

And in a different way the then-recent history also may have contributed to the particular circumstances of its publication. The destruction wreaked by the fire upon the publishers located around St. Paul's seems to

---

[50] Ellwood, *The History of the Life of Thomas Ellwood, Written by his own Hand* (London, 1714), p. 199.

[51] von Maltzahn argues that "in 1667 with the government in retreat and licensers under pressure, the focus in controlling the press needed narrowing to those who raised more present fears and encouraged sedition" (p. 486).

[52] Toland, "The Life of John Milton" (1698), in Darbishire (ed.), *The Early Lives of Milton*, p. 180. The imprimatur itself survives on the otherwise blank verso of the first leaf of the manuscript of Book 1 at the Pierpont Morgan Library in New York.

have led Milton to Samuel Simmons, a relatively obscure stationer, whose shop in Aldergate Street had escaped the devastation. Perhaps it was its proximity to Milton's home in Artillery Walk that suggested Simmons in particular, especially if Jacob Tonson's assertion that Milton "did not trust wholly to the printer" is true; or perhaps it was family loyalty, as Simmons' father had printed *The Tenure of Kings and Magistrates* in 1649 as well as several other tracts by Milton.[53] Or maybe Simmons was the only stationer willing to take the risk of publishing a long work by the notorious poet.

For whatever reason, it was Simmons, primarily a printer rather than a publisher, who arranged with Milton to publish the poem. The surviving contract is the earliest between a writer and publisher that has come to light, and Simmons, at least to later generations, has been often criticized for taking advantage of the blind and disgraced Milton with an agreement that paid the poet £5 for the copy and promised an additional £5 when 1,300 copies (of an edition limited to 1,500) were sold, and also a further £5 for each of a second and third edition (also to be paid when 1,300 copies were sold). All additional "benefit proffitt & advantage" from the poem were ceded to the publisher.[54] Thomas Newton, for example, sniffed, in his "Life of Milton," prefaced to his edition of the poem in 1749, "How much more do others get by the work of great authors, than the authors themselves do."[55]

Nonetheless, if these sums seem paltry today, in the context of literary publication at the time they are probably reasonable. Dryden, for example, is reported to have received £20 from Jacob Tonson for *Troilus and Cressida*,[56] the exact amount Milton eventually received for *Paradise Lost*. It is possible that Milton additionally received some copies for his own use—to sell or to give as presentation copies. Indeed, in some cases this was the only compensation an author would receive and it was not an uncommon supplement to an author's payment. But the suggestion, recently made, that Milton was given the two hundred copies remaining from the print runs of the first three editions after the first 1,300 copies of each were sold seems

---

[53] Tonson's remarks are in a letter that was preserved with the manuscript of Book 1; see Darbishire (ed.), *The Manuscript of Milton's "Paradise Lost," Book 1*, p. xii; on the Simmons family, see McKenzie.

[54] The contract is reproduced in French, vol. 4, pp. 429–31. For a full analysis of the contract in the context of the 17th-century book trade, see Peter Lindenbaum, "Milton's Contract," in *Cardoza Arts & Entertainment Law Journal* 10 (1992): 439–54, reprinted in *Construction of Authorship: Textual Appropriations in Law and Literature*, ed. Martha Woodmansee and Peter Jaszi (Durham, NC, and London: Duke University Press, 1994), pp. 175–90.

[55] Newton (ed.), *Paradise Lost* (London, 1749), vol. 1, xxxvii.

[56] *Critical and Miscellaneous Prose Work of John Dryden*, ed. Edmond Malone (London, 1800), vol. 1, pp. 522–23.

unlikely.[57] It is far too many copies either for Simmons to part with or for Milton profitably to use. If Milton had for his own use anything like that number, we would expect a significant number of presentation copies to survive, but this is not the case. The specification of 1,300 copies merely marks the point at which Simmons was responsible to make payment; Milton would not have to wait until the entire impression had sold out to get his money.

The contract was signed on April 27, 1667, and Simmons entered the poem in the Stationers' register on August 20. Probably by early October *Paradise Lost* was available for sale. Simmons had arranged with various booksellers to carry the poem as much to spread the financial risk as to broaden the distribution. Peter Parker, with a shop "under *Creed* Church neer *Aldgate*," Robert Boulter "at the *Turks Head* in *Bishopgate-Street*," and Matthias Walker, "Under St. *Dunstons* Church in *Fleet-Street*," are all named on the title pages of the earliest impressions (see Fig. 7). Later impressions add two more booksellers—S. Thompson and H. Mortlack—and by 1669 T. Helder, "at the Angel in *Little Britain*," is the only bookseller listed. Interestingly, the earliest printings of the title page do not mention Simmons' name at all, perhaps his acknowledgment that a stationer, whom Tonson called "a strict dissenter" and who had been at various times charged with printing "seditious" books,"[58] might discourage sales of a poem, already in danger of seeming too-readily identified with unpopular causes. But by 1668, Simmons' name does appear on the newly printed title page.

The book was simply, if capably, printed on paper probably made in France, and with some sheets, in a nice irony, showing the orb and cross watermark that usually identifies the paper maker as a Catholic. It is a neat quarto, appearing first with no prefatory matter at all. It consists of forty-three gatherings (signatures A-Tt⁴–Vv²), each printed on the front and back of a single sheet of paper, folded twice and cut to produce the eight pages of the individual signatures. There is a boxed running head on each page of text, reading "*Paradise lost*." and the book number (e.g., "Book III.") printed in roman. The poem is printed in a single column, usually of thirty-two lines. The outer edge of the page has a double rule enclosing numbers for every tenth line, seemingly the first English poem to be numbered. The left-hand margin of the text is set close against the left rule, except where the beginning of a verse paragraph is indented. It is a clean and attractive page layout, but decidedly understated. An ornamental border

---

[57] See Dobranski, p. 35, which in other regards is extremely useful.

[58] Darbishire (ed.), *The Manuscript of Milton's "Paradise Lost,"* p. xi; *CSPD: Charles II*, 1664, p. 148.

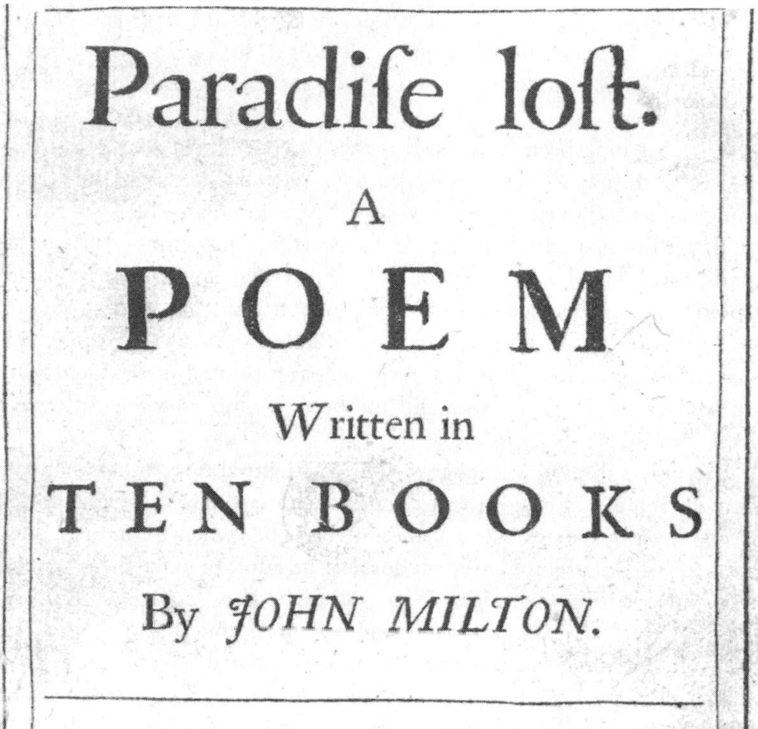

Paradise loſt.

A
POEM

Written in

TEN BOOKS

By *JOHN MILTON*.

Licenſed and Entred according
to Order.

L O N D O N

Printed, and are to be ſold by *Peter Parker*
under *Creed* Church neer *Aldgate*; And by
Robert Boulter at the *Turks Head* in *Biſhopſgate-ſtreet*;
And *Matthias Walker*, under St. *Dunſtons* Church
in *Fleet-ſtreet*, 1667.

Fig. 7. Title page of *Paradise Lost*, the first, ten-book version of 1667.

below the lower rule of the top box does run across the first page of each
book, and a decorated initial capital is used for its first word; otherwise the
type throughout is a common, modified Garamond, with many pieces
obviously worn.

What has long been recognized is that the poem sold slowly and that
different title pages were issued both to reflect changing bookselling
arrangements and to encourage new sales. Seven different title pages exist of
the first edition of the poem. Two, however, are just minor variants of
others, and probably not independently set, so there are actually five sepa-
rate printings of the page—two in 1667, one in 1668, and two in 1669.[59]
But the different title pages do not mark different *editions* of the poem.
That is, the poem itself was not reset; the pages printed in the late spring
and summer of 1667 are what fill the book behind whatever title page
greets the reader.

The only substantive change within this first edition, other than the
normal variation through press corrections unsystematically distributed
across its various states, came sometime in 1668, when Simmons added
fourteen pages of preliminaries, no doubt in an effort to make the poem less
coldly intimidating to readers. In an address to the "Courteous Reader,"
Simmons admits that originally "There was no Argument, . . . but for the
satisfaction of many that have desired it, it is procured." The arguments to
each book were then printed sequentially. Simmons also added Milton's
paragraph on "The Verse," and a short errata sheet was included. In 1669,
when yet again a new title page was printed, the poem was presented in this
form, though Simmons reprinted signatures Z and Vv, probably because
there were inadequate remaining quantities of these gatherings to make up
complete copies of the poem. Copies of this final state were soon available,
and on April 26, 1669, Simmons paid Milton the £5 he was owed when
1,300 copies of this first edition had been sold.[60]

It may have been the slowness with which the poem sold out its first edi-
tion that made Simmons wait to publish a second, or perhaps it was that
Milton himself delayed it, desirous of making changes. In any case, it was
not until 1674 that a second edition appeared. On July 6, 1674, the Term
Catalogues of the Stationers' Company record: "*Paradise* Lost. A Poem, in
Twelve Books; Revised and Augmented by the Author, **John Milton**, Price
3s." The title page is similarly worded, noting that the poem is "The Sec-
ond Edition" and that it was "Printed by *S. Simmons* next door to the
Golden Lion in *Aldersgate-street*, 1674" (see Fig. 8). The ten books of the
original have been expanded to twelve by dividing the original Book 7 into

---

[59] Moyles, pp. 4–12.

[60] The receipt survives in the Christ College, Cambridge Library, catalogued as MS 8.

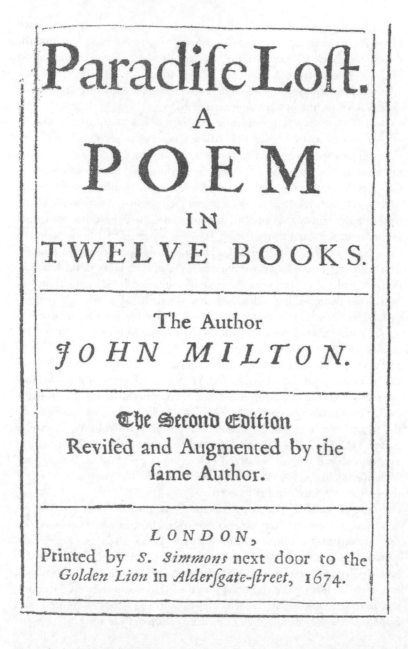

Paradiſe Loſt.

A POEM

IN TWELVE BOOKS.

The Author
JOHN MILTON.

𝕿𝖍𝖊 𝕾𝖊𝖈𝖔𝖓𝖉 𝕰𝖉𝖎𝖙𝖎𝖔𝖓
Reviſed and Augmented by the
ſame Author.

LONDON,
Printed by *S. Simmons* next door to the
Golden Lion in *Alderſgate-ſtreet,* 1674.

Fig. 8. Title page of the second edition of *Paradise Lost*, the twelve-book version of 1674.

Books 7 and 8, with Book 8 of the original now becoming Book 9. Four new lines of poetry appear at the beginning of the new Book 8. Similarly, the original Book 10 is divided into Books 11 and 12, with five lines added to the beginning of Book 12 to accomplish the transition. There are a few other local revisions, and the arguments, now printed before each book, were divided for the new arrangement of 1674.

The 1674 edition is an octavo (meaning that it is comprised of gatherings of sixteen pages formed by folding a sheet of paper three times, enabling eight pages to be printed on each side) rather than a quarto like the first edition. The sheets used for this new edition were, however, larger than the sheets used in 1667, so the finished book, while smaller, is not substantially so. Nonetheless, the pages seem cramped compared with those of the first edition. The type is smaller, and normally there are thirty-four lines (rather than the usual thirty-two of 1667) to a page. The edition lacks the rules, both horizontal and vertical, of the first, and omits the line numbers. The decorated initial letters for the first word of each book in the first edition are replaced in the second by undistinguished large capitals, and in general the edition is less welcoming than the first.

It is, however, better printed than 1667, probably from the fact that it is set seemingly from a corrected copy of the first edition rather than from manuscript (which simplifies the compositor's task). It also includes two prefatory poems (see pp. 1–4 below), one in Latin by Samuel Barrow (though signed only "*S. B.* M. D." and one in English by Andrew Marvell (signed "*A. M.*"), and a portrait of Milton, bound as a verso to face the title page. The portrait was engraved by William Dolle, and closely modeled on the frontispiece engraving by William Faithorne in Milton's *History of Britain* (1670). Dolle's portrait appeared first in the 1672 edition of *Artis Logicae*, and was slightly reworked before it was printed for *Paradise Lost*. The self-effacing presentation of the poem in 1667 has given way to something more confident and self-assertive.

Marvell's prefatory poem remarks the "slender book" in which Milton's "vast design" unfolds. The compact octavo published by Samuel Simmons first enabled Milton's final version of that vast design to reach his readers, however "fit" or "few." Sometime in the summer of 1674, Milton's *Paradise Lost* appeared in print essentially in the form the poet had come to imagine it. On the eighth of November Milton died. His poem, however, did not, and lives still, honing its readers' alertness to the need for honesty and courage in the face of the often dispiriting realities of the world.

BIBLIOGRAPHY

Editions (in chronological order):

Paradise Lost. London, 1667.

Paradise Lost. London, 1674.

Paradise Lost. London, 1688.

Paradise Lost, ed. P[atrick] H[ume]. London, 1695.

Paradise Lost, ed. Richard Bentley. London, 1732.

Paradise Lost, ed. Thomas Newton. London, 1749.

The Manuscript of Milton's "Paradise Lost," Book 1, ed. Helen Darbishire. Oxford: Clarendon Press, 1931.

The Works of John Milton, gen. ed. Frank Allen Patterson. New York: Columbia University Press, 1931–1938.

John Milton's Complete Poetical Works, Reproduced in Photographic Facsimile, ed. Harris F. Fletcher. 4 vols. Urbana: University of Illinois Press, 1943–1948.

The Poetical Works of John Milton, ed. Helen Darbishire. 2 vols. Oxford: Clarendon Press, 1952–1955.

Milton: Poems, ed. B. A. Wright. London: Dent, 1956.

John Milton: Complete Poems and Major Prose, ed. Merritt Y. Hughes. New York: Odyssey, 1957.

The Complete Poetry of John Milton, ed. John T. Shawcross. Garden City, NY: Anchor-Doubleday, 1971.

Paradise Lost and Paradise Regained, ed. Christopher Ricks. New York: New American Library, 1968.

Paradise Lost, ed. Alastair Fowler. London: Longmans, 1968, revised 1971; new edition 1998.

Paradise Lost, ed. Scott Elledge. New York: Norton, 1975.

John Milton, eds. Stephen Orgel and Jonathan Goldberg. Oxford: Oxford University Press, 1990.

Paradise Lost, ed. Roy Flannagan. New York: Macmillan, 1993.

Paradise Lost, ed. John Leonard. London: Penguin, 2000.

John Milton, *Paradise Lost*, ed. Merritt Y. Hughes, 1962; rpt. Indianapolis and Cambridge, MA: Hackett, 2003.

Paradise Lost, ed. Gordon Teskey. New York: Norton, 2005.

Biographies:

Brown, Cedric. *John Milton: A Literary Life*. London: St. Martin's Press, 1995.

Darbishire, Helen (ed.). *The Early Lives of Milton*. London: Constable, 1932.

Lewalski, Barbara. *The Life of John Milton: A Critical Biography*. Oxford: Blackwell, 2001.

Masson, David. *The Life of John Milton: Narrated in Connexion with the Political, Ecclesiastical, and Literary History of His Time*. 7 vols. London: Macmillan, 1859–1894.

Parker, William Riley. *Milton: A Biography*. ed. Gordon Campbell. 2 vols, revised version. Oxford: Oxford University Press, 1996.

Winstanley, William. *Lives of the Most Famous English Poets*. London, 1687.

Critical Works:

Achinstein, Sharon. *Milton and the Revolutionary Reader*. Princeton: Princeton University Press, 1994.

Armitage, David, Armand Himy, and Quentin Skinner (eds). *Milton and Republicanism*. Cambridge: Cambridge University Press, 1995.

Barker, Arthur. *Milton and the Puritan Dilemma, 1641–1660*. Toronto: University of Toronto Press, 1942.

Bennett, Joan. *Reviving Liberty: Radical Christian Humanism in Milton's Great Poems*. Cambridge, MA: Harvard University Press, 1989.

Blessington, Francis C. *"Paradise Lost" and the Classical Epic*. London: Routledge & Kegan Paul, 1979.

Boesky, Amy. "Milton, Galileo, and Sunspots: Optics and Certainty in *Paradise Lost*." *Milton Studies* 34 (1997): 23–44.

Broadbent, John. *Some Graver Subject: An Essay on "Paradise Lost."* London: Chatto & Windus, 1960.

Burden, Dennis H. *The Logical Epic: A Study of the Argument of "Paradise Lost."* London: Routledge & Kegan Paul, 1967.

Burrow, Colin. *Epic Romance: Homer to Milton*. Oxford: Clarendon Press, 1993.

Cope, Jackson I. *The Metaphoric Structure of "Paradise Lost."* Baltimore, MD: Johns Hopkins University Press, 1962.

Corns, Thomas N. *Milton's Language*. Oxford: Blackwell, 1990.

Creaser, John. "Editorial Problems in Milton." *Review of English Studies* 34 (1983): 279–303, and 35 (1984): 45–60.

Curry, Walter Clyde. *Milton's Ontology, Cosmogony and Physics*. Lexington: University Press of Kentucky, 1957.

Danielson, Dennis (ed). *The Cambridge Companion to Milton*. 1989; 2nd ed. Cambridge: Cambridge University Press, 1999.

————. *Milton's Good God: A Study in Literary Theodicy.* Cambridge: Cambridge University Press, 1982.

Diekhoff, John S. "Rhyme in *Paradise Lost.*" *PMLA* 49 (1934): 539–43.

Dobranski, Stephen B. *Milton, Authorship, and the Book Trade.* Cambridge: Cambridge University Press, 1999.

————, and John Rumrich (eds.). *Milton and Heresy.* Cambridge: Cambridge University Press, 1998.

DuRocher, Richard. *J. Milton and Ovid.* Ithaca, NY: Cornell University Press, 1985.

Empson, William. *Milton's God.* 1961; rev. ed. London: Chatto & Windus, 1965.

Evans, J. Martin. *"Paradise Lost" and the Genesis Tradition.* Oxford: Clarendon Press, 1968.

————. *Milton's Imperial Epic: "Paradise Lost" and the Discourse of Colonialism.* Ithaca, NY: Cornell University Press, 1991.

Fallon, Robert Thomas. *Divided Empire: Milton's Political Imagery.* University Park: Pennsylvania State University Press, 1995.

Fallon, Stephen M. *Milton Among the Philosophers: Poetry and Materialism in Seventeenth-Century England.* Ithaca, NY: Cornell University Press, 1991.

Ferry, Anne D. *Milton's Epic Voice: The Narrator in "Paradise Lost."* Cambridge, MA: Harvard University Press, 1963.

Fish, Stanley Eugene. *How Milton Works.* Cambridge, MA: Harvard University Press, 2001.

————. *Surprised by Sin: The Reader in "Paradise Lost."* 1967; rev. ed. Cambridge, MA: Harvard University Press, 1998.

Flannagan, Roy. "Art, Artists, Galileo, and Concordances." *Milton Quarterly* 20 (1986): 103–5.

French, J. Milton. *The Life Records of John Milton.* 5 vols. New Brunswick: Rutgers University Press, 1949–1958.

Froula, Christine. "When Eve Reads Milton: Undoing the Canonical Economy." *Critical Inquiry* 10 (1983): 321–47.

Frye, Northrop. *The Return of Eden: Five Essays on Milton's Epics.* Toronto: University of Toronto Press, 1965.

Gardner, Helen. *A Reading of "Paradise Lost."* Oxford: Oxford University Press, 1965.

Greene, Thomas. *The Descent from Heaven: A Study in Epic Continuity.* New Haven, CT, and London: Yale University Press, 1963.

Gregerson, Linda. *The Reformation of the Subject: Spenser, Milton, and The English Protestant Epic.* Cambridge: Cambridge University Press, 1995.

Grossman, Marshall. *Authors to Themselves: Milton and the Revelation of History.* Cambridge: Cambridge University Press, 1987.

Haskin, Dayton. *Milton's Burden of Interpretation*. Philadelphia: University of Pennsylvania Press, 1994.

Helgerson, Richard. *Self-Crowned Laureates: Spenser, Jonson, Milton, and the Literary System*. Berkeley: University of California Press, 1983.

Hill, Christopher. *Milton and the English Revolution*. London: Faber and Faber, 1977.

Hollander, John. *The Figure of Echo: A Mode of Allusion in Milton and After*. Berkeley: University of California Press, 1981.

Hunter, William B. "The Provenance of the *Christian Doctrine*: Addenda from the Bishop of Salisbury." *SEL* 33 (1993): 191–207.

———. *The Descent of Urania: Studies in Milton, 1946–1988*. Lewisburgh, PA: Bucknell University Press, 1989.

———. "Milton's Power of Matter." *JHI* 13 (1952): 55–62.

Kelley, Maurice. *This Great Argument: A Study of Milton's "De Doctrina Christiana" as a Gloss on "Paradise Lost."* Princeton: Princeton University Press, 1941.

Kerrigan, William. *The Sacred Complex: On the Psychogenesis of "Paradise Lost."* Cambridge, MA: Harvard University Press, 1983.

———. *The Prophetic Milton*. Charlottesville: University of Virginia Press, 1974.

King, John M. *Milton and Religious Controversy: Satire and Polemic in "Paradise Lost."* Cambridge: Cambridge University Press, 2000.

Knoppers, Laura Lunger. *Historicizing Milton: Spectacle, Power, and Poetry in Restoration England*. Athens: University of Georgia Press, 1994.

Kolbrener, William. *Milton's Warring Angels: A Study of Critical Engagements*. Cambridge: Cambridge University Press, 1997.

Leonard, John. *Naming in Paradise: Milton and the Language of Adam and Eve*. Oxford: Clarendon Press, 1990.

Lewalski, Barbara K. *"Paradise Lost" and the Rhetoric of Literary Form*. Princeton: Princeton University Press, 1985.

———. "Milton on Women—Yet Once More." *Milton Studies* 6 (1974): 3–20.

Lewis, C. S. *A Preface to "Paradise Lost."* London: Oxford University Press, 1942, rpt. 1961.

Lieb, Michael. *Milton and the Culture of Violence*. Ithaca, NY: Cornell University Press, 1994.

———. *Poetics of the Holy: A Reading of "Paradise Lost."* Chapel Hill: University of North Carolina Press, 1981.

Loewenstein, David. *Milton and the Drama of History*. Cambridge: Cambridge University Press, 1990.

———. "The Radical Religious Politics of *Paradise Lost*." In *A Companion to Milton*, ed. Thomas N. Corns. Oxford: Blackwell, 2001.

Lovejoy, Arthur O. "Milton and the Paradox of the Fortunate Fall." *ELH* 4 (1937): 161–79.

MacCaffery, Isabel. *"Paradise Lost" as Myth.* Cambridge, MA: Harvard University Press, 1959.

Martin, Catherine Gimelli (ed.). *Milton and Gender.* Cambridge: Cambridge University Press, 2004.

Martindale, Charles. *John Milton and the Transformation of Ancient Epic.* New York: Barnes and Noble, 1986.

McColley, Diane K. *Milton's Eve.* Urbana: University of Illinois Press, 1983.

McKenzie, D. F. "Milton's Printers: Matthew, Mary, and Samuel Simmons." *Milton Quarterly* 14 (1980): 87–91.

Moyles, R. G. *The Text of "Paradise Lost": A Study in Editorial Procedure.* Toronto, Buffalo, NY, and London: University of Toronto Press, 1985.

Murrin, Michael. *History and Warfare in the Renaissance Epic.* Chicago: University of Chicago Press, 1994.

Norbrook, David. *Writing the English Republic: Poetry, Rhetoric and Politics, 1627–1660.* Cambridge: Cambridge University Press, 1999.

Nyquist, Mary, and Margaret W. Ferguson (eds.). *Re-membering Milton: Essays on Texts and Traditions.* London: Methuen, 1987.

Patrides, C. A. *Milton and the Christian Tradition.* Oxford: Clarendon Press, 1966.

Porter, William M. *Reading the Classics and "Paradise Lost."* Lincoln: University of Nebraska Press, 1993.

Prince, F. T. *The Italian Element in Milton's Verse.* Oxford: Oxford University Press, 1954.

Quint, David. *Epic and Empire: Politics and Generic Form from Virgil to Milton.* Princeton: Princeton University Press, 1993.

Radzinowicz, Mary Ann. *Milton's Epics and the Book of Psalms.* Princeton: Princeton University Press, 1989.

Rajan, Balachandra. *"Paradise Lost" and the Seventeenth-Century Reader.* London: Chatto & Windus, 1947.

Revard, Stella Purce. *The War in Heaven: "Paradise Lost" and the Tradition of Satan's Rebellion.* Ithaca, NY: Cornell University Press, 1980.

Ricks, Christopher. *Milton's Grand Style.* Oxford: Clarendon Press, 1963.

Riggs, William. *The Christian Poet in "Paradise Lost."* Berkeley: University of California Press, 1972.

Rogers, John. *The Matter of Revolution: Science, Poetry, and Politics in the Age of Milton.* Ithaca, NY: Cornell University Press, 1996.

Rosenblatt, Jason P. *Torah and Law in "Paradise Lost."* Princeton: Princeton University Press, 1994.

Rosenheim, James M. "An Early Appreciation of *Paradise Lost.*" *MP* 75 (1978): 280–82.

Rumrich, John Peter. *Matter of Glory: A New Preface to "Paradise Lost."* Pittsburgh: University of Pittsburgh Press, 1987.

———. *Milton Unbound: Controversy and Reinterpretation*. Cambridge: Cambridge University Press, 1996.

Schwartz, Regina. *Remembering and Repeating: Biblical Creation in "Paradise Lost."* Cambridge: Cambridge University Press, 1988.

Sewell, Arthur. *A Study in Milton's Christian Doctrine.* London: Oxford University Press, 1939.

Shawcross, John. "Orthography and the Text of *Paradise Lost.*" In *Language and Style in Milton*, eds. Ronald Emma and John T. Shawcross. New York: Ungar, 1967.

——— (ed.). *Milton 1732–1801: The Critical Heritage.* London and Boston: Routledge & Kegan Paul, 1972.

Smith, Nigel. *Literature and Revolution in England, 1640–1660.* New Haven, CT: Yale University Press, 1994.

———. "*Paradise Lost* from Civil War to Restoration." In *Writing of the English Revolution,* ed. N. H. Keeble. Cambridge: Cambridge University Press, 2001.

Sprott, Ernest S. *Milton's Art of Prosody.* Oxford: Blackwell, 1953.

Starnes, DeWitt T., and Ernest William Talbert. *Classical Myth and Legend in Renaissance Dictionaries.* Chapel Hill: University of North Carolina Press, 1955.

Steadman, John M. *Epic and Tragic Structure in "Paradise Lost."* Chicago: University of Chicago Press, 1976.

———. *Milton and the Renaissance Hero.* Oxford: Clarendon Press, 1967.

———. *Milton's Biblical and Classical Imagery.* Pittsburgh: Duquesne University Press, 1984.

Stein, Arnold. *Answerable Style: Essays on "Paradise Lost."* Seattle and London: University of Washington Press, 1953.

Summers, Joseph. *The Muse's Method: An Introduction to "Paradise Lost."* Cambridge, MA: Harvard University Press, 1962.

Tayler, Edward W. *Milton's Poetry: Its Development in Time.* Pittsburgh: Duquesne University Press, 1979.

Treip, Mindele. *Milton's Punctuation and Changing English Usage, 1582–1676.* London: Methuen, 1970.

Turner, James Grantham. *One Flesh: Paradisal Marriage and Sexual Relations in the Age of Milton.* Oxford: Clarendon Press, 1987.

von Maltzahn, Nicholas. "The First Reception of *Paradise Lost.*" *RES* 47 (1996): 479–99.

Waldock, A. J. A. *"Paradise Lost" and Its Critics*. Cambridge, MA: Harvard University Press, 1947.

Walker, Julia. "Milton and Galileo." *Milton Studies* 25 (1989): 109–23.

——— (ed.). *Milton and the Idea of Women*. Urbana and Chicago: University of Illinois Press, 1988.

Webber, Joan. *Milton and His Epic Tradition*. Seattle: University of Washington Press, 1979.

West, Robert H. *Milton and the Angels*. Athens: University of Georgia Press, 1955.

Williams, Arnold. *The Common Expositor: An Account of the Commentaries on Genesis, 1527–1633*. Chapel Hill: University of North Carolina Press, 1948.

Wittreich, Joseph A., Jr. *The Feminist Milton*. Ithaca, NY: Cornell University Press, 1987.

———. *Visionary Poetics: Milton's Tradition and His Legacy*. San Marino, CA: Huntington Library, 1979.

Woodhouse, A. S. P. *The Heavenly Muse: A Preface to Milton*. Toronto: University of Toronto Press, 1972.

Worden, Blair. "Milton's Republicanism and the Tyranny of Heaven," in *Machiavelli and Republicanism*, eds. Gisela Bock, Quentin Skinner, and Maurizio Viroli. Cambridge: Cambridge University Press, 1990.

TEXTUAL INTRODUCTION

This volume is intended as a revision of Merritt Y. Hughes' justly praised edition of *Paradise Lost*. Although both editions provide a modernized text of the poem as it appeared some four months before Milton died in 1674, the modernization here is more thoroughgoing than that of Hughes' version. Even while he accepted the logic of modernizing the early text's spelling and some slight modification of its punctuation, Hughes was unwilling to sacrifice the traditional look of Milton's poem. His printed text, therefore, retained the idiosyncratic deployment of the capitals of the original and preserved other "seventeenth century typographical peculiarities, especially the italicization of proper names and place names."[1]

I am less ambivalent about modernizing here than Hughes seems to have been, but no less concerned that the text be as fully responsible to Milton's poem as it is to Milton's readers. This Textual Introduction is intended both to make clear my procedures in attempting to achieve this goal and to offer a rationale for them. I have modernized archaic *spellings* in the original but not archaic *forms* of words (thus I have changed "justifie" to "justify" at 1.26 and "smoak" to "smoke" at 1.237, but have retained "embryon" at 2.900). The distinction, to be sure, is not always easy to make sharply (is "enow" at 2.504 an old form or an old spelling of the modern "enough"?). I have regularized, for ease of identification, the spelling of proper names where the modernization does not effect pronunciation or meter (for example, Milton's "Cusco" [11.407] is here "Cuzco," as it is always rendered today). I have marked sounded 'èd's in the final syllable of past tense and participial verb forms that in modern pronunciation would not normally be pronounced but that are clearly demanded by the poem's meter (e.g., "squarèd" at 1.758), and I have concomitantly expanded the elisions (e.g., "receiv'd" at 1.174) designed to mark the unstressed forms. In general, I have expanded elided forms where the elision does not obviously clarify pronunciation or stress. Does "swoll'n," for example, really mark a distinct pronunciation of the word? Most readers would not equally stress the two syllables in any case, and the unstressed *e* results in a pronunciation not sufficiently unlike the elided form to merit a typographic indication that implies far greater

---

[1] Milton, *Paradise Lost*, ed. Hughes (2003), p. vii. Hughes' text was originally prepared for his edition of the poem published by Doubleday in 1935.

certainty about Milton's pronunciation—and about the principles of his prosody—than in fact we have. I have also normalized the use of capitals, which in the original are frequent but hardly systematic or necessarily expressive (as at 2.620: "many a Frozen, many a fierie Alpe"). I distinguish between "Heaven," referring to God's empyreal seat, and "heaven" or the "heavens" of the created universe. I have eliminated the conventional italics for proper names, and I have added quotation marks where there is direct address. I have throughout cautiously modernized the punctuation, normalizing and regularizing the pointing of the original. Milton, for example, often introduces similes, such as "Thir glory withered. As when Heavens Fire . . . " (1.612), with periods as here, but he also uses semicolons, colons, and commas; all of these I have changed to commas as modern usage would demand.

Little of this, I hope, will seem deeply controversial (the emphasis here is of course on "deeply"), though admittedly many editions, including Hughes' original, have adopted more conservative principles (literally conserving more of the texture of the original). It is perhaps worth noting, however, that the impulse to modernize began soon after Milton's death. In 1688 Jacob Tonson published a new edition of *Paradise Lost*, the first to be published by someone other than Milton's original publisher, Samuel Simmons. Tonson's edition began the process of standardizing most spelling according to the norms of the age, for example removing redundant *e*'s at the ends of words like "faire" and normalizing the spellings of words like "suttle" and "perfet."

The first step in understanding the logic for any set of editorial decisions is to consider the nature of the text. In this case, only three early versions of the poem make any serious claim upon a modern editor's attention. *Paradise Lost* appeared in two printed editions in Milton's lifetime, both published by Samuel Simmons. The first appeared in 1667 as "Paradise lost. A POEM Written in TEN BOOKS By JOHN MILTON," and a second edition, "Revised and Augmented by the same Author," was published in 1674, just a few months before Milton died. The only bibliographically significant manuscript to survive is a copy of Book 1 (now in the Pierpont Morgan Library in New York City), not, however, in Milton's hand but in that of a professional scribe, with evidence also of the attention of various correctors and retaining the printers' marks that reveal it to be the manuscript from which the first book was printed in 1667.[2]

Since the edition of 1674 shows unmistakable evidence of Milton's involvement in the preparation of its text—and becomes, therefore, the most

[2] An extremely useful facsimile, transcription, and account of the manuscript can be found in Darbishire (ed.), *The Manuscript of Milton's "Paradise Lost," Book 1.*

authoritative record of his last and most fully considered intentions[3]—it has seemed to most editors (including me) the logical version upon which to base a modern edition, though editors inevitably consult both the Morgan manuscript and the 1667 text and occasionally adopt readings from one or both. Although the 1674 edition does not show evidence of Milton's careful supervision of the printing (the compositor, for example, takes his text in at least two places from *uncorrected* sheets of the 1667 edition), the 1674 publication unquestionably records Milton's latest sense of the form in which the poem should appear. Milton's second edition expanded the ten-book structure of the original by dividing 1667's Book 7 into Books 7 and 8 and 1667's Book 10 into Books 11 and 12, also adding a few lines at the beginning of both the new Books 8 and 12. In four other places there is evidence of substantive revision: at 1.504–5; at 5.636–41, replacing three lines from the edition of 1667; adding three lines following 11.484; and at 11.581–82, replacing 1667's 10.548). It is in this revised form that almost all readers since 1674 have encountered *Paradise Lost*. The 1674 edition was capably printed according to the standards of the time. Very few substantive readings need to be recovered from beneath "the veil of print," as editors sometimes understand their task,[4] and those that do readily suggest themselves—for example, at 7.321, where both early printed editions have "the smelling Gourd." As Richard Bentley noted in 1732, the correct reading of the adjective is "swelling" (a familiar classical epithet), the compositor's eye caught by the occurrence of "smelling" two lines earlier and this duplication evidence itself that "smelling" was not the intended reading.

Nonetheless, recognizing the authority of the 1674 edition does not solve all problems facing an editor. It determines the most obvious issues of the language and structure of the poem, but much else remains unsettled. Although one famous bibliographer notoriously claimed that editing *Paradise Lost* was "a safe, sane, and slightly dull occupation,"[5] it seems to me the truth is almost the exact reverse. None of those adjectives applies. The idiosyncratic spelling, unsystematic capitalization, and seemingly desultory punctuation of Milton's poem—multiplied by their existence in two published texts and a manuscript of one book, so that there are thousands of

---

[3] See G. Thomas Tanselle, "The Editorial Problem of Final Intention," in *Studies in Bibliography* 29 (1976): 167–211. "Final intentions" are, of course, not the only grounds on which we might prefer one text to another; indeed authorial intentions, final or otherwise, have come under scrutiny in the last few decades as both theoreticians and textual scholars have insisted that we see the limitations of understanding the author as the single and sovereign source of the meanings of a work.

[4] Fredson Bowers, *On Editing Shakespeare* (Charlottesville: University of Virginia Press, 1966), p. 87.

[5] Bowers, p. 72.

variants to be considered—present endless difficulties for an editor, not least those arising from the question of whether these aspects were at any stage fully in the control of a poet who was blind.

My analysis suggests that there is no convincing case to be made that any one of these texts clearly demonstrates Milton's own habits of spelling or punctuation, and none of the texts shows evidence of his careful supervision of these aspects in its preparation.[6] This is not unusual. Writers of the period usually ceded responsibility for the accidentals of their text to the printers and scribes who prepared them. In 1683, Joseph Moxon noted as "a task and duty incumbent on the *Compositer* . . . to discern and amend the bad *Spelling* and *Pointing* of his Copy"; and Milton's nephew, Edward Phillips, reports that upon his visits to the poet he would regularly be shown "a parcel" of verse that had been copied out in various hands and that Phillips would assume responsibility for their "correction as to the orthography and pointing."[7] But even if Milton's intentions in these matters were accurately registered in some text or could be confidently reconstructed, it is fair to ask what value these mechanical idiosyncrasies offer a modern reader. Is there a subtle system of meaning here, perhaps imperfectly realized, which we should recognize and restore (e.g., is there a significant difference between "he" and "hee" or between "only" and "onely")? Or are these mere "accidentals," in the often misunderstood term of the great bibliographer W. W. Greg,[8] that is, the conventions of composition, arbitrary or unconscious habits, not void of significance but detachable from the substantive achievement of the poem—and possibly not Milton's in any case, but those of the scribes who prepared the manuscripts or the compositors in the printing house? Put differently, the question is: for a modern reader, do these accidentals clarify Milton's intentions, or do they obscure them?

Merely asking the question prevents us from automatically deciding to reproduce the 1674 text exactly as it appeared, though certainly that would make the editorial task easier—or, more precisely, that would make the editorial task unnecessary. One could simply print what appeared on the page

---

[6] Among the various excellent textual studies of *Paradise Lost*, see Moyles, *The Text of "Paradise Lost"*; Creaser, "Editorial Problems in Milton"; and Shawcross, "Orthography and the Text of *Paradise Lost.*"

[7] See Joseph Moxon, *Mechanick Exercises on the Whole Art of Printing*, eds. Herbert Davis and Harry Carter, 2nd ed. (London: Oxford University Press, 1962), p. 192; and see Edward Phillips, "The Life of Milton," (1694), p. 421 below.

[8] W. W. Greg, "The Rationale of Copy-Text," in *Studies in Bibliography* 3 (1950–1951), 19–36; reprinted in *The Collected Papers of Sir Walter W. Greg*, ed. J. C. Maxwell (Oxford: Clarendon Press, 1966), pp. 374–91. Greg's term, used to differentiate the spelling, capitalization, and punctuation from the "substantives" (i.e., the words and their arrangement) has sometimes led to the misconception that he implies that these do not, or cannot, affect meaning.

in 1674 and there would be no need to exert any editorial intelligence at all. Indeed, there are many good reasons to reproduce the poem as it appeared in 1674, but if that is what is desired, arguably it would be better to have a facsimile of the 1674 poem rather than a modern, printed transcription, allowing a modern reader the benefit of reading the same text that a reader in Milton's own time read. But even if the facsimile were available, various other aspects of the physical book would not be the same, aspects that register on the consciousness of a reader, insuring that the fundamental experience would be different (if only because the 17th-century reader was reading a book that in every way seemed contemporary, while the modern reader would be reading a book that could only seem antiquated or quaint, a self-conscious anachronism instead of a state-of-the-art product of the book trade).

But if maintaining the accidentals of the early texts would indeed deliver *Paradise Lost* to a reader in the precise form Milton intended, a powerful argument could be made for either following the text exactly as it appeared in 1674 or emending the text in order to restore those intentions. Although some have seen the idiosyncratic spelling and punctuation as either expressive or, at least, characteristic (that is, as either a deliberate part of the poem's system of meaning or as evidence of Milton's own unconscious habits of composition), the accidentals of the 1674 edition are so inconsistently deployed that it is difficult to see how they reveal anything more than Milton's own merely "casual" interest in them.[9] If in places Milton's work seems to exhibit both spelling and punctuation preferences, these preferences are not systematically reflected in either of the early published texts of *Paradise Lost* or in the manuscript copy of Book 1, and one may indeed wonder if they are preferences at all.

At best, one can make the case in the early texts of the poem only for an imperfectly realized system of accidentals,[10] although the argument for any system at all always risks becoming circular: Milton's presumed principles become evident only after the inconsistencies of the given text have been "reformed" according to the dictates of the presumed system. Nonetheless,

---

[9] The quoted word belongs to Moyles, who insists that "there is no evidence to show that Milton supervised the accidentals—the spelling and the punctuation—in more than a casual way" (p. 28).

[10] Helen Darbishire, who believes that she has identified a carefully worked out system of accidentals that Milton expected the printers to follow to the best of their ability, admits: "That best was still imperfect: the copy would sometimes be faulty, their own vigilance not unsleeping." Her confidence in Milton's effective supervision of the accidentals of the poem is perhaps undermined by the very incongruity of her language in thinking about the activity of the blind poet as "he saw it through the press." See her edition of *Paradise Lost* in *The Poetical Works of John Milton*, vol. 1, p. xviii.

one could endeavor to recover and restore to the text the system Milton may
have intended. This is a legitimate editorial undertaking, and indeed Helen
Darbishire has attempted just this in her much admired edition of the
poem.[11] Yet even if one felt confident that one had recovered Milton's in-
tended practices of spelling and punctuation from the vagaries of the
processes of textual transmission, one might reasonably ask what advantage
this offers most students of the poem. What is the value for nonspecialist
readers in being forced to decide whether the distinction between "supreme"
and "supream" is indeed an indication of a metrical variation ("supream" ac-
cented on the second syllable), as some have claimed, especially since at 2.210
"Supream" seems clearly to demand an accent on the first syllable; or to won-
der if "gate" is the modern "gate" (as at 4.542) or in fact "gait" (as at 4.568);
or attempt to find significance in the inconsistency of capitalization in a line
like "our prison strong, this huge convex of Fire" (2.434). Even if it can be
shown that Milton generally preferred certain spellings, what, if anything, is a
student to make of obviously idiosyncratic forms like "highth" (2.190), espe-
cially as they are not consistently rendered in the text (in this case, one also
finds in the 1674 text "hight," "higth," and "heighth," and it is not at all clear
if even a minor pronunciation difference is being signaled).

The basic choices available to an editor then are these: one can print the
accidentals of the poem as they appeared in 1674, print them as one con-
jectures Milton hoped they would appear, or choose to modernize the acci-
dentals as the procedure for modern readers that makes the text most
accessible, producing the least syntactic confusion and visual distraction as
it presents the poem's sound and sense. Each of these choices reflects an in-
telligible and responsible editorial position, and each might well produce a
text of use to a particular set of readers. It is, however, the third choice that
seems best to serve the greatest number of readers of the poem, and, for an
edition primarily designed for students, it is the choice I have made here.
Although there may be a number of (good) reasons to want to read the
poem exactly as it appeared in 1674 (or in 1667, or as one thinks Milton
would have wished it to appear), most readers require a text that accurately
presents the poem in the form Milton conceived it but also in a manner
that does not create interpretative obstacles Milton did not intend. This is
the text I have endeavored to provide.

If, however, this goal seems reasonable (though not, of course, in-
evitable), I am aware that the treatment of punctuation here, even if it can
be seen to advance my aim, may still appear to many scholars a controversial,

---

[11] Darbishire includes a thoughtful rationale for her editorial procedures; ibid., pp. ix–xxxv;
for a similar editorial understanding, see also Wright, in his "Textual Introduction" to *Milton:
Poems* (1956), pp. v–xxxiii.

if not actually misguided, decision. Many editors of the poem have confidently modernized spelling and normalized capitalization, but the poem's punctuation has generally been left alone. My (no longer) secret sense has been that its retention is more pragmatic than principled: modernization of the punctuation of Milton's meandering sentences and verse paragraphs is extremely difficult. Editors have rationalized keeping the original punctuation, even where spelling has been modernized, by insisting that spelling and punctuation perform different linguistic functions, justifying their different treatments in the text: spelling is merely denotative, allowing a reader to identify a particular lexical intention, but punctuation is a grammatical marker and thus an essential structure of meaning.

Spelling and punctuation are, of course, two separate conventions of language, but the sharp functional opposition that many have insisted upon is misleading, based in large part upon an anachronistic understanding of 17th-century punctuation. Modern punctuation indeed is essentially grammatical, although it also marks rhythmical pauses; the specific mark is determined by the effort to express the syntactic relations between elements (e.g., a comma after a clause articulates a different logical relation than a semicolon; a semicolon something different than a colon). In the 17th century, punctuation functioned almost in the opposite way. Some syntactic relations are of course expressed, but much is intended as a rhythmical guide. Commas and semicolons, for example, are differentiated less by the logical relation they mediate than by the heaviness of the pause they call for. Milton's punctuation works essentially this way. It is designed more for the ear than for the mind, more to allow the rhythm be experienced by the reader than the sentenced parsed. Mindele Treip, even while acknowledging that Milton's "grammar is frequently vague, elliptical, or ambiguous," insists upon the value of Milton's punctuation in *Paradise Lost*, because it "tunes our ear to have further expectations beyond those of grammar."[12]

This might be taken as a compelling reason to reproduce Milton's punctuation, however alien it may seem; he is, after all, a poet. Two things, however, militate against this seemingly sensible position. Not only is Milton's punctuation virtually impossible to disentangle from the punctuation habits of the compositors who set the two early printed editions of *Paradise Lost* or from those of the scribe who copied out the manuscript of Book 1, but also, and more fundamental here, it is inevitably misleading to modern readers, who are used to having punctuation marks guide them through the syntax of a sentence. We come to a text anticipating that the punctuation we encounter signals logical relations. If this is an error, it is not one that

---

[12] Treip, pp. 96, 114.

Milton expects us to make. He could not know how punctuation or the expectations of readers would change in the centuries after he wrote.

Especially in a text where the grammar is often "vague, elliptical, or ambiguous," nonspecialist readers need signposts to negotiate the syntax, and it hardly seems in their interest to insist on a system of punctuation that at best can be shown to approximate Milton's intentions and that, because of the changed function of punctuation in modern English, will inevitably make the meaning of the poem less rather than more clear to a modern reader. Milton, for example, contrary to modern usage, often uses periods rather than colons to introduce speech, and colons rather than semicolons to separate independent clauses. In both cases, simple substitution of the modern mark preserves and signals Milton's grammatical intentions with very little loss. Admittedly not all such modernization is either so simple or so benign; there is in many cases some loss of the expressive rhythms of the original once the grammatical relations are marked according to our current methods of punctuation. In 1674, lines 80–97 in Book 7 read as one long sentence:

> But since thou hast voutsaf't
> Gently for our instruction to impart
> Things above Earthly thought, which yet concernd
> Our knowing, as to highest wisdom seemd,
> Deign to descend now lower, and relate
> What may no less perhaps availe us known,
> How first began this Heav'n which we behold
> Distant so high, with moving Fires adornd
> Innumerable, and this which yeelds or fills
> All space, the ambient Aire wide interfus'd
> Imbracing round this florid Earth, what cause
> Mov'd the Creator in his holy Rest
> Through all Eternitie so late to build
> In *Chaos*, and the work begun, how soon
> Absolv'd, if unforbid thou maist unfould
> What wee, not to explore the secrets aske
> Of his Eternal Empire, but the more
> To magnifie his works, the more we know.

Modernized, it reads:

> But since thou hast vouchsafed
> Gently for our instruction to impart
> Things above earthly thought which yet concerned
> Our knowing, as to highest wisdom seemed,

> Deign to descend now lower and relate
> What may no less perhaps avail us known:
> How first began this heaven which we behold
> Distant so high with moving fires adorned
> Innumerable, and this which yields or fills
> All space, the ambient air, wide interfused
> Embracing round this florid earth? What cause
> Moved the creator in his holy rest
> Through all eternity so late to build
> In chaos, and, the work begun, how soon
> Absolved, if unforbid thou mayst unfold
> What we, not to explore the secrets ask
> Of his eternal empire, but the more
> To magnify his works the more we know?

Arguably (but only arguably) the commas separating clauses in the original can be seen as a grammatical index to Adam's breathless wonder, but I am not convinced that clarifying the syntax is not a greater aid to nonspecialist readers. It is impossible in punctuating the text for modern readers to respect equally Milton's rhythmical intentions and his syntactic ones. Because of the historical shift in punctuation practice, attending to one inevitably involves some distortion of the other. With the necessity to choose, this edition has opted for modern punctuation that will both acknowledge and clarify Milton's complex syntax, respecting his grammatical intentions, even at the price of some muting of his rhythmical intent. But we may limit even that small price, since, for most readers, the syntactic clarity achieved helps reveal the poem's "true musical delight,"[13] allowing students to read and hear the verse more easily than when they are forced to struggle with a system of punctuation that unintentionally complicates and confuses Milton's poetic design.

[13] The phrase appears in Milton's note on "The Verse," which he wrote at the request of the publisher Simmons and that was first appended to the fourth issue of the first edition of the poem (1668), there as what "rhyme" denies poetry; see pp. 4–5 below.

TEXTUAL NOTES

The notes below record the few substantive changes from the 1674 edition. They do not record modernizations of spelling or punctuation. The reading adopted in this edition appears in boldface, followed by the rejected reading from 1674. Where the emendation comes from the 1667 edition or the Pierpont Morgan manuscript, that fact is indicated parenthetically immediately following the emendation (i.e., 2.483: **their** (1667) her). Where both early printed texts have the same rejected reading, this too is indicated parenthetically.

1.432:	**these** (MS) those (1667 and 1674)
2.483:	**their** (1667) her
2.527:	**his** (1667) this
4.472:	**shalt** shall (1667 and 1674)
4.928:	**The** (1667) Thy
6.326:	**sheared** shared (1667 and 1674)
7.321:	**swelling** smelling (1667 and 1674)
7.451:	**soul** Fowle (Foul in 1667)
7.494:	**Needless** Needlest (1667 and 1674)
8.269:	**as** (1667) and
9.213:	**hear** (1667) bear
9.394:	**Likest** (1667) likeliest
9.437:	**Embroidered** Imborderd
9.1019:	**we** (1667) me
9.1092:	**for** (1667) from
9.1093:	**from** (1667) for
10.550:	**fair** (1667) omitted in 1674
10.989:	**So death** [In 1667 and 1674, the metrically deficient line ends after "remain," and "So death" begins 10.990, which then itself is hypermetrical.]
11.344:	**hither** (1667) thither
11.427:	**that sin** (1667) that
12.534:	**Will** (1667) Well

ABBREVIATIONS

In general, titles are spelled out for the convenience of readers. The exceptions are conventional. Books of the bible are abbreviated with shortened forms of the familiar title, e.g., 1 Cor. for 1 Corinthians. Milton's own works are spelled out in full, with the exception of:

PL	*Paradise Lost*
PR	*Paradise Regained*
SA	*Samson Agonistes*

Milton's prose works and early poetry are cited from *The Works of John Milton,* gen. ed. Frank Allen Patterson. New York: Columbia University Press, 1931–38, which is abbreviated as *Works.*

Other abbreviations:

CSPD	*Calendar of State Papers Domestic*
ELH	*English Literary History* (but now officially *ELH*)
JEGP	*Journal of English and Germanic Philology*
JHI	*Journal of the History of Ideas*
MLN	*Modern Language Notes*
MP	*Modern Philology*
OED	*Oxford English Dictionary* (2nd edition)
PQ	*Philological Quarterly*
RES	*Review of English Studies*
SEL	*Studies in English Literature*
SP	*Studies in Philology*
TLS	*Times Literary Supplement*

PARADISE
LOST

In Paradisum Amissam
Summi Poetæ Johannis Miltoni

Qui legis Amissam Paradisum, grandia magni
Carmina Miltoni, *quid nisi cuncta legis?*
Res cunctas, & cunctarum primordia rerum,
Et fata, & fines continet iste liber.
Intima panduntur magni penetralia mundi,   5
Scribitur & toto quicquid in Orbe latet.
Terræque, tractusque maris, coelumque profundum
Sulphureumque Erebi, *flammivomumque specus.*
Quæque colunt terras, Portumque & Tartara cæca,
Quæque colunt summi lucida regna Poli.   10
Et quodcunque ullis conclusum est finibus usquam,
Et sine fine Chaos, & sine fine Deus:
Et sine fine magis, si quid magis est sine fine,
In Christo erga homines conciliatus amor.
Hæc qui speraret quis crederet esse futurum?   15
Et tamen hæc hodie terra Britanna *legit.*
O quantos in bella Duces! quæ protulit arma!
Quæ canit, & quanta prælia dira tuba.
Coelestes acies! atque in certamine Coelum!
Et quæ Coelestes pugna deceret agros!   20
Quantus in ætheriis tollit se Lucifer *armis!*
Atque ipso graditur vix Michaele *minor!*
Quantis, & quam funestis concurritur iris
Dum ferus hic stellas protegit, ille rapit!
Dum vulsos Montes ceu Tela reciproca torquent,   25
Et non mortali desuper igne pluunt:
Stat dubius cui se parti concedat Olympus,
Et metuit pugnæ non superesse suæ.
At simul in coelis Messiæ insignia fulgent,
Et currus animes, armaque digna Deo,   30
Horrendumque rotæ strident, & sæva rotarum
Erumpunt torvis fulgura luminibus,
Et flammæ vibrant, & vera tonitrua rauco
Admistis flammis insonuere Polo
Excidit attonitis mens omnis, & impetus omnis   35

Et cassis dextris irrita Tela cadunt.
Ad poenas fugiunt, & ceu foret Orcus asylum
Infernis certant condere se tenebris.
Cedite Romani Scriptores, cedite Graii
Et quos fama recens vel celebravit anus.   40
Hæc quicunque leget tantum cecinesse putabit
Mæonidem ranas, Virgilium *culices.*[1]

S. B., *M.D.*

[trans: On the *Paradise Lost* of John Milton, Most Excellent Poet]

You who read *Paradise Lost,* the magnificent poem by the great Milton, what do you read but the story of everything? The book includes all things, and the origins of all things, and their destinies and ends. The innermost secrets of the great universe are revealed, and whatever lies hidden in the entire world is there set out: the land and the breadth of the sea, and the depths of the sky and the sulphurous fire-vomiting den of Erebus—all that lives on earth and in the sea, and everything that lives in dark Tartarus and in the bright kingdoms of Heaven above; whatever is included anywhere within any boundaries, and also that which is without boundary: chaos and infinite God, and what is even more without limit, if there is anything that is more without limit, the love toward mankind embodied in Christ. Who that had ever hoped for such a poem could have believed it would exist? And yet this is what the land of Britain reads today. O how great the generals, what deeds of arms are here put forth! What fearsome battles are sung and celebrated with how resonant a trumpet! Heavenly armies, and Heaven at war, and fighting that is suited for the fields of Heaven! How huge Lucifer seems as he rises up armed in the heavens, hardly inferior to Michael himself! With what furious and deadly rage they fight; while one fiercely defends the stars, the other would pull them down. While they pluck up mountains and throw them at each other like spears and rain down inhuman fires from above, Olympus stands uncertain to which side to yield and fears that it may not survive the war. But as soon as the signs of the Messiah gleam in the sky and his living chariot and his armor assemble for God, as soon as its wheels horribly grind and shoot out their fierce lightning, and the flames flash and bellow, mixed with the thunder and lightning from the hoarse skies, from his awestruck foes all courage, all resistance, departs, and

---

[1] Added only in 1674, the poem is probably by Milton's friend, Doctor Samuel Barrow.

their useless weapons fall from their feeble hands. They run to their punishments, and, as if Orcus were a refuge, they attempt to hide themselves in the hellish darkness. Make way you writers of Rome, make way you writers of Greece, and everyone else, whether modern or ancient, whom fame has celebrated. Anyone who will read this poem will think that Homer only sang of frogs, Virgil only of gnats.

On *Paradise Lost*

When I beheld the poet blind, yet bold,
In slender book his vast design unfold,
Messiah crowned, God's reconciled decree,
Rebelling angels, the forbidden tree,
Heaven, hell, earth, chaos, all; the argument   5
Held me a while misdoubting his intent,
That he would ruin (for I saw him strong)
The sacred truths to fable and old song
(So Samson groped the temple's posts in spite)
The world o'erwhelming to revenge his sight.   10
    Yet as I read, soon growing less severe,
I liked his project, the success did fear;
Through that wide field how he his way should find
O'er which lame faith leads understanding blind;
Lest he perplexed the things he would explain,   15
And what was easy he should render vain.
    Or if a work so infinite he spanned
Jealous I was that some less skillful hand
(Such as disquiet always what is well,
And by ill imitating would excel)   20
Might hence presume the whole creation's day
To change in scenes, and show it in a play.
    Pardon me, mighty poet, nor despise
My causeless, yet not impious, surmise.
But I am now convinced, and none will dare   25
Within thy labors to pretend a share.
Thou hast not missed one thought that could be fit,
And all that was improper dost omit:
So that no room is here for writers left,
But to detect their ignorance or theft.   30
    That majesty which through thy work doth reign
Draws the devout, deterring the profane.
And things divine thou treat'st of in such state

As them preserves, and thee, inviolate.
At once delight and horror on us seize,　　　　　　　　　　35
Thou sing'st with so much gravity and ease;
And above humane flight dost soar aloft
With plume so strong, so equal, and so soft.
The bird named from that Paradise you sing
So never flags, but always keeps on wing.　　　　　　　　40
　　　Where couldst thou words of such a compass find?
Whence furnish such a vast expense of mind?
Just Heaven thee like Tiresias to requite
Rewards with prophecy thy loss of sight.
　　　Well might'st thou scorn thy readers to allure　　　45
With tinkling rhyme, of thy own sense secure;
While the Town-Bayes writes all the while and spells,
And like a packhorse tires without his bells:
Their fancies like our bushy-points appear,
The poets tag them, we for fashion wear.　　　　　　　　50
I too transported by the mode offend,
And while I meant to praise thee must commend.
Thy verse created like thy theme sublime,
In number, weight, and measure, needs not rhyme.[2]

A. M.

The Printer to the Reader

Courteous Reader, there was no argument at first intended to the book, but, for the satisfaction of many that have desired it, I have procured it, and withal a reason of that which stumbled many others: why the poem rhymes not.

The Verse

The measure is English heroic verse without rhyme, as that of Homer in Greek and Virgil in Latin, rhyme being no necessary adjunct or true ornament of poem or good verse, in longer works especially, but the invention

---

[2] This second prefatory poem, by Andrew Marvell, was, like the Latin tribute above, also added in the second edition in 1674. It appears in the first edition of Marvell's verse, *Miscellaneous Poems* (1681). Lines 18–26 refer to John Dryden's opera, *The State of Innocence*, published in 1677 but never performed, and "Bayes," in line 47 also refers to Dryden, who had been satirized in Buckingham's *Rehearsal* by that name (bays, referring to the laurel and thus Dryden's laureate ambitions).

of a barbarous age to set off wretched matter and lame meter; graced indeed since by the use of some famous modern poets carried away by custom, but much to their own vexation, hindrance, and constraint to express many things otherwise, and for the most part worse than else they would have expressed them. Not without cause, therefore, some both Italian and Spanish poets of prime note have rejected rhyme both in longer and shorter works, as have also long since our best English tragedies, as a thing of itself, to all judicious ears, trivial and of no true musical delight, which consists only in apt numbers, fit quantity of syllables, and the sense variously drawn out from one verse into another, not in the jingling sound of like endings, a fault avoided by the learned ancients both in poetry and all good oratory. This neglect, then, of rhyme so little is to be taken for a defect, though it may seem so perhaps to vulgar readers, that it rather is to be esteemed an example set, the first in English, of ancient liberty recovered to heroic poem from the troublesome and modern bondage of rhyming.

BOOK 1

The Argument

This first book proposes, first in brief, the whole subject: man's disobedience and the loss thereupon of Paradise wherein he was placed; then touches the prime cause of his fall, the serpent, or rather Satan in the serpent, who, revolting from God and drawing to his side many legions of angels, was by the command of God driven out of Heaven with all his crew into the great deep. Which action passed over, the poem hastes into the midst of things, presenting Satan with his angels now fallen into hell, described here, not in the center (for Heaven and earth may be supposed as yet not made, certainly not yet accursed) but in a place of utter darkness, fitliest called chaos. Here Satan, with his angels lying on the burning lake, thunderstruck and astonished, after a certain space recovers, as from confusion, calls up him who next in order and dignity lay by him. They confer of their miserable fall. Satan awakens all his legions, who lay till then in the same manner confounded. They rise: their numbers, array of battle, their chief leaders named, according to the idols known afterward in Canaan and the countries adjoining. To these Satan directs his speech, comforts them with hope yet of regaining Heaven, but tells them lastly of a new world and new kind of creature to be created, according to an ancient prophecy or report in Heaven (for that angels were long before this visible creation was the opinion of many ancient Fathers). To find out the truth of this prophecy, and what to determine thereon, he refers to a full council. What his associates thence attempt. Pandaemonium, the palace of Satan, rises, suddenly built out of the deep; the infernal peers there sit in council.

Of man's first disobedience and the fruit

1–4. *Of man's . . . man: man* is repeated in a way that recalls the stress upon the corresponding words in the opening lines of Homer's *Odyssey* and Virgil's *Aeneid*, as well as the conviction of Renaissance poets that epic poetry should portray a "virtuous man," as Spenser (in his letter to Raleigh in *The Faerie Queene*) said that Homer did "in the persons of Agamemnon and Ulysses." Here *man's . . . disobedience* is that of Adam in par-

ticular and mankind's in general, while the *one greater man,* line 4, is Jesus, who redeems what Adam lost; cf. Rom. 5:19: "as by one man's disobedience many were made sinners, so by the obedience of one shall many be made righteous." The word for "man" in Hebrew is "Adam."

1. *first disobedience* identifies disobedience itself as the poem's major subject (as opposed to the heroism of the traditional epic),

6

Of that forbidden tree, whose mortal taste
Brought death into the world and all our woe,
With loss of Eden, till one greater man
Restore us and regain the blissful seat,   5
Sing heavenly muse, that on the secret top
Of Oreb, or of Sinai, didst inspire
That shepherd who first taught the chosen seed
In the beginning how the heavens and earth
Rose out of chaos; or if Sion hill   10
Delight thee more, and Siloa's brook that flowed
Fast by the oracle of God, I thence
Invoke thy aid to my adventurous song,
That with no middle flight intends to soar
Above the Aonian mount while it pursues   15
Things unattempted yet in prose or rhyme.

and *first* suggests that Adam and Eve's *dis-obedience* will be followed by others. *fruit:* both the literal fruit of the tree and the consequences of the action of eating from it

2. *forbidden tree:* See Gen. 2:17; also Samuel Daniel, *The Complaint of Rosamund* (1592): "The wanton taste of that forbidden tree" (line 748).   *mortal:* fatal, but also that which introduces mortality into human history

5. *regain:* i.e., regain for mankind *seat:* throne (i.e., home)

6–7. *Sing . . . Sinai:* The *heavenly muse,* the Urania of Book 7, recalls the muse invoked by classical poets for inspiration but here ambitiously is identified as God himself, the voice that speaks to Moses (*That shepherd,* line 8) in Exod. 3:1 and 19:20 on *Oreb* or *Sinai;* cf. 12.227–30.

6. *Sing:* Note the long delay of the verb in the first sentence.

8. *first:* Note the repetition of *first* in lines 1, 8, 19, 27, 28, and 33.   *the chosen seed:* the Israelites; see 1 Chron. 16:13: "O seed of Israel his servant, ye children of Jacob, his chosen ones."

9. *In the beginning:* the first three words of Genesis and also of John

9–10. *how . . . chaos:* chaos is the original unformed matter that God endows with

form. In the poem, chaos sometimes (as here) refers to the matter itself, sometimes refers to the area in which this unformed matter resides (Cf. 2.890–1053), and sometimes is personified as the ruler or residing spirit of this area. Traditionally God creates *ex nihilo,* out of nothing, so this is a heterodox assertion; see pp. xxxvii–xxxviii above.

10. *Sion hill:* Mount Zion, the site on which the Temple of Solomon was located

11. *Siloa's brook:* a small river that flowed near the Temple, with whose waters Jesus restored a blind man's sight (John 9)

12. *oracle:* the sanctuary in the Temple of Solomon for the ark in which the holy texts were kept (1 Kings 6:9; also Ps. 28.2: "I lift up my hands towards the holy oracle"), but suggesting as well the oracle of Apollo at Delphi.

13. *adventurous song:* Milton admits the extraordinary ambition of his undertaking; see pp. xxvi–xxviii above.

15. *Aonian mount:* Helicon, the mountain on which the classical muses lived

16. *Things unattempted . . . rhyme:* The line translates the opening of Ludovico Ariosto's 1532 epic, *Orlando Furioso* (*cosa non detta in prosa mai né in rima,*" line 2), ironically in that it chooses to make its own assertion of originality via a quotation. The claim is explained in 9.28–32.

And chiefly thou, O spirit, that dost prefer
Before all temples the upright heart and pure,
Instruct me, for thou know'st; thou from the first
Wast present, and, with mighty wings outspread,   20
Dove-like sat'st brooding on the vast abyss
And mad'st it pregnant. What in me is dark
Illumine, what is low raise and support,
That to the height of this great argument
I may assert eternal providence   25
And justify the ways of God to men.
   Say first, for Heaven hides nothing from thy view,
Nor° the deep tract of hell, say first what cause   *not even*
Moved our grand parents in that happy state,
Favored of Heaven so highly, to fall off   30
From their creator and transgress his will
For one restraint, lords of the world besides.
Who first seduced them to that foul revolt?
The infernal serpent, he it was, whose guile,

17. *chiefly:* seems to refer to "thou" as punctuated in the manuscript and in the early printed texts, but could possibly refer to "instruct" in line 19.   *spirit:* the Holy Spirit, a manifestation of God's creative power (usually pronounced as one syllable, "spirt")

21. *abyss:* the word used by the translators of the Old Testament into Greek for the Hebrew word translated as "the deep" in Gen. 1:2; cf. 2.405.

22. *What . . . dark:* what I do not know (but Milton had been totally blind since 1652)

24. *argument:* subject (as more evidently in 9.2), not referring only to the justification of God's ways

25. *providence:* God's purposeful shaping of human history

26. *justify:* In the poet's claim that he will *justify* God's actions lies the remarkable assertion not only that he is able to do this but also that God's ways are in need of justification. Richard Baxter wrote: "Justification . . . implyeth Accusation" in his *Aphorismes of Justification* (London, 1649), p. 135.

28. *what cause:* echoes *Aeneid* 1.8, *Musa, mihi causas memora:* "tell me the cause, o muse."

29. *grand parents:* i.e., Adam and Eve, both our ultimate grandparents in the biological regress and our distinguished ancestors

30–31. *fall off From:* abandon, become estranged from (the first use of *fall* in the poem)

32. *For one restraint:* except for the single prohibition (not to eat the fruit of the Tree of Knowledge; cf. line 2)

33. *Who first . . . revolt:* Homer (*Iliad* 1.8) asks who it was that first brought discord among the Greeks and instantly answers that it was Apollo.

34. *The infernal serpent:* here, as in 12.383, refers to "that old serpent, which is the Devil, and Satan" (Rev. 20:2–3) more distinctly than to the serpent seducer of Eve. He is *infernal* in the literal sense that he is doomed to the punishment of hell or "the bottomless pit," where Milton imagines all the devils as dramatically turned into serpents (10.509–40).

Stirred up with envy and revenge, deceived   35
The mother of mankind, what time his pride
Had cast him out from Heaven with all his host°   army
Of rebel angels, by whose aid aspiring
To set himself in glory above his peers,
He trusted to have equaled the most high,   40
If he opposed, and with ambitious aim
Against the throne and monarchy of God
Raised impious war in Heaven and battle proud
With vain attempt. Him the almighty power
Hurled headlong flaming from the ethereal sky   45
With hideous ruin and combustion down
To bottomless perdition, there to dwell
In adamantine chains and penal fire,
Who durst defy the omnipotent to arms.
Nine times the space that measures day and night   50
To mortal men, he with his horrid crew
Lay vanquished, rolling in the fiery gulf,
Confounded° though immortal; but his doom   defeated
Reserved him to more wrath, for now the thought

35. *deceived:* Adam falls "not deceived" (9.998)

36. *what time:* when

38–39. *aspiring . . . peers:* This is in essence the charge that Satan levels against God (see 5.794–97) as well as the very claim leveled against the English king in the attack on monarchy in the 1640s. (Line 38 is the first of the very few lines in the poem [see lines 98, 102, and 606] with a "feminine" ending, an unstressed, extra syllable.)

40. *the most high:* translation of one of the Hebrew names for God: *Elohim;* see Isa. 14:14–15: "I will be like the most High. Yet thou shalt be brought down to hell."

43. *impious war:* translates literally the Latin *bellum impium,* the phrase used for "civil war"; see also *Henry 5,* 3.3.15: "impious war."

45–47. *Hurled . . . perdition:* The lines blend biblical associations such as Isa. 14:12: "How art thou fallen from heaven, O Lucifer, son of the morning," and classical accounts, like Homer's description of Hep-

haestus "hurled" from heaven in *Iliad* 1.591. (*ruin,* line 46, keeps its etymological sense of "fall"; Latin *ruina.*)

45. *ethereal:* heavenly; literally, like the element (ether) that supposedly makes up the furthest regions of the universe

48. *adamantine chains:* unbreakable chains made of what legend holds to be the hardest substance known (adamant, from Greek *adamas* = invincible); Jude 1:6 speaks of the fallen "angels which kept not their first estate" bound "in everlasting chains"; in Phineas Fletcher's *Purple Island* (1633) the dragon is "bound in adamantine chain" (12.64).

50–51. *Nine . . . men:* Here and in 6.871 the devils fall for as many days as Hesiod (*Theogony* 664–735) gives for the Titans' fall from heaven after their overthrow by the Olympian gods.

52. *fiery gulf:* See Rev. 19:20, where "the beast" and "the false prophet" are "cast alive into a lake of fire burning with brimstone."

Both of lost happiness and lasting pain   55
Torments him; round he throws his baleful eyes
That witnessed huge affliction and dismay
Mixed with obdurate pride and steadfast hate.
At once as far as angels' ken he views
The dismal situation waste and wild,   60
A dungeon horrible, on all sides round
As one great furnace flamed, yet from those flames
No light, but rather darkness visible
Served only to discover sights of woe,
Regions of sorrow, doleful shades, where peace   65
And rest can never dwell, hope never comes
That comes to all, but torture without end
Still urges, and a fiery deluge fed
With ever-burning sulfur unconsumed.
Such place eternal justice had prepared   70
For those rebellious, here their prison ordained
In utter darkness and their portion set
As far removed from God and light of Heaven
As from the center thrice to the utmost pole.
O how unlike the place from whence they fell!   75
There the companions of his fall, o'erwhelmed
With floods and whirlwinds of tempestuous fire
He soon discerns, and weltering° by his side   *wallowing*
One next himself in power, and next in crime,
Long after known in Palestine and named   80
Beelzebub. To whom the arch-enemy,

56. *baleful:* 1) malignant; 2) sorrowful

57. *witnessed:* 1) saw; 2) bore witness to

59. *angels' ken:* Early editions do not use an apostrophe to indicate the possessive case. It is inserted here on the assumption that ken is a noun meaning "sight" and is used as it is in 11.379, though it could be a verb (= "are able to see") following *angels.*

63. *darkness visible:* The thought goes back to Job's description of the world of the dead as a realm where "the light is as darkness" (Job 10:22).

66. *hope never comes:* perhaps an echo of Dante's inscription over hell's gate: "All hope abandon ye who enter here" (*Inferno* 3.9: *lasciate ogne speranza, voi ch'intrate*)

68. *Still urges:* constantly incites

72. *portion:* fate, lot; cf. Luke 12:46: "The lord of that servant . . . will appoint him his portion with the unbelievers."

73–74. *As . . . pole:* The *center* here is the earth; the *pole* is one extreme point of the entire universe. The conception of the universe is Ptolemaic. In a passage of Aratus' *Phaenomena,* which Cicero paraphrased in *On the Nature of the Gods* (II, xl–xli), heaven similarly towers up to the celestial north pole, but the scene also directly recalls Virgil's picture of Avernus as twice as far under the earth as heaven is above (*Aeneid* 6.577–79).

81. *Beelzebub:* literally, "lord of the flies" (perhaps derived from Middle Eastern deities who were worshipped as deliverers

And thence in Heaven called Satan, with bold words
Breaking the horrid silence thus began:
    "If thou beest he—but O how fallen! how changed
From him, who in the happy realms of light   85
Clothed with transcendent brightness didst outshine
Myriads though bright; if he whom mutual league,
United thoughts and counsels, equal hope
And hazard in the glorious enterprise,
Joined with me once, now misery hath joined   90
In equal ruin; into what pit thou seest
From what height fallen, so much the stronger proved
He with his thunder; and till then who knew
The force of those dire arms? Yet not for those,
Nor what the potent victor in his rage   95
Can else inflict do I repent or change,
Though changed in outward luster; that fixed mind
And high disdain, from sense of injured merit,
That with the mightiest raised me to contend,
And to the fierce contention brought along   100
Innumerable force of spirits armed
That durst dislike his reign, and me preferring,
His utmost power with adverse power opposed
In dubious battle on the plains of Heaven

from insect pests) and related etymologically to the Philistine god, Baal. For Milton's readers, *Beelzebub* was vaguely the prince of the first order of demons that Robert Burton made him in his *Anatomy of Melancholy* (1621, 1.2.1–2) or the monarch of burning hell that Marlowe made him in Faustus' first invocation in *Doctor Faustus* (1.3). The traditions behind Beelzebub's title "chief of the devils" in Matt. 10:24 (cf. Mark 3:22 and Luke 11:15) were skeptically reviewed by John Selden in his *De Dis Syris syntagmata* II, (London, 1617), p. 207.

82. *Satan:* In Hebrew, Satan means "enemy" or "adversary"; this is how he is known in Heaven, rather than as Lucifer, his old name, meaning "bringer of light" which was forfeited with his fall.

84–85. *If . . . him:* Satan's first words recall Aeneas' vision of the ghost of Hector on the night of Troy's fall, so "changed from the living Hector" (*Aeneid* 2.275–76). Cf.

Isa. 14:12: "How art thou fallen . . . O Lucifer." Satan's shift from "fallen" to "changed" suggests an unwillingness to admit what has happened.

94–97. *Yet . . . luster:* A possible echo of Capaneus' boast in *Inferno* 14.52–91, that Jove's thunder would never break his blasphemous spirit, or of the warning of Aeschylus' Prometheus to Hermes (*Prometheus* 987–96) that he would never yield to Zeus though the god might forever buffet him with thunder and snow.

98. *injured merit:* Contrast Satan's assertion of merit here and in 2.5 and 21 with the merit that makes Christ "more than birthright Son of God" (3.309) and entitles him to reign in heaven (6.43).

102. *preferring:* 1) liking better; 2) advancing in rank, promoting

104. *dubious:* of uncertain outcome (though uncertain to whom?)

And shook his throne. What though the field be lost?   105
All is not lost; the unconquerable will,
And study of revenge, immortal hate,
And courage never to submit or yield—
And what is else not to be overcome?
That glory never shall his wrath or might   110
Extort from me. To bow and sue for grace
With suppliant knee and deify his power,
Who from the terror of this arm so late
Doubted his empire, that were low indeed,
That were an ignominy and shame beneath   115
This downfall, since by fate the strength of gods
And this empyreal substance cannot fail,
Since through experience of this great event
In arms not worse, in foresight much advanced,
We may with more successful hope resolve   120
To wage by force or guile eternal war,
Irreconcilable to our grand foe,
Who now triumphs° and in the excess of joy   *celebrates*
Sole reigning holds the tyranny of Heaven."
    So spake the apostate angel, though in pain,   125
Vaunting aloud, but racked with deep despair;
And him thus answered soon his bold compeer:

---

105. *shook his throne:* But see 6.833–34, where we are told that everything in heaven "shook," except "the throne itself of God."

107. *study:* carries with it the Latin sense of *studium* = zeal, desire

109. *what . . . overcome:* i.e., what else can "not being overcome" mean?

112. *deify:* the irony of the word is obvious; God's power does not need to be deified.

114. *Doubted:* feared for (the subject of the verb is *God*)

115. *ignominy:* disgrace; probably pronounced "ignomy" here and in 2.207, though not in 6.383. "Ignomy" was a common spelling, though the elision may come at the end of the word before "and."

116–117. *since . . . fail:* Compare the unwilling recognition of the supremacy of fate by Belial (2.197), Mammon (2.231–33), and Beelzebub (2.393) with Sin's certainty

that fate has doomed her and Death to a common end (2.805–07) and God's declaration that his "will is fate" (7.173). Though the angels are sometimes called "gods" (even by God himself in 3.341), Satan's use of the word here reflects his consistent misunderstanding of the singular nature of God, anticipating Satan's claim (5.853–66) that the devils are self-begotten and his promise to Eve (9.708) that by eating the forbidden fruit she and Adam should "be as gods."

117. *empyreal substance:* the pure fire of which angels are composed; see Heb. 1:7: "who maketh his angels spirits, and his ministers a flame of fire."

124. *tyranny of Heaven:* This is the central claim of the rebellious angels: that God's rule is *tyranny*, the imposition of rule over one's equals (belied by the fact that they are created by God); see p. xxxii above.

"O prince, O chief of many thronèd powers,
That led the embattled° seraphim to war   *ready for battle*
Under thy conduct, and, in dreadful deeds   130
Fearless, endangered Heaven's perpetual king
And put to proof his high supremacy,
Whether upheld by strength, or chance, or fate;
Too well I see and rue the dire event°   *outcome*
That with sad overthrow and foul defeat   135
Hath lost us Heaven, and all this mighty host
In horrible destruction laid thus low,
As far as gods and heavenly essences
Can perish, for the mind and spirit remains
Invincible and vigor soon returns,   140
Though all our glory extinct and happy state
Here swallowed up in endless misery.
But what if he our conqueror (whom I now
Of force believe almighty, since no less
Than such could have o'erpowered such force as ours)   145
Have left us this our spirit and strength entire°   *undiminished*
Strongly to suffer and support° our pains   *endure*
That we may so suffice his vengeful ire
Or do him mightier service as his thralls°   *slaves*
By right of war, whate'er his business be: 150
Here in the heart of hell to work in fire
Or do his errands in the gloomy deep.
What can it then avail, though yet we feel
Strength undiminished or eternal being,
To undergo eternal punishment?"   155
Whereto with speedy words the arch-fiend replied:
        "Fallen cherub, to be weak is miserable,
Doing or suffering, but of this be sure,

---

128. *powers:* one of the nine orders of angels, like *seraphim* in line 129 (the other seven are: cherubim, thrones, dominations, virtues, principalities, archangels, and angels)

131. *perpetual:* Beelzebub's admission that God has been *king* from the beginning (*perpetual* = continuous) perhaps is intended subtly to suggest that his rule is not necessarily eternal, a familiar philosophical distinction.

144. *Of force:* 1) necessarily; 2) by his power

148–150. *may so suffice . . . be:* Beelzebub's words recall the description of the fallen angels in *Christian Doctrine* (I, ix; in *Works* 15, 109) as "sometimes permitted to wander throughout the whole earth, the air, the heaven itself, to execute the judgments of God" (*suffice* = satisfy).

152. *deep:* the region filled by chaos; see 7.92–93.

158. *Doing or suffering:* whether active or passive, perhaps here parodying the two

To do aught good never will be our task,
But ever to do ill our sole delight,   160
As being the contrary to his high will
Whom we resist. If then his providence
Out of our evil seek to bring forth good,
Our labor must be to pervert that end
And out of good still to find means of evil,   165
Which oft times may succeed° so as perhaps   *ensue, follow*
Shall grieve him, if I fail not, and disturb°   *divert*
His inmost counsels from their destined aim.
But see the angry victor hath recalled
His ministers of vengeance and pursuit   170
Back to the gates of Heaven; the sulphurous hail,
Shot after us in storm, o'erblown hath laid°   *calmed*
The fiery surge, that from the precipice
Of Heaven received us falling, and the thunder,
Winged with red lightning and impetuous rage,   175
Perhaps hath spent his shafts and ceases now
To bellow through the vast and boundless deep.
Let us not slip° the occasion, whether scorn   *let slip, miss*
Or satiate° fury yield it from our foe.   *satisfied*
Seest thou yon dreary plain, forlorn and wild,   180
The seat of desolation, void of light,
Save what the glimmering of these livid flames
Casts pale and dreadful? Thither let us tend
From off the tossing of these fiery waves;
There rest, if any rest can harbor there,   185

---

kinds of religious life, the active and contemplative, or contrasting the energy of Satan with the suffering of Christ; cf. 2.199, n., and *PR*, 3.195.

160–168. *ever . . . aim:* Satan's dramatic resolve and self-characterization here and in 9.118–30, prepare for the final discovery, in Adam's words, that God shall produce all the good to be worked in the world by the Son's redemption of Adam's sin, and so "evil turn to good" (12.471).

167. *fail not:* am not mistaken

176. *his:* its (and at line 572; "its" in line 254 in its modern sense is an unusual usage for Milton)

180–183. *yon dreary . . . dreadful:* The *livid* darkness recalls other literary descriptions of hell, such as Statius' picture of the shadowy *Styx livida* (*Thebaid* I, 57), Dante's picture of the place where all light is "silent" (*Inferno* 5.28), and the fiery but lightless land described in Caedmon's *Genesis* (333–34). *dreary* = 1) gloomy; 2) blood-covered

182. *livid:* blue (the color of burning sulphur)

185–186. *rest . . . powers:* for the play on *rest*, compare Shakespeare, *Richard II*, 5.1.5–6: "Here let us rest, if this rebellious earth, / Have any rest for her true king's queen."

And, reassembling our afflicted powers,
Consult how we may henceforth most offend°   *harm*
Our enemy, our own loss how repair,
How overcome this dire calamity,
What reinforcement we may gain from hope,   190
If not what resolution from despair."
    Thus Satan, talking to his nearest mate,
With head uplift above the wave and eyes
That sparkling blazed; his other parts besides,
prone on the flood, extended long and large,   195
Lay floating many a rood, in bulk as huge
As whom the fables name of monstrous size,
Titanian, or Earth-born, that warred on Jove,
Briareos or Typhon, whom the den
By ancient Tarsus held, or that sea beast   200
Leviathan, which God of all his works
Created hugest that swim the ocean stream.
Him haply slumbering on the Norway foam
The pilot of some small night-foundered skiff,
Deeming° some island, oft, as seamen tell,   *believing*
With fixèd anchor in his scaly rind
Moors by his side under the lee,° while night   *shelter*

---

186. *afflicted powers:* defeated armies
191. *If not:* or else
196. *rood:* i.e., rod, a unit of variable linear measurement, six to eight yards
199. *Briareos or Typhon:* In the war of the Titans with the Olympian gods, the hundred-armed *Briareos* is described by Hesiod (*Theogony* 713–16) as helping to defeat his brother Titans. For the parallel with the revolt of Satan's angels, see Hesiod's story of Typhon, or Typhoeus, as the most frightful of Earth-born monsters (*Theogony* 819–85) whom Zeus hurled back from Olympus and Ovid's description of him as buried alive under Etna and neighboring mountains (*Metamorphoses* 5.346–58). The mythological revolts were allegorized by Natale Conti (*Mythologiae* [1551] liber 6.xxii) as symbolizing ambition that assails even heaven itself.
200. *Tarsus:* The connection of Typhon with Tarsus stems from Pindar's reference to

Typhon, in *Pythian Odes* I, 28–39, as having been born in a cave in Cilicia, of which Tarsus was the capital.
201–208. *Leviathan . . . delays:* Of all the biblical references to the mysterious sea-monster *Leviathan*, the closest to Milton's use is Isaiah's prophecy that the Lord "shall punish Leviathan, the piercing serpent, even Leviathan, that crooked serpent; and he shall slay the dragon that is in the sea" (Isa. 28:1). The tale of the mariners who mistake the leviathan for an island is widespread: e.g., in the story of Sinbad the sailor in the *Arabian Nights,* in Olaus Magnus' *Historia de gentibus septentrionalibus* (Rome, 1555), in Caxton's *Mirrour of the World* (II, ix), in Bartholemew's *De proprietatibus rerum* (xiii, 26), etc. See J. H. Pitman, "Milton and the Physiologus," in *MLN*, 40 (1925), 439. Cf. the unfallen "leviathan" at 7.412–16.
204. *night-foundered:* engulfed by night; i.e., lost in the darkness; cf. *Comus,* line 483.

Invests° the sea, and wishèd morn delays,   *covers, envelops*
So stretched out huge in length the arch-fiend lay
Chained on the burning lake, nor ever thence   210
Had risen or heaved his head, but that the will
And high permission of all-ruling Heaven
Left him at large° to his own dark designs,   *free, at liberty*
That with reiterated crimes he might
Heap on himself damnation while he sought   215
Evil to others and, enraged, might see
How all his malice served but to bring forth
Infinite goodness, grace, and mercy shown
On man by him seduced, but on himself
Treble confusion,° wrath, and vengeance poured.   *ruin, distress*
Forthwith upright he rears from off the pool
His mighty stature; on each hand the flames
Driven backward slope their pointing spires and, rolled
In billows, leave i' th' midst a horrid vale.
Then with expanded wings he steers his flight   225
Aloft, incumbent on the dusky air
That felt unusual weight, till on dry land
He lights,° if it were land that ever burned   *sets down, alights*
With solid, as the lake with liquid fire,
And such appeared in hue,° as when the force   *aspect, form*
Of subterranean wind transports a hill
Torn from Pelorus or the shattered side
Of thundering Etna, whose combustible
And fueled entrails thence conceiving fire,
Sublimed with mineral fury, aid the winds   235

210–215. *nor ever . . . damnation:* See Milton's discussion of scriptural evidence for the doctrine of God's blamelessness in permitting the crimes of the wicked in *Christian Doctrine* I, viii; *Works* 15, esp. pp. 67–91.

224. *horrid:* horrible or frightening, but also with its etymological sense of spiky or bristling (like the pointed flames)

226. *incumbent on:* leaning upon, lying on

230–237. *force . . . smoke:* The lines recall Virgil's picture of Mount Etna darkening the promontory of *Pelorus* in Sicily with its smoke (*Aeneid* 3.570–77) and Ovid's account of the rending of Sicily from Italy by

winds bursting out of the earth (*Metamorphoses* 15.296–377). Ovid's seismology was still acceptable when Burton suggested in his *Anatomy of Melancholy* (2.2.3) that the earth might "be full of wind, or sulfurous, innate fire, as our Meteorologists inform us, which, sometimes breaking out, causeth horrible earthquakes."

232. *Pelorus:* Cape Faro in Sicily, near Mount Etna

235. *Sublimed:* turned to vapor (an alchemical image of purifying substances by first exposing them to extreme heat in which they are converted to a gas and then resolidified in a purer form upon cooling)

And leave a singèd bottom all involved°   *wreathed, enveloped*
With stench and smoke: such resting found the sole
Of unblessed feet. Him followed his next mate,
Both glorying to have scaped the Stygian flood
As gods, and by their own recovered strength,   240
Not by the sufferance of supernal° power.   *heavenly*
  "Is this the region, this the soil, the clime,"
Said then the lost archangel, "this the seat°   *residence*
That we must change° for Heaven, this mournful gloom   *exchange*
For that celestial light? Be it so, since he   245
Who now is sovereign can dispose and bid
What shall be right. Farthest from him is best
Whom reason hath equaled, force hath made supreme
Above his equals. Farewell happy fields
Where joy forever dwells. Hail horrors, hail   250
Infernal world, and thou profoundest hell
Receive thy new possessor: one who brings
A mind not to be changed by place or time.
The mind is its own place and in itself
Can make a Heaven of hell, a hell of Heaven.   255
What matter where, if I be still the same
And what I should be, all but less than he
Whom thunder hath made greater? Here at least
We shall be free. The almighty hath not built
Here for his envy, will not drive us hence;   260

239. *Stygian:* The word is often used without explicit reference to the Styx, the most famous of hell's rivers, generally to mean "infernal," but usually it particularly connotes darkness, as here and in *Elegy* 4, line 95.

241. *sufferance:* permission (see line 213 above)

242. *clime:* region (cf. 1.297, 2.572, 10.678, and 12.636)

246. *sovereign:* For Satan, God's sovereignty is not essential; God merely "now is sovereign." "Sovran" was Milton's preferred spelling of the word, hence pronounced with two syllables.

254–259. *The mind . . . free:* Satan's heresy is traced by D. C. Allen in *MLN*, LXXI (1956), 325, to Amaury de Bene, who was burned early in the thirteenth century for arguing that Heaven and hell were states of mind rather than actual places. The wider roots of Satan's boast can be traced to Renaissance distortions of the Stoic doctrine that the mind is master of its fate, and to the interpretation of Christ's teaching that "the kingdom of God is within you" by Jakob Boehme and his disciples as meaning that "we have heaven and hell in ourselves" (*The Threefold Life of Man* [1620], 14.72); on *its*, see note on line 176.

257. *all but less than:* all but equal to (but the contorted phrasing suggests Satan's anxiety about the claim)

260. *for his envy:* i.e., so he might envy us (see the similar usage at 4.516–7 and 8.494)

Here we may reign secure, and in my choice
To reign is worth ambition though in hell:
Better to reign in hell than serve in Heaven.
But wherefore let we then our faithful friends,
The associates and copartners of our loss,   265
Lie thus astonished on the oblivious pool
And call them not to share with us their part
In this unhappy mansion,° or once more   *dwelling place*
With rallied arms to try what may be yet
Regained in Heaven or what more lost in hell?"   270
     So Satan spake, and him Beelzebub
Thus answered: "Leader of those armies bright,
Which but the omnipotent none could have foiled,
If once they hear that voice, their liveliest° pledge   *most vital*
Of hope in fears and dangers, heard so oft   275
In worst extremes and on the perilous edge
Of battle when it raged, in all assaults
Their surest signal, they will soon resume
New courage and revive, though now they lie
Groveling and prostrate on yon lake of fire,   280
As we erewhile,° astounded and amazed—   *previously*
No wonder, fallen such a pernicious° height."   *destructive*
     He scarce had ceased when the superior fiend
Was moving toward the shore, his ponderous shield,
Ethereal temper, massy, large, and round,   285
Behind him cast; the broad circumference
Hung on his shoulders like the moon, whose orb
Through optic glass the Tuscan artist views

263. *Better . . . Heaven:* The passage
contrasts with Abdiel's warning to Satan in
Heaven that his reign in hell will be mere
bondage (6.178–88). It parodies a remark
attributed to Julius Caesar by Plutarch (*Lives*,
"Life of Caesar," 11.2) that he would rather
be the first man in a Spanish village than sec-
ond in Rome. Cf. Ps. 84:10: "I had rather be
a doorkeeper in the house of my God, than
to dwell in the tents of wickedness." Also
note Phineas Fletcher, *Purple Island:* "In
heav'n they scorn'd to serve, so now in hell
they reigne" (7.10).
     265. *The associates . . . loss:* Cf. *As You
Like It*, 2.1.1: "Now, my co-mates and broth-
ers in exile."

266. *the oblivious pool:* suggests the un-
derworld river Lethe in Greek mythology, a
drink of whose waters made the spirits of the
dead forget their earthly life (*oblivious* = caus-
ing oblivion), though Satan and the fallen
angels are pointedly unable to forget their
fate; cf. 2.606–14.
     269. *rallied arms:* restored forces
     276. *edge:* decisive moment, but also
the front line of battle (as in 6.108)
     285. *Ethereal temper:* hardened in the
ether (the element supposedly existing above
the earth)
     288. *the Tuscan artist:* i.e., Galileo, the
first astronomer to use a telescope (*optic glass*)
capable of revealing the real nature of the

At evening from the top of Fiesole
Or in Valdarno to descry new lands,   290
Rivers, or mountains in her spotty globe.
His spear, to equal which the tallest pine
Hewn on Norwegian hills, to be the mast
Of some great admiral, were but a wand,
He walked with to support uneasy steps   295
Over the burning marl, not like those steps
On Heaven's azure, and the torrid clime
Smote on him sore besides, vaulted with fire;
Nathless° he so endured, till on the beach   *nevertheless*
Of that inflamèd sea he stood and called   300
His legions, angel forms, who lay entranced,
Thick as autumnal leaves that strew the brooks
In Vallombrosa, where the Etrurian shades
High overarched embower; or scattered sedge
Afloat, when with fierce winds Orion armed   305
Hath vexed the Red Sea coast, whose waves o'erthrew
Busiris and his Memphian chivalry
While with perfidious hatred they pursued

moon's surface. In *Areopagitica* (*Works* 4, 330), Milton recalls a visit to him at *Fiesole* in the Tuscan hills above the Arno, whose valley is the *Valdarno* (line 290). Interestingly, Galileo was blind at the time of Milton's visit, but Milton never mentions the fact.

292–294. *to equal . . . wand:* The simile establishes a ratio: spear is to pine as pine is to wand (i.e., small stick). By the time the reader reaches the end of the simile the spear becomes a sign of weakness.

294. *admiral:* admiral's flagship, the primary ship in a fleet. The spelling 'ammiral" in the early texts probably indicates Milton's preferred pronunciation, and might reflect a supposed etymological link to "emir" (cf. line 348).

296. *burning marl:* brimstone (*marl* = soil or earth)

302–304. *Thick . . . embower:* Perhaps a memory of Dante's spirits numberless as autumn leaves (*Inferno*, 3.112–14) or of the same image (as C. M. Bowra notes in *From Virgil to Milton,* 240–41) in Homer, Bacchylides, Virgil, and Tasso. Milton may have

visited *Vallombrosa* (literally, shady valley) during his stay in Tuscany. Cf. Isa. 34:4, where it is said that "all the host of heaven" shall "fall down, as the leaf falleth off from the vine."

303. *Etrurian shades:* Tuscan foliage (with a play on *shades* = spirits)

304–311. *scattered sedge . . . wheels:* The rapidly compounding simile fuses Virgilian descriptions of the constellation Orion as cloudy and stormy (*Aeneid* 1.535; 7.719) with biblical references to the masses of seaweed (*sedge*) in the Red Sea, which in turn recalls the destruction there of Pharaoh's chariots and horsemen (the *Memphian chivalry*) that it overwhelmed as they tried to stop the flight of the Hebrews across it from the Land of *Goshen* in Egypt to safety on the eastern shore.

307. *Busiris:* Milton identifies the mythical Busiris with the Pharaoh of Exodus, who had long been recognized by commentators as a type of Satan, *vera daemonis figura,* as he is called in the Prologue to the *Rule of St. Benedict.*

The sojourners of Goshen, who beheld
From the safe shore their floating carcasses   ° 310
And broken chariot wheels, so thick bestrewn
Abject° and lost lay these, covering the flood,   *defeated, dispirited*
Under amazement of their hideous change.
He called so loud that all the hollow deep
Of hell resounded: "Princes, potentates,   315
Warriors: the flower of Heaven once yours, now lost,
If such astonishment as this can seize
Eternal spirits; or have ye chosen this place
After the toil of battle to repose°   *restore*
Your wearied virtue° for the ease you find   *strength*
To slumber here as in the vales of Heaven?
Or in this abject posture have ye sworn
To adore the conqueror, who now beholds
Cherub and seraph rolling in the flood
With scattered arms and ensigns, till anon   325
His swift pursuers from Heaven gates discern
The advantage and, descending, tread us down
Thus drooping, or with linkèd thunderbolts
Transfix us to the bottom of this gulf?
Awake, arise, or be for ever fallen."   330
      They heard and were abashed, and up they sprung
Upon the wing, as when men wont to watch
On duty, sleeping found by whom they dread,
Rouse and bestir themselves ere well awake.
Nor did they not perceive the evil plight   335
In which they were or the fierce pains not feel,
Yet to their general's voice they soon obeyed
Innumerable. As when the potent rod
Of Amram's son in Egypt's evil day
Waved round the coast up called a pitchy° cloud   *black (like pitch)*

---

309. *sojourners of Goshen:* See Genesis
47:27: "Israel dwelt in the land of Egypt, in
the country of Goshen."

314. *deep:* The manuscript of Book 1
reads "deeps," perhaps the correct reading
designed to suggest the reverberation of
sound.

325. *arms and ensigns:* weapons and
banners

335–336. *Nor . . . feel:* The sentence
has two double negatives (*Nor . . . not per-*

ceive; Nor . . . not feel), so they do *perceive*
and *feel.*

339. *Amram's son:* i.e., Moses, who
called down a plague of locusts upon the
Egyptians, so that it covered "the face of the
whole earth, so that the land was darkened"
(Exod. 10:12–15); cf. 12.176–99.

340. *Waved round the coast:* Milton's
version of the description of Moses, who
"stretched forth his rod over the land of
Egypt" (Exod. 10:13); *coast* = region

Of locusts, warping on the eastern wind,
That o'er the realm of impious Pharaoh hung
Like night and darkened all the land of Nile,
So numberless were those bad angels seen
Hovering on wing under the cope° of hell   *canopy, roof*
'Twixt upper, nether, and surrounding fires,
Till, as a signal given, the uplifted spear
Of their great sultan waving to direct
Their course, in even balance down they light
On the firm brimstone and fill all the plain: 350
A multitude like which the populous north
Poured never from her frozen loins to pass
Rhine or the Danube when her barbarous sons
Came like a deluge on the south and spread
Beneath Gibraltar to the Libyan sands.   355
Forthwith from every squadron and each band
The heads and leaders thither haste where stood
Their great commander: godlike shapes and forms
Excelling human, princely dignities,
And powers that erst° in Heaven sat on thrones,   *formerly, once*
Though of their names in heavenly records now
Be no memorial, blotted out and razed
By their rebellion from the books of life.
Nor had they yet among the sons of Eve
Got them new names, till wandering o'er the earth,   365
Through God's high sufferance, for the trial of man,
By falsities and lies the greatest part
Of mankind they corrupted to forsake

341. *warping:* whirling about, swarming
349. *even balance:* perfect formation
353–355. *Rhine . . . sands:* The simile comparing the reinvigorated fallen angels to the Barbarian invasion may derive from Machiavelli's opening of *The Florentine History* (anonymous translation of 1674): "The people inhabiting the Regions Northwards from the rivers *Rhyne* and *Danube*, living in a healthful clime, and apt for Generation ofttimes increase to such vast multitudes, that part of them are constrained to forsake their Native Country, and seek new places to dwell in. . . .These people were they, who destroyed the Roman Empire" (pp. 1–2). The crossing of the Vandals into North Africa (*the*

Libyan sands) is prominent on the following pages of Machiavelli's *History* (pp. 4–5).
363. *books of life:* The phrase is biblical for the recording of the names of the faithful; see Ps. 69:28, Rev. 3:5, and the "Lamb's book of life" in Rev. 21:27, into which came nothing "that defileth, neither whatsoever, worketh abomination or maketh a lie."
367–371. *By falsities . . . brute:* The lines recall Paul's contempt for pagan religions that "changed the truth of God into a lie" (Rom. 1:25) and "changed the glory of the incorruptible God into an image made like to corruptible man, and to birds, and fourfooted beasts, and creeping things" (Rom. 1:25, 23).

God their creator and the invisible
Glory of him that made them to transform   370
Oft to the image of a brute adorned
With gay religions full of pomp and gold,
And devils to adore for deities.
Then were they known to men by various names
And various idols through the heathen world.   375
Say, muse, their names then known, who first, who last,
Roused from the slumber on that fiery couch
At their great emperor's call, as next in worth
Came singly where he stood on the bare strand,°   *beach, shore*
While the promiscuous crowd stood yet aloof?   380
The chief were those who, from the pit of hell
Roaming to seek their prey on earth, durst fix
Their seats long after next the seat of God,
Their altars by his altar, gods adored
Among the nations round, and durst abide   385
Jehovah thundering out of Sion, throned
Between the cherubim, yea, often placed
Within his sanctuary itself their shrines,
Abominations, and with cursèd things
His holy rites and solemn feasts profaned,   390
And with their darkness durst affront° his light.   *confront, defy*
First Moloch, horrid king, besmeared with blood

372. *gay religions:* ostentatious rituals

373. *devils . . . deities:* Cf. Deut. 32:17:
"They sacrificed unto devils, not to God."
Milton's phrasing balances both terms by the
alliteration of "devils" and "deities" and the
internal rhyme in "adore" and "for."

376. *Say, muse . . . last:* The line echoes
Homer's introduction of the catalogue of
ships in the *Iliad* (2.484) with the plea to the
Muse to tell him who were the commanders
and lords of the Greeks. See also *Aeneid*
7.641ff.

377. *fiery couch:* i.e., the burning lake

380. *promiscuous:* disordered, randomly
mixed together

384–388. *Their altars . . . their shrines:*
1 and 2 Kings tell the stories of various apos-
tate kings of Judah who "did that which was
evil in the sight of the Lord" (2 Kings 21:2)

by setting up altars to pagan gods in and
around the Temple; see also Ezek. 43:8.

386. *thundering out of Sion:* follows
Amos 1:2: "The Lord will roar from Zion"

386–387. *throned . . . cherubim:* Gold
cherubim stood at each side of the ark of the
covenant on Mount Sion; see 2 Kings 19:15:
"O Lord God of Israel, which dwellest be-
tween the cherubims," and Ps. 80:1: "Shep-
herd of Israel . . . thou that dwellest between
the cherubims." (The King James transla-
tions make an English plural out of the al-
ready plural Hebrew "cherubim.")

389. *Abominations:* idols (see 401–3n.)

392. *Moloch:* The Hebrew name liter-
ally means "king." He was a god of the Am-
monites, who worshipped him in the form of
a hollow idol filled with fire into which chil-
dren were thrown for sacrifices.

Of human sacrifice and parents' tears,
Though for the noise of drums and timbrels loud
Their children's cries unheard that passed through fire   395
To his grim idol. Him the Ammonite
Worshipped in Rabba and her watery plain,
In Argob and in Basan, to the stream
Of utmost Arnon. Nor content with such
Audacious neighborhood,° the wisest heart   *location*
Of Solomon he led by fraud to build
His temple right against the temple of God
On that opprobrious hill and made his grove
The pleasant valley of Hinnom, Tophet thence
And black Gehenna called, the type of hell.   405
Next Chemos, the obscene° dread of Moab's sons,   *repulsive, loathsome*
From Aroer to Nebo, and the wild
Of southmost Abarim; in Hesebon
And Horonaim, Seon's realm, beyond

394–395. *for the noise . . . fire:* I.e., the noise of the drums drowned out the cries of the children sacrificed.

397. *Rabba:* Rabba (or Rabbath, modern Ammon in Jordan), the Ammonite capital, was conquered by David (2 Sam. 12:27).

398–399. *Agrob . . . Arnon:* Two towns that lay near the Moabite border stream of Arnon, where the Israelites destroyed the "children of Ammon" (Deut. 3:1–13).

401–403. *Of Solomon . . . hill:* Beguiled by his wives, Solomon built "an high place for Chemosh (Chemos), the abomination of Moab, in the hill that is before Jerusalem, and for Moloch, the abomination of Ammon" (1 Kings 11:7). The hill was the Mount of Olives, *that opprobrious hill,* the "mount of corruption" of 2 Kings 23:13, and the "hill of scandal" of line 416 and the "offensive mountain" of line 443 below.

404–405. *valley of Hinnom . . . Gehenna called:* In Jer. 19:5–6 the apostate Israelites burn "their sons with fire for burnt offerings unto Baal" in the valley of the "son of Hinnom." The Greek word "Gehenna," as St. Jerome wrote in his *Commentary on the Gospel of Matthew,* is not biblical, but under

that name he identified the valley and associated it with the Baal-worship of the neighboring valley of Tophet, which was known as " the monument to the dead."

405. *type:* figure, foreshadowing, symbol

406. *Chemos:* a fertility God of the Moabites; in Num. 21:29, the Moabites are called the "people of Chemosh." He is not identified in Selden's *De Dis Syris,* and Thomas Fuller was in doubt whether the "Babylonish Deity Bell" was " the same with Chemosh and Baal-Peor (which is the opinion of St. Jerome) and if not, wherein lay the difference" (*A Pisgah-Sight of Palestine,* 1650, p. 64).

407–408. *From Aroer . . . Horonaim:* Moabite towns and geographical features conspicuous on Thomas Fuller's map of the land of the tribe of Reuben (*A Pisgah-Sight of Palestine,* p. 55), together with the other places that are named in lines 398 and 406 and 410–18 below.

409. *Seon's realm:* Seon (Sihon), King of the Ammorites, conquered Moab and was in turn conquered by Moses. The defeat of Seon is celebrated in Num. 21:25; cf. Ps. 135:11 and 136:18–19, and Isa. 15:4.

The flowery dale of Sibma clad with vines,   410
And Eleale to the Asphaltic Pool;
(Peor his other name, when he enticed
Israel in Sittim on their march from Nile
To do him wanton rites, which cost them woe).
Yet thence his lustful orgies he enlarged   415
Even to that hill of scandal, by the grove
Of Moloch homicide, lust hard by hate,
Till good Josiah drove them thence to hell.
With these came they who, from the bordering flood
Of old Euphrates to the brook that parts   420
Egypt from Syrian ground, had general names
Of Baalim and Ashtaroth, those male,
These feminine. For spirits when they please
Can either sex assume or both, so soft
And uncompounded is their essence pure,   425
Not tied or manacled with joint or limb,
Nor founded on the brittle strength of bones,
Like cumbrous° flesh, but in what shape they choose,   *cumbersome, unwieldy*
Dilated° or condensed, bright or obscure,   *enlarged*
Can execute their airy purposes   430

410–411. *Sibma . . . Eleale:* Close to the city of Eleale on Fuller's 1650 map, *Sibma* (or Sibmah) is marked by a vine, and in his text the valley is described as filled with vineyards for whose destruction the prophets later mourned (cf. Isa. 16:8–9, and Jer. 48:32).

411. *the Asphaltic Pool:* i.e., The Dead Sea, which is described in a famous passage of Diodorus Siculus' *Library* (19.98) as producing a floating island of solid asphalt every year (actually a dark scum that forms from the mineral deposits left as the waters evaporate)

412–413. *Peor . . . Nile:* On the exodus from Egypt to Canaan "Israel abode in Shittim, and the people began to commit whoredom with the daughters of Moab. . . . And Israel joined himself unto Baal-peor" (Num. 25:1–3).

417. *hard by:* next to

418. *good Josiah:* King Josiah, reforming king of Judah, destroyed the idols of

Moloch, Chemos, and Baal (2 Kings 23:4–20).

420. *Euphrates to the brook:* The *Euphrates* bounded Palestine on the east, and the "*brook* Besor" (1 Sam. 30:10) marked the Egyptian frontier.

422. *Baalim and Ashtaroth:* plural forms of the names of pagan gods: cf. the singular *Astoreth* in line 438 below. Baal-peor (line 412) was only one of several local Baals in Scripture.

425. *uncompounded:* undifferentiated into parts

428. *in what shape they choose:* In attributing protean powers to the devils and angels, Milton possibly had in mind a passage in Michael Psellus' work of the tenth century, the *De operatione daemonum* (5.8–9), published in Paris in 1615 and widely quoted by writers on witchcraft to explain spirits appearing in the forms of beasts, men, or angels. Cf. 3.636, 4.800, and 6.327–92.

And works of love or enmity fulfill.
For these the race of Israel oft forsook
Their living strength and unfrequented left
His righteous altar, bowing lowly down
To bestial gods, for which their heads as low   435
Bowed down in battle, sunk before the spear
Of despicable foes. With these in troop
Came Astoreth, whom the Phoenicians called
Astarte, Queen of Heaven, with crescent horns,
To whose bright image nightly by the moon   440
Sidonian virgins paid their vows and songs,
In Sion also not unsung, where stood
Her temple on the offensive mountain, built
By that uxorious king whose heart, though large,
Beguiled by fair idolatresses, fell   445
To idols foul. Thammuz came next behind,
Whose annual wound in Lebanon allured
The Syrian damsels to lament his fate
In amorous ditties all a summer's day,
While smooth Adonis from his native rock   450
Ran purple to the sea, supposed with blood
Of Thammuz yearly wounded; the love tale
Infected Sion's daughters with like heat,
Whose wanton passions in the sacred porch
Ezekiel saw, when by the vision led   455

433–434. *unfrequented . . . altar:* cf. Ovid's *Metamorphoses*: "The unfrequented Altar without fire" (1.374, Sandys' trans.)

438–439. *Astoreth . . . Astarte:* a Phoenician fertility goddess with the head of a horned bull; cf. "Nativity Ode," line 200: "mooned Ashtaroth, Heaven's queen."

441. *Sidonian:* i.e., Phoenicia (Sidon was the major city of Phoenicia.)

443. *offensive mountain:* see 401–3n.

444. *that uxorious king:* i.e., Solomon, who, overfond of his 700 wives (uxorious), was led to follow pagan gods (1 Kings 11: 1–4); for his *large* heart, see 1 Kings 4:29 where God gives him "largeness of heart" (i.e., intellect).

446–452. *Thammuz . . . wounded:* Public mourning for the death of *Thammuz* (conflated with Adonis) took place annually

in July, when the river Adonis in Lebanon ran red (with mud from red clay but supposedly with the god's blood). The story was popular and could be found in works as heterogeneous as Sir Walter Raleigh's *History of the World* (1614), George Sandys' *Relation of a Journey* (1615), and Charles Stephanus' *Dictionarium Historicum* (1553) in forms so close to Milton's passage that all of them have been mentioned as possible sources. Thammuz' story gets popularly retold in *amorous ditties* (line 448) and as a *love tale* (line 452), because Astarte and Thammuz were lovers in mythology and were later identified with Venus and Adonis.

454–55. *sacred . . . saw:* See Ezek. 8:13–14, where the prophet sees "women weeping for Thammuz" at "the door to the gate of the Lord's house."

His eye surveyed the dark idolatries
Of alienated Judah. Next came one
Who mourned in earnest when the captive ark
Maimed his brute image, head and hands lopped off
In his own temple, on the groundsel edge,   460
Where he fell flat and shamed his worshippers;
Dagon his name, sea monster, upward man
And downward fish, yet had his temple high
Reared in Azotus, dreaded through the coast
Of Palestine, in Gath and Ascalon   465
And Accaron and Gaza's frontier bounds.
Him followed Rimmon, whose delightful seat
Was fair Damascus, on the fertile banks
Of Abbana and Pharphar, lucid streams.
He also against the house of God was bold;   470
A leper once he lost, and gained a king,
Ahaz, his sottish conqueror, whom he drew
God's altar to disparage and displace
For one of Syrian mode whereon to burn
His odious offerings and adore the gods   475
Whom he had vanquished. After these appeared
A crew who under names of old renown,

457. *alienated Judah:* the Jews alienated from God (by their idolatry)

457–466. *Next . . . bounds:* The story of the miraculous fall of the image of the fish-deity Dagon "upon his face to the ground before the ark of the Lord" so that "the head of Dagon and both the palms of his hands were cut off upon the threshold" (1 Sam. 5:3–4) was well known. George Sandys, John Selden, Samuel Purchas, Raleigh, and Alexander Ross, in his *Pansebeia, or, A View of all Religions of the World* (1653), all describe Dagon's fall and represent his image as human from the waist up but fishlike below. Cf. *SA* 13 ff.

460. *groundsel edge:* threshold

464. *Azotus:* the Greek form given on Abraham Ortelius' maps (1570) for Ashdod, the form in *SA*, line 981, where "Accaron" (line 466) is called Ekron. All five Philistine cities lay on or near the Mediterranean coast.

467–469. *Rimmon . . . Pharphar:* Rim-mon was a Babylonian God; *Damascus*, at the confluence of the rivers *Abbana* and *Pharphar*, was the site of the chief temple dedicated to him.

471. *A leper . . . lost:* The *leper* is the Syrian general Naaman, whose leprosy was cured when Elisha told him to wash "seven times" in the Jordan (2 Kings 5: 1–19) and who then rejected Rimmon and embraced the God of Israel. The imagery of lines 467–71 was sufficiently well known that Ralph Cudworth, in his *Sermon before the Commons* (1647), could write: "The Gospel is not like Abbana and Pharphar, those common rivers of Damascus, that could only cleanse the outside; but is a true Jordan" (p. 31).

471–474. *gained . . . mode:* King Ahaz of Judah, after conquering Damascus, rejected Judaism and became a follower of Rimmon and ordered an altar made in the *Syrian mode* and placed in the temple; see 2 Kings 16: 7–18; *sottish* = foolish.

Osiris, Isis, Orus and their train,
With monstrous shapes and sorceries abused°   *deceived*
Fanatic Egypt and her priests to seek   480
Their wandering gods disguised in brutish forms
Rather than human. Nor did Israel scape
The infection when their borrowed gold composed
The calf in Oreb, and the rebel king
Doubled that sin in Bethel and in Dan,   485
Likening his maker to the grazèd ox,
Jehovah, who, in one night when he passed
From Egypt marching, equaled with one stroke
Both her first born and all her bleating gods.
Belial came last, than whom a spirit more lewd   490
Fell not from Heaven or more gross to love
Vice for itself. To him no temple stood
Or altar smoked, yet who more oft than he
In temples and at altars, when the priest
Turns atheist, as did Eli's sons, who filled   495

478. *Osiris, Isis, Orus:* Isis, the Egyptian moon goddess, mother of Orus, and wife of the sun god Osiris; cf. the rout of the Egyptian gods by "the dreaded Infant's hand" in "Nativity Ode" 211–15.

481. *disguised . . . forms:* Ovid (*Metamorphoses* 5.319–31) writes that the Olympian gods left Greece for Egypt, where they took animal forms, which the Egyptians worshipped.

482–484. *Israel . . . Oreb:* refers to the golden calf worshipped by the Israelites in the desert; the gold is borrowed because Aaron made the idol from the "golden earrings" of the Israelites (Exod. 32:2–4).

484–489. *rebel king . . . gods:* When Jeroboam (the *rebel king,* line 484) led the secession of the Ten Tribes from the Judaean kingdom, he set up golden calves in the key cities of Samaria, Bethel, and Dan, and proclaimed, "Behold thy gods, O Israel, which brought thee up out of the land of Egypt" (1 Kings 12:28). Milton contrasts the miraculous slaying of the firstborn children and cattle, including the sacred Egyptian animals (the "bleating gods," line 489) on the night of Israel's escape from Egypt.

485. *Doubled:* 1) repeated; 2) made "two calves of gold" (1 Kings 12:28–29)

486. *Likening . . . ox:* See Ps. 106:20: "they changed their glory into the similitude of an ox that eateth grass."

487. *passed:* i.e., passed through and passed over, the event related in Exod. 12: 12–13, when God promises to "pass through the land of Egypt . . . and will smite all the firstborn," but to "pass over" the houses of the Jews, sparing their children

488. *equaled:* i.e., killed (made equal in death)

490. *Belial:* The name derives from Judges 19:22 and 20:13, where it appears in the Hebrew as an abstract noun meaning "profligacy" or "shamelessness." The biblical phrase, "the sons of Belial" (see lines 501–2), was widely current in Puritan writings, meaning "dissipated men" or "enemies of God." In the New Testament "Belial" gets personified (as in 2 Cor. 6:15), and in reformation biblical drama Belial often appeared as a character, as he also does in Burton's *Anatomy of Melancholy,* where he is a prince of the third order of devils, who were "the vessels of anger and inventors of all mischief" (1:2.1–2).

495–496. *Eli's sons . . . God:* See 1 Samuel 2:12–22: "the sons of Eli were sons of Belial; they knew not the Lord . . . [and]

With lust and violence the house of God?
In courts and palaces he also reigns,
And in luxurious° cities, where the noise   *unchaste, wanton, self-indulgent*
Of riot° ascends above their loftiest towers,   *debauchery*
And injury and outrage; and when night   500
darkens the streets, then wander forth the sons
Of Belial, flown with insolence and wine.
Witness the streets of Sodom, and that night
In Gibeah, when the hospitable door
Exposed a matron to avoid worse rape.   505
These were the prime in order and in might.
The rest were long to tell though far renowned:
The Ionian gods, of Javan's issue held
Gods, yet confessed later than Heaven and Earth,
Their boasted parents. Titan, Heaven's first born,   510
With his enormous° brood, and birthright seized   *monstrous*
By younger Saturn; he, from mightier Jove
His own and Rhea's son, like measure° found;   *retribution*
So Jove usurping reigned. These, first in Crete
And Ida known, thence on the snowy top   515
Of cold Olympus ruled the middle air,
Their highest heaven; or on the Delphian cliff,

lay with the women that assembled at the
door of the tabernacle of the congregation."
    497. *In courts . . . reigns:* overtly marks
Milton's hostility to the restored monarchy;
cf. *PR* 2.182–83.
    502. *flown with:* 1) aroused by; 2)
puffed up with
    503. *Sodom:* In Genesis 18–19, Sodom,
with Gomorrah, are cities of extreme wicked-
ness, upon which God "rained . . . brimstone
and fire" (19:24).
    504–505. *In Gibeah . . . rape:* See
Judges 19:22–25, where a Levite avoids a ho-
mosexual (*worse*) rape by giving up his con-
cubine to be raped by "certain sons of
Belial." The irony of *hospitable* is patent.
    508–509. *The Ionian . . . Gods:* The
identification of the Ionians (Greeks) as de-
scendants of Javan, the son of Japhet (Gene-
sis 10:2), Noah's son, goes back as far as the
translation of the Old Testament into Greek
in the third century B.C. Cf. 4.717, and *SA*
716. (*held* = held to be, believed)

    509–510. *confessed later . . . parents:*
manifestly younger than *Heaven and Earth*
(Uranus and Ge), who according to Greek
mythology were the parents of the Titans
(but if God created *Heaven and Earth* these
are obviously false gods).
    510–514. *Titan . . . reigned:* Titan, the
oldest of Uranus' children, was overthrown
by Saturn, who was in turn overthrown by
his son, Jove (i.e., *Rhea's son*).
    510. *Heaven's first born:* first born not
of Milton's Heaven (Light is arguably
Heaven's first born) but merely of Heaven
(Uranus), the father of the Titans
    514–519. *These . . . land:* Milton re-
hearses the story of the rearing of Jove (or
Zeus) on Mount Ida in Crete and of his
worship at Delphi, in the grove of Dodona
in Epeirus and all through Greece (*Doric
land*).
    516. *middle air:* the second of three lev-
els of the atmosphere that medieval science
thought surrounded the earth

Or in Dodona, and through all the bounds
Of Doric land, or who with Saturn old
Fled over Adria to the Hesperian fields,   520
And o'er the Celtic roamed the utmost isles.
All these and more came flocking, but with looks
Downcast and damp,° yet such wherein appeared   *depressed*
Obscure some glimpse of joy to have found their chief
Not in despair, to have found themselves not lost   525
In loss itself, which on his countenance cast
Like doubtful hue; but he his wonted° pride   *accustomed, usual*
Soon recollecting,° with high words that bore   *recovering, summoning*
Semblance of worth, not substance, gently raised
Their fainting courage and dispelled their fears;   530
Then straight° commands that at the warlike sound   *at once*
Of trumpets loud and clarions° be upreared   *trumpets*
His mighty standard. That proud honor claimed
Azazel as his right, a cherub tall,
Who forthwith from the glittering staff unfurled   535
The imperial ensign, which, full high advanced,
Shone like a meteor streaming to the wind
With gems and golden luster rich emblazed,
Seraphic arms and trophies, all the while
Sonorous metal blowing martial sounds,   540
At which the universal host upsent°   *shot upward*
A shout that tore hell's concave,° and beyond   *canopy, roof*
Frighted the reign of Chaos and old Night.
All in a moment through the gloom were seen
Ten thousand banners rise into the air   545
With orient colors waving; with them rose
A forest huge of spears, and thronging helms

519–521. *who . . . isles:* those who went with Saturn, who, after being deposed by Jove / Zeus, *fled* across the Adriatic Sea (*Adria*) to Italy (the *Hesperian fields*), then to France (*Celtic*), and finally to *the utmost isles* (Great Britain and Ireland)

534. *Azazel:* In the Hebrew text of Leviticus 16:10, *Azazel* is the word signifying the scapegoat that annually carried the sins of Israel into the wilderness, but in Jewish tradition as represented by the Book of Enoch (10:4) the name is given to a prince of the devils whom Raphael binds "to await the great day of fire."

538. *emblazed:* adorned (with heraldic images)

543. *reign of Chaos:* realm of Chaos; cf. 2.895 and 2.907, where Chaos is used to signify both the region of disorganized matter between hell and Heaven and the ruler of that realm.   *Night:* a personification of the darkness in the regions of informed matter; see 2.961–3.

546. *orient colors:* the radiant pinks and yellows of the sky at daybreak

Appeared, and serried shields in thick array
Of depth immeasurable. Anon they move
In perfect phalanx to the Dorian mood   550
Of flutes and soft recorders, such as raised
To height of noblest temper heroes old
Arming to battle, and, instead of rage,
Deliberate valor breathed, firm and unmoved
With dread of death to flight or foul retreat,   555
Nor wanting power to mitigate and swage°   *comfort, assuage*
With solemn touches troubled thoughts, and chase
Anguish and doubt and fear and sorrow and pain
From mortal or immortal minds. Thus they,
Breathing united force with fixèd thought,   560
Moved on in silence to soft pipes that charmed
Their painful steps o'er the burnt soil; and now
Advanced in view they stand, a horrid front
Of dreadful length and dazzling arms, in guise
Of warriors old with ordered spear and shield,   565
Awaiting what command their mighty chief
Had to impose. He through the armèd files
Darts his experienced eye, and soon traverse
The whole battalion views, their order due,
Their visages and stature as of gods;   570
Their number last he sums. And now his heart
Distends with pride, and hardening in his strength
Glories; for never, since created man,
Met such embodied force as named with these
Could merit more than that small infantry   575

548. *serried:* shoulder to shoulder, in close order (French *serrer* = lock, close up)

550–567. *Dorian . . . impose:* In the background is Plato's teaching in the *Republic* III, 399A that music in the quietly firm Dorian style best prepares men for battle, composing their emotions. In Peter White-horne's translation of Machiavelli's *Arte of Warre* (1560), p. 126, the Spartan practice of using flutes to accompany soldiers is contrasted with the Roman use of the trumpet in battle. The *perfect phalanx* (line 550) is the formation of soldiers in an exact square; see line 758, "squarèd regiment," below.

554–555. *unmoved . . . death:* only apparent *valor,* since angels do not die

563. *horrid:* retains its etymological sense of "bristling" (Latin *horridus*), here with "a forest huge of spears" (line 548)

568. *traverse:* across (i.e., in rank [width] rather than in file [depth])

573. *since created man:* since the creation of man

575–576. *small infantry . . . cranes:* refers to the war between the pygmies and the cranes in Homer's *Iliad* 3.1–5; Milton is probably punning on infant-ry, as Joseph Addison first noted in 1712 (see also Jonson's *Time Vindicated,* line 177: "Infantery").

Warred on by cranes, though all the giant brood
Of Phlegra with the heroic race were joined
That fought at Thebes and Ilium, on each side
Mixed with auxiliar° gods, and what resounds   *assisting, helpful*
In fable or romance of Uther's son   580
Begirt with British and Armoric knights,
And all who since, baptized or infidel,
Jousted in Aspramont or Montalban,
Damasco, or Marocco, or Trebizond,
Or whom Bizerte sent from Afric shore   585
When Charlemagne with all his peerage fell
By Fuentarabia. Thus far these beyond
Compare of mortal prowess yet observed
Their dread commander. He, above the rest
In shape and gesture proudly eminent,   590
Stood like a tower; his form had yet not lost
All her original brightness nor appeared

576–578. *though all . . . Ilium:* I.e., even if the giants and gods who fought at *Phlegra* were combined with all the heroes and gods who fought at Thebes and Troy; (the sulfurous plain of Phlegra in Italy seems to be intended here, as it was by Ovid in *Metamorphoses* 5.352, rather than the Macedonian Phlegra in Thessaly where Pindar located the battle in *Nemean Odes* I, 100.)

578. *Thebes and Ilium:* the sites of heroic action in Statius' *Thebaid* and Homer's *Iliad* (*Ilium* = Troy) respectively, actions in which the gods are often portrayed as intervening

580–581. *Uther's son . . . knights: Uther's son* is King Arthur, who had both *British and Armoric* (i.e., from Brittany) *knights* attending him.

583. *Aspramont or Montalban: Aspramont*, in Calabria, gave its name to an Italian romance by Barbarino, published in 1516, which narrates Charlemagne's repulse of a Saracen invasion. *Montalban* is Rinaldo's castle in Luigi Pulci's *Il Morgante Maggiore* (1483), Matteo Maria Boiardo's *Orlando Innamorato* (1495), and Ariosto's *Orlando Furioso*.

584. *Damasco . . . Trebizond:* In Ariosto's *Orlando Furioso* 17 *Damascus* is the scene of a tournament of Christian and

pagan knights. *Marocco* here may refer to Morocco, as most editors have assumed, but as the other two places are famous Middle Eastern cities, Milton seems more likely to intend the city now known as Marrakesh, as Fowler suggests (1998). The Byzantine city of *Trebizond*, on the south shore of the Black Sea, was captured by the Turks in 1461.

585. *Bizerte:* a port (pronounced with three syllables) in Tunisia, where King Agramont resides in *Orlando Furioso* 18, 158; and from which Troiano mounts the invasion of Spain in Boiardo's *Orlando Inammorato* II

586–587. *Charlemagne . . . Fuentarabia:* The climax of the *Song of Roland*, the massacre of Charlemagne's rear-guard troops in the Pyrenees by the Saracens, actually took place at Roncesvalles; Fuentarabia, on the Spanish coast, is some forty miles away. In 1659, Charles II went to Fuentarabia to try to get both France and Spain to support his return to the England. Perhaps the unexplained reference reflects Milton's political wish for a King named Charles.

588. *observed:* It is syntactically ambiguous whether Satan is the one observing or observed here.

592. *her:* refers to *form*, and reflects the fact that in Latin it is a feminine noun (*forma*)

Less than archangel ruined and the excess
Of glory obscured, as when the sun new risen
Looks through the horizontal misty air   595
Shorn of his beams, or from behind the moon
In dim eclipse disastrous twilight sheds
On half the nations and, with fear of change,
Perplexes° monarchs. Darkened so, yet shone   *troubles, torments*
Above them all the archangel, but his face   600
Deep scars of thunder had entrenched,° and care   *furrowed, cut into*
Sat on his faded cheek, but under brows
Of dauntless courage and considerate° pride   *deliberate, calculating*
Waiting revenge; cruel his eye, but cast
Signs of remorse and passion to behold   605
The fellows of his crime, the followers rather
(Far other once beheld in bliss) condemned
Forever now to have their lot in pain,
Millions of spirits for his fault amerced
Of Heaven and from eternal splendors flung   610
For his revolt; yet faithful how they stood,
Their glory withered, as when Heaven's fire
Hath scathed the forest oaks or mountain pines,
With singèd top their stately growth though bare
Stands on the blasted heath. He now prepared   615
To speak, whereat their doubled ranks they bend
From wing to wing and half enclose him round
With all his peers. Attention held them mute.
Thrice he assayed,° and thrice, in spite of scorn,   *tried*
Tears such as angels weep burst forth; at last   620
Words interwove with sighs found out their way:
     "O myriads of immortal spirits, O powers

594–599. *sun . . . monarchs:* Milton
must have intended his readers to think of
similar comparisons of doomed rulers to the
rising sun in clouds or eclipse such as Shake-
speare's simile for the appearance of Richard
II, like "the blushing, discontented sun /
From out the fiery portal of the east, / When
he perceives the envious clouds are bent / To
dim his glory" (*Richard II,* 3.3.662–66). The
simile adumbrates Satan's final defeat as the
eclipse in 11.181–84 adumbrates the effect
of man's sin on the world. Charles II's censor
is said to have objected to the lines as a veiled

threat to the King, perhaps unsurprisingly, as
Eikonoklastes speaks of "those who beeing
exalted in high place above thir merit, fear all
change" (*Works* 5, 220).
     595. *horizontal:* on the horizon
     597. *disastrous:* etymologically "astro-
logically unfavorable" (Latin *dis* + *astrum* =
star)
     609–610. *amerced Of:* deprived of, pe-
nalized by
     615. *blasted heath:* echoes *Macbeth,*
1.3.77: "Upon this blasted heath you stop
our way"

Matchless but with the almighty, and that strife
Was not inglorious, though the event° was dire,   *outcome*
As this place testifies, and this dire change   625
Hateful to utter; but what power of mind
Foreseeing or presaging, from the depth
Of knowledge past or present, could have feared
How such united force of gods, how such
As stood like these, could ever know repulse?   630
For who can yet believe, though after loss,
That all these puissant legions, whose exile
Hath emptied Heaven, shall fail to reascend
Self-raised and repossess their native seat?
For me be witness, all the host of Heaven,   635
If counsels different or danger shunned
By me have lost our hopes. But he who reigns
Monarch in Heaven, till then as one secure
Sat on his throne, upheld by old repute,
Consent, or custom, and his regal state   640
Put forth at full, but still° his strength concealed,   *always*
Which tempted our attempt and wrought our fall.
Henceforth his might we know and know our own,
So as not either to provoke or dread
New war, provoked; our better part remains   645
To work in close° design, by fraud or guile,   *secret, hidden*
What force effected not, that he no less
At length from us may find, who overcomes
By force hath overcome but half his foe.
Space may produce new worlds, whereof so rife   650
There went a fame in Heaven that he ere long

633. *Hath emptied Heaven:* Satan exaggerates; in 2.692, even Death says that Satan only "Drew after him the third part of Heaven's sons."

634. *native seat:* original homeland

636. *different:* differing, disagreeing; some editions have argued that the word here means "deferring"

639–640. *upheld . . . custom:* Satan gives three explanations for God's continuance on the throne (none of course the right one): the fame of the institution (*repute*), the agreement of the angels (*Consent*), and tradition (*custom*). All of these were invoked in the discussion of monarchy in mid-17th-century England, though God in fact rules by virtue of the fact that he is, as creator, of a superior order of being than any of his creatures.

642. *tempted our attempt:* Cf. the similar pun in 9.648. The claim that God is responsible for their rebellion by not revealing his full strength is a telling evasion of Satan's own responsibility.

650. *Space:* i.e., chaos, the region of unformed matter; but note that "may produce" suggests that *Space* is not just the neutral material of creation but the very agent of creation, not God

651. *fame:* rumor; cf. 2.345–53, 2.830–35, and 10.481.

Intended to create and therein plant
A generation whom his choice regard
Should favor equal to the sons of Heaven.
Thither, if but to pry, shall be perhaps   655
Our first eruption, thither or elsewhere,
For this infernal pit shall never hold
Celestial spirits in bondage, nor the abyss
Long under darkness cover. But these thoughts
Full counsel must mature. Peace is despaired,   660
For who can think submission? War, then, war
Open or understood must be resolved."
    He spake, and to confirm his words, outflew
Millions of flaming swords drawn from the thighs
Of mighty cherubim; the sudden blaze   665
Far round illumined hell. Highly they raged
Against the highest and fierce with graspèd arms
Clashed on their sounding shields the din of war,
Hurling defiance toward the vault of Heaven.
    There stood a hill not far whose grisly top   670
Belched fire and rolling smoke; the rest entire
Shone with a glossy scurf,° undoubted sign   *crust, cover*
That in his womb was hid metallic ore,
The work of sulphur. Thither, winged with speed,
A numerous brigade hastened, as when bands   675
Of pioneers with spade and pickaxe armed
Forerun the royal camp to trench a field
Or cast a rampart. Mammon led them on,

---

654. *favor equal:* Cf. "favored more"
2.350.
    656. *eruption:* sallying forth (*OED* 3,
but with a lurking sense of the medical use of
"breaking out," as a rash)
    660. *despaired:* is despaired of, aban-
doned as a possibility
    662. *Open or understood:* overt or unde-
clared (like Belial's "open or concealed" at
2.187)
    666. *Highly:* 1) loudly; 2) arrogantly
    669. *Hurling defiance:* The verb recalls
the angels themselves "hurled" from Heaven
(line 45).
    674. *The work of sulphur:* metals were
often thought to consist of two combined el-
ements: mercury and sulphur; Ben Jonson,

Alchemist, 2.3.153–54: "sulphur or quicksil-
ver, who are the parents of all other metals";
cf. 6.509–15.
    675. *brigade:* The early texts' spelling,
"brigad," indicates the accent on the first syl-
lable.
    676. *pioneers:* laborers responsible for
building roads and military fortification
    677–678. *Forerun . . . rampart:* go be-
fore the main body of troops to dig trenches
or build some fortification
    678. *Mammon:* an Aramaic word mean-
ing riches; it enters the bible in Matthew 6:24,
and Luke 16:13. Mediaeval tradition per-
sonified it, and *Mammon* became the prince
of the lowest of the nine orders of demons, in-
terested only in material wealth.

Mammon, the least erected spirit that fell
From Heaven, for even in Heaven his looks and thoughts   680
Were always downward bent, admiring more
The riches of Heaven's pavement, trodden gold,
Than aught divine or holy else enjoyed
In vision beatific. By him first,
Men also, and by his suggestion taught,   685
Ransacked the center, and with impious hands
Rifled the bowels of their mother earth
For treasures better hid. Soon had his crew
Opened into the hill a spacious wound
And digged out ribs of gold. Let none admire   690
That riches grow in hell; that soil may best
Deserve the precious bane. And here let those
Who boast in mortal things and wondering tell
Of Babel and the works of Memphian kings
Learn how their greatest monuments of fame,   695
And strength, and art are easily outdone
By spirits reprobate,° and in an hour   *rejected by God*
What in an age they with incessant toil
And hands innumerable scarce perform.
Nigh on the plain in many cells prepared,   700
That underneath had veins of liquid fire
Sluiced from the lake, a second multitude
With wondrous art found out the massy ore,

679. *least erected:* of spirit, as the leader of the lowest order of demons; also, the least high minded and most bent over, since the riches in the ground were his major concern. Cf. the uprightness of Adam and Eve at 4.288.

682. *riches of Heaven's pavement:* follows Rev. 21:21: "the street of the city was pure gold."

684. *vision beatific:* mystical experience of God. In Dante's *Paradiso,* it is the fulfillment of the promise that "the pure in heart . . . shall see God" (Matthew 5:8), and is as much a part of the imaginative background of *PL* as it is of the *Divine Comedy.* Cf. 5.613. In "On Time," line 18, it becomes a "happy-making sight."

686–691. *Ransacked . . . hell:* Milton alludes to Ovid's classic statement of this commonplace (*Metamorphoses* 1.137–42). Cf. 6.470–520, and *Comus,* lines 732–35; *ribs,* line 690 = vein of ore, but parodies Adam's rib in 8.467, as *wound* (line 689) anticipates Christ's wound on the cross.

690. *admire:* wonder (see also *Admiring* = wondering at line 731)

692. *precious bane: bane* = poison; the oxymoron reflects the commonplace that the love of wealth is the root of all evil.

694. *Babel . . . kings:* two of the famous building projects of the ancient world: the Tower of Babel (Genesis 11:1–9) and the great pyramids at Memphis (Martial, *De Spectaculis* I.1: "let not barbaric Memphis tell of her pyramids).

703. *found out:* i.e., separated from the rock in which it is embedded; the reading of the manuscript of Book 1 and of the 1667

Severing° each kind, and scummed the bullion dross;   *separating*
A third as soon had formed within the ground   705
A various mold and from the boiling cells
By strange conveyance filled each hollow nook,
As in an organ from one blast of wind
To many a row of pipes the soundboard breathes.
Anon out of the earth a fabric° huge   *building*
Rose like an exhalation,° with the sound   *mist*
Of dulcet symphonies and voices sweet,
Built like a temple, where pilasters° round   *rectangular columns*
Were set and Doric pillars overlaid
With golden architrave; nor did there want   715
Cornice or frieze with bossy sculptures graven;
The roof was fretted gold. Not Babylon
Nor great Alcairo such magnificence
Equaled in all their glories to enshrine
Belus or Serapis their gods or seat   720
Their kings, when Egypt with Assyria strove
In wealth and luxury. The ascending pile
Stood fixed her stately height, and straight the doors,
Opening their brazen folds, discover wide

---

edition is "founded," which has been followed by many editors, but which has the disadvantage of anticipating the process of founding metal described in lines 705–9.

704. *bullion dross:* the impurities that rise to the top as the ore is purified by boiling

706. *various:* complex (as it would have to be for the "mold" to permit the temple to be cast)

709. *soundboard:* the surface that deflects the air from the bellows into an organ's pipes. Pandaemonium, like Troy and Camelot, is built to music.

710–717. *fabric huge . . . gold:* The passage has resemblances to Ovid's description of the palaces of the gods (*Metamorphoses* 1.171–72, and 4.762–64) and especially to the technical architectural terms in his description of the palace built by Vulcan for Apollo. It also compares interestingly with a description of a masque performed at court in 1637: "the *earth open'd*, and there rose up a richly-adorned pallace, seeming all of goldsmith's work, with porticos vaulted, on pi-

lasters of rich rustick work; their bases and capitols of gold. Above these ran an architrave freese, and coronis of the same—the freese enrich'd with jewels" (quoted by Todd in his 1698 edition of *PL*)

714. *Doric pillars:* rounded, fluted columns

715–716. *architrave . . . frieze:* the three pieces of the decorative entablature above the columns supporting a roof: the *architrave* was the lowest, resting on the column, the *frieze* was in the middle, and the *cornice* on top.

716. *bossy:* embossed, carved in relief

717. *fretted:* decorated with carvings or reliefs

718. *Alcairo:* i.e., the ancient city of Memphis, between Upper and Lower Egypt

720. *Belus or Serapis:* Belus is a variant of Baal (cf. line 422 above). *Serapis* (usually, though not here, accented on the second syllable) was a name given to Osiris as lord of the underworld and patron of the land's fertility.

724. *brazen folds:* brass panels

Within her ample spaces o'er the smooth   725
And level pavement; from the archèd roof,
Pendant by subtle magic, many a row
Of starry lamps and blazing cressets fed
With naphtha and asphaltus yielded light
As from a sky. The hasty multitude   730
Admiring entered, and the work some praise
And some, the architect: his hand was known
In Heaven by many a towered structure high,
Where sceptered angels held their residence
And sat as princes, whom the supreme King   735
Exalted to such power and gave to rule
Each in his hierarchy the orders bright.
Nor was his name unheard or unadored
In ancient Greece; and in Ausonian land
Men called him Mulciber, and how he fell   740
From Heaven they fabled, thrown by angry Jove
Sheer o'er the crystal battlements; from morn
To noon he fell, from noon to dewy eve,
A summer's day, and with the setting sun
Dropped from the zenith like a falling star   745
On Lemnos the Aegean isle: thus they relate,
Erring; for he with this rebellious rout
Fell long before, nor aught availed him now
To have built in Heaven high towers, nor did he scape
By all his engines, but was headlong sent   750
With his industrious crew to build in hell.
Meanwhile the wingèd heralds, by command
Of sovereign power, with awful° ceremony   *awesome*
And trumpets' sound throughout the host proclaim
A solemn council forthwith to be held   755
At Pandaemonium, the high capital

728–729. *cressets . . . asphaltus:* iron baskets containing flammable materials like *naphtha* and *asphaltus* (bitumen), which were suspended as lights

739. *Ausonian land:* i.e., Italy, here given its ancient Greek name

740. *Mulciber:* the "founder of metal," more commonly called Vulcan in Latin, and in Greek, Hephaestus. Homer's story (*Iliad* 1.588–95) that Zeus hurled him out of Heaven in drunken rage, and that he was all day long in falling onto the island of Lemnos

in the Aegean Sea, was condemned as frivolous by Plato (*Republic* II, 378d).

747. *Erring:* After seven lines of verse, Milton belatedly announces that the classical myth is false. It is his own account, based on the Bible, that is true.

748. *nor aught availed:* nor did it help him

750. *engines:* 1) weapons; 2) strategies

756. *Pandaemonium:* The name is Milton's invention, from Greek (*pan* = all; *daemon* = supernatural being), although the

Of Satan and his peers. Their summons called
From every band and squarèd regiment
By place or choice the worthiest. They anon
With hundreds and with thousands trooping came   760
Attended; all access was thronged, the gates
And porches wide, but chief the spacious hall
(Though like a covered field, where champions bold
Wont° ride in armed, and at the soldan's chair   *were accustomed to*
Defied the best of paynim° chivalry   *pagan*
To mortal combat or career° with lance)   *gallop (i.e., joust)*
Thick swarmed, both on the ground and in the air,
Brushed with the hiss of rustling wings. As bees
In spring time, when the sun with Taurus rides,
Pour forth their populous youth about the hive   770
In clusters, they among fresh dews and flowers
Fly to and fro, or on the smoothèd plank,
The suburb of their straw-built citadel,
New rubbed with balm, expatiate and confer
Their state affairs, so thick the airy crowd   775
Swarmed and were straitened° till the signal given.   *packed together, confined*
Behold a wonder! They but now who seemed
In bigness to surpass earth's giant sons,
Now less than smallest dwarfs in narrow room
Throng numberless, like that pygmean race   780

---

conception seems indebted to Henry More's word "*pandaemoniothen,*" in his "Psychozoia" in *Psychodia Platonica* (Cambridge, 1642), p. 40, which signifies the dominion of the devils in this world.

757. *peers:* nobles (but also implies, what Satan denies, that all the fallen angels are equal, at least in their moral quality); see 2.445.

759. *By place or choice:* by virtue of rank or by election

761. *all access:* every entrance

764. *soldan's chair:* sultan's throne

768–775. *bees . . . affairs:* The simile echoes well-known comparisons of throngs of people to bees by Homer (*Iliad* 2.87–90) and Virgil (*Aeneid* 1.430–36 and *Georgics* 4.149–227). Milton discusses Virgil's account in the *Georgics* of bees possessing cities and laws in the *First Defense* (*Works* 7,

85–87) in his scornful reply to Salmasius' assertion that the respect of bees for their "kings" was a divine example of absolute monarchy worthy of human imitation. It is perhaps also worth noting, as R. W. Smith points out in her comparison of Pandaemonium with St. Peter's in Rome (*MP*, 29 [1931], 187–98) that the bee was the emblem of the Barberini Pope Urban VIII, who dedicated the basilica in 1636, and that "his followers were often referred to as bees."

769. *with Taurus rides:* Taurus, the bull, is the second zodiacal sign, and entered by the sun in April; hence, in spring.

774. *expatiate:* wander about (the original Latin sense of the word), but also, speak at length

780–781. *pygmean race . . . mount:* Cf. line 575 above, and the allusion to the Himalayas as "the Indian steep" in *Comus*, line 139.

Beyond the Indian mount or fairy elves,
Whose midnight revels by a forest side
Or fountain some belated peasant sees,
Or dreams he sees, while overhead the moon
Sits arbitress and nearer to the earth   785
Wheels her pale course; they, on their mirth and dance
Intent, with jocund music charm his ear.
At once with joy and fear his heart rebounds.
Thus incorporeal spirits to smallest forms
Reduced their shapes immense and were at large,   790
Though without number still, amidst the hall
Of that infernal court. But far within
And in their own dimensions like themselves
The great seraphic lords and cherubim
In close recess and secret conclave sat,   795
A thousand demigods on golden seats,
Frequent and full. After short silence then
And summons read, the great consult° began.   *consultation*

The End of the First Book.

781–787. *fairy elves . . . ear:* Comparison with *A Midsummer Night's Dream* 2.1 is perhaps inevitable, but the note of mystery is characteristically Miltonic, like the sound of "sands and shores and desert wildernesses" in *Comus,* lines 208–9. There is also, in *sees / Or dreams he sees,* a reminiscence of Virgil's picture of Aeneas in the Elysian Fields, seeing or thinking that he sees Dido, "like the fugitive moon among clouds" (*Aeneid* 6.450–55).

785. *arbitress:* etymologically, one who goes to see; hence, witness; cf. the "arbitrator" at 2.359

790. *at large:* free, but in relation to the image of them reduced "to smallest forms" (line 789) the pun is unmistakable and demeaning

795. *close recess:* private meeting place *conclave:* governing council (Latin *conclave* = a room that can be locked)

797. *Frequent and full:* packed together in great numbers

BOOK 2

The Argument

The consultation begun, Satan debates whether another battle be to be hazarded for the recovery of Heaven; some advise it, others dissuade. A third proposal is preferred, mentioned before by Satan: to search the truth of that prophecy or tradition in Heaven concerning another world and another kind of creature equal or not much inferior to themselves, about this time to be created. They doubt who shall be sent on this difficult search; Satan, their chief, undertakes alone the voyage, is honored and applauded. The council thus ended, the rest betake them several ways and to several employments, as their inclinations lead them, to entertain the time till Satan return. He passes on his journey to hell gates, finds them shut, and who sat there to guard them, by whom at length they are opened, and discover to him the great gulf between hell and Heaven; with what difficulty he passes through, directed by Chaos, the power of that place, to the sight of this new world which he sought.

High on a throne of royal state, which far
Outshone the wealth of Hormuz and of Ind,
Or where the gorgeous East with richest hand
Showers on her kings barbaric pearl and gold,
Satan exalted sat, by merit raised   5
To that bad eminence, and, from despair

1–4. *High . . . gold:* The scene may have been intended to recall Spenser's more symbolic description of the throne of Lucifera, incarnate Pride: "High above all a cloth of state was spred, / And a rich throne, as bright as sunny day" (*Faerie Queene* 1.4.8,1–2). But see also Milton's discussion of Charles I "sitting upon his throne under the golden and silken heaven of his canopy of state" in *Angli Pro Populo Anglicano Defensio* (*The First Defense, Works* 7, 481).

2. *Hormuz:* the island port of Hormuz at the mouth of the Persian Gulf; Milton's spelling was "Ormus," suggesting its pronunciation. Fulke Greville used the port city as the setting of his tragedy of *Alaham* (posthumously published in 1633); in the last scene, his usurping hero cries: "Is this Ormus? Or is Ormus my hell, / Where only Furies, and not Men, doe dwell?" See also 1.348, where Satan is compared to an Eastern "sultan."

4. *barbaric:* uncivilized or exotic; the term used originally for all nations not Greek or Roman; cf. *Aeneid* 2.504: "barbaric gold"

5. *by merit raised:* on Satan's *merit,* see line 21, below, and 1.98; see also Christ's "right of merit" (6.43 and 3.309).

Thus high uplifted beyond hope, aspires
Beyond thus high, insatiate to pursue
Vain war with Heaven, and by success untaught
His proud imaginations° thus displayed: *schemes, plots*
    "Powers and dominions, deities of Heaven,
For since no deep within her gulf can hold
Immortal vigor, though oppressed and fallen,
I give not Heaven for lost. From this descent
Celestial virtues rising will appear   15
More glorious and more dread than from no fall,
And trust themselves to fear no second fate.
Me though just right and the fixed laws of Heaven
Did first create your leader, next, free choice,
With what besides, in counsel or in fight,   20
Hath been achieved of° merit, yet this loss,   *by*
Thus far at least recovered, hath much more
Established in a safe, unenvied throne
Yielded with full consent. The happier state
In Heaven, which follows dignity, might draw   25
Envy from each inferior, but who here
Will envy whom° the highest place exposes   *him whom*
Foremost to stand against the thunderer's aim
Your bulwark, and condemns to greatest share
Of endless pain? Where there is then no good   30
For which to strive, no strife can grow up there
From faction; for none sure will claim in hell
Precedence, none, whose portion is so small

---

7. *Beyond:* 1) greater than; 2) past the possibility of

9. *Vain:* 1) hopeless; 2) motivated by vanity   *success:* outcome; cf. *success* in line 123 below; the irony of using this word for a negative outcome is unmistakable.

11. *Powers and dominions:* two of the nine orders of angels; see line 128n. See also *virtues* in line 15, though each of the terms here is more generic than specific, referring generally to the assembly of fallen angels. See Col. 1:16: "For by him were all things created . . . whether they be thrones, or dominions, or principalities, or powers."

14. *I give . . . lost:* I do not consider Heaven lost.

14–16. *From . . . fall:* a parody of the fortunate fall, the *felix culpa;* cf. 12.50–65.

18–21. *Me . . . merit:* Satan anxiously and incoherently claims rule on every possible basis: *right,* necessity (*fixed laws*), *free choice,* and *merit;* but cf. lines 32–33 where he claims that in Hell "none . . . will claim . . . Precedence."

28. *thunderer's aim:* recalls Ovid's repeated attribution of the thunderbolt to Jove as his emblem (*Metamorphoses* 1.154, 170, and 197). Satan uses the symbol of power to suggest that God is a tyrant, who rules by force rather than right.

Of present pain that with ambitious mind
Will covet more. With this advantage then   35
To union and firm faith and firm accord,
More than can be in Heaven, we now return
To claim our just inheritance of old,
Surer to prosper than prosperity
Could have assured us, and by what best way,   40
Whether of open war or covert guile,
We now debate; who can advise, may speak."
    He ceased, and next him Moloch, sceptered king,
Stood up, the strongest and the fiercest spirit
That fought in Heaven, now fiercer by despair.   45
His trust was with the eternal to be deemed
Equal in strength, and rather than be less
Cared not to be at all; with that care lost
Went all his fear: of God, or hell, or worse
He recked° not, and these words thereafter spake: *cared*
    "My sentence is for open war: Of wiles,
More unexpert, I boast not; them let those
Contrive who need or when they need, not now.
For while they sit contriving shall the rest,
Millions that stand in arms and longing wait   55
The signal to ascend, sit lingering here,
Heaven's fugitives, and for their dwelling place
Accept this dark opprobrious° den of shame,   *disgraceful, ignominious*
The prison of his tyranny who reigns
By our delay? No, let us rather choose   60
Armed with hell flames and fury all at once
O'er Heaven's high towers to force resistless° way,   *irresistible*
Turning our tortures into horrid arms
Against the torturer, when to meet the noise
Of his almighty engine he shall hear   65

---

40. *what best way:* In spite of the preceding praise of hell, Satan assumes they will return to Heaven and need only debate the means.

41. *open . . . guile:* In Tasso's *Gerusalemme Liberata*, Satan urges "open force, or secret guile" (trans. Fairfax [1600], 4.16).

43. *Moloch:* the "furious king" of the battle in heaven (6.357) is *sceptered* as the kings often are in Homeric councils (e.g., *Iliad* 2.86, and *Odyssey* 2.231)

50. *thereafter:* accordingly, therefore

51. *sentence:* decision, opinion; cf. line 291 below.

52. *unexpert:* inexperienced; cf. *expert* in 6.233.

63. *horrid arms:* terrible weapons (but *horrid* also carries Latin sense of bristling [here, with flames])

65. *engine:* machine used in warfare (here, God's thunder)

Infernal thunder, and for lightning see
Black fire and horror shot with equal rage
Among his angels and his throne itself
Mixed with Tartarean sulfur and strange fire,
His own invented torments. But perhaps   70
The way seems difficult and steep to scale
With upright wing against a higher foe.
Let such bethink them, if the sleepy drench°   *drink, potion*
Of that forgetful lake benumb not still,
That in our proper motion we ascend   75
Up to our native seat; descent and fall
To us is adverse. Who but felt of late,
When the fierce foe hung on our broken rear
Insulting, and pursued us through the deep,
With what compulsion and laborious flight   80
We sunk thus low? The ascent is easy then;
The event° is feared: should we again provoke   *outcome*
Our stronger, some worse way his wrath may find
To our destruction, if there be in hell
Fear to be worse destroyed. What can be worse   85
Than to dwell here, driven out from bliss, condemned
In this abhorrèd deep to utter woe,
Where pain of unextinguishable fire
Must exercise us without hope of end
The vassals of his anger, when the scourge   90

69. *Tartarean:* hellish, derived from
Tartarus, the name for the place of torment
in the classical underworld
74. *that forgetful lake:* i.e., the river
Lethe, whose waters make those who drink
forget their earthly lives (see the "oblivious
pool" in 1.266); Moloch's contempt for his
companions' forgetfulness of their glory in
heaven suggests the reference of the ghost in
Hamlet (1.5.32–33) to the "dullness" of "the
fat weed / That roots itself in ease on Lethe
wharf."
75. *in . . . ascend:* i.e., it is our nature to
ascend (but see lines 932–35, where Satan
enters chaos and "plumb down he drops");
proper = natural.
78. *broken rear:* defeated rearguard
79. *Insulting:* exulting (but also with
sense of attacking)

81. *ascent is easy:* Cf. Virgil, *Aeneid*
6.126–29: "the descent to Avernus is easy
. . . but to retrace one's steps and escape to
the upper air, this is the task, this is the toil."
Appropriately, Book 2 makes over twenty
references to *Aeneid* 6, Virgil's book of the
underworld.
83. *Our stronger:* Moloch admits that
God is *stronger*, but does not admit the essen-
tial distinction (creator v. created) between
God and the angels.
87. *utter:* 1) complete; 2) give voice to
89. *exercise:* torment, afflict (from Latin
exerceo = vex)
90. *vassals:* servants, slaves, in *Of Refor-
mation* (*Works* 3, part 1, 79); "downe-
trodden Vassels of Perdition"; but Bentley
(1732) suggested that the proper word might
be "vessels," and that the allusion is to

Inexorably, and the torturing hour
Calls us to penance? More destroyed than thus
We should be quite abolished and expire.
What fear we then? What doubt we to incense
His utmost ire, which to the height enraged   95
Will either quite consume us and reduce
To nothing this essential, happier far
Than miserable to have eternal being?
Or if our substance be indeed divine
And cannot cease to be, we are at worst   100
On this side nothing; and by proof° we feel   experience
Our power sufficient to disturb his Heaven,
And with perpetual inroads to alarm,
Though inaccessible, his fatal throne,
Which, if not victory, is yet revenge."   105
      He ended frowning, and his look denounced°   proclaimed
Desperate revenge and battle dangerous
To less than gods. On the other side up rose
Belial, in act more graceful and humane;
A fairer person lost not Heaven. He seemed   110
For dignity composed and high exploit,
But all was false and hollow though his tongue
Dropped manna and could make the worse appear
The better reason to perplex and dash
Maturest counsels, for his thoughts were low,   115
To vice industrious but to nobler deeds
Timorous and slothful; yet he pleased the ear,

"vessels of wrath fitted to destruction" in
Rom. 9:22.

    91. *Inexorably:* irresistibly (literally, un-
able to be moved by prayer; and notice
"scourge" in line 90 and "penance" in line 92)

    94. *what doubt we:* why do we hesitate

    97. *essential:* The adjective is here used
as a noun meaning "essence"; cf. 1.138.

    100–101. *at worst . . . nothing:* already as
bad off as things can be, short of annihilation

    104. *fatal:* fated, upheld by fate; but
also deadly; cf. the meanings of fate and gods
in 1.116.

    109. *Belial . . . humane:* Cf. Belial's first
appearance in 1.490, and his later ones in

6.620–27 (and also *PR* 2.150–73). For his
bearing, Milton may have been indebted to
the tradition that he "taketh the form of a
beautifull angel, he speaketh faire," as in
Reginald Scot's *Discoveries of Witchcraft*
(1584), 15.2; but the characterization is Mil-
ton's own. (*humane* = elegant, refined)

    113. *manna:* sweet matter, but here
ironic in contrast with the manna miracu-
lously dropped to feed the Israelites in Exod.
16:15–22 and referred to in Ps. 78:24–25.

    113–114. *could . . . reason:* echoes the
charge against Socrates in Plato's *Apology*
(19b), who is said to be skilled at "making
the weaker argument stronger"

And with persuasive accent thus began:
   "I should be much for open war, O peers,
As not behind in hate, if what was urged   120
Main reason to persuade immediate war
Did not dissuade me most and seem to cast
Ominous conjecture on the whole success,
When he who most excels in fact of arms,
In what he counsels and in what excels   125
Mistrustful, grounds his courage on despair
And utter dissolution, as the scope°   *target*
Of all his aim, after some dire revenge.
First, what revenge? The towers of Heaven are filled
With armèd watch that render all access   130
Impregnable; oft on the bordering deep
Encamp their legions or with obscure wing
Scout far and wide into the realm of night,
Scorning surprise. Or could we break our way
By force, and at our heels all hell should rise   135
With blackest insurrection to confound
Heaven's purest light, yet our great enemy
All incorruptible would on his throne
Sit unpolluted, and the ethereal mold
Incapable of stain would soon expel   140
Her mischief and purge off the baser fire
Victorious. Thus repulsed, our final hope
Is flat° despair; we must exasperate   *absolute, complete*
The almighty victor to spend all his rage,
And that must end us, that must be our cure,   145
To be no more. Sad cure; for who would lose,
Though full of pain, this intellectual being,
Those thoughts that wander through eternity,

---

124. *fact of arms:* act of bravery, martial feat

139–141. *the ethereal . . . fire:* In part, the passage rests on the conception of God as "a consuming fire" (Deut. 4:24) and of "his angels" as "a flaming fire" (Ps. 104:4), and in part it rests on the distinction between the pure *ethereal mold* (i.e., heavenly substance, pure fire) and *the baser fire* of earth. Cf. 1.117 and 11.48–53.

146–151. *To be . . . motion:* Editors reg-ularly quote Claudio's dread of death, when "This sensible warm motion" will "become / A kneaded clod" (*Measure for Measure* 3.1.120–21), but the thought also parallels Seneca's (*De consolatione* 11.7) about the soul as kindred to the gods and at home in every world and every age because its thought ranges through all heaven and through all past and future time. Milton repeats the thought in *Areopagitica:* "minds that can wander be-yond all limit and satiety" (*Works* 55, 320).

To perish rather, swallowed up and lost
In the wide womb of uncreated Night,   150
Devoid of sense° and motion? And who knows   *sensation*
Let this be good, whether our angry foe
Can give it or will ever? How he can
Is doubtful; that he never will is sure.
Will he, so wise, let loose at once his ire,   155
Belike through impotence, or unaware,
To give his enemies their wish and end
Them in his anger, whom his anger saves
To punish endless? 'Wherefore cease we then?'
Say they who counsel war; 'we are decreed,   160
Reserved, and destined to eternal woe;
Whatever doing, what can we suffer more,
What can we suffer worse?' Is this then worst,
Thus sitting, thus consulting, thus in arms?
What when we fled amain,° pursued and struck   *at full speed*
With Heaven's afflicting thunder, and besought
The deep to shelter us? This hell then seemed
A refuge from those wounds. Or when we lay
Chained on the burning lake? That sure was worse.
What if the breath that kindled those grim fires   170
Awaked should blow them into sevenfold rage
And plunge us in the flames, or from above
Should intermitted vengeance arm again
His red right hand to plague us? What if all
Her stores were opened, and this firmament   175
Of hell should spout her cataracts of fire,
Impendent horrors, threatening hideous fall
One day upon our heads, while we perhaps

---

150. *wide . . . Night:* Compare Spenser's
"in the wide wombe of the world there lyes, /
In hatefull darkenesse and in deepe horrore, /
An huge eternall Chaos" (*Faerie Queene* 3.6.36).

153. *it:* i.e., annihilation (which might
be impossible for angels made of "ethereal
substance," 6.330)

156. *Belike through impotence:* perhaps
from a lack of self-control

165. *What:* what was it

169. *Chained . . . lake:* Cf. Rev. 20:10:
"And the devil that deceived them was cast
into the lake of fire and brimstone." See 1.210.

170. *breath that kindled:* See Isa. 30:33,
where hell is described as a pile thereof fire,
and "the breath of the Lord, like a stream of
brimstone, doth kindle it."

174. *right red hand:* translates Horace's
rubente dextera as an attribute of an angry
Jove in *Odes* 1.2.1–4

176. *cataracts:* literally, floodgates; here
used figuratively to mean "outpouring"

Designing or exhorting glorious war,
Caught in a fiery tempest shall be hurled   180
Each on his rock transfixed, the sport and prey
Of racking whirlwinds, or forever sunk
Under yon boiling ocean, wrapped in chains,
There to converse with everlasting groans,
Unrespited, unpitied, unreprieved,   185
Ages of hopeless end? This would be worse.
War therefore, open or concealed, alike
My voice dissuades; for what can force or guile
With him, or who deceive his mind, whose eye
Views all things at one view? He from Heaven's height   190
All these our motions° vain sees and derides,   *proposals, plans*
Not more almighty to resist our might
Than wise to frustrate all our plots and wiles.
Shall we then live thus vile, the race of Heaven
Thus trampled, thus expelled to suffer here   195
Chains and these torments? Better these than worse
By my advice, since fate inevitable
Subdues us, and omnipotent decree,
The victor's will. To suffer, as to do,
Our strength is equal, nor the law unjust   200
That so ordains; this was at first resolved,
If we were wise, against so great a foe
Contending, and so doubtful what might fall.
I laugh when those who at the spear are bold
And venturous, if that fail them, shrink and fear   205
What yet they know must follow: to endure
Exile, or ignominy, or bonds, or pain,

181–182. *the sport . . . whirlwinds:* Cf. *Aeneid* 6.75: "the sport of rushing winds."

182. *racking:* driving, fierce (but also with the sense of tormenting)

186. *hopeless end:* no end to hope for

189. *With him:* do against him

190–191. *He . . . derides:* Belial anticipates Ps. 2:4: "He that sitteth in the heavens shall laugh: the Lord shall have them in derision."

199–200. *To suffer . . . equal:* i.e., our ability to endure is equal to our strength to

attack. *To suffer, as to do* translates the words of Mucius Scaevola as he thrust his hand into the fire to give his Etruscan captors an example of what a Roman could endure, after he had been seized in an attempt to assassinate their king (Livy, *Ab Urbe Condita*, 2.12), though the irony here is that Belial wants to avoid the fire; see also 1.157–8.

201. *resolved:* accepted, understood (as a possibility)

207. *ignominy:* humiliation; for the pronunciation see 1.115n.

The sentence of their conqueror. This is now
Our doom, which, if we can sustain and bear,
Our supreme foe in time may much remit°   *abate, give up*
His anger and perhaps, thus far removed,
Not mind us not offending, satisfied
With what is punished, whence these raging fires
Will slacken, if his breath stir not their flames.
Our purer essence then will overcome   215
Their noxious vapor or, inured,° not feel,   *accustomed to*
Or, changed at length and to the place conformed
In temper and in nature, will receive
Familiar the fierce heat and void of pain;
This horror will grow mild, this darkness light,   220
Besides what hope the never-ending flight
Of future days may bring, what chance, what change
Worth waiting, since our present lot appears
For happy though but ill, for ill not worst,
If we procure not to ourselves more woe."   225
        Thus Belial, with words clothed in reason's garb,
Counseled ignoble ease and peaceful sloth,
Not peace. And after him thus Mammon spake:
        "Either to disenthrone the king of Heaven
We war, if war be best, or to regain   230
Our own right lost; him to unthrone we then
May hope when everlasting fate shall yield
To fickle chance, and Chaos judge the strife.

---

212. *mind:* call to mind, be concerned about

213. *what is punished:* i.e., the punishment

213–219. *whence . . . pain:* The thought is allied to that attributed to Augustine by Thomas Heywood in his *Hierarchie of the Blessed Angels* (1635) 4, p. 211: "For in Saint Austines Comment you may finde, / The subtile essence of the Angels (pure / At first, that they more fully might endure / The sence of Fire) was grossed in their Fall, / Of courser temper, then th'Originall."

218. *temper:* loosely equivalent to "temperament"; it was used physiologically to mean the balance of physical "humors" in

the body, variations in which caused various individual natures or characters. Cf. line 276 below.

220. *light:* 1) bright; 2) easy to bear

224. *For happy:* from the point of view of happiness

226. *words . . . garb:* compare *Comus* 758: "false rules prancked in reason's garb"

228. *Mammon:* See 1.678 and note.

229. *disenthrone the king of Heaven:* Richard Holdsworth, in *An Answer Without a Question* (1649), writes of the regicides: "they combine with Hell to disenthrone / The King of Heaven, as they have done their own" (p. 8).

232. *fate:* See *fate* in 1.116.

The former, vain to hope, argues as vain
The latter, for what place can be for us   235
Within Heaven's bound, unless Heaven's lord supreme
We overpower? Suppose he should relent
And publish grace to all on promise made
Of new subjection; with what eyes could we
Stand in his presence humble and receive   240
Strict laws imposed, to celebrate his throne
With warbled hymns and to his godhead sing
Forced hallelujahs, while he lordly sits
Our envied sovereign and his altar breathes
Ambrosial odors and ambrosial flowers,   245
Our servile offerings? This must be our task
In Heaven, this our delight; how wearisome
Eternity so spent in worship paid
To whom we hate. Let us not then pursue,
By force impossible, by leave obtained   250
Unacceptable, though in Heaven, our state
Of splendid vassalage, but rather seek
Our own good from ourselves, and from our own
Live to ourselves, though in this vast recess,
Free and to none accountable, preferring   255
Hard liberty before the easy yoke
Of servile pomp. Our greatness will appear

234–235. *The former . . . The latter:* i.e., to "disenthrone the king" and "to regain / Our own right"

238–239. *publish . . . subjection:* With the restoration, Charles II did *publish grace to all,* issuing general pardons upon the promise of future loyalty (*new subjection*).

243. *Forced hallelujahs:* songs of praise that they are forced to sing; *hallelujahs* is the plural form of the transliteration of the Hebrew phrase for "Praise ye the Lord." Robert Sanderson said (*Ten Sermons Preached,* 1627, p. 115) that the Psalms could all be summed up in the words "Hosannah" and "Hallelujah." Cf. the "Unfeigned hallelujahs" at 6.744.

245. *Ambrosial:* worthy of the gods, divine; in the *Iliad* 4.3–4, Hebe pours out ambrosia for the gods, but it is usually mentioned as their food, cf. the "celestial food, divine, / Ambrosial" of *PR* 4.588–89.

249. *pursue:* try to obtain; its object is *state* (line 251)

250–251. *by leave . . . Unacceptable:* i.e., that which we would not want even if we were allowed it

255–257. *preferring . . . pomp:* This Miltonic principle is restated in *SA* 268–71, where "strenuous liberty" is preferred to "bondage with ease." It makes both classical and biblical reference: Sallust's account of the closing words of the invective of the Consul Aemilius Lepidus against the tyrant Cornelius Sulla in 78 B.C. (*Oration to the Roman People*); and also Matt. 11:28–30: "Come unto me . . . for my yoke is easy." It, however, would no doubt have been read most immediately as Milton's comment on the *pomp* of the pageantry greeting the restoration of Charles II.

Then most conspicuous when great things of small,
Useful of hurtful, prosperous of adverse,
We can create and in what place soe'er   260
Thrive under evil and work ease out of pain
Through labor and endurance. This deep world
Of darkness do we dread? How oft amidst
Thick clouds and dark doth Heaven's all-ruling sire
Choose to reside, his glory unobscured,   265
And with the majesty of darkness round
Covers his throne, from whence deep thunders roar
Mustering their rage, and Heaven resembles hell?
As he our darkness, cannot we his light
Imitate when we please? This desert soil   270
Wants not her hidden luster—gems and gold—
Nor want we skill or art from whence to raise
Magnificence; and what can Heaven show more?
Our torments also may in length of time
Become our elements, these piercing fires   275
As soft as now severe, our temper° changed   *bodily constitution, nature*
Into their temper, which must needs remove
The sensible of pain. All things invite
To peaceful counsels and the settled state
Of order, how in safety best we may   280
Compose our present evils, with regard
Of what we are and were, dismissing quite
All thoughts of war. Ye have what I advise."

---

264. *Thick clouds and dark:* At the dedi-
cation of Solomon's temple, the sanctuary was
covered by a cloud: "the glory of the Lord had
filled the house of God. Then said Solomon,
the Lord hath said that he would dwell in the
thick darkness" (2 Chron. 5:13–6:1). Cf. Ps.
18:11–13: "He made darkness his secret
place: his pavilion round about him were
dark waters and thick clouds of the skies. . . .
The Lord also thundered in the heavens."

271. *Wants not:* does not lack

275. *elements:* natural environment; tra-
ditionally, the devils were assigned to the
various *elements* and might be classified, as
they were by Burton in the *Anatomy of
Melancholy* (1.2.1.2), into Fiery Spirits or

Devils, Aerial Spirits or Devils, Water-devils,
Terrestrial and Sub-Terrestrial devils. Cf. the
"Daemons" of "fire, air, flood, or under-
ground" in "Il Penseroso," lines 93–94.

278. *The sensible of pain:* the element
capable of feeling pain, or perhaps merely the
sensation itself; in either case, Mammon be-
trays his character by his indifference to all
except the physical pains of hell.

281. *Compose:* adjust to, gain compo-
sure in the face of

282. *were:* In 1667 this reads "where,"
which also makes sense; it seems that 1674
corrects the earlier version, making the issue
one of temporal change rather than spatial,
but either is possible.

He scarce had finished when such murmur filled
The assembly as when hollow rocks retain   285
The sound of blustering winds, which all night long
Had roused the sea, now with hoarse cadence lull
Seafaring men o'erwatched, whose bark by chance
Or pinnace anchors in a craggy bay
After the tempest. Such applause was heard   290
As Mammon ended, and his sentence° pleased,   *opinion*
Advising peace, for such another field°   *battlefield*
They dreaded worse than hell, so much the fear
Of thunder and the sword of Michael
Wrought still within them and, no less, desire   295
To found this nether empire, which might rise
By policy and long process of time
In emulation opposite to Heaven.
Which when Beelzebub perceived, than whom,
Satan except, none higher sat, with grave   300
Aspect° he rose and in his rising seemed   *expression*
A pillar of state; deep on his front° engraven   *forehead*
Deliberation sat, and public care
And princely counsel in his face yet shone,
Majestic though in ruin. Sage he stood   305
With Atlantean shoulders fit to bear
The weight of mightiest monarchies; his look
Drew audience and attention still as night
Or summer's noontide air while thus he spake:
     "Thrones and imperial powers, offspring of Heaven,   310

284–290. *when . . . tempest:* There are several classical parallels, the closest that in the *Aeneid* 10.96–99, where the gods in council assent to Juno's violent appeal like winds threatening storm to sailors.

288. *o'erwatched:* exhausted from their long watch

294. *the sword of Michael:* An anticipation of Michael's command of the heavenly host in Book 6; cf. Rev. 12:7: "And there was war in Heaven: Michael and his angels fought against the dragon." Though without specific biblical warrant, the sword is used in visual arts iconographically to identify the archangel; see also 6.250.

295. *Wrought still:* continued to operate

296. *nether:* lower (belonging to hell)

297. *policy:* statecraft, strategy (often with a negative connotation of deviousness)

298. *opposite to:* 1) totally different from; 2) antagonistic to

306. *Atlantean shoulders:* Atlas' shoulders, which in mythology were forced to carry the universe; see the reference to Atlas, "whom the Gentiles feign to bear up Heav'n" in *SA*, line 150. The familiar image suggested a comparison to "pillars of state" to Spenser when he described England as supported by Lord Burleigh, "As the wide compasse of the firmament / On Atlas mighty shoulders is upstayd" (Sonnets Dedicatory to the *Faerie Queene*).

Ethereal virtues—or these titles now
Must we renounce and, changing style, be called
Princes of hell? For so the popular vote
Inclines, here to continue and build up here
A growing empire. Doubtless; while we dream   315
And know not that the king of Heaven hath doomed
This place our dungeon, not our safe retreat
Beyond his potent arm to live exempt
From Heaven's high jurisdiction, in new league
Banded against his throne, but to remain   320
In strictest bondage, though thus far removed,
Under the inevitable curb° reserved   *restraint*
His captive multitude: for he, be sure,
In height or depth, still first and last will reign
Sole king and of his kingdom lose no part   325
By our revolt, but over hell extend
His empire and with iron scepter rule
Us here, as with his golden, those in Heaven.
What° sit we then projecting peace and war?   *why*
War hath determined us and foiled with loss   330
Irreparable; terms of peace yet none
Vouchsafed° or sought, for what peace will be given   *offered*
To us enslaved but custody severe,
And stripes,° and arbitrary punishment   *whippings*
Inflicted? And what peace can we return   335
But, to our power, hostility and hate,
Untamed reluctance,° and revenge though slow,   *resistance, struggle*
Yet ever plotting how the conqueror least
May reap his conquest and may least rejoice

312. *style:* title (*OED* 18a)

315. *Doubtless:* Standing between semi-colons as it does in the early editions, *Doubtless* marks a flash of sarcasm between Beelzebub's irony and his ensuing earnest argument.

324. *first . . . reign:* The words attributed to God in the Apocalypse, "I am Alpha and Omega, the beginning and the end, the first and the last" (Rev. 22:13; see also 1:11 and 21:6), here inspire Beelzebub's despair, as later they inspire the joy of God's faithful creatures "to extol / Him first, him last" (5.165).

327. *iron scepter:* recalls Rev. 19:15: "he

shall rule them with a rod of iron" (see also Ps. 2:9). Iron was a traditional symbol of enmity, as gold was the symbol of friendship (see line 328) or of justice and mercy, an iconography that recurs in Abdiel's warning to Satan (5.886–88).

330. *determined us:* 1) brought us to this condition; 2) decided our course

334. *arbitrary:* undeserved, capricious (but note an alternative meaning of *arbitrary:* at the discretion of an authority or arbitrator)

336. *to our power:* to the extent of our power

In doing what we most in suffering feel?   340
Nor will occasion want nor shall we need
With dangerous expedition to invade
Heaven, whose high walls fear no assault or siege
Or ambush from the deep. What if we find
Some easier enterprise? There is a place   345
(If ancient and prophetic fame in Heaven
Err not), another world, the happy seat
Of some new race called man, about this time
To be created like to us, though less
In power and excellence but favored more   350
Of him who rules above; so was his will
Pronounced among the gods and by an oath,
That shook Heaven's whole circumference, confirmed.
Thither let us bend all our thoughts to learn
What creatures there inhabit, of what mold
Or substance, how endued, and what their power,
And where their weakness, how attempted best,
By force or subtlety. Though Heaven be shut
And Heaven's high arbitrator sit secure
In his own strength, this place may lie exposed,   360
The utmost border of his kingdom, left
To their defense who hold it. Here perhaps
Some advantageous act may be achieved
By sudden onset, either with hell fire
To waste his whole creation or possess   365
All as our own and drive, as we were driven,

---

346. *ancient and prophetic fame:* See Satan's reference to this *fame* in 1.651.

348–350. *some new race . . . more:* Milton makes use of Origen's assertion (rejected by Saint Thomas in the *Summa Theologica* 1.961.a.33) that God created the world after the revolt of the angels.

349–350. *less . . . excellence:* Compare Ps. 8.5: "For thou hast made him a little lower than the angels, and hast crowned him with glory and honour."

352. *gods:* Here and in 3.341, 5.60 and 117, 9.164, and 10.90, "gods" refers to the angels, for, as Milton explains in *Christian Doctrine* I.v, "the name of God is not infrequently ascribed, by the will and concession of God the Father, even unto angels and men" (*Works*, 14, 245).

352–353. *by an oath . . . circumference:* See Isa: 13:12–13: "I will make a man more precious than fine gold. . . . Therefore I will shake the heavens." The reference also combines biblical representations of God taking an oath by himself "because he could swear by no greater" (Heb. 6:13), with Zeus' vow to Thetis (*Iliad* 1.530) or his promise to Cybele (*Aeneid* 9.106).

356. *substance:* matter, material; see pp. xxxvii–xli above.   *how endued:* supplied with what qualities

357. *attempted:* attacked (but with "tempted" inevitably heard as well)

The puny habitants, or if not drive,
Seduce them to our party that their God
May prove their foe and with repenting hand
Abolish his own works. This would surpass   370
Common revenge and interrupt his joy
In our confusion,° and our joy upraise   *destruction*
In his disturbance when his darling sons,
Hurled headlong to partake with us, shall curse
Their frail original and faded bliss,   375
Faded so soon. Advise if this be worth
Attempting, or to sit in darkness here
Hatching vain empires." Thus Beelzebub
Pleaded his devilish counsel, first devised
By Satan and in part proposed: for whence,   380
But from the author of all ill could spring
So deep a malice, to confound° the race   *ruin, destroy*
Of mankind in one root, and earth with hell
To mingle and involve,° done all to spite   *entangle*
The great creator? But their spite still serves   385
His glory to augment. The bold design
Pleased highly those infernal states, and joy
Sparkled in all their eyes; with full assent

367. *puny:* weak, but it may have its et-
ymological meaning of "new born" (French,
puis né), here, "newly created." Some ver-
sions of the revolt based the motivation of
the angels on their resentment of the honor
that God commanded them to pay to the
"puny" (in both senses) race of man; thus, in
an infernal council in *Psyche* (1648), Joseph
Beaumont has Beelzebub ask rhetorically:
"Was't not enough, against the righteous Law
/ Of Primogeniture, to throw us down /
From that bright home, which all the world
do's know / Was by confest inheritance our
own: / But, to our shame, Man, that vile
worm, must dwell / In our fair Orbs, and
Heav'n with Vermin fill" (1.24).

368–370. *God . . . works:* echoes Gen.
6:7, where God nearly does what Beelzebub
wishes: "and the Lord said, I will destroy
man whom I have created from the face of
the earth . . . for it repenteth me that I have
made [him]."

374. *Hurled headlong:* repeats the phrase

of 1.45, so in Beelzebub's imagination
mankind would "partake" of the exact fate of
the fallen angels

375. *original:* origin (not "original
state" as in 9.150, but referring to Adam as
the origin of humankind). The 1667 first
edition reads "Originals."

375–376. *faded bliss . . . soon:* See
9.893, when Adam drops his garland and "all
the faded roses shed," the first sign of the
decay that accompanies the fall.

377–378. *sit . . . Hatching:* Compare
God's spirit that "Dove-like, sat'st brooding
on the vast abyss / And mad'st it pregnant."
(1.21–22).

379–380. *first . . . proposed:* See
1.651–54. The phrase reveals Satan's manip-
ulation of the council.

387. *states:* dignitaries, though here it
may refer to the estates of the realm. The par-
liaments of England and France traditionally
consisted of the three estates: lords, clergy,
and commons.

They vote, whereat his speech he thus renews:
   "Well have ye judged, well ended long debate,   390
Synod of gods and, like to what ye are,
Great things resolved, which from the lowest deep
Will once more lift us up, in spite of fate,
Nearer our ancient seat, perhaps in view
Of those bright confines, whence with neighboring arms   395
And opportune excursion we may chance
Re-enter Heaven, or else in some mild zone
Dwell, not unvisited of Heaven's fair light,
Secure and, at the brightening orient beam,
Purge off this gloom; the soft delicious air,   400
To heal the scar of these corrosive fires,
Shall breathe her balm. But first, whom shall we send
In search of this new world? Whom shall we find
Sufficient? Who shall tempt with wandering feet
The dark unbottomed° infinite abyss   *limitless*
And, through the palpable obscure, find out
His uncouth way or spread his airy flight
Upborn with indefatigable wings
Over the vast abrupt, ere he arrive
The happy isle? What strength, what art, can then   410
Suffice or what evasion bear him safe
Through the strict sentries and stations thick
Of angels watching round? Here he had need
All circumspection, and we now no less
Choice in our suffrage, for on whom we send   415

391. *Synod:* assembly (usually ecclesiastical, but sometimes used for a conjunction of stars)

394. *our ancient seat:* Cf. "seat," in the sense of "established home," as in 1.5.

402. *first . . . send:* Cf. Isa. 6:8: "I heard the voice of the Lord, saying, Whom shall I send, and who will go for us."

403. *this new world:* establishes earth as a "new world" awaiting its discovery and colonization

404. *tempt:* venture into, attempt (though hardly a neutral choice of word in this poem)

406. *palpable obscure:* echoes the "darkness which may be felt" which God sent to plague the Egyptians (Exod. 10:21)

407. *uncouth:* unknown; cf. line 827 below.

409. *abrupt:* an adjective used as a noun, here with its Latin meaning of "a breach" (*abruptus* = broken off). It refers to the chasm between hell and heaven.

410. *The happy isle:* i.e., earth, imagined as an island (the name here probably derived from the Isles of the Blessed in Greek mythology)

412. *sentries and stations:* guards and guard posts; the meter demands three syllables for *sentries*, and the early spelling, "senteries" reflects this pronunciation.
thick: numerous and close together

415. *Choice . . . suffrage:* care in our vote

The weight of all and our last hope relies."
    This said, he sat, and expectation held
His look suspense, awaiting who appeared
To second, or oppose, or undertake
The perilous attempt; but all sat mute,   420
Pondering the danger with deep thoughts, and each
In other's countenance read his own dismay,
Astonished. None among the choice and prime
Of those Heaven-warring champions could be found
So hardy as to proffer° or accept   *volunteer*
Alone the dreadful voyage, till at last
Satan, whom now transcendent glory raised
Above his fellows, with monarchal pride
Conscious of highest worth, unmoved, thus spake:
    "O progeny of Heaven, empyreal thrones,   430
With reason hath deep silence and demur
Seized us, though undismayed. Long is the way
And hard that out of hell leads up to light;
Our prison strong, this huge convex of fire,
Outrageous to devour, immures us round   435
Ninefold, and gates of burning adamant
Barred over us prohibit all egress.
These passed, if any pass, the void profound
Of unessential Night receives him next
Wide gaping, and with utter loss of being   440

---

418. *suspense:* suspended, hanging; i.e., doubtful or in suspense (here an adjective modifying "look")

420. *all sat mute:* Cf. "all . . . stood mute" in 3.217.

423. *choice and prime:* best and most highly regarded

428. *monarchal pride:* Compare Christ's "meek aspect" at the parallel moment in 3.266. Milton's anti-royalism is unmistakable in the assignment of the adjective to Satan's pride. Etymologically, *monarchal* means of single rule, and for Milton only God, by virtue of his unique status as creator, can properly said to merit the term, as at 4.960: "Heaven's awful monarch"; see pp. xxviii–xxxiii above.

432–433. *Long . . . hard:* The thought harks back to the Sibyl's warning to Aeneas (*Aeneid* 6.126–29) that the descent to Avernus is easy, and perhaps also to Virgil's warning to Dante (*Inferno* 39.95), as they prepare to ascend from the center of the earth toward Purgatory, that the way is hard. Cf. 3.21.

434. *convex:* canopy, dome (referring to the sphere surrounding Hell); cf. 3.419.

435. *Outrageous to devour:* brutally destructive

435–436. *immures . . . Ninefold:* recalls "the nine-fold circles" of the Styx that imprison the underworld in the *Aeneid* (6.439), as the *gates of burning adamant* recall the columns of unbreakable adamant supporting the gates of Tartarus (*Aeneid* 6.552). (*immures* = encloses within walls)

439. *unessential:* without actual being, formless, uncreated, as in line 150 above.

Threatens him, plunged in that abortive gulf.
If thence he scape into whatever world
Or unknown region, what remains him less
Than unknown dangers and as hard escape?
But I should ill become this throne, O peers,   445
And this imperial sovereignty, adorned
With splendor, armed with power, if aught proposed
And judged of public moment in the shape
Of difficulty or danger could deter
Me from attempting. Wherefore do I assume   450
These royalties° and not refuse to reign,   *royal prerogatives*
Refusing to accept as great a share
Of hazard as of honor, due alike
To him who reigns, and so much to him due
Of hazard more as he above the rest   455
High honored sits? Go therefore, mighty powers,
Terror of Heaven though fallen; intend at home,
While here shall be our home, what best may ease
The present misery and render hell
More tolerable, if there be cure or charm   460
To respite or deceive° or slack the pain   *elude, beguile*
Of this ill mansion.° Intermit no watch   *dwelling place*
Against a wakeful foe, while I abroad,
Through all the coasts of dark destruction, seek
Deliverance for us all; this enterprise   465
None shall partake with me." Thus saying, rose
The monarch and prevented all reply,
Prudent, lest from his resolution raised,°   *emboldened*
Others among the chief might offer now
(Certain to be refused) what erst° they feared,   *at first*
And, so refused, might in opinion stand
His rivals, winning cheap the high repute
Which he through hazard huge must earn. But they
Dreaded not more the adventure than his voice
Forbidding, and at once with him they rose;   475

The negative form of the word anticipates
abortive, line 441, which may mean
"aborted" (lifeless) or "monstrous" (and
therefore terrifying), or "abortion-causing"
(see Chaos as a "womb," line 150).

   443–444. *him less Than:* for him apart
from

448. *moment:* importance; the word
here has the Latin force that it still has in the
adjective "momentous"

452. *Refusing:* i.e., if I refuse

457. *intend at:* consider, think about

462. *intermit no watch:* do not relax
your guard

Their rising all at once was as the sound
Of thunder heard remote. Towards him they bend
With awful° reverence prone and as a god   *awestruck, inspiring awe*
Extol him equal to the highest in Heaven.
Nor failed they to express how much they praised   480
That for the general safety he despised
His own, for neither do the spirits damned
Lose all their virtue, lest bad men should boast
Their specious deeds on earth which glory excites,
Or close° ambition varnished o'er with zeal.   *secret*
Thus they, their doubtful consultations dark,
Ended rejoicing in their matchless chief,
As when from mountain tops the dusky clouds
Ascending, while the north wind sleeps, o'erspread
Heaven's cheerful face, the louring element   490
Scowls o'er the darkened landscape snow or shower,
If chance the radiant sun with farewell sweet
Extend his evening beam, the fields revive,
The birds their notes renew, and bleating herds
Attest their joy, that° hill and valley rings.   *so that*
O shame to men! Devil with devil damned
Firm concord holds; men only disagree
Of creatures rational, though under hope
Of heavenly grace and God proclaiming peace,
Yet live in hatred, enmity, and strife   500
Among themselves and levy cruel wars,
Wasting the earth, each other to destroy,
As if (which might induce us to accord)
Man had not hellish foes enow° besides,   *enough*
That day and night for his destruction wait.   505
    The Stygian council thus dissolved, and forth
In order came the grand infernal peers.°   *nobles*
Midst came their mighty paramount° and seemed   *leader*
Alone the antagonist of Heaven, nor less

490. *louring element:* darkening (threat-
ening) sky
    491. *landscape:* Milton writes "land-
skip," which I have here modernized.
    496–502. *Devil . . . earth:* The lines re-
state an orthodox doctrine that is found in
Antonio Rusca's *De Inferno et Statu Dae-
monum* (Milan, 1621), pp. 505–7. Rusca

does not refer to the *cruel wars* of the 17th
century, as Milton does here, but he says ex-
plicitly that the devils avoid civil strife and
maintain orders and ranks among themselves
so as to tempt mankind most efficiently;
Wasting = destroying, laying waste to.
    506. *Stygian:* hellish (from the river
Styx, the river that led to Hades)

Than hell's dread emperor with pomp supreme   510
And godlike imitated state; him round
A globe of fiery seraphim enclosed
With bright emblazonry and horrent° arms.   *bristling*
Then, of their session ended, they bid cry
With trumpets' regal sound the great result.   515
Toward the four winds four speedy cherubim
Put to their mouths the sounding alchemy
By herald's voice explained; the hollow abyss
Heard far and wide, and all the host of hell,
With deafening shout, returned them loud acclaim.   520
Thence more at ease their minds and somewhat raised
By false presumptuous hope, the rangèd powers°   *armies arrayed in ranks*
Disband, and, wandering, each his several way
Pursues, as inclination or sad choice
Leads him perplexed, where he may likeliest find   525
Truce to his restless thoughts and entertain
The irksome hours till his great chief return.
Part on the plain, or in the air sublime
Upon the wing, or in swift race contend,
As at the Olympian games or Pythian fields;   530
Part curb their fiery steeds, or shun the goal
With rapid wheels, or fronted brigades form.
As when to warn proud cities war appears

511. *imitated:* hence artificial and false, but implying Satan's nostalgia for Heaven *state:* magnificent display (*OED* 17)

512. *globe:* a phalanx of soldiers; *OED* cites Giles Fletcher the younger's lines: "out there flies / A globe of winged angels, swift as thought" ("Christ's Triumph after Death," 1610, lines 101–2). Cf. *PR* 4.581.

513. *emblazonry:* heraldic display

517. *sounding alchemy:* trumpets of brass (Sir Francis Bacon, in *Articles of Questions Touching Metals and Minerals* in the posthumous 1664 edition of *Sylva Sylvarum*, said "Bell-metal they call alchemy"); cf. 1 Cor. 13:1, where, in the absence of love, even the "tongues of . . . angels" become "sounding brass."

528–565. *Part . . . philosophy:* The diversions of the demons are entertainments like the activities of the dead heroes in the *Aeneid* 6.642: "some disport their limbs on the grassy wrestling ground, vie in sports, and grapple on the yellow sand; some trip it in the dance and chant songs"; cf. also the funeral games at the tomb of Anchises in *Aeneid* 5.103–603.

531. *shun the goal:* The image is of Roman charioteers skillfully driving their teams to avoid the posts planted in the arena, as Horace describes them in the opening lines of his first book of *Odes*; also see *Aeneid* 6.653–55.

532. *fronted brigades:* i.e., opposing (confronting) teams

533–535. *As . . . clouds:* Perhaps there is a reflection of the "chariots and troops of soldiers in their armour running about among the clouds" that Josephus mentions among

Waged in the troubled sky and armies rush
To battle in the clouds, before each van°   *vanguard*
Prick forth the airy knights and couch their spears
Till thickest legions close; with feats of arms
From either end of Heaven the welkin° burns.   *sky*
Others with vast Typhoean rage more fell°   *fierce*
Rend up both rocks and hills and ride the air   540
In whirlwind. Hell scarce holds the wild uproar,
As when Alcides, from Oechalia crowned
With conquest, felt the envenomed robe and tore,
Through pain, up by the roots Thessalian pines,
And Lichas from the top of Oeta threw   545
Into the Euboic Sea. Others, more mild,
Retreated in a silent valley, sing,
With notes angelical to many a harp,
Their own heroic deeds and hapless fall
By doom° of battle and complain that fate   *judgment*
Free virtue should enthrall to force or chance.
Their song was partial, but the harmony
(What could it less when spirits immortal sing?)
Suspended hell and took° with ravishment   *enraptured*
The thronging audience. In discourse more sweet   555
(For eloquence, the soul; song charms the sense)
Others apart sat on a hill, retired
In thoughts more elevate, and reasoned high
Of providence, foreknowledge, will, and fate,

the portents seen by the Jews before the fall of Jerusalem (*Wars* 6.5.3.), though similar portents in England from 1640–1660 were widely reported; and indeed Hume (1695) claimed these lines as an allusion to "our Civil Wars."

536. *Prick forth:* ride towards each other   *couch:* lower into an attacking position

539. *Typhoean:* See the note on *Typhoean* in 1.197. The name Typhon or Typhoeus meant "whirlwind" (line 541), and the Greek word has influenced (but is not cognate with) the English word "typhoon" (which is of Arabian or Persian origin).

542–546. *As when Alcides . . . Sea:* The passage retells an episode of the legend of Hercules (*Alcides*), who, following a victory

in Oechalia and returning to the island of Euboea (off the Attic coast), slew his friend Lichas in blind rage brought on by *the envenomed robe* of Nessus, which Lichas had innocently given him to wear. The story is treated by Sophocles in the *Trachiniae* and by Seneca in *The Mad Hercules*; cf. Ovid's version (*Metamorphoses* 9.134 ff.), on which Milton depends, though Ovid places Mount *Oeta* in Thessaly, rather than Euboea, the scene of the action here.

552. *partial:* i.e., favorable to their own view of their quarrel with God as a struggle against tyrannic force, but also musically, "in parts, or harmonized"

554. *Suspended:* held rapt, but also deferred, precisely enacted by the parentheses of line 552   *took:* captivated

Fixed fate, free will, foreknowledge absolute,   560
And found no end, in wandering mazes lost.
Of good and evil much they argued then,
Of happiness and final misery,
Passion and apathy, and glory and shame:
Vain wisdom all, and false philosophy,   565
Yet with a pleasing sorcery could charm
Pain for a while or anguish, and excite
Fallacious hope, or arm the obdurèd° breast   *hardened*
With stubborn patience as with triple steel.
Another part in squadrons and gross° bands,   *massed, tight*
On bold adventure to discover wide
That dismal world, if any clime perhaps
Might yield them easier habitation, bend
Four ways their flying march, along the banks
Of four infernal rivers that disgorge   575
Into the burning lake their baleful streams:
Abhorrèd Styx, the flood of deadly hate;
Sad Acheron of sorrow, black and deep;
Cocytus, named of lamentation loud
Heard on the rueful stream; fierce Phlegeton,   580
Whose waves of torrent fire inflame with rage.
Far off from these a slow and silent stream,
Lethe, the river of oblivion, rolls
Her watery labyrinth, whereof who drinks
Forthwith his former state and being forgets,   585
Forgets both joy and grief, pleasure and pain.

564. *apathy:* See the condemnation of the Stoic ideal of apathy or absolute mastery of all the passions as the opposite of Christian patience in *Christian Doctrine* II, x (*Works* 17, 251), and the contempt in *PR* 4.300–1, for the Stoic's "Philosophic pride, by him call'd virtue."

565. *Vain . . . philosophy:* Like Henry More in his *Immortality of the Soul* (1659, 3.17.8), Milton found it natural that there should be "students of philosophy" among the demons, who are "divided into sects and opinions, as we are here." But cf. Col. 2:8: "Beware lest any man spoil you through philosophy and vain deceit, after the tradition of men, after the rudiments of the world."

577–581. *Styx . . . rage:* The lines translate the meanings of the Greek names of the four rivers of hell. Though they flow into the "lake of fire and brimstone" of Rev. 20:10, they bound a hell that is like Virgil's (*Aeneid* 6.656–59) or Spenser's. In the *Faerie Queene* 2.8.20, Spenser described the allegorically "bitter wave / Of hellish Styx"; in 2.7.57, he named Cocytus, whose sad waves echoed with "piteous cryes and yelling shrightes"; in 2.6.50, he mentioned "flaming Phlegethon", and in 1.5.33, "the bitter waves of Acheron."

583. *Lethe:* the "forgetful lake" of line 74 above

Beyond this flood a frozen continent
Lies dark and wild, beat with perpetual storms
Of whirlwind and dire hail, which on firm land
Thaws not, but gathers heap° and ruin seems   *into heaps*
Of ancient pile; all else deep snow and ice,
A gulf profound as that Serbonian bog
Betwixt Damietta and Mount Casius old
Where armies whole have sunk; the parching air
Burns frore, and cold performs the effect of fire.   595
Thither by harpy-footed furies haled
At certain revolutions° all the damned   *seasons*
Are brought and feel by turns the bitter change
Of fierce extremes, extremes by change more fierce,
From beds of raging fire to starve in ice   600
Their soft ethereal warmth, and there to pine
Immovable, infixed,° and frozen round,   *firmly planted*
Periods of time, thence hurried back to fire.
They ferry over this Lethean sound
Both to and fro, their sorrow to augment,   605
And wish and struggle, as they pass, to reach
The tempting stream, with one small drop to lose
In sweet forgetfulness all pain and woe,
All in one moment, and so near the brink;
But fate withstands and, to oppose the attempt,   610
Medusa, with gorgonian terror, guards
The ford, and of itself the water flies
All taste of living wight,° as once it fled   *person*

591. *ancient pile:* The accumulated *hail* (line 589) seems like the ruin of a marble *pile* (i.e., building).

592–593. *Serbonian bog . . . Casius old:* On Thomas Fuller's map of the route of the Hebrews from Egypt to Palestine (*A Pisgah-Sight of Palestine*, 1650, p. 43) and on some maps by Ortelius the *Serbonian Bog* (Lake Serbonis) lies between *Damietta* (on the mouth of the Phatnitic branch of the Nile, on the right bank) and *Mount Casius*. In Diodorus Siculus' *Library* 1.3.5–7, and several 17th-century histories are accounts of "whole armies" sinking in its quicksands.

595. *frore:* frozen; cf. Claudio's fear that in hell his soul might "bathe in fiery floods"

or "reside / In thrilling region of thick-ribbed ice" (*Measure for Measure* 3.1.121–22).

596. *harpy-footed:* with sharp talons; Virgil anticipated Milton in attributing the claws of the harpies to the Furies, or Eumenides, goddesses who avenged crimes like Orestes' slaying of his mother (*Aeneid* 3.217).   *haled:* dragged, hauled (for play on "hailed," see line 589)

600. *starve:* in its original, general sense of "die" for any cause, here by freezing

604. *Lethean sound:* the river Lethe (see lines 74 and 583 above); *sound* = waterway

611. *Medusa:* one of the monstrous, snake-haired gorgons that could turn people to stone with a look

The lip of Tantalus. Thus roving on
In confused march forlorn, the adventurous bands   615
With shuddering horror pale and eyes aghast
Viewed first their lamentable lot and found
No rest; through many a dark and dreary vale
They passed, and many a region dolorous,
O'er many a frozen, many a fiery alp,°   *any high mountain*
Rocks, caves, lakes, fens, bogs, dens, and shades of death,
A universe of death, which God by curse
Created evil, for evil only good,
Where all life dies, death lives, and nature breeds
Perverse, all monstrous, all prodigious things,   625
Abominable, inutterable, and worse
Than fables yet have feigned or fear conceived,
Gorgons and hydras and chimeras dire.
　　　Meanwhile the adversary of God and man,
Satan, with thoughts inflamed of highest design,   630
Puts on swift wings and toward the gates of hell
Explores his solitary flight; sometimes
He scours the right hand coast, sometimes the left,
Now shaves° with level wing the deep, then soars   *skims over*
Up to the fiery concave, towering high.   635
As when far off at sea a fleet descried
Hangs in the clouds, by equinoctial° winds   *at the equator*
Close sailing from Bengala or the isles

614. *Tantalus:* In Tartarus (*Odyssey* 11.582–92) Ulysses saw *Tantalus* fixed in a pool of water that forever fell below the reach of his thirsty lips; "thirsty Tantalus hung by the chin," as Spenser describes him (*Faerie Queene* 1.5.35). Above him laden fruit trees are just out of his reach.

628. *Gorgons and hydras and chimeras:* *Gorgons* were female monsters with snakes for hair, like *Medusa* (line 611); the many-headed *hydras* and the flame-spitting *chimeras* are vague monsters like the "un-numbered specters" of Virgil's hell, where "horrid Hydra stands, / And Briareus with all his hundred hands, / Gorgons, Geryon with his triple frame; / And vain Chimera vomits empty flame (*Aeneid* 6.286–89, Dryden's translation).

629. *adversary:* the literal meaning of Satan; see 1 Pet. 5:8; "your adversary the devil."

632. *Explores:* retains its Latin meaning of "tests" or "tries out"

636–640. *As . . . drugs:* The simile reflects the interest in the new spice trade. English ships carried spices back to Europe from the Moluccas, or Spice Islands, of which *Ternate* and *Tidore* were the best known, by sailing through the *Ethiopian* Sea (the Indian Ocean off East Africa), around the *Cape* of Good Hope into the Atlantic. In Milton's time *Bengala* (Bengal) was part of the Mogul empire.

637. *Hangs in the clouds:* seems to be floating in the air

638. *Close sailing:* sailing as close to the wind as the ships will go to enable the most direct route

Of Ternate and Tidore, whence merchants bring
Their spicy drugs, they on the trading flood   640
Through the wide Ethiopian to the Cape
Ply,° stemming nightly toward the pole, so seemed   *steadily sail*
Far off the flying fiend. At last appear
Hell bounds high reaching to the horrid roof
And thrice threefold the gates; three folds were brass,   645
Three iron, three of adamantine rock
Impenetrable, impaled° with circling fire   *fenced in, enclosed*
Yet unconsumed. Before the gates there sat
On either side a formidable shape;
The one seemed woman to the waist and fair,   650
But ended foul in many a scaly fold,
Voluminous and vast, a serpent armed
With mortal sting. About her middle round
A cry° of hell hounds never ceasing barked   *pack*
With wide Cerberean mouths full loud, and rung   655
A hideous peal; yet, when they list, would creep,
If aught disturbed their noise, into her womb
And kennel there, yet there still barked and howled
Within unseen. Far less abhorred than these
Vexed Scylla bathing in the sea that parts   660
Calabria from the hoarse Trinacrian shore,
Nor uglier follow the night-hag, when, called
In secret, riding through the air she comes,
Lured with the smell of infant blood, to dance
With Lapland witches while the laboring moon   665

---

640. *spicy drugs:* spices used medicinally
641. *wide Ethiopian:* i.e., the Indian Ocean
642. *stemming:* making headway
650–659. *The one . . . unseen:* The lines become completely clear only in light of lines 762–67 below. Milton's Sin owes her serpentine nether parts to conceptions like Spenser's Error: "Halfe like a serpent horribly displaide, / But th'other halfe did womans shape retaine" (*Faerie Queene* 1.1.14); but the dogs around Sin's waist, and especially their *Cerberean mouths,* echo Ovid's description of *Scylla* (see line 660), the lovely nymph whose body Circe transformed into a mass of yelping hounds from the waist down

(*Metamorphoses* 14.50–74). (Cerberus was the multiheaded dog that guarded hell.)
652. *Voluminous:* coiled (like a scroll, Latin *volumen*)
660–661. *parts . . . Trinacrian shore:* separates Calabria (the toe of the Italian mainland) from Sicily
662. *the night-hag:* probably Hecate whose charms were used by Circe to bewitch Scylla. Popular superstition made Hecate the witches' queen, as in *Macbeth* (3.5 and 4.1).
662–663. *called In secret:* conjured, magically summoned
665. *Lapland witches:* Lapland was notoriously a home of witches; see *Comedy of Errors* 4.3.11: "Lapland sorcerers."

Eclipses at their charms. The other shape—
If shape it might be called that shape had none
Distinguishable in member, joint, or limb,
Or substance might be called that shadow seemed,
For each seemed either—black it stood as night,   670
Fierce as ten furies, terrible as hell,
And shook a dreadful dart;° what seemed his head   *spear*
The likeness of a kingly crown had on.
Satan was now at hand, and from his seat
The monster moving onward came as fast   675
With horrid strides; hell trembled as he strode.
The undaunted fiend what this might be admired—
Admired, not feared; God and his Son except,
Created thing naught valued he nor shunned,
And with disdainful look thus first began: 680
     "Whence and what art thou, execrable° shape,   *accursed, abhorrent*
That darest, though grim and terrible, advance
Thy miscreated° front athwart my way   *misshapen face*
To yonder gates? Through them I mean to pass,
That be assured, without leave asked of thee;   685
Retire, or taste thy folly and learn by proof,°   *experience*
Hell-born, not to contend with spirits of Heaven."
     To whom the goblin, full of wrath, replied:
"Art thou that traitor angel, art thou he
Who first broke peace in Heaven and faith, till then   690
Unbroken, and in proud rebellious arms
Drew after him the third part of Heaven's sons
Conjured against the highest, for which both thou
And they, outcast from God, are here condemned
To waste eternal days in woe and pain?   695

laboring: in eclipse; in the *Georgics* (2.478) Virgil speaks of the labors (*labores*) of the moon in this sense, though the word here also suggests the action of pregnancy and childbirth.

671. *furies:* See line 596 above and note.

673. *a kingly crown:* another unmistakable anti-monarchical touch; Milton invokes John's vision of the king of terrors, when "a crown was given unto him [Death]: and he went forth conquering, and to conquer" (Rev. 6:2).

677. *admired:* here (and in line 678) has its Latin force of "wondered at"

692. *the third part of Heaven's sons:* echoes John's dragon, whose "tail drew the third part of the stars of heaven, and did cast them to the earth" (Rev. 12:3–4). Cf. 1.632–33, where it is claimed heaven has been "emptied" and 9.141–42, where the claim for the rebel angels is "well-nigh half."

693. *Conjured:* conspired, bound together by an oath (Latin *con* = with + *jurare* = to swear)

And reckon'st thou thyself with spirits of Heaven,
Hell-doomed, and breath'st defiance here and scorn
Where I reign king, and, to enrage thee more,
Thy king and lord? Back to thy punishment,
False fugitive, and to thy speed add wings,   700
Lest with a whip of scorpions I pursue
Thy lingering, or with one stroke of this dart
Strange horror seize thee and pangs unfelt before."
    So spake the grisly terror, and in shape,
So speaking and so threatening, grew ten-fold   705
More dreadful and deform; on the other side,
Incensed with indignation, Satan stood
Unterrified and like a comet burned,
That fires the length of Ophiucus huge
In the Arctic sky, and from his horrid hair   710
Shakes pestilence and war. Each at the head
Leveled his deadly aim; their fatal hands
No second stroke intend, and such a frown
Each cast at the other, as when two black clouds,
With Heaven's artillery fraught, come rattling on   715
Over the Caspian, then stand front to front,
Hovering a space, till winds the signal blow
To join their dark encounter in mid air.
So frowned the mighty combatants that hell
Grew darker at their frown, so matched they stood,   720
For never but once more was either like
To meet so great a foe; and now great deeds
Had been achieved whereof all hell had rung,
Had not the snaky sorceress that sat

701. *whip of scorpions:* See 1 Kings 12:11: "my father hath chastised you with whips, but I will chastise you with scorpions."

708. *like . . . burned:* Aeneas' helmet similarly shines like a portentous comet as his ship approaches Turnus' camp (*Aeneid* 10.272–75).

709. *Ophiucus:* one of the largest constellations in the northern sky, known as The Serpent Bearer; its name and situation both are relevant to Satan, who is the "infernal serpent" (1.34) and who raises the revolt in the north of Heaven (5.689).

710. *horrid hair:* hair bristling (in

anger); the word "comet" (line 708) comes from a Greek word meaning "long haired."

714. *two black clouds:* Orlando and the Tartar king Agricane encounter each other like thunder clouds in Boiardo's *Orlando Innamorato* 1.16.

715. *With Heaven's artillery fraught:* laden with lightning and thunder

716. *the Caspian:* The Caspian Sea was proverbial for storms as early as the reference to it as such by Horace in *Odes* 2.9.2.

721. *but once more:* refers to Christ's ultimate victory over "the last enemy . . . death" (1 Cor. 15:26); see also Heb. 2:14.

Fast by hell gate and kept the fatal key   725
Risen and with hideous outcry rushed between.
    "O father, what intends thy hand," she cried,
"Against thy only son? What fury, O son,
Possesses thee to bend that mortal dart
Against thy father's head? And know'st for whom?   730
For him who sits above and laughs the while
At thee, ordained his drudge° to execute   *servant*
Whate'er his wrath, which he calls justice, bids,
His wrath which one day will destroy ye both."
    She spake, and at her words the hellish pest   735
Forbore; then these to her Satan returned:
    "So strange thy outcry, and thy words so strange
Thou interposest, that my sudden hand
Prevented spares to tell thee yet by deeds
What it intends till first I know of thee   740
What thing thou art, thus double-formed, and why
In this infernal vale first met thou call'st
Me 'father,' and that phantasm call'st my son.
I know thee not, nor ever saw till now
Sight more detestable than him and thee."   745
    To whom thus the portress° of hell gate replied: *female gatekeeper*
"Hast thou forgot me then, and do I seem
Now in thine eye so foul, once deemed so fair
In Heaven, when at the assembly and, in sight
Of all the seraphim, with thee combined   750
In bold conspiracy against Heaven's king,
All on a sudden miserable pain
Surprised thee, dim thine eyes, and dizzy swum
In darkness, while thy head flames thick and fast
Threw forth, till on the left side opening wide,   755
Likest to thee in shape and countenance bright,
Then shining heavenly fair, a goddess armed

---

725. *fatal key:* the opposite of the keys of Saint Peter (Matt. 16:19) that open the doors to Heaven

736. *these:* i.e., these words

738–739. *my . . . spares to:* i.e., my hand, usually quick to strike, was held back and thus refrains from

752–758. *All on . . . sprung:* The myth of Athena's (Minerva's) birth from the head of Zeus in Hesiod's *Theogony* (920–29) is fused with an ancient allegory stemming from James' words (James 1:15): "When lust hath conceived, it bringeth forth sin: and sin, when it is finished, bringeth forth death." See also John Gower's personification of Sin as the incestuous mother of Death in the *Mirrour de l'Omme* (c. 1380, lines 205–37).

Out of thy head I sprung? Amazement seized
All the host of Heaven; back they recoiled afraid
At first and called me 'Sin' and for a sign   760
Portentous held me; but familiar grown
I pleased, and with attractive graces won
The most averse, thee chiefly, who full oft
Thyself in me thy perfect image viewing
Becam'st enamored, and such joy thou took'st   765
With me in secret that my womb conceived
A growing burden. Meanwhile war arose,
And fields° were fought in Heaven, wherein remained   *battles*
(For what could else) to our almighty foe
Clear victory, to our part loss and rout   770
Through all the empyrean. Down they fell,
Driven headlong from the pitch° of Heaven, down   *summit, zenith*
Into this deep, and in the general fall
I also, at which time this powerful key
Into my hand was given with charge to keep   775
These gates forever shut, which none can pass
Without my opening. Pensive here I sat
Alone, but long I sat not, till my womb,
Pregnant by thee and now excessive grown,
Prodigious motion felt and rueful throes.   780
At last this odious offspring whom thou seest,
Thine own begotten, breaking violent way
Tore through my entrails, that,° with fear and pain   *so that*
Distorted, all my nether shape thus grew
Transformed; but he, my inbred enemy,   785
Forth issued, brandishing his fatal dart
Made to destroy. I fled and cried out 'Death!'
Hell trembled at the hideous name, and sighed
From all her caves, and back resounded 'Death!'
I fled, but he pursued (though more, it seems,   790
Inflamed with lust than rage), and, swifter far,
Me overtook, his mother all dismayed,
And in embraces forcible and foul
Engendering with me, of that rape begot
These yelling monsters that with ceaseless cry   795

795–799. *These yelling . . . return:* Both
the allegory and the details resemble
Spenser's Error: "of her there bred / A thou-
sand young ones, which she dayly fed, /
Sucking upon her poisnous dugs, . . . Soone
as the uncouth light upon them shone, / Into

Surround me, as thou saw'st, hourly conceived
And hourly born, with sorrow infinite
To me; for, when they list, into the womb
That bred them they return, and howl and gnaw
My bowels, their repast, then bursting forth   800
Afresh, with conscious terrors vex me round,
That rest or intermission none I find.
Before mine eyes in opposition sits
Grim Death, my son and foe, who sets them on,
And me, his parent, would full soon devour   805
For want of other prey, but that he knows
His end with mine involved and knows that I
Should prove a bitter morsel and his bane
Whenever that shall be; so fate pronounced.
But thou, O father, I forewarn thee, shun   810
His deadly arrow; neither vainly hope
To be invulnerable in those bright arms,
Though tempered heavenly, for that mortal dint,
Save he who reigns above, none can resist."
     She finished, and the subtle fiend, his lore°   *lesson*
Soon learned, now milder, and thus answered smooth:
"Dear daughter, since thou claim'st me for thy sire
And my fair son here show'st me (the dear pledge
Of dalliance had with thee in Heaven, and joys
Then sweet, now sad to mention through dire change   820
Befallen us unforeseen, unthought of) know
I come no enemy, but to set free
From out this dark and dismal house of pain
Both him and thee and all the heavenly host
Of spirits that in our just pretenses° armed   *legal claims*
Fell with us from on high; from them I go
This uncouth° errand sole, and one for all   *strange, unpleasant*
Myself expose, with lonely steps to tread
The unfounded deep and through the void immense

her mouth they crept, and suddain all were gone" (*Faerie Queene* 1.1.15.4–9; cf. lines 649–60 above).

801. *conscious terrors:* living monsters, but also the *terrors* resulting from the consciousness of sin

813. *mortal dint:* fatal blow

818–819. *pledge Of dalliance:* token of lovemaking

823. *house:* See Job 30:23: "thou wilt bring me to death, to the house appointed for all living."

826–828. *I . . . expose:* parodies Christ's *errand* in becoming mortal, which also involves *one* sacrificing *for all.*

829. *unfounded:* bottomless, without foundation

To search, with wandering quest, a place foretold   830
Should be—and, by concurring signs, ere now
Created vast and round—a place of bliss
In the purlieus° of Heaven, and therein placed   *outskirts*
A race of upstart creatures to supply
Perhaps our vacant room, though more removed,   835
Lest Heaven surcharged° with potent multitude   *overcrowded*
Might hap to move new broils. Be this or aught
Than this more secret now designed, I haste
To know, and this once known shall soon return,
And bring ye to the place where thou and Death   840
Shall dwell at ease and up and down unseen
Wing silently the buxom air, embalmed°   *fragrant, scented*
With odors; there ye shall be fed and filled
Immeasurably: all things shall be your prey."
He ceased, for both seemed highly pleased, and Death   845
Grinned horrible a ghastly smile to hear
His famine should be filled and blessed his maw
Destined to that good hour; no less rejoiced
His mother bad, and thus bespake° her sire: *said to*
    "The key of this infernal pit by due   850
And by command of Heaven's all-powerful king
I keep, by him forbidden to unlock
These adamantine gates; against all force
Death ready stands to interpose his dart,
Fearless to be o'ermatched by living might.   855
But what owe I to his commands above
Who hates me and hath hither thrust me down
Into this gloom of Tartarus profound
To sit in hateful office° here confined,   *service*
Inhabitant of Heaven and heavenly born,   860
Here in perpetual agony and pain,
With terrors and with clamors compassed round
Of mine own brood, that on my bowels feed?
Thou art my father, thou my author, thou
My being gav'st me; whom should I obey   865
But thee, whom follow? Thou wilt bring me soon

840–844. *bring ye . . . prey:* Satan's
promise is fulfilled in 10.397–409.
   842. *buxom:* yielding, pliant; cf. 5.270.
   847. *famine:* hunger; cf. 10.991.

865–866. *whom . . . thee:* Sin decides to
obey as the natural and necessary behavior of
child to father, the first (and ironic) occur-
rence of the word and idea in the poem.

To that new world of light and bliss among
The gods who live at ease, where I shall reign
At thy right hand voluptuous, as beseems
Thy daughter and thy darling, without end."   870
    Thus saying, from her side the fatal key,
Sad instrument of all our woe, she took,
And, toward the gate rolling her bestial train,
Forthwith the huge portcullis° high updrew,   *outer gate*
Which but° herself not all the Stygian powers   *except for*
Could once have moved; then in the keyhole turns
The intricate wards, and every bolt and bar
Of massy iron or solid rock with ease
Unfastens. On a sudden, open fly
With impetuous recoil and jarring sound   880
The infernal doors, and on their hinges grate
Harsh thunder, that the lowest bottom shook
Of Erebus. She opened, but to shut
Excelled her power; the gates wide open stood
That with extended wings a bannered host   885
Under spread ensigns marching might pass through
With horse and chariots ranked in loose array;
So wide they stood, and like a furnace mouth
Cast forth redounding° smoke and ruddy flame.   *surging, billowing*
Before their eyes in sudden view appear   890
The secrets of the hoary° deep, a dark   *ancient*
Illimitable ocean without bound,
Without dimension, where length, breadth, and height,
And time and place are lost; where eldest Night
And Chaos, ancestors of Nature, hold   895

---

869. *At . . . voluptuous:* Sin imagines herself enthroned at the right hand of her father, Satan, just as the Son is seated at his Father's right hand in 3.62–3. Satan, Sin, and Death form an infernal Trinity in contrast with its heavenly counterpart.

872. *all our woe:* echoes 1.3

877. *wards:* the projections on a key, which in correspondence with the incisions on the plate of a lock will permit the device to open

883. *Erebus:* hell; in Hesiod's account of the generation of the oldest Gods (*Theogony* 123), in a line that Milton quotes

in his first *Prolusion* (*Works* 12, 127), *Erebus* is named as the first child of Chaos, while Night is the second.

884–888. *the gates . . . stood:* See Matt. 7:13: "wide is the gate, and broad is the way, that leadeth to destruction, and many there be which go in thereat."

885–886. *bannered host . . . ensigns:* armies marching with banners waving

891. *secrets:* secret places

895–903. *Chaos . . . sands:* The conception of *Chaos* stems from both Hesiod's mythological account and Ovid's rationalized treatment of the primeval chaotic mass

Eternal anarchy amidst the noise
Of endless wars and by confusion stand.
For hot, cold, moist, and dry, four champions fierce,
Strive here for mastery, and to battle bring
Their embryon atoms; they around the flag   900
Of each his faction, in their several clans,
Light-armed or heavy, sharp, smooth, swift, or slow,
Swarm populous, unnumbered as the sands
Of Barca or Cyrene's torrid soil,
Levied to side with warring winds and poise°   *add weight to*
Their lighter wings. To whom these most adhere,
He rules a moment. Chaos umpire sits
And, by decision, more embroils the fray
By which he reigns; next him high arbiter
Chance governs all. Into this wild abyss,   910
The womb of nature and perhaps her grave,
Of neither sea, nor shore, nor air, nor fire,
But all these in their pregnant causes mixed
Confusedly, and which thus must ever fight
Unless the almighty maker them ordain   915
His dark materials to create more worlds.
Into this wild abyss the wary fiend
Stood on the brink of hell and looked awhile,
Pondering his voyage, for no narrow frith°   *estuary, firth*

of "warring seeds of things" before the world began (*Metamorphoses* 1.5–20). The conception influenced Renaissance thought so deeply that the orthodox Du Bartas imagined Chaos as corresponding to the formless void of Gen. 1:2, and described its "brawling Elements" as lying "jumbled all together, / Where hot and cold were jarring each with either; / The blunt with sharp, the dank against the drie, / The hard with soft" (Sylvester's translation of Du Bartas' *Divine Weeks*, 1608, p. 8). The war of the elements and its resolution by love went back to Empedocles but had been Christianized in the eclectic tradition that gave Spenser his view of it as ended when "their Almightie Maker . . . . bound them with inviolable bands; / Else would the waters overflow the lands, / And fire devour the ayre, and hell them quight" (*Faerie Queene* 4.10.5).

898. *hot, cold, moist, and dry:* the qualities of the four primal elements (fire, air, water, earth) that were thought to combine in various ways to form all matter

900. *embryon atoms:* basic units of unformed matter; cf. *pregnant causes,* line 913.

904. *Barca . . . soil:* Barca and Cyrene were both cities on the Cyranaican plateau in modern Libya.

905. *Levied:* both "uplifted" and "drafted into service"

911. *The womb . . . grave:* The line is a translation of Lucretius' *De rerum natura* 5.259, but his prophecy of the world's destruction is felt here as harmonious with the Christian doctrine that (in Sylvester's translation of Du Bartas' words) "This world to Chaos shall again return" (*Divine Weeks,* "The Schisme," 1608, p. 111).

He had to cross. Nor was his ear less pealed   920
With noises loud and ruinous (to compare
Great things with small) than when Bellona storms
With all her battering engines, bent to raze
Some capital city; or less than if this frame°   *structure*
Of Heaven were falling, and these elements   925
In mutiny had from her axle torn
The steadfast earth. At last his sail-broad vans°   *wings*
He spreads for flight and, in the surging smoke
Uplifted, spurns the ground; thence many a league,
As in a cloudy chair ascending, rides   930
Audacious but, that seat soon failing, meets
A vast vacuity. All unawares,
Fluttering his pennons vain, plumb down he drops
Ten thousand fathom deep, and to this hour
Down had been falling had not by ill chance   935
The strong rebuff of some tumultuous cloud
Instinct with fire and niter hurried him
As many miles aloft; that fury stayed,
Quenched in a boggy Syrtis, neither sea
Nor good dry land; nigh foundered on he fares,   940
Treading the crude consistence, half on foot,

920. *pealed:* assailed or deafened by noise. Cf. 3.329, and *SA* 235.

921–922. *to compare . . . small:* Virgil uses the phrase and indeed compares great things with small things like bees (e.g., *Georgics* 4.176); Milton's *small* here marks the destruction of a city or the very disintegration of the universe.

922. *Bellona:* the Roman goddess of war

930. *cloudy chair:* the stage machinery of a court masque that allowed the gods to rise seemingly on a cloud

933. *pennons vain:* useless wings

936–938. *strong rebuff . . . aloft:* Milton describes some powerful current that reorients Satan. Contemporary science explained thunderclouds as occurring when, in the words of J. A. Comenius' *Synopsis of Physics*, the earth's "sulphury exhalations are mixed with nitrous (the first of a hot nature, the second most cold), they endure one another so long, as till the sulphur takes fire. But as

soon as that is done, presently there follows the same effect as in gun-powder, (whose composition is the same of Sulphur and Nitre) a fight, a rupture, a noise, a violent casting forth of the matter." The passage, from the English translation (1651) of Comenius' *Physicae ad Lumen Divinum reformatae Synopsis* (Amsterdam, 1643), is quoted by E. H. Duncan in *PQ,* 30 (1951), 442–43.

937. *Instinct:* infused, animated; cf. 6.752.   *niter:* a volatile compound related to saltpeter

939. *boggy Syrtis:* The classical description of the two vast tidal marshes called the *Syrtis* is in Pliny, 5.4. On the northern coast of Africa near Carthage, the bogs are described by Lucan (*Pharsalia* 9.303) as being "ambiguous between sea and land."

941. *crude consistence:* half-formed matter; *consistence* = "solidity or firmness sufficient to maintain its form" (*OED* 4)

Half flying; behooves him now both oar and sail.
As when a griffin through the wilderness
With wingèd course o'er hill or moory° dale,   *marshlike*
Pursues the Arimaspian, who by stealth   945
Had from his wakeful custody purloined
The guarded gold, so eagerly the fiend
O'er bog or steep, through strait, rough, dense, or rare,
With head, hands, wings, or feet pursues his way
And swims, or sinks, or wades, or creeps, or flies.   950
At length a universal hubbub wild
Of stunning° sounds and voices all confused   *deafening*
Borne through the hollow dark assaults his ear
With loudest vehemence; thither he plies,°   *makes his way*
Undaunted, to meet there whatever power   955
Or spirit of the nethermost abyss
Might in that noise reside, of whom to ask
Which way the nearest coast of darkness lies
Bordering on light; when straight behold the throne
Of Chaos and his dark pavilion spread   960
Wide on the wasteful deep; with him enthroned
Sat sable-vested° Night, eldest of things,   *clad in black*
The consort of his reign, and by them stood
Orcus and Ades, and the dreaded name
Of Demogorgon; Rumor next and Chance,   965
And Tumult and Confusion all embroiled,
And Discord with a thousand various mouths.
     To whom Satan, turning boldly, thus: "Ye powers
And spirits of this nethermost abyss,
Chaos and ancient Night, I come no spy   970

943–947. *griffin . . . gold:* refers to the popular story (which goes back to Herodotus, 3.116, of the gold which the Arimaspians, a "one-eyed people" living in what is now Siberia, steal from the griffins, the mythological creatures—half eagle, half lion—who guarded the mines.

948. *O'er . . . rare:* Note the ten monosyllables, perhaps intended to provide a rhythmical indication of the difficulty of the voyage; cf. Sir William Alexander's abuse of this device in *Jonathan* (1637) 1.556, describing a duel between Jonathan and Nahas: they "Urg'd, shunn'd, forc'd, fayn'd, bow'd, rais'd, hand, leg, left, right. "

961. *wasteful deep:* desolate chaos

964. *Orcus and Ades:* i.e., Hades, two of various names for the ruler of the underworld

965. *Demogorgon:* Milton, in *Prolusion* 1, calls him the "ancestor of all the gods" and notes that he "was also called Chaos by antiquity" (*Works* 12, 127). The name is probably a corruption of Plato's Demiourgos in the *Timaeus*. Spenser writes of "*Demogorgon*, in dull darknesse pent, / Farr from the view of gods and heauens blis" (*Faerie Queene* 4.2.47).

970. *I come no spy:* Cf. lines 354–58 above.

With purpose to explore or to disturb
The secrets of your realm, but, by constraint,
Wandering this darksome desert, as my way
Lies through your spacious empire up to light,
Alone and without guide, half lost, I seek   975
What readiest path leads where your gloomy bounds
Confine with Heaven; or if some other place
From your dominion won, the ethereal king
Possesses lately, thither to arrive
I travel this profound;° direct my course.   *deep abyss*
Directed, no mean recompense it brings
To your behoof° if I that region lost,   *benefit, advantage*
All usurpation thence expelled, reduce
To her original darkness and your sway
(Which is my present journey) and once more   985
Erect the standard there of ancient Night;
Yours be the advantage all, mine the revenge."
        Thus Satan; and him thus the anarch old
With faltering speech and visage incomposed°   *disturbed, disordered*
Answered: "I know thee, stranger, who thou art,   990
That mighty leading angel, who of late
Made head against Heaven's king, though overthrown.
I saw and heard, for such a numerous host
Fled not in silence through the frighted° deep   *pervaded with fear*
With ruin upon ruin, rout on rout,   995
Confusion worse confounded; and Heaven gates
Poured out by millions her victorious bands
Pursuing. I upon my frontiers here
Keep residence; if all I can will serve
That little which is left so° to defend,   *in this way*
Encroached on still through our intestine broils,
Weakening the scepter of old Night—first hell,
Your dungeon, stretching far and wide beneath;
Now lately heaven and earth, another world

977. *Confine with:* border upon
988. *the anarch:* Chaos, personified as ruler of his lawless realm; cf. lines 896 and 907–10 above.
990. *I know . . . art:* See Mark 1:24: "I know thee who thou art, the Holy One of God."

992. *Made head against:* rose in insurrection
1001. *our intestine broils:* the civil war in Heaven; perhaps *our* should be, as Pearce suggested in 1733, "your."
1004. *heaven:* here meaning "the sky" (not the Heaven of line 1006)

Hung o'er my realm, linked in a golden chain   1005
To that side Heaven from whence your legions fell.
If that way be your walk, you have not far;
So much the nearer danger. Go and speed;
Havoc° and spoil and ruin are my gain."   *destruction*
    He ceased, and Satan stayed not to reply,   1010
But, glad that now his sea should find a shore,
With fresh alacrity and force renewed
Springs upward like a pyramid of fire
Into the wild expanse, and, through the shock
Of fighting elements on all sides round   1015
Environed, wins his way, harder beset
And more endangered, than when Argo passed
Through Bosphorus betwixt the jostling rocks,
Or when Ulysses on the larbord shunned
Charybdis and by the other whirlpool steered.   1020
So he with difficulty and labor hard
Moved on, with difficulty and labor he;
But he once passed, soon after when man fell,
Strange alteration! Sin and Death amain°   *immediately*
Following his track, such was the will of Heaven,   1025
Paved after him a broad and beaten way
Over the dark abyss, whose boiling gulf
Tamely endured a bridge of wondrous length,
From hell continued reaching to the utmost orb
Of this frail world, by which the spirits perverse   1030
With easy intercourse pass to and fro
To tempt or punish mortals, except whom
God and good angels guard by special grace.

1005. *in a golden chain:* For Milton's use of the Homeric story of the *golden chain* with which Zeus boasted that he could draw earth and all its seas up to heaven *(Iliad* 8.3–24), see line 1051 and note below.

1008. *danger:* keeps its obsolete sense of "damage, mischief, or harm"

1017. *Argo:* the ship of Jason and his crew, the Argonauts, when they escaped death between the floating islands in the Bosphorus, or Straits of Constantinople, as Apollonius of Rhodes told the tale in his *Argonautica* 2.552–611.

1019–1020. *Ulysses . . . steered: Charybdis* is the whirlpool on the Sicilian side of the Straits of Messina, to Ulysses' *larboard* (port or left side) as he sailed westward in Homer's account of his escape from Charybdis and *the other whirlpool,* the still more frightful Scylla (see note at 2.650–659; cf. *Odyssey* 12.234–59).

1026. *broad . . . beaten way:* wide and heavily travelled road; see lines 884–89 and note.

1029. *utmost orb:* outermost sphere

1033. *special grace:* not just the sufficient grace universally available to the faithful, but the grace directed at the elect; cf. "peculiar grace" at 3.183.

But now at last the sacred influence
Of light appears and from the walls of Heaven   1035
Shoots far into the bosom of dim night
A glimmering dawn; here nature first begins
Her farthest verge,° and Chaos to retire   *boundary*
As from her outmost works a broken foe,
With tumult less and with less hostile din,   1040
That Satan with less toil and now with ease
Wafts on the calmer wave by dubious° light   *weak, wavering*
And like a weather-beaten vessel holds°   *makes for*
Gladly the port, though shrouds and tackle torn;
Or in the emptier waste resembling air   1045
Weighs° his spread wings, at leisure to behold   *holds steady, hovers*
Far off the empyreal Heaven, extended wide
In circuit, undetermined square or round,
With opal towers and battlements adorned
Of living sapphire, once his native seat,   1050
And fast by, hanging in a golden chain,
This pendant world, in bigness as a star
Of smallest magnitude close by the moon.
Thither full fraught with mischievous revenge,
Accursed, and in a cursèd hour he hies.   1055

The End of the Second Book.

1037. *here nature first begins:* nature, in Milton's use here, means the created world as distinct from the surrounding chaos, where not even the first of God's creations, light, is known.

1039. *her outmost works:* i.e., nature's most distant fortifications

1044. *shrouds and tackle:* the sails and rigging of a ship

1048. *undetermined:* not certainly, undeterminable (by Satan's eye), though Rev. 21:16 calls it "foursquare"

1050. *Of living sapphire:* John speaks of one of the foundations of Heaven's wall as of sapphire (Rev. 21:19); *living* = as it is found in nature; see 4.605 and pp. xxxviii–xxxix above.

1051. *golden chain:* Cf. Milton's use of the golden chain of Zeus in *Prolusion 2* (*Works* 12, 151) as a symbol of divine design penetrating the entire universe. The conception runs from Plato's *Theaetetus* (153c) to Chaucer's "Knight's Tale" (1.A.2987–93): "The Firste Moevere of the cause above, / When he first made the faire cheyne of love, / Greet was th'effect, and heigh was his entente. / Wel wiste he why, and what thereof he mente; / For with that faire cheyne of love he bond / The fyr, the eyr, the water, and the lond / In certeyn boundes, that they may nat flee."

1052. *This pendant world:* i.e., the entire spherical universe hanging in space (see 3.419), which Satan has yet to penetrate (not merely the earth)

BOOK 3

The Argument

God sitting on his throne sees Satan flying toward this world, then newly created; shows him to the Son who sat at his right hand; foretells the success of Satan in perverting mankind; clears his own justice and wisdom from all imputation, having created man free and able enough to have withstood his tempter, yet declares his purpose of grace toward him, in regard he fell not of his own malice, as did Satan, but by him seduced. The Son of God renders praises to his Father for the manifestation of his gracious purpose toward man, but God again declares that grace cannot be extended toward man without the satisfaction of divine justice. Man hath offended the majesty of God by aspiring to godhead and therefore, with all his progeny devoted to death, must die, unless some one can be found sufficient to answer for his offence and undergo his punishment. The Son of God freely offers himself a ransom for man; the Father accepts him, ordains his incarnation, pronounces his exaltation above all names in heaven and earth, commands all the angels to adore him; they obey and, hymning to their harps in full choir, celebrate the Father and the Son. Meanwhile Satan alights upon the bare convex of this world's outermost orb, where wandering he first finds a place since called the Limbo of Vanity; what persons and things fly up thither; thence comes to the gate of heaven, described ascending by stairs, and the waters above the firmament that flow about it. His passage thence to the orb of the sun; he finds there Uriel, the regent of that orb, but first changes himself into the shape of a meaner angel and, pretending a zealous desire to behold the new creation and man whom God had placed here, inquires of him the place of his habitation, and is directed; alights first on Mount Niphates.

Hail holy light, offspring of Heaven firstborn;
Or of the eternal coeternal beam

1. *Hail holy light:* These words mark the poem's transition to Heaven from the darkness of hell and chaos, the first two words repeating the alliteration that ends Book 2.
1–2. *offspring . . . beam:* The poet conjectures that *light* is either the *firstborn* of Heaven (see also 7.243–4, where light is called "the first of things") or that light may have existed always and simultaneously with God; both accounts conflict with Genesis 1:1–3, where God creates light after creating the heavens and the earth.

May I express thee unblamed, since God is light,
And never but in unapproachèd light
Dwelt from eternity, dwelt then in thee,   5
Bright effluence° of bright essence increate?   *stream, outpouring*
Or hear'st thou rather pure ethereal stream,
Whose fountain who shall tell? Before the sun,
Before the heavens thou wert, and at the voice
Of God, as with a mantle, didst invest°   *cover, envelop*
The rising world of waters dark and deep,
Won from the void and formless infinite.
Thee I revisit now with bolder wing,
Escaped the Stygian pool, though long detained
In that obscure sojourn, while in my flight   15
Through utter and through middle darkness borne
With other notes than to the Orphean lyre
I sung of Chaos and eternal Night,
Taught by the heavenly muse to venture down
The dark descent and up to reascend,   20
Though hard and rare; thee I revisit safe

---

3. *unblamed:* refers to the narrator (rather than *thee*), asking if he can thus describe light without being criticized (*unblamed*) for the unorthodoxy of the conception; see 1–2 and note.   *God is light:* the assertion of 1 John 1:5 that justifies Milton's revision of the Genesis narrative

4. *unapproachèd:* inaccessible; see 1 Tim. 6:16: "the light which no man can approach unto."

6. *essence increate:* eternal essence (of God)

7. *hear'st thou rather:* would you prefer to be called

8. *Whose . . . tell:* from an unnamable source

11. *world . . . deep:* an almost exact quotation of *Faerie Queene,* 1.1.39: "the world of waters wide and deepe"

12. *void and formless infinite:* i.e., chaos; cf. 7.233 and n.

13–14. *with . . . pool:* Milton's claim that now he *with bolder wing* moves beyond his previous focus on hell (*Escaped the Stygian pool*) is unnervingly parallel to the por-

trait of Satan "glorying to have scaped the Stygian flood" (1.239); see p. xxvii above.

14. *Stygian pool:* the river Styx, the river of the classical Hades

16. *utter and . . . middle darkness:* i.e., hell and chaos; cf. 1.72 and 6.614.

17. *Orphean:* of Orpheus, who traveled to the underworld to reclaim Eurydice and whose music convinced Pluto to release her. Milton no doubt also thought of the tradition of Orpheus as the first interpreter of the physical and spiritual secrets of hell, "a man most learned in divinity," as Natale Conti called him in *Mythologiae* 7.14.

19. *the heavenly muse:* Editors often see this as referring specifically to Urania, the muse of astronomy, as in 7.1, but cf. 1.6 and note, where it is made clear that Milton's muse is heavenly in a more radical sense.

20–21. *The dark . . . rare:* Cf. the Sibyl's warning that the ascent from hell is hard (*Aeneid* 6.128) and its earlier echo here in 2.432–3; (*rare* = both "unusual" and "through rarified air").

And feel thy sovereign vital lamp, but thou
Revisit'st not these eyes, that roll in vain
To° find thy piercing ray and find no dawn,   *in order to*
So thick a drop serene hath quenched their orbs   25
Or dim suffusion veiled. Yet not the more
Cease I to wander where the muses haunt
Clear spring, or shady grove, or sunny hill,
Smit° with the love of sacred song, but chief   *smitten*
Thee, Sion, and the flowery brooks beneath,   30
That wash thy hallowed feet and warbling flow,
Nightly I visit; nor sometimes forget
Those other two equaled with me in fate,
So° were I equaled with them in renown: *if only*
Blind Thamyris and blind Maeonides,   35
And Tiresias and Phineus, prophets old.
Then feed° on thoughts that voluntary move   *would I feed*
Harmonious numbers, as the wakeful bird

22–24. *but . . . dawn:* Milton was entirely blind by 1652.

25. *drop serene:* translates *gutta serena,* the Latin medical term for all forms of blindness in which the eye retains a normal appearance. Milton was proud that his eyes, as the portrait-frontispiece of *PL* in 1674 proved, betrayed so little "external appearance of injury," and were "as clear and bright, without the semblance of a cloud, as the eyes of those whose sight is the most perfect" (*Second Defense, Works* 8, 61).

26. *dim suffusion veiled:* The narrator wonders if his sight may not be totally *quenched* (line 25) but perhaps only partially *veiled; dim suffusion* translates *suffusio nigra,* another Latin medical term for a disease of the eye that clouds the eyeball with cataracts.

30. *Sion . . . beneath:* Instead of the Castalian spring "where the muses haunt" (line 27) on Mount Parnassus, Milton prefers the sacred Mount *Sion* in Jerusalem and its *flowery brooks,* Kidron and Siloa.

35. *Thamyris:* a blind Thracian poet; Homer (*Iliad* 2.594–600) says he was blinded by the gods for hubristically claiming he could sing better than the muses.   *Maeo-*

nides: i.e., Homer (supposedly born in Maeonia), whose blind eyes were well known, "turn'd upwards," as George Chapman described them in *Euthymiae Raptus* (1609), lines 36–38, because he was "outward blind; But, inward; past and future things he sawe; / And was to both, and present times, their lawe."

36. *Tiresias and Phineus:* both blind seers; Milton, in *De Idea Platonica,* lines 25–26, refers to *Tiresias* as "the Theban seer whose blindness proved his great illumination." Milton, in his *Second Defense* (*Works* 8, 64), quoted Apollonius on the Thracian king and prophet *Phineus:* "Fearless, though Jove might rage, he showed / The arcane purposes of heaven to us; / Endless old age the gods on him bestowed / And made him strong, but blind and piteous."

37. *voluntary move:* spontaneously give rise to

38. *Harmonious numbers:* pleasingly metrical verse; see the "true musical delight" of "apt numbers" in Milton's prefatory note on the verse of *PL* (p. 5 above).   *wakeful bird:* i.e., the nightingale

Sings darkling and, in shadiest covert hid,
Tunes her nocturnal note. Thus with the year   40
Seasons return, but not to me returns
Day, or the sweet approach of ev'n or morn,
Or sight of vernal° bloom or summer's rose,   *springtime*
Or flocks, or herds, or human face divine,
But cloud instead, and ever-during dark   45
Surrounds me, from the cheerful ways of men
Cut off, and for the book of knowledge fair
Presented with a universal blank
Of nature's works, to me expunged and razed,
And wisdom at one entrance quite shut out.   50
So much the rather thou celestial light
Shine inward and the mind through all her powers
Irradiate; there plant eyes; all mist from thence
Purge and disperse, that I may see and tell
Of things invisible to mortal sight.   55
      Now had the almighty Father from above,
From the pure empyrean where he sits
High throned above all height, bent down his eye,
His own works and their works at once to view:
About him all the sanctities of Heaven   60
Stood thick as stars and from his sight received
Beatitude past utterance; on his right
The radiant image of his glory sat,

39. *darkling:* in the dark, at night (not a participle but an adverb; see *King Lear* 1.4.240: "So out went the candle and we were left darkling.")

45. *ever-during:* everlasting

47. *book of knowledge fair:* i.e., the beautiful created world, the book of God's works rather than his words

48. *blank:* void (but also suggesting a *blank* page in the "book of knowledge")

50. *entrance:* portal of sense perception (i.e., the eyes)

51–55. *So much . . . sight:* The lines assert the possibility of a sharpened inner vision as compensation for blindness.

53–54. *all mist . . . disperse:* Cf. 2.399–400, where Beelzebub hopes the fallen angels can "purge off this gloom."

56. *Now:* God exists in an eternal present (viewing all things "at once," line 59), as

the difficulty of exactly specifying the effect of this adverb makes clear.

57. *pure empyrean:* heavenly region of pure light

59. *their:* i.e., the works of God's work

60. *the sanctities of Heaven:* the hierarchies of angels; Shakespeare uses the exact phrase in *Henry IV, Part Two* (4.2.21).

61. *his sight:* the sight of God (but also the fact of being seen by him). *Christian Doctrine* speaks of the enjoyment of the "sight" of God as the supreme joy of the righteous in heaven (I, xxxiii; *Works* 16, 375). Cf. *PL,* 1.684.

62. *on his right:* See Hebrews 1:3, where Christ "sat down on the right hand of the Majesty on high."

63. *radiant image of his glory:* condenses Heb. 1:3: "the brightness of his glory, and the express image of his person"

His only Son; on earth he first beheld
Our two first parents, yet° the only two   *still*
Of mankind, in the happy garden placed,
Reaping immortal fruits of joy and love,
Uninterrupted joy, unrivalled love
In blissful solitude; he then surveyed
Hell and the gulf between, and Satan there   70
Coasting the wall of Heaven on this side night
In the dun air sublime, and ready now
To stoop with wearied wings and willing feet
On the bare outside of this world, that seemed
Firm land embosomed without firmament,   75
Uncertain which, in ocean or in air.
Him God beholding from his prospect high,
Wherein past, present, future he beholds,
Thus to his only Son foreseeing spake:
    "Only begotten Son, seest thou what rage   80
Transports our adversary, whom no bounds
Prescribed, no bars of hell, nor all the chains
Heaped on him there, nor yet the main° abyss   *vast*
Wide interrupt can hold, so bent he seems
On desperate revenge that shall redound   85
Upon his own rebellious head. And now,
Through all restraint broke loose, he wings his way
Not far off Heaven, in the precincts° of light,   *region*
Directly toward the new created world
And man there placed, with purpose to assay°   *test*
If him by force he can destroy or, worse,

---

64. *His only son:* See line 80, and John 1:14: "the only begotten of the Father."

67. *immortal fruits:* heavenly benefits (but inevitably recalling the fruit "whose mortal taste / Brought death into the world" [1.2–3])

70–73. *Satan . . . wings:* Satan flies *sublime* (aloft) through the upper limits of chaos and close to the wall of heaven in the dusky, twilight atmosphere (*dun air*), ready to *stoop* (dive like a hawk) upon the universe.

74. *world:* not the earth, but the universe; cf. lines 418–19 below, 2.434, and 7.269.

75. *embosomed without firmament:* i.e., directly exposed to chaos without the protection of the firmament (and also, outside the firmament)

76. *Uncertain:* an impersonal and absolute construction: it is *uncertain*, i.e., hard to see, whether the chaos around the floating universe is more like water or like air

81. *Transports:* i.e., carries away, in both a physical and a psychological sense

83. *abyss:* i.e., chaos

84. *Wide interrupt:* forming a large gulf; *interrupt* keeps its Latin meaning and participial form, and means "broken open."

By some false guile pervert; and shall pervert,
For man will hearken to his glozing lies
And easily transgress the sole command,
Sole pledge of his obedience; so will fall,   95
He and his faithless progeny. Whose fault?
Whose but his own? Ingrate, he had of me
All he could have; I made him just and right,
Sufficient to have stood though free to fall.
Such I created all the ethereal powers   100
And spirits, both them who stood and them who failed;
Freely they stood who stood and fell who fell.
Not free, what proof could they have given sincere
Of true allegiance, constant faith, or love,
Where only what they needs must do appeared,   105
Not what they would? What praise could they receive?
What pleasure I from such obedience paid,
When will and reason (reason also is choice)
Useless and vain, of freedom both despoiled,

92. *pervert.* turn from his rightful direction

93. *glozing:* flattering; cf. "glozed" at 9.549.

94. *sole command:* the prohibition to touch the tree of knowledge (Gen. 3:3: "Ye shall not eat of it, neither shall ye touch it, lest ye die")

95. *pledge of his obedience:* This is the true importance of the tree, not a source of some forbidden knowledge, but a *pledge* of *obedience,* a sign of man's relationship with God.

96. *He and his faithless progeny:* not only that Adam and future generations will prove disloyal, but also more radically: Adam breaks faith with God by his act of disobedience and thereby, without sense of "the welfare of his offspring" (as in *Christian Doctrine* I, xi; *Works* 15, 183), involves them all in his breach of faith; cf. 3.209.

97. *Ingrate:* either an adjective (ungrateful) or a noun   *had:* Since God sees all time at once, verb tenses are arbitrary; here a future action is announced as past, just as *ingrate* defines behavior that has not yet occurred.

98–102. *I made . . . fell:* Milton insists upon God's freedom from responsibility in spite of his foreknowledge of the fall, arguing that God had provided both Adam and Eve and the angels not only with *Sufficient* grace to withstand to resist evil, but also with free will, so that their standing faithful or falling might depend upon their own volition. Thus, as in *Christian Doctrine* (I, iii), all the evil that ensued from man's fall was entirely "contingent upon man's will" (*Works* 14, 77–81). Cf. Satan's confession in 4.63–68, and the stress on the angels' guilt in 5.525–43.

103–106. *Not free . . . receive:* Cf. *Christian Doctrine* I, iv: "The acceptableness of duties done under a law of necessity is diminished, or rather is annihilated altogether" (*Works* 14, 141); cf. lines 173–89 below.

108. *reason also is choice:* i.e., reason is as free as will, allowed and revealing itself in the choices it justifies; see *Areopagitica:* "When God gave him reason, he gave him freedom to choose, for reason is but choosing" (*Works* 4, 319).

109. *Useless and vain:* unused and empty (i.e., in name only)

Made passive both, had served necessity,   110
Not me? They therefore as to right belonged,
So were created, nor can justly accuse
Their maker, or their making, or their fate,
As if predestination overruled
Their will, disposed by absolute decree   115
Or high foreknowledge; they themselves decreed
Their own revolt, not I. If I foreknew,
Foreknowledge had no influence on their fault,
Which had no less proved certain unforeknown.
So without least impulse, or shadow of fate,   120
Or aught by me immutably foreseen,
They trespass, authors to themselves in all,
Both what they judge and what they choose, for so
I formed them free and free they must remain
Till they enthrall themselves. I else° must change   *otherwise*
Their nature and revoke the high decree
Unchangeable, eternal, which ordained
Their freedom; they themselves ordained their fall.
The first sort by their own suggestion° fell,   *temptation*
Self-tempted, self-depraved; man falls deceived   130
By the other first; man therefore shall find grace,
The other, none. In mercy and justice both,
Through Heaven and earth, so shall my glory excel,
But mercy first and last shall brightest shine."
    Thus while God spake, ambrosial fragrance filled   135
All Heaven and, in the blessèd spirits elect,
Sense of new joy ineffable° diffused.   *inexpressible*

---

112. *So:* i.e., free and rational

119. *no . . . unforeknown:* The long chapter "On Predestination" in *Christian Doctrine* I, iv, is devoted to proof that "the prescience of God seems to have no connection with the principle or essence of predestination" (*Works* 14, 125). The claim is that as God sees "past, present, and future" at once (line 78), his foreknowledge is no different than human memory: what happens is known but not caused.

125–128. *I . . . fall:* similar to the claim in *Christian Doctrine* I, iii, which insists that "God is not mutable, so long as he decrees nothing absolutely which could happen oth-

erwise through the liberty that he assigns to man. He would indeed be mutable if he were to obstruct by another decree that liberty which he had already decreed, or were to darken it with the least shadow of necessity" (*Works* 14, 77).

129. *The first sort:* i.e., the angels who revolted

136. *spirits elect:* the unfallen angels; *Christian Doctrine* (I, ix) insists that "the good angels stand by their own strength," pointing to the fact that "the elect angels" of 1 Tim. 5:21, means only "those who have not revolted" (*Works* 15, 99). Cf. line 184 below.

Beyond compare the Son of God was seen
Most glorious; in him all his Father shone
Substantially expressed, and in his face   140
Divine compassion visibly appeared,
Love without end and, without measure, grace,
Which uttering thus he to his Father spake:
   "O Father, gracious was that word which closed
Thy sovereign sentence: that man should find grace;   145
For which both Heaven and earth shall high extol
Thy praises, with the innumerable sound
Of hymns and sacred songs wherewith thy throne
Encompassed shall resound thee ever blessed.
For should man finally be lost, should man,   150
Thy creature late° so loved, thy youngest son,   *lately*
Fall circumvented thus by fraud, though joined
With his own folly? That be from thee far,
That far be from thee, Father, who art judge
Of all things made and judgest only right.   155
Or shall the adversary thus obtain
His end and frustrate thine? Shall he fulfill
His malice, and thy goodness bring to naught,
Or proud return, though to his heavier doom°   *condemnation*
Yet with revenge accomplished, and to hell   160
Draw after him the whole race of mankind
By him corrupted? Or wilt thou thyself
Abolish thy creation and unmake,
For him,° what for thy glory thou hast made?   *Satan*
So should thy goodness and thy greatness both   165
Be questioned and blasphemed without defense."
   To whom the great creator thus replied:
"O Son, in whom my soul hath chief delight,
Son of my bosom, Son who art alone

---

140. *Substantially expressed:* not a qual-
ification but a theological commitment that
in Christ God's very nature is made present
and visible; see 6.681–82. In *Christian
Doctrine* (I, v) Milton, however, insists that
although "the father remains in him," this
"does not denote unity of essence but only
intimacy of communion" (*Works* 14, 213).
  153–155. *That be . . . right:* See Gen.
18:25: "that the righteous should be as the

wicked, that be far from thee: Shall not the
Judge of all the earth do right?"
  158. *naught:* 1) nothing; 2) wickedness
  166. *blasphemed:* defamed, insulted
  168–169. *O Son . . . bosom:* The lines
echo the words from heaven at Christ's bap-
tism: "This is my beloved Son, in whom I am
well pleased" (Matt. 3:17), and the naming of
Christ as "the only begotten Son, which is in
the bosom of the Father" (John 1:18).

My word, my wisdom, and effectual might,   170
All hast thou spoken as my thoughts are, all
As my eternal purpose hath decreed.
Man shall not quite be lost, but saved who will,
Yet not of will in him but grace in me
Freely vouchsafed;° once more I will renew   *given, entrusted*
His lapsed powers, though forfeit and enthralled
By sin to foul exorbitant° desires;   *erring*
Upheld by me, yet once more he shall stand
On even ground against his mortal° foe,   *deadly*
By me upheld that he may know how frail   180
His fallen condition is and to me owe
All his deliverance, and to none but me.
Some I have chosen of peculiar grace
Elect above the rest: so is my will.
The rest shall hear me call, and oft be warned   185
Their sinful state, and to appease betimes°   *early*
The incensèd deity while offered grace

170. *word . . . wisdom . . . effectual might:* The triad defines the interlocking roles in which Christ manifests God's glory: 1) the creative *word* in John 1:1 (and see 7.208–9); 2) Paul calls Christ "the wisdom of God" in 1 Cor. 1:24 (see 7.9–10); 3) God's *effectual might:* i.e., the instrumental agent of God's power; cf. "Christ the power of God" (1 Cor. 1:24; see 6.710–14).

173–174. *saved . . . me:* The distinction between God's *grace* and man's *will* points to the two parts of the efficient cause of salvation: human will as the impelling, agential part, and God's grace as the instrumental cause. Milton, unlike Calvin, insists upon the co-operation of the two. (*of* = through)

176. *lapsed:* (literally) fallen, and therefore diminished   *forfeit:* i.e., forfeited; anticipates the legal view of the penalty to be paid by Adam in line 210 below

178. *yet once more:* See the opening line of "Lycidas" (and cf. Heb. 12:26–27).

180. *know how frail:* See Ps. 39:4: "Lord, make me to know my end . . . that I may know how frail I am."

183–201. *Some . . . fall:* A systematic, soteriological account, dividing souls into

three distinct categories: 1) the special elect (line 183); 2) those who accept the general offer of grace (lines 185–90), and those who reject grace and are damned (lines 199–201). It was this kind of systematizing that led to Alexander Pope's famous condemnation of Milton ("Epistle to Augustus," line 102) for creating moments in which "God the Father turns a School-divine."

183. *peculiar grace:* in contrast to "sufficient grace" (line 99), which is available to all (see lines 185–90 below); those few *of peculiar grace* are "Elect" (line 184), in Calvin's sense (i.e., in that their own will is irrelevant to their salvation).

185–190. *The rest. . . due:* Milton distils the essence of the chapter "On Predestination" in *Christian Doctrine* (I, iv), which rejects the general application of the Calvinistic doctrine that "before the foundation of the world." God, for his own glory, "without any foresight of faith and good works, or perseverance in either of them," had "predestined certain souls to salvation and ordained others to dishonor and wrath for their sin." God's "election" of men is here explained in terms of his "sufficient grace" and their free

Invites, for I will clear their senses dark,
What may suffice, and soften stony hearts
To pray, repent, and bring obedience due.   190
To prayer, repentance, and obedience due,
Though but endeavored with sincere intent,
Mine ear shall not be slow, mine eye not shut.
And I will place within them as a guide
My umpire conscience, whom if they will hear   195
Light after light well used they shall attain
And, to the end persisting, safe arrive.
This my long sufferance and my day of grace
They who neglect and scorn shall never taste,
But hard be hardened, blind be blinded more,   200
That they may stumble on and deeper fall;
And none but such from mercy I exclude.
But yet all is not done: man disobeying,
Disloyal breaks his fealty° and sins   *loyalty*
Against the high supremacy of Heaven,   205
Affecting godhead, and so, losing all,
To expiate his treason hath naught left,
But, to destruction sacred and devote,
He with his whole posterity must die;
Die he or justice must, unless for him   210
Some other, able and as willing, pay
The rigid satisfaction, death for death.

acceptance of it. So "none can be reprobated, except they do not believe or continue in the faith, and even this as a consequence rather than a decree" (*Works* 14, 141).

189. *stony hearts:* See Ezek. 11:19: "I will take the stony heart out of their flesh, and will give them an heart of flesh." See also 11.4–5.

195. *conscience:* constantly equated with reason and individual judgment in *Christian Doctrine*. In the end, Milton says in the chapter on the Last Judgment (I, xxxiii in *Works* 16, 357), man shall be judged according to the response of his conscience to "the measure of light which he has enjoyed."

200. *hard . . . more:* The hardening and blinding are not the causes of sin but the results; cf. *Christian Doctrine* I, viii, which insists that it is God "who hardens [the sinner's] heart, who blinds his understanding," but that God is not "in the smallest instance the author of sin" (*Works* 15, 71–73).

206. *Affecting godhead:* aspiring to or assuming divinity; it is to be a "goddess among gods" with which Satan tempts Eve (9.547) and succeeds: "nor was godhead from her thought" (9.790).

208. *sacred and devote:* set apart and condemned; both adjectives keep their Latin meanings of "dedicated to a deity" for some holy purpose (here, sacrifice).

211. *as willing:* i.e., as willing as he is able

212. *rigid satisfaction:* strict fulfillment of the claims of justice

Say heavenly powers, where shall we find such love,
Which of ye will be mortal to redeem
Man's mortal crime, and just the unjust to save?   215
Dwells in all Heaven charity so dear?"
    He asked, but all the heavenly choir stood mute,
And silence was in Heaven; on man's behalf
Patron or intercessor none appeared,
Much less that durst upon his own head draw   220
The deadly forfeiture and ransom set.
And now without redemption all mankind
Must have been lost, adjudged to death and hell
By doom° severe, had not the Son of God,   *sentence, judgment*
In whom the fullness dwells of love divine,   225
His dearest mediation thus renewed:
    "Father, thy word is past:° man shall find grace,   *uttered, pledged*
And shall grace not find means, that finds her way,
The speediest of thy wingèd messengers,
To visit all thy creatures, and to all   230
Comes unprevented, unimplored, unsought,
Happy for man, so coming? He her aid
Can never seek, once dead in sins and lost;
Atonement for himself or offering meet,°   *appropriate*
Indebted and undone, hath none to bring.   235
Behold me, then: me for him, life for life
I offer; on me let thine anger fall;
Account me man; I for his sake will leave

---

215. *just . . . save:* See 1 Pet. 3:18: "For Christ also hath once suffered for sins, the just for the unjust, that he might bring us to God."

216. *dear:* loving but also "expensive," picking up the economic language of "pay" (line 211), "satisfaction" (line 212), and "redeem" (line 214)

217. *stood mute:* Saint John says that there was silence in heaven when the seventh seal was opened (Rev. 8:1); cf. 2.420.

219. *Patron or intercessor: Patron* is used here in its Latin sense of an advocate in a court of law, and, like *intercessor,* reflects the conception of Christ in 1 John 2:1: "And if any man sin, we have an advocate with the Father, Jesus Christ the righteous."

225. *In whom . . . divine:* Derives from

Col. 2:9: "For in him dwelleth all the fullness of the Godhead bodily."

231. *unprevented, unimplored, unsought:* unanticipated, not asked for, freely given; *unprevented* = not preceded (by prayer), reflecting its Latin etymology from *praevenio* = to precede

232. *her:* i.e., grace's

233. *dead in sins:* echoes the language of Paul in Eph. 2:1–5, who says that "by grace" our souls may be "quickened" even "when we were dead in sins"

236–238. *Behold . . . man:* Christ grammatically couches his heroism predominately as an object, rather than as a self-assertive subject: "me" not "I"; cf. Satan's "I should ill become this throne . . . Wherefore do I assume . . . While I abroad, . . . seek deliverance for us all (2.445–65).

Thy bosom, and this glory next to thee
Freely put off, and for him lastly die   240
Well pleased; on me let death wreak all his rage.
Under his gloomy power I shall not long
Lie vanquished; thou hast given me to possess
Life in myself forever; by thee I live,
Though now to death I yield and am his due,   245
All that of me can die, yet, that debt paid,
Thou wilt not leave me in the loathsome grave
His prey, nor suffer my unspotted soul
Forever with corruption there to dwell,
But I shall rise victorious and subdue   250
My vanquisher, spoiled of his vaunted° spoil;   *boasted about*
Death his death's wound shall then receive and stoop
Inglorious, of his mortal sting disarmed.
I through the ample air in triumph high
Shall lead hell captive maugre° hell, and show   *in spite of*
The powers of darkness bound. Thou, at the sight
Pleased, out of Heaven shalt look down and smile,
While by thee raised I ruin all my foes,
Death last, and with his carcass glut the grave;
Then with the multitude of my redeemed   260
Shall enter Heaven, long absent, and return,
Father, to see thy face, wherein no cloud
Of anger shall remain, but peace assured
And reconcilement; wrath shall be no more
Thenceforth, but in thy presence joy entire."   265
     His words here ended, but his meek aspect
Silent yet spake and breathed immortal love
To mortal men, above which only shone

246. *All . . . die:* As Christ he is immortal; only his human nature can die (see line 282 below on his double "nature").

247–249. *Thou . . . corruption:* Ps. 16:10 says "Thou wilt not leave my soul in hell; neither wilt thou suffer thine Holy One to see corruption."

252–256. *Death . . . bound:* Milton seems to have been influenced by Jacopo Sannazaro, the first book of whose epic on the birth of Christ, *De Partu Virginis* (1526), develops a similar network of biblical texts forming a prophecy put into the mouth of David. Pluto (Satan) is foreseen as led captive to Tartarus, while Christ conquers the powers of the air (the fiends) and subdues Death and hell.

254–256. *I . . . bound:* The lines echo Eph. 4:8: "When he ascended up on high, he led captivity captive"; see also Ps. 68:18.

258. *ruin:* overthrow, destroy (Latin *ruere* = to throw down)

259. *Death last:* reflects Paul's "The last enemy that shall be destroyed is death" (1 Cor. 15:26).

Filial obedience; as a sacrifice
Glad to be offered, he attends the will   270
Of his great Father. Admiration° seized   *astonishment*
All Heaven, what this might mean and whither tend
Wondering; but soon the almighty thus replied:
   "O thou in Heaven and earth the only peace
Found out for mankind under wrath, O thou   275
My sole complacence, well thou know'st how dear
To me are all my works, nor man the least
Though last created, that for him I spare
Thee from my bosom and right hand to save,
By losing thee awhile, the whole race lost.   280
Thou therefore whom thou only canst redeem,
Their nature also to thy nature join
And be thyself man among men on earth,
Made flesh, when time shall be, of virgin seed
By wondrous birth. Be thou in Adam's room°   *place*
The head of all mankind though Adam's son.
As in him perish all men, so in thee,
As from a second root, shall be restored
As many as are restored; without thee, none.
His crime makes guilty all his sons; thy merit   290
Imputed shall absolve them who renounce
Their own both righteous and unrighteous deeds
And live in thee transplanted and from thee
Receive new life. So man, as is most just,

270. *attends:* waits (for an expression of his Father's will)

276. *complacence:* satisfaction, source of pleasure

280. *lost:* i.e., which would otherwise be lost

281. *thou only canst redeem:* But cf. lines 211–12, where God seems to imply that any of the angels could "pay the rigid satisfaction."

283–285. *be . . . birth:* Similarly, in Matt. 1:23 Isaiah's birth oracle (Isa. 7:14), "Behold, a virgin shall conceive, and bear a son, and shall call his name Immanuel," is interpreted as a prophecy of the birth of Christ. Cf. 10.74.

284. *when time shall be:* i.e., when time as humans understand it shall begin (i.e., with the creation of the heavens on day four of creation)

286. *The head of all mankind:* derived from 1 Cor. 11:3: "The head of every man is Christ."

288–289. *As . . . restored:* Cf. "For as in Adam all die, even so in Christ shall all be made alive" (1 Cor. 15:22); *root* picks up the organic metaphor in "seed" in line 284 above and continued with "transplanted" in line 293; see also 1.4–5.

291. *Imputed:* passed on, vicariously transferred (here, the theological doctrine of "imputed righteousness," which transfers Christ's righteousness to the Christian faithful; see 12.295 and note).

Shall satisfy for man, be judged and die,   295
And dying rise, and, rising with him, raise
His brethren ransomed with his own dear life.
So heavenly love shall outdo hellish hate,
Giving to death and dying to redeem,
So dearly to redeem, what hellish hate   300
So easily destroyed and still destroys
In those who, when they may, accept not grace.
Nor shalt thou by descending to assume
Man's nature lessen or degrade thine own.
Because thou hast, though throned in highest bliss   305
Equal to God and equally enjoying
Godlike fruition,° quitted all to save   *joy*
A world from utter loss and hast been found
By merit more than birthright Son of God,
Found worthiest to be so by being good   310
Far more than great or high, because in thee
Love hath abounded more than glory abounds,
Therefore thy humiliation shall exalt
With thee thy manhood also to this throne;
Here shalt thou sit incarnate, here shalt reign   315
Both God and man, Son both of God and man,
Anointed universal king; all power
I give thee: reign forever and assume°   *take possession of*
Thy merits; under thee as head supreme
Thrones, princedoms, powers, dominions I reduce.   320

297. *ransomed:* echoes Matt. 20:28, which says that Christ came "to give his life a ransom for many"

299. *Giving:* yielding (and giving to)

301. *destroyed and still destroys:* The future events are spoken of as both past and present by God, who sees all time concurrently.

306. *Equal to God:* Milton's Trinitarian thought is complex and unorthodox; here he asserts the equality of the Son and the Father (not their identity), but elsewhere in the poem he endorses the opinion of *Christian Doctrine* (I, v) that "the Son himself and his apostles acknowledge throughout the whole of their discourses and writings, that the Fa-

ther is greater than the Son in all things" (*Works* 14, 219).

307. *quitted:* 1) renounced; 2) redeemed

309. *By merit:* Cf. Satan's "by merit raised" (2.5); also note Ovid, *Metamorphoses* 2.42–43, where Apollo says to his son, Phaeton: "by merit, as by birth, to thee is due that name [of son]."

317–318. *Anointed . . . thee:* The lines fuse God's words to the Son in Heb. 1:9: "God, even thy God, hath anointed thee with the oil of gladness above thy fellows," and Christ's saying that "All power is given unto me" (Matt. 28:18), a line with obvious anti-Trinitarian implications.

All knees to thee shall bow of them that bide
In Heaven, or earth, or under earth in hell
When thou, attended° gloriously from Heaven,   *accompanied*
Shalt in the sky appear and from thee send
The summoning archangels to proclaim   325
Thy dread tribunal; forthwith from all winds
The living and forthwith the cited° dead   *summoned*
Of all past ages to the general doom
Shall hasten, such a peal shall rouse their sleep.
Then all thy saints assembled, thou shalt judge   330
Bad men and angels; they arraigned shall sink
Beneath thy sentence; hell, her numbers full,
Thenceforth shall be forever shut. Meanwhile
The world shall burn and from her ashes spring
New Heaven and earth, wherein the just shall dwell   335
And, after all their tribulations long,
See golden days, fruitful of golden deeds,
With joy and love triumphing and fair truth.
Then thou thy regal scepter shalt lay by,
For regal scepter then no more shall need:°   *be needed*
God shall be all in all. But all ye gods,
Adore him who, to compass all this, dies;
Adore the Son and honor him as me."
    No sooner had the almighty ceased, but all
The multitude of angels, with a shout   345
Loud as from numbers without number, sweet
As from blessèd voices, uttering joy, Heaven rung

321–322. *All . . . hell:* The promise
stems from Phil. 2:10: "That at the name of
Jesus every knee should bow, of things in
heaven, and things in earth, and things
under the earth."

323. *gloriously:* can modify either *at-
tended,* or *appear* in line 324

326. *all winds:* all directions

328. *general doom:* Judgment Day

330. *saints:* the elect (see Matt. 24:31)

335. *New . . . earth:* See Rev. 21:1: "and
I saw a new heaven and a new earth"; cf.
12.547–51 below.

339. *regal scepter . . . by:* Monarchy is
abandoned, no longer even an appropriate
metaphor for Christ's relation to God's cre-
ations when all things become one with God
(see lines 340–41 below).

341. *God . . . all in all:* Cf. "and when
all things shall be subdued unto him, then
shall the Son also himself be subject unto
him that put all things under him, that God
may be all in all" (1 Cor. 15:28).

341–342. *all ye gods, Adore him:* For
gods = angels, see 2.352; but cf. God's gracious
ascription of the term with Satan's temptation
of Eve: "ye shall be as gods" (9.708–14).

343. *honor him as me:* transfers to the
angels the charge of John 5:23: "All men
should honour the Son, even as they honour
the Father."

347. *rung:* rang; Heaven is what is ring-
ing, filled with the angels' "jubilee" (= sounds
of jubilation; from the Hebrew word mean-
ing "ram's horn") and "hosannahs" (cries of
praise; from the Hebrew for "save now").

With jubilee, and loud hosannas filled
The eternal regions; lowly reverent
Toward either throne they bow, and to the ground   350
With solemn adoration down they cast
Their crowns inwove with amaranth and gold,
Immortal amaranth, a flower which once
In Paradise, fast by the tree of life,
Began to bloom, but soon, for° man's offence,   *on account of*
To Heaven removed where first it grew, there grows
And flowers aloft shading the fount of life
And where the river of bliss through midst of Heaven
Rolls o'er Elysian flowers her amber stream;
With these that never fade, the spirits elect   360
Bind their resplendent locks enwreathed with beams;
Now in loose garlands thick thrown off, the bright
Pavement, that like a sea of jasper shone
Impurpled, with celestial roses smiled.
Then, crowned again, their golden harps they took,   365
Harps ever tuned that glittering by their side
Like quivers hung, and with preamble sweet
Of charming symphony they introduce
Their sacred song and waken raptures high;
No voice exempt,° no voice but well could join   *left out*
Melodious part, such concord is in Heaven.
    "Thee Father," first they sung, "Omnipotent,
Immutable, immortal, infinite,
Eternal king; thee, author of all being,

352. *amaranth:* an imagined, unfading flower, often identified in Christian commentary with the saints' "inheritance incorruptible, and undefiled, and that fadeth not away," in 1 Pet. 1:4. Cf. "Lycidas," line 149.

358. *the river of bliss:* Cf. John's "pure river of water of life, clear as crystal" (Rev. 22:1), though Milton's river of bliss flows over "Elysian flowers" (line 359).

360. *these:* i.e., the amaranth flowers

362. *thick:* in great number (like the fallen angels who lay "thick as autumnal leaves" [1.302]).

363–364. *like a sea . . . roses:* The colors are those of the "sea of glass like unto crystal" (Rev. 4:6) and the "light . . . like unto a stone most precious, even like a jasper stone, clear

as crystal" (Rev. 21:11) that John saw around the throne of God.

373–382. *Immutable . . . eyes:* The lines recall Moses' accounts of God speaking to him on Sinai when "a cloud covered the mount" (Exod. 24:15) and Isaiah's vision (Isa. 6:1–4) of "the Lord sitting upon a throne" with the seraphim veiling their eyes about him in the temple. Theologically, the lines reflect the idea that as an uncaused cause God is knowable and definable only by his attributes. The conception was familiar and appears, for example, in superficially similar language in Josiah Sylvester's translation of Du Bartas' *Divine Weeks* (1608, p. 2): "Before all Time, all Matter, Form, and Place, / God all in all, and all in God it was: / Immutable, immortal, infinite, /

Fountain of light, thyself invisible   375
Amidst the glorious brightness where thou sit'st
Throned inaccessible, but° when thou shad'st   *except*
The full blaze of thy beams and through a cloud
Drawn round about thee like a radiant shrine,
Dark with excessive bright thy skirts appear   380
Yet dazzle Heaven that° brightest seraphim   *so that*
Approach not but with both wings veil their eyes.
Thee," next they sang, "of all creation first,
Begotten son, divine similitude,
In whose conspicuous countenance, without cloud   385
Made visible, the almighty Father shines
Whom else no creature can behold; on thee
Impressed the effulgence of his glory abides;
Transfused on thee his ample spirit rests.
He Heaven of Heavens and all the powers therein   390
By thee created, and by thee threw down
The aspiring dominations; thou that day
Thy Father's dreadful thunder didst not spare
Nor stop thy flaming chariot wheels that shook
Heaven's everlasting frame, while o'er the necks   395
Thou drov'st of warring angels disarrayed.
Back from pursuit thy powers with loud acclaim
Thee only extolled, Son of thy Father's might,
To execute fierce vengeance on his foes.

Incomprehensible, all spirit, all light, / All Majestie, all-self-Omnipotent / Invisible." Cf. 2.264 and 5.599.

380. *skirts:* the aura of light surrounding his being

383. *of all creation first:* As God's efficient agent, Christ is necessarily the first of God's creations, but if he is a *creation,* one must then ask, as *Christian Doctrine,* I, vii does, "How therefore can he be himself God?" (*Works* 15, 11). Though some have used Col. 1:15 to avoid the implication here of what was known as Arianism, the anti-Trinitarian heresy that denied the essential unity of the Father, Son, and Holy Spirit, here and in line 384 it is hard to escape.

384. *Begotten son:* Although the phrase,

familiar from John 1:18, is used at line 80 above, the anti-Trinitarian thought is more insistent here: Christ is clearly *Begotten*; only God is not. *Christian Doctrine* firmly held that "he . . . who did not beget, but was begotten, is not the first cause, but the effect, and therefore is not the Supreme God" (I, v; *Works* 14, 313).   *divine similitude:* perfect image of God

389. *his ample spirit:* Here, as in 1.17 and 7.165, 7.209, and 7.235, the reference is to God's power rather than to the Holy Spirit, the third person of the Trinity.

391–392. *By thee . . . dominations:* The Son's triumph over the *aspiring dominations* or rebellious angels of Satan is the theme of 6.824–92.

396. *disarrayed:* in confusion (literally with their battle ranks, "array," in confusion)

Not so on man; him through their malice fallen,   400
Father of mercy and grace, thou didst not doom
So strictly but much more to pity incline.
No sooner did thy dear and only Son
Perceive thee purposed not to doom frail man
So strictly, but much more to pity inclined,   405
He,° to appease thy wrath and end the strife   *then he*
Of mercy and justice in thy face discerned,
Regardless° of the bliss wherein he sat   *disregarding*
Second to thee, offered himself to die
For man's offence. O unexampled love,   410
Love nowhere to be found less than divine!
Hail Son of God, savior of men, thy name
Shall be the copious matter of my song
Henceforth, and never shall my harp thy praise
Forget, nor from thy Father's praise disjoin."   415
      Thus they in Heaven, above the starry sphere,
Their happy hours in joy and hymning spent.
Meanwhile upon the firm opacous° globe   *opaque*
Of this round world, whose first convex divides   *universe*
The luminous inferior orbs, enclosed   420
From chaos and the inroad of darkness old,
Satan alighted walks. A globe far off
It seemed, now seems a boundless continent
Dark, waste, and wild, under the frown of night
Starless exposed and ever-threatening storms   425
Of chaos blustering round, inclement sky,
Save on that side which from the wall of heaven,
Though distant far, some small reflection gains
Of glimmering air less vexed with tempest loud.
Here walked the fiend at large in spacious field.   430
As when a vulture on Imaus bred,

---

404. *purposed not to doom:* intending
not to pronounce judgment

413–414. *my song . . . my harp:* i.e., the
angelic song and harp, but easily seen to refer
to Milton's poem as well

416. *starry sphere:* the shell of the uni-
verse on which Satan has landed in line 74
above. The empyreal Heaven of the angels is
outside and *above* it.

419. *first convex:* outer shell, "the bare
outside of this world" at line 74

429. *vexed:* tossed around (Latin *vexare*
= shake)

431. *vulture on Imaus:* The vulture was
described in Batman's version of Bartholo-
maeus' *Book of Nature* (*De proprietatibus
rerum*, 1582, sig. Gg1r) as able to scent its
prey across whole continents. *Imaus* is the
name given to a mountain range in central
Asia running northeast from Afghanistan to
the Arctic Ocean, and is sometimes the name
of a single mountain in the range.

Whose snowy ridge the roving Tartar bounds,
Dislodging from a region scarce of prey
To gorge the flesh of lambs or yeanling° kids   *newborn*
On hills where flocks are fed, flies toward the springs   435
Of Ganges or Hydaspes, Indian streams,
But in his way lights on the barren plains
Of Sericana,° where Chineses drive   *China*
With sails and wind their cany wagons light,
So on this windy sea of land the fiend   440
Walked up and down alone bent on his prey,
Alone, for other creature in this place
Living or lifeless to be found was none—
None yet, but store° hereafter from the earth   *plenty*
Up hither like aerial vapors flew   445
Of all things transitory and vain, when Sin
With vanity had filled the works of men:
Both all things vain and all who in vain things
Built their fond° hopes of glory, or lasting fame,   *foolish*
Or happiness in this or the other life.   450
All who have their reward on earth, the fruits
Of painful° superstition and blind zeal,   *painstaking*
Naught seeking but the praise of men, here find
Fit retribution empty as their deeds;
All the unaccomplished° works of nature's hand,   *imperfect*
Abortive, monstrous, or unkindly° mixed,   *unnaturally*
Dissolved on earth, fleet° hither and, in vain   *drift, float*
Till final dissolution, wander here,
Not in the neighboring moon as some have dreamed.

432. *roving Tartar bounds:* confines the nomadic (or marauding) Tartar

436. *Hydaspes:* a river in Kashmir, now known as the Jhelum, a tributary of the Indus

437. *the barren plains:* i.e., the Gobi Desert

438–439. *Chineses . . . light:* Several geographers confirmed the story of the Chinese wind-wagons, e.g., Robert Parke's translation of the Spanish Jesuit Juan Gonzalez de Mendoza's *Historie of the Great and Mighty Kingdome of China* (1588, p. 22); *cany* = made of cane or bamboo

445–496. *Up hither . . . fools:* Though Milton (line 471), like Dante (*Inferno* 5.138), puts *Empedocles* into *limbo*, his para-

dise of fools has little in common with Dante's circle of the great poets, philosophers, and heroes. It is more indebted to Ariosto's Limbo of Vanity (*Orlando Furioso* 34.70), which includes "A mighty mass of things strangely confus'd, / Things that on earth were lost, or were abus'd," as Milton translated it in *Of Reformation in England* (*Works* 3, part 1, 27).

456. *Abortive:* prematurely born

458. *final dissolution:* Milton's "mortalism" insists that the soul dies with the body and is resurrected with it at the final judgment, rather than existing on its own.

459. *in the neighboring . . . dreamed:* Various writers, including Giordano Bruno

Those argent° fields more likely habitants,   *silver*
Translated saints or middle spirits, hold
Betwixt the angelical and human kind.
Hither of ill-joined sons and daughters born
First from the ancient world those giants came
With many a vain exploit though then renowned.   465
The builders next of Babel on the plain
Of Sennaar, and still with vain design
New Babels, had they wherewithal, would build.
Others came single: he who, to be deemed
A god, leaped fondly into Etna flames,   470
Empedocles, and he who, to enjoy
Plato's Elysium, leaped into the sea,
Cleombrotus, and many more too long:
Embryos and idiots, eremites° and friars   *hermits*
White, black and gray, with all their trumpery.°   *deceit, worthless ideas*
Here pilgrims roam that strayed so far to seek
In Golgotha him dead who lives in Heaven;
And they who, to be sure of Paradise,

and Henry More, had postulated lunar life; Ariosto satirized the idea by locating his fool's paradise on the moon (*Orlando Furioso* 34.56–68).

461. *Translated saints:* holy men miraculously transported to Heaven before their deaths, like Enoch in Gen. 5:24 or Elijah in 2 Kings 2

464. *giants:* Gen. 6:4 tells of a race of giants born "when the sons of God came in unto the daughters of men"; see also 11.573–97n.

466. *Babel:* The Tower of Babel (Gen. 11:1–9), built to reach Heaven, was a type of arrogant human pride; see 12.38–62.

467. *Sennaar:* the vulgate spelling of Shinar, the plain on which the Tower of Babel was erected (Gen. 11:2)

469–471. *he . . . Empedocles:* Cf. Horace, *Ars Poetica* 464–66: "Empedocles, eager to be thought a god immortal, coolly leapt into burning Etna"; the plan failed when the volcano spit out one of his shoes.

471–473. *he . . . Cleombrotus:* Inspired

by Plato's account of the happiness of the soul after death, Cleombrotus jumped into the sea. Callimachus, in Epigram 25, writes: "Farewell, O sun, said Cleombrotus of Ambracia and leapt from a lofty wall into Hades. No evil had he seen worthy of death, but he had read one writing of Plato's "On the Soul [i.e., *The Phaedo*]."

473. *too long:* i.e., too numerous to list

474–480. *Embryos . . . disguised:* examples of the many kinds of delusive hope offered by the Catholic Church and its teachings

474. *Embryos and idiots:* Because they could not be responsible morally, their souls were held by Catholic theologians not to be damned—even though they still bore the stain of original sin—but to inhabit a limbo above the earth.

474–475. *friars . . . gray:* The White Friars are the Carmelites; the Black, the Dominicans; and the Grey, Franciscans, from the color of their habits (and here insultingly linked with "embryos and idiots").

477. *Golgotha:* the hill near Jerusalem where Christ was crucified (John 19:17)

Dying put on the weeds of Dominic,
Or in Franciscan think to pass disguised;   480
They pass the planets seven and pass the fixed,
And that crystalline sphere whose balance weighs
The trepidation talked, and that first moved;
And now Saint Peter at Heaven's wicket seems
To wait them with his keys, and now at foot   485
Of Heaven's ascent they lift their feet, when, lo,
A violent crosswind from either coast
Blows them transverse° ten thousand leagues awry   *sideways*
Into the devious air; then might ye see
Cowls, hoods, and habits with their wearers tossed   490
And fluttered into rags, then relics, beads,°   *rosary beads*
Indulgences, dispenses, pardons, bulls,
The sport of winds; all these upwhirled aloft
Fly o'er the backside of the world far off
Into a limbo large and broad, since° called   *in future times*
The paradise of fools, to few unknown
Long after, now unpeopled and untrod.

479. *weeds:* robes; illustrations of the practice of such efforts to ensure salvation are given by Johan Huizinga in *The Waning of the Middle Ages* (London, 1924), pp. 164–65; also see Dante's *Inferno* 27.67–129.

481–483. *They . . . moved:* i.e., they pass the seven planetary spheres, the sphere of the *fixed* stars, and the *crystalline sphere,* whose scales (i.e., the sign of Libra, the *balance*) measure the amount of oscillation (*trepidation*) that was much discussed (*talked*); and they pass the outermost tenth sphere, the *primum mobile* (i.e., *that first moved*). Milton here follows a Ptolemaic conception of the heavens.

484. *wicket:* gate; a further mocking literalization and diminution of the process of salvation, which for Milton could only come through grace and faith. Perhaps in "wicket" one is meant to hear a hint of "wicked."

486. *ascent:* stairway (see lines 501–22 below)

487–488. *crosswind . . . Blows them:* Burton, in his *Anatomy of Melancholy*, speaks of those easily led and "apt to be carried about by the blast of every wind" (3.4.1.2).

489. *devious:* 1) remote, far away (*OED* 1); 2) blowing about, following an unpredictable course (but also with its moral sense of swerving from the right course)

490–497. *Cowls . . . untrod:* Milton's mockery of the forms of Catholic devotion. An illuminating parallel to this passage is in Burton's *Anatomy of Melancholy*, which anticipates phrases like *the sports of winds* and *Indulgences, dispenses, pardons, bulls,* and declares that the availability of such exemptions and licenses has "so fleeced the commonalty, and spurred on this free superstitious horse, that he runs himself blind, and is an Ass to carry burdens" (ibid., 3.4.1.2).

492. *Indulgences, dispenses, pardons:* various exemptions or absolutions stipulated by the Catholic Church that might be purchased to free one from either the penalty for one's sins or the requirement to fulfill some obligation.   *bulls:* papal edicts, so called because fastened with a seal, or *bulla*

494. *backside:* far side (with the obvious pun; also note *winds* in line 493)

All this dark globe the fiend found as he passed,
And long he wandered, till at last a gleam
Of dawning light turned thitherward in haste   500
His traveled° steps; far distant he descries,   *weary with travel*
Ascending by degrees° magnificent   *steps (of a stairway)*
Up to the wall of Heaven, a structure high,
At top whereof, but far more rich, appeared
The work as of a kingly palace gate   505
With frontispiece of diamond and gold
Embellished; thick with sparkling orient° gems   *lustrous*
The portal shone, inimitable on earth
By model or by shading pencil drawn.
The stairs were such as whereon Jacob saw   510
Angels ascending and descending, bands
Of guardians bright, when he from Esau fled
To Padan-Aram, in the field of Luz,
Dreaming by night under the open sky,
And waking cried, "This is the gate of Heaven."   515
Each stair mysteriously was meant, nor stood
There always but drawn up to heaven sometimes
Viewless,° and underneath a bright sea flowed   *invisible*
Of jasper or of liquid pearl, whereon
Who° after came from earth, sailing arrived,   *those who*
Wafted by angels, or flew o'er the lake
Rapt in a chariot drawn by fiery steeds.

506. *frontispiece:* façade of (or pediment over) heaven's gate, the *wicket* of line 484 above

510–515. *Jacob . . . Heaven:* In Gen. 28:10–17, Jacob flees after cheating his brother, Esau, out of their father's blessing; one night he dreams of a ladder that "reached to heaven," with "the angels of God ascending and descending on it." The dream begins Jacob's regeneration.

513. *To Padan-Aram. . . Luz:* The syntax can confuse, hence the comma after *Padan-Aran*; it is in the field of Luz (which Jacob later renames Bethel) that Jacob has his dream, as he sleeps one night on his way to Padan-Aram (i.e., Syria).

516. *mysteriously:* symbolically, allegorically; Jacob's dream was often allegorically interpreted by Christian commentators; for example, Nicholas of Lyre (c. 1300), a French Franciscan, writes in his *Postillae* that Jacob's ladder "signified the steps of the generations through which Christ descended through the flesh from Abraham to the Virgin Mary, who bore him"; other allegorizations focus on the gradual ascent of the soul toward perfection.

518–519. *sea . . . Of jasper:* the "waters above the Firmament," which the Argument to this book says "flow about" the "gate of heaven"; cf. line 574 below and 7.261.

521–522. *Wafted . . . steeds:* Cf. the parable of the flight of the beggar Lazarus to heaven in the arms of angels (Luke 16:22) and Elijah's translation to heaven in a "chariot of fire" drawn by "horses of fire" (2 Kings 2:11).

The stairs were then let down, whether° to dare   *either*
The fiend by easy ascent or aggravate°   *intensify*
His sad exclusion from the doors of bliss.   525
Direct against, which opened from beneath,
Just o'er the blissful seat of Paradise,
A passage down to the earth, a passage wide,
Wider by far than that of aftertimes
Over Mount Sion and, though that were large,   530
Over the promised land to God so dear,
By which to visit oft those happy tribes
On high behests his angels to and fro
Passed frequent, and° his eye with choice regard   *and so did*
From Paneas, the fount of Jordan's flood,   535
To Beersaba, where the holy land
Borders on Egypt and the Arabian shore;
So wide the opening seemed, where bounds were set
To darkness, such as bound the ocean wave.
Satan from hence, now on the lower stair   540
That scaled by steps of gold to Heaven gate,
Looks down with wonder at the sudden view
Of all this world at once, as when a scout,
Through dark and desert ways with peril gone
All night, at last by break of cheerful dawn   545
Obtains° the brow of some high-climbing hill,   *reaches*
Which to his eye discovers° unaware   *reveals*
The goodly prospect of some foreign land
First seen, or some renowned metropolis
With glistering spires and pinnacles adorned,   550
Which now the rising sun gilds with his beams.
Such wonder seized, though after Heaven seen,
The spirit malign, but much more envy seized
At sight of all this world beheld so fair.
Round he surveys, and well might, where he stood   555

---

530. *Mount Sion:* Cf. *Sion* in 1.86, 1.442, and 3.30.

534. *choice regard:* careful judgment

535–536. *Paneas . . . Beersaba: Paneas,* the Greek name of the city of Dan, near the source of the Jordan in the north of Canaan, and *Beersaba* (Beersheba) in the extreme south, are often mentioned as the bounds of the country (e.g., 1 Kings 4:25).

539. *bound the ocean wave:* i.e., parted the Red Sea

548. *goodly prospect:* attractive sight

552. *though after Heaven seen:* though he had seen Heaven

555–579. *Round . . . far:* Entering the universe at the point where it is suspended from heaven by the golden chain (cf. 2.1051), Satan sees the panorama of the stars

So high above the circling canopy
Of night's extended shade, from eastern point
Of Libra to the fleecy star that bears
Andromeda far off Atlantic seas
Beyond the horizon; then from pole to pole   560
He views in breadth, and without longer pause
Down right into the world's first region throws
His flight precipitant and winds with ease
Through the pure marble air his oblique way
Amongst innumerable stars that shone,   565
Stars distant,° but nigh hand seemed other worlds;   *at a distance*
Or° other worlds they seemed or happy isles,   *either*
Like those Hesperian gardens famed of old,
Fortunate fields, and groves, and flowery vales,
Thrice happy isles, but who dwelt happy there   570
He stayed not to inquire. Above them all
The golden sun, in splendor likest Heaven,
Allured his eye; thither his course he bends
Through the calm firmament, but up or down
By center or eccentric, hard to tell,   575
Or longitude, where the great luminary,

stretching from *Libra* at the eastern end of the Zodiac to the constellation of Aries (the Ram, *the fleecy star*), with that of *Andromeda*, which seems to ride on it at the western end, below the Atlantic *horizon*. He plunges through the upper air or *world's first region*, through the orbs of the *primum mobile*, the crystalline sphere and the fixed stars (all in the reverse order from that in which they are named in lines 481–83 above), and then, entering the lower region of the planets, is attracted by the sun, whose orb in the geocentric, Ptolemaic astronomy was below that of the fixed stars. The *golden sun is above* the stars only in the sense that it is more splendid than they and dispenses light to them, as it is said again to do in 5.23.

556–557. *circling canopy . . . shade:* i.e., the dark side of the earth, above the canonical shadow it presumably casts

562–563. *throws . . . precipitant:* quickly makes his way

564. *marble:* gleaming (reflecting the derivation of "marble" from a Greek word

meaning "gleaming")   *oblique:* indirect (also with the sense of "perverse")

566. *nigh hand:* near at hand

568. *Hesperian gardens:* Here, as in *Comus* lines 981–82, the *Hesperian gardens* are in the Happy Isles, or Hesperides, which were vaguely identified with the Canary Islands or sometimes with the British Isles. In classical myth, the gardens had golden apples guarded by dragons; Hercules killed the dragons and stole the apples; cf. 4.249–50.

571. *Above:* not in spatial location but "in splendor" (line 572)

573. *bends:* 1) directs; 2) swerves

575. *hard to tell:* Milton here refuses to decide between the Ptolemaic and Copernican views of the orbits of the planets; see 4.592–94 for a similar reluctance.

576. *longitude:* distance along the ecliptic, the supposed orbit of the sun around the earth (thus a measurement of Satan's horizontal movement in relation to the earth, the opposite of our present sense of the word). *great luminary:* i.e., the sun

Aloof° the vulgar constellations thick   *away from*
That from his lordly eye keep distance due,
Dispenses light from far; they, as they move
Their starry dance in numbers that compute   580
Days, months, and years, toward his all-cheering lamp
Turn swift their various motions, or are turned
By his magnetic beam that gently warms
The universe, and to each inward part
With gentle penetration, though unseen,   585
Shoots invisible virtue° even to the deep,   *influence, power*
So wondrously was set his station bright.
There lands the fiend, a spot like which perhaps
Astronomer in the sun's lucent orb
Through his glazed optic tube yet never saw.   590
The place he found beyond expression bright
Compared with aught on earth, metal or stone,
Not all parts like, but all alike informed°   *imbued*
With radiant light, as glowing iron with fire;
If metal, part seemed gold, part silver clear;   595
If stone, carbuncle most or chrysolite,
Ruby, or topaz, to the twelve that shone
In Aaron's breastplate and a stone besides
Imagined rather oft then elsewhere seen:
That stone, or like to that which here below   600
Philosophers in vain so long have sought,
In vain though by their powerful art they bind
Volatile Hermes and call up unbound

577. *vulgar:* crowded (Latin *vulgus* = crowd)

580. *numbers that compute:* rhythms that define

583. *magnetic beam:* refers to the idea that the sun's magnetic force determined the orbits of the planets (a theory published by Kepler in 1609)

588–590. *a spot . . . saw:* Galileo's sighting of sun spots with his *glazed optic tube* (telescope), published in 1613, was one of the most exciting astronomical discoveries of the century, though here the *spot* is pointedly something Galileo *never* saw. (*lucent* = shining, bright)

596. *carbuncle . . . chrysolite:* respectively, red and green gemstones

597–598. *the twelve . . . breastplate:* See Exod. 28:17–20 for the twelve jewels of *Aaron's breastplate,* which correspond to the twelve tribes of Israel.

599. *Imagined . . . seen:* i.e., much more often imagined than anywhere seen

600. *stone:* the philosopher's stone, which alchemists believed would turn base metals to gold

602. *bind:* here, an alchemical term referring to the mixing of mercury with other elements to make it less *volatile*

603. *Volatile Hermes:* literally, winged Hermes (*volatile* = able to fly [*OED* 2a]) but Hermes symbolized the element mercury, important to the alchemical processes, which is volatile in another sense (i.e., evaporating rapidly [*OED* 3a]).

In various shapes old Proteus from the sea,
Drained through a limbeck to his native form.   605
What wonder, then, if fields and region here°   *in the sun*
Breathe forth elixir pure and rivers run
Potable° gold, when with one virtuous touch   *drinkable*
The archchemic° sun, so far from us remote,   *chief alchemist*
Produces with terrestrial humor° mixed   *moisture*
Here in the dark so many precious things
Of color glorious and effect so rare?
Here matter new to gaze the devil met
Undazzled; far and wide his eye commands,
For sight no obstacle found here nor shade,   615
But all sunshine, as when his beams at noon
Culminate from the equator, as they now
Shot upward still direct, whence no way round
Shadow from body opaque can fall, and the air,
Nowhere so clear, sharpened his visual ray   620
To objects distant far, whereby he soon
Saw within ken a glorious angel stand,
The same whom John saw also in the sun.
His back was turned, but not his brightness hid
Of beaming sunny rays; a golden tiar°   *tiara, crown (halo)*
Circled his head, nor less his locks behind
Illustrious on his shoulders fledge° with wings   *feathered*
Lay waving round; on some great charge employed
He seemed, or fixed in cogitation deep.
Glad was the spirit impure as now in hope   630
To find who might direct his wandering flight
To Paradise, the happy seat of man,

604. *Proteus:* the sea god capable of changing into *various shapes,* hence a metaphor for the alchemists' dream of transforming substances

605. *limbeck:* alembic, the distilling apparatus of the alchemists

607. *elixir pure:* the final refinement in the alchemical process. The word *elixir,* which was the drink of the gods in Homer, was the basis of the medieval medical term "elixir of life," a life-prolonging substance akin to, or the liquid form of, the "philosopher's stone."

608. *virtuous:* powerful, energizing

617. *Culminate from the equator:* fall from the highest point of the orbit, the celestial equator (not that of earth)

620. *sharpened his visual ray:* Satan's sight is sharpened because no shadows fall anywhere when the sun culminates, or reaches the meridian over the equator. Though this happens only at the spring and autumn equinoxes, Milton thought of it as happening daily before the sun, as a result of Adam's sin, was pushed "from the equinoctial road" (10.672).

622. *within ken:* in his range of vision

622–623. *a glorious angel . . . sun:* The *glorious angel,* Uriel (line 648), though he is never mentioned in the Bible, is here said to be the angel whom *John* saw "standing in the sun" (Rev. 19:17).

His journey's end and our beginning woe.
But first he casts to change his proper shape,
Which else might work him danger or delay: 635
And now a stripling cherub he appears,
Not of the prime, yet such as in his face
Youth smiled celestial and to every limb
Suitable grace diffused, so well he feigned;
Under a coronet his flowing hair   640
In curls on either cheek played; wings he wore
Of many a colored plume sprinkled with gold,
His habit fit for speed succinct, and held
Before his decent steps a silver wand.
He drew not nigh unheard; the angel bright,   645
Ere he drew nigh, his radiant visage turned,
Admonished by his ear, and straight was known
The archangel Uriel, one of the seven
Who in God's presence nearest to his throne
Stand ready at command, and are his eyes   650
That run through all the heavens or down to the earth
Bear his swift errands over moist and dry,
O'er sea and land; him Satan thus accosts:
    "Uriel, for thou, of those seven spirits that stand
In sight of God's high throne gloriously bright   655
The first, art wont his great authentic° will   *authoritative*
Interpreter° through highest Heaven to bring   *as an interpreter*
Where all his sons thy embassy attend;
And here art likeliest by supreme decree
Like honor to obtain and, as his eye,   660

---

634. *casts:* 1) schemes, contrives; 2) throws off (shape or clothes)

637. *Not of the prime:* not actually young (though he "appears" to be a "stripling cherub," line 636); less likely here, *of the prime* could mean "of the first rank" or "one of the primary angels."

643. *succinct:* close fitting or tucked in (modifies *habit*)

644. *decent:* graceful, dignified (see "Suitable grace," line 639)

648. *Uriel:* Though Uriel is never mentioned in the bible, Jewish mystics (based on the apocryphal 2 Esd. 4:36) made him one of the four great archangels, along with Michael, Gabriel, and Raphael, who ruled the four quarters of the world—Uriel's quarter being the south. The name in Hebrew means "fire of God."

648–649. *one . . . throne:* Milton had in mind "the seven Spirits" whom John saw before God's throne (Rev. 1:4) and of whom Zechariah wrote (Zech. 4:10): they are the eyes of the Lord, which run to and fro through the whole earth." The apocryphal 1 Enoch 22:1 puts Uriel first among these.

658. *sons:* Like the writer of Job, Milton calls the angels *sons* of God and thinks of them as living scattered through the provinces of Heaven, except on the days when they must "present themselves before the Lord" (Job 2:1).

To visit oft this new creation round;
Unspeakable desire to see and know
All these his wondrous works, but chiefly man,
His chief delight and favor,° him for whom   *favorite*
All these his works so wondrous he ordained,   665
Hath brought me from the choirs of cherubim
Alone thus wandering. Brightest seraph, tell
In which of all these shining orbs hath man
His fixèd seat, or fixèd seat hath none,
But all these shining orbs his choice to dwell,   670
That I may find him and with secret gaze
Or open admiration him behold
On whom the great creator hath bestowed
Worlds, and on whom hath all these graces poured,
That both in him and all things, as is meet,   675
The universal maker we may praise,
Who justly hath driven out his rebel foes
To deepest hell, and to repair that loss
Created this new happy race of men
To serve him better; wise are all his ways."   680
So spake the false dissembler unperceived,
For neither man nor angel can discern
Hypocrisy, the only evil that walks
Invisible, except to God alone,
By his permissive will through heaven and earth;   685
And oft, though wisdom wake, suspicion sleeps
At wisdom's gate and to simplicity
Resigns her charge, while goodness thinks no ill
Where no ill seems, which now for once beguiled
Uriel, though regent° of the sun and held   *deputy*
The sharpest sighted spirit of all in Heaven,
Who to the fraudulent impostor foul
In his uprightness answer thus returned:
     "Fair angel, thy desire which tends° to know   *is directed*
The works of God, thereby to glorify   695

682–684. *For neither . . . Invisible:* At
very least this forces an alert reader to ask
how, if an archangel cannot discern Satan's
hypocrisy, Adam and Eve can be expected to
recognize it—though, in fact, it is not
through Satan's hypocrisy that they fall.
     685. *By his permissive will:* The distinc-
tion between God's permissive will and his
active will avoids making him responsible for
evil; cf. 1.211.
     689. *which:* i.e., hypocrisy
     694. *Fair:* Neither 1667 nor 1674 in-
dents here, but, following most modern edi-
tions, I have indicated the new verse
paragraph with the change of speaker that is
the poem's normal practice.

The great work-master, leads to no excess
That reaches blame but rather merits praise
The more it seems excess, that led thee hither
From thy empyreal mansion thus alone,
To witness with thine eyes what some, perhaps   700
Contented with report, hear only in Heaven;
For wonderful indeed are all his works,
Pleasant to know and worthiest to be all
Had in remembrance always with delight;
But what created mind can comprehend   705
Their number or the wisdom infinite
That brought them forth but hid their causes deep?
I saw when at his word the formless mass,
This world's material mold, came to a heap;
Confusion heard his voice, and wild uproar   710
Stood ruled, stood vast infinitude confined,
Till at his second bidding darkness fled,
Light shone, and order from disorder sprung;
Swift to their several quarters hasted then
The cumbrous elements, earth, flood, air, fire,   715
And this ethereal quintessence of Heaven
Flew upward, spirited with various forms

696–697. *no excess . . . blame:* It was an expressed principle of Renaissance Neoplatonism (e.g., Giordano Bruno's *De Gli Eroici Furori,* 1585, Part 1, Dialogue 2) that no extreme in the contemplation of God and his works could violate Aristotle's principle (in the *Nicomachean Ethics*) that virtue consists in avoiding extremes.

702–704. *For wonderful . . . delight:* Several psalms are echoed: e.g., 8:3–4 and 111:4: "he hath made his wonderful works to be remembered."

705–706. *what . . . number:* insists that all things created by God have limits to their comprehension, including the angels and "even the Son, [who] knows not all things absolutely; there being some secret purposes, the knowledge of which the Father has reserved to himself alone" (*Christian Doctrine* 1.5; *Works* 14, 317).

706. *wisdom infinite:* See Prov. 3:19: "The Lord by wisdom hath founded the earth; by understanding hath he established

the heavens." "Wisdom" in this passage was often interpreted as referring to Christ, relating Milton's usage here to the creative Word by which the world is created in 7.208–21.

709. *material mold:* constituent matter

712. *second bidding:* i.e., "Let there be light" (Gen. 1:3); this is the *second bidding* because "in the beginning God created the heaven and the earth (Gen. 1:1); but see lines 1–4 above.

713–719. *order . . . move:* The conception of creation as ending the war of "embryon atoms" in chaos (cf. 2.900, above) by the separating out of the four elements reflects Plato's picture of creation (in the *Timaeus* 30a) as a divine transformation of disorder into order. The idea of an *ethereal quintessence,* or fifth element called ether, rising from chaos to form the imperishable substance of heaven and the stars stems from Ovid's account of the creation (*Metamorphoses* 1.21–27), and from Aristotle's account in *On the Heavens* (1.3.270b).

717. *spirited with:* animated by

That rolled orbicular° and turned to stars   *in spherical orbits*
Numberless, as thou seest, and how they move.
Each had his place appointed, each his course;   720
The rest in circuit walls this universe.
Look downward on that globe whose hither side
With light from hence, though but reflected, shines;
That place is earth, the seat of man; that light
His day, which else, as the other hemisphere,   725
Night would invade, but there the neighboring moon
(So call that opposite fair star) her aid
Timely interposes, and her monthly round
Still ending, still renewing through midheaven,
With borrowed light her countenance triform   730
Hence fills and empties to enlighten the earth,
And in her pale dominion checks the night.
That spot to which I point is Paradise,
Adam's abode; those lofty shades his bower.
Thy way thou canst not miss; me mine requires."   735
     Thus said, he turned, and Satan, bowing low,
As to superior spirits is wont in Heaven,
Where honor due and reverence none neglects,
Took leave and, toward the coast° of earth beneath,   *side*
Down from the ecliptic, sped with hoped success,   740
Throws his steep flight in many an airy wheel,
Nor stayed, till on Niphates' top he lights.

The End of the Third Book.

721. *in circuit:* orbiting an outer sphere
723. *hence:* from here (i.e., the sun)
730. *triform:* having three aspects, as in Horace's phrase "triform goddess," recognizing the moon's three visible phases and its personification as three separate divinities—Luna, Diana, and Hecate (*Odes* 3.22.4); see also Ovid's invocation of the "triple power" of the moon (*Metamorphoses* 7.177, trans. Sandys).
731. *Hence:* i.e., from the sun
732. *checks:* restrains, holds in check (but possibly also "dapples," "adds variegated colors")
736–737. *Satan, bowing . . . Heaven:* Clearly there are hierarchies that are observed in Heaven.

740. *Down . . . ecliptic:* Satan now plunges earthward from the *ecliptic,* the sun's orbit around the earth in the Ptolemaic astronomy, and from the sun itself, where he has been talking with Uriel; cf. lines 617–21 above.
741. *Throws . . . wheel:* adjusts his flight with a series of loops; cf. Satan "circling," 9.65. Atalante's hippogriff similarly flies *con larghe ruote* (with large circles) before landing to pursue Bradamante in Ariosto's *Orlando Furioso* (4.24).
742. *on Niphates' top:* Mount *Niphates* was in the Taurus range in Armenia, near Assyria, as Milton says in 4.126.

BOOK 4

The Argument

Satan, now in prospect of Eden and nigh the place where he must now attempt the bold enterprise which he undertook alone against God and man, falls into many doubts with himself and many passions: fear, envy, and despair; but at length confirms himself in evil, journeys on to Paradise, whose outward prospect and situation is described, overleaps the bounds, sits in the shape of a cormorant on the Tree of Life, as highest in the garden, to look about him. The garden described; Satan's first sight of Adam and Eve: his wonder at their excellent form and happy state but with resolution to work their fall; overhears their discourse, thence gathers that the Tree of Knowledge was forbidden them to eat of, under penalty of death, and thereon intends to found his temptation by seducing them to transgress; then leaves them awhile, to know further of their state by some other means. Meanwhile Uriel, descending on a sunbeam, warns Gabriel, who had in charge the gate of Paradise, that some evil spirit had escaped the deep and passed at noon by his sphere in the shape of a good angel down to Paradise, discovered after by his furious gestures in the Mount. Gabriel promises to find him ere morning. Night coming on, Adam and Eve discourse of going to their rest; their bower described; their evening worship. Gabriel, drawing forth his bands of night-watch to walk the round of Paradise, appoints two strong angels to Adam's bower, lest the evil spirit should be there doing some harm to Adam or Eve sleeping; there they find him at the ear of Eve, tempting her in a dream, and bring him, though unwilling, to Gabriel; by whom questioned, he scornfully answers, prepares resistance, but, hindered by a sign from Heaven, flies out of Paradise.

O for that warning voice, which he who saw
The Apocalypse heard cry in Heaven aloud
Then, when the dragon, put to second rout,

1–3. *O . . . Then:* A wish for a *warning voice* now, like that which John heard in heaven in his vision of the last days; see Rev. 12:7–9.

2. *The Apocalypse:* the Greek title of the book of Revelation, meaning "the unveiling"

3. *dragon, put to second rout:* See Rev. 12:7–9, where John prophesies war in Heaven (which will end with the *second rout* of Satan, after his initial fall): "And there was war in heaven: Michael and his angels fought against the dragon; and the dragon fought

Came furious down to be revenged on men—
"Woe to the inhabitants on earth"—that now,   5
While time was, our first parents had been warned
The coming of their secret foe and scaped,
Haply so scaped, his mortal snare; for now
Satan, now first inflamed with rage, came down,
The tempter ere the accuser of mankind,   10
To wreak° on innocent frail man his loss   *avenge*
Of that first battle and his flight to hell;
Yet not rejoicing in his speed, though bold
Far off and fearless, nor with cause to boast,
Begins his dire attempt which, nigh the birth   15
Now rolling, boils in his tumultuous breast
And like a devilish engine back recoils
Upon himself; horror and doubt distract
His troubled thoughts and from the bottom stir
The hell within him, for within him hell   20
He brings, and round about him, nor from hell
One step no more than from himself can fly
By change of place. Now conscience wakes despair
That slumbered, wakes the bitter memory
Of what he was, what is, and what must be   25
Worse; of worse deeds worse sufferings must ensue.

and his angels. . . . And the great dragon was cast out, that old serpent, called the Devil, and Satan, which deceiveth the whole world: he was cast out into the earth, and his angels were cast out with him."

5. *Woe . . . earth:* See Rev. 12:12: "Woe to the inhabiters of the earth . . . for the devil is come down unto you, having great wrath, because he knoweth that he hath but a short time."

6. *While time was:* while there was still time

10. *accuser:* betrayer; but translates the Greek *diabolus*; cf. Rev. 12.10: "the accuser of our brethren is cast down."

11. *his:* i.e., Satan's

15–16. *nigh . . . rolling:* which now moving to its inception

17. *devilish engine:* i.e., cannon; see 6.518 (but also, diabolical plot, which also *back recoils* on its inventor; see 1.50).

18. *distract:* 1) draw in different directions; 2) drive mad

20–23. *The hell . . . place:* The most famous of many assertions of the doctrine is by Marlowe's Mephistopheles: "Hell hath no limits, nor is circumscribed / In any one self place; for where we are is hell, / And where hell is, there must we ever be" (*Doctor Faustus*, [2.1], lines 513–5). Similarly Bonaventura said that "the devils carry the fire of hell wherever they go" (*Sentences* 2.d.6.2), and Thomas Aquinas declared (*Summa Theologica* 1, q. 64, art. 4) that they are "bound with the fire of hell while they are in the dark atmosphere of this world." Cf. 1.255 and 6.181.

24–26. *memory . . . worse:* Cf. Francesca's cry to Dante: "No greater pain than the recollection of happiness in misery" (*Inferno* 5.121–22). The commonplace may derive from Book 2 of Boethius' *Consolation*

Sometimes toward Eden, which now in his view
Lay pleasant, his grieved look he fixes sad,
Sometimes toward Heaven and the full-blazing sun,
Which now sat high in his meridian° tower;   *noon*
Then much revolving, thus in sighs began:
    "O thou that, with surpassing glory crowned,
Look'st from thy sole dominion like the god
Of this new world, at whose sight all the stars
Hide their diminished heads, to thee I call,   35
But with no friendly voice, and add thy name,
O sun, to tell thee how I hate thy beams
That bring to my remembrance from what state
I fell, how glorious once above thy sphere,
Till pride and worse ambition threw me down,   40
Warring in Heaven against Heaven's matchless king.
Ah wherefore? He deserved no such return
From me, whom he created what I was
In that bright eminence, and with his good
Upbraided none; nor was his service hard.   45
What could be less than to afford him praise,
The easiest recompense, and pay him thanks,
How due? Yet all his good proved ill in me
And wrought but malice; lifted up so high
I 'sdained° subjection and thought one step higher   *disdained*
Would set me highest and, in a moment, quit°   *cancel*
The debt immense of endless gratitude,
So burdensome, still° paying, still to owe,   *continually*
Forgetful what from him I still received

---

of Philosophy, which Chaucer renders: "The worste kynde of infortune is this, / A man to han ben in prosperitee, / And it remembren, when it passed is" (*Troilus and Criseyde* 3, 1626–28).

    27–28. *Eden . . . pleasant:* The word "Eden" derives from the Hebrew word for "delight"; cf. *grieved* and *sad*.

    31. *revolving:* pondering (turning over thoughts in his mind); "much" can either be an adverb or a noun, the object of *revolving*

    32–41. *O thou . . . king:* For Edward Phillips' statement that these lines were written "several years before the poem was begun," and intended for a tragedy on the fall, see his "Life of Milton," on pp. 420–21

below. Their resemblance to the openings of Euripides' *Phoenissae* and Aeschylus' *Prometheus Bound* cannot have been accidental.

    33. *sole:* unique, but suggests "sol," the sun

    37. *hate thy beams:* See John 3:20: "Every one that doeth evil hateth the light."

    43. *whom he created what I was:* The admission here undercuts his justification of the revolt; if he is created by God, he cannot be God's equal (see 1.40 and 5.794–96), hence his insistence at 5.860 that the angels are "self-begot."

    45. *Upbraided none:* Cf. James 1:5: "God, that giveth to all men liberally, and upbraideth not."

And understood not that a grateful mind   55
By owing° owes not but still pays, at once   *acknowledging*
Indebted and discharged; what burden then?
O had his powerful destiny ordained
Me some inferior angel, I had stood
Then happy; no unbounded hope had raised   60
Ambition. Yet why not? Some other power°   *celestial being*
As great might have aspired and me, though mean,
Drawn to his part; but other powers as great
Fell not, but stand unshaken from within
Or from without, to all temptations armed.   65
Hadst thou the same free will and power to stand?
Thou hadst. Whom hast thou then or what to accuse,
But Heaven's free love dealt equally to all?
Be then his love accursed, since, love or hate,
To me alike, it deals eternal woe.   70
Nay, cursed be thou, since against his thy will
Chose freely what it now so justly rues.
Me miserable! Which way shall I fly
Infinite wrath and infinite despair?
Which way I fly is hell; myself am hell,   75
And in the lowest deep a lower deep
Still threatening to devour me opens wide,
To which the hell I suffer seems a Heaven.
O then at last relent; is there no place
Left for repentance, none for pardon left?   80
None left but by submission, and that word
Disdain forbids me, and my dread of shame
Among the spirits beneath, whom I seduced
With other promises and other vaunts
Than to submit, boasting I could subdue   85
The omnipotent. Ay me, they little know
How dearly I abide that boast so vain,

---

56. *still:* nevertheless
59. *stood:* 1) remained; 2) stood faithful
62. *mean:* low-ranking, unimportant
66–72. *Hadst . . . rues:* Cf. God's statement that the devils fell "freely" (3.102) and Raphael's insistence on the free obedience of the good angels (5.525–40).
66, 67, 71. *thou:* i.e., Satan
75. *Which . . . am hell:* Cf. 1.255, 9.122–23, and especially line 20 above.

79. *at last relent:* Milton's God denies the possibility of forgiveness for Satan and the fallen angels; see 3.129–32 and 5.615.
79–80. *no . . . repentance:* echoes Hebrews 12:17, speaking of Esau, who "found no place of repentance, though he sought it carefully with tears"
81. *that word:* i.e., submission
87. *abide:* 1) live with; 2) suffer for

Under what torments inwardly I groan;
While they adore me on the throne of hell
With diadem° and scepter high advanced,   *crown*
The lower still I fall, only supreme
In misery; such joy ambition finds.
But say I could repent and could obtain
By act of grace my former state: how soon
Would height recall high thoughts, how soon unsay   95
What feigned submission swore; ease would recant
Vows made in pain as violent and void,
For never can true reconcilement grow
Where wounds of deadly hate have pierced so deep,
Which would but lead me to a worse relapse   100
And heavier fall. So should I purchase dear
Short intermission bought with double smart.
This knows my punisher; therefore as far
From granting he, as I from begging, peace;
All hope excluded thus, behold, instead   105
Of us outcast, exiled, his new delight
Mankind created, and for him this world.
So farewell hope and, with hope, farewell fear;
Farewell remorse. All good to me is lost.
Evil be thou my good; by thee at least   110
Divided empire with Heaven's king I hold,
By thee, and more than half perhaps will reign,°   *govern*
As man ere long and this new world shall know."
         Thus while he spake, each passion° dimmed his face,   *emotion*
Thrice changed with pale—ire, envy, and despair—   115
Which marred his borrowed visage and betrayed
Him counterfeit, if any eye beheld,
For Heavenly minds from such distempers foul
Are ever clear. Whereof he soon aware,
Each perturbation smoothed with outward calm,   120

94. *act of grace:* formal pardon
97. *violent:* not voluntary, extorted by force
102. *double smart:* multiplied pain
110. *Evil be thou my good:* But compare Isa. 5:20: "Woe unto them that call evil good, and good evil." Cf. 1.165 and 9.122–23.
110, 112. *By thee:* i.e., by evil
115. *pale:* pallor; it is perhaps tempting to read "pale ire," but Satan's face is *Thrice changed with pale*, paling as each of the three passions, *ire, envy, and despair*, registers on it. Cf. *Faerie Queene* 1.916: "his visage wexed pale, / And chaunge of hew great passion did bewray."
116. *his borrowed visage:* i.e., that of a "stripling cherub" at 3.636
118. *distempers:* diseases or disorders (from an improper mixture of humors)

Artificer of fraud, and was the first
That practiced falsehood under saintly show,
Deep malice to conceal, couched° with revenge;   *which lay hidden*
Yet not enough had practiced to deceive
Uriel once warned, whose eye pursued him down   125
The way he went and on the Assyrian mount
Saw him disfigured more than could befall
Spirit of happy sort; his gestures fierce
He marked and mad demeanor, then alone,
As he supposed, all unobserved, unseen.   130
So on he fares and to the border comes
Of Eden, where delicious Paradise,
Now nearer, crowns with her enclosure green,
As with a rural mound the champaign° head   *level, open country*
Of a steep wilderness, whose hairy sides   135
With thicket overgrown, grotesque and wild,
Access denied; and overhead up grew
Insuperable height of loftiest shade,
Cedar, and pine, and fir, and branching palm,
A sylvan scene, and as the ranks ascend   140
Shade above shade, a woody theater
Of stateliest view. Yet higher than their tops
The verdurous° wall of Paradise up sprung,   *green, overgrown with plants*
Which to our general sire gave prospect large

121. *Artificer of fraud:* Satan as "father of lies." Cf. 3.683.

126. *Assyrian mount:* Mount Niphates; see 3.742.

129. *He:* i.e., Uriel

130, 131. *he:* i.e., Satan

132–135. *Eden . . . wilderness:* Milton's Eden exists as an enclosed garden (the etymological meaning of "paradise") on the plateau (*champaign head*) at the top of a *steep,* heavily wooded hill. The *delicious Paradise* takes its name from the *hortus deliciarum,* as the early Church fathers defined paradise, which, in the King James translation, becomes "the garden of Eden." Milton's synthetic details owe something to the "divine forest" of Dante's Earthly Paradise crowning the Mount of Purgatory (*Purgatorio* 28.2), and something more to Spenser's Garden of Adonis: "With mountains rownd

about environed, / And mightie woodes, which did the valley shade, / And like a stately theatre it made" (*Faerie Queene* 3.6.39).

136. *grotesque:* with tangled branches; the form of the word is French though it originally comes from the Italian *grotto,* a cave. In Milton's time it referred mainly to painting or sculpture in which tangled foliage was often prominent.

137. *Access denied:* It is *access* from below to Eden that it is *denied* by the *steep wilderness* that grows on the hill on the top of which the garden sits.

140. *sylvan scene:* echoes Virgil's "*silvis scaena*" (*Aeneid* 1.164), but picks up a specific theatrical sense from "woody theater" in line 141

144. *general sire:* i.e., Adam, the father of the race (*general* derives from Latin *genus* = race, stock)

Into his nether empire neighboring round.   145
And higher than that wall a circling row
Of goodliest trees loaden with fairest fruit,
Blossoms and fruits at once of golden hue
Appeared with gay enameled° colors mixed,   *lustrous, bright*
On which the sun more glad impressed his beams   150
Than in fair evening cloud or humid bow,
When God hath showered the earth; so lovely seemed
That landscape. And of° pure now purer air   *from*
Meets his approach and to the heart inspires°   *breathes in*
Vernal delight and joy, able to drive°   *drive away*
All sadness but despair. Now gentle gales°   *winds (not storms)*
Fanning their odoriferous wings dispense
Native perfumes and whisper whence they stole
Those balmy spoils. As when to them who sail
Beyond the Cape of Hope and now are past   160
Mozambique, off at sea northeast winds blow
Sabean odors from the spicy shore
Of Araby the blessed, with such delay
Well pleased they slack their course, and many a league
Cheered with the grateful° smell old Ocean smiles,   *pleasing*
So entertained° those odorous sweets the fiend   *received*
Who came their bane, though with them better pleased
Than Asmodeus with the fishy fume
That drove him, though enamored, from the spouse

151. *humid bow:* rainbow (anticipates 11.865–67)

158. *Native perfumes:* sweet smells occurring naturally in Paradise (and not luxury imports, as in 17th-century England)

158–159. *whisper . . . spoils:* Perhaps because the sibilant at the end of "paradise" sounds like the breeze.

160. *Cape of Hope:* the Cape of Good Hope

161. *Mozambique:* In Milton's time, a province of Portuguese East Africa and its island capital, off the southeast coast of Africa. It was so fertile that "all the Armadas and Fleetes that sayle from Portugall to the Indies, if they cannot finish and performe their Voyage, will goe and Winter. . . in this Iland of Mozambique" (Samuel Purchas, *Pilgrimes* [1625] Part 2, p. 1023).

162. *Sabean:* from Sheba (Saba), modern Yemen

163. *Araby the blessed:* Arabia Felix, modern Yemen, the land described by the Greek historian Diodorus as swept by winds that "waft the air from off that land, perfumed with sweet odours of myrrh and other odoriferous plants, to the adjacent parts of the sea" (*Library of History,* 3.44)

165. *old Ocean:* Oceanus, one of the Titans, and, according to Homer, father of the Olympian gods (*Iliad* 14.201 ff.)

167. *bane:* poison; in Old English the word means "murderer."

168–171. *Asmodeus . . . bound:* In the apocryphal book of Tobit, *Tobit's son* (Tobias) travels to Media where he marries Sarah, who had previously lost seven husbands, all murdered on her wedding nights

Of Tobit's son and with a vengeance sent   170
From Media post to Egypt, there fast bound.
      Now to the ascent of that steep savage hill
Satan had journeyed on, pensive and slow,
But further way found none, so thick entwined,
As one continued brake,° the undergrowth   *thicket*
Of shrubs and tangling bushes had perplexed
All path of man or beast that passed that way.
One gate there only was, and that looked east
On the other side, which when the arch-felon saw
Due entrance he disdained and, in contempt,   180
At one slight bound high overleaped all bound
Of hill or highest wall, and sheer within
Lights on his feet. As when a prowling wolf,
Whom hunger drives to seek new haunt for prey,
Watching where shepherds pen their flocks at eve   185
In hurdled cotes amid the field secure,
Leaps o'er the fence with ease into the fold,
Or, as a thief bent to unhoard the cash
Of some rich burgher,° whose substantial doors   *citizen*
Cross-barred and bolted fast fear no assault,   190
In at the window climbs or o'er the tiles,
So clomb this first grand thief into God's fold;
So since into his Church lewd hirelings climb.

by her demon lover *Asmodeus* (or Asmadai, as he is called in 6.365). He would also have slain Tobias, if the angel Raphael had not instructed the youth to burn the heart and liver of a fish in his chamber, "The which smell when the evil spirit has smelled, he fled into the utmost parts of Egypt, and the angel bound him" (Tobit 8:3).

172. *savage:* here mainly in its original sense of "woody" or "wild" (from Italian *selvaggio,* Latin *silvaticus*) and means simply that the hill was covered with trees

176. *had perplexed:* would have entangled (Latin *plectare* = to braid)

178. *east:* It was on the "east of the garden of Eden" (Genesis 3:24) that God posted the cherubs to prevent Adam and Even from re-entering it after their banishment.

182. *sheer:* entirely (but also with the sense of perpendicularly, i.e., straight up and down)

183–193. *As when . . . climb:* John's warning that "he that entereth not by the door into the sheepfold, but climbeth up some other way, the same is a thief and a robber" (John 10:1) underlies the passage as clearly as it does in Milton's "Lycidas," lines 114–15: "such as for their bellies sake, / Creep and intrude, and climb into the fold."

186. *hurdled cotes:* fenced-in enclosures

188. *unhoard:* i.e., steal (remove from a hoard)

192. *clomb:* archaic past tense of "climb"

193. *lewd hirelings:* i.e., unprincipled clergy; Milton in 1659 had written a pamphlet *Considerations Touching the Likeliest Means to Remove Hirelings Out of the Church* as part of his ongoing attack on the mercenary clergy, who devour the "flocks" they should protect.

Thence up he flew and on the Tree of Life,
The middle tree and highest there that grew,   195
Sat like a cormorant, yet not true life
Thereby regained but sat devising death
To them who lived; nor on the virtue° thought   *power, strength*
Of that life-giving plant but only used
For prospect what well used had been the pledge   200
Of immortality. So little knows
Any but God alone to value right
The good before him but perverts best things
To worst abuse or to their meanest use.
Beneath him with new wonder now he views   205
To all delight of human sense exposed
In narrow room nature's whole wealth, yea more,
A Heaven on earth, for blissful Paradise
Of God the garden was, by him in the east
Of Eden planted; Eden stretched her line°   *boundary*
From Auran eastward to the royal towers
Of great Seleucia, built by Grecian kings,
Or where the sons of Eden long before
Dwelt in Telassar. In this pleasant soil
His far more pleasant garden God ordained;   215
Out of the fertile ground he caused to grow
All trees of noblest kind for sight, smell, taste;
And all amid them stood the Tree of Life,
High eminent, blooming° ambrosial fruit   *bearing*

194–195. *Tree of Life . . . grew:* See
Genesis 2:9: "Out of the ground made the
Lord God to grow every tree that is pleasant
to the sight, and good for food; the tree of
life also in the midst of the garden, and the
tree of knowledge of good and evil."

196. *cormorant:* The cormorant (liter-
ally, "crow of the sea") was a traditional sym-
bol of greed and greedy men. See also the
vulture simile in 3.431, and compare the
simile likening Raphael to the phoenix in
5.271–72.

199–200. *only used For prospect:* i.e.,
used only as a perch to look from (rather
than *well used,* as it was intended for Adam
and Eve, as a *pledge* of faithfulness, which
would have maintained their "immortality"
(line 201)

209–210. *by him . . . planted:* "And the
Lord God planted a garden eastward in
Eden; and there he put the man whom he
had formed" (Gen. 2:8). Cf. line 132
above.

211. *Auran:* a province in Canaan, vari-
ously spelled (e.g., Haran and Hauran),
where Abraham once lived (Gen. 11:31).

212. *Seleucia:* Alexander's general Se-
leucus Nicator, founded Seleucia as the seat
of his Greek kingdom in western Asia on the
Tigris, about fifteen miles south of modern
Baghdad.

214. *Telassar:* a city of Eden mentioned
in Isa. 37:12 and in 2 Kings 19:12 (where it
is spelled "Thelasar")

Of vegetable° gold; and next to Life,   *living, growing*
Our death, the Tree of Knowledge, grew fast° by: *near*
Knowledge of good bought dear by knowing ill.
Southward through Eden went a river large,
Nor changed his course but through the shaggy° hill   *heavily wooded*
Passed underneath engulfed, for God had thrown   225
That mountain as his garden mold high raised
Upon the rapid current, which, through veins
Of porous earth with kindly° thirst up drawn,   *natural*
Rose a fresh fountain and with many a rill
Watered the garden; thence united fell   230
Down the steep glade and met the nether flood,
Which from his darksome passage now appears,
And now divided into four main streams
Runs diverse,° wandering many a famous realm   *in various directions*
And country whereof here needs no account,   235
But rather to tell how, if art could tell,
How from that sapphire fount the crispèd° brooks,   *rippling*
Rolling on orient pearl and sands of gold,
With mazy error under pendant shades
Ran nectar, visiting each plant, and fed   240
Flowers worthy of Paradise, which not nice° art,   *delicate, exquisite*
In beds and curious knots, but nature boon°   *bountiful*
Poured forth profuse on hill and dale and plain,
Both where the morning sun first warmly smote
The open field, and where the unpierced shade   245
Embrowned the noontide bowers. Thus was this place,
A happy rural seat of various view:

222. *Knowledge . . . ill:* See the statement in *Areopagitica* (*Works* 4, 311) that "perhaps this is that doom which Adam fell into of knowing good and evil, that is to say, of knowing good by evil."

223. *a river:* i.e., the Tigris (named at 9.71)

226. *garden mold:* top soil, earth good for gardening

227–228. *through . . . drawn:* Before the fall, water is supplied in Eden by being *drawn* up from the earth, rather than by rain; see Gen. 2:6: "there went up a mist from the earth, and watered the whole face of the ground."

229–233. *a fresh fountain . . . streams:*

The passage follows Gen. 2:10: "a river went out of Eden to water the garden: and from thence it was parted, and became into four heads."

237. *sapphire fount:* the "fresh fountain" of line 229, probably blue, reflecting the sky, rather than actually of sapphire

239. *mazy error:* meandering; *error* here only has its Latin force of "wandering." The *OED* cites Ben Jonson's *Discoveries,* calling the wanderings of Aeneas his "error by sea."

242. *curious knots:* complex designs

246. *Embrowned:* darkened, as in 9.1088

247. *of various view:* with views of a variety of landscapes

Groves whose rich trees wept odorous gums and balm,
Others whose fruit burnished with golden rind
Hung amiable (Hesperian fables true,   250
If true, here only) and of delicious taste.
Betwixt them lawns or level downs, and flocks
Grazing the tender herb were interposed,
Or palmy hillock or the flowery lap
Of some irriguous° valley spread her store,   *well watered*
Flowers of all hue and without thorn the rose.
Another side, umbrageous grots and caves
Of cool recess, o'er which the mantling° vine   *enveloping*
Lays forth her purple grape and gently creeps
Luxuriant; meanwhile murmuring waters fall   260
Down the slope hills, dispersed, or in a lake,
That to the fringèd bank with myrtle crowned
Her crystal mirror holds, unite their streams.
The birds their choir apply; airs, vernal airs,
Breathing the smell of field and grove, attune   265
The trembling leaves, while universal Pan
Knit° with the Graces and the Hours in dance   *clasping hands*
Led on the eternal spring. Not that fair field
Of Enna, where Proserpine gathering flowers,
Herself a fairer flower by gloomy Dis   270

250. *Hesperian fables:* the well-known legends of the golden apples of Hesperides, which if eaten conferred immortality; see 3.568.

251. *If true, here only:* i.e., if these fable are true, it is only as they describe Eden

252. *Betwixt them lawns:* between the groves (were) open spaces, glades (not *lawns* in its modern sense as areas of manicured grass)   *downs:* wide tracts of open land

254. *lap:* valley, hollow (*OED* 1.5b), but a mark of the benign, human scale of Eden

256. *without thorn the rose:* a patristic tradition based on Gen. 3:18 held that thorns appeared on the rose only after the fall; see Robert Herrick's epigram, "The Rose": "Before man's fall the Rose was born, / Saint Ambrose says, without the thorn."

257. *umbrageous grots:* shady grottoes

264. *apply:* 1) join; 2) add (to the scene) *airs:* 1) breezes; 2) melodies

266–267. *universal Pan . . . dance:* In Greek, "pan" can mean "all," leading to the elevation of Pan the wood nymph to one *universal Pan,* the god of all nature. The *Graces*—Euphrosyne, Agalaia, and Thalia— are Venus' attendants; the *Hours* are the *horai,* the goddesses who preside over the seasons; cf. the dance of "The Graces and the rosy-bosom'd Hours" in *Comus* line 986.

268–287. *Not . . . strange:* The passage describes four mythical paradises that Milton says cannot be compared with Eden.

268. *eternal spring:* Until the earth tilts on its axis as a result of the fall (see 10.651–91), the seasons do not change.

269–272. *Enna . . . world:* Ovid writes of Proserpine's kidnap by Dis in the Sicilian grove of *Enna* (*Metamorphoses* 5.385–91). The Homeric *Hymn to Demeter* (ninth cen-

Was gathered, which cost Ceres all that pain
To seek her through the world, nor that sweet grove
Of Daphne by Orontes and the inspired
Castalian spring might with this Paradise
Of Eden strive; nor that Nyseian isle   275
Girt with the river Triton, where old Cham,
Whom gentiles Ammon call and Libyan Jove,
Hid Amalthea and her florid son,
Young Bacchus, from his stepdame Rhea's eye;
Nor where Abassin kings their issue° guard,   *children*
Mount Amara, though this by some supposed
True Paradise, under the Ethiop line
By Nilus' head, enclosed with shining rock,
A whole day's journey high, but wide remote
From this Assyrian garden where the fiend   285
Saw undelighted all delight, all kind
Of living creatures new to sight and strange.
Two of far nobler shape, erect and tall,
Godlike erect, with native honor clad
In naked majesty, seemed lords of all,   290
And worthy seemed, for in their looks divine
The image of their glorious maker shone:
Truth, wisdom, sanctitude severe° and pure,   *austere*
Severe, but in true filial freedom placed,
Whence true authority in men, though both   295

tury B.C.) describes Ceres' quest of her
daughter, wandering for nine days and not
eating or drinking as she searched.
    273–274. *Daphne . . . spring:* The gar-
dens of *Daphne* on the *Orontes* River in Syria
had in them a temple dedicated to Apollo
and a *spring* named after the Castalian spring
on Mount Parnassus (cf. 3.30). It was *in-
spired* because its waters traditionally gave
prophetic power.
    275–279. *Nyseian isles . . . eye:* Nysa was
an island in the River Triton near modern
Tunis, where (according to a widely-known
passage in Diodorus' *Library* 3.67) Saturn's
son *Ammon,* fearing the jealousy of his wife,
Rhea, hid his lover, the nymph *Amalthea,*
and their child, *Bacchus.* Ammon was identi-
fied by mythographers with both *Jove* and
Noah's son *Cham* (Ham).

    280. *Abassin:* Abyssinian
    281–284. *Mount Amara . . . high:* Peter
Heylyn, in *Cosmographie* (1652) 4.64, writes
that on top of "The hill of Amara . . . are
thirty-four palaces in which the younger sons
of the emperor are continually enclosed to
avoid sedition: . . . [it is] not much distant
from the Equator if not plainly under it, yet
blessed with such a temperate air that some
have taken it (but mistaken it) for the place
of Paradise." *Ethiop line* = the equator
    283. *Nilus' head:* the head or source of
the Nile
    285. *this Assyrian garden:* i.e., the Gar-
den of Eden
    286. *delight:* "delight" is the meaning of
the Hebrew word "Eden"
    295. *Whence:* i.e., from God

Not equal, as their sex not equal seemed:
For contemplation he and valor formed,
For softness she and sweet attractive grace;
He for God only, she for God in him.
His fair large front and eye sublime declared   300
Absolute rule, and hyacinthine locks
Round from his parted forelock manly hung
Clustering but not beneath his shoulders broad;
She as a veil down to the slender waist
Her unadornèd golden tresses wore   305
Disheveled,° but in wanton ringlets waved   *hanging down*
As the vine curls her tendrils, which implied
Subjection, but required with gentle sway
And by her yielded, by him best received,
Yielded with coy° submission, modest pride,   *shy*
And sweet, reluctant, amorous delay.
Nor those mysterious parts were then concealed;
Then was not guilty shame, dishonest° shame   *unchaste*
Of nature's works, honor dishonorable,
Sin-bred. How have ye troubled all mankind   315
With shows instead, mere shows of seeming pure,
And banished from man's life his happiest life,
Simplicity and spotless innocence!
So passed they naked on, nor shunned the sight
Of God or angel, for they thought no ill;   320
So hand in hand they passed, the loveliest pair
That ever since in love's embraces met:
Adam, the goodliest man of men since born

---

296. *their sex not equal seemed:* Does *seemed* undo the claim of inequality, as many have argued? But see 8.561–78 and 10.145–56. Some editors claim that *equal* only means "identical," but it cannot easily escape its political meaning. See pp. xxxiii–xxxvi above.

300. *large   front:* broad forehead *sublime:* noble (but also "upraised")

301. *hyacinthine:* curled; Homer writes that Odysseus' hair "hung down like hyacinthine petals" (*Odyssey* 6.231).

301–305. *locks . . . wore:* Milton's portraits derive from Paul: "if a man have long hair, it is a shame unto him. . . . But if a woman have long hair, it is a glory unto her:

for her hair is given unto her for a covering" (1 Cor. 11:14–15). Long hair for men was politically coded: Royalists were often attacked in tracts like Thomas Hall's *The Loathsomnesse of Long Haire* (1654).

306. *wanton:* luxuriant, but with no sense of the pejorative meanings that Milton sometimes attaches to it, for example, in line 768

312. *mysterious:* secret (but also with the sense of "sacred")

321. *hand in hand:* Compare the other moments where they are hand in hand, for example, 9.385–86, 9.1037, and 12.648.

323–324. *of men . . . sons:* of all men since born as his descendents

His sons, the fairest of her daughters Eve.
Under a tuft of shade that on a green   325
Stood whispering soft by a fresh fountain side
They sat them down, and after no more toil
Of their sweet gardening labor than sufficed
To recommend cool zephyr and made ease
More easy, wholesome thirst and appetite   330
More grateful, to their supper fruits they fell,
Nectarine fruits, which the compliant boughs
Yielded them, sidelong as they sat recline°   *reclining*
On the soft downy bank damasked with flowers.
The savory pulp they chew and in the rind,   335
Still as they thirsted, scoop the brimming stream;
Nor gentle purpose nor endearing smiles
Wanted,° nor youthful dalliance as beseems   *were lacking*
Fair couple linked in happy nuptial league,
Alone as they. About them frisking played   340
All beasts of the earth, since wild, and of all chase
In wood or wilderness, forest or den;
Sporting the lion ramped and in his paw
Dandled the kid; bears, tigers, ounces,° pards   *lynxes*
Gamboled before them; the unwieldy elephant   345
To make them mirth used all his might and wreathed
His lithe proboscis; close the serpent sly,
Insinuating, wove with Gordian twine
His braided train° and of his fatal guile   *length*
Gave proof unheeded; others on the grass   350

---

324. *the fairest . . . Eve:* Eve, the fairest
of all women born as her daughters

329. *recommend cool zephyr:* make a
cool breeze enjoyable

332. *Nectarine:* filled with (or sweet as)
nectar

334. *damasked:* richly adorned (like
silks from Damascus)

337. *purpose:* conversation; Spenser has
Una and Red Cross sit together and "fitting
purpose frame" (*Faerie Queene* 1.12.13.9).

341. *since wild:* After the fall they will
become wild; see 10.710.   *all chase:*
habitants

343. *ramped:* reared up on hind legs

344. *Dandled the kid:* gently bounced
the baby goat   *pards:* leopards; the
whole scene reflects the image of the peace-
able kingdom derived from Isa. 11:6: "the
leopard shall lie down with the kid; and the
calf and the young lion and the fatling to-
gether."

347. *lithe proboscis:* flexible snout (i.e.,
trunk)

348. *Insinuating:* moving sinuously (in-
evitably suggesting, but here to be rejected,
the sense of "gaining someone's confidence
through devious means")   *Gordian
twine:* convoluted coils like the Gordian
knot that Alexander the Great cut; cf. 9.436.

Couched and, now filled with pasture, gazing sat
Or bedward ruminating, for the sun
Declined was hasting now with prone career
To the Ocean Isles, and in the ascending scale
Of heaven the stars that usher evening rose;   355
When Satan, still in gaze as first he stood,
Scarce thus at length failed speech recovered sad:
    "O hell! What do mine eyes with grief behold?
Into our room of bliss thus high advanced
Creatures of other mold,° earth-born perhaps,   *bodily form*
Not spirits, yet to heavenly spirits bright
Little inferior, whom my thoughts pursue
With wonder, and could love, so lively shines
In them divine resemblance, and such grace
The hand that formed them on their shape hath poured.   365
Ah gentle pair, ye little think how nigh
Your change approaches, when all these delights
Will vanish and deliver ye to woe,
More woe the more your taste is now of joy;
Happy, but for so happy ill secured   370
Long to continue, and this high seat, your heaven,
Ill fenced for Heaven to keep out such a foe
As now is entered; yet no purposed foe
To you whom I could pity thus forlorn,
Though I unpitied. League with you I seek   375
And mutual amity so strait,° so close,   *intimate*
That I with you must dwell, or you with me
Henceforth; my dwelling haply may not please,
Like this fair Paradise, your sense, yet such
Accept your maker's work; he gave it me,   380
Which I as freely give; hell shall unfold
To entertain you two her widest gates
And send forth all her kings; there will be room,

352. *bedward ruminating:* chewing the cud on their way to bed
353. *with prone career:* in a sharp descent
354. *Ocean Isles:* the Azores, as line 592 below indicates, a group of nine islands in the Atlantic west of Portugal.
359. *room:* place; cf. the reference to the "vacant room" left by the fallen angels in 7.190.

361–362. *to heavenly . . . inferior:* Satan paraphrases Psalm 8:5, which says that God has made man "a little lower than the angels and . . . crowned him with glory and honour."
370. *for so happy:* for people as happy as you
379. *your sense:* the object of "please" in line 378   *such:* i.e., hell (Satan's "dwelling," line 378)

Not like these narrow limits, to receive
Your numerous offspring; if no better place,   385
Thank him who puts me, loath to this revenge
On you who wrong me not, for° him who wronged.   *instead of*
And should I at your harmless innocence
Melt,° as I do, yet public reason just,   *weep*
Honor and empire with revenge enlarged   390
By conquering this new world, compels me now
To do what else,° though damned, I should abhor."   *otherwise*
    So spake the fiend and with necessity,
The tyrant's plea, excused his devilish deeds.
Then from his lofty stand on that high tree   395
Down he alights among the sportful herd
Of those four-footed kinds, himself now one,
Now other, as their shape served best his end°   *purpose*
Nearer to view his prey and unespied
To mark what of their state he more might learn   400
By word or action marked. About them round
A lion now he stalks with fiery glare,
Then as a tiger, who by chance hath spied
In some purlieu two gentle fawns at play,
Straight couches close, then rising changes oft   405
His couchant watch, as one who chose his ground
Whence rushing he might surest seize them both
Gripped in each paw, when Adam, first of men,
To first of women, Eve, thus moving speech,

384. *limits:* boundaries (both geographic and moral)

386. *puts me loath:* pushes me reluctantly

389. *public reason:* reason of state; in *The Contra-Replicant* (1643, p. 19) Henry Parker condemned the Royalists for too frequent appeals to "public reason." In the *Advancement of Learning* (1605, 1.2.3), Francis Bacon recalled that its abuse in Italy under the name *ragione di stato* had been condemned by Pius V as an invention "against religion and the moral virtues." In *Adamo Caduto* (1647, 5.2), Serafino Della Salandra has Satan tell the devils that they are going to corrupt mankind by inventing *ragione di stato*.

402–408. *A lion . . . paw:* In Du Bartas' *Divine Weeks* (trans. Sylvester, 1608), Satan, "a mischiefe to effect," transforms himself into various animals before finally assuming the shape of the serpent: "Thinks now the beauty of a Horse to borrow; / Anon to creep into a Haifer's side, / Then in a Cock, or in a Dog to hide; / Then in a nimble Hart himself to shroud; / Then in the starr'd plumes of a Peacock proud" (p. 250). Cf. this image of predatory animals with the peaceable kingdom in lines 339–47.

404. *purlieu:* outlying area (see 2.833)

406. *couchant:* crouching (a heraldic term)

Turned him all ear to hear new utterance flow: 410
    "Sole partner and sole part of all these joys,
Dearer thyself than all, needs must the power
That made us and, for us, this ample world
Be infinitely good, and of his good
As liberal and free as infinite,   415
That raised us from the dust and placed us here
In all this happiness, who at his hand
Have nothing merited nor can perform
Aught whereof he hath need, he who requires
From us no other service than to keep   420
This one, this easy charge, of all the trees
In Paradise that bear delicious fruit
So various, not to taste that only Tree
Of Knowledge, planted by the Tree of Life,
So near grows death to life, whate'er death is,   425
Some dreadful thing no doubt; for well thou know'st
God hath pronounced it death to taste that tree,
The only sign of our obedience left
Among so many signs of power and rule
Conferred upon us, and dominion given   430
Over all other creatures that possess
Earth, air, and sea. Then let us not think hard
One easy prohibition, who enjoy
Free leave so large to all things else and choice
Unlimited of manifold delights;   435
But let us ever praise him and extol
His bounty, following our delightful task
To prune these growing plants and tend these flowers,
Which, were it toilsome, yet with thee were sweet."
    To whom thus Eve replied: "O thou for whom   440
And from whom I was formed flesh of thy flesh,

---

410. *him:* refers to Satan, who is *all ear* to catch what Adam will say

411. *Sole . . . sole:* only . . . unique; see also line 487 below.

414–415. *of his good . . . infinite:* i.e., God's gifts are as generously and freely given as they are never-ending

425. *whate'er death is:* Before the fall they have no knowledge of death; it is for

them only an abstract negative concept ("Some dreadful thing no doubt," line 426; also see 9.695).

430–432. *dominion . . . sea:* See God's words of man at the creation: "Let us make man in our image . . . and let them have dominion over the fish of the sea, and over the fowl of the air, and over the cattle, and over all the earth" (Gen. 1:26).

And without whom am to no end, my guide
And head, what thou hast said is just and right.
For we to him indeed all praises owe
And daily thanks—I chiefly, who enjoy   445
So far the happier lot, enjoying thee
Preeminent by so much odds, while thou
Like° consort to thyself canst no where find.   *similar*
That day I oft remember, when from sleep
I first awaked and found myself reposed   450
Under a shade of flowers, much wondering where
And what I was, whence thither brought and how.
Not distant far from thence a murmuring sound
Of waters issued from a cave and spread
Into a liquid plain, then stood unmoved   455
Pure as the expanse of Heaven; I thither went
With unexperienced thought and laid me down
On the green bank to look into the clear
Smooth lake that to me seemed another sky.
As I bent down to look, just opposite,   460
A shape within the watery gleam appeared,
Bending to look on me; I started back;
It started° back. But pleased I soon returned;   *jumped*
Pleased it returned as soon with answering looks
Of sympathy and love. There I had fixed   465
Mine eyes till now and pined with vain desire
Had not a voice thus warned me: 'What thou seest,
What there thou seest, fair creature, is thyself;
With thee it came and goes; but follow me,
And I will bring thee where no shadow stays   470
Thy coming and thy soft embraces; he
Whose image thou art, him thou shalt enjoy
Inseparably thine, to him shalt bear

---

442. *am to no end:* have no purpose
443. *head:* Cf. Paul: "The head of the woman is the man" (1 Cor. 11:3).
447. *by so much odds:* by such a large difference; but the syntax makes it ambiguous if it is his preeminence or her enjoyment (line 446) that is so superior
457–468. *laid . . . thyself:* This is like Ovid's account of Narcissus lying beside a pool, fascinated by his reflection but pining away because he never learns that what he

sees and loves is himself (*Metamorphoses* 3.402–510); unlike Narcissus, Eve is *warned* (lines 467–68) that what she sees is her *self*.
466. *vain:* futile (but, although the *OED* says the sense of "given to or indulging in personal vanity" can be dated only from 1692, clearly it is also in play here).
470. *shadow:* image (Ovid, *Metamorphoses* 3.417, uses the same word *umbra* = shadow.)   *stays:* waits for (but the meaning "hinders" lurks here).

Multitudes like thyself and thence be called
"Mother of human race."' What could I do   475
But follow straight,° invisibly thus led?   *at once*
Till I espied thee, fair indeed and tall,
Under a platan,° yet methought less fair,   *sycamore (or plane) tree*
Less winning soft, less amiably mild,
Than that smooth watery image; back I turned;   480
Thou, following, cried'st aloud, 'Return, fair Eve;
Whom fly'st thou? Whom thou fly'st, of him thou art,
His flesh, his bone; to give thee being I lent
Out of my side to thee, nearest my heart,
Substantial life to have thee by my side   485
Henceforth an individual solace dear;
Part of my soul I seek thee, and thee claim
My other half.' With that, thy gentle hand
Seized mine; I yielded, and from that time see
How beauty is excelled by manly grace   490
And wisdom, which alone is truly fair."
    So spake our general mother, and, with eyes
Of conjugal attraction unreproved°   *innocent, irreproachable*
And meek surrender, half embracing leaned
On our first father; half her swelling breast   495
Naked met his, under the flowing gold
Of her loose tresses hid. He in delight
Both of her beauty and submissive charms
Smiled with superior love, as Jupiter
On Juno smiles when he impregns the clouds   500
That shed May flowers, and pressed her matron° lip   *wifely*
With kisses pure. Aside the devil turned

475. *Mother . . . race:* Gen. 3:20 says
that "Adam called his wife's name Eve; be-
cause she was the mother of all living."

475–491. *What . . . fair:* Cf. Adam's ac-
count of these events in 8.481–520.

483. *His flesh, his bone:* The phrase
echoes Adam's claim in Gen. 2:23 that Eve is
"bone of my bones, and flesh of my flesh."

486. *individual:* inseparable, indivisible
(though the opposite meaning of the word,
"single" or "singular," generally thought to be
a later development, can also be heard here).

492. *general:* universal, collective (see
line 144 above)

499–500. *Jupiter . . . clouds:* Jupiter,

god of the sky, and Juno, goddess of the air,
allow for a comforting image of union and
fecundity (as in Virgil's *Georgics* 2.325), but
it is not Juno who is impregnated here but *the
clouds,* particularly disturbing since in Pindar
(*Pythian Odes* 2.21 ff.) the monstrous Centau-
rus is born when Ixion, enamored with Hera
(Juno), impregnates a cloud that Zeus
(Jupiter) had shaped to look like his wife.

502–503. *Aside . . . envy:* Satan's envy of
the love of Adam and Eve was traditional.
The devils know desire (but only unfulfilled)
but not love; see lines 509–11. Line 502
marks the first time Milton calls Satan "the
devil."

For envy, yet with jealous leer malign
Eyed them askance, and to himself thus plained:°   *complained*
    "Sight hateful, sight tormenting! Thus these two   505
Imparadised in one another's arms,
The happier Eden, shall enjoy their fill
Of bliss on bliss, while I to hell am thrust,
Where neither joy nor love but fierce desire,
Among our other torments not the least,   510
Still unfulfilled with pain of longing pines;°   *makes me suffer*
Yet let me not forget what I have gained
From their own mouths; all is not theirs it seems:
One fatal tree there stands, of Knowledge called,
Forbidden them to taste. Knowledge forbidden?   515
Suspicious, reasonless. Why should their Lord
Envy them that? Can it be a sin to know?
Can it be death? And do they only stand
By ignorance? Is that their happy state,
The proof of their obedience and their faith?   520
O fair foundation laid whereon to build
Their ruin! Hence I will excite their minds
With more desire to know and to reject
Envious commands, invented with design
To keep them low whom knowledge might exalt   525
Equal with gods; aspiring to be such,
They taste and die; what likelier can ensue?
But first with narrow search I must walk round
This garden and no corner leave unspied;
A chance but chance may lead where I may meet   530
Some wandering spirit of Heaven, by fountain side
Or in thick shade retired, from him to draw
What further would be learned. Live while ye may,
Yet happy pair; enjoy, till I return,
Short pleasures, for long woes are to succeed."   535
    So saying, his proud step he scornful turned,
But with sly circumspection, and began

---

513. *From their own mouths:* i.e., by overhearing what they have said; but the bitter irony here is that what he gains will come *from their own mouths* in a different sense as they bite of the apple (see line 527 below).

521–522. *build Their ruin:* The gleeful paradox of building a ruin points to the fundamental perversity of Satan's ambitions.

526. *Equal with gods:* Cf. Satan's temptation of Eve in 9.547–48, but this is Satan's own ambition; see 1.40.

530. *A chance but chance:* i.e., there is a possibility that luck

Through wood, through waste, o'er hill, o'er dale, his roam.
Meanwhile in utmost longitude, where heaven
With earth and ocean meets, the setting sun   540
Slowly descended and, with right aspect
Against the eastern gate of Paradise,
Leveled his evening rays. It was a rock
Of alabaster, piled up to the clouds,
Conspicuous far, winding with one ascent   545
Accessible from earth, one entrance high;
The rest was craggy cliff that overhung
Still as it rose, impossible to climb.
Betwixt these rocky pillars Gabriel sat,
Chief of the angelic guards, awaiting night;   550
About him exercised heroic games
The unarmed youth of Heaven, but nigh at hand
Celestial armory, shields, helms, and spears,
Hung high with diamond flaming and with gold.
Thither came Uriel, gliding through the ev'n°   *evening*
On a sunbeam, swift as a shooting star
In autumn thwarts the night, when vapors fired
Impress the air, and shows the mariner
From what point of his compass to beware
Impetuous winds; he thus began in haste: 560
  "Gabriel, to thee thy course° by lot hath given   *duty*
Charge and strict watch that to this happy place

539. *utmost longitude:* i.e., the farthest west

541. *with right aspect:* at right angles, with a direct view; the setting sun shines straight upon the inner side of the eastern gate of Paradise.

543–549. *rock . . . sat:* The description of the *rock* is seemingly indebted to Samuel Purchas' account of Mount Amara: "some taking this for our fore-fathers Paradise," which looks "to him that stands beneath, like a high wall, whereon the heaven is as it were propped: & at the top, ouer-hanged with rocks, jutting forth of the sides the space of a mile, bearing out like mushromes, so that it is impossible to ascend it" (*Purchas His Pilgrimage,* 1613, pp. 565–66); *alabaster* is defined in Cockeram's *English Dictionarie* (1623) as "a very cold Marble, white and clear."

545. *Conspicuous far:* capable of being seen from far away

549. *Gabriel:* Though none of the scriptural mentions of Gabriel (Dan. 8:16 and 9:21; and Luke 1:19) implies his "Charge and strict watch" (line 562) of Paradise, perhaps his name, meaning "strength of God," encouraged the tradition (see the apocryphal 1 Enoch 20:7) of his guardianship.

556–560. *swift . . . winds:* Uriel appears as *a shooting star,* which early astronomers explained as an exhalation of vapors that ignite (*vapors fired*) and then in its trajectory marks the sky (*impress the air*), and by many was thought an omen predicting storms (*shows the mariner . . . to beware / Impetuous winds*).

557. *thwarts:* flies across (but also, frustrates)

No evil thing approach or enter in;
This day at height of noon came to my sphere
A spirit, zealous, as he seemed, to know   565
More of the almighty's works, and chiefly man
God's latest image. I described his way
Bent all on speed and marked his airy gait;
But in the mount that lies from Eden north,
Where he first lighted, soon discerned his looks   570
Alien from Heaven, with passions foul obscured.
Mine eye pursued him still, but under shade
Lost sight of him; one of the banished crew,
I fear, hath ventured from the deep to raise
New troubles; him thy care must be to find."   575
    To whom the wingèd warrior thus returned:
"Uriel, no wonder if thy perfect sight,
Amid the sun's bright circle where thou sit'st,
See far and wide. In at this gate none pass
The vigilance here placed but such as come   580
Well known from Heaven, and since meridian hour
No creature thence. If spirit of other sort
So minded have o'erleaped these earthy bounds
On purpose, hard thou know'st it to exclude
Spiritual substance with corporeal bar.°   *barrier, impediment*
But if within the circuit of these walks,
In whatsoever shape, he lurk of whom
Thou tell'st, by morrow dawning I shall know."
    So promised he, and Uriel to his charge
Returned on that bright beam, whose point now raised   590
Bore him slope downward to the sun now fallen
Beneath the Azores, whither the prime orb,
Incredible how swift, had thither rolled
Diurnal° or this less voluble earth   *in a day*

567. *God's latest image:* i.e., man; the first *image* was the Son; cf. 3.63 and 3.384. *described:* saw, descried (it is possible that "descried" is indeed the intended word here; see 9.60).

568. *Bent all:* concentrating totally *airy gait:* 1) path across the sky; 2) angelic means of locomotion

580. *vigilance:* The abstract word stands for the vigilant Gabriel himself.

589–592. *Uriel . . . Azores:* Uriel slides down the sunbeam to the sun, which is now below the western horizon (see "Azores" in line 354 and note) and therefore, at least visibly, lower than the earth (hence its *point now raised*).

592–595. *whither . . . there:* Milton leaves open the question of whether it is the sun or earth that moves.

592. *prime orb:* the sun

594. *voluble:* swiftly rotating

By shorter flight to the east had left him there   595
Arraying with reflected purple and gold
The clouds that on his western throne attend.
Now came still evening on, and twilight gray
Had in her sober livery all things clad;
Silence accompanied, for beast and bird,   600
They to their grassy couch, these to their nests
Were slunk, all but the wakeful nightingale;
She all night long her amorous descant° sung;   *melodious song*
Silence was pleased. Now glowed the firmament
With living sapphires: Hesperus that led   605
The starry host rode brightest, till the moon,
Rising in clouded majesty, at length
Apparent queen, unveiled her peerless light
And o'er the dark her silver mantle threw.
    When Adam thus to Eve: "Fair Consort, the hour   610
Of night and all things now retired to rest
Mind° us of like repose, since God hath set   *remind*
Labor and rest, as day and night, to men
Successive, and the timely dew of sleep
Now falling with soft slumbrous weight inclines   615
Our eyelids. Other creatures all day long
Rove idle unemployed and less need rest;
Man hath his daily work of body or mind
Appointed, which declares his dignity
And the regard of Heaven on all his ways,   620
While other animals unactive range,
And of their doings God takes no account.
Tomorrow ere fresh morning streak the east
With first approach of light, we must be risen
And at our pleasant labor to reform   625
Yon flowery arbors, yonder alleys green,
Our walk at noon, with branches overgrown

---

600. *accompanied:* joined with their company (but with a playful musical sense of "sang or played along with," especially given that it is *Silence;* cf. Silence enchanted by the Lady's music in *Comus* lines 557–60, and in "Il Penseroso" lines 55–56, "the mute Silence" to be broken only by the nightingale's song).

605. *living sapphires:* i.e., the stars shone as brilliant jewels, but see 2.1050; *liv-*ing = natural, uncut   *Hesperus:* Venus, the evening "star"; cf. 9.49.

608. *Apparent:* clearly visible (with a play with "queen" on "heir apparent")

620. *regard:* 1) attention; 2) esteem

623–632. *Tomorrow . . . ease:* Milton's Adam and Eve do not live a purely contemplative life, following Donne, in Sermon 19, "Adam was not put into Paradise, only in that Paradise to contemplate the future Paradise, but to dress and keep the present."

That mock our scant manuring and require
More hands than ours to lop their wanton growth.
Those blossoms also, and those dropping gums,   630
That lie bestrewn unsightly and unsmooth,
Ask riddance if we mean to tread with ease;
Meanwhile, as nature wills, night bids us rest."
　　To whom thus Eve, with perfect beauty adorned:
"My author and disposer, what thou bidd'st   635
Unargued I obey, so God ordains;
God is thy law, thou mine; to know no more
Is woman's happiest knowledge and her praise.
With thee conversing I forget all time,
All seasons and their change; all please alike.   640
Sweet is the breath of morn, her rising sweet
With charm of earliest birds; pleasant the sun
When first on this delightful land he spreads
His orient° beams on herb, tree, fruit, and flower,   *bright*
Glistering with dew; fragrant the fertile earth   645
After soft showers, and sweet the coming on
Of grateful evening mild; then silent night
With this her solemn bird, and this fair moon,
And these the gems of heaven, her starry train;
But neither breath of morn when she ascends   650
With charm of earliest birds, nor rising sun
On this delightful land, nor herb, fruit, flower,
Glistering with dew, nor fragrance after showers,
Nor grateful evening mild, nor silent night
With this her solemn bird, nor walk by moon   655
Or glittering starlight, without thee is sweet.
But wherefore all night long shine these? For whom
This glorious sight, when sleep hath shut all eyes?"
　　To whom our general ancestor replied:
"Daughter of God and man, accomplished Eve,   660
Those have their course to finish, round the earth

---

628. *manuring:* cultivation; the word has its Latin meaning of "working with the hands."

632. *Ask riddance:* ask to be removed

635. *author and disposer:* i.e., originator and supervisor

640. *seasons and their change:* different occasions (not the seasons of the year, which began only after Adam and Eve's fall)

641–656. *Sweet . . . sweet:* A remarkable example of epanadiplosis, a rhetorical figure that begins and ends with the same word

642. *charm:* the blended singing of a group of birds, though not excluding the familiar meanings: "attractiveness" or "appeal," or even "magic spell"

648. *solemn bird:* i.e., the nightingale

657–658. *But . . . eyes:* Eve voices the first human request for knowledge.

660. *accomplished:* 1) full of accomplishments; 2) complete, perfect

By morrow evening, and from land to land
In order, though to nations yet unborn,
Ministering light prepared they set and rise,
Lest total darkness should by night regain   665
Her old possession and extinguish life
In nature and all things, which these soft fires
Not only enlighten but with kindly° heat   *natural*
Of various influence foment and warm,
Temper or nourish, or in part shed down   670
Their stellar virtue on all kinds° that grow   *species*
On earth, made hereby apter to receive
Perfection from the sun's more potent ray.
These then, though unbeheld in deep of night,
Shine not in vain, nor think, though men were none,   675
That Heaven would want spectators, God want praise;
Millions of spiritual creatures walk the earth
Unseen, both when we wake and when we sleep;
All these with ceaseless praise his works behold
Both day and night. How often from the steep   680
Of echoing hill or thicket have we heard
Celestial voices to the midnight air,
Sole or responsive each to others note,
Singing their great creator? Oft in bands
While they keep watch or nightly rounding walk,   685
With heavenly touch of instrumental sounds
In full harmonic number joined, their songs
Divide the night and lift our thoughts to Heaven."
     Thus talking, hand in hand alone they passed
On to their blissful bower; it was a place   690
Chosen by the sovereign planter when he framed°   *fashioned*
All things to man's delightful use; the roof
Of thickest covert was inwoven shade,

---

669. *foment:* warm (*OED* 2: "cherish with heat"), but more generally, nurture

675. *though men were none:* even if there were no people

682–688. *Celestial voices . . . Heaven:* The angelic singers seem like the Muses in Hesiod's *Theogony* 3–21 and 35–52, who sing the greatness of their father Zeus, the earth, and heaven, in ceaseless concert as they mount the cloudy slope of Olympus in the darkness.

685. *rounding:* making their rounds (but inevitably also suggesting singing in rounds)

688. *Divide the night:* mark off the angels' different night-watches (but perhaps also in a musical sense: "perform antiphonally," "in divided choirs")

690. *blissful bower:* Cf. Venus' "blisfull bowre of joy" in Spenser's *Faerie Queene* 3.6.95, and also the "Bower of Bliss" in 2.7.

Laurel and myrtle, and what higher grew
Of firm and fragrant leaf; on either side   695
Acanthus and each odorous bushy shrub
Fenced up the verdant wall; each beauteous flower,
Iris all hues, roses, and jessamine,°   *jasmine*
Reared high their flourished° heads between and wrought   *blossoming*
Mosaic; underfoot the violet,   700
Crocus, and hyacinth with rich inlay
Broidered° the ground more colored than with stone   *decorated, embroidered*
Of costliest emblem. Other creature here,
Beast, bird, insect, or worm, durst enter none;
Such was their awe of man. In shady bower   705
More sacred and sequestered, though but feigned,
Pan or Silvanus never slept, nor Nymph
Nor Faunus haunted. Here in close recess
With flowers, garlands, and sweet-smelling herbs
Espousèd Eve decked first her nuptial bed,   710
And heavenly choirs the hymenaean sung,
What day the genial angel to our sire
Brought her in naked beauty more adorned,
More lovely than Pandora whom the Gods
Endowed with all their gifts, and, O too like   715
In sad event, when to the unwiser son
Of Japhet brought by Hermes, she ensnared
Mankind with her fair looks to be avenged
On him who had stole Jove's authentic° fire.   *original*
Thus at their shady lodge arrived, both stood,   720
Both turned, and under open sky adored
The God that made both sky, air, earth, and heaven

703. *Of costliest emblem:* inlaid with precious metal and gems

706. *feigned:* imagined (implies that myths of "Pan," "Sylvanus," and "Faunus" [lines 707–8], all half-man, half-goat pastoral gods, were merely pagan fabrications)

708. *close recess:* a secluded place

711. *hymenaean:* marriage song (Hymen was the classical god of marriage.)

712. *genial:* "concerned with nuptials or generation" (*OED* 1)

714–719. *Pandora . . . fire:* Pandora, whose name means "all gifts," was given by the gods to Epimetheus, *the unwiser son Of Japhet,* in order *to be avenged on* his brother, Prometheus, for stealing *fire* from the heavens. Epimetheus married Pandora and opened the sealed casket that the gods sent with her, but found it full of all life's ills, which were then released into the world. In classical myth, the brothers were sons of the Titan Iapetos, who was often identified with Noah's son *Japhet* (or Japheth; see Gen. 9:27 and 10:1), the father of Javan, the founder of the Greek race, who is mentioned in 1.508.

Which they beheld, the moon's resplendent globe,
And starry pole: "Thou also mad'st the night,
Maker omnipotent, and thou the day,   725
Which we in our appointed work employed
Have finished happy in our mutual help
And mutual love, the crown of all our bliss
Ordained by thee, and this delicious place,
For us too large, where thy abundance wants   730
Partakers and, uncropped, falls to the ground.
But thou hast promised from us two a race
To fill the earth, who shall with us extol
Thy goodness infinite, both when we wake
And when we seek, as now, thy gift of sleep."   735
      This said unanimous,° and other rites   *with one mind*
Observing none but adoration pure,
Which God likes best, into their inmost bower
Handed° they went and, eased the putting off   *hand in hand*
These troublesome disguises which we wear,   740
Straight side by side were laid, nor turned, I ween,°   *guess, presume*
Adam from his fair spouse, nor Eve the rites
Mysterious of connubial love refused.
Whatever hypocrites austerely talk
Of purity and place° and innocence,   *fitting occasion*
Defaming as impure what God declares
Pure and commands to some, leaves free to all.
Our maker bids increase; who bids abstain

---

724. *pole:* stands here for the entire sky, as it does in *Comus,* line 99

724–735. *Thou . . . sleep:* The passage draws upon Ps. 74:16: "The day is thine, the night also is thine," and Ps. 127:2: "he giveth his beloved sleep"; but the gift of sleep is often mentioned in Homer and Virgil in passages like Aeneas' reference to the quiet of evening coming to bring the most welcome gift of the gods (*Aeneid* 2.269).

739. *eased the putting off:* not needing to remove

742–743. *rites . . . love:* i.e., sex; compare Joseph Beaumont's *Psyche* (1648), 1.203–6: "Except the venerable Temples, what / Place is more reverend than the Nuptial Bed? / Nay, heav'n has made a Temple

too of that / For Chastitie's most secret rites." (*mysterious* = sacred, awe-inspiring)

744–747. *Whatever . . . all:* reflects 1 Tim. 4:1–3: "in the latter times some shall depart from the faith . . . Speaking lies in hypocrisy . . . Forbidding to marry, and commanding to abstain from meats, which God hath created to be received with thanksgiving of them which believe and know the truth."

747. *commands to some:* In 1 Cor. 7:9, Paul enjoins those who are unable to restrain their sexual appetite, to marry, "for it is better to marry than to burn."

748. *Our . . . increase:* i.e., God's command to "Be fruitful, and multiply, and replenish the earth" (Gen. 1:28)

But our destroyer, foe to God and man?
Hail wedded love, mysterious law, true source   750
Of human offspring, sole propriety
In Paradise, of all things common else.
By thee adulterous lust was driven from men
Among the bestial herds to range; by thee
Founded in reason, loyal, just, and pure,   755
Relations dear and all the charities°   *love, kindness*
Of father, son, and brother, first were known.
Far be it that I should write thee sin or blame,
Or think thee unbefitting holiest place,
Perpetual fountain of domestic sweets,°   *pleasures*
Whose bed is undefiled and chaste pronounced,
Present or past, as saints and patriarchs used.
Here Love his golden shafts employs; here lights
His constant lamp and waves his purple° wings,   *brilliant*
Reigns here and revels, not in the bought smile   765
Of harlots, loveless, joyless, unendeared,
Casual fruition,° nor in court amours,   *pleasure (often sexual)*
Mixed dance, or wanton masque, or midnight ball,
Or serenade, which the starved lover sings
To his proud fair, best quitted with disdain.   770
These, lulled by nightingales, embracing slept,
And on their naked limbs the flowery roof
Showered roses, which the morn repaired. Sleep on

750. *mysterious law:* principle both sacred and symbolic; probably derived from Eph. 5:31–2: "For this cause shall a man leave his father and mother, and shall be joined unto his wife, and they two shall be one flesh. This is great mystery: but I speak concerning Christ and the church."

751–752. *sole propriety . . . else:* the one exclusive possession (*propriety* = property) that each holds, since (before the fall) there was no other kind of property

761. *bed is undefiled:* echoes Heb. 13:4: "Marriage is honourable in all, and the bed undefiled."

762. *saints and patriarchs used:* Some saints and many of the Hebrew bible's patriarchs were married, offering further evidence that celibacy is not a requirement of a virtuous life.

763. *Love . . . employs:* Cupid uses his golden arrow; Ovid describes Cupid with an arrow of gold, inspiring love, and another of lead, which banished it (*Metamorphoses* 1.467–70).

768. *Mixed . . . ball:* Cf. Milton's attack on the bishops for encouraging "gaming, jigging, wassailing, and mixed dancing" in *Of Reformation* (*Works* 3, part 1, 53); *Mixed dance* = men and women dancing together; *masque* = a form of richly symbolic and ostentatious court entertainment of the Stuart monarchs

769. *starved:* deprived, pining (the conventional attribute of the lovelorn)

773. *repaired:* restored and replaced in the earth; there is no death, even for decorative flowers, in Eden.

Blessèd pair; and O yet happiest if ye seek
No happier state and know to know no more.   775
    Now had night measured with her shadowy cone
Halfway up hill this vast sublunar vault,
And from their ivory port the cherubim
Forth issuing at the accustomed hour stood armed
To their night watches in warlike parade,   780
When Gabriel to his next in power° thus spake: *rank*
    "Uzziel, half these draw off and coast° the south   *follow the coastline of*
With strictest watch; these other wheel° the north;   *encircle*
Our circuit meets full west." As flame they part,
Half wheeling to the shield, half to the spear.   785
From these, two strong and subtle spirits he called
That near him stood and gave them thus in charge:
    "Ithuriel and Zephon, with winged speed
Search through this garden; leave unsearched no nook,
But chiefly where those two fair creatures lodge,   790
Now laid perhaps asleep secure° of harm.   *with no fear*
This evening from the sun's decline arrived
Who tells of some infernal spirit seen
Hitherward bent° (who could have thought?) escaped   *bound, directed*
The bars of hell, on errand bad no doubt;   795
Such where ye find, seize fast and hither bring."
    So saying, on he led his radiant files,
Dazzling the moon; these to the bower direct
In search of whom they sought; him there they found,
Squat like a toad, close at the ear of Eve,   800
Assaying by his devilish art to reach

---

775. *know to know no more:* be wise
enough to seek no more knowledge (i.e., of
good and evil); cf. 7.120; with the "No" at
the beginning of the line, four monosyllables
sound identically.

776–777. *Now . . . vault:* The cone of
the earth's shadow cast by the sun at an angle
Halfway between the horizon and the zenith
indicates that it is nine o'clock. When the
point of the cone reaches the zenith, it will
be midnight.

778. *ivory port:* gate of ivory; in the
Odyssey (14.562–65), this is the source of
false dreams, or dreams whose "message is
never accomplished."

782. *Uzziel:* means "strength of God"
and occurs in the Bible only as a human
name (Exod. 6:18; and Num. 3:19). For the
angelic names here and in line 788, see
Robert West, "The Names of Milton's An-
gels," *SP* 47 (1950): 211–23.

788. *Ithuriel and Zephon:* The Hebrew
name *Ithuriel* ("discovery of God") does not
occur in the Bible, and *Zephon* ("look-out"
or "searcher") occurs only as a human name
(Num. 26:15).

793. *Who:* i.e., someone who

797. *radiant files:* rows of angels

798. *these:* i.e., Ithuriel and Zephon

The organs of her fancy° and with them forge   *imagination*
Illusions as he list, phantasms and dreams,
Or if, inspiring venom, he might taint
The animal spirits that from pure blood arise   805
Like gentle breaths from rivers pure, thence raise
At least distempered, discontented thoughts,
Vain hopes, vain aims, inordinate desires
Blown up with high conceits engendering pride.
Him thus intent Ithuriel with his spear   810
Touched lightly, for no falsehood can endure
Touch of celestial temper but returns
Of force to its own likeness. Up he starts
Discovered and surprised. As when a spark
Lights on a heap of nitrous powder laid
Fit for the tun some magazine to store
Against a rumored war, the smutty° grain   *black*
With sudden blaze diffused inflames the air,
So started up in his own shape the fiend.
Back stepped those two fair angels half amazed   820
So sudden to behold the grisly king,
Yet thus, unmoved with fear, accost him soon:
   "Which of those rebel spirits adjudged to hell
Com'st thou, escaped thy prison and transformed?
Why sat'st thou like an enemy in wait   825
Here watching at the head of these that sleep?"
   "Know ye not," then said Satan, filled with scorn,
"Know ye not me? Ye knew me once no mate
For you, there sitting where ye durst not soar;
Not to know me argues° yourselves unknown,   *proves*
The lowest of your throng; or if ye know,

---

804. *inspiring venom:* breathing venom into [her]

805. *animal spirits . . . arise:* Elizabethan psychology identified three sources of motivation: animal (i.e., spiritual, from Latin *anima* = soul), natural, and vital spirits. Animal spirits, transmitted through the blood, as Robert Burton explained (*Anatomy of Melancholy* 1.1.2.2), "brought up to the brain, and diffused by the nerves, to the subordinate members, give sense and motion to them all."

809. *high conceits:* ambitious notions

812. *celestial temper:* i.e., Ithuriel's spear (line 810), tempered in celestial ether (see 2.813) though also *temper* as temperament (and contrasted with Satan's "distempered" thoughts, line 807)

815. *nitrous powder:* gunpowder

815–817. *laid . . . Against:* ready for use (*Fit for the tun*), an ammunition dump (*magazine*) stored up in anticipation of

828. *no mate:* no equal (i.e., superior)

Why ask ye and superfluous° begin   *with superfluous words*
Your message, like to end as much in vain?"
To whom thus Zephon, answering scorn with scorn:
"Think not, revolted spirit, thy shape the same,   835
Or undiminished brightness, to be known
As when thou stood'st in Heaven upright and pure;
That glory then, when thou no more wast good,
Departed from thee, and thou resemblest now
Thy sin and place of doom obscure and foul.   840
But come, for thou, be sure, shalt give account
To him who sent us, whose charge is to keep
This place inviolable and these from harm."
    So spake the cherub, and his grave rebuke
Severe in youthful beauty added grace   845
Invincible. Abashed the devil stood,
And felt how awful goodness is, and saw
Virtue in her shape how lovely, saw, and pined°   *suffered for*
His loss, but chiefly to find here observed
His luster visibly impaired, yet seemed   850
Undaunted. "If I must contend," said he,
"Best with the best, the sender not the sent,
Or all at once; more glory will be won,
Or less be lost." "Thy fear," said Zephon bold,
"Will save us trial what the least can do   855
Single against thee wicked, and thence weak."
    The fiend replied not, overcome with rage,
But, like a proud steed reined, went haughty on,
Champing his iron curb. To strive or fly
He held it vain; awe from above had quelled   860
His heart, not else dismayed. Now drew they nigh
The western point, where those half-rounding guards
Just met and closing stood in squadron joined,
Awaiting next command. To whom their chief,
Gabriel, from the front thus called aloud: 865
    "O friends, I hear the tread of nimble feet

840. *obscure:* has its Latin force, "dark"
(but also, and more galling to Satan, "un-
known")
843. *these:* the sleeping Adam and Eve
847. *awful:* awe-inspiring (as at line
960)
856. *Single:* alone, in single combat

862. *half-rounding:* completing the half-
circle of the garden, some having swung
north, the others south, so as to meet in the
west
866. *I hear . . . feet:* Compare *Comus*: "I
hear the tread / of hateful steps" (lines
91–92)

Hasting this way and now by glimpse discern
Ithuriel and Zephon through the shade,°   *trees*
And with them comes a third, of regal port°   *bearing*
But faded splendor wan, who, by his gait   870
And fierce demeanor seems the prince of hell,
Not likely to part hence without contest;
Stand firm, for in his look defiance lours."
    He scarce had ended, when those two approached
And brief related whom they brought, where found,   875
How busied, in what form and posture couched.
    To whom with stern regard thus Gabriel spake:
"Why hast thou, Satan, broke the bounds prescribed
To thy transgressions and disturbed the charge
Of others, who approve° not to transgress   *recommend themselves*
By thy example but have power and right
To question thy bold entrance on this place,
Employed it seems to violate sleep and those
Whose dwelling God hath planted here in bliss?"
    To whom thus Satan with contemptuous brow: 885
"Gabriel, thou hadst in Heaven the esteem of wise,
And such I held thee; but this question asked
Puts me in doubt. Lives there who loves his pain?
Who would not, finding way, break loose from hell,
Though thither doomed? Thou wouldst thyself, no doubt,   890
And boldly venture to whatever place
Farthest from pain, where thou might'st hope to change
Torment with ease and soonest recompense
Dole° with delight, which in this place I sought.   *sorrow, pain*
To thee no reason, who know'st only good   895
But evil hast not tried. And wilt object
His will who bound us? Let him surer bar
His iron gates if he intends our stay
In that dark durance:° thus much what was asked.   *imprisonment*
The rest is true: they found me where they say,   900

---

876. *couched:* hidden (see line 123 above)

879. *transgressions:* sins (but also boundary violations) *charge:* i.e., Adam and Eve, with whose protection Gabriel's troop is charged

886. *esteem of wise:* reputation for wisdom

895. *To thee no reason:* Avoiding pain is not a reason that Gabriel would understand, since he has never felt it.

896. *object:* raise the objection (that the devils are confined to hell by God's will)

899. *thus . . . asked:* i.e., this is all I have to say in answer to what was asked

But that implies not violence or harm."
    Thus he in scorn. The warlike angel, moved,°   *moved to anger*
Disdainfully half-smiling thus replied:
"O loss of one in Heaven to judge of wise
Since Satan fell, whom folly overthrew,   905
And now returns him from his prison scaped,
Gravely in doubt whether to hold them wise
Or not who ask what boldness brought him hither
Unlicensed from his bounds in hell prescribed;
So wise he judges it to fly from pain,   910
However,° and to scape his punishment.   *by whatever means*
So judge thou still, presumptuous, till the wrath
Which thou incurr'st by flying meet thy flight
Sevenfold, and scourge that wisdom back to hell,
Which taught thee yet no better, that no pain   915
Can equal anger infinite provoked.
But wherefore° thou alone? Wherefore with thee   *why*
Came not all hell broke loose? Is pain to them
Less pain, less to be fled, or thou than they
Less hardy to endure? Courageous chief,   920
The first in flight from pain, hadst thou alleged
To thy deserted host this cause of flight,
Thou surely hadst not come sole fugitive."
    To which the fiend thus answered, frowning stern:
"Not that I less endure or shrink from pain,   925
Insulting angel; well thou know'st I stood
Thy fiercest when in battle to thy aid
The blasting volleyed thunder made all speed
And seconded thy else° not dreaded spear.   *otherwise*
But still thy words at random, as before,   930
Argue thy inexperience what behooves
From hard assays° and ill successes past   *attacks*

904. *O loss:* O what a loss (to lose such a judge of what is wise as Satan)

906. *him:* himself (i.e., Satan), though it also can be the object of "returns" with "folly" as the subject

914. *Sevenfold:* Probably echoing Gen. 4:15: "vengeance shall be taken on him sevenfold."

926. *stood:* withstood or confronted, stood up against; a flashback in time but a look forward in the poem to the battle in heaven in 6.56–879

927. *Thy fiercest:* your fiercest assault

928–929. *The blasting . . . seconded:* i.e., the volleys of God's powerful thunder rushed to your aid and strengthened

930. *at random:* to no purpose, wide of the mark

932. *From:* after

A faithful leader: not to hazard all
Through ways of danger by himself untried.
I therefore, I alone first undertook   935
To wing the desolate abyss and spy
This new created world, whereof in hell
Fame° is not silent, here in hope to find   *rumor*
Better abode, and my afflicted powers
To settle here on earth or in mid air;   940
Though for possession put to try once more
What thou and thy gay legions dare against,
Whose easier business were to serve their Lord
High up in Heaven with songs to hymn his throne
And practiced distances to cringe, not fight."   945
  To whom the warrior angel soon replied:
"To say and straight unsay, pretending first
Wise to fly pain, professing next the spy,
Argues no leader but a liar traced,°   *discovered*
Satan; and could'st thou 'faithful' add? O name,   950
O sacred name of faithfulness profaned!
Faithful to whom? To thy rebellious crew?
Army of fiends; fit body to fit head!
Was this your discipline and faith engaged,
Your military obedience, to dissolve   955
Allegiance to the acknowledged power supreme?
And thou, sly hypocrite, who now wouldst seem
Patron of liberty, who more than thou
Once fawned, and cringed, and servilely adored
Heaven's awful monarch? Wherefore but in hope   960
To dispossess him and thyself to reign?
But mark what I aread° thee now: avaunt;   *advise*
Fly thither whence thou fled'st. If from this hour
Within these hallowed limits thou appear,
Back to the infernal pit I drag thee chained   965
And seal thee so, as henceforth not to scorn
The facile gates of hell too slightly barred."

939. *afflicted powers:* defeated armies; echoes Satan's "afflicted powers" in 1.186

940. *mid air:* Satan is called the "prince of the power of the air" in Eph. 2:2.

941. *put to try:* forced to test

942. *gay:* ostentatious (compare the "bright legions" at 6.64)

945. *practiced distances:* with customary deferential behavior

958. *Patron:* advocate, supporter; cf. the similar use of *Patron* in 3.219.

962. *avaunt:* be gone

967. *facile:* easily opened; see 2.874–84.

So threatened he, but Satan to no threats
Gave heed but waxing more in rage replied:
    "Then, when I am thy captive, talk of chains,   970
Proud limitary cherub, but ere then
Far heavier load thyself expect to feel
From my prevailing arm, though Heaven's king
Ride on thy wings, and thou with thy compeers,
Used to the yoke, draw'st his triumphant wheels   975
In progress° through the road of Heaven star-paved."   *triumphal procession*
    While thus he spake, the angelic squadron bright
Turned fiery red, sharpening in moonèd horns
Their phalanx and began to hem him round
With ported spears, as thick as when a field   980
Of Ceres, ripe for harvest, waving bends
Her bearded grove of ears which way the wind
Sways them; the careful° plowman doubting stands,   *anxious*
Lest on the threshing floor his hopeful sheaves
Prove chaff. On the other side Satan alarmed,   985
Collecting all his might, dilated stood
Like Tenerife or Atlas unremoved;
His stature reached the sky, and on his crest
Sat horror plumed, nor wanted in his grasp
What seemed both spear and shield. Now dreadful deeds   990
Might have ensued; nor only Paradise
In this commotion, but the starry cope°   *canopy, cover*
Of heaven perhaps, or all the elements
At least had gone to wrack, disturbed and torn
With violence of this conflict, had not soon   995
The eternal, to prevent such horrid fray,
Hung forth in heaven his golden scales, yet seen

969. *waxing more in rage:* 1) getting angrier; 2) swelling up larger in his anger

971. *limitary:* "boundary-protecting" is the meaning, but perhaps there is an overtone suggesting that Gabriel is presuming too much in setting bounds to Satan's movements

975. *triumphant wheels:* looks forward to 6.770–71

978. *moonèd horns:* crescent-shaped formations

980. *ported:* pointed forward ready to strike (rather than "at port," held across the chest)

981. *Ceres:* the goddess of agriculture, here representing the grain itself

983. *doubting:* apprehensive, fearful

985. *alarmed:* ready for battle, but also "worried"

987. *Tenerife:* a mountain in the Canary Islands   *Atlas unremoved:* the Atlas Mountains in Morocco (*unremoved* = immovable)

991–995. *nor only . . . conflict:* Cf. 6.668–70, where similarly Heaven threatens to go to "wrack."

997. *golden scales:* i.e., the constellation Libra, or The Scales; Milton no doubt re-

Betwixt Astrea and the scorpion sign,
Wherein all things created first he weighed,
The pendulous round earth with balanced air   1000
In counterpoise, now ponders all events,
Battles, and realms. In these he put two weights,
The sequel° each of parting and of fight;   *outcome*
The latter quick up flew and kicked the beam,
Which Gabriel spying, thus bespake° the fiend: *spoke to*
    "Satan, I know thy strength, and thou know'st mine:
Neither our own but given. What folly then
To boast what arms can do, since thine no more
Than Heaven permits, nor mine, though doubled now
To trample thee as mire. For proof look up,   1010
And read thy lot in yon celestial sign
Where thou art weighed and shown how light, how weak,
If thou resist." The fiend looked up and knew
His mounted scale aloft; nor more, but fled
Murmuring, and with him fled the shades of night.   1015

The End of the Fourth Book.

membered the golden scales in which Zeus weighed the destinies of the Greeks against those of the Trojans (*Iliad* 8.69–72), and of Hector against Achilles (*Iliad* 22.209), or the weighing of Aeneas' fate against that of Turnus (*Aeneid* 12.725–27), but he gives the conception cosmic scope by identifying the scales with the constellation, which can be seen "Betwixt Astraea [i.e., Virgo] and the scorpion sign [i.e., Scorpio]" (line 998).

998–1002. *he weighed . . . realms:* Cf. Isa. 40:12: God is he "Who hath measured the waters in the hollow of his hand, and meted out heaven with the span, and comprehended the dust of the earth in a measure, and weighed the mountains in scales, and the hills in a balance."

1001. *ponders:* considers, but also retaining its literal Latin meaning, "weighs"

1004. *The latter . . . flew:* i.e., "parting" is the heavier, more worthy alternative; "fight" *up flew,* as it, as an option, lacks weight or value.

1011–1012. *read . . . light:* Milton draws upon Daniel's account (Dan. 5:27) of God's use of the figure of the scales to warn the Babylonian king, Belshazzar: "Thou art weighed in the balances, and art found wanting."

1014. *nor more:* he said no more

1015. *with him . . . night:* Like Book 2, Book 4 ends with a transition from darkness to day.

BOOK 5

The Argument

Morning approached, Eve relates to Adam her troublesome dream; he likes it not, yet comforts her. They come forth to their day labors: their morning hymn at the door of their bower. God to render man inexcusable sends Raphael to admonish him of his obedience, of his free estate, of his enemy near at hand—who he is, and why his enemy—and whatever else may avail Adam to know. Raphael comes down to Paradise: his appearance described, his coming discerned by Adam afar off sitting at the door of his bower. He goes out to meet him, brings him to his lodge, entertains him with the choicest fruits of Paradise got together by Eve; their discourse at table. Raphael performs his message, minds Adam of his state and of his enemy, relates at Adam's request who that enemy is and how he came to be so, beginning from his first revolt in Heaven and the occasion thereof: how he drew his legions after him to the parts of the north and there incited them to rebel with him, persuading all but only Abdiel, a seraph, who in argument dissuades and opposes him, then forsakes him.

Now morn, her rosy steps in the eastern clime
Advancing, sowed the earth with orient pearl,
When Adam waked, so customed, for his sleep
Was airy light, from pure digestion bred
And temperate vapors bland, which the only sound   5
Of leaves and fuming rills, Aurora's fan,
Lightly dispersed and the shrill matin song

---

1. *rosy steps:* The phrase is Milton's transformation of the signature "rosy-fingered dawn" of Homer, *Iliad* 1.77; cf. 6.524, and 7.29–30.

2. *sowed . . . orient pearl:* covered the earth with lustrous light (picking up *orient* = eastern); see Ps. 97:11: "light is sown for the righteous."

3–4. *sleep . . . bred:* Cf. their "grosser" sleep after eating the apple (9.1049).

5. *vapors bland:* soothing exhalations, the residue of the process of digestion; cf. the "exhilarating vapor bland" that follows digestion of the forbidden apple (9.1047). *which:* refers to "sleep" (line 3) which is "Lightly dispersed" (line 7) by the morning breeze.

6. *fuming rills, Aurora's fan:* i.e., the leaves, stirred by the breeze of the goddess of morning, Aurora

7–8. *shrill . . . bough:* Cf. Robert Herrick: "When all the birds have matins said / And sung their thankful hymns" ("Corrina's Going A-Maying").

Of birds on every bough; so much the more
His wonder was to find unwakened Eve,
With tresses discomposed and glowing cheek   10
As through unquiet rest. He, on his side
Leaning half-raised, with looks of cordial love
Hung over her enamored and beheld
Beauty, which whether waking or asleep,
Shot forth peculiar° graces; then with voice   *solely belonging (to Eve)*
Mild, as when Zephyrus on Flora breathes,
Her hand soft touching, whispered thus: "Awake
My fairest, my espoused, my latest found,
Heaven's last best gift, my ever-new delight,
Awake; the morning shines and the fresh field   20
Calls us; we lose the prime to mark how spring
Our tended plants, how blows the citron grove,
What drops the myrrh, and what the balmy reed,
How nature paints her colors, how the bee
Sits on the bloom extracting liquid sweet."   25
    Such whispering waked her, but with startled eye
On Adam, whom embracing, thus she spake:
    "O sole, in whom my thoughts find all repose,
My glory, my perfection, glad I see
Thy face and morn returned, for I this night,   30
Such night till this I never passed, have dreamed,
If dreamed, not, as I oft am wont, of thee,
Works of day passed, or morrows next design,
But of offence and trouble, which my mind
Knew never till this irksome night; methought   35
Close at mine ear one called me forth to walk
With gentle voice; I thought it thine; it said,

---

12. *cordial:* heart-felt (but also "restorative," [*OED* 2])

16. *Zephyrus on Flora breathes:* the west wind blows gently over flowers; similarly Zephyrus fans Paradise in 4.329. *Flora*, goddess of flowers, is half personification and half metonymy, as Ceres is in 4.981.

17–25. *Awake . . . sweet:* an aubade, or morning song, transforming the Song of Solomon 2:10–13: "Rise up, my love, my fair one, and come away. . . . The flowers appear on the earth; the time of the singing of

birds is come, . . . and the vines with the tender grape give a good smell."

21. *prime:* the first daylight hour, as at line 170 below; in Paradise, always six o'clock (see 10.651–706); perhaps also carries with it the ecclesiastical sense of the first of the canonical hours of prayer.

22. *blows:* blooms; cf. 7.319 and 9.629.

23. *balmy reed:* balsam-bearing tree

28. *sole:* i.e., one and only, but plays on "soul" (see line 610 below: "United as one individual soul").

'Why sleep'st thou Eve? Now is the pleasant time,
The cool, the silent, save where silence yields
To the night-warbling bird that now awake   40
Tunes sweetest his love-labored song; now reigns
Full-orbed the moon and with more pleasing light
Shadowy sets off the face of things, in vain
If none regard; heaven wakes with all his eyes,
Whom to behold but thee, nature's desire,   45
In whose sight all things joy with ravishment
Attracted by thy beauty still° to gaze?'   *always*
I rose as at thy call but found thee not;
To find thee I directed then my walk,
And on, methought, alone I passed through ways   50
That brought me on a sudden to the tree
Of interdicted knowledge. Fair it seemed,
Much fairer to my fancy than by day;
And as I wondering looked, beside it stood
One shaped and winged like one of those from Heaven   55
By us oft seen; his dewy locks distilled
Ambrosia. On that tree he also gazed,
And 'O fair plant,' said he, 'with fruit surcharged,
Deigns none to ease thy load and taste thy sweet,
Nor god nor man? Is knowledge so despised,   60
Or envy, or what reserve forbids to taste?
Forbid who will, none shall from me withhold
Longer thy offered good; why else set here?'
This said, he paused not, but with venturous arm
He plucked; he tasted. Me damp horror chilled   65

---

41. *love-labored:* made with love and for love

42. *with more pleasing light:* It is not surprising that Satan would find the moon's light *more pleasing* than the sunlight that it merely reflects, as this echoes his own anxious relationship to God, his own originator.

44. *all his eyes:* as in Spenser (and many other poets) where the stars are the "many eyes" with which "High heaven beholdes" mankind (*Faerie Queene* 3.11.45.7–8)

45–90. *Whom to behold . . . exaltation:* anticipates (though with a different result) the temptation of Eve in 9.532–732.

56–57. *dewy locks . . . Ambrosia:* Milton recalls Virgil's description of Venus' "dishevell'd hair, / Which flowing from her shoulders reach'd the ground, / And widely spread ambrosial scents around" (*Aeneid* 1.403–4, Dryden's translation). (*Ambrosia* = heavenly fragrance)

58. *surcharged:* overflowing (but the Satanic claim of excess denies the fundamental harmony of Eden; cf. *Comus*, line 728).

60. *god:* here means "angel," as in 2.352 and line 117 below

61. *Or envy . . . reserve:* i.e., whose envy or what restriction

65. *damp horror:* the sweat of fear; cf. *Aeneid* 2.120–1.

At such bold words vouched° with a deed so bold,   *confirmed*
But he thus, overjoyed: 'O fruit divine,
Sweet of thyself, but much more sweet thus cropped,
Forbidden here, it seems, as only fit
For gods, yet able to make gods of men—   70
And why not gods of men, since good the more
Communicated° more abundant grows,   *shared, imparted*
The author not impaired but honored more?
Here, happy creature, fair angelic Eve,
Partake thou also; happy though thou art,   75
Happier thou mayst be, worthier canst not be.
Taste this and be henceforth among the gods
Thyself a goddess, not to earth confined,
But sometimes in the air as we sometimes
Ascend to Heaven, by merit thine, and see   80
What life the gods live there, and such live thou.'
So saying, he drew nigh and to me held,
Even to my mouth, of that same fruit held part
Which he had plucked; the pleasant savory smell
So quickened appetite, that I, methought,   85
Could not but taste. Forthwith up to the clouds
With him I flew and underneath beheld
The earth outstretched immense, a prospect wide
And various, wondering at my flight and change
To this high exaltation; suddenly   90
My guide was gone, and I, methought, sunk down
And fell asleep; but O how glad I waked
To find this but a dream!" Thus Eve her night
Related, and thus Adam answered sad:
    "Best image of myself and dearer half,   95
The trouble of thy thoughts this night in sleep
Affects me equally; nor can I like
This uncouth° dream, of evil sprung I fear;   *unpleasant, strange*

70–71. *gods:* The use of the word "gods" to imply that there can be more than one figures in Satan's temptation of Eve in 9.705–12, as it has in his speech to Beelzebub in 1.116.

79. *as we:* Milton exploits the ambiguity of the syntax here: does *as we* refer to "Ascend to Heaven" (line 78) or to *in the air*?

84. *savory:* appetizing, but here and throughout plays with a secondary meaning—"edifying, especially of spiritual matters" (*OED* 2b)

86–89. *Forthwith . . . various:* Eve imagines a view, like God's, of earth from a vantage point above time.

94. *sad:* soberly, seriously (unlike at line 116)

Yet evil whence? In thee can harbor none,
Created pure. But know that in the soul   100
Are many lesser faculties that serve
Reason as chief; among these fancy next
Her office holds: of all external things,
Which the five watchful senses represent,
She forms imaginations,° airy shapes,   *images*
Which reason, joining or disjoining, frames°   *fashions, forms into*
All what we affirm or what deny and call
Our knowledge or opinion, then retires
Into her private cell when nature rests.
Oft in her absence, mimic fancy wakes   110
To imitate her, but, misjoining shapes,
Wild work produces oft, and most in dreams,
Ill-matching words and deeds long past or late.°   *recent*
Some such resemblances methinks I find
Of our last evening's talk in this thy dream,   115
But with addition strange, yet be not sad.
Evil into the mind of God or man
May come and go, so unapproved, and leave
No spot or blame behind, which gives me hope
That what in sleep thou didst abhor to dream,   120
Waking thou never wilt consent to do.
Be not disheartened then, nor cloud those looks

99. *evil whence:* translates Tertullian's famous *unde malum;* see pp. xxii–xxiii above.

100–116. *know . . . strange:* The passage summarizes early modern "faculty psychology" comparing the activities of *fancy*—the unconscious imagination, which *forms imaginations, airy shapes*—with those of *reason,* which should rule and organize the mental processes.

104. *represent:* make present to the mind

108–113. *then retires . . . late:* Unlike fancy, which is always active, reason is interrupted by sleep, allowing fancy to produce disjointed and disturbing dreams; thus John Bramhall, in his *Castigations of Mr. Hobbes* (1658), writes: "In the time of sleep . . . when the imagination is not governed by reason, we see what absurd and monstrous and inconsistent shapes and phansies it doth collect, remote from true deliberation" (p. 341).

108. *retires:* The subject of *retires* is "reason," line 106.

109. *cell:* compartment (of the brain)

117–119. *Evil . . . behind: god* here seems to mean "angel," as it does in line 60 above; but Milton may be appealing to the accepted view of God's omniscience as implying that divine knowledge extends to the potential, accidental evil in good things because, as Aquinas explains (*Summa Theologica.* I, q. 14, a.10), "God would not know good things perfectly unless he knew evil things." The central issue, however, is the claim that the thought of evil is not itself evil; only approval of the thought is.

118. *so:* 1) thus, in this case; 2) so long as it is   *unapproved:* 1) not consented to or approved of; 2) not experienced or put to proof

That wont° to be more cheerful and serene   *are accustomed*
Than when fair morning first smiles on the world,
And let us to our fresh employments rise   125
Among the groves, the fountains, and the flowers
That open now their choicest bosomed° smells   *enclosed*
Reserved from night and kept for thee in store."
    So cheered he his fair spouse, and she was cheered,
But silently a gentle tear let fall   130
From either eye and wiped them with her hair;
Two other precious drops that ready stood,
Each in their crystal sluice, he, ere they fell,
Kissed, as the gracious signs of sweet remorse
And pious awe that feared to have offended.   135
    So all was cleared, and to the field they haste.
But first from under shady arborous roof
Soon as they forth were come to open sight
Of day-spring and the sun, who, scarce up risen
With wheels yet hovering o'er the ocean brim,   140
Shot parallel to the earth his dewy ray,
Discovering° in wide landscape all the east   *revealing*
Of Paradise and Eden's happy plains,
Lowly they bowed adoring and began
Their orisons,° each morning duly paid   *prayers*
In various style; for neither various style
Nor holy rapture wanted they to praise
Their maker in fit strains pronounced or sung
Unmeditated, such prompt eloquence
Flowed from their lips, in prose or numerous verse,   150

---

125. *fresh:* 1) refreshing; 2) new

133. *crystal sluice:* i.e., Eve's eye; cf. Shakespeare's *Venus and Adonis:* "She veiled her eyelids, who like sluices stopped / The crystal tide that from her two cheeks fair / In the sweet channel of her bosom dropped" (lines 956–58).

135. *pious awe:* devoted care (but its stronger sense of "devout reverence" anticipates 10.145)

136. *cleared:* meanings include cleared up, cleared away, and "cleared" in a juridical sense

139. *day-spring:* cf. Luke 1:78: "The dayspring from on high hath visited us."

140. *wheels:* assumes the metaphor of the chariot of the sun, beginning its daily journey

146–152. *In various style . . . sweetness:* They pray in diverse ways, with both formal variations and spontaneous emotion; Milton's point here is that in the unfallen world sincere prayer was creative and individual and not dependent upon set forms of worship.

147. *holy rapture:* religious ecstasy

150. *numerous:* rhythmical, metrical; see the "Harmonious numbers" of 3.38.

More tunable° than needed lute or harp   *sweet sounding, melodious*
To add more sweetness, and they thus began:
   "These are thy glorious works, parent of good,
Almighty, thine this universal frame
Thus wondrous fair; thyself how wondrous then!   155
Unspeakable,° who sit'st above these heavens   *inexpressible*
To us invisible or dimly seen
In these thy lowest works, yet these declare
Thy goodness beyond thought and power divine.
Speak ye who best can tell, ye sons of light,   160
Angels, for ye behold him and with songs
And choral symphonies, day without night,
Circle his throne rejoicing, ye in Heaven;
On earth join all ye creatures to extol
Him first, him last, him midst, and without end.   165
Fairest of stars, last in the train of night,
If better thou belong not to the dawn,
Sure pledge of day, that crown'st the smiling morn
With thy bright circlet, praise him in thy sphere
While day arises, that sweet hour of prime.   170
Thou Sun, of this great world both eye and soul,
Acknowledge him thy greater, sound his praise
In thy eternal course, both when thou climb'st
And when high noon hast gained, and when thou fall'st.

153–208. *These . . . dark:* The hymn of praise is loosely based on Ps. 148 and 104.

154. *frame:* creation, structure, as it in Hamlet's "goodly frame, the earth" (*Hamlet* 2.2.298).

158–159. *these . . . goodness:* echoes Ps. 19:1: "The heavens declare the glory of God."

165. *Him . . . end:* See Rev. 1:11 (and 22:13): "I am Alpha and Omega, the first and last."

166. *Fairest . . . night:* Hesperus (or Venus) is named as the fairest star in Heaven in the *Iliad* 22.318. In the pre-sunrise sky it was the last body to disappear (*last in the train of light*). In its appearance in the early morning sky, it was often known as Lucifer ("light-bringer").

169. *praise him . . . sphere:* here and throughout the hymn the natural world is said to *praise* God simply by being what it is; but cf. Satan's anxious understanding of praise in 4.46–53.

170. *prime:* light; see line 21 and note.

171. *Sun . . . soul:* Similarly Donne conceived the sun in a metaphor that made it the eye of the world and the male force inspiriting it: "Thee, eye of heaven, this great Soule envies not, / By thy male force, is all wee have begot" ("Progress of the Soul"). The conception of the sun as the soul of the world goes back to Pliny (*Natural History* 2.4) and was developed by Conti (*Mythologiae* 5.17) into a synthesis of many solar myths signifying that the sun was "lord of the stars and giver of life to mortals, since he is the author of light to the other stars and by him all things flourish." Cf. 4.667–73 and 8.94–97.

Moon, that now meet'st the orient° sun, now fly'st   *in the east*
With the fixed stars, fixed in their orb that flies,
And ye five other wandering fires that move
In mystic dance not without song resound
His praise, who out of darkness called up light.
Air and ye elements, the eldest birth   180
Of nature's womb, that in quaternion run
Perpetual circle, multiform, and mix
And nourish all things, let your ceaseless change
Vary to our great maker still new praise.
Ye mists and exhalations that now rise   185
From hill or steaming lake, dusky or gray,
Till the sun paint your fleecy skirts with gold
In honor to the world's great author, rise,
Whether to deck with clouds the uncolored° sky   *monochromatic (all blue)*
Or wet the thirsty earth with falling showers,   190
Rising or falling still advance his praise.
His praise, ye winds that from four quarters blow
Breathe soft or loud; and wave your tops, ye pines,
With every plant, in sign of worship wave.
Fountains and ye that warble as ye flow   195
Melodious murmurs, warbling tune his praise.
Join voices all ye living souls; ye birds,
That singing up to Heaven gate ascend,
Bear on your wings and in your notes his praise;
Ye that in waters glide, and ye that walk   200
The earth and stately tread or lowly creep
Witness if I be silent, morn or ev'n,
To hill or valley, fountain or fresh shade

176. *orb that flies:* revolving sphere (of *the fixed stars*)

177. *five other wandering fires:* i.e., Mercury, Mars, Jupiter, Saturn, plus either Venus (though already mentioned) or Earth; *wandering* reflects the etymology of "planet" from the Greek word "to wander," that is, changing their relation to the earth.

178. *not without song:* i.e., accompanied by the music of the spheres (which, traditionally, as in "Arcades," lines 61–73, cannot be heard by fallen creatures)

180. *eldest:* i.e., earth, water, and fire

(all mentioned in Genesis before the fourth "element," air)

181–183. *in . . . things:* a familiar account of the orderly interactions of the four basic elements (the *quaternion*) that underlies all material being; see Cicero: "As there are four sorts of bodies, the continuance of nature is caused by their reciprocal changes. . . . Thus by their continual motions . . . the conjunction of the several parts of the universe is preserved" (*De natura deorum* 2.33). See also lines 415–18 below, and the contrasting account of the warring elements, which in chaos strive "for mastery" at 2.898–916.

Made vocal by my song and taught his praise.
Hail universal lord, be bounteous still°   *always*
To give us only good; and if the night
Have gathered aught of evil or concealed,
Disperse it, as now light dispels the dark."
    So prayed they innocent, and to their thoughts
Firm peace recovered soon and wonted calm.   210
On to their morning's rural work they haste,
Among sweet dews and flowers, where any row
Of fruit trees overwoody reached too far
Their pampered boughs and needed hands to check
Fruitless embraces; or they led the vine   215
To wed her elm: she spoused about him twines
Her marriageable arms and with her brings
Her dower, the adopted clusters, to adorn
His barren leaves. Them thus employed beheld
With pity Heaven's high king and to him called   220
Raphael, the sociable spirit, that deigned
To travel with Tobias and secured
His marriage with the seven-times-wedded maid.
    "Raphael," said he, "thou hear'st what stir on earth
Satan, from hell scaped through the darksome gulf,   225
Hath raised in Paradise and how disturbed
This night the human pair, how he designs
In them at once to ruin all mankind.
Go therefore; half this day as friend with friend
Converse with Adam, in what bower or shade   230
Thou find'st him from the heat of noon retired

---

204. *Made vocal by:* made to echo with
205–206. *be . . . good:* The lines may
echo Socrates' prayer "for good gifts, for the
gods know best what things are good," as
Xenophon reports it in *Memorabilia* 1.22;
but more immediately suggest Matt. 7:11:
"If ye then, being evil, know how to give
good gifts unto your children, how much
more shall your Father which is in Heaven
give good things to them that ask him."
213. *overwoody:* with overly luxuriant
growth; Eden is not self-regulating
215–216. *vine . . . elm:* The figure of
the climbing *vine* wedding a tree was tradi-
tional when Spenser wrote of the "vine-prop

elme" (*Faerie Queene* 1.1.8.7) perhaps from
Horace, *Odes* 2.15.4 and 4.5.31.
221. *Raphael:* The name "Raphael"
means "medicine of God." He accompanies
Tobias in the apocryphal book of Tobit, and,
along with Michael, Gabriel, and Uriel, is
one of "the four angels of the presence" of
God in Jewish tradition.
221–223. *deigned . . . maid:* With the
help of the angel, Tobias married Sara, whose
previous seven husbands had been killed by
the spirit Asmodeus; see 4.167–71.
229. *friend with friend:* cf. Exodus
33:11: "And the Lord spake unto Moses face
to face, as a man speaketh unto his friend."

To respite his day-labor with repast
Or with repose, and such discourse bring on
As may advise° him of his happy state,   *inform*
Happiness in his power left free to will,   235
Left to his own free will, his will though free
Yet mutable; whence warn him to beware
He swerve not too secure; tell him withal
His danger and from whom, what enemy,
Late-fallen himself from Heaven, is plotting now   240
The fall of others from like state of bliss:
By violence, no, for that shall be withstood,
But by deceit and lies; this let him know,
Lest willfully transgressing he pretend
Surprisal, unadmonished, unforewarned."   245
    So spake the eternal Father and fulfilled
All justice. Nor delayed the wingèd saint°   *angel*
After his charge received but from among
Thousand celestial ardors where he stood
Veiled with his gorgeous wings up springing light°   *lightly, nimbly*
Flew through the midst of Heaven; the angelic choirs,
On each hand parting, to his speed gave way
Through all the empyreal road, till at the gate
Of Heaven arrived, the gate self-opened wide
On golden hinges turning, as by work   255
Divine the sovereign architect had framed.
From hence (no cloud or, to obstruct his sight,
Star interposed, however small) he sees,
Not unconform° to other shining globes,   *unlike*
Earth and the garden of God with cedars crowned   260
Above all hills, as when by night the glass
Of Galileo, less assured,° observes   *clear, certain*
Imagined lands and regions in the moon,

---

238. *swerve not too secure:* does not go
astray by being overconfident (*secure* is liter-
ally "without care"). Cf. 4.186 and *SA*, line
55: "Proudly secure, yet liable to fall"

244–245. *pretend Surprisal:* offer as an
excuse that he was taken by surprise

246–247. *fulfilled All justice:* did
everything that the claims of justice de-
manded

249. *celestial ardors:* angels of light
(from Latin *ardere* = to burn); the Hebrew

"seraph" similarly comes from a root mean-
ing "to burn."

253. *empyreal:* heavenly, of the highest
heaven

256. *sovereign architect:* i.e., God; cf.
Du Bartas' "Eden": "Heaven's great architect"
(Sylvester trans., 2.1.448).

261–262. *glass Of Galileo:* telescope; see
1.287–91 and 3.590. This mention of
Galileo is the only time a contemporary of
Milton is named in the poem.

Or pilot from amidst the Cyclades,
Delos or Samos first appearing, kens   265
A cloudy spot. Down thither prone° in flight   *horizontal, bent forward*
He speeds and through the vast ethereal sky
Sails between worlds and worlds with steady wing,
Now on the polar winds, then with quick fan°   *flutter, flapping*
Winnows the buxom air till, within soar   270
Of towering eagles, to all the fowls he seems
A phoenix, gazed by all, as that sole bird
When to enshrine his relics in the sun's
Bright temple to Egyptian Thebes he flies.
At once on the eastern cliff of Paradise   275
He lights and to his proper shape returns:
A seraph winged. Six wings he wore to shade
His lineaments divine: the pair that clad
Each shoulder broad came mantling o'er his breast
With regal ornament; the middle pair   280
Girt like a starry zone° his waist and round   *belt*
Skirted his loins and thighs with downy gold
And colors dipped in Heaven; the third his feet
Shadowed from either heel with feathered mail

264. *Cyclades:* a chain of islands in the southern Aegean

265. *Delos . . . Samos: Delos* is an island in the center of the Cyclades; *Samos,* the easternmost island in the Aegean, off the coast of Turkey.

266–274. *Down . . . flies:* The scene is designed to recall the descent of Mercury in *Aeneid* 4.241. Raphael plunges earthward by the same passage or route that Satan has followed in 3.528–87, but without pausing at the sun.

269. *Now on the polar winds:* first on the strong winds emanating from the poles (though it is possible that *winds* here is a verb, as at 3.563, parallel to "Winnows" in line 270, with "the polar" functioning as a proper noun; the meaning is not substantially changed).

270. *buxom air:* unresisting air nearer the earth (gentler than the polar winds)

270–271. *within . . . eagles:* entering the altitude that highest-flying eagles can reach

272–274. *phoenix . . . flies:* Milton knew many accounts of the *phoenix,* the legendary unique (*sole*) bird that every 500 years immolates itself and is reborn as fledgling from its own ashes. According to Ovid (*Metamorphoses* 15.391–407) the reborn phoenix would "carry its own cradle and its father's tomb" to Heliopolis (identified by Milton and others as *Thebes*), where the ashes were placed in the Temple of Apollo (*the sun's Bright temple*). Cf. *SA*, lines 1699–1707.

277. *seraph . . . wore:* Milton understands Raphael's "proper shape" (line 276) to be that of the seraphim in Isa. 6:2, each with "six wings; with twain he covered his face, and with twain he covered his feet, and with twain he did fly."

279. *mantling:* covering like a mantle (a loose, sleeveless cloak)

284. *mail:* plumage (but suggesting "armor")

Sky-tinctured grain. Like Maia's son he stood   285
And shook his plumes that° heavenly fragrance filled   *so that*
The circuit wide. Straight knew him all the bands
Of angels under watch and to his state
And to his message high in honor rise,
For on some message high they guessed him bound.   290
Their glittering tents he passed and now is come
Into the blissful field through groves of myrrh,
And flowering odors, cassia, nard, and balm,
A wilderness of sweets, for Nature here
Wantoned as in her prime and played at will   295
Her virgin fancies, pouring forth more sweet,
Wild above rule or art, enormous bliss.
Him through the spicy° forest onward come   *fragrant*
Adam discerned, as in the door he sat
Of his cool bower, while now the mounted sun   300
Shot down direct his fervid rays to warm
Earth's inmost womb, more warmth than Adam needs;
And Eve within, due° at her hour prepared   *duly, fittingly*
For dinner savory fruits of taste to please
True appetite, and not disrelish thirst   305
Of nectarous draughts between from milky stream,
Berry or grape; to whom thus Adam called:
    "Haste hither, Eve, and worth thy sight behold
Eastward among those trees what glorious shape

---

285. *Sky-tinctured grain:* colored sky blue (*grain* was originally a crimson dye but came to mean any permanent dye) *Maia's son:* i.e., Mercury (son of Maia and Jupiter)

287. *bands:* troops (see 4.684–85)

288. *state:* rank, dignity; cf. 1.640 and 2.511, and line 353 below.

289. *message:* mission (as God's emissary)

292. *blissful field:* i.e., Paradise; cf. "bliss" in line 297 below.

293. *cassia, nard, and balm:* aromatic plants; *cassia* has an especially fragrant bark, a sweet-smelling ointment was made from the root of *nard,* and *balm* is balsam.

295. *Wantoned . . . will:* frolicked . . . and happily imitated; negative connotations lurk in *Wantoned* (i.e., behaved lasciviously)

and *will* (i.e., sexual desire) to be heard by postlapsarian readers but not yet properly attaching to the descriptions of prelapsarian Eden; see 9.1015.

297. *Wild:* This too is totally innocent here; nature is wild, uncontrolled by human "rule or art," but as yet not needing that control.

299–300. *in . . . bower:* Adam sits like Abraham, who, sitting in his "tent door in the heat of the day," saw three angels coming and, with Sara, hastened to prepare a meal for them (Gen. 18:2–8).

306. *nectarous draughts between:* sweet drinks between courses of fruit (*draughts* is pronounced "drafts")   *milky stream:* nectar, juice ("milky," *OED* 1b)

308. *worth thy sight:* worth seeing

Comes this way moving; seems another morn   310
Risen on mid-noon; some great behest from Heaven
To us perhaps he brings and will vouchsafe
This day to be our guest. But go with speed
And what thy stores contain bring forth and pour
Abundance fit to honor and receive   315
Our heavenly stranger; well we may afford
Our givers their own gifts and large bestow
From large bestowed where nature multiplies
Her fertile growth and by disburdening grows
More fruitful, which instructs us not to spare."   320
    To whom thus Eve: "Adam, earth's hallowed mold,°   *pattern, form*
Of God inspired,° small store will serve where store,   *animated, inspirited*
All seasons, ripe for use hangs on the stalk,
Save what by frugal storing firmness gains
To nourish and superfluous moist consumes;   325
But I will haste and from each bough and break,
Each plant and juiciest gourd, will pluck such choice
To entertain our angel guest, as he
Beholding shall confess that here on earth
God hath dispensed his bounties as in Heaven."   330
    So saying, with dispatchful° looks in haste   *purposeful*
She turns, on hospitable thoughts intent
What choice to chose for delicacy best,
What order so contrived as not to mix
Tastes not well joined, inelegant, but bring   335
Taste after taste upheld with kindliest change;
Bestirs her then, and from each tender stalk
Whatever earth, all-bearing mother, yields
In India east or west, or middle shore
In Pontus or the Punic Coast, or where   340
Alcinous reigned, fruit of all kinds, in coat

---

317. *large:* liberally (and at line 318)

322. *store . . . store:* stockpile . . . abundance

323. *All seasons:* Before the fall there was only one season, but see 4.640 and note.

324. *frugal:* The word derives from Latin *frux* = fruit.

336. *upheld with kindliest change:* sustained with the most natural variety

340. *Pontus or the Punic Coast:* The *Pontus* coast is the southern shore of the Black Sea; the *Punic Coast* is the Carthaginian coast of the Mediterranean off modern Tunis.

340–341. *where Alcinous reigned:* i.e., the mythical island of Scheria (possibly modern Corfu), where, in the *Odyssey* (7.115–28) Ulysses found a paradisal garden of perpetual springtime and plenty in the palace of King Alcinous; see 9.440–41 below.

Rough or smooth rined, or bearded husk, or shell,
She gathers, tribute large, and on the board
Heaps with unsparing hand; for drink, the grape
She crushes, inoffensive must, and meads   345
From many a berry, and from sweet kernels pressed
She tempers° dulcet creams, nor these to hold   *mixes, blends*
Wants her fit vessels pure, then strews the ground
With rose and odors from the shrub unfumed.
Meanwhile our primitive° great sire, to meet   *primary, original*
His godlike guest, walks forth without more train
Accompanied than with his own complete
Perfections; in himself was all his state
More solemn than the tedious pomp that waits
On princes when their rich retinue long   355
Of horses led and grooms besmeared with gold
Dazzles the crowd and sets them all agape.
Nearer his presence, Adam, though not awed,
Yet with submiss° approach and reverence meek   *submissive*
As to a superior nature, bowing low,   360
       Thus said: "Native of Heaven, for other place
None can than Heaven such glorious shape contain,
Since, by descending from the thrones above,
Those happy places thou hast deigned awhile
To want,° and honor these, vouchsafe with us   *do without*
Two only, who yet by sovereign gift possess
This spacious ground, in yonder shady bower
To rest and what the garden choicest bears
To sit and taste, till this meridian° heat   *midday*
Be over and the sun more cool decline."   370
       Whom thus the angelic virtue answered mild:
"Adam, I therefore came, nor art thou such

---

342. *rined:* rinded (i.e., having a rind)

345. *inoffensive must, and meads:* non-alcoholic grape juice and honey-sweetened drinks

349. *unfumed:* unburned (i.e., from the fresh plant, not from its burning as an incense, since before the fall there was no fire; see also line 396 below)

353–357. *in himself . . . agape:* Adam's *solemn* (i.e., awe-inspiring) natural majesty is compared with the meretricious display of a

modern ruler like Charles II who *dazzles the crowd* with his *tedious pomp.*

366. *sovereign gift:* both the *gift* from their sovereign, God, and the *gift* of their sovereignty over nature

371. *virtue:* one of the lower orders of angels; as a seraph or one of the supreme rank in the heavenly hierarchy, Raphael may have the title of any of the inferior orders (thus at 7.41, Raphael is an archangel)

Created, or such place hast here to dwell,
As may not oft invite, though spirits of Heaven,
To visit thee; lead on then where thy bower   375
O'ershades, for these mid-hours till evening rise
I have at will." So to the sylvan lodge
They came, that like Pomona's arbor smiled
With flowerets decked and fragrant smells; but Eve
Undecked, save with herself, more lovely fair   380
Than wood-nymph or the fairest goddess feigned
Of three that in Mount Ida naked strove,
Stood to entertain her guest from Heaven; no veil
She needed, virtue-proof, no thought infirm
Altered her cheek. On whom the angel "hail"   385
Bestowed, the holy salutation used
Long after to blessed Mary, second Eve.

   "Hail, mother of mankind, whose fruitful womb
Shall fill the world more numerous with thy sons
Than with these various fruits the trees of God   390
Have heaped this table." Raised of grassy turf
Their table was, and mossy seats had round,
And on her ample square from side to side
All autumn piled, though spring and autumn here
Danced hand in hand. Awhile discourse they hold,   395
No fear lest dinner cool, when thus began
Our author: "Heavenly stranger, please to taste
These bounties which our nourisher, from whom
All perfect good unmeasured out descends

374. *though spirits of Heaven:* even heavenly spirits

378. *Pomona's:* the Roman goddess of flowers to whom Eve is again compared at 9.393

382. *three . . . strove:* Hera, Aphrodite, and Athena *strove* to win the apple of discord that bore the inscription, "For the fairest." *Mount Ida,* overlooking ancient Troy, was the site of Paris' judgment—awarding the apple to Aphrodite as the "fairest goddess" (line 381), and inadvertently setting in motion the events that led to the Trojan War.

384. *virtue-proof:* invulnerable (to evil) through her virtue

385–387. *On whom . . . Eve: hail* is the greeting of the angel of the Annunciation to Mary (Luke 1:28). Mary is also named the *second Eve* in 10.183; for Eve as *mother of mankind,* see Gen. 3:20 and 11.158 below. It was common, though not often by Protestants, "to derive *Ave,* the first word of the Angels salutation to Maria of *Eva,* invented because shee repaired what was lost by *Eva*" (Andrew Willet, *Hexapla* [London, 1608], p. 54).

396. *No fear . . . cool:* Since fire is a consequence of the fall (see 10.1078–81), food was not cooked; early critics were sometimes put off by the "lowness" of the expression here.

398–399. *nourisher . . . descends:* Milton's line recalls James 1:17: "Every good and every perfect gift is from above, and cometh down from the Father of lights."

To us for food and for delight, hath caused   400
The earth to yield; unsavory food perhaps
To spiritual natures, only this I know,
That one celestial father gives to all."
    To whom the Angel: "Therefore what he gives
(Whose praise be ever sung) to man, in part   405
Spiritual, may of purest spirits be found
No ingrateful° food, and food alike those pure   *unacceptable, unwelcome*
Intelligential substances require
As doth your rational; and both contain
Within them every lower faculty   410
Of sense whereby they hear, see, smell, touch, taste,
Tasting concoct, digest, assimilate,
And corporeal to incorporeal turn.
For know, whatever was created needs
To be sustained and fed; of elements   415
The grosser feeds the purer: earth, the sea;
Earth and the sea feed air; the air, those fires
Ethereal; and, as lowest, first the moon,
Whence in her visage round those spots, unpurged
Vapors not yet into her substance turned;   420
Nor doth the moon no nourishment exhale
From her moist continent to higher orbs.

401–403. *unsavory . . . all:* Adam's curiosity about angelic diets gives way to certainty about God's goodness.

407–409. *food . . . rational:* Raphael tells Adam that angels (*pure Intelligential substances*) require food as much as do humans (*your rational* [natures]); Milton here rejects the notion that angels are immaterial (see also lines 438–39 and 8.622–29 below).

412. *Tasting . . . assimilate:* i.e., once tasting, [they] concoct, digest, assimilate (the three phases of digestion, according to 17th-century physiology, as the food enters the stomach, is digested, and finally assimilated)

414–426. *needs . . . ocean:* The idea that the natural world is sustained in the same way as the physical body was familiar from classical times. Justus Lipsius, in *Physiologiae Stoicorum* (Antwerp, 1637) 2.14, p. 540, offers countless authorities, among them Homer, Cicero, Seneca, and especially Pliny (*Natural History* 2.9) for the idea

that the stars "feed on the vapors of the earth that the sun sups on the waters of the great ocean, and the moon on those of rivers and brooks." Milton was aware of contemporary revivals of the doctrine, like that of Robert Fludd in *Utriusque cosmi historia* (Frankfort, 1617), where an engraving (1.5–6) shows the sun actually "supping with the ocean" at sunset.

419–420. *in . . . turned:* i.e., the *spots* that can be seen on the surface (*visage*) of the moon are the still unassimilated *Vapors;* however, in 1.287–89, Milton mentions the moon seen through the newly-discovered telescope, which revealed the lunar spots to be geological features on the surface.

422. *moist continent:* refers to the belief that the moon drew up vapors from the earth; cf. *Hamlet* 1.1.118, where the moon is called "the moist star."   *higher orbs:* successive planetary spheres; the moon's was the "lowest"(line 418), nearest to earth.

The sun, that light imparts to all, receives
From all his alimental recompense
In humid exhalations and at ev'n   425
Sups with the ocean; though in Heaven the trees
Of life ambrosial fruitage bear, and vines
Yield nectar, though from off the boughs each morn
We brush mellifluous° dews and find the ground   *honey-like*
Covered with pearly grain; yet God hath here   430
Varied his bounty so with new delights
As may compare with Heaven, and to taste
Think not I shall be nice."° So down they sat   *overly refined, fastidious*
And to their viands fell, nor seemingly
The angel, nor in mist, the common gloss°   *explanation*
Of theologians, but with keen dispatch
Of real hunger and concoctive heat
To transubstantiate; what redounds transpires
Through spirits with ease, nor wonder, if by fire
Of sooty coal the empiric alchemist   440
Can turn or holds it possible to turn
Metals of drossiest ore to perfect gold
As from the mine. Meanwhile at table Eve
Ministered naked and their flowing cups
With pleasant liquors crowned. O innocence   445
Deserving Paradise! If ever, then,
Then had the sons of God excuse to have been
Enamored at that sight; but in those hearts

---

424. *alimentary recompense:* nourishing food offered to the sun in the form of *humid exhalations* (line 425) in return for the *light* that it *imparts* (line 423)

430. *grain:* drops (though exploits the familiar association of dew with manna, which in Ps. 78:24 is called "corn of heaven")

434. *nor seemingly:* not just in appearance

435. *in mist:* 1) in vapor; 2) symbolically

437–438. *concoctive . . . transubstantiate:* in the digestive process, to be turned into a subtler material form; *transubstantiate* is the technical term used by Catholics to describe the transformation of bread and wine into the body and blood of Christ, its use here a characteristic anti-Catholic hit, pointing to the true transubstantiation in Eden.

438–439. *redounds . . . ease:* A typically Miltonic willingness to put full pressure on the logic of his formulations, here, as he moves from thinking of angels eating to the inevitability of some form of angelic excretion; *redounds:* cannot be assimilated, or remains as excess

440. *the empiric alchemist:* any dabbler in alchemy

445. *crowned:* filled; the cups of Apollo's worshippers are "crowned" with wine in *Iliad* 1.470, and Virgil's peasants "crown" their cups in *Georgics* 2.528.

447. *sons of God:* angels; see Gen. 6:2.

448. *those:* i.e., Adam and Eve's

Love unlibidinous° reigned nor jealousy   *untainted by lust*
Was understood, the injured lover's hell.   450
    Thus when with meats and drinks they had sufficed
Not burdened, nature, sudden mind° arose   ·*resolve*
In Adam not to let the occasion pass
Given him by this great conference to know
Of things above his world and of their being   455
Who dwell in Heaven, whose excellence he saw
Transcend his own so far, whose radiant forms,
Divine effulgence,° whose high power so far   *radiant splendor*
Exceeded human, and his wary speech
Thus to the empyreal minister he framed: 460
    "Inhabitant with God, now know I well
Thy favor in this honor done to man,
Under whose lowly roof thou hast vouchsafed
To enter and these earthly fruits to taste,
Food not of angels, yet accepted so   465
As that more willingly thou couldst not seem
At Heaven's high feasts to have fed, yet what compare?"
    To whom the wingèd hierarch replied:
"O Adam, one almighty is, from whom
All things proceed and up to him return   470
If not depraved from good, created all
Such to perfection, one first matter all,
Endued with various forms, various degrees
Of substance, and, in things that live, of life,
But more refined, more spiritous, and pure,   475
As nearer to him placed or nearer tending,
Each in their several active spheres assigned,
Till body up to spirit work in bounds
Proportioned to each kind. So from the root
Springs lighter the green stalk, from thence the leaves   480

467. *what compare:* how can they be comparable (to meals in Heaven)

469–490. *one almighty . . . same:* The view expressed here is of all things having their origin and end in God; each created form is placed on a *gradual* (i.e., graduated) *scale* of being nearer or farther from God by virtue of the relative refinement of its nature, differing in nature not in *kind* but only *in degree* of its similarity to the divine essence.

472. *one first matter all:* Creation, for Milton, is not *ex nihilo,* but there is an "original matter" (*Christian Doctrine* I, vii; *Works* 15, 17) that is given shape and purpose by God in the act of creation; see pp. xxxvii–xli above.

478. *in bounds:* 1) within the limits; 2) quickly (in leaps and bounds)

More airy, last the bright consummate flower
Spirits odorous breathes; flowers and their fruit,
Man's nourishment, by gradual scale sublimed,
To vital spirits aspire, to animal,
To intellectual, give both life and sense,   485
Fancy and understanding, whence the soul
Reason receives, and reason is her being,
Discursive or intuitive: discourse
Is oftest yours, the latter most is ours,
Differing but in degree, of kind the same.   490
Wonder not, then, what God for you saw good
If I refuse not, but convert, as you,
To proper° substance; time may come when men   *my own*
With angels may participate and find
No inconvenient diet nor too light fare;   495
And from these corporal nutriments perhaps
Your bodies may at last turn all to spirit,
Improved by tract of time, and, winged, ascend
Ethereal as we, or may at choice
Here or in heavenly paradises dwell,   500
If ye be found obedient and retain
Unalterably firm his love entire
Whose progeny you are. Meanwhile enjoy
Your fill what happiness this happy state
Can comprehend,° incapable of more."   *contain, circumscribe*
      To whom the patriarch of mankind replied:
"O favorable spirit, propitious° guest,   *gracious*
Well hast thou taught the way that might direct
Our knowledge and the scale of nature set

483. *sublimed:* raised (an alchemical term referring to the change of a solid object to a gas)

488. *Discursive or intuitive:* The distinction marks the different intellectual processes of humans and angels: humans use reason to piece together understandings that angels can immediately intuit whole. The principle had theological authority. Zanchius, for example, declared in *De Operibus Dei* (Neustadt, 1591) 3.6, that "angels do not know by rationating, combining and dividing data" as humans do. For Milton, however, the distinction is not absolute, as he indicates with "oftest" and "most" in line 489.

498. *tract:* interval, duration; Adam and Eve were capable of dwelling in Eden only for a probationary period before they would *ascend* to Heaven (see 7.157–61).

503. *progeny:* Adam and Eve are not God's offspring, as this suggests, but his creations or creatures; the word is used metaphorically, as in Acts 17:28: "we are also his offspring."

509. *scale of nature:* i.e., the great chain of being, an image deriving perhaps originally from Plato's *Timaeus,* of the organiza-

From center to circumference whereon   510
In contemplation of created things
By steps we may ascend to God. But say,
What meant that caution joined, 'if ye be found
Obedient'? Can we want obedience then
To him, or possibly his love desert   515
Who formed us from the dust and placed us here
Full to the utmost measure of what bliss
Human desires can seek or apprehend?"°   *experience, feel*
    To whom the angel: "Son of Heaven and earth,
Attend: that thou art happy, owe to God;   520
That thou continu'st such, owe° to thyself,   *attribute, ascribe*
That is, to thy obedience; therein stand.
This was that caution given thee; be advised.
God made thee perfect, not immutable,
And good he made thee; but to persevere   525
He left it in thy power, ordained thy will
By nature free, not overruled by fate
Inextricable or strict necessity;
Our voluntary service he requires,
Not our necessitated; such with him   530
Finds no acceptance, nor can find, for how
Can hearts, not free, be tried° whether they serve   *tested*
Willing or no, who will but what they must
By destiny and can no other choose?
Myself and all the angelic host that stand   535
In sight of God enthroned, our happy state
Hold, as you yours, while our obedience holds,
On other surety° none. Freely we serve   *ground of certainty*
Because we freely love, as in our will
To love or not; in this we stand or fall;   540
And some are fallen, to disobedience fallen,
And so from Heaven to deepest hell: O fall
From what high state of bliss into what woe!"
    To whom our great progenitor: "Thy words,

---

tion of the universe as a ladder reaching from
the lowest form of created matter up to God;
the "golden chain" of 2.1005 is one of its
symbols, as is Jacob's ladder (3.510–18).

    511. *In contemplation . . . things:* by
thinking about the natural world (and recog-
nizing the divine plan in this book of na-

ture); Adam shows himself "for contempla-
tion . . . formed" (4.297).

    538–540. *Freely . . . fall:* Cf. *Christian
Doctrine* I, iii (*Works* 14, 81): "in assigning
the gift of free will God suffered both men
and angels to stand or fall at their own un-
controlled choice."

Attentive and with more delighted ear,   545
Divine instructor, I have heard than when
Cherubic songs by night from neighboring hills
Aerial° music send. Nor knew I not   *heavenly, angelic*
To be both will and deed created free;
Yet that we never shall forget to love   550
Our maker and obey him whose command
Single is yet so just, my constant thoughts
Assured me and still assure, though what thou tell'st
Hath passed in Heaven some doubt within me move
But more desire to hear, if thou consent,   555
The full relation, which must needs be strange,
Worthy of sacred silence to be heard;
And we have yet large day, for scarce the sun
Hath finished half his journey and scarce begins
His other half in the great zone of heaven."   560
    Thus Adam made request, and Raphael,
After short pause assenting, thus began:
    "High matter thou enjoin'st me, O prime of men,
Sad task and hard, for how shall I relate
To human sense the invisible exploits   565
Of warring spirits, how without remorse
The ruin of so many glorious once
And perfect while they stood, how last unfold
The secrets of another world perhaps
Not lawful to reveal? Yet for thy good   570

---

547. *Cherubic songs:* the songs of the cherubim guarding Eden, which Adam describes at 4.680–88

554. *move:* provokes (applies both to *doubt* in this line and "desire" in the next)

556–560. *The full . . . heaven:* Raphael's *full relation* in the significant amount of remaining daylight (*large day*) will include the war in heaven (Book 6), the creation of the universe (Book 7), and a short discussion of the stars (8.1–178). The *sacred silence* is a reminiscence of the silence of the spirits in the underworld as Horace imagined them (*Odes* 2.13.29–30) listening to the songs, "*sacro digna silentio,*" of the shades of the poets, though Horace goes on to say that the listeners in fact prefer tales of battles and

exiled tyrants ("*sed magis / pugnas et exactus tyrannos*").

563–570. *High . . . reveal:* The angel's preamble is similar to Aeneas' beginning in his tale to Dido of the fall of Troy, which fills the first two books of the *Aeneid:* "Great Queen, what you command me to relate / Renews the sad remembrance of our fate. / An empire from its old foundations rent, / And every woe the Trojans underwent. (2.3–6, Dryden's translation).

563. *prime:* 1) original; 2) most excellent

566. *without remorse:* It is possible that Raphael is announcing that he will tell the story of the ruin of the disobedient angels *without remorse* (i.e., pity) because they deserved their fall; or it may be that he is

This is dispensed, and what surmounts the reach
Of human sense I shall delineate so
By likening spiritual to corporal forms
As may express them best—though what if earth
Be but the shadow of Heaven, and things therein   575
Each to other like, more than on earth is thought?
　　"As yet this world was not, and Chaos wild
Reigned where these Heavens now roll, where earth now rests
Upon her center poised, when on a day
(For time, though in eternity, applied   580
To motion, measures all things durable
By present, past, and future), on such day
As heaven's great year brings forth, the empyreal host
Of angels, by imperial summons called,
Innumerable before the almighty's throne,   585
Forthwith from all the ends of Heaven appeared

worrying here that he may not be able to tell it without being overcome by remorse (i.e., sadness; see "sad task" in line 564) for what has been lost.

571. *dispensed:* permitted, done with dispensation

573. *corporal:* corporeal; Milton often distinguishes the two words: *corporal* reserved for "relating to the body" and "corporeal" meaning "with a body" (as opposed to spiritual), but here, most likely for metrical reasons, the subtle distinction is not maintained. The fourth edition of the poem in 1688 does read "corporeal."

574–576. *what . . . thought:* Though the conception of earth as the shadow of Heaven has been traced to various sources, it stems most directly from Plato's doctrine (*Republic* 10) that the phenomenal universe bears the same relation to eternal Ideas as the shadow to reality, and from Cicero's understanding of Plato's thought (in *Timaeus ex Platone* 2.39–41) as implying that "the world which we see is a simulacrum of an eternal one." More than either, Milton allows that earth and Heaven may be even more alike than *on earth is thought.*

578–579. *earth . . . poised:* See the fuller account of the earth "self-balanced on her center" at 7.242.

579. *on a day:* marks the earliest moment of the poem's chronology

580–582. *For . . . future:* Milton engages the philosophical debate about whether time existed before creation. Arguing in *Christian Doctrine* (I, vii) that it seems "probable that the apostasy which caused the expulsion of so many thousands [of angels] from heaven, took place before the foundations of the world were laid," Milton attacked "the common opinion that motion and time (which is the measure of motion) could not, according to the ratio or priority and subsequence, have existed before world was made." He was thinking of Plato's account of the divine creation of the "sun, the moon, and the five other planets" as indicators of time (*Timaeus* 38c–e), and Milton went on to argue that "Aristotle, who teaches that no ideas of motion and time can be formed except in reference to this world, nevertheless pronounces the world itself to be eternal" (*Works* 15, 35).

583. *heaven's great year:* The conception of the *great year,* the length of time it took all the heavenly bodies to complete their revolution in the heavens, originates also in the *Timaeus* (39d). Plato seems to suggest that it was the equivalent of 36,000 earthly years.

Under their hierarchs in orders bright;
Ten thousand thousand ensigns high advanced,
Standards and gonfalons twixt van° and rear   *vanguard*
Stream in the air and for distinction serve   590
Of hierarchies, of orders, and degrees;
Or in their glittering tissues° bear emblazed   *fabrics*
Holy memorials, acts of zeal and love
Recorded eminent. Thus when in orbs
Of circuit inexpressible they stood,   595
Orb within orb, the Father infinite,
By whom in bliss embosomed sat the Son,
Amidst as from a flaming mount whose top
Brightness had made invisible, thus spake:
"'Hear all ye angels, progeny of light,   600
Thrones, dominations, princedoms, virtues, powers,
Hear my decree, which unrevoked shall stand.
This day I have begot whom I declare
My only Son, and on this holy hill
Him have anointed, whom ye now behold   605
At my right hand; your head I him appoint,
And by myself have sworn to him shall bow
All knees in Heaven and shall confess him Lord.
Under his great vicegerent reign abide

587. *orders:* i.e., the nine orders of angels

589. *gonfalons:* banners (usually hung from a horizontal piece at the top of a pole, and used in formal processions)

590–591. *for distinction . . . degrees:* Heaven is thoroughly hierarchical.

594. *eminent:* can modify either "acts" (line 593) or *recorded*. In the former it functions as an adjective; in the latter, as an adverb.

597. *in bliss embosomed:* Cf. 3.169: "son of my bosom."

599. *Brightness . . . invisible:* like the aura surrounding God at 3.380 that is "Dark with excessive bright"; contrast the "darkness visible" of hell at 1.63.

603–615. *This day . . . end:* Milton begins the chronological action of *Paradise Lost* by dramatizing the revelation of the

exaltation of Christ to the angels, a tradition that stems from Heb. 1:1–6 and had orthodox theological support such as Aquinas gives to it (*Summa Theologica* I, q. 57, a.5). The word *begot* is not literal; Christ is not born on this day, but exalted (cf. Ps. 2:7 and its interpretation in Hebrews 1 or in Acts 13:33; and see also *Christian Doctrine* 1.5, which discusses the exaltation and uses "begotten" to mean "made him a king").

605. *anointed:* the literal meaning of "messiah"

606. *At my right hand:* See Ps. 110:1: "The Lord said unto my Lord, sit thou at my right hand."   *head:* See Col. 2:9: "ye are complete in him, which is the head of all principality and power."

607. *by myself . . . sworn:* So God swears by himself to Abraham (Gen. 22:16; see also Isa. 45:23).

United as one individual soul   610
Forever happy; him who disobeys
Me disobeys, breaks union, and that day,
Cast out from God and blessèd vision, falls
Into utter darkness, deep engulfed, his place
Ordained without redemption, without end.'   615
    "So spake the omnipotent, and with his words
All seemed well pleased; all seemed, but were not all.
That day, as other solemn° days, they spent   *holy, sacred*
In song and dance about the sacred hill,
Mystical dance, which yonder starry sphere   620
Of planets and of fixed° in all her wheels   *fixed stars*
Resembles nearest, mazes intricate,
Eccentric, intervolved,° yet regular   *interlocking*
Then most when most irregular they seem,
And in their motions harmony divine   625
So smoothes her charming tones that God's own ear
Listens delighted. Evening now approached
(For we have also our evening and our morn,
We ours for change delectable, not need),
Forthwith from dance to sweet repast they turn   630
Desirous; all in circles as they stood,
Tables are set and on a sudden piled
With angels' food, and rubied nectar flows
In pearl, in diamond, and massy gold,
Fruit of delicious vines, the growth of Heaven.   635
On flowers reposed and with fresh flowerets crowned,
They eat, they drink, and in communion sweet

610. *individual:* indivisible, inseparable (the word's usual meaning at this time, especially as referring to the Trinity, as at 4.486)

613. *blessèd vision:* i.e., of God; see 1.684.

620. *Mystical dance:* Milton could count on his readers to know both Plato's conception of the orderly movement of the stars as a dance and its literary trail in poems like Sir John Davies' *Orchestra: Or a Poeme of Dauncing* (1596): "What if to you these sparks disordered seeme / As if by chaunce they had been scattered there / The Gods a solemne measure doe it deeme / And see a just proportion euery where" (36.1–4).

623. *Eccentric:* has the astronomical application, as a noncircular orbit, that it has in 3.575 and 8.83.

630–637. *to sweet . . . drink:* The description of the meal is remarkably physical, perhaps inconsistent with the idea of the refinement of matter ("sublimed," line 483) as one nears God, although possibly evidence merely of the metaphorical necessity Raphael admits at lines 572–73 above.

637. *communion:* fellowship; the angels sit in "fellowships of joy" in 11.79–80. In 1667, the word here was "refection" (i.e., refreshment); Milton's revision seems to emphasize the meal as both communal and naturally sacramental.

Quaff immortality and joy, secure
Of surfeit where full measure only bounds
Excess, before the all-bounteous king, who showered   640
With copious hand, rejoicing in their joy.
Now when ambrosial° night with clouds exhaled   *fragrant*
From that high mount of God, whence light and shade
Spring both, the face of brightest Heaven had changed
To grateful twilight (for night comes not there   645
In darker veil), and roseate dews disposed
All but the unsleeping eyes of God to rest,
Wide over all the plain and wider far
Than all this globose° earth in plain outspread   *spherical*
(Such are the courts of God), the angelic throng,   650
Dispersed in bands and files,° their camp extend   *detachments of soldiers*
By living streams among the trees of life,
Pavilions numberless and sudden reared,
Celestial tabernacles, where they slept
Fanned with cool winds, save those who in their course   655
Melodious hymns about the sovereign throne
Alternate all night long. But not so waked
Satan, so call him now; his former name
Is heard no more in Heaven; he, of the first,
If not the first archangel, great in power,   660
In favor and preeminence, yet fraught
With envy against the Son of God, that day
Honored by his great Father and proclaimed
Messiah, king anointed, could not bear,
Through pride, that sight and thought himself impaired.   665
Deep malice thence conceiving and disdain,
Soon as midnight brought on the dusky hour
Friendliest to sleep and silence, he resolved
With all his legions to dislodge and leave

642. *ambrosial:* fragrant; see 2.245 above.

645. *night comes not there:* The description echoes the prophecy of Rev. 21:25, that "there shall be no night there." See line 162 above.

646. *roseate:* rose-scented (but punning, Latin *ros* = dew)

647. *unsleeping eyes of God:* follows Ps. 121:4: "he that keepeth Israel shall neither slumber nor sleep"

655. *course:* appointed task, as in 4.561

658–659. *former name . . . Heaven:* See the explanation in 1.361–63, that the names of the fallen angels are "blotted out" of "heavenly records."

664. *Messiah:* In Hebrew the word literally means "anointed." See 605 and note.

665. *impaired:* i.e., lowered in rank in the heavenly hierarchy (see line 73 above)

669. *dislodge:* can either refer to Satan's decision to *dislodge* (i.e., remove) himself

Unworshipped, unobeyed, the throne supreme,   670
Contemptuous, and his next subordinate
Awakening, thus to him in secret spake:
    "'Sleep'st thou, companion dear? What sleep can close
Thy eyelids? And remember'st what decree
Of yesterday so late hath passed the lips   675
Of Heaven's almighty? Thou to me thy thoughts
Wast wont, I mine to thee was wont to impart;
Both waking we were one; how then can now
Thy sleep dissent? New laws thou see'st imposed;
New laws from him who reigns, new minds° may raise   *intentions*
In us who serve, new counsels to debate
What doubtful may ensue; more in this place
To utter is not safe. Assemble thou
Of all those myriads which we lead the chief;
Tell them that by command ere yet dim night   685
Her shadowy cloud withdraws I am to haste,
And all who under me their banners wave,
Homeward with flying march where we possess
The quarters of the north, there to prepare
Fit entertainment to receive our king,   690
The great Messiah, and his new commands,
Who speedily through all the hierarchies
Intends to pass triumphant and give laws.'
    "So spake the false archangel and infused
Bad influence into the unwary breast   695
Of his associate; he together calls,

---

from the immediate environs of God (see 683–90 below) or to the futile effort to *dislodge* (i.e., displace) God from his "throne" (line 670)

671. *his next subordinate:* i.e., Beelzebub; see 2.299–300 (probably unnamed either because his prelapsarian name is not given in the bible or because Raphael here would not speak it).

689. *quarters of the north:* The association of Satan with the north is primarily based on Isa. 14:13: "I will ascend into heaven, I will exalt my throne above the stars of God: I will sit also upon the mount of the congregation, in the sides of the north." Augustine rationalized the tradition (in *Epistle*

140.55) by suggesting that, because the devils have turned their backs on the warmth of charity and are far advanced in pride and envy, they are torpid in icy hardness, "And hence through a figure they are put in the north." See also lines 726 and 755 below.

690. *entertainment:* Behind the overt lie is a sardonic pun from an alternative meaning of *entertainment,* which can also connote a military confrontation ("entertain," *OED* 9c).

694. *infused:* Here it is "Bad influence" (line 695) that is *infused,* but cf. 7.236, where it is "vital virtue" that is "infused" at creation.

696. *he:* i.e., Beelzebub, the *associate*

Or several° one by one, the regent powers,   *separately*
Under him regent, tells, as he was taught,
That the most high commanding now ere night,
Now ere dim night had disencumbered Heaven,   700
The great hierarchal standard was to move,
Tells the suggested cause and casts° between   *contrives, plots*
Ambiguous words and jealousies to sound°   *test, measure*
Or taint integrity; but all obeyed
The wonted signal and superior voice   705
Of their great potentate, for great indeed
His name and high was his degree in Heaven;
His countenance, as the morning star that guides
The starry flock, allured them and with lies
Drew after him the third part of Heaven's host.   710
Meanwhile the eternal eye, whose sight discerns
Abstrusest° thoughts, from forth his holy mount   *most hidden*
And from within the golden lamps that burn
Nightly before him, saw, without their light,
Rebellion rising, saw in whom, how spread   715
Among the sons of morn, what multitudes
Were banded to oppose his high decree
And smiling to his only Son thus said:
    " 'Son, thou in whom my glory I behold
In full resplendence, heir of all my might,   720
Nearly° it now concerns us to be sure   *urgently*
Of our omnipotence and with what arms
We mean to hold what anciently we claim
Of deity or empire, such a foe
Is rising, who intends to erect his throne   725
Equal to ours throughout the spacious north;

699. *the most high:* The angels are meant to understand this as referring to God, but it is the role Satan would claim, and does, for the disobedient angels; see Isa. 14:14: "I will be like the most High."

700. *dim night:* See lines 642–45 above.

708. *the morning star:* another allusion to "Lucifer, son of the morning" (Isa. 14:12), the name given to the morning appearance of the star Hesperus or Venus (see line 166n. above); but cf. Rev. 22:16, where Jesus names himself "the bright and morning star."

710. *third part . . . host:* On the fraction of Heaven that rebels against God, see 2.692 and note.

713. *the golden lamps:* Milton refers to the "seven lamps of fire burning before the throne" (Rev. 4:5), a passage perhaps related to the "seven eyes" mentioned in Zech. 3:9, which figure in 3.648–50.

716. *sons of morn:* angels (see lines 708–9 above); see also Job 38:7: "the morning stars sang together, and all the sons of God shouted for joy."

719–720. *Son . . . resplendence:* See 3.63–4.

Nor so content, hath in his thought to try
In battle what our power is or our right.
Let us advise, and to this hazard draw
With speed what force is left, and all employ   730
In our defense, lest unawares we lose
This our high place, our sanctuary, our hill.'
    "To whom the Son with calm aspect and clear,
Lightning divine, ineffable, serene,
Made answer: 'Mighty Father, thou thy foes   735
Justly hast in derision and secure
Laugh'st at their vain designs and tumults vain,
Matter to me of glory, whom their hate
Illustrates,° when they see all regal power   *makes glorious or illustrious*
Given me to quell their pride and in event   740
Know whether I be dexterous to subdue
Thy rebels or be found the worst in Heaven.'
    "So spake the Son, but Satan with his powers
Far was advanced on wingèd speed, an host
Innumerable as the stars of night   745
Or stars of morning, dewdrops which the sun
Impearls on every leaf and every flower.
Regions they passed, the mighty regencies°   *dominions, provinces*
Of seraphim and potentates and thrones
In their triple degrees, regions to which   750
All thy dominion, Adam, is no more
Than what this garden is to all the earth
And all the sea, from one entire globose
Stretched into longitude; which having passed,
At length into the limits of the north   755
They came, and Satan to his royal seat
High on a hill far blazing, as a mount

731–732. *lest unawares . . . hill:* But an omniscient God could not be taken *unawares;* perhaps this is why the whole speech is introduced with the picture of God "smiling" (line 718); see also lines 736–7 below.

736–737. *Justly . . . Laugh'st:* The language comes from Ps. 2:4: "He that sitteth in the heavens shall laugh: the Lord shall have them in derision"; cf. 2.191.

740. *in event:* by the outcome (*event* keeps its Latin meaning [e = *out; venire* = to come], as in 2.82)

741. *dexterous:* skillful, but punning on Christ at the "right hand" (*ad dextram*) of God; see 3.279 and line 606 above.

743. *powers:* here most likely means "armies" (and not, as at 1.128, a collective term for the various orders of angels)

753. *globose:* sphere (an adjective for a noun); see line 649

754. *Stretched into longitude:* spread out or projected onto a flat plane (like most maps)

Raised on a mount, with pyramids and towers
From diamond quarries hewn and rocks of gold,
The palace of great Lucifer (so call   760
That structure in the dialect of men
Interpreted) which, not long after, he,
Affecting° all equality with God,   *pretending to, claiming*
In imitation of that mount whereon
Messiah was declared in sight of Heaven,   765
The Mountain of the Congregation called;
For thither he assembled all his train,
Pretending so commanded to consult
About the great reception of their king
Thither to come, and with calumnious art   770
Of counterfeited truth thus held their ears:
    "'Thrones, dominations, princedoms, virtues, powers,
If these magnific titles yet remain
Not merely titular, since by decree
Another now hath to himself engrossed°   *monopolized*
All power and us eclipsed under the name
Of King anointed, for whom all this haste
Of midnight march and hurried meeting here,
This only to consult how we may best
With what may be devised of honors new   780
Receive him coming to receive from us
Knee-tribute yet unpaid, prostration vile,
Too much to one, but double how endured,
To one and to his image now proclaimed?
But what if better counsels might erect   785

---

758. *pyramids and towers:* architectural
forms that Milton associates with ambition
and pride; see 1.694.
    760–762. *The palace . . . Interpreted:*
The use of the name "Lucifer" is appropriate
for Satan only before his fall, but Milton ad-
mits that the name is nonetheless used *in the
dialect of men.*
    764. *that mount:* the "flaming mount"
in line 598
    768–770. *Pretending . . . come:* See lines
685–91 above.
    772–774. *Thrones . . . titular:* The list
of angelic titles echoes God's speech at line
601 above, but what has rendered the titles

merely titular is not the exaltation of Christ
but their own disobedience.
    777. *King anointed:* i.e., Messiah; see
line 664.
    781–783. *coming . . . endured:* Here
Satan finds the thought of praising Christ un-
endurable, but cf. Gabriel's memory of Satan's
actual servility in Heaven at 4.958–60.
    783–784. *Too much . . . proclaimed:*
Satan sees the elevation of Christ as doubling
his own obligations of gratitude, revealing
his misunderstanding of the nature of grati-
tude as well as of the relation of Christ and
God. In calling Christ God's "image," how-
ever, he merely echoes 3.63, though miscon-
struing what this implies; see 3.139–40.

Our minds and teach us to cast off this yoke?
Will ye submit your necks and choose to bend
The supple knee? Ye will not, if I trust
To know ye right, or if ye know yourselves
Natives and sons of Heaven possessed before   790
By none, and, if not equal all, yet free,
Equally free; for orders and degrees
Jar not with liberty but well consist.
Who can in reason, then, or right assume
Monarchy over such as live by right   795
His equals if, in power and splendor less,
In freedom equal? Or can introduce
Law and edict on us who, without law,
Err not, much less for this to be our lord
And look for adoration to the abuse   800
Of those imperial titles which assert
Our being ordained to govern, not to serve?'
      "Thus far his bold discourse without control
Had audience,° when among the seraphim   *hearing, acceptance*
Abdiel, than whom none with more zeal adored   805
The deity and divine commands obeyed,
Stood up, and in a flame of zeal severe
The current of his fury thus opposed:
      "'O argument blasphemous, false and proud!
Words which no ear ever to hear in Heaven   810
Expected, least of all from thee, ingrate,

788. *The supple knee:* recalls "the tribute of his supple knee" in Shakespeare's *Richard II*, 1.4.33 and other examples that reveal the proverbial character of this image of submissiveness.

791–802. *if not equal . . . serve:* For Milton, hierarchy and freedom can coexist; he is not a radical leveler (and for that matter neither is Satan, though on different grounds). Here Satan twists the truth that Milton asserted in *Christian Doctrine* 1.9 and detailed in his conception of human order and liberty in *The Reason of Church Government* (*Works* 3, part 1, 185) as patterned upon "the angels themselves, in whom no disorder is feared, as the apostle that saw them in his rapture describes . . . [as] distinguished and quaternioned into their celestial

princedoms and satrapies, according as God himself has writ his imperial decrees through the great provinces of heaven."

794–796. *Who can . . . equals:* This is the central political claim of Satan, that it is unjust to *assume Monarchy over* those who are by right one's *equals*. If God has indeed established rule over those who are his equals, then God is a tyrant; but see lines 831–37 below, and 4.42–44, where Satan admits the fact of his created nature (thus differentiating Satan's politics from Milton's).

797. *Or can:* i.e., or who can

805. *Abdiel:* The name means "servant of God," and it appears in the bible only as a human name (1 Chron. 5:15).

808. *his:* i.e., Satan's

811. *ingrate:* Cf. 3.97.

In place thyself so high above thy peers.
Canst thou with impious obloquy° condemn   *abusive speech*
The just decree of God, pronounced and sworn,
That to his only Son, by right endued   815
With regal scepter, every soul in Heaven
Shall bend the knee, and in that honor due
Confess him rightful king? Unjust, thou say'st,
Flatly unjust, to bind with laws the free,
And equal over equals to let reign,   820
One over all with unsucceeded power.
Shalt thou give law to God? Shalt thou dispute
With him the points of liberty, who made
Thee what thou art and formed the powers of Heaven
Such as he pleased and circumscribed their being?   825
Yet by experience taught we know how good,
And of our good and of our dignity
How provident he is, how far from thought
To make us less, bent rather to exalt
Our happy state under one head more near   830
United. But, to grant it thee unjust
That equal over equals monarch reign,
Thyself though great and glorious dost thou count,
Or all angelic nature joined in one,
Equal to him, begotten Son, by whom   835
As by his word the mighty Father made
All things, even thee, and all the spirits of Heaven
By him created in their bright degrees,
Crowned them with glory, and to their glory named

816–818. *every soul . . . king:* echoes
Phil. 2.10–11: "At the name of Jesus every
knee should bow . . . and . . . every tongue
should confess that Jesus Christ is Lord."

821. *unsucceeded:* with no successor
(i.e., eternal)

822–824. *Shalt thou . . . art:* Cf. Rom.
9:20: "O man, who art thou that repliest
against God? Shall the thing formed say to
him that formed it, Why hast thou made me
thus?"

829. *bent:* determined, but suggesting
bending down, bent over, in order to raise
(*exalt*) mankind (an anticipation of Christ's
incarnation)

833–837. *Thyself . . . thee:* Here Abdiel
exposes the fallacy of Satan's political posi-
tion: Satan is not God's equal, because he
was created by God; there's an ontological
difference between the two of them as cre-
ator and creature that radically justifies God's
power and authority.

835–842. *by whom . . . made:* echoes
Col. 1:16–17: "For by him were all things
created, that are in heaven, and that are in
earth, visible and invisible, whether they be
thrones, or dominions, or principalities, or
powers: all things were created by him, and
for him: and he is before all things, and by
him all things consist."

Thrones, dominations, princedoms, virtues, powers,   840
Essential powers, nor by his reign obscured
But more illustrious made since he, the head,
One of our number thus reduced becomes,
His laws our laws; all honor to him done
Returns our own. Cease then this impious rage   845
And tempt not these; but hasten to appease
Th' incensèd Father and the incensèd Son,
While pardon may be found in time besought.'
      "So spake the fervent angel, but his zeal
None seconded as out of season judged   850
Or singular and rash, whereat rejoiced
The apostate and more haughty thus replied:
'That we were formed then, say'st thou? And the work
Of secondary hands, by task transferred
From Father to his Son? Strange point and new!   855
Doctrine which we would know whence learned: who saw
When this creation was? Remember'st thou
Thy making while the maker gave thee being?
We know no time when we were not as now;
Know none before us, self-begot, self-raised   860
By our own quickening power when fatal course
Had circled his full orb, the birth mature
Of this our native Heaven, ethereal sons.
Our puissance° is our own; our own right hand   *power, strength*
Shall teach us highest deeds by proof to try   865
Who is our equal. Then thou shalt behold
Whether by supplication we intend
Address and to begirt the almighty throne
Beseeching or besieging. This report,
These tidings carry to the anointed king,   870
And fly, ere evil intercept thy flight.'

853–858. *That we . . . being:* As early as 1.116, Satan casts doubt upon the article of faith that Milton formulated in *Christian Doctrine* I, vii (*Works* 15, 33) in the words: "the angels were created at some particular period." The challenge to Abdiel is made on the grounds of an unanswerable empiricism, but 1) Satan's own claim to being "self-begot" is thus similarly unverifiable; and 2) cf. Adam's rhetorical question, "who himself

beginning knew" (8.251), and the account of his self-awareness and instinctive sense that he was made "by some great maker" whom he should "adore" (8.270–80).

861. *fatal:* inevitable, ordained by fate

864. *our own right hand:* our collective might (but the irony of the synecdoche is clear in the inevitable comparison with the might of Christ, God's "right hand"; see line 606 above).

"He said, and, as the sound of waters deep,
Hoarse murmur echoed to his words applause
Through the infinite host; nor less for that
The flaming seraph fearless though alone,   875
Encompassed round with foes, thus answered bold:
    "'O alienate from God, O spirit accursed,
Forsaken of all good; I see thy fall
Determined and thy hapless crew involved
In this perfidious fraud, contagion spread   880
Both of thy crime and punishment; henceforth
No more be troubled how to quit the yoke
Of God's Messiah: those indulgent laws
Will not now be vouchsafed. Other decrees
Against thee are gone forth without recall;   885
That golden scepter which thou didst reject
Is now an iron rod to bruise and break
Thy disobedience. Well thou didst advise,
Yet not for thy advice or threats I fly
These wicked tents devoted, lest the wrath   890
Impendent raging into sudden flame
Distinguish not; for soon expect to feel
His thunder on thy head, devouring fire.
Then who created thee lamenting learn,
When who can uncreate thee thou shalt know.'   895
    "So spake the seraph Abdiel, faithful found,
Among the faithless, faithful only he;
Among innumerable false, unmoved,
Unshaken, unseduced, unterrified,
His loyalty he kept, his love, his zeal;   900
Nor number nor example with him wrought
To swerve from truth or change his constant mind

---

872. *as the sound of waters deep:* In Rev.
14:2 (see also Rev. 19:6), "a voice from
heaven" is heard as "the voice of many
waters"; perhaps the simile here declares the
distance from true worship.

887. *iron rod:* Cf. the "iron scepter"
that the devils fear in 2.327.

890. *wicked tents devoted:* Abdiel resem-
bles Moses urging the Jews to abandon the
blasphemous rebels Korah, Dathan, and Abi-
ram: "Depart, I pray you, from the tents of

these wicked men . . . lest ye be consumed in
all their sins" (Num. 16:26). (*devoted* here
has its Latin sense of "doomed.")

891. *Impendent:* hanging (over the rebel
angels' heads)

892. *Distinguish not:* not make the dis-
tinction (between the rebellious and the
faithful)

901. *Nor . . . nor:* neither . . . nor
with him wrought: persuaded him

Though single. From amidst them forth he passed,
Long way through hostile scorn, which he sustained
Superior, nor of violence feared aught;   905
And with retorted scorn his back he turned
On those proud towers to swift destruction doomed."

The End of the Fifth Book.

903. *single:* alone (Abdiel becomes the type of the one just man who will be saved; e.g., Enoch and Noah)

906. *retorted:* answering (but "retorted" literally means "turned back" and so plays also on *back he turned*).

BOOK 6

The Argument

Raphael continues to relate how Michael and Gabriel were sent forth to battle against Satan and his angels. The first fight described. Satan and his powers retire under night; he calls a council, invents devilish engines, which in the second day's fight put Michael and his angels to some disorder, but they at length, pulling up mountains, overwhelmed both the force and machines of Satan. Yet the tumult not so ending, God on the third day sends Messiah, his Son, for whom he had reserved the glory of that victory; he, in the power of his Father coming to the place and causing all his legions to stand still on either side, with his chariot and thunder driving into the midst of his enemies, pursues them, unable to resist, toward the wall of Heaven, which, opening, they leap down with horror and confusion into the place of punishment prepared for them in the deep. Messiah returns with triumph to his Father.

"All night the dreadless angel unpursued
Through Heaven's wide champaign° held his way till morn,   *level, open country*
Waked by the circling hours, with rosy hand
Unbarred the gates of light. There is a cave
Within the mount of God, fast by his throne,
Where light and darkness in perpetual round
Lodge and dislodge by turns, which makes through Heaven
Grateful vicissitude, like day and night:
Light issues forth, and at the other door
Obsequious darkness enters till her hour   10

---

1. *the dreadless angel:* i.e., Abdiel (*dreadless* = without fear)

3. *circling hours:* the passing of time, both in a mechanistic sense of time's repetition and as a personification, the Horae, goddesses of the seasons (see Spenser's *Faerie Queene* 7.7.45: "The Howres, faire daughters of high Jove, / . . . who did them Porters make / Of heaven's gate")

4–8. *There is . . . night:* In Hesiod's *Theogony*, there is a cave in the abyss in

which night and day similarly alternate in residence (744–54); here, however, it is *Within the mount of God.*

5. *fast by:* next to

8. *Grateful vicissitude:* enjoyable alternation; see 7.350–51.

10. *Obsequious:* obedient (reflecting the Latin meaning of *obsequor* = following); cf. the *Obsequious darkness* here with the "grateful twilight" of 5.645.

To veil the Heaven, though darkness there might well
Seem twilight here. And now went forth the morn
Such as in highest Heaven, arrayed in gold
Empyreal; from before her vanished night,
Shot through with orient beams, when all the plain   15
Covered with thick embattled° squadrons bright,   *ready for battle*
Chariots and flaming arms and fiery steeds,
Reflecting blaze on blaze, first met his view:
War he perceived, war in procinct, and found
Already known what he for news had thought   20
To have reported; gladly then he mixed
Among those friendly powers, who him received
With joy and acclamations loud, that one
That of so many myriads fallen, yet one,
Returned not lost. On to the sacred hill   25
They led him high applauded and present
Before the seat supreme, from whence a voice
From midst a golden cloud thus mild was heard:
    "'Servant of God, well done; well hast thou fought
The better fight, who single hast maintained   30
Against revolted multitudes the cause
Of truth, in word mightier than they in arms,

11–12. *darkness . . . here:* See 5.645–46 for an earlier statement on the absence of darkness in Heaven.

14. *Empyreal:* purest, as from the highest heaven; the word makes reference to its derivation from the Greek word for "fire," but see the distinction of heavenly and earthly fire in 2.138–42

15. *Shot through:* both "pierced" and "varied in color"; perhaps an obvious metaphor in context, but part of the extraordinary intermingling of material and immaterial in Raphael's (if not also Milton's) descriptions of Heaven

18. *Reflecting blaze on blaze:* The image is a *mise en abyme* of fiery surfaces reflecting each other.

19. *procinct:* readiness; see George Chapman's use of the term in his translation of *Iliad* 12.88–89: "each chariot and steed . . . to be kept in all procinct of warre."

21. *gladly:* After the stunning anticlimax of lines 19–21, Abdiel feels no disappointment but *gladly* mingles with angels.

26. *present:* a verb (as an adjective it would be tautological) with the understood object "him," but in the present tense; narratively inappropriate after *led*, but to God past, present, and future appear at once

29. *Servant of God:* the literal translation of the Hebrew "Abdiel," see 5.805n. This and the next phrase echo Matt. 25:21: "Well done, thou good and faithful servant."

29–30. *fought . . . fight:* echoes the proverb "to fight the good fight," but here it marks more than merely fighting well: it is fighting for the right cause. That is what makes this act *better;* see 1 Tim. 6:12: "Fight the good fight of faith."

30. *single:* the word, echoing its use in 5.903, emphasizes Abdiel's heroism, *single* in the senses of being both unmatched and unaided.

32. *truth . . . arms:* The idea that truth is mightier than the sword is proverbial,

And for the testimony of truth hast born
Universal reproach, far worse to bear
Than violence; for this was all thy care   35
To stand approved in sight of God, though worlds
Judged thee perverse. The easier conquest now
Remains thee, aided by this host of friends,
Back on thy foes more glorious to return
Than scorned thou didst depart, and to subdue   40
By force, who reason for their law refuse,
Right reason for their law, and for their king
Messiah, who by right of merit reigns.
Go, Michael, of celestial armies prince
And thou, in military prowess next,   45
Gabriel, lead forth to battle these my sons
Invincible, lead forth my armèd saints°   *angels*
By thousands and by millions ranged for fight,
Equal in number to that godless crew
Rebellious; them with fire and hostile arms   50
Fearless assault and, to the brow° of Heaven   *edge, verge*
Pursuing, drive them out from God and bliss
Into their place of punishment, the gulf
Of Tartarus, which ready opens wide

though the singular *word* here is perhaps surprising, especially as Milton makes the contrasting term plural (*arms*); but the line both explains and enacts the singleness of Abdiel against the "revolted multitudes" (line 31).

33–34. *testimony . . . reproach:* echoes Ps. 69.7: "For thy sake I have borne reproach."

35–36. *all . . . God:* See 2 Tim. 2:15: "study to shew thyself approved unto God."

42. *Right reason . . . law:* in contrast to the disobedience of Satan and his followers, "who reason for their law refuse" (line 41); "right reason" translates the Stoic *recta ratio; Right* = upright, meaning "with rectitude," and, thus, also the opposite of "fallen." In *Christian Doctrine* (I, ii), Milton speaks of "conscience, or right reason" (*Works* 14, 29).

43. *by right of merit:* Cf. 2.5–6, where "Satan exalted sat, by merit raised / To that bad eminence"; see also his claim (2.21) that

his rule is justified by what "Hath been achieved of merit."

44. *Michael . . . prince:* In Jewish and Christian tradition Michael (the "godlike" or "strength of God") is the foremost of the angels (sometimes even conflated with Christ): in Rev. 12:7, it is "Michael and his angels" who "fought against the dragon"; and he is "the great prince which standeth for the children of thy people" in Dan. 12:1.

46. *Gabriel:* See 4.549–50.

49. *Equal in number to:* Many commentators, troubled by the fact that Satan has taken with him only a third of the angels of Heaven (2.692), gloss this as meaning "easily the equal of"; however, God is saying that Michael should only take with him a force of angels *Equal in number to* the angels that rebelled. The inconclusive fighting on the first two days confirms this parity; see lines 684–94.

53–54. *gulf Of Tartarus:* abyss of Hell

His fiery chaos to receive their fall.'   55
   "So spake the sovereign voice, and clouds began
To darken all the hill, and smoke to roll
In dusky wreaths, reluctant flames, the sign
Of wrath awaked; nor with less dread the loud
Ethereal trumpet from on high 'gan blow,   60
At which command the powers militant
That stood for Heaven in mighty quadrate joined
Of union irresistible, moved on
In silence their bright legions to the sound
Of instrumental harmony that breathed   65
Heroic ardor to adventurous deeds
Under their godlike leaders in the cause
Of God and his Messiah. On they move
Indissolubly firm; nor obvious hill,
Nor straitening ¡ vale, nor wood, nor stream divides   *confining*
Their perfect ranks, for high above the ground
Their march was, and the passive air upbore
Their nimble tread. As when the total kind
Of birds in orderly array on wing
Came summoned over Eden to receive   75
Their names of thee, so over many a tract

56–59. *clouds . . . awaked:* The scene resembles Mount Sinai when it was "altogether on a smoke, because the Lord descended upon it in fire; and the smoke thereof ascended as the smoke of a furnace" (Exod. 19:18); *reluctant,* therefore, does not mean that the flames are hesitant to display God's awakened *wrath* but that they are writhing (*OED* 1, and 10.515 below) as they flicker or glow in the dark (also punning perhaps on the Latin *reluceo* = to glow).

62. *stood for:* upheld, defended (but also, committed to); *stood,* throughout this poem about the fall, is always a charged word, carrying the implication of "stood faithful," i.e., as opposed to fallen   *quadrate:* square battle formation, like the "perfect phalanx" of 1.550. The military formations in Heaven are similar to those in hell; both are in the four-sided configurations based on the *agmen quadratum* of the Romans.

63–65. *moved on . . . . harmony:* cf. 1.561, where the fallen angels "Moved on in

silence to soft pipes"; in both Heaven and hell, the angels are inspired by *instrumental harmony.* Some editors have tried to differentiate the martial music of Heaven and hell, but Milton makes them oddly similar: in Hell the music is "such as raised / To height of noblest temper heroes old" (1.551–52); in Heaven, the music breathes "Heroic ardor to adventurous deeds" (5.66). Perhaps this reflects Milton's own deep suspicion of the traditional terms of heroism, or merely indicates that the value of heroic action rests not in the action itself but on the ends it serves.

69. *obvious:* primarily has its literal, Latin meaning of "standing in the way"

72. *passive air upbore:* The air's passivity is immediately denied by its action, *upbore,* perhaps suggesting the fundamental productivity of everything in heaven.

73–76. *As when . . . thee:* Adam names the creatures, including *the total kind* (i.e., all the species) of birds, in Gen. 2:20 and

Of Heaven they marched and many a province wide,
Tenfold the length of this terrene. At last,
Far in the horizon to the north appeared
From skirt to skirt a fiery region stretched   80
In battailous° aspect and, nearer view   *warlike*
Bristled with upright beams innumerable
Of rigid spears, and helmets thronged, and shields
Various with boastful argument portrayed,
The banded powers of Satan hasting on   85
With furious expedition; for they weened°   *expected, reckoned*
That selfsame day by fight or by surprise
To win the mount of God, and on his throne
To set the envier of his state, the proud
Aspirer, but their thoughts proved fond and vain   90
In the midway, though strange to us it seemed
At first that angel should with angel war
And in fierce hosting meet, who wont to meet
So oft in festivals of joy and love
Unanimous,° as sons of one great sire   *of one mind*
Hymning the eternal Father. But the shout
Of battle now began, and rushing sound
Of onset ended soon each milder thought.
High in the midst, exalted as a god,
The apostate in his sun-bright chariot sat,   100
Idol of majesty divine, enclosed
With flaming cherubim and golden shields;
Then lighted from his gorgeous throne, for now

8.343–51 below; Homer (*Iliad* 2.459–63) and Virgil (*Aeneid* 7.699–701) both compare mustering troops to flights of birds.

78. *terrene:* the earth (adjective used as a noun), though spheres can't properly be said to have *length*

79. *to the north:* See the mustering of the devils in "the quarters of the north" in 5.689.

80. *skirt to skirt:* side to side

82. *beams:* here means spears ("beam," as length of timber)

83. *rigid spears . . . shields:* Milton's angels have weaponry, unlike those in Thomas Heywood's *Hierarchie of the Blessed Angels* (1635), where "No Lances, Swords, nor Bombards they had then, / Or other

weapons now in use with men . . . only spiritual Armes" (p. 341).

84. *argument:* the heraldic emblem or motto on the shields. There may be an allusion to the boastfully inscribed shields of the seven doomed kings in the assault on Thebes in Euripides' *Phoenician Maidens*, 1108–40.

86. *expedition:* speed

91. *midway:* i.e., well before they could be realized

93. *hosting:* 1) hostility (*host* = army); 2) hospitality, ironic with *fierce*

100. *his sun-bright chariot:* Cf. Christ's "chariot of paternal deity / Flashing thick flames," lines 750–51 below.

101. *Idol:* false image (as in the arrogations of line 100 above and 102 below)

'Twixt host and host but narrow space was left,
A dreadful interval, and front to front   105
Presented stood in terrible array
Of hideous length. Before the cloudy van
On the rough edge° of battle ere it joined,   *line of battle*
Satan with vast and haughty strides advanced,
Came towering, armed in adamant and gold;   110
Abdiel that sight endured not, where he stood
Among the mightiest, bent on highest deeds,
And thus his own undaunted heart explores:
    "'O Heaven, that such resemblance of the highest
Should yet remain where faith and realty   115
Remain not. Wherefore should not strength and might
There fail where virtue fails, or weakest prove
Where boldest, though to sight unconquerable?
His puissance,° trusting in the almighty's aid,   *power, strength*
I mean to try, whose reason I have tried°   *proved by trial, tested*
Unsound and false; nor is it aught but just
That he who in debate of truth hath won
Should win in arms, in both disputes alike
Victor, though brutish that contest and foul
When reason hath to deal with force, yet so   125
Most reason is that reason overcome.'
    "So pondering, and from his armèd peers
Forth stepping opposite, halfway he met
His daring foe, at this prevention° more   *obstruction, obstacle*
Incensed, and thus securely° him defied: *confidently*
    "'Proud, art thou met? Thy hope was to have reached
The height of thy aspiring unopposed,
The throne of God unguarded, and his side
Abandoned at the terror of thy power
Or potent tongue. Fool, not to think how vain   135
Against the omnipotent to rise in arms,

---

105. *interval:* space (Latin *intervallum* = the space between two armed camps)

107. *cloudy van:* dismaying vanguard (of the army)

110. *adamant:* See 1.48 and note.

111. *he:* i.e., Satan

113. *And . . . explores:* The line echoes Homer's introduction of Hector's soliloquy as he goes out to face Achilles in the single combat in which he finally is slain (*Iliad* 22.98); *explores* = pours out.

115. *realty:* sincerity (if it is not a misprint for "fealty" [i.e., loyalty], as some have speculated)

118. *to sight:* apparently (characteristically for Milton, *sight* here is unreliable).

126. *Most reason is:* the most reasonable outcome is

Who out of smallest things could without end
Have raised incessant armies to defeat
Thy folly, or, with solitary hand
Reaching beyond all limit, at one blow   140
Unaided could have finished thee and whelmed
Thy legions under darkness. But thou seest
All are not of thy train; there be who faith
Prefer and piety to God, though then
To thee not visible when I alone   145
Seemed in thy world erroneous to dissent
From all. My sect thou seest; now learn too late
How few sometimes may know when thousands err.'
    "Whom the grand foe with scornful eye askance
Thus answered: 'Ill for thee, but in wished hour   150
Of my revenge first sought, for thou return'st
From flight, seditious angel, to receive
Thy merited reward, the first assay°   assault
Of this right hand provoked, since first that tongue
Inspired with contradiction durst oppose   155
A third part of the gods in synod met
Their deities to assert, who, while they feel
Vigor divine within them, can allow
Omnipotence to none. But well thou com'st
Before thy fellows, ambitious to win   160
From me some plume,° that thy success may show   trophy
Destruction to the rest; this pause between
(Unanswered lest thou boast) to let thee know.
At first I thought that liberty and Heaven
To heavenly souls had been all one, but now   165
I see that most through sloth had rather serve,

---

143. *there be:* there are those

147. *sect:* kind, sort; though *sect* and its synonym "sectary," were used, mostly pejoratively, for any of the denominations into which Protestantism was splintering. In the Preface to *Eikonoklastes* (*Works* 5, 73) Milton protested against the "odious names of Schism and Sectarism," and insisted that "they who adhere to wisdom and to truth are not therefore to be blam'd for being so few as to seem a sect or faction."

156. *third part:* See 2.692 and note. *synod:* assembly (as in 2.391 and note)

160. *ambitious:* an adjective modifying "com'st" in line 159, but Satan's followers are indeed *fellows, ambitious,* as the syntax momentarily tempts us

161. *success:* fortune, result (here presumed to be bad)

162. *this pause:* i.e., between this conversation and your defeat

163. *Unanswered lest thou boast:* lest you boast that I could not answer you

165. *all one:* the same thing

166. *most . . . serve:* Cf. *SA*, lines 268–71: "But what more oft in nations grown cor-

Ministering spirits trained up in feast and song.
Such hast thou armed, the minstrelsy of Heaven,
Servility with freedom to contend,
As both their deeds compared this day shall prove.'   170
    "To whom in brief thus Abdiel stern replied:
'Apostate, still thou err'st, nor end wilt find
Of erring, from the path of truth remote.
Unjustly thou deprav'st° it with the name   *perverts, distorts*
Of servitude to serve whom God ordains   175
Or nature: God and nature bid the same
When he who rules is worthiest and excels
Them whom he governs. This is servitude:
To serve the unwise or him who hath rebelled
Against his worthier, as thine now serve thee,   180
Thyself not free but to thyself enthralled,
Yet lewdly darest our ministering upbraid.
Reign thou in hell, thy kingdom; let me serve
In Heaven God ever blessed and his divine
Behests obey, worthiest to be obeyed.   185
Yet chains in hell, not realms, expect; meanwhile
From me returned, as erst thou said'st, from flight,
This greeting on thy impious crest receive.'
    "So saying, a noble stroke he lifted high,
Which hung not, but so swift with tempest fell   190
On the proud crest of Satan that no sight
Nor motion of swift thought, less could his shield,
Such ruin intercept; ten paces huge
He back recoiled, the tenth on bended knee

rupt . . . Than to love bondage more than
liberty / Bondage with ease than strenuous
liberty."
    167–168. *Ministering spirits . . . Heaven:*
Satan mocks the obedient angels as servile
and weak (*minstrelsy* = group of minstrels).
Cf. line 182 below, and Heb. 1:14, where of
the angels it is asked: "are they not all minis-
tering spirits."
    176. *nature:* For Milton, *nature* is "the
mysterious power and efficacy of the divine
voice which went forth in the beginning, and
to which, as to a perpetual command, all
things have since paid obedience" (*Christian
Doctrine* I, viii [*Works* 15, 93]). See Hooker,

Laws of Ecclesiastical Polity (1593, 1.3.1–4),
where *nature* is similarly understood as
"God's instrument."
    178–181. *This is . . . enthralled:* So
servitude is defined in 12.90–101, and *PR*
2.463–72.
    182. *lewdly:* 1) vilely; 2) ignorantly
    183–184. *Reign thou . . . blessed:* Abdiel
precisely reverses the Satanic insistence that
it is "Better to reign in hell than serve in
Heaven (1.263).
    189. *a noble stroke he lifted high:* The
noun *stroke* here oddly anticipates the action
of the verb, and *noble* assumes the value of
the yet-to-be-completed action.

His massy spear upstayed, as if on earth   195
Winds under ground or waters forcing way
Sidelong had pushed a mountain from his seat
Half sunk with all his pines. Amazement seized
The rebel thrones, but greater rage to see
Thus foiled their mightiest; ours joy filled and shout,   200
Presage of victory and fierce desire
Of battle, whereat Michael bid sound
The archangel trumpet. Through the vast of Heaven
It sounded, and the faithful armies rung
'Hosanna' to the highest; nor stood at gaze   205
The adverse legions nor less hideous joined
The horrid shock. Now storming fury rose
And clamor such as heard in Heaven till now
Was never: arms on armor clashing brayed
Horrible discord, and the madding° wheels   *whirling (spinning madly)*
Of brazen chariots raged; dire was the noise
Of conflict; overhead the dismal hiss
Of fiery darts in flaming volleys flew
And flying vaulted either host with fire.
So under fiery cope together rushed   215
Both battles main with ruinous assault
And inextinguishable rage; all Heaven
Resounded, and had earth been then, all earth
Had to her center shook. What wonder, when
Millions of fierce encountering angels fought   220
On either side, the least of whom could wield
These elements and arm him with the force

---

196. *Winds under ground:* popularly
thought to be the cause of earthquakes, as at
1.230–37 (cf. Dante, *Purgatoria* 21.55–56,
where earthquakes come from "wind that is
hidden in the earth.")

199. *thrones:* one of the nine angelic or-
ders, here used synecdochically for all the
rebel angels

200. *ours:* i.e., our angels

203. *vast:* boundless space (cf. Shake-
speare, *The Tempest* 1.2.327: "vast of night.")

204–205. *faithful armies rung 'Hosanna':*
Cf. Mammon's reluctance to "sing / Forced
hallelujahs" (2.242–3).

213. *fiery darts:* echoes Eph. 6:16,

where Paul endorses the "shield of faith,
wherewith ye shall be able to quench all the
fiery darts of the wicked."

215. *cope:* sky (as in 4.992); Hesiod de-
scribes it as darkened by missiles in the strug-
gle of the giants with the gods (*Theogony*
716–17).

216. *battles main:* the main body of the
armies, as opposed to their "vans" or the
"wings"

222. *These elements:* i.e., the earth itself
(where Raphael and Adam are, hence *These*),
to be composed of the four elements—air,
water, fire, and earth—which "the least" of
the angels could throw (line 221).

Of all their regions? How much more of power
Army against army numberless to raise
Dreadful combustion° warring and disturb,   *tumult, confusion*
Though not destroy, their happy native seat,
Had not the eternal king omnipotent
From his stronghold of Heaven high overruled
And limited their might, though numbered such
As each divided legion might have seemed   230
A numerous host, in strength each armèd hand
A legion. Led in fight, yet leader seemed
Each warrior, single as in chief, expert
When to advance, or stand, or turn the sway
Of battle, open when, and when to close   235
The ridges° of grim war; no thought of flight,   *ranks (of soldiers)*
None of retreat, no unbecoming deed
That argued fear; each on himself relied,
As only in his arm the moment lay
Of victory; deeds of eternal fame   240
Were done, but infinite, for wide was spread
That war and various. Sometimes on firm ground
A standing fight, then soaring on main° wing   *powerful*
Tormented all the air; all air seemed then
Conflicting fire. Long time in even scale   245
The battle hung, till Satan, who that day
Prodigious power had shown and met in arms
No equal, ranging through the dire attack
Of fighting seraphim confused, at length
Saw where the sword of Michael smote and felled   250
Squadrons at once; with huge two-handed sway°   *force, effort*
Brandished aloft the horrid edge came down
Wide wasting; such destruction to withstand
He hasted and opposed the rocky orb
Of tenfold adamant, his ample shield   255

---

223. *their:* the elements (see 3.714–15)

229. *numbered such:* so numerous

232–233. *Led in fight . . . chief:* Though they had leaders, every individual acted with the skill and confidence of an experienced commander.

239. *moment:* 1) outcome; 2) incremental weight that could tip the balance of a scale (see line 245)

254–255. *rocky orb . . . adamant:* i.e., Satan's *ample shield,* which is *rocky* because it is made of adamant, the mythical, unbreakable substance here imagined as being further (and unnecessarily) strengthened by being folded ten times to multiply its thickness. The armor of the angels is made of the same substance (line 542 below).

A vast circumference. At his approach
The great archangel from his warlike toil
Surceased, and glad, as hoping here to end
Intestine war in Heaven, the arch-foe subdued
Or captive dragged in chains, with hostile frown   260
And visage all enflamed first thus began:
    "'Author of evil, unknown till thy revolt,
Unnamed in Heaven, now plenteous, as thou seest
These acts of hateful strife, hateful to all,
Though heaviest by just measure on thyself   265
And thy adherents. How hast thou disturbed
Heaven's blessèd peace and into nature brought
Misery, uncreated till the crime
Of thy rebellion! How hast thou instilled
Thy malice into thousands, once upright   270
And faithful, now proved false! But think not here
To trouble holy rest; Heaven casts thee out
From all her confines. Heaven, the seat of bliss,
Brooks not the works of violence and war.
Hence, then, and evil go with thee along,   275
Thy offspring, to the place of evil, hell,
Thou and thy wicked crew. There mingle broils
Ere this avenging sword begin thy doom
Or some more sudden vengeance winged from God
Precipitate thee with augmented pain.'   280
    "So spake the prince of angels; to whom thus
The adversary: 'Nor think thou with wind
Of airy threats to awe whom yet with deeds
Thou canst not. Hast thou turned the least of these
To flight, or, if to fall, but that they rise   285
Unvanquished, easier to transact with me
That thou shouldst hope, imperious, and with threats
To chase me hence? Err not that so shall end

---

259. *Intestine war:* civil war

263. *Unnamed . . . plenteous:* These adjectives modify "evil" (line 262), not "revolt."

267. *into nature brought:* Nature is treated as having been created free from all discord, until the fall of the angels disturbs *Heaven's blessèd peace,* as man's fall further disturbs nature in 9.782–4; Milton conceives of Heaven not as supernatural but as part of nature, though celestial.

275–276. *evil . . . Thy offspring:* See the account of Satan's progeny in 2.741–58.

277. *mingle broils:* start fights

282. *adversary:* not just "opponent," but the literal meaning of Satan; see 3.81 and 3.156.

286. *transact with:* deal with (as in the phrase, "I'll deal with you")

288. *Err not:* Do not think

The strife which thou call'st evil, but we style
The strife of glory, which we mean to win   290
Or turn this Heaven itself into the hell
Thou fablest, here, however, to dwell free,
If not to reign. Meanwhile thy utmost force,
And join him named Almighty to thy aid,
I fly not but have sought thee far and nigh.'   295
    "They ended parle° and both addressed for fight   *discussion, parley*
Unspeakable (for who, though with the tongue
Of angels, can relate or to what things
Liken on earth conspicuous° that may lift   *visible*
Human imagination to such height   300
Of godlike power?), for likest gods they seemed,
Stood they or moved, in stature, motion, arms,
Fit to decide the empire of great Heaven.
Now waved their fiery swords and in the air
Made horrid circles; two broad suns their shields   305
Blazed opposite, while Expectation stood
In horror. From each hand with speed retired,
Where erst was thickest fight, the angelic throng
And left large field unsafe within the wind
Of such commotion, such as, to set forth   310
Great things by small, if, nature's concord broke,°   *broken*
Among the constellations war were sprung,
Two planets rushing from aspect malign
Of fiercest opposition in mid-sky
Should combat, and their jarring spheres confound.   315
Together both, with next to almighty arm
Uplifted imminent,° one stroke they aimed   *threatening*
That might determine,° and not need repeat,   *end (the matter)*

289. *which thou call'st:* In line 268 above Michael has called Satan's disturbance of the peace a "crime." See also 262.

296. *addressed:* prepared, made ready

302. *Stood . . . moved:* whether standing still or moving

305. *suns their shields:* In 1.287, Satan's shield was "like the moon."

306. *Expectation:* a personification of the mood of the apprehensive angels; see Shakespeare's *Henry V,* where "now sits Expectation in the air" (2.Chorus.8).

308. *erst:* formerly (as at line 187 above)

311. *Great things by small:* though the *small* here are cosmic events, suggesting the enormity of the battle in Heaven

313–314. *aspect malign . . . opposition:* opposed positions in the zodiac (and hence *malign* in their influence on humans)

315. *their jarring spheres confound:* the colliding planets demolish (also with an aural sense of the harsh discord disrupting the music of the spheres)

318. *repeat:* repetition

As not of power, at once; nor odds appeared
In might or swift prevention;° but the sword   *anticipation*
Of Michael from the armory of God
Was given him tempered so, that neither keen
Nor solid might resist that edge. It met
The sword of Satan with steep force to smite
Descending and in half cut sheer, nor stayed,   325
But with swift wheel reverse, deep entering sheared
All his right side. Then Satan first knew pain,
And writhed him to and fro convolved,° so sore   *contorted*
The griding° sword with discontinuous wound   *painfully cutting*
Passed through him; but the ethereal substance closed   330
Not long divisible, and from the gash
A stream of nectarous humor issuing flowed
Sanguine, such as celestial spirits may bleed,
And all his armor stained erewhile so bright.
Forthwith on all sides to his aid was run   335
By angels many and strong who interposed
Defense, while others bore him on their shields
Back to his chariot, where it stood retired
From off the files of war; there they him laid
Gnashing for anguish and despite and shame   340
To find himself not matchless and his pride
Humbled by such rebuke, so far beneath
His confidence to equal God in power.
Yet soon he healed, for spirits that live throughout

319. *at once:* immediately (modifies "determine" in 318)

321. *armory of God:* The image comes from Jer. 50.25: "the Lord hath opened up his armoury, and hath brought forth the weapons of his indignation."

322–323. *tempered . . . edge:* echoes the description of Artegal's word in Spenser's *Faerie Queene* 5.1.10: "of most perfect metals it was made / Tempered with Adamant . . . / For there no substance was so firme and hard, / But it would pierce or cleave, where so it came."

327. *Satan first knew pain:* Sin, however, says (2.752) that Satan earlier felt "a sudden miserable pain" at the assembly in Heaven where "Messiah was declared" (5.765).

328. *sore:* painfully

329. *discontinuous:* open, gaping (*OED* 1: "breaking the continuity or solidity of the body")

330–331. *the ethereal substance . . . divisible:* Renaissance commentators on angelology held that angelic *substance* was capable of damage but immediately healed itself, thus rendering the military aspect of the battle pointless.

332–333. *nectarous humor . . . Sanguine:* the internal fluid (*nectarous* because of the angelic diet) flowed like blood; cf. Homer's account of the "ichor" that flows from Aphrodite's wound (*Iliad* 5.339–42).

335–336. *was run By:* i.e., ran, hurried (in imitation of Latin syntax; see 10.229)

Vital in every part—not as frail man   345
In entrails, heart or head, liver or reins°—   *kidneys*
Cannot but by annihilating die,
Nor in their liquid texture mortal wound
Receive no more than can the fluid air;
All heart they live, all head, all eye, all ear,   350
All intellect, all sense, and as they please
They limb themselves, and color, shape, or size
Assume as likes them best, condense or rare.
　　"Meanwhile in other parts like deeds deserved
Memorial: where the might of Gabriel fought,   355
And with fierce ensigns pierced the deep array
Of Moloch, furious king, who him defied
And at his chariot wheels to drag him bound
Threatened, nor from the holy one of Heaven
Refrained° his tongue blasphemous, but anon,   *restrained, bridled*
Down cloven to the waist, with shattered arms
And uncouth° pain fled bellowing. On each wing   *unfamiliar*
Uriel and Raphael his vaunting foe,
Though huge and in a rock of diamond armed,
Vanquished Adramelec and Asmadai,   365
Two potent thrones, that to be less than gods
Disdained but meaner thoughts learned in their flight,
Mangled with ghastly wounds through plate and mail;
Nor stood unmindful Abdiel to annoy

351–353. *as they . . . rare:* See
1.423–31.
　352. *limb:* i.e., form, shape (provide
limbs); some editors have emended to
"limn," meaning "paint" or "adorn," but this
seems no less metaphoric than what both
early texts print.
　353. *condense or rare:* solid or vaporous
　354–362. *Meanwhile . . . bellowing:*
Scholars have seen a resemblance here to the
comic battle between devils and Saracens in
Matteo Maria Boiardo's *Orlando Innamorato*
(1495) 2.22.50–54, but the suggestion ig-
nores the degree to which early readers took
the war seriously; see Samuel Barrow's prefa-
tory poem, pp. 1–2 above.
　356. *ensigns:* divisions of troops (each
identified by an *ensign* or banner)   *deep
array:* thick rows of troops

359–360. *nor from . . . blasphemous:*
The language reflects 2 Kings 19:22; "Whom
hast thou reproached and blasphemed? and
against whom hast thou exalted thy voice,
and lifted up thine eyes on high? even against
the Holy One of Israel."
　365. *Adramelec and Asmadai: Andra-
malec* was a local name for the Babylonian
sun god; 2 Kings 17:31 says that children
were burned on his altar. *Asmadai* is *As-
modeus,* the evil spirit of 4.168 and the book
of Tobit; but medieval tradition made him
chief of the fourth order of fallen angels,
hence his role here as one of their leaders.
　366. *gods:* Here the word is ironic, re-
ferring to the divine ambitions of the devils
that Satan flatters by calling them "gods" in
2.391 and line 156 above.

The atheist crew, but with redoubled blow   370
Ariel and Arioch and the violence
Of Ramiel, scorched and blasted, overthrew.
I might relate of thousands, and their names
Eternize here on earth, but those elect
Angels, contented with their fame in Heaven,   375
Seek not the praise of men; the other sort,
In might though wondrous and in acts of war,
Nor of renown less eager, yet by doom
Cancelled from Heaven and sacred memory,
Nameless in dark oblivion let them dwell.   380
For strength from truth divided and from just,
Illaudable, naught merits but dispraise
And ignominy, yet to glory aspires
Vainglorious, and through infamy seeks fame:
Therefore eternal silence be their doom.   385
    "And now their mightiest quelled, the battle swerved
With many an inroad gored; deformèd rout
Entered and foul disorder; all the ground
With shivered armor strewn, and on a heap
Chariot and charioteer lay overturned   390
And fiery foaming steeds; what stood recoiled
O'erwearied through the faint satanic host
Defensive scarce or with pale fear surprised,
Then first with fear surprised and sense of pain
Fled ignominious, to such evil brought   395

370. *atheist:* impious (but since the devils disbelieve in God's nature as transcending their own, they may be termed *atheist* in a stricter sense)

371. *Ariel and Arioch:* Milton uses both as names of rebellious angels: *Ariel,* "lion of God" or "light of God," is an epithet for "the city where David dwelt" in Isa. 29:1; *Arioch* ("lion-like") is the name of one of the kings with whom Abram (Abraham) fights in defense of Lot (Gen. 14.1), but it is also the name of the captain of Nebuchadnezzar's guard in Babylon (Dan. 2.14). Both names, however, turn up in medieval and renaissance works of demonology.

372. *Ramiel:* another rebellious angel; *Ramiel* means "thunder of God," and is a name that appears in 1 Enoch 6:7 as an angel who is denied Heaven for fornicating with "the daughters of men."

374–376. *elect . . . men:* Although Raphael does speak his own name in the account of the war of Heaven (line 363), he never identifies himself by name to Adam and Eve, so cannot be thought to be seeking *the praise of men.*

379. *Cancelled:* blotted out; cf. 1.361–62.

381. *just:* i.e., justice

382. *Illaudable:* not worthy of praise (Latin *illaudatus* = without fame, obscure)

383. *ignominy:* The word literally means "namelessness," a sense particularly relevant here.

386. *battle swerved:* army fell back

391. *what stood:* those who still stood

393. *Defensive scarce:* hardly able to defend themselves

By sin of disobedience, till that hour
Not liable to fear or flight or pain.
Far otherwise the inviolable saints
In cubic phalanx firm advanced entire,
Invulnerable, impenetrably armed;   400
Such high advantages their innocence
Gave them above their foes not to have sinned,
Not to have disobeyed; in fight they stood
Unwearied, unobnoxious° to be pained   *not liable, unable*
By wound, though from their place by violence moved.   405
    "Now Night her course began and, over Heaven
Inducing darkness, grateful truce imposed
And silence on the odious din of war.
Under her cloudy covert both retired,
Victor and vanquished; on the foughten field   410
Michael and his angels prevalent,°   *victorious, having prevailed*
Encamping, placed in guard their watches round,
Cherubic waving fires; on the other part
Satan with his rebellious disappeared,
Far in the dark dislodged, and, void of rest,   415
His potentates to council called by night
And in the midst thus undismayed began:
    "'O now in danger tried, now known in arms
Not to be overpowered, companions dear,
Found worthy not of liberty alone,   420
Too mean pretense, but what we more affect,
Honor, dominion, glory, and renown,
Who have sustained one day in doubtful fight
(And if one day, why not eternal days?)
What Heaven's lord had powerfullest to send   425

398. *inviolable saints:* the loyal angels, who are immune to harm

399. *cubic phalanx:* like the "quadrate" in line 62; this is a cube rather than a square perhaps because as angels fight in the air their formation displays obvious height as well as length and depth.

409. *her:* i.e., Night's (line 406)

410. *foughten field:* battlefield (an archaic usage already by Milton's time; cf. Shakespeare, *Henry V* 4.6.18: "As in this glorious and well-foughten field")

415. *dislodged:* as at 5.669, either "moved camp" or "driven from their positions"; the first they do, the second is done to them, the ambiguity crystallizing the central question about the nature of fate in the poem.

421. *mean pretense:* trivial ambition (but *pretense* also means "dissimulation") *affect:* similarly ambiguous: both "aspire to" and "assume a false appearance"

423. *doubtful:* indecisive, uncertain (though only to Satan and his followers— even the reader has been told the outcome as early as 1.44–45)

Against us from about his throne, and judged
Sufficient to subdue us to his will,
But proves not so! Then fallible, it seems,
Of future we may deem him, though till now
Omniscient thought. True is, less firmly armed,   430
Some disadvantage we endured and pain,
Till now not known, but known, as soon contemned,
Since now we find this our empyreal form
Incapable of mortal injury
Imperishable and, though pierced with wound,   435
Soon closing and by native vigor healed.
Of evil then so small as easy think
The remedy: perhaps more valid arms,
Weapons more violent, when next we meet
May serve to better us and worse° our foes,   *make worse*
Or equal what between us made the odds,
In nature none. If other hidden cause
Left them superior, while we can preserve
Unhurt our minds and understanding sound,
Due search and consultation will disclose.'   445
      "He sat; and in the assembly next upstood
Nisroch, of principalities the prime;
As one he stood escaped from cruel fight,
Sore toiled, his riven arms to havoc hewn
And, cloudy in aspect, thus answering spake: 450
'Deliverer from new lords, leader to free
Enjoyment of our right as gods, yet hard
For gods and too unequal work we find
Against unequal arms to fight in pain
Against unpained, impassive,° from which evil   *insensitive to pain*
Ruin must needs ensue; for what avails
Valor or strength, though matchless, quelled with pain,
Which all subdues and makes remiss° the hands   *weak, incapable of action*

---

429. *Of future:* either "in the future" or
"about the future," either way, a mark of how
fallible Satan is in thinking about God

430. *True is:* it is true that

432. *known, as soon contemned:* despised
as soon as it is known

438. *valid:* powerful (Latin *validus* =
strong)

441–442. *what . . . none:* whatever gave
them advantage today, though nature has
given them none

444. *sound:* either a verb (= seek out) or
an adjective (= healthy)

447. *Nisroch:* an Assyrian deity in
whose temple Sennacherib was murdered by
his sons (2 Kings 19:37)

449. *to havoc hewn:* cut to pieces

Of mightiest? Sense of pleasure we may well
Spare out of life perhaps, and not repine   460
But live content, which is the calmest life;
But pain is perfect misery, the worst
Of evils, and, excessive, overturns
All patience. He who therefore can invent
With what more forcible we may offend   465
Our yet unwounded enemies, or arm
Ourselves with like defence to me deserves
No less than for deliverance what we owe.'
    "Whereto with look composed Satan replied:
'Not uninvented that, which thou aright   470
Believ'st so main° to our success, I bring;   *essential*
Which of us who beholds the bright surface
Of this ethereous mold whereon we stand,
This continent of spacious Heaven adorned
With plant, fruit, flower ambrosial, gems and gold—   475
Whose eye so superficially surveys
These things as not to mind° from whence they grow   *remember, give heed to*
Deep underground, materials dark and crude,
Of spiritous and fiery spume, till, touched
With Heaven's ray and tempered, they shoot forth   480
So beauteous, opening to the ambient° light?   *surrounding*
These in their dark nativity the deep
Shall yield us pregnant with infernal flame,

465. *offend:* here retains its Latin sense force of "strike at" or "injure"

467. *to me:* in my opinion

468. *for deliverance . . . owe:* i.e., what we owe Satan for our deliverance

473. *ethereous mold:* i.e., Heaven, which is made of ether; *ethereous* is a neologism, perhaps coined to emphasize the potency of this "ethereal" matter.

477–481. *grow . . . beauteous:* This account of the origins of minerals is indebted to Aristotle's theory of the origin of metals in the *Meteorologica* 1.4.341b and 3.6.348z, Metals here *grow* organically like plants, and the *spiritous and fiery spume* is simply the exhalation of fire and water underground, by whose evaporation under the influence of *Heaven's ray* (i.e., sunshine) metals of all kinds were supposed to "originate from the impris-

onment of the vaporous exhalation in the earth and especially in stones." Cf. 3.583–85, 3.609–12, and *Comus*, lines 732–36.

482. *nativity:* The obvious irony of the word points up the contrast between Satanic destruction and God's grace.

483. *infernal flame:* though *infernal* in a sense Satan cannot yet suspect; he means only that it is from the "deep" (line 482).

483–491. *infernal . . . bolt:* Satan imagines he can gain technological superiority over God's thunderbolts with the invention of the cannon. Spenser similarly identifies "that divelish yron Engin wrought / In deepest Hell" (*Faerie Queene* 1.7.13). Ariosto's comic account of Cimasco's invention of the arquebus in *Orlando Furioso* 9.28–29 is another frequently cited source, though the idea was a commonplace, as in Samuel

Which into hollow engines long and round
Thick-rammed, at the other bore° with touch of fire   *the touchhole, or fuse*
Dilated and infuriate shall send forth
From far with thundering noise among our foes
Such implements of mischief as shall dash
To pieces and o'erwhelm whatever stands
Adverse, that they shall fear we have disarmed   490
The thunderer of his only° dreaded bolt.   *unique*
Nor long shall be our labor, yet ere dawn
Effect shall end our wish. Meanwhile revive;
Abandon fear; to strength and counsel° joined   *judgment*
Think nothing hard, much less to be despaired.'   495
He ended, and his words their drooping cheer
Enlightened and their languished hope revived.
The invention all admired, and each, how he
To be the inventor missed, so easy it seemed
Once found, which yet unfound, most would have thought   500
Impossible; yet haply° of thy race   *by chance*
In future days if malice should abound
Someone intent on mischief or inspired
With devilish machination might devise
Like instrument to plague the sons of men   505
For sin, on war and mutual slaughter bent.
Forthwith from council to the work they flew:
None arguing stood; innumerable hands
Were ready; in a moment up they turned
Wide the celestial soil and saw beneath   510
The originals° of nature in their crude   *raw materials*
Conception: sulphurous and nitrous foam
They found, they mingled, and with subtle art
Concocted and adusted they reduced
To blackest grain and into store conveyed.   515
Part hidden veins digged up (nor hath this earth

Daniel's *Civil Wars*: "Artillerie, the infernall   498. *admired:* as the verb of which "all"
instrument / New-brought from Hell" (6.26).   is the subject, it means "looked upon with
   485. *touch:* 1) contact; 2) touch pow-   admiration"; as the (implicit) verb with
der, a fine gunpowder   "each" as its subject, it means "wondered" or
   486. *Dilated and infuriate:* violently ex-   "marveled" (in narcissistic surprise that he
ploding (*dilated* = expanding; *infuriate* = rag- was not its inventor, lines 498–99).
ing, maddened)   514. *Concocted and adusted:* heated and
   493. *Effect . . . wish:* i.e., we will accom- dried out
plish what we have wished for   516–519. *Part . . . part:* Some . . . others

Entrails unlike) of mineral and stone,
Whereof to found their engines and their balls
Of missive ruin; part incentive reed
Provide, pernicious with one touch to fire.   520
So all ere day-spring, under conscious° night   *witnessing*
Secret they finished and in order set,
With silent circumspection unespied.
Now when fair morn orient in Heaven appeared,
Up rose the victor angels and to arms   525
The matin° trumpet sung; in arms they stood   *morning*
Of golden panoply, refulgent host,
Soon banded; others from the dawning hills
Looked round, and scouts each coast light-armed scour
Each quarter to descry the distant foe,   530
Where lodged, or whither fled, or if for fight
In motion or in halt. Him soon they met
Under spread ensigns moving nigh in slow
But firm battalion; back with speediest sail
Zophiel, of cherubim the swiftest wing,   535
Came flying and in midair aloud thus cried:
    "'Arm, warriors, arm for fight; the foe at hand,
Whom fled we thought, will save us long pursuit
This day; fear not his flight. So thick a cloud
He comes, and settled in his face I see   540
Sad resolution and secure. Let each
His adamantine coat gird well, and each
Fit well his helm, grip fast his orbèd shield,
Borne even or high, for this day will pour down,
If I conjecture aught, no drizzling shower   545
But rattling storm of arrows barbed with fire.'
So warned he them, aware themselves, and soon

518. *found . . . balls:* manufacture their artillery and cannonballs

519. *missive ruin:* message of destruction (with play on *missive* = missile)   *incentive reed:* the kindling or match used to ignite the cannon (*incentive* = flammable)

520. *pernicious:* destructive, but it also keeps a secondary Latin meaning (from *pernix*) of "swift" (i.e., in almost immediate response to the match)

527. *panoply:* full armor (as at line 760) *refulgent host:* shining army

532. *Him:* the army of the rebellious angels (similarly, "He" and "his" in line 540)

535. *Zophiel:* The name is found nowhere in the Bible, but the Hebrew means "spy of God."

538. *Whom fled we thought:* whom we thought had fled

541. *Sad . . . secure:* steadfast . . . confident

544. *even or high:* in front of the body or over the head

547. *aware themselves:* already wary

In order, quit of all impediment,
Instant without disturb they took alarm
And onward move embattled,° when behold   *ready for battle*
Not distant far with heavy pace the foe
Approaching gross and huge, in hollow cube
Training° his devilish enginery, impaled   *dragging*
On every side with shadowing squadrons deep
To hide the fraud. At interview both stood
Awhile, but suddenly at head appeared
Satan, and thus was heard commanding loud:
   "'Vanguard, to right and left the front unfold
That all may see who hate us how we seek
Peace and composure and, with open breast,   560
Stand ready to receive them, if they like
Our overture and turn not back perverse;
But that I doubt. However, witness Heaven,
Heaven witness thou anon, while we discharge
Freely our part. Ye who appointed stand   565
Do as you have in charge, and briefly touch
What we propound, and loud, that all may hear.'
   "So scoffing in ambiguous words he scarce
Had ended, when to right and left the front
Divided and to either flank retired.   570
Which to our eyes discovered, new and strange,

---

548. *quit of all impediment:* unencumbered by any equipment

549. *Instant . . . alarm:* immediately with no loss of composure they responded to the call to arms (*took alarm*)

552. *gross:* compact (see 2.570)   *hollow cube:* mimicking the "cubic phalanx" (line 399) of the faithful angels, but *hollow* to hide the cannon.

553. *enginery:* artillery (see line 518) *impaled:* enclosed, surrounded

555. *At interview:* facing one another

558. *unfold:* open to view (i.e., the forward troops move aside, unfolding, as a wing)

560. *Peace . . . breast:* In this line and throughout the speech, Satan puns, "scoffing in ambiguous words" (line 568): *Peace* plays on "piece," as a piece of ordnance, and *composure* means both "agreement" and "construction" (i.e., the cannon they have built); *breast* means "heart" but also "the forward line of a military formation."

562. *overture:* both "proposal" and "the bore" of a cannon or gun; cf. the "hideous orifice" at line 577.

564. *discharge:* another example of the play of "ambiguous words": both *discharge* (i.e., perform) their duty and *discharge* (i.e., fire) their weapons.

565. *appointed:* more punning: 1) chosen; 2) equipped

566. *have . . . touch:* still more puns; *have in charge:* 1) have been ordered; 2) are armed and ready to fire; *briefly touch: touch* as "touch upon" (i.e., "mention") and as "touch off" (i.e., "ignite")

567. *propound:* send forth, as both "propose" and "shoot out"

A triple-mounted row of pillars laid
On wheels (for like to pillars most they seemed,
Or hollowed bodies made of oak or fir,
With branches lopped, in wood or mountain felled)   575
Brass, iron, stony mold, had not their mouths
With hideous orifice gaped on us wide,
Portending hollow truce; at each behind
A seraph stood and in his hand a reed
Stood waving, tipped with fire, while we, suspense,   580
Collected stood within our thoughts amused
Not long, for sudden all at once their reeds
Put forth and to a narrow vent applied
With nicest touch. Immediate in a flame,
But soon obscured with smoke, all Heaven appeared   585
From those deep-throated engines belched, whose roar
Embowelled° with outrageous noise the air   *filled, packed*
And all her entrails tore, disgorging foul
Their devilish glut: chained thunderbolts and hail
Of iron globes, which on the victor host   590
Leveled, with such impetuous fury smote,
That whom they hit none on their feet might stand,
Though standing else as rocks, but down they fell
By thousands; angel on archangel rolled
The sooner for their arms; unarmed they might   595
Have easily as spirits evaded swift
By quick contraction or remove, but now
Foul dissipation° followed and forced rout,   *scattering*

---

572. *triple-mounted row:* The rebellious angels have invented a gigantic version of a 17th-century weapon known as an "orgue," a gun with three tiers, capable of sustained and rapid firing; and here a demonic parody of Christ's "three-bolted thunder" at line 764.

576. *mold:* made from, molded out of

576–589. *mouths . . . glut:* The physiological emphasis—*mouths, orifice, behind, narrow vent, deep-throated, belched, Embowelled, entrails, disgorging . . . glut*—diminishes their technology to mere flatulence, defecation, and vomit.

578. *hollow truce:* insincere peace terms (but, as punning seems to be catching, also

the hollow cannon that they will face; cf. line 574)

579–581. *A seraph . . . stood:* Note the three uses of the verb *stood*, each with a different subject.

580. *suspense:* unsure, tentative (*OED* 2)

581. *amused:* puzzled, musing, preoccupied (as at line 623)

587. *outrageous:* violent

589. *chained thunderbolts:* cannonballs chained together, known as "chain shot" and capable of inflicting terrible damage as it swept through rank of troops

597. *quick contraction or remove:* recalls the ability to change size and shape attributed to the angels in 11.428–29

Nor served it to relax their serried files.
What should they do? If on they rushed, repulse   600
Repeated and indecent overthrow
Doubled would render them yet more despised
And to their foes a laughter, for in view
Stood ranked of seraphim another row
In posture to displode their second tire   605
Of thunder; back defeated to return
They worse abhorred. Satan beheld their plight
And to his mates thus in derision called:
     "'O friends, why come not on these victors proud?
Erewhile they fierce were coming, and when we,   610
To entertain them fair with open front
And breast (what could we more?), propounded terms
Of composition, straight they changed their minds,
Flew off, and into strange vagaries° fell,   *motions, movements*
As they would dance, yet for a dance they seemed   615
Somewhat extravagant and wild, perhaps
For joy of offered peace. But I suppose
If our proposals once again were heard
We should compel them to a quick result.'
     "To whom thus Belial in like gamesome mood: 620
'Leader, the terms we sent were terms of weight,
Of hard contents, and full of force urged home,
Such as we might perceive amused them all
And stumbled many; who receive them right,
Had need from head to foot well understand;   625

---

599. *Nor . . . serried files:* Nor did it
help to spread out their tight formations
(*serried* = in close order)

601. *indecent:* shameful, but also keeps
its Latin force of "ugly" or "graceless"

604. *seraphim:* here the rebel seraphs

605. *In posture . . . tire:* in position to
fire their second volley

611. *entertain:* receive, welcome (but
also in a military sense, "engage")

611–612. *front And breast:* 1) face and
heart; 2) forward lines of troops (see lines
560 and 569 above)

613. *composition:* 1) truce; 2) (chemi-
cal) composition

615. *As they would dance:* Satan's mock-
ery, which Joseph Addison regarded (in *Spec-*

tator 279, January 19, 1712) as in the worst
possible taste, has reminded most editors of
Patroclus' mocking praise of the "skilful
dance" of Hector's charioteer in his death
agony in *Iliad* 16.744–45.

620–627. *in like . . . upright:* Belial, *in
like gamesome mood,* continues the scornful
punning of Satan's speech; e.g., *terms of
weight* = 1) substantive negotiating positions
and 2) heavy cannonballs; *stumbled* = 1) con-
fused and 2) knocked down.

625. *understand:* punning on the famil-
iar, cognitive meaning of *understand* and its
now obsolete meaning of "support" (as when
Viola says, "My legs do better understand
me, sir, than I understand what you mean,"
in *Twelfth Night* 3.1.90)

Not understood, this gift they have besides:
They show us when our foes walk not upright.'
  "So they among themselves in pleasant vein
Stood scoffing, heightened in their thoughts beyond
All doubt of victory; eternal might   630
To match with their inventions they presumed
So easy, and of his thunder made a scorn
And all his host derided while they stood
Awhile in trouble; but they stood not long.
Rage prompted them at length and found them arms   635
Against such hellish mischief fit to oppose.
Forthwith (behold the excellence, the power
Which God hath in his mighty angels placed!)
Their arms away they threw and to the hills
(For earth hath this variety from Heaven,   640
Of pleasure situate in hill and dale)
Light° as the lightning glimpse they ran; they flew;   *swiftly*
From their foundations loosening to and fro
They plucked the seated hills with all their load,
Rocks, waters, woods, and, by the shaggy tops   645
Uplifting, bore them in their hands; amaze,°   *astonishment, amazement*
Be sure, and terror seized the rebel host
When coming toward them so dread° they saw   *terrifying*
The bottom of the mountains upward turned,
Till on those cursèd engines' triple-row   650
They saw them whelmed and all their confidence
Under the weight of mountains buried deep,
Themselves invaded° next and on their heads   *attacked*
Main° promontories flung, which in the air   *enormous, massive*
Came shadowing and oppressed° whole legions armed; *crushed, buried*
Their armor helped their harm, crushed in and bruised
Into their substance pent,° which wrought them pain   *confined*
Implacable and many a dolorous groan,
Long struggling underneath, ere they could wind
Out of such prison, though spirits of purest light,   660

---

627. *walk . . . upright:* 1) deal honestly;
2) stay on their feet
640. *from Heaven:* derived from Heaven,
resembling Heaven
643–646. *From . . . hands:* Similarly
the giants in Hesiod's *Theogony* (713–20)

fight for Zeus against the Titans by up-
rooting the hills and hurling them at their
enemies.
650. *engines' triple-row:* the three-tiered
cannon described in lines 572–73
651. *them:* i.e., the cannon

Purest at first, now gross by sinning grown.
The rest in imitation to like arms
Betook them and the neighboring hills uptore:
So hills amid the air encountered hills
Hurled to and fro with jaculation° dire,   *throwing*
That underground they fought in dismal shade,
Infernal noise. War seemed a civil° game   *refined*
To° this uproar; horrid confusion heaped   *compared to*
Upon confusion rose; and now all Heaven
Had gone to wrack, with ruin overspread,   670
Had not the almighty Father, where he sits
Shrined in his sanctuary of Heaven secure
Consulting on the sum of things, foreseen
This tumult and permitted all, advised
That his great purpose he might so fulfill   675
To honor his anointed Son avenged
Upon his enemies and to declare°   *make manifest*
All power on him transferred, whence to his Son,
The assessor of his throne, he thus began:
    "'Effulgence of my glory, Son beloved,   680
Son in whose face invisible is beheld
Visibly what by deity I am
And in whose hand what by decree I do,
Second omnipotence, two days are past,
Two days as we compute the days of Heaven,   685
Since Michael and his powers went forth to tame

661. *gross:* corporeal, material (with the sense of "unwholesome" and "repugnant")

665. *dire:* frightening, horrible

669–70. *all Heaven . . . wrack:* cf. 4.993–94.

670. *Had:* would have

671. *sits:* present tense because God is eternally present

673. *Consulting . . . things:* deliberating about all that has occurred or will happen (*sum of things* literally translates *summa rerum,* often used in Roman political texts to mean "the greatest good")

674–675. *advised That:* knowingly (advisedly) so that

679. *assessor:* assistant, partner, "one who sits beside" (*OED* 1); the word is still used in England of associate judges as "shar-ers of the seat" of a chief judge, and of associate officials generally.

680. *Effulgence . . . glory:* See Hebrews 1:3: "the brightness of his glory and the express image of his person"; see also 3.388.

681–682. *invisible . . . Visibly:* the paradox is explained in Col. 1:15, where Christ is called "the image of the invisible God"; see also *Christian Doctrine* I, v: "God was manifest in the flesh, namely, in the Son, his image; in any other way he is invisible" (*Works* 14, 265).

684. *Second omnipotence:* i.e., Christ, who "can do nothing of himself, but what he seeth the Father do" (John 5:19)

685. *as we . . . Heaven:* calls attention to the difficulty of narrating celestial events to a human audience

These disobedient; sore hath been their fight,
As likeliest was when two such foes met armed,
For to themselves I left them, and, thou know'st,
Equal in their creation they were formed   690
Save what sin hath impaired, which yet hath wrought
Insensibly, for I suspend their doom
Whence in perpetual fight they needs must last
Endless and no solution will be found.
War, wearied, hath performed what war can do   695
And to disordered rage let loose the reins
With mountains as with weapons armed, which makes
Wild work in Heaven and dangerous to the main.°   *whole expanse of Heaven*
Two days are therefore° passed; the third is thine: *in that manner*
For thee I have ordained it and thus far   700
Have suffered,° that the glory may be thine   *permitted*
Of ending this great war since none but thou
Can end it. Into thee such virtue and grace
Immense I have transfused that all may know
In Heaven and hell thy power above compare,   705
And this perverse commotion governed thus
To manifest thee worthiest to be heir
Of all things, to be heir and to be king
By sacred unction, thy deservèd right.
Go then, thou mightiest in thy Father's might,   710
Ascend my chariot, guide the rapid wheels
That shake Heaven's basis, bring forth all my war,
My bow and thunder, my almighty arms
Gird on, and sword upon thy puissant thigh.
Pursue these sons of darkness; drive them out   715
From all Heaven's bounds into the utter deep;
There let them learn, as likes° them, to despise   *pleases*
God and Messiah, his anointed king.'
    "He said and on his Son with rays direct
Shone full; he all his Father full expressed   720

---

692. *Insensibly:* imperceptibly, i.e., not so as to have significantly weakened the strength of the rebel angels

707. *heir:* cf. Heb. 1:2: "his Son, whom he hath appointed heir of all things"; see also 5.720.

709. *sacred unction:* ritual anointing; see line 718 below.

712. *war:* i.e., power (weapons of war), as in 12.214

714. *Gird . . . thigh:* Cf. Ps. 45:3: "Gird thy sword upon thy thigh."

715. *sons of darkness:* Cf. 5.716: "sons of morn."

720–721. *full expressed Ineffably:* another paradox, like that at lines 681–82; here

Ineffably into his face received,
And thus the filial godhead answering spake:
    "'O Father, O supreme of heavenly thrones,
First, highest, holiest, best, thou always seek'st
To glorify thy Son, I always thee,   725
As is most just; this I my glory account,
My exaltation and my whole delight,
That thou, in me well pleased, declar'st thy will
Fulfilled, which to fulfill is all my bliss.
Scepter and power, thy giving, I assume   730
And gladlier shall resign when in the end
Thou shalt be all in all and I in thee
Forever, and in me all whom thou lov'st.
But whom thou hat'st, I hate and can put on
Thy terrors as I put thy mildness on,   735
Image of thee in all things, and shall soon,
Armed with thy might, rid Heaven of these rebelled,
To their prepared ill mansion driven down
To chains of darkness and the undying worm,
That from thy just obedience could revolt,   740
Whom to obey is happiness entire.
Then shall thy saints unmixed, and from the impure
Far separate, circling thy holy mount,
Unfeignèd hallelujahs to thee sing,
Hymns of high praise, and I among them chief.'   745
So said, he, o'er his scepter bowing, rose
From the right hand of glory where he sat,
And the third sacred morn began to shine
Dawning through Heaven. Forth rushed with whirlwind sound

that God's ineffable (i.e., inexpressible) na-
ture can be fully expressed in Christ's face
    728. *well pleased:* Cf. the voice from
heaven at Christ's baptism and again at the
transfiguration: "This is my beloved Son, in
whom I am well pleased" (Matt. 3:17 and
17:5).
    731–733. *in the end . . . lov'st:* The vi-
sion of the end of time when all things loved
by Christ will return to God for eternity; see
1 Cor. 15:24–28: "Then cometh the end . . .
And when all things shall be subdued unto
him . . . God may be all in all." See also
3.341.

    734. *But . . . hat'st:* transfigures Ps.
139:21: "Do not I hate them, O Lord, that
hate thee?"
    739. *chains of darkness . . . worm:* the
torments of hell: as in 1.47–48 and 4.965;
cf. 2 Pet. 2:4: "God spared not the angels
that sinned, but cast them down to hell, and
delivered them into chains of darkness";
while *the undying worm* echoes Mark 9:44,
"their worm dieth not," which commenta-
tors understood as the eternal pains of gnaw-
ing conscience.
    744. *Unfeignèd hallelujahs:* Cf. 2.243:
Mammon's sense of "forced hallelujahs."

The chariot of paternal deity   750
Flashing thick flames, wheel within wheel, undrawn,
Itself instinct with spirit, but convoyed
By four cherubic shapes. Four faces each
Had wondrous, as with stars their bodies all
And wings were set with eyes, with eyes the wheels   755
Of beryl and careering° fires between.   *moving back and forth*
Over their heads a crystal firmament,
Whereon a sapphire throne inlaid with pure
Amber and colors of the showery arch.
He in celestial panoply all armed   760
Of radiant urim, work divinely wrought,
Ascended; at his right hand Victory
Sat eagle-winged, beside him hung his bow
And quiver with three-bolted thunder stored,
And from about him fierce effusion° rolled   *smoke*
Of smoke and bickering flame and sparkles dire;
Attended with ten thousand thousand saints,
He onward came; far off his coming shone,
And twenty thousand (I their number heard)
Chariots of God, half on each hand were seen.   770
He on the wings of cherub rode sublime

750–759. *The chariot . . . arch:* The fiery chariot with *wheel within wheel* and *convoyed* [i.e., accompanied] / *By four cherubic shapes* comes from Ezek. 1 and 10.

750. *chariot of paternal diety:* Here the Son is able to drive the Father's chariot, unlike the story of Phaeton attempting to drive the chariot of his father, the sun god.

751–752. *undrawn . . . spirit:* not drawn by horses but animated (*instinct,* as in 2.937) by *spirit*

759. *showery arch:* i.e., rainbow

761. *radiant urim:* gems serving as symbols of holy office; in Exod. 28:30, "the Urim and the Thummim" are placed onto Aaron's high-priestly "breastplate of judgment." Their radiance here is part of the symbolism of the spiritual light incarnate in the Son as God's judge and executioner. See 3.597–98.

762. *Ascended:* In the edition of 1667, this word began the second half of the poem.

762–763. *Victory eagle-winged: Victory* is personified and visualized like the statuettes on the war chariots of the Greeks; cf. Shakespeare *Richard II* 5.3.351: "Victory sits on our helms."

764. *three-bolted thunder:* In Ovid's *Metamorphoses* 2.325, Jupiter throws a three-forked (*trifidia*) thunderbolt at Phaeton.

766. *bickering:* destructive (parallel to "fierce" in the previous line); cf. Milton's use of the word in *Eikonoklastes* as the equivalent of "slashing" (*Works* 5, 114).

769–770. *twenty thousand . . . Chariots of God:* drawn from Ps. 68:17: "The chariots of God are twenty thousand"

771. *He . . . sublime:* The line echoes David's cry: God "rode upon a cherub, and did fly; and he was seen upon the wings of the wind" (2 Sam. 22:11). (*sublime* = literally "lifted up," but a recollection of that divine flight)

On the crystalline sky in sapphire throned.
Illustrious° far and wide, but by his own   *shining*
First seen: them unexpected joy surprised,
When the great ensign of Messiah blazed   775
Aloft by angels borne, his sign in Heaven,
Under whose conduct Michael soon reduced
His army, circumfused on either wing,
Under their head embodied all in one.
Before him power divine his way prepared;   780
At his command the uprooted hills retired
Each to his place; they heard his voice and went
Obsequious;° Heaven his wonted face renewed,   *obedient*
And with fresh flowerets hill and valley smiled.
This saw his hapless foes but stood obdured   785
And to rebellious fight rallied their powers
Insensate,° hope conceiving from despair.   *senselessly*
In heavenly spirits could such perverseness dwell?
But to convince the proud what signs avail,
Or wonders move the obdurate to relent?   790
They, hardened more by what might most reclaim,
Grieving to see his glory, at the sight
Took envy and, aspiring to his height,
Stood re-embattled° fierce, by force or fraud   *ready again to fight*
Weening° to prosper and at length prevail   *foolishly hoping*
Against God and Messiah, or to fall
In universal ruin last;° and now   *at last*
To final battle drew, disdaining flight
Or faint retreat, when the great Son of God
To all his host on either hand thus spake: 800
      "'Stand still in bright array, ye saints; here stand

772. *in sapphire throned:* derives from Ezek. 1:26: "the likeness of a throne, as the appearance of sapphire stone"

773. *his own:* i.e., the faithful angel

776. *his sign in Heaven:* The *sign* recalls the promise that at the end of the world there "shall appear the sign of the Son of Man in heaven" (Matt. 24:30).

777. *reduced:* led back (the word's basic Latin meaning, *re* = back; *ducere* = to lead)

778. *circumfused on either wing:* spread out on both flanks

779. *embodied all in one:* reformed into a single body of troops

785. *obdured:* hardened (with a sense of the hardening of the heart against grace, see 3.200 and note); see also lines 790 and 791 below.

788. *In heavenly . . . dwell:* The line transfigures Virgil's question at the end of his account of Juno's malice against Aeneas: "Can such anger dwell in a divine being" (*Aeneid* 1.11); see also 9.729–30: "can envy dwell / In heavenly breasts?"

791. *what might most reclaim:* i.e., Christ

801. *Stand still . . . stand: Stand,* of course, is a loaded word in *PL,* and begins

Ye angels armed; this day from battle rest.
Faithful hath been your warfare and of God
Accepted, fearless in his righteous cause,
And, as ye have received, so have ye done   805
Invincibly. But of this cursèd crew
The punishment to other hand belongs;
Vengeance is his or whose he sole appoints.
Number to this day's work is not ordained
Nor multitude; stand only and behold   810
God's indignation on these godless poured
By me. Not you but me they have despised,
Yet envied; against me is all their rage,
Because the Father, to whom in Heaven supreme
Kingdom and power and glory appertains,   815
Hath honored me according to his will.
Therefore to me their doom he hath assigned,
That they may have their wish to try with me
In battle which the stronger proves: they all
Or I alone against them, since by strength   820
They measure all, of other excellence
Not emulous, nor care who them excels;
Nor other strife with them do I vouchsafe.'°   *allow, permit*
    "So spake the Son and into terror changed
His countenance, too severe to be beheld   825
And full of wrath bent on his enemies.
At once the four spread out their starry wings
With dreadful shade contiguous, and the orbs
Of his fierce chariot rolled as with the sound
Of torrent floods or of a numerous host.   830
He on his impious foes right onward drove
Gloomy as night; under his burning wheels

and ends this line; the defining action of the
saints is to *stand still,* i.e., remain always
faithful. Cf. Moses at the Red Sea: "stand
still, and see the salvation of the Lord, which
he will shew to you to day" (Exod. 14:13).
    808. *Vengeance is his:* Cf. "Vengeance is
mine; I will repay, saith the Lord" (Rom.
12:19).
    812. *Not you . . . despised:* See 1 Sam.
8:7: "And the Lord said to Samuel . . . they
have not rejected thee, but they have rejected
me, that I should not reign over them." The
verse was often cited by anti-royalists as evi-

dence that kingship was a form of idolatry
and a rejection of God.
    815. *Kingdom . . . power . . . glory:* Matt.
6:13: "For thine is the kingdom, and the
power, and the glory, for ever."
    827. *the four . . . wings:* i.e., the cheru-
bim of line 753 above and line 845 below
    828. *contiguous:* adjoining, modifies
"wings" in line 827, not *shade;* see Ezek. 1:9:
"their wings were joined one to another."
    832. *Gloomy as night:* In the *Iliad*
(12.462), Hector, though splendidly armed,
is similarly described with his face like

The steadfast empyrean shook throughout,
All but the throne itself of God. Full soon
Among them he arrived, in his right hand   835
Grasping ten thousand thunders,° which he sent   *thunderbolts*
Before him such as in their souls infixed
Plagues;° they, astonished, all resistance lost,   *afflictions*
All courage; down their idle weapons dropped;
O'er shields and helms and helmèd heads he rode   840
Of thrones and mighty seraphim prostrate,
That wished the mountains now might be again
Thrown on them as a shelter from his ire.
Nor less on either side tempestuous fell
His arrows from the fourfold-visaged four,   845
Distinct° with eyes and, from the living wheels,   *adorned*
Distinct alike with multitude of eyes.
One spirit in them ruled, and every eye
Glared lightning and shot forth pernicious fire
Among the accursed that withered all their strength   850
And of their wonted vigor left them drained,
Exhausted, spiritless, afflicted, fallen.
Yet half his strength he put not forth but checked
His thunder in mid-volley, for he meant
Not to destroy but root them out of Heaven.   855
The overthrown he raised and, as a herd
Of goats or timorous flock together thronged,

"sudden night" as he attacks his foes. *Gloomy* does not mean "depressed" or "dispirited" but rather "dark," a sign of Christ's ferocity (see lines 824–26).

833. *steadfast empyrean:* As opposed to the fiery regions of the upper air, Heaven has a solid (*steadfast*) foundation that here "shook throughout," as in 2 Sam. 22:8: "the foundations of heaven moved and shook, because he was wroth."

834. *All . . . God:* Compare Satan's boast that the revolt "shook [God's] throne" (1.105).

842–843. *That wished . . . ire:* The line evokes the cry of the wicked at the last judgment, saying "to the mountains and rocks, fall on us, and hide us from the face of him

that sitteth on the throne" (Rev. 6:16, echoing Hosea 10:8).

845. *four-fold visaged:* derives from Ezek. 10:14, where every wheel "had four faces" (a cherub, a man, a lion, and an eagle)

849. *pernicious:* both "destructive" and "swift" (as at line 520 above)

856–857. *as a herd . . . thronged:* The image is demeaning, the end of a process of diminution from the heroic pretensions of the first books: early editors often excused what some felt was the bad taste of this simile on the ground that Homer compares the Greek hosts to flies around a milk pail, but the image mainly draws upon the apocalyptic separation of the sheep from the goats, which were sent "into everlasting fire, prepared for the devil and his angels" (Matt. 25:41).

Drove them before him thunderstruck, pursued
With terrors and with furies to the bounds
And crystal wall of Heaven, which, opening wide,   860
Rolled inward and a spacious gap disclosed
Into the wasteful° deep; the monstrous sight   *desolate, empty*
Struck them with horror backward but far worse
Urged them behind; headlong themselves they threw
Down from the verge of Heaven; eternal wrath   865
Burnt after them to the bottomless pit.
    "Hell heard the unsufferable noise; hell saw
Heaven ruining from Heaven and would have fled
Affrighted, but strict fate had cast too deep
Her dark foundations, and too fast had bound.   870
Nine days they fell; confounded, Chaos roared
And felt tenfold confusion in their fall
Through his wild anarchy, so huge a rout
Encumbered him with ruin. Hell at last
Yawning received them whole and on them closed,   875
Hell, their fit habitation, fraught with fire
Unquenchable, the house of woe and pain.
Disburdened, Heaven rejoiced and soon repaired
Her mural breach, returning whence it rolled.
Sole victor, from the expulsion of his foes,   880
Messiah his triumphal chariot turned.
To meet him all his saints, who silent stood
Eyewitnesses of his almighty acts,
With jubilee advanced, and, as they went

858. *thunderstruck:* both literally and metaphorically

864. *headlong themselves they threw:* The phrase returns the action of the poem to the beginning of the poem; see 1.44–49. The image emphasizes the fallen angels' own choice of damnation.

866. *the bottomless pit:* Cf. Rev. 20:1: "The key of the bottomless pit"

867. *unsufferable noise:* See Chaos' report of the angels who "Fled not in silence through the frightened deep" (2.994).

868. *ruining:* falling; cf. "ruin" in 1.46.

871. *Nine days they fell:* In Hesiod's *Theogony,* the Titans fell "nine nights and days" (722); also cf. 1.50–51, where the fallen angels lay on the burning lake "nine

times the space that measures day and night / To mortal men."

871–874. *Chaos . . . ruin:* Cf. 2.995–96, where Chaos reports that at the fall he heard: "ruin upon ruin, rout on rout, / Confusion worse confounded."

879. *Her mural breach:* the gap in her walls

880–892. *Sole victor . . . bliss:* The apocalyptic echoes here culminate in the final allusion to Paul's vision of the Son "Upholding all things by the word of his power" and sitting down "on the right hand of the Majesty on high" (Heb. 1:3).

884–885. *With jubilee . . . palm:* The victorious entry is designed also to suggest Christ's entry into Jerusalem (Matt. 21:5–9).

Shaded with branching palm, each order bright   885
Sung triumph and him sung victorious king,
Son, heir, and lord, to him dominion given,
Worthiest to reign. He, celebrated, rode
Triumphant through mid-Heaven into the courts
And temple of his mighty Father throned   890
On high, who into glory him received
Where now he sits at the right hand of bliss.
     "Thus, measuring things in Heaven by things on earth,
At thy request and that thou mayst beware
By what is past, to thee I have revealed   895
What might have else to human race been hid:
The discord which befell, and war in Heaven
Among the angelic powers, and the deep fall
Of those too high aspiring who rebelled
With Satan, he who envies now thy state,   900
Who now is plotting how he may seduce
Thee also from obedience, that, with him
Bereaved of happiness, thou mayst partake
His punishment, eternal misery,
Which would be all his solace and revenge,   905
As a despite done against the most high,
Thee once to gain companion of his woe.
But listen not to his temptations; warn
Thy weaker; let it profit thee to have heard
By terrible example the reward   910
Of disobedience; firm they might have stood,
Yet fell; remember, and fear to transgress."

                          The End of the Sixth Book.

898. *powers:* can mean either "angels" (*OED* 8) or "armies" (*OED* 9)

909. *Thy weaker:* the "weaker vessel" of 1 Pet. 3:7. Juan Luis Vives voiced what was a commonplace, seeing woman as "a frayle thyng, and of weake discreacion, and that maie lyghtly be deceived, whiche thyng our fyrste mother Eve sheweth, whome the devyll caught with a lyght argument" (Richard Hyde's 1557 translation of Vives' *Instruction of a Christian Woman* (sig. D1ʳ). Some critics are surprised only that Raphael would say this with Eve present (see 7.50–51), but she has "overheard" the conversation from a "shady nook" (9.276–77).

BOOK 7

The Argument

Raphael, at the request of Adam, relates how and wherefore this world was first created: that God, after the expelling of Satan and his angels out of Heaven, declared his pleasure to create another world and other creatures to dwell therein; sends his Son with glory and attendance of angels to perform the work of creation in six days; the angels celebrate with hymns the performance thereof, and his reascension into Heaven.

Descend from Heaven, Urania, by that name
If rightly thou art called, whose voice divine
Following, above the Olympian hill I soar,
Above the flight of Pegasean wing.
The meaning, not the name I call: for thou   5
Nor of the muses nine nor on the top
Of old Olympus dwell'st, but heavenly born,
Before the hills appeared or fountain flowed,
Thou with eternal Wisdom didst converse,°   *dwell*
Wisdom thy sister, and with her didst play   10
In presence of the almighty Father, pleased
With thy celestial song. Up led by thee

1. *Descend from Heaven:* translates the "*Descende caelo*" of Horace's invocation to the muse Calliope in *Odes* 3.4.1.

1–2. *Urania . . . called: Urania*, the classical muse of astronomy, would be an appropriate agent to invoke for Milton's poem, though the narrator raises the question if this is her proper name—and then goes on to deny the identification in lines 5–7 (even though Du Bartas in *L'Uranie* [1567] had claimed her as a specifically Christian muse).

3–4. *above . . . wing:* The narrator claims that his epic ambitions are greater than those of the classical poets: *the Olympian hill,* Mount Olympus (like "the Aonian mount" in 1.15), was the haunt of the classical Muses (reduced here to a *hill*),

and Pegasus, the flying horse, was often used as an image of poetic inspiration. Milton denigrates the classical muse as inadequate for his poetic need.

5. *The meaning . . . call:* "Urania" means "the heavenly one," and it is that, rather than the classical muse, that Milton invokes; cf. 1.6–10.

6. *Nor . . . nor:* neither . . . nor

8–12. *Before . . . song:* Milton's muse, "heavenly born" (line 7), is described as the *sister* of *Wisdom,* both existing long before Mount Olympus or its sacred spring was created, existing indeed before creation itself. *Wisdom* comes from Prov. 8:25–30: "Before the mountains were settled, before the hills was I brought forth . . . Then I was by him . . .

Into the Heaven of Heavens I have presumed,
An earthly guest, and drawn empyreal° air,   *heavenly*
Thy tempering; with like safety guided down   15
Return me to my native element,
Lest from this flying steed unreined (as once
Bellerophon, though from a lower clime)
Dismounted on the Aleian field I fall
Erroneous there to wander and forlorn.   20
Half yet remains unsung but narrower bound
Within the visible diurnal sphere;
Standing on earth, not rapt above the pole,
More safe I sing with mortal voice, unchanged
To hoarse or mute though fallen on evil days,   25
On evil days though fallen and evil tongues,
In darkness and with dangers compassed round
And solitude. Yet not alone while thou
Visit'st my slumbers nightly or when morn
Purples the east. Still govern° thou my song,   *guide*
Urania, and fit audience find, though few.
But drive far off the barbarous dissonance

was daily his delight, rejoicing always before him." Scholars have argued about the identification of the *sister,* but probably Milton means the creative Word itself.

13. *presumed:* ventured (though the unavoidable suggestion of presumption identifies the poetic voice, as it has been from the beginning [see 1.13–16], with an ambition that sometimes sounds unnervingly like Satan's; see pp. xxvi–xxviii above).

15. *Thy tempering:* i.e., the air tempered (i.e., modified, made breathable) by you

16. *native element:* the earth

18–19. *Bellerophon . . . fall*: Bellerophon angered the gods when he tried to fly to Heaven on Pegasus; a gadfly, sent by Jove, stung the horse, and Bellerophon fell onto the *Aleian field* (*Iliad* 6.200–02; *Aleian* derives from the Greek for "wandering," as "Erroneous" in line 20 does from Latin); *clime* = region, with a pun on "climb"

20. *Erroneous:* As it modifies *to wander,* it means "aimlessly"; as it modifies "fall" (line 19), it means "having erred" (in the presumption of his flight).

21–22. *Half . . . sphere:* The narrator announces both the beginning of the second half of his poem and that it will focus not on Heaven and hell but on *the visible diurnal sphere* (the visible universe in which earth exists and that seems, from earth's perspective, daily, i.e., *diurnal,* to revolve around it).

23. *rapt above the pole:* in rapturous contemplation of things above the earth (hence, now he will "sing with mortal voice," line 24)

25–27. *though fallen . . . round:* The narrative voice becomes intensely personal as Milton laments the *evil days* of both the failed revolution (which left Milton at risk for his life at the King's restoration; *with dangers compassed round*) and his complete blindness after 1652 (*In darkness*); see pp. xix–xxii above.

29. *Visit'st . . . nightly:* Cf. the nightly visits of the muse in 3.32 and 9.22; and Ps. 17:3: "thou hast visited me in the night."

31. *fit . . . though few:* In the Preface to *Eikonoklastes* (*Works* 5, 65) Milton says that publication allows the tract "to find out her

Of Bacchus and his revelers, the race
Of that wild rout that tore the Thracian bard
In Rhodope, where woods and rocks had ears   35
To rapture till the savage clamor drowned
Both harp and voice, nor could the muse defend
Her son. So fail not thou who thee implores,
For thou art Heavenly, she an empty dream.
    Say, goddess, what ensued when Raphael,   40
The affable archangel, had forewarned
Adam by dire example to beware
Apostasy by what befell in Heaven
To those apostates lest the like befall
In Paradise to Adam or his race,   45
Charged not to touch the interdicted tree,
If they transgress and slight° that sole command   *disregard*
So easily obeyed amid the choice
Of all tastes else to please their appetite,
Though wandering. He with his consorted Eve   50
The story heard attentive and was filled
With admiration and deep muse° to hear   *thoughts, meditation*

own fit readers: few perhaps, but those few, such of value and substantial worth, as truth and wisdom, not respecting numbers and big names, have been ever wont in all ages to be contented with." But the attitude was a commonplace; see, for example, Joachim du Bellay, who advised the poet "who aspires to a more than vulgar glory to separate himself from inept admirers . . . and to content himself with few readers" in *La deffence et illustration de la langue francoys* (1549) 2.6.

33. *Bacchus and his revelers:* Orpheus, "the Thracian bard" of line 34, was torn apart by drunken followers of the god Bacchus (see Ovid, *Metamorphoses* 11.1–60). Milton identifies these with the royalists in *The Readie and Easie Way* (1660) seeing the backsliding English now with their "necks yoked with tigers of Bacchus" (*Works* 6, 139).

35. *Rhodope:* the mountain range in Thrace where Orpheus was killed; (pronounced with three syllables)

36–37. *drowned . . . voice:* follows Ovid: "his head and harp they into Hebrus

flung" (*Metamorphoses* 11.51; trans. Sandys, 1626); "Hebrus" = a river in Thrace.

37–38. *nor could . . . son:* Orpheus' mother was the muse of poetry, Calliope, but she was unable to *defend Her son* from the Bacchanalian mob; see Milton's "Lycidas" lines 58–63.

43. *Apostasy:* renunciation of faith or principle, rebellion (literally, "standing apart," from Greek *apo* = away from + *stenai* = to stand)

46. *the interdicted tree:* i.e., the Tree of Knowledge, *interdicted* (i.e., forbidden) to Adam and Eve: "But of the tree of the knowledge of good and evil, thou shalt not eat of it: for in the day that thou eatest thereof, thou shalt surely die" (Gen. 2:17)

50–51. *He . . . attentive:* Here Adam and Eve both seem to be listening together, though at 9.275–78, Eve claims that she only accidentally "overheard" what the "parting angel" said.

50. *consorted:* wedded (united as consorts, from Latin *con* = with + *sors* = fate)

52. *admiration:* amazement, wonder

Of things so high and strange, things to their thought
So unimaginable as hate in Heaven
And war so near the peace of God in bliss   55
With such confusion, but the evil soon
Driven back redounded as a flood on those
From whom it sprung, impossible to mix
With blessedness; whence Adam soon repealed°   *abandoned*
The doubts that in his heart arose and now   60
Led on, yet sinless, with desire to know
What nearer might concern him—how this world
Of heaven and earth conspicuous first began,
When and whereof created, for what cause,
What within Eden or without was done   65
Before his memory—as one whose drought°   *thirst*
Yet scarce allayed still eyes the current° stream,   *flowing*
Whose liquid murmur heard new thirst excites,
Proceeded thus to ask his heavenly guest:
   "Great things and full of wonder in our ears,   70
Far differing from this world, thou hast revealed,
Divine interpreter, by favor sent
Down from the empyrean to forewarn
Us timely of what might else have been our loss,
Unknown, which human knowledge could not reach,   75
For which to the infinitely good we owe
Immortal thanks and his admonishment
Receive with solemn purpose to observe
Immutably his sovereign will, the end
Of what we are. But since thou hast vouchsafed°   *been willing, deigned*
Gently for our instruction to impart
Things above earthly thought which yet concerned
Our knowing, as to highest wisdom seemed,°   *seemed good*
Deign to descend now lower and relate
What may no less perhaps avail us known: 85

---

57. *redounded:* returned, rebounded (Latin *re* = back + *undare* = to surge as waves)

61. *yet sinless:* still (not "nevertheless," since the "desire to know" is in itself innocuous) innocent; see 9.659: "Eve yet sinless."

63. *conspicuous:* visible (in contrast to the unseen heaven of the angels)

72. *Divine interpreter:* The epithet recalls Virgil's title for Mercury as "*intrepes divum,*" interpreter for the gods (*Aeneid* 4.378).

79. *end:* purpose, telos; cf. God's glorification as "the chief end of man" in the *Shorter Catechism.*

How first began this heaven which we behold
Distant so high with moving fires adorned
Innumerable, and this which yields or fills
All space, the ambient air, wide interfused
Embracing round this florid earth? What cause   90
Moved the creator in his holy rest
Through all eternity so late to build
In chaos and, the work begun, how soon
Absolved, if unforbid thou mayst unfold
What we, not to explore the secrets ask   95
Of his eternal empire, but the more
To magnify his works the more we know?
And the great light of day yet wants to run
Much of his race though steep, suspense in Heaven
Held by thy voice; thy potent voice he hears   100
And longer will delay to hear thee tell
His generation and the rising birth
Of nature from the unapparent deep.
Or if the star of evening and the moon
Haste to thy audience,° night with her will bring   *hearing*
Silence, and sleep, listening to thee, will watch,°   *stay awake, keep vigil*
Or we can bid his absence till thy song
End and dismiss thee ere the morning shine."
    Thus Adam his illustrious guest besought,
    And thus the godlike angel answered mild: 110

86–94. *How . . . Absolved:* Adam's curiosity is reportorial: he wants to know "how" (*How first began . . .*); "why" (*what cause Moved . . .*); *and* "when" (*how soon Absolved*). Although Calvin (*Institutes*, 1.14.1), said that "why God delayed so long [to create the universe] it is neither fit nor lawful to inquire," Adam's questions address the creation as something more directly motivated than as compensation for the loss of the rebellious angels; see lines 145–56 below.

90. *florid:* flourishing (both "teeming" and "luxuriant")

94. *Absolved:* here has its Latin force of "finished" or "completed"

97. *To magnify his works:* echoes Job 36:24: "Remember that thou magnify his work"

98–99. *great . . . steep:* The sun still has hours to shine, though it has begun its descent.

99. *suspense:* both "suspended" and "attentive; in suspense" (i.e., refusing to set, so it can hear Raphael's account; see "Held by thy voice," line 100)

102. *His generation:* of his creation

103. *unapparent deep:* i.e., chaos, *unapparent* (indiscernible) both because it is outside the visible universe and because Milton regarded it, until creation, as "Matter unformed and void" (line 233 below)

104. *star of evening:* Hesperus

107. *his:* i.e., sleep's

109. *illustrious:* distinguished (but also "radiant," keeping its etymological sense from the Latin *illustrare*, "to make light")

"This also thy request with caution asked
Obtain, though to recount almighty works
What words or tongue of seraph can suffice,
Or heart of man suffice to comprehend?
Yet what thou canst attain which best may serve   115
To glorify the maker and infer°   *make*
Thee also happier shall not be withheld
Thy hearing, such commission from above
I have received to answer thy desire
Of knowledge within bounds; beyond abstain   120
To ask nor let thine own inventions hope
Things not revealed which the invisible king,
Only omniscient, hath suppressed in night,
To none communicable in earth or Heaven:
Enough is left besides to search and know.   125
But knowledge is as food and needs no less
Her temperance over appetite to know
In measure what the mind may well contain,
Oppresses else with surfeit and soon turns
Wisdom to folly, as nourishment to wind.   130
    "Know, then, that after Lucifer from Heaven
(So call him, brighter once amidst the host
Of angels than that star the stars among)
Fell with his flaming legions through the deep
Into his place and the great Son returned   135
Victorious with his saints, the omnipotent
Eternal Father from his throne beheld
Their multitude and to his Son thus spake:
    "'At least our envious foe hath failed, who thought
All like himself rebellious, by whose aid   140

---

121. *inventions hope:* speculations hope for; cf. Ps. 106:29: "Thus they provoked him to anger with their inventions."

126–130. *knowledge . . . wind:* The extended comparison of *knowledge* with *food* was familiar; editors regularly cite Davenant's *Gondibert* (1651): "For though books serve as diet for the mind, / If knowledge, early got, self-value breeds, / By false digestion it is turned to wind, / And what would nourish on the eater feeds" (2.8.22–25).

131. *Know:* The imperative is notable after Raphael's warning about Adam's "desire / Of knowledge" (lines 119–20 above).

132. *So call him:* alludes to Satan's loss of his angelic name; see 1.361–63 and 5.658–59.

133. *that star:* i.e., Lucifer, the morning star, bringing or heralding the day, as the name literally signifies

135. *Into his place:* In Acts 1:25, Judas is described as having fallen "by transgression . . . that he might go to his own place."

136. *saints:* i.e., the faithful angels, as in 6.767

This inaccessible high strength, the seat
Of deity supreme, us dispossessed,
He trusted to have seized and into fraud
Drew many, whom their place knows here no more;
Yet far the greater part have kept, I see,   145
Their station; Heaven yet populous retains
Number sufficient to possess her realms
Though wide, and this high temple to frequent
With ministeries due and solemn rites.
But lest his heart exalt him in the harm   150
Already done to have dispeopled Heaven
(My damage fondly° deemed) I can repair   *foolishly*
That detriment, if such it be to lose
Self-lost, and in a moment will create
Another world, out of one man a race   155
Of men innumerable there to dwell,
Not here, till by degrees of merit raised
They open to themselves at length the way
Up hither, under long obedience tried,
And earth be changed to Heaven, and Heaven to earth,   160
One kingdom, joy and union without end.
Meanwhile inhabit lax, ye powers of Heaven,

142. *us dispossessed:* after dispossessing us

143. *fraud:* error (Latin *fraudem* = error, mistake); see 9.643–44, where Satan "into fraud / Led Eve."

144. *their place . . . more:* The line echoes the words of Job (7:10) about the lot of the dead: "He shall return no more to his house, neither shall his place know him any more."

145. *far the greater part:* Satan claims that his rebellion had "emptied heaven" (1.633), and later that "well-nigh half" of the angels followed him; yet even Sin admits he only "drew after him the third part of Heaven's sons" (2.692).

149. *ministeries:* religious observances; the modern form of the word is "ministries," but Milton's spelling is more common in the 17th century and clearly here it has four syllables.

150–151. *lest . . . done:* An oddly negative motivation for the creation, and surprisingly similar to what Satan claims in 9.143–51.

152–156. *I can . . . innumerable:* Cf. Augustine, *City of God* 22.1: "by gathering so many vnto this grace as should supply the places of the falne Angels, and so preserue (and perhaps augment) the number of the heavenly Inhabitants" (trans. John Healy, 1610, p. 877).

154. *Self-lost:* lost, or ruined, by their own act and to themselves rather than to God

159–160. *under . . . to earth:* The line tallies with Raphael's account of the plan for man's development in 5.469–79.

162. *inhabit lax:* spread out, settle widely (through the regions, which have lost a third of their inhabitants in Satan's revolt)

And thou my word, begotten Son, by thee
This I perform: speak thou and be it done.
My overshadowing spirit and might with thee   165
I send along; ride forth and bid the deep
Within appointed bounds be heaven and earth,
Boundless the deep, because I am who fill
Infinitude, nor vacuous the space.
Though I, uncircumscribed myself, retire   170
And put not forth my goodness, which is free
To act or not, necessity and chance
Approach not me, and what I will is fate.'
    "So spake the almighty, and to what he spake
His word, the filial godhead, gave effect.   175
Immediate are the acts of God, more swift
Than time or motion, but to human ears
Cannot without process of speech be told,
So told as earthly notion° can receive.   *understanding, intellect*
Great triumph and rejoicing was in Heaven   180
When such was heard declared the almighty's will;
Glory they sung to the most high, good will
To future men, and in their dwellings peace;
Glory to him whose just avenging ire

163–164. *thou . . . done:* On Milton's view of Christ as the instrument of God's creation and for the potential heterodoxy of his Trinitarian understanding, see 3.169–73, 6.680–83, and *Christian Doctrine* I, v: "The Son was the first of the whole creation, by whom afterwards all other things were made both in heaven and earth" (*Works* 14, 181).

165. *overshadowing spirit:* In lines 235–37 below, "the spirit of God" spreads his wings over chaos to infuse it with form and purpose; see also Luke 1:35: "the power of the highest shall overshadow thee."

168–169. *I . . . Infinitude:* See Jer. 23:24: "Do not I fill heaven and earth?"

170–172. *Though . . . not:* God has removed himself from the deep to "this high temple" (line 148), leaving formless and purposeless matter (which is ruled by "necessity and chance"), and until now has not chosen to exercise his *goodness* upon it.

173. *what I will is fate:* In *Christian Doctrine* I, ii (*Works* 14, 27) Milton defines *fate* as "either the essence of a thing or that general law which is the origin of everything, and under which everything acts; . . . fate can be nothing but a divine decree emanating from some almighty power."

176–179. *Immediate . . . receive:* Jewish and Christian bible commentary often argued that creation was actually instantaneous rather than the sequential account of Genesis; thus Du Bartas' line: "His Word and Deed, all in an instant wrought" (*Divine Weeks*, trans. Sylvester, 1608, p. 164); the limits of human understanding (*earthly notion*), however, demand the temporal ordering of narrative to understand it.

182. *Glory . . . high:* There is an echo both of the angels' song to the shepherds at Christ's birth, "Glory to God in the highest" (Luke 2:14) and of their shouting "for joy before God at the creation" in Job 38:7.

Had driven out the ungodly from his sight   185
And the habitations of the just; to him
Glory and praise whose wisdom had ordained
Good out of evil to create, instead
Of spirits malign, a better race to bring
Into their vacant room and thence diffuse   190
His good to worlds and ages infinite.
So sang the hierarchies. Meanwhile the Son
On his great expedition now appeared,
Girt with omnipotence, with radiance crowned
Of majesty divine, sapience, and love   195
Immense, and all his Father in him shone.
About his chariot, numberless were poured
Cherub and seraph, potentates and thrones,
And virtues, wingèd spirits, and chariots wingèd,
From the armory of God, where stand of old   200
Myriads between two brazen mountains lodged
Against° a solemn day, harnessed at hand,   *in preparation for*
Celestial equipage,° and now came forth   *chariots*
Spontaneous, for within them spirit lived,
Attendant on their lord. Heaven opened wide   205
Her ever-during° gates, harmonious sound   *everlasting*
On golden hinges moving, to let forth
The king of glory in his powerful word
And spirit coming to create new worlds.
On Heavenly ground they stood, and from the shore   210
They viewed the vast immeasurable abyss
Outrageous° as a sea, dark, wasteful, wild,   *agitated, roiling*
Up from the bottom turned by furious winds
And surging waves, as mountains to assault

185. *the habitations of the just:* In
Proverbs 3:33, God "blesseth the habitation
of the just."

192. *hierarchies:* orders of angels (see
5.587), the term itself confirming the gradu-
ated distinctions of Heaven's social order

196. *all . . . shone:* See 3.138: "in him
all his Father shone"; and 6.719–21.

197. *poured:* arrayed, spread about (like
the Latin *effundo*)

199–201. *chariots . . . lodged:* The scene
draws both upon both the language of
Zechariah's vision of four chariots coming

"out from between two mountains; and the
mountains were mountains of brass" (6:1)
and Jeremiah's claim in 1:25 that "the Lord
hath opened his armory."

204. *Spontaneous . . . lived:* On the vitality
of Heavenly matter, see pp. xxxvii–xli above.

205–209. *Heaven . . . worlds:* follows
Psalm 24:9: "Lift up your heads, O ye gates;
even left them up, ye everlasting doors; and
the King of glory shall come in."

206–207. *harmonious . . . moving:* Cf.
the "jarring sound" as "the infernal doors" of
hell open (2.880–81).

Heaven's height and with the center mix the pole.   215
    "'Silence, ye troubled waves, and thou deep, peace,'
Said then the omnific° word; 'your discord end.'   *all-creating*
    "Nor stayed, but, on the wings of cherubim
Uplifted, in paternal glory rode
Far into chaos and the world unborn;   220
For chaos heard his voice; him all his train
Followed in bright procession to behold
Creation and the wonders of his might.
Then stayed the fervid wheels, and in his hand
He took the golden compasses, prepared   225
In God's eternal store, to circumscribe
This universe and all created things.
One foot he centered and the other turned
Round through the vast profundity obscure
And said, 'thus far extend, thus far thy bounds,   230
This be thy just° circumference, O world.'   *exact*
Thus God the heaven created, thus the earth,
Matter unformed and void. Darkness profound
Covered the abyss, but on the watery calm
His brooding wings the spirit of God outspread   235
And vital virtue° infused and vital warmth   *power*
Throughout the fluid mass, but downward purged
The black tartareous cold infernal dregs

216–217. *Silence . . . end:* echoes Mark 4:39: "And he arose, and rebuked the wind, and said unto the sea, 'Peace, be still.' And the wind ceased, and there was a great calm."

218. *Nor stayed:* Cf. the "wary" Satan in much the same position in 2.917–18, who "Stood on the brink of hell and looked awhile."

221. *him:* i.e., Christ

224. *fervid:* burning (see 6.832)

225–230. *compasses . . . bounds:* The image originates in Wisdom's account of the creation in Proverbs 8:27: "When he prepared the heavens, I was there: when he set a compass upon the face of the depth." Commentators often held that a literal compass was used in creation, with one foot on the earth and the other describing the surrounding heavens. This is the image in Dante's *Paradiso* (19.40–42) of turning a compass to

mark the limits of the world (*stremo del mundo*), more fully elaborated in Godfrey Goodman's *The Fall of Man* (1616): "In the beginning God did square and proportion the heauens for the earth, vsing his rule, leauell, and compasse; the earth as a center, and the heauens for the circumference" (p. 16).

233–235. *Matter . . . outspread:* Echoes Gen. 1:2: "And the earth was without form, and void; and darkness was upon the face of the deep. And the spirit of God moved upon the face of the waters"; (*Matter unformed* is the "first matter" in 5.472, which God in creation endows with form).

237–239. *downward . . . life:* God *downward* purges those things *Adverse to life* in an image that suggests defecation and leaves the created universe all good; (*tartareous* = crusty; but suggesting Tartarus, hell).

Adverse to life; then founded, then conglobed
Like things to like, the rest to several place   240
Disparted,° and between spun out the air   *distributed*
And earth self-balanced on her center hung.
    "'Let there be light,' said God, and forthwith light
Ethereal, first of things, quintessence pure,
Sprung from the deep and from her native east   245
To journey through the airy gloom began,
Sphered in a radiant cloud, for yet the sun
Was not; she in a cloudy tabernacle
Sojourned the while. God saw the light was good
And light from darkness by the hemisphere   250
Divided: light, "the day" and darkness, "night"
He named. Thus was the first day, ev'n, and morn.
Nor passed uncelebrated nor unsung
By the celestial choirs when orient° light   *brilliant*
Exhaling° first from darkness they beheld,   *rising (like a mist)*
Birthday of heaven and earth; with joy and shout
The hollow universal orb they filled
And touched their golden harps and hymning praised
God and his works: "creator" him they sung,
Both when first evening was and when first morn.   260
    "Again God said: 'Let there be firmament
Amid the waters, and let it divide

239. *founded, then conglobed:* formed, then conjoined

242. *earth . . . hung:* The image comes most immediately from Job 26:7: "He hangeth the earth upon nothing"; but appears in classical sources as well, e.g., Ovid's "self-poiz'd Earth" in *Metamorphoses* 1.12 (trans. Sandys); see also Milton's "On the Morning of Christ's Nativity," line 122: "The well-balanced world on hinges hung."

243–252. *Let . . . named:* God's command, *Let there be light,* and his division of the light from the darkness occur on the first day of creation (Gen. 1–5), while it is on the fourth day that the "two great lights; the greater light to rule the day, and the lesser light to rule the night, . . . [and] the stars also," are created (Gen. 1:16).

248. *she:* i.e., light (the sun does not yet exist; theologians sometimes worried about

how there could be light before it source, and escaped the seeming contradiction by referring to 1 Tim. 6:16, where God dwells "in the light no man can approach unto"). *tabernacle:* temporary shelter; see Ps. 19:4: "a tabernacle for the sun."

252. *ev'n and morn:* complete, a full day measured, as the Jews do, from sundown to sunrise

261–271. *Let . . . ocean:* In Gen. 1:6–8, God says "Let there be a firmament in the midst of the water . . . And God made the firmament, and divided the waters which were under the firmament from the waters which were above the firmament . . . And God called the firmament Heaven." Milton conceives of the *firmament* as the mass of air and vapor between the earth and *the uttermost convex* of the created universe. The waters above it then become the *Crystalline*

The waters from the waters; and God made
The firmament, expanse of liquid, pure,
Transparent, elemental air diffused   265
In circuit to the uttermost convex
Of this great round, partition firm and sure,
The waters underneath from those above
Dividing; for, as earth, so he the world°   *universe*
Built on circumfluous° waters calm in wide   *flowing around*
Crystalline ocean and the loud misrule
Of chaos far removed, lest fierce extremes
Contiguous might distemper° the whole frame.   *disrupt, disarrange*
And 'heaven' he named the firmament; so ev'n
And morning chorus sung the second day.   275
    "The earth was formed, but, in the womb as yet
Of waters, embryon immature involved,
Appeared not; over all the face of earth
Main ocean flowed, not idle, but with warm
Prolific humor softening all her globe,   280
Fermented the great mother to conceive,
Satiate with genial° moisture, when God said: *fertilizing, life-enhancing*
'Be gathered now ye waters under heaven
Into one place and let dry land appear.'
Immediately the mountains huge appear   285
Emergent, and their broad bare backs upheave
Into the clouds, their tops ascend the sky.
So high as heaved the tumid° hills, so low   *swollen*

ocean of line 271 (i.e., "the sea of jasper" in 3.518–19).

266. *convex:* dome (though we would be more likely to imagine it as "concave")

267. *great round:* the sphere of the universe (like "world" in line 269) in which the earth exists at the center

274. *heaven:* God names the firmament "heaven" rather than the other way around; Gen. 1:8: "And God called the firmament Heaven."

277. *embryon immature involved:* an undeveloped embryo enveloped (by the waters)

279. *Main:* unbroken; before the continental landmasses appeared, the ocean existed as a continuous belt of water around the earth.

280. *Prolific humor:* life-giving liquid; the image of the generative sea is less biblical (though see Ps. 24:2) than it is classical: see Ovid's account of creation (*Metamorphoses* 1.1–51) and Lucretius' theory of organic life (*De rerum natura* 5.783–820), but it is in harmony with Milton's conception of the impregnating spirit brooding on the waters in 1.21 and 7.235–37.

283–290. *Be . . . waters:* The lines fuse the picture of the mountains and valleys going up and down "unto the place which thou has founded for them" in Ps. 104:8, with the command of God in Gen. 1:9: "Let the waters under the heaven be gathered together unto one place, and let the dry land appear."

Down sunk a hollow bottom broad and deep,
Capacious bed of waters; thither they   290
Hasted with glad precipitance,° uprolled   *swift downward movement*
As drops on dust conglobing° from the dry;   *forming spheres*
Part rise in crystal wall or ridge direct
For haste, such flight the great command impressed
On the swift floods. As armies at the call   295
Of trumpet (for of armies thou hast heard)
Troop to their standard, so the watery throng,
Wave rolling after wave, where way they found,
If steep, with torrent rapture, if through plain,
Soft-ebbing; nor withstood them rock or hill,   300
But they, or underground or circuit wide
With serpent error wandering, found their way
And on the washy ooze deep channels wore,
Easy ere God had bid the ground be dry,
All but within those banks where rivers now   305
Stream and perpetual draw their humid train.
The dry land, 'earth,' and the great receptacle
Of congregated waters he called 'seas,'
And saw that it was good and said: 'Let the earth
Put forth the verdant grass, herb yielding seed   310
And fruit tree yielding fruit after her kind
Whose seed is in herself upon the earth.'
He scarce had said, when the bare earth, till then
Desert and bare, unsightly, unadorned,
Brought forth the tender grass whose verdure clad   315
Her universal face with pleasant green,
Then herbs of every leaf that sudden flowered,
Opening their various colors and made gay

293. *in crystal . . . direct:* In 12.197, the Red Sea is described as parting into "crystal walls"; part of the waters so divide, the rest swell and crash like waves (*ridge direct*). Du Bartas similarly describes the passage through the sea as a "valley . . . flanked all along / With walls of crystal" (trans. Sylvester, 1608, p. 476).

299. *torrent rapture:* the powerful movement of a swollen mountain stream

301. *or . . . or:* either . . . or

302. *With serpent error wandering:* gently winding with serpentine curves (but the language, though merely descriptive here for the as yet unfallen Adam and Eve cannot help but anticipate their fall; cf. "mazy error" in 4.239).

306. *humid train:* liquid flow

307–312. *the great. . . earth:* Compare Gen. 1:10–11: "the gathering together of the waters called he Seas: and God saw that it was good. And God said, 'Let the earth bring forth grass, the herb yielding seed, and the fruit tree yielding fruit after his kind, whose seed is in itself, upon earth.'"

Her bosom, smelling sweet; and, these scarce blown,°   *blossomed*
Forth flourished thick the clustering vine, forth crept   320
The swelling gourd, up stood the corny reed
Embattled in her field and the humble shrub
And bush with frizzled hair implicit; last
Rose, as in dance, the stately trees and spread
Their branches hung with copious fruit or gemmed   325
Their blossoms. With high woods the hills were crowned,
With tufts the valleys and each fountain side,
With borders long the rivers. That earth now
Seemed like to Heaven, a seat where gods might dwell
Or wander with delight and love to haunt   330
Her sacred shades. Though God had yet not rained
Upon the earth, and man to till the ground
None was, but from the earth a dewy mist
Went up and watered all the ground and each
Plant of the field, which, ere it was in the earth,   335
God made, and every herb, before it grew
On the green stem. God saw that it was good;
So ev'n and morn recorded° the third day.   *registered, witnessed*
        "Again the Almighty spake: 'Let there be lights
High in the expanse of heaven to divide   340
The day from night, and let them be for signs,
For seasons and for days and circling years,
And let them be for lights as I ordain
Their office in the firmament of heaven
To give light on the earth': and it was so.   345
And God made two great lights, great for their use
To man, the greater to have rule by day,

321. *swelling gourd:* In the early texts, this read "smelling gourd," and some editors have defended that reading; but see "Textual Introduction," p. lxix above. *corny reed:* grain-bearing stalks, wheat sheaves

322. *Embattled:* standing tall (as the army with "ported spears" is described like a field of tall-standing grain in 4.980–83). *humble:* here meaning "low growing"

323. *frizzled hair implicit:* curly branches intertwined

325. *gemmed:* put forth (Latin *gemmare*

= to bud); but also in the sense of "adorned, as with gems"

331–334. *God . . . ground:* adapts Gen. 2:5–6: "God had not caused it to rain upon the earth, and there was not a man to till the ground. Bur there went up a mist from the earth, and watered the whole face of the ground."

335–337. *Plant . . . stem:* Compare God's creation of "every plant of the field before it was in the earth, and every herb of the field before it grew" in Gen. 2:5.

339–352. *Let . . . divide:* These lines closely paraphrase Gen. 1:14–19.

The less by night altern,° and made the stars   *alternately*
And set them in the firmament of heaven
To illuminate the earth and rule the day   350
In their vicissitude and rule the night,
And light from darkness to divide. God saw,
Surveying his great work, that it was good:
For, of celestial bodies first, the sun
A mighty sphere he framed, unlightsome first,   355
Though of ethereal mold, then formed the moon
Globose° and every magnitude of stars,   *round*
And sowed with stars the heaven thick as a field.
Of light by far the greater part he took,
Transplanted from her cloudy shrine, and placed   360
In the sun's orb, made porous to receive
And drink the liquid light, firm to retain
Her gathered beams, great palace now of light.
Hither, as to their fountain, other stars
Repairing, in their golden urns draw light,   365
And hence the morning planet gilds her horns;
By tincture° or reflection they augment   *absorption*
Their small peculiar, though from human sight
So far remote with diminution° seen.   *dimmed brightness*
First in his east the glorious lamp was seen,   370
Regent of day, and all the horizon round
Invested with bright rays, jocund to run
His longitude through heaven's high road; the gray

351. *vicissitude:* alternation (see the similar use in 6.8)

355. *unlightsome first:* It is not until the fourth day that the sun, a potential source of light, actually emits it.

356. *ethereal mold:* heavenly matter (i.e., ether, which naturally gives off light; see 3.7).

358. *sowed . . . field:* The image comes from Spenser's "Hymn of Heavenly Beauty": "All sowd with glistring stars more thicke then grasse" (53).

359–363. *Of light . . . light:* The light that was stored in the "cloudy tabernacle" in line 248 above) is now placed in the sun, imagined as hollow and porous (but *firm,* so the liquid light doesn't all leak out).

364–365. *as to . . . light:* The stars and planets come to the sun to *draw* light, as people come to a *fountain* with *urns* to get water.

366. *gilds her horns:* refers to Galileo's discovery that Venus has phases like those of the moon, whose horns were a traditional description of its crescent phase.

368. *small peculiar:* own small portion of light

372. *jocund to run:* joyful at the opportunity to run; cf. Ps. 19:4–5, where the sun is imagined "as a bridegroom coming out of his chamber" and rejoicing "as a strong man to run a race." The image, of course, presumes a geocentric conception of the universe.

373. *longitude:* course across the sky (i.e., distance from east to west, a measurement opposite to the word's modern use); cf. 3.576.

Dawn and the Pleiades before him danced,
Shedding sweet influence. Less bright the moon,   375
But opposite in leveled west, was set
His° mirror, with full face borrowing her light   *i.e., the sun's*
From him, for other light she needed none
In that aspect and still that distance keeps
Till night; then in the east her turn she shines,   380
Revolved on heaven's great axle, and her reign
With thousand lesser lights dividual holds,
With thousand thousand stars that then appeared
Spangling the hemisphere; then first adorned
With their bright luminaries that set and rose,   385
Glad evening and glad morn crowned the fourth day.
     "And God said: 'Let the waters generate
Reptile with spawn° abundant, living soul,   *offspring*
And let fowl fly above the earth with wings
Displayed° on the open firmament of heaven.'   *spread out*
And God created the great whales and each
Soul living, each that crept, which plenteously
The waters generated by their kinds,°   *species*
And every bird of wing after his kind;
And saw that it was good and blessed them, saying,   395
'Be fruitful, multiply, and in the seas
And lakes and running streams the waters fill;
And let the fowl be multiplied on the earth.'
Forthwith the sounds and seas, each creek and bay,
With fry° innumerable swarm, and shoals   *hatchlings, offspring*
Of fish that with their fins and shining scales
Glide under the green wave in schools that oft
Bank the mid-sea. Part, single or with mate,
Graze the seaweed their pasture and through groves
Of coral stray or, sporting with quick glance,   405
Show to the sun their waved coats dropped° with gold   *spotted, flecked*
Or, in their pearly shells at ease, attend°   *wait for*
Moist nutriment or under rocks their food

374–375. *Pleiades... influence:* There is
an allusion to "the sweet influence of
Pleiades" (Job 38:31); the Pleiades were
Atlas' seven daughters, who were elevated to
seven stars in the constellation Taurus.

379. *In that aspect:* i.e., when full

382. *dividual:* shared, divided (modifies
"reign" in line 381)

387–398. *Let... earth:* The lines para-
phrase Gen. 1:20–22.

388. *Reptile:* i.e., all creatures that
crawl, creep, or swim   *living soul:* ani-
mate creatures

403. *Bank the mid-sea:* seem to make a
ledge (bank) with their numbers in mid-
ocean

In jointed armor watch; on smooth the seal,
And bended dolphins play. Part, huge of bulk   410
Wallowing unwieldy, enormous in their gait,
Tempest° the ocean: there leviathan,   *stir up, roil*
Hugest of living creatures, on the deep,
Stretched like a promontory, sleeps or swims
And seems a moving land, and at his gills   415
Draws in and at his trunk spouts out a sea.
Meanwhile the tepid° caves and fens and shores   *damp*
Their brood as numerous hatch, from the egg that soon
Bursting, with kindly° rupture forth disclosed   *natural*
Their callow° young; but feathered soon and fledge   *immature, unfeathered*
They summed their pens and, soaring the air sublime,°   *above, up high*
With clang despised the ground under a cloud
In prospect; there the eagle and the stork
On cliffs and cedar tops their aeries build.
Part loosely wing the region, part, more wise,   425
In common ranged, in figure wedge their way,
Intelligent of seasons, and set forth
Their airy caravan high over seas
Flying and over lands with mutual wing
Easing their flight: so steers the prudent crane   430
Her annual voyage, borne on winds; the air
Floats as they pass, fanned with unnumbered plumes.

409. *jointed armor:* i.e., the exoskeleton of crustacea   *on smooth:* on a stretch of smooth sea

412–416. *leviathan . . . sea:* describes an enormous sea creature—part whale, part elephant, but not yet monstrous or dangerous; cf. 1.200–10. In the 1688 edition of *PL*, the engraving introducing Book 6 shows a double-spouting whale.

420–421. *fledge . . . pens:* fit to fly now with their plumage complete; (*pens* = pinion feathers necessary for flight)

422. *clang:* screeches, the harsh cries of shore birds; see 11.835: "sea mews' clang *despised:* looked down upon (literal, with no suggestion of contempt)

422–423. *under . . . prospect:* From the perspective of the earth (*In prospect*), the great number of birds seems to be a cloud.

424. *cedar tops:* Cf. Ps. 104:17: "as for the stork, the fir trees are her house."

425. *Part loosely:* some individually

425–426. *part . . . common:* others, more prudently, flocked together

427. *Intelligent of seasons:* But there are no *seasons* as we know them until after the fall (10.651–91); perhaps Raphael's knowledge of what will happen slips out, or perhaps the reference is to Jer. 8:7, where the stork "knoweth her appointed times; and the turtle[dove] and the crane and the swallow observe the time of their coming" as opposed to the people who "know not the judgment of the Lord."

430. *Easing their flight:* Elizabethan naturalists, following Pliny (*Natural History* 10.32.63), believed that flocking birds rested on the bird in front; the leader would cycle to the rear when tired, with the next in line moving up.

432. *Floats:* undulates, is fanned into waves

From branch to branch the smaller birds with song
Solaced the woods and spread their painted wings
Till ev'n, nor then the solemn nightingale   435
Ceased warbling, but all night tuned her soft lays.
Others on silver lakes and rivers bathed
Their downy breast: the swan, with archèd neck
Between her white wings mantling proudly, rows
Her state with oary feet; yet oft they quit   440
The dank and, rising on stiff pennons, tower
The mid-aerial sky. Others on ground
Walked firm: the crested cock, whose clarion sounds
The silent hours, and the other, whose gay train
Adorns him colored with the florid hue   445
Of rainbows and starry eyes. The waters thus
With fish replenished and the air, with fowl,
Evening and morn solemnized the fifth day.
     "The sixth, and of creation last, arose
With evening harps and matin, when God said: 450
'Let the earth bring forth soul living in her kind,
Cattle and creeping things and beast of the earth,
Each in their kind.' The earth obeyed and straight,
Opening her fertile womb, teemed at a birth
Innumerous living creatures, perfect forms,   455
Limbed and full grown: out of the ground uprose,
As from his lair, the wild beast where he wons°   *lives*
In forest wild, in thicket, brake, or den.
Among the trees in pairs they rose; they walked:
The cattle in the fields and meadows green,   460
Those rare and solitary, these in flocks
Pasturing at once and in broad herds upsprung.

435–436. *nor then . . . lays:* In the un-
fallen world, the nightingale sang all through
the night, rather than stopping at nightfall.
     439. *mantling:* with wings forming a
mantle or cloak; see 5.279.
     441. *dank:* water (of the "lakes and
rivers," l. 436)   *pennons:* pinion feath-
ers (see 420–21)
     441–442. *tower The mid-aerial sky:* soar
into the middle air
     444. *the other:* i.e., the peacock
     447. *replenished:* fully furnished, stocked
(though for the first time, as at 8.371)

450. *matin:* morning (modifying "harps")
     451. *Let . . . kind:* The command of
God is based on Gen. 1:24–25.
     451. *soul:* Bentley's 1732 emendation
of "Fowle" (which appears in the early
editions) to "soul" seems inevitable; *soul* =
animate creature, as in line 388 above, and
corresponds to "living creature" in Gen.
1:24.
     454. *teemed at a birth:* gave birth in a
single delivery to
     462. *at once:* all at the same time

The grassy clods now calved: now half appeared
The tawny lion, pawing to get free
His hinder parts, then springs as broke from bonds   465
And rampant shakes his brinded mane; the ounce,°   *lynx*
The leopard, and the tiger, as the mole
Rising, the crumbled earth above them threw
In hillocks; the swift stag from underground
Bore up his branching head; scarce from his mold   470
Behemoth, biggest born of earth, upheaved
His vastness; fleeced the flocks and bleating rose
As plants; ambiguous between sea and land,
The river horse and scaly crocodile.
At once came forth whatever creeps the ground,   475
Insect or worm:° those waved their limber fans   *any crawling reptile*
For wings and smallest lineaments exact
In all the liveries decked of summer's pride
With spots of gold and purple, azure and green;
These as a line their long dimension drew,   480
Streaking the ground with sinuous trace. Not all
Minims° of nature: some of serpent kind,   *tiniest creatures*
Wondrous in length and corpulence,° involved   *bulk*
Their snaky folds and added wings. First crept
The parsimonious emmet, provident   485
Of future, in small room large heart enclosed,
Pattern of just equality perhaps
Hereafter, joined in her popular tribes

466. *brinded:* brindled, streaked with different colors

471. *Behemoth:* A marginal note on Job 40:15–24 in the Geneva Bible (1560) says: "The Hebrues say Behemoth signifieth Elephant, so called for his hugenesse, by the whiche may be understood the deuyl." Before the fall, however, the creature does not have this figurative significance.

473. *ambiguous between sea and land:* i.e., amphibious

474. *river horse:* a literal translation of the Greek "hippopotamus"

480. *These:* i.e., the creeping insects and worms at line 476.

483–484. *involved . . . wings:* coiled their reptilian bodies

485. *parsimonious emmet:* thrifty ant

486. *large heart:* capacious intellect (see 1.444 and 1 Kings 4:29, where Solomon's "largeness of heart" translates the Hebrew for "intellect").

487. *Pattern of just equality:* The supposed democracy of the ants (see Prov. 6), who, unlike bees, have no queen (or king), was often used by 17th-century republican thinkers as an example for human political ordering. Milton comments upon the ant providing an example "of a frugal and self governing democratie or Commonwealth, safer and more thriving in the joint providence and counsel of many industrious equals, then under the single domination of one imperious Lord" (*The Readie and Easie Way* [1660], in *Works* 6, 122).

Of commonalty; swarming next appeared
The female bee that feeds her husband drone   490
Deliciously and builds her waxen cells
With honey stored. The rest are numberless,
And thou their natures know'st and gav'st them names,
Needless to thee repeated; nor unknown
The serpent, subtlest beast of all the field,   495
Of huge extent sometimes, with brazen eyes
And hairy mane terrific, though to thee
Not noxious but obedient at thy call.
Now heaven in all her glory shone and rolled
Her motions, as the great first mover's hand   500
First wheeled their course; earth in her rich attire
Consummate lovely smiled: air, water, earth,
By fowl, fish, beast, was flown, was swum, was walked
Frequent. And of the sixth day yet remained;
There wanted yet the master work, the end   505
Of all yet done: a creature who, not prone
And brute as other creatures but endued
With sanctity of reason, might erect
His stature and, upright with front° serene,   *forehead, face*
Govern the rest, self-knowing, and from thence   510
Magnanimous to correspond with Heaven,

490. *The female . . . drone:* Milton ig-
nores the structure of the bee colony around
a queen.

493. *thou . . . names:* as in Gen.
2:19–20, and at 8.349–54 above

495–498. *serpent . . . call:* Compare
Gen. 3:1: "the serpent was more subtil than
any beast of the field." Before its curse (see
10.175–78) it was a splendid and intelligent
creature—*terrific* (i.e., terrifying) but *Not
noxious* (i.e., harmful); for its *hairy mane*
Milton perhaps recalled the sea serpents that
Virgil describes as devouring Laocoon and
his sons (*Aeneid* 2.203–7). Cf. 9.494–502.

504. *Frequent:* keeps its Latin meaning
of "abundantly" or "in throngs" (*frequens* =
crowded).

505–506. *There wanted . . . done:*
echoes Ovid in *Metamorphoses* 1.76–77:
"The nobler Creature, with a mind possest, /

Was wanting yet, that should command the
rest" (trans. Sandys).

505. *end:* 1) the last piece; 2) the *telos,*
the ultimate purpose

506–510. *creature . . . self-knowing:* The
belief in man's upright attitude as a symbol
of both his superiority to the beasts and his
kinship with God runs through classical lit-
erature from Plato (*Timaeus* 90a) to Cicero
(*On the Nature of the Gods* 2.56) and Ovid
(*Metamorphoses* 1.76–86), and it runs
through hexameral literature in many pas-
sages like Du Bartas' description of Adam
with "not his Face down to the earthward
bending, / Like beasts that but regard their
belly, . . . / . . . but towards the Azure Skyes"
(*Divine Weeks,* trans. Sylvester, 1608, p. 165).

511. *Magnanimous to correspond:* great
of spirit to 1) be in contact and 2) be in har-
mony

But grateful to acknowledge whence his good
Descends, thither with heart and voice and eyes
Directed in devotion, to adore
And worship God supreme, who made him chief   515
Of all his works. Therefore the omnipotent
Eternal Father (for where is not he
Present?) thus to his Son audibly spake:
'Let us make now man in our image, man
In our similitude, and let them rule   520
Over the fish and fowl of sea and air,
Beast of the field, and over all the earth
And every creeping thing that creeps the ground.'
This said, he formed thee, Adam, thee, O man,
Dust of the ground, and in thy nostrils breathed   525
The breath of life; in his own image he
Created thee, in the image of God
Express, and thou becam'st a living soul.
Male he created thee, but thy consort
Female for race, then blessed mankind and said: 530
'Be fruitful, multiply, and fill the earth,
Subdue it, and, throughout, dominion hold
Over fish of the sea and fowl of the air
And every living thing that moves on the earth.'
Wherever thus created, for no place   535
Is yet distinct by name, thence, as thou know'st,
He brought thee into this delicious grove,

519–520. *Let . . . similitude:* echoes
Gen. 1.26, where God says "Let us make
man in our image, after our likeness." Bibli-
cal commentary traditionally interpreted the
passage as meaning (as Sir Walter Raleigh
says in *The History of the World*, 1621, 1.2.2)
that man is in the image of God's "reasonable
and understanding nature" (p. 23).

520–534. *let . . . earth:* The lines para-
phrase Gen. 1.26–28. The command to
Adam to "have dominion over the fish of the
sea, and over the fowl of the air, and over
every living thing that moveth upon the
earth" rang through 17th-century literature
in countless passages like Burton's glorifica-
tion of man as the "Sovereigne Lord of the
Earth, Viceroy of the World, sole Com-

mander and Governour of all the creatures in
it" (*Anatomy of Melancholy* 1.1.1; cf.
8.338–41 and 8.381–82).

524. *Adam, thee, O man:* Raphael ad-
dresses only Adam; cf. line 50 above and note.

526–530. *in his own image . . . race:*
Compare Gen. 1.27: "in the image of God
created he them; male and female created he
them'; in *PL* Eve is created first as Adam's
consort, and only secondarily for *race* (i.e.,
propagation); see 8.363–451.

528. *Express:* exact, accurate; Christ is
said to be in "the express image of God" in
Heb. 1:3; see also *Comus,* line 69: "the ex-
press resemblance of the gods."

535–538. *Wherever . . . God:* Adam is
made somewhere else and *brought . . . into*

This garden, planted with the trees of God,
Delectable both to behold and taste,
And freely all their pleasant fruit for food   540
Gave thee. All sorts are here that all the earth yields,
Variety without end, but of the tree
Which tasted works knowledge of good and evil,
Thou mayst not: in the day thou eat'st, thou diest;
Death is the penalty imposed; beware,   545
And govern well thy appetite, lest Sin
Surprise thee, and her black attendant Death.
Here finished he, and all that he had made
Viewed and, behold, all was entirely good.
So ev'n and morn accomplished the sixth day,   550
Yet not till the creator from his work
Desisting, though unwearied, upreturned
Up to the Heaven of Heavens his high abode
Thence to behold this new created world,
The addition of his empire, how it showed   555
In prospect from his throne, how good, how fair,
Answering his great idea. Up he rode
Followed with acclamation and the sound
Symphonious of ten thousand harps that tuned°   *played*
Angelic harmonies. The earth, the air   560
Resounded (thou remember'st, for thou heard'st),
The heavens and all the constellations rung,
The planets in their station listening stood
While the bright pomp° ascended jubilant.   *procession*
'Open, ye everlasting gates,' they sung;   565
'Open, ye Heavens, your living doors; let in
The great creator from his work returned
Magnificent, his six days work: a world;
Open, and henceforth oft, for God will deign
To visit oft the dwellings of just men   570

---

this delicious grove; Gen. 2:15, says that God "took the man, and put him into the garden of Eden."

544. *Thou mayst not:* demands "taste" to complete the prohibition

557. *idea:* as in Plato (*Timaeus* 37c), the essential form, ideal conception; see *Christian Doctrine* I, iii (*Works* 14, 65),

which speaks of God's foreknowledge and wisdom as "that idea of everything, which he had in his mind, to use the language of men, before he decreed anything."

565–567. *Open . . . creator:* Cf. Ps. 24:7: "Lift up your heads, O ye gates; and be ye lift up, ye everlasting doors; and the King of glory shall come in"; cf. lines 205–9 above.

Delighted, and with frequent intercourse
Thither will send his wingèd messengers
On errands of supernal grace.' So sung
The glorious train ascending. He through Heaven,
That opened wide her blazing° portals, led   *radiant*
To God's eternal house direct the way,
A broad and ample road whose dust is gold
And pavement, stars, as stars to thee appear,
Seen in the galaxy, that Milky Way
Which nightly as a circling zone thou seest   580
Powdered with stars. And now on earth the seventh
Evening arose in Eden, for the sun
Was set, and twilight from the east came on,
Forerunning night, when at the holy mount
Of Heaven's high-seated top, the imperial throne   585
Of godhead, fixed forever firm and sure,
The filial power arrived and sat him down
With his great Father (for he also went
Invisible, yet stayed: such privilege
Hath omnipresence) and the work ordained,   590
Author and end of all things, and, from work
Now resting, blessed and hallowed the seventh day,
As resting on that day from all his work,
But not in silence holy kept: the harp
Had work and rested not, the solemn pipe   595
And dulcimer, all organs of sweet stop,
All sounds on fret by string or golden wire

572. *messengers:* The Latin *angelus* literally means "messenger."

577–581. *broad . . . stars:* The lines resemble Ovid's description of the Milky Way (*Metamorphoses* 1.166–69) as the road to Jove's court. The *broad and ample road* is an innocent figure of "the broad and beaten way" (2.1026) that Sin and Death pave from Hell to earth.

581. *Powdered with stars:* Sylvester's Du Bartas similarly has "Poudred with Starrs" (*Divine Works*, 1608, p. 101).

584–585. *holy mount . . . top:* See 5.643: "that high mount of God."

588. *he:* i.e., God the Father

592. *blessed . . . the seventh day:* The blessing of the Sabbath is based on Gen. 2:2–3 and Exod. 20:11.

594. *But . . . kept:* The Sabbath is a day of rest, but making music is not considered work, a rejection of the strictest forms of Sabbatarianism; for Milton, worship was to be joyful and spontaneous, not required or formal. See "thus was Sabbath kept" in line 634.

597. *sounds on fret:* musical notes determined by the position of the fingers in relation to the ridges (frets) on the fingerboard of a guitar, lute, or similar stringed instrument

Tempered soft tunings intermixed with voice
Choral or unison. Of incense, clouds
Fuming from golden censers hid the mount.   600
Creation and the six days acts they sung:
'Great are thy works, Jehovah; infinite
Thy power! What thought can measure thee or tongue
Relate thee, greater now in thy return
Than from the giant angels? Thee that day   605
Thy thunders magnified, but to create
Is greater than created to destroy.
Who can impair° thee, mighty king, or bound   *diminish*
Thy empire? Easily the proud attempt
Of spirits apostate and their counsels vain   610
Thou hast repelled, while impiously they thought
Thee to diminish and from thee withdraw
The number of thy worshippers. Who seeks
To lessen thee against his purpose serves
To manifest the more thy might; his evil   615
Thou usest and from thence creat'st more good.
Witness this new-made world, another Heaven
From Heaven gate not far, founded in view
On the clear hyaline, the glassy sea
Of amplitude almost immense,° with stars   *immeasurable*
Numerous and every star perhaps a world

598. *Tempered soft tunings:* made sweet, harmonious sounds

599. *Choral or unison:* in harmonious parts or all singing a single melody

599–600. *incense . . . censers:* The worship sounds oddly Catholic for the fiercely Protestant Milton, but registers Rev. 8:3, where an "angel came and stood at the altar, having a golden censer [a vessel in which incense is burned]; and there was given unto him much incense, that he should offer it with the prayers of all saints upon the golden alter which was before the throne." In Heaven this is worship; on earth, for Milton, it is idolatry (similar to his view of Heaven's obvious royalism).

605. *giant angels:* the fallen angels; as in 6:643–66, Milton seemingly has the revolt of the giants against Zeus in mind, suggesting that the Greek myth is an imperfect memory of the actual war in Heaven; compare, however, Shakespeare's *Henry VIII* 1.2.199, "A giant traitor," where "giant" means "overweening" or "ambitious" rather than indicating size or consequence.

606–607. *to create . . . destroy:* This is the fundamental fact differentiating God from Satan and establishing the moral hierarchy of the poem: not just that Satan destroys and God creates—for that could lead to a heretical dualism—but that God creates and Satan is *created*.

619. *hyaline, the glassy sea:* the "Crystalline ocean" in line 271 above; the waters above the firmament; "hyaline" translates the Greek word meaning "glassy." See the "sea of glass like unto crystal" in Rev. 4:6.

621–622. *a world . . . destined habitation:* The controversial idea that the stars may be inhabited goes back to Plato's

Of destined habitation—but thou know'st
Their seasons—among these the seat of men,
Earth, with her nether ocean circumfused,
Their pleasant dwelling place. Thrice happy men,   625
And sons of men whom God hath thus advanced,
Created in his image, there to dwell
And worship him, and in reward to rule
Over his works on earth, in sea, or air,
And multiply a race of worshippers   630
Holy and just—thrice happy if they know
Their happiness and persevere upright.'
      "So sung they, and the empyrean rung
With hallelujahs: thus was Sabbath kept.
And thy request think now fulfilled, that asked   635
How first this world and face of things began,
And what, before thy memory, was done
From the beginning, that posterity
Informed by thee might know; if else thou seek'st
Aught not surpassing human measure, say."   640

The End of the Seventh Book.

Timaeus 41. Cf. 3.565–71, and 8.144–48 and 8.175–76, where Milton allows that other worlds might be inhabited.

622–623. *thou know'st Their seasons:* See Acts 1:7: "it is not for you to know the times or the seasons, which the father hath put in his own power."

624. *nether ocean circumfused:* the waters below the firmament (as opposed to "the glassy sea" in line 619), which were regarded by ancient geographers as joined together and encircling the continents; see lines 261–73 above.

628–629. *to rule . . . works:* in addition to Gen. 1.26–28, see Ps. 8:6: "Thou madest him to have dominion over the works of thy hands; thou hast put all things under his feet."

632. *persevere upright:* remain obedient; cf. Raphael's repeated warning to Adam to persevere in 8.639. To *persevere upright* is, literally, not to fall.

636. *face of things:* visible nature; cf. line 63 above and 5.43. Milton's readers were familiar with the transition from man's creation in the image of God to his introduction to the marvels of nature. In his translation of *Aristotles politiques, or Discourses of gouernment,* Louis le Roy wrote: "Man is begotten . . . after the image and similitude of God . . . to celebrate his honour . . . to the end that he may view the order of the celestiall bodies, and keepe . . . the habitation of this middle terrestrial globe" (I.D.'s translation, [London, 1598], p. 18).

BOOK 8

The Argument

Adam inquires concerning celestial motions, is doubtfully answered and ex-
horted to search rather things more worthy of knowledge; Adam assents
and, still desirous to detain Raphael, relates to him what he remembered
since his own creation: his placing in Paradise, his talk with God concern-
ing solitude and fit society, his first meeting and nuptials with Eve, his dis-
course with the angel thereupon, who after admonitions repeated departs.

The angel ended and in Adam's ear
So charming left his voice that he awhile
Thought him still speaking, still stood fixed to hear,
Then, as new-waked, thus gratefully replied:
"What thanks sufficient or what recompense   5
Equal have I to render thee, divine
Historian, who thus largely hast allayed
The thirst I had of knowledge and vouchsafed
This friendly condescension to relate
Things else by me unsearchable, now heard   10
With wonder but delight, and, as is due,
With glory attributed to the high
Creator? Something yet of doubt remains
Which only thy solution° can resolve: *explanation*

1–4. *The angel . . . replied:* These lines
were added in the second edition when
Milton divided the original Book 7 at line
640 to make the present Books 7 and 8. The
original line 641 read: "To whom thus Adam
gratefully repli'd . . ." Adam thinking
Raphael *still speaking* perhaps recalls Socrates
hearing the incarnate laws echoing the close
of Plato's *Crito.*

2. *charming:* enchanting (in both the
familiar metaphoric and the literal sense of
the word)

3. *him:* i.e., Raphael

8. *thirst:* The word again associates
"knowledge" with appetites that must be
controlled, as at 7.126–30.

9. *condescension:* willingness (with none
of the modern patronizing overtones); also
includes the etymological sense of "voluntary
descent" obviously relevant here to the angel

11. *With wonder but:* with admiration
but also with; the reassuring *but* (rather than
an unproblematic "and") reminds us that the
revelations from Raphael are not the familiar
stories as we inevitably hear them, but radical
new information about the world in which
Adam finds himself.

236

When I behold this goodly frame, this world   15
Of heaven and earth consisting, and compute°   *consider*
Their magnitudes, this earth a spot, a grain,
An atom, with the firmament compared
And all her numbered stars that seem to roll
Spaces incomprehensible (for such   20
Their distance argues and their swift return
Diurnal)° merely to officiate light   *daily*
Round this opacous° earth, this punctual spot,   *shadowy, dark*
One day and night, in all their vast survey
Useless besides, reasoning I oft admire   25
How nature wise and frugal could commit
Such disproportions with superfluous hand
So many nobler bodies to create,
Greater so manifold, to this one use,
For aught appears, and on their orbs impose   30
Such restless revolution day by day
Repeated, while the sedentary earth,
That better might with far less compass° move,   *motion*
Served by more noble than herself, attains
Her end without least motion and receives   35
As tribute, such a sumless° journey brought   *immeasurable*
Of incorporeal speed, her warmth and light,

15. *this goodly frame:* this magnificent universe; compare *Hamlet* 2.2.298: "this goodly frame, the earth"; cf. 5.154 and 7.273.

19. *numbered:* numerous (as in *Cymbeline* 1.6.37: "the numbered beach"); but also counted or accounted for, as in Ps. 147:4: "He telleth the number of the stars; he calleth them all by their names."

22. *officiate:* provide (with a lingering religious sense from the word meaning "perform a religious service")

23. *punctual:* tiny (a mere point, but probably also with the modern sense that earth's movements can be exactly timed); Copernican astronomers stressed the small size of the earth in the widening astronomical spaces and, for theologians like Jerome Zanchius, the fact that the earth was "less than a point" in the universe became a prime reason for glorifying God (*De operibus Dei* 2.2.5 [Neustadt, 1591]).

25–29. *reasoning . . . use:* Adam wonders (*I oft admire*) about the seeming *disproportions* in the heavens that provide more stars than are necessary to light the earth (*this one use*). Eve had asked a similar question of Adam at 4.657–58, and his restatement of it to the angel here suggests Adam's uncertainty about his answer to her at 4.660–80.

29. *Greater so manifold:* so many times greater

30. *For aught appears:* for so it seems

30–38. *on their orbs . . . fails:* Adam wonders further about the economy of the heavens: why so many heavenly bodies are made to circle the *sedentary* (i.e., motionless) earth rather than having the *earth*, which could *with far less compass move*, circle them.

37. *Of incorporeal speed:* i.e., faster than corporeal bodies can be imagined moving; cf. line 110: "Speed almost spiritual."

Speed to describe whose swiftness number fails."
  So spake our sire and by his countenance seemed
Entering on studious thoughts abstruse, which Eve   40
Perceiving, where she sat retired in sight,
With lowliness majestic from her seat,
And grace that won who saw to wish her stay,
Rose and went forth among her fruits and flowers
To visit° how they prospered, bud and bloom,   *inspect*
Her nursery; they at her coming sprung
And, touched by her fair tendance,° gladlier grew.   *care, tending*
Yet went she not as not with such discourse
Delighted or not capable her ear
Of what was high; such pleasure she reserved,   50
Adam relating, she sole auditress:
Her husband the relater she preferred
Before the angel, and of him to ask
Chose rather: he, she knew, would intermix
Grateful digressions and solve high dispute   55
With conjugal caresses; from his lip
Not words alone pleased her. O when meet now
Such pairs in love and mutual honor joined?
With goddesslike demeanor forth she went
Not unattended, for on her as queen   60
A pomp of winning graces waited still
And from about her shot darts of desire
Into all eyes to wish her still in sight.
And Raphael now to Adam's doubt proposed
Benevolent and facile° thus replied: *gracious, approachable*
  "To ask or search I blame thee not, for heaven

40–44. *Eve . . . flowers:* Eve's departure differentiates Book 8 from Book 7 and permits Adam the opportunity to discuss with Raphael his own desire for a mate and Eve's creation (lines 354–594).

43. *that won who saw:* which convinced those who saw her

46. *Her nursery:* both the objects in her care and the activity itself

52–57. *Her husband . . . her:* Eve *Chose* to learn from Adam rather than the Angel, not least because of the *conjugal caresses* that break up the account, naturalizing the Pauline injunction of 1 Cor. 14:35, that if

women "will learn anything, let them ask their husbands at home."

55. *high dispute:* lofty-minded or complex discussion (see "high" in line 50)

61. *pomp:* procession (as at 7.564)

62. *darts of desire:* i.e., looks expressing their desire to see her (rather than of lascivious sexual desire); the word order, delaying the explanation, raises the issue of the potential danger here; cf. *Hamlet* 1.3.35: "Out of the shot and danger of desire."

64. *doubt proposed:* question raised; cf. line 13 above.

Is as the book of God before thee set
Wherein to read his wondrous works and learn
His seasons, hours, or days, or months, or years.
This to attain, whether heaven move or earth,   70
Imports not if thou reckon right; the rest
From man or angel the great architect
Did wisely to conceal and not divulge
His secrets to be scanned° by them who ought   *examined*
Rather admire; or, if they list to try   75
Conjecture, he his fabric of the heavens
Hath left to their disputes, perhaps to move
His laughter at their quaint opinions wide
Hereafter, when they come to model heaven
And calculate the stars: how they will wield   80
The mighty frame, how build, unbuild, contrive
To save appearances, how gird the sphere
With centric and eccentric scribbled o'er,
Cycle and epicycle, orb in orb.
Already by thy reasoning this I guess,   85
Who art to lead thy offspring, and supposest
That bodies bright and greater should not serve
The less not bright nor heaven such journeys run,
Earth sitting still, when she alone receives
The benefit. Consider first that great   90
Or bright infers° not excellence: the earth,   *implies*

67. *the book of God:* i.e., the book of nature (God's revelation no less than the bible) was a traditional metaphor among theologians; see, for example, Thomas Browne, *Religio Medici* (London, 1642): "Thus there are two bookes from whence I collect my Divinity; besides that written one of God, another of his servant Nature" (p. 26).

70–71. *whether Heaven . . . not:* Raphael does not resolve the question of whether the universe is geo- or heliocentric; rather he dismisses questions about the "fabric of the heavens" (line 76) as ultimately trivial (see lines 77–78).

75. *admire:* feel awe (corrects the sense in which Adam uses the word at line 25 above)

78. *wide:* i.e., wide of the mark, mistaken

82. *save appearances:* account for the anomalies, explain away the contradictions; the term was often adopted specifically for the attempts of astronomers to reconcile the complex movements of the heavenly bodies with their scientific theories.

83. *centric and eccentric:* circular and parabolic orbits around the earth (or sun)

84. *epicycle:* "A small circle, having its center on the circumference of a greater circle. In the Ptolemaic system . . . each of the 'seven planets' was supposed to revolve in an epicycle, the center of which moved along a greater circle called a deferent" (*OED*).

90. *Consider first:* Compare Raphael's patient instruction of Adam here with Michael's more abrupt corrections of his errors of interpretation in Books 11 and 12.

Though, in comparison of heaven, so small,
Nor glistering, may of solid good contain
More plenty than the sun that barren shines,
Whose virtue on itself works no effect   95
But in the fruitful earth; there first received
His beams, unactive else, their vigor find.
Yet not to earth are those bright luminaries
Officious but to thee, earth's habitant.
And for the heaven's wide circuit, let it speak   100
The maker's high magnificence, who built
So spacious and his line stretched out so far
That man may know he dwells not in his own,
An edifice too large for him to fill,
Lodged in a small partition, and the rest   105
Ordained for uses to his Lord best known.
The swiftness of those circles° attribute,   *planets, orbiting bodies*
Though numberless, to his omnipotence,
That to corporeal substances could add
Speed almost spiritual; me thou think'st not slow,   110
Who since the morning hour set out from Heaven
Where God resides and ere mid-day arrived
In Eden, distance inexpressible
By numbers that have name. But this I urge,
Admitting motion in the heavens, to show   115
Invalid that which thee to doubt it moved,

93. *glistering:* sparkling, shining; cf.
Merchant of Venice 2.7.65: "All that glisters is
not gold."

94. *barren:* The life-giving rays of the
sun do not generate life there, but are effica-
cious only "in the fruitful earth" (line 96).

99. *Officious:* serviceable, of use (com-
pare "officiate" in line 22 above)

100–102. *let it speak . . . far:* The lines
answer God's question to Job about the
earth: "Who hath laid the measures thereof,
if thou knowest? or who hath stretched the
line upon it?" (Job 38:5); *speak* = bespeak,
witness to.

103–106. *That man . . . known:* Implic-
itly an argument that the heavens do serve
human need: though they are uneconomi-
cally structured if their purpose were only to
provide light for earth, they are so designed

That man may know his proper place in
God's infinitude. See lines 119–22 below.

107. *attribute:* pay tribute

108. *numberless:* immeasurable (modi-
fies "swiftness" in line 107)

110. *Speed almost spiritual:* the speed of
the Heavenly spirits that were thought to
move the planets; compare Donne's "the in-
telligence that moves" in "Good Friday
1613, Riding Westward"; see also line 37
above.

111–112. *Heaven Where God resides:*
this *Heaven* differs from the "heaven"
Raphael is discussing, which is merely the
spheres of the fixed stars and planets (see
3.416).

114–116. *But . . . moved:* i.e., but even
if, for the sake of argument, I will agree that
the heavenly bodies move, the premise that

Not that I so affirm, though so it seem
To thee who hast thy dwelling here on earth.
God, to remove his ways from human sense,
Placed heaven from earth so far that earthly sight,   120
If it presume, might err in things too high
And no advantage gain. What if the sun
Be center to the world,° and other stars,   *universe*
By his attractive virtue and their own
Incited, dance about him various rounds?   125
Their wandering course now high, now low, then hid,
Progressive, retrograde, or standing still
In six thou seest; and what if, seventh to these,
The planet earth, so steadfast though she seem,
Insensibly three different motions move,   130
Which else to several spheres thou must ascribe,
Moved contrary with thwart obliquities?
Or save the sun his labor, and that swift
Nocturnal and diurnal rhomb supposed,
Invisible else above all stars, the wheel   135
Of day and night, which needs not thy belief,

you drew from that fact (that the divine economy is wasteful) isn't valid

117–118. *Not . . . earth:* Raphael quickly denies that he does accept Adam's proto-Ptolemaic view, though he admits it looks that way from the vantage point of the earth.

124. *attractive virtue:* power of attraction (see the sun's "magnetic beam" in 3.583)

125. *rounds:* dances where the participants move in a circle (*OED* III.11.a); but *rounds* could itself mean "planets" (*OED* I.1); see 5.177–78.

126. *wandering:* elliptical; but particularly appropriate for the orbit of planets, as the word "planet" comes from the Greek word for "wanderer"

127. *Progressive, retrograde:* moving west to east, moving east to west (i.e., in a direction either in or contrary to the order of the signs of the zodiac)

128–130. *what . . . move:* i.e., what if the earth is the *seventh* planet (rather than the unmoving center of the system), and it

imperceptibly (*Insensibly*) moves in *three different* ways: rotation (daily motion), orbital revolution (annual motion), and the Copernican "third motion," intended to account for the fact that the earth's axis was thought always to align with the same point in the celestial sphere. (The more usual explanation of the third motion is that it refers to the revolution of the earth's north pole around that of the ecliptic, causing the seasons with precession of the equinoxes, but precession, Milton says explicitly in 10.668–71, began with the fall.)

131–132. *Which else . . . obliquities:* which (unless you posit the motions of the earth) you can either (*else*) explain the observed motion of the planets and stars by ascribing to them irregular and incompatible movements (*thwart obliquities*)

133–136. *Or save the sun . . . night:* i.e., Or you could ignore the sun's role and then have to explain night and day by reference to the *Nocturnal and diurnal rhomb,* which Ptolemaic astronomers *supposed* the invisible,

If earth, industrious of herself, fetch day
Travelling east and with her part averse
From the sun's beam meet night, her other part
Still luminous by his ray. What if that light,   140
Sent from her through the wide transpicuous air,
To the terrestrial moon be as a star
Enlightening her by day, as she by night
This earth? Reciprocal, if land be there,
Fields and inhabitants: her spots thou seest   145
As clouds, and clouds may rain, and rain produce
Fruits in her softened soil for some to eat
Allotted there. And other suns perhaps
With their attendant moons thou wilt descry°   *discover*
Communicating male and female light,   150
Which two great sexes animate the world,
Stored in each orb perhaps with some that live.
For such vast room in nature unpossessed
By living soul, desert and desolate,
Only to shine, yet scarce to contribute   155
Each orb a glimpse of light, conveyed so far
Down to this habitable, which returns
Light back to them, is obvious to dispute.

outer sphere (or *primum mobile*), which re-
volved around the universe in a day. (A
rhomb is a spinning wheel.)

137. *industrious:* active, i.e., moving,
not stationary

141. *transpicuous:* clear, transparent
(but with an additional sense of being clearly
understood, which the technical language
and complex syntax must make difficult)

142. *terrestrial:* 1) belonging to the
earth; 2) inhabitable like the earth

144. *Reciprocal:* i.e., mutually support-
ive, contributing light to one another   *if
land be there:* the conditional reflects the un-
certainty about the material makeup of the
moon; the full reciprocity Raphael imagines
exists only if the moon has "Fields and in-
habitants" (line 145) like the earth.

148–149. *other suns . . . moons:* In
1610, Galileo had discovered four of the
moons of Jupiter (known now as the
Galilean moons), though the image is more

of fixed stars (*suns*) being attended by orbit-
ing planets, as in our solar system.

150. *male and female light:* That the
moon and the sun might be so gendered can
be traced to Pliny's *Natural History*
(2.100–1), where the sun is described as
"Masculine" and the moon as "a planet
Feminine" (1601, trans. P. Holland, p. 44).
But here the distinction is primarily that be-
tween direct (*male*) and reflected (*female*)
light, with all the obvious implications for
Raphael's gender politics.

151–152. *two . . . live:* Milton imagines
"male and female light" to be sexually active
and fecund, animating the universe (*world*)
and *perhaps* populating the planets (*each orb*).

155. *Only to shine:* i.e., merely for the
sake of illumination

157. *habitable:* i.e., habitable planet

158. *obvious to dispute:* open to argu-
ment; in his *Seventh Prolusion* Milton asked
his audience of Cambridge undergraduates

But whether thus these things or whether not,
Whether the sun predominant in heaven   160
Rise on the earth or earth rise on the sun,
He from the east his flaming road begin
Or she from west her silent course advance
With inoffensive pace that spinning sleeps°   *turns gently*
On her soft axle, while she paces even   165
And bears the soft with the smooth air along,
Solicit° not thy thoughts with matters hid;   *trouble, unsettle*
Leave them to God above; him serve and fear.
Of other creatures as him pleases best,
Wherever placed, let him dispose; joy thou   170
In what he gives to thee: this Paradise
And thy fair Eve. Heaven is for thee too high
To know what passes there; be lowly wise.
Think only what concerns thee and thy being;
Dream not of other worlds, what creatures there   175
Live, in what state, condition, or degree,
Contented that thus far hath been revealed
Not of earth only but of highest Heaven."
    To whom thus Adam, cleared of doubt, replied:
"How fully hast thou satisfied me, pure   180
Intelligence of Heaven, angel serene,
And freed from intricacies, taught to live
The easiest way, nor with perplexing thoughts
To interrupt the sweet of life, from which
God hath bid dwell far off all anxious cares   185
And not molest us, unless we ourselves
Seek them with wandering thoughts and notions vain.

whether they could believe that the "great spaces of the enormous firmament, illuminated and adorned by the everlasting fires . . . that they may furnish light for ignorant and stooping men" (*Works* 12, 257).

164. *inoffensive:* unobstructed (but also retains its familiar meaning, "harmless")

165–166. *soft . . . soft:* Milton repeats the word in two different grammatical forms: first as an adjective, then as an adverb; cf. 9.386 where the single word functions in both capacities.

168. *him serve and fear:* Ecclesiastes defines "the whole duty of man" as the obligation to "Fear God and keep his commandments" (Eccles. 12:13).

173. *be lowly wise:* echoes Du Bartas: "Be sober wise: so, bound thy frail desire: / And, what thou canst not comprehend, admire" (*Divine Weeks*, 1608, trans. Sylvester, p. 447).

181. *Intelligence of Heaven:* angelic being; George Puttenham spoke of poets as the first students of "Celestial courses, by reason of the continuall motion of the heavens, searching after the first mover, and from thence by degrees comming to know and consider of the substances separate & abstract, which we call the divine intelligences or good Angels" (*The Arte of English Poesie* [London, 1589], p. 4).

But apt the mind or fancy is to rove
Unchecked, and of her roving is no end
Till warned or by experience taught she learn   190
That not to know at large of things remote
From use, obscure and subtle, but to know
That which before us lies in daily life
Is the prime wisdom; what is more is fume,°   *vapor*
Or emptiness, or fond impertinence,   195
And renders us in things that most concern
Unpracticed, unprepared, and still to seek.
Therefore from this high pitch° let us descend   *summit*
A lower flight and speak of things at hand
Useful, whence haply° mention may arise   *perhaps*
Of something not unseasonable to ask
By sufferance° and thy wonted favor deigned.   *permission*
Thee I have heard relating what was done
Ere my remembrance; now hear me relate
My story, which perhaps thou hast not heard,   205
And day is yet not spent; till then thou seest
How subtly to detain thee I devise,
Inviting thee to hear while I relate,
Fond, were it not in hope of thy reply.
For while I sit with thee I seem in Heaven,   210
And sweeter thy discourse is to my ear
Than fruits of palm tree pleasantest to thirst
And hunger both, from labor, at the hour
Of sweet repast; they satiate and soon fill,
Though pleasant, but thy words with grace divine   215
Imbued bring to their sweetness no satiety."
     To whom thus Raphael answered heavenly meek:
"Nor are thy lips ungraceful, sire of men,
Nor tongue ineloquent, for God on thee
Abundantly his gifts hath also poured,   220

188–197. *apt . . . seek:* The thought was
increasingly familiar; in Ralph Cudworth's
words: "We think it a gallant thing to be flut-
tering up to Heaven with our wings of Knowl-
edge and Speculation; wheras the highest
mystery of a Divine Life here, and of perfect
Happiness hereafter, consisteth in nothing but
mere Obedience to the Divine Will" (*A Ser-
mon Preached before the Honorable House of
Commons . . . March 31, 1647*, sig. D2r).

195. *fond impertinence:* foolish irrele-
vance (see also "Fond" in line 209).

197. *still to seek:* always seeking (never
finding) solutions

207. *How subtly:* a mark of just how
unsubtle the unfallen Adam in fact is

213. *from labor:* coming *from labor*

218. *ungraceful:* See Ps. 45:2: "Grace is
poured into thy lips."

Inward and outward both, his image fair.
Speaking or mute all comeliness and grace
Attends thee, and each word, each motion forms.
Nor less think we in Heaven of thee on earth
Than of our fellow servant and inquire   225
Gladly into the ways of God with man:
For God we see hath honored thee and set
On man his equal love. Say therefore on,
For I that day was absent, as befell,°   *as it happened*
Bound on a voyage uncouth and obscure,   230
Far on excursion toward the gates of hell,
Squared in full legion (such command we had)
To see that none thence issued forth a spy
Or enemy while God was in his work,
Lest he, incensed at such eruption bold,   235
Destruction with creation might have mixed.
Not that they durst without his leave attempt,
But us he sends upon his high behests
For state, as sovereign king, and to inure
Our prompt obedience. Fast we found, fast shut   240
The dismal gates and barricadoed° strong;   *barred, barricaded*
But long ere our approaching heard within
Noise other than the sound of dance or song,
Torment and loud lament and furious rage.
Glad we returned up to the coasts of light   245
Ere sabbath evening; so we had in charge.
But thy relation now, for I attend
Pleased with thy words no less than thou with mine."

---

221. *Inward . . . fair:* Compare the stress upon man as God's image in 7.519 and 7.627, but note that what prevents *fair* from carrying negative overtones (as in "fair enticing fruit" at 9.996) is that the God's *image fair* is instilled *Inward and outward both.*"

225–226. *inquire . . . man:* The angels' unanxious query contrasts interestingly with 1.26.

228. *equal love:* equal to his love of the angels (see 1.652–54); but also compare Beelzebub's complaint (2.348–51) that "man [is] favored more / Of him who rules above."

230. *uncouth and obscure:* unfamiliar and remote

232. *Squared:* in a square formation (see 1.550, 1.758, and 6.62)

237–240. *Not . . . obedience:* Raphael understands that the activity of the angels is not needed by God to achieve his purposes but is the medium of their relationship with him; that is, God doesn't need the angels' efforts, but the angels do.

239. *For state:* for ceremony   *inure:* discipline, strengthen by exercise

244. *Torment . . . rage:* perhaps the rage of the fallen angels in 1.666; the noise recalls the " woeful mourning, plaints, and cries" that Astolfo hears at "the mouth of Hell" in *Orlando Furioso* (34.4, 1591, trans. Harrington).

    So spake the godlike power, and thus our sire:
"For man to tell how human life began   250
Is hard, for who himself beginning knew?
Desire with thee still longer to converse
Induced me. As new-waked from soundest sleep,
Soft on the flowery herb I found me laid
In balmy sweat, which with his beams the sun   255
Soon dried and on the reeking moisture fed.
Straight toward Heaven my wondering eyes I turned
And gazed awhile the ample sky, till, raised
By quick instinctive motion, up I sprung
As thitherward endeavoring and upright   260
Stood on my feet; about me round I saw
Hill, dale, and shady woods and sunny plains
And liquid lapse of murmuring streams; by these,
Creatures that lived and moved and walked or flew,
Birds on the branches warbling; all things smiled;   265
With fragrance and with joy my heart o'erflowed.
Myself I then perused and limb by limb
Surveyed, and sometimes went and sometimes ran
With supple joints as lively vigor led;
But who I was, or where, or from what cause   270
Knew not; to speak I tried and forthwith spake;
My tongue obeyed and readily could name
Whate'er I saw. 'Thou sun,' said I, 'fair light,
And thou enlightened earth so fresh and gay,°   *brightly colored*
Ye hills and dales, ye rivers, woods, and plains,   275

---

251. *who himself beginning knew:* Satan
chides Abdiel with this same question in
5.857–58, but, where Satan disingenuously
uses the fact to deny Abdiel's insistence that
they were created (5.836–38), Adam intuits
that he came "Not of myself" but "by some
great maker" (line 278 below).

256. *on . . . fed:* fed on vapors (see
5.415); *reeking* = steaming

260. *upright:* Uprightness differentiates
mankind from other species, and has, of
course, an unavoidable moral sense as well;
cf. 7.506–11.

263. *lapse:* flow (derived from the verb
"to lap," but the word also can mean "error"
or "fall," as at 12.83, a sense Adam cannot

intend but that for a reader anticipates the
fall to come).

268. *went:* walked; cf. *The Tempest*
3.2.18–19: "We'll not run . . . Nor go
neither."

271–273. *to speak . . . saw:* Gen. 2:19
says that "whatsoever Adam called every liv-
ing creature, that was the name thereof" ; cf.
lines 342–54 below. Though it was com-
monly thought that Adam spontaneously
spoke Hebrew, Milton, in his *Art of Logic*
1.24 (*Works* 11, 221), says only that the lan-
guage "which Adam received in Eden," like
the languages that followed, "perhaps derived
from the first," was "without doubt divinely
given."

And ye that live and move, fair creatures, tell,
Tell, if ye saw, how came I thus, how here?
Not of myself; by some great maker, then,
In goodness and in power preeminent;
Tell me, how may I know him, how adore,   280
From whom I have that thus I move and live
And feel that I am happier than I know?'
While thus I called and strayed I knew not whither
From where I first drew air and first beheld
This happy light, when answer none returned,   285
On a green shady bank profuse of flowers
Pensive I sat me down; there gentle sleep
First found me and with soft oppression seized
My drowsèd sense untroubled, though I thought
I then was passing to my former state   290
Insensible, and forthwith to dissolve;
When suddenly stood at my head a dream
Whose inward apparition° gently moved   *appearance*
My fancy to believe I yet had being
And lived: one came, methought, of shape divine   295
And said, 'Thy mansion wants thee, Adam; rise,
First man, of men innumerable ordained
First father; called by thee I come thy guide
To the garden of bliss, thy seat prepared.'
So saying, by the hand he took me raised   300
And over fields and waters, as in air
Smooth sliding without step, last led me up
A woody mountain, whose high top was plain,
A circuit wide enclosed, with goodliest trees
Planted, with walks and bowers, that what I saw   305
Of earth before scarce pleasant seemed. Each tree
Loaden with fairest fruit that hung to the eye

---

281. *From . . . live:* The line evokes Acts 17:28: "For in him we live, and move, and have our being," which echoes the prayer to Zeus in the opening lines of Aratus of Soli's third century B.C. *Phaenomena.*

288. *with soft oppression seized:* gently overwhelmed (but compare 9.1044–45: "dewy sleep / Oppressed them," and 9.1037, "Her hand he seized," as a measure of how much will change with their disobedience).

292. *stood . . . dream:* In the *Iliad*, Onieros (which means "dream") stands at Agammemnon's head, appearing as Nestor (2.20); cf. Eve's dream (5.9–93) and Adam's following comment (5.100–13).

296. *mansion wants:* dwelling place lacks (Eden is not where Adam was created; see 7.535–38, and Gen. 2:8 and 2:15).

302. *sliding:* gliding; cf. 6.71–3.

Tempting stirred in me sudden appetite
To pluck and eat; whereat I waked and found
Before mine eyes all real as the dream   310
Had lively shadowed. Here had new begun
My wandering had not he who was my guide
Up hither from among the trees appeared,
Presence divine. Rejoicing, but with awe,
In adoration at his feet I fell   315
Submiss;° he reared me and 'Whom thou sought'st, I am,'   *submissive*
Said mildly, 'author of all this thou seest
Above or round about thee or beneath.
This Paradise I give thee; count it thine
To till and keep° and of the fruit to eat.   *care for*
Of every tree that in the garden grows
Eat freely with glad heart; fear here no dearth;
But of the tree whose operation° brings   *effect*
Knowledge of good and ill, which I have set
The pledge of thy obedience and thy faith,   325
Amid the garden by the Tree of Life,
Remember what I warn thee: shun to taste
And shun the bitter consequence; for know,
The day thou eat'st thereof, my sole command
Transgressed, inevitably thou shalt die,   330
From that day mortal, and this happy state
Shalt lose, expelled from hence into a world
Of woe and sorrow.' Sternly he pronounced
The rigid interdiction,° which resounds   *prohibition*
Yet dreadful in mine ear, though in my choice   335
Not to incur; but soon his clear aspect

311. *lively shadowed:* vividly represented, made appear like the living reality

319–322. *This . . . dearth:* Milton's version of Gen. 2:15–16: "And the Lord took the man, and put him into the garden of Eden to dress it and keep it. And the Lord God commanded the man, saying, Of every tree of the garden thou mayest freely eat."

323–330. *But . . . die:* Milton's elaboration of Gen. 2:17: "But of the tree of the knowledge of good and evil, thou shalt not eat of it: for in the day that thou eatest thereof thou shalt surely die."

325. *pledge:* It is only as a *pledge* that the interdiction matters; the pledge, not the tree, is the test of the relationship with God; see 3.95 and 4.428.

331. *mortal:* Milton's word *mortal* (i.e., subject to death) tries to reconcile God's promise that "in the day" that Adam eats the apple he shall "surely die" (Gen. 2:17) with the fact that Adam lived 930 years after he ate of the apple.

335–336. *in my choice . . . incur:* i.e., in my control not to be liable to the punishment; Adam intuits his own freedom.

Returned, and gracious purpose° thus renewed:
'Not only these fair bounds° but all the earth   *lands, territories*
To thee and to thy race I give; as lords
Possess it and all things that therein live   340
Or live in sea or air: beast, fish, and fowl.
In sign whereof each bird and beast behold
After their kinds; I bring them to receive
From thee their names and pay thee fealty
With low subjection; understand the same   345
Of fish within their watery residence,
Not hither summoned since they cannot change
Their element to draw the thinner air.'
As thus he spake, each bird and beast behold
Approaching two and two: these cowering low   350
With blandishment, each bird stooped on his wing.
I named them as they passed and understood
Their nature (with such knowledge God endued
My sudden apprehension). But in these
I found not what methought I wanted still   355
And to the heavenly vision thus presumed:°   *dared speak*

      "'O by what name, for thou above all these,
Above mankind or aught than mankind higher,
Surpassest far my naming, how may I
Adore thee, author of this universe   360
And all this good to man, for whose well-being
So amply and with hands so liberal
Thou hast provided all things? But with me

337. *purpose:* speech, discourse (see 4.337)

343–344. *I bring . . . names:* In Adam's intuitive ability to give names to the animals, many commentators on Genesis saw that Adam was "endued with natural wisdom," since, as *Christian Doctrine* argues, "without extraordinary wisdom he could not have given names to the whole animal creation with such sudden intelligence" (I, vii; *Works* 15, 53). Francis Bacon found proof of man's essential enjoyment of the contemplative life in the fact that "the first acts that man performed in Paradise consisted of the two summary parts of knowledge; the view of the creatures, and the impo-

sition of Names" (*Advancement of Learning* 1.6.6). But see 11.277 for Eve's parallel role.

350. *Approaching . . . two:* anticipates the entrance of the animals "two and two . . . into the ark" (Gen. 7:9) before the flood.

350–351. *cowering . . . blandishment:* bowing as a sign of respect or flattery; but there is a technical meaning of *cowering* perhaps relevant here: "in falconry, the quivering of young hawks, who shake their wings, in sign of obedience to the old ones" (*OED*, "cower," b).

351. *stooped . . . wing:* flew down (with the sense also of "bowed down"); cf. "stooped" at 11.185.

I see not who partakes. In solitude
What happiness? Who can enjoy alone   365
Or, all enjoying, what contentment find?'
Thus I presumptuous, and the vision bright,
As with a smile more brightened, thus replied:
  "'What call'st thou solitude? Is not the earth
With various living creatures, and the air,   370
Replenished, and all these at thy command
To come and play before thee? Know'st thou not
Their language and their ways? They also know,°   *have understanding*
And reason not contemptibly. With these
Find pastime and bear rule; thy realm is large.'   375
So spake the universal Lord and seemed
So ordering. I, with leave of speech implored
And humble deprecation, thus replied:
  "'Let not my words offend thee, heavenly power;
My maker be propitious while I speak: 380
Hast thou not made me here thy substitute,°   *deputy*
And these inferior far beneath me set?
Among unequals what society
Can sort, what harmony or true delight,
Which must be mutual, in proportion due   385
Given and received? But in disparity,
The one intense, the other still remiss,
Cannot well suit with either but soon prove
Tedious alike. Of fellowship I speak
Such as I seek, fit to participate°   *participate in, share*
All rational delight, wherein the brute
Cannot be human consort; they rejoice

364–365. *In solitude What happiness:* But for God there is "blissful solitude" (3.69), a mark of the difference between man and God.

371. *Replenished:* fully stocked (as at 7.447)

373. *language:* not human speech (the animals are "mute to all articulate sound," 9.557), but the sounds they make

380. *propitious:* gracious, favorably disposed

383–384. *Among unequals. . . sort:* Adam wants an equal partner; if Eve is created *unequal,* God has frustrated his request. Adam at least cannot be charged with misogyny before the fall; see also line 426 below; *society* = companionship; see pp. xxxiii–xxxvi above.   *sort:* be appropriate or satisfying.

387. *intense . . . remiss:* taut and slack; with "harmony" (line 384), a musical metaphor begins that continues through *intense* and *remiss* as the taut (high-pitched) and slack (low-pitched) strings on an instrument.

392. *consort:* companion (but continuing the musical metaphor begun at line 384)

Each with their kind, lion with lioness,
So fitly them in pairs thou hast combined;
Much less can bird with beast, or fish with fowl   395
So well converse,° nor with the ox the ape,   *associate*
Worse, then, can man with beast, and least of all.'
Whereto the almighty answered, not displeased:
'A nice° and subtle happiness I see   *discriminating*
Thou to thyself proposest in the choice   400
Of thy associates, Adam, and wilt taste
No pleasure, though in pleasure, solitary.
What think'st thou, then, of me and this my state?
Seem I to thee sufficiently possessed
Of happiness, or not, who am alone   405
From all eternity, for none I know
Second to me or like, equal much less?
How have I, then, with whom to hold converse
Save with the creatures which I made, and those
To me inferior, infinite descents   410
Beneath what other creatures are to thee?'
      "He ceased; I lowly answered: 'To attain
The height and depth of thy eternal ways
All human thoughts come short, supreme of things;
Thou in thyself art perfect, and in thee   415
Is no deficience found; not so is man,
But° in degree, the cause of his desire   *except*
By conversation with his like to help
Or solace° his defects. No need that thou   *alleviate*
Shouldst propagate, already infinite,   420
And through all numbers absolute, though one;

---

402. *in pleasure:* Eden literally means "pleasure" or "delight."

406–407. *none . . . less:* The line echoes Horace's allusion to the supreme deity, "than whom no greater exists, and to whom there is none similar or second" (*Odes*, 1.12.17–18), but the thought of the entire passage reflects Aristotle's demonstration of the unity of the divine nature (unlike Adam's unity or solitary oneness in line 425 below, which disqualifies him for happiness in that state) and its capacity for eternal happiness in the contemplation of unchanging truth (*Nicomachean Ethics* 7.14.8).

415–419. *Thou . . . defects:* Adam reasons well here, recognizing that God's singular perfection does not require or permit a mate, but that human nature differs precisely in this; God's love is thus gratuitous, unneeded by him; but human love is necessary to achieve the form of perfection available to the race.

421. *numbers:* here used in its Latin sense of "parts," but in line 422 "number" has its ordinary meaning. God is perfect in all respects because he is absolute, but man fulfills himself only in society.

But man by number is to manifest
His single imperfection and beget
Like of his like, his image multiplied,
In unity° defective, which requires   *being alone*
Collateral° love and dearest amity.   *shared, mutual*
Thou in thy secrecy,° although alone,   *seclusion*
Best with thyself accompanied, seek'st not
Social communication, yet, so pleased,
Canst raise thy creature to what height thou wilt   430
Of union or communion, deified;
I by conversing cannot these erect
From prone nor in their ways complacence find.'
Thus I emboldened spake and freedom used
Permissive and acceptance found, which gained   435
This answer from the gracious voice divine:
    "'Thus far to try thee, Adam, I was pleased
And find thee knowing not of beasts alone,
Which thou hast rightly named, but of thyself,
Expressing well the spirit within thee free,   440
My image, not imparted to the brute,
Whose fellowship therefore unmeet for thee
Good reason was thou freely shouldst dislike,
And be so minded still. I, ere thou spak'st,
Knew it not good for man to be alone   445
And no such company as then thou saw'st
Intended thee, for trial only brought
To see how thou could'st judge of fit and meet.
What next I bring shall please thee, be assured,

423. *single imperfection:* imperfection in being alone, lack of true self-sufficiency

428. *Best . . . accompanied:* Cf. Cicero's famous thought that Scipio Africanus was never so little alone than when by himself (*De officiis*, 3.1.1), said by Abraham Cowley, in his essay "Of Solitude," to be "a very vulgar saying": "Every Man and almost every Boy for these seventeen hundred years, has had it in his mouth" (*Works*, London, 1680, sig. Qqq1ʳ).

431. *deified:* through grace, participant in the divine nature

432–433. *these erect From prone:* make these animals that crawl or walk on all fours (*prone*) stand upright (see 7.505–11).

433. *complacence:* satisfaction, pleasure (see 3.276, where Christ is God's "sole complacence," precisely confirming in the Trinitarian paradox the distinction Adam draws).

435. *Permissive:* allowed, permitted; modifies "freedom," line 434

437. *try:* test; like a Socratic teacher, God tests Adam, tempting him to error and leading him to discover the truth himself.

444–445. *I . . . alone:* See Gen. 2:18: "It is not good that the man should be alone."

448. *To see . . . meet:* Cf. Prov. 17:3: "The fining pot is for silver, and the furnace for gold: but, the Lord trieth the hearts."

Thy likeness, thy fit help, thy other self,   450
Thy wish exactly to thy heart's desire.'
    "He ended, or I heard no more, for now
My earthly by his heavenly overpowered,
Which it had long stood under, strained to the height
In that celestial colloquy sublime   455
As with an object that excels the sense,
Dazzled and spent, sunk down, and sought repair
Of sleep, which instantly fell on me, called
By nature as in aid, and closed mine eyes.
Mine eyes he closed but open left the cell   460
Of fancy, my internal sight, by which
Abstract, as in a trance, methought I saw,
Though sleeping where I lay, and saw the shape
Still glorious before whom awake I stood,
Who, stooping, opened my left side and took   465
From thence a rib, with cordial spirits warm
And life blood streaming fresh; wide was the wound,
But suddenly with flesh filled up and healed.
The rib he formed and fashioned with his hands;
Under his forming hands a creature grew,   470
Manlike but different sex, so lovely fair

450–451. *Thy likeness . . . Thy wish:*
The first three terms define Adam's *wish*, ex-
pressed in his discussion with God, for the
"Collateral love and dearest amity" (line 426)
that define an egalitarian and companionate
marriage.

450. *thy fit . . . self:* In addition to the
biblical term for wife, "helpmeet" (*fit help*),
Milton adds the classical term for an ideal
friend, an *other self* (*alter ego* in Latin).

453. *earthly:* i.e., earthly nature

460–471. *Mine . . . fair:* Milton elabo-
rates on Gen. 2:21–22: "The Lord God
caused a deep sleep to fall upon Adam and he
slept: and he took one of his ribs, . . . And
the rib, which the Lord God had taken from
man, made he a woman, and brought her
unto the man."

460–461. *cell Of fancy:* organ of fancy;
Milton translates a term used by medieval
philosophers, like Nicholas Cusanus, for a
lobe in the brain, the *cellula phantastica,* where

the information from the senses was thought
to be assembled; Adam has explained the role
of *fancy* in dreams in 5.102–13.

462. *Abstract:* withdrawn from con-
sciousness (Latin *ab* = from; *tractus* = drawn
methought I saw: Cf. Milton's Sonnet 19:
"Methought I saw my late espoused Saint"

465. *left side:* Gen. 2:21 does not specify
from which side of Adam God took the rib;
tradition made it the *left* either because that
was closer to Adam's heart (see 4.483–84) or,
in the misogynist version, which a fallen Adam
will anticipate (10.884–86), because the left
(Latin *sinister*) is readily denigrated. In *Tetra-
chordon* (*Works* 4, 91), Milton says: "That
there was a nearer alliance between *Adam* and
Eve, than could be ever after between man and
wife, is visible to any. For no other woman was
ever moulded out of her husband's rib."

466. *cordial spirits:* the "vital spirits"
that the heart (Latin, *cor*) was supposed to
distribute to the body; cf. 5.484.

That what seemed fair in all the world seemed now
Mean, or in her summed up, in her contained,
And in her looks, which from that time infused
Sweetness into my heart unfelt before,   475
And into all things from her air inspired°   *breathed*
The spirit of love and amorous delight.
She disappeared and left me dark; I waked
To find her or forever to deplore
Her loss and other pleasures all abjure;   480
When out of hope, behold her not far off,
Such as I saw her in my dream, adorned
With what all earth or heaven could bestow
To make her amiable.° On she came   *lovely*
Led by her heavenly maker, though unseen,   485
And guided by his voice, nor uninformed
Of nuptial sanctity and marriage rites.
Grace was in all her steps, Heaven in her eye,
In every gesture dignity and love.
I, overjoyed, could not forbear aloud: 490
    " 'This turn hath made amends; thou hast fulfilled
Thy words, creator bounteous and benign,
Giver of all things fair, but fairest this
Of all thy gifts, nor enviest. I now see
Bone of my bone, flesh of my flesh, myself   495
Before me; woman is her name, of man
Extracted; for this cause he shall forgo
Father and mother and to his wife adhere;
And they shall be one flesh, one heart, one soul.'
    "She heard me thus and, though divinely brought,   500
Yet innocence and virgin modesty,

---

476. *air:* manner, appearance (*OED* 3)

481. *When out of:* i.e., when I had given up

490. *forbear aloud:* resist crying aloud

494. *nor enviest:* nor do you give grudgingly (in contrast to the Greek gods, who often envied men their happiness)

495–499. *Bone . . . soul:* Both Matt. 19: 4–6 and Mark 10:6–8 repeat Gen. 2:23–24: "And Adam said, 'This is now bone of my bones, and flesh of my flesh: she shall be called Woman, because she was taken out of Man. Therefore shall a man leave his father and his mother, and shall cleave unto his wife, and they shall be one flesh.' "

499. *one flesh . . . soul:* Compare this threefold elaboration of the single word *flesh* with Gen. 2:24, no doubt to erase any overly narrow interpretation of the word; hence Andrus Willet: "They shall be one flesh, not only in respect of carnal copulation . . . but in respect of their perpetual society" (*Hexapla* [London, 1608] p. 39).

500. *brought:* led (see line 485 above)

Her virtue and the conscience° of her worth,   *consciousness*
That would be wooed and not unsought be won,
Not obvious,° not obtrusive, but retired,   *bold, outgoing*
The more desirable, or, to say all,   505
Nature herself, though pure of sinful thought,
Wrought in her so that seeing me she turned;
I followed her; she what was honor knew
And with obsequious majesty approved
My pleaded reason. To the nuptial bower   510
I led her blushing like the morn; all heaven
And happy constellations on that hour
Shed their selectest influence; the earth
Gave sign of gratulation,° and each hill;   *rejoicing, congratulation*
Joyous the birds; fresh gales and gentle airs   515
Whispered it to the woods, and from their wings
Flung rose, flung odors from the spicy shrub,
Disporting till the amorous bird of night
Sung spousal and bid haste the evening star
On his hilltop to light the bridal lamp.   520
Thus I have told thee all my state and brought
My story to the sum of earthly bliss,
Which I enjoy, and must confess to find
In all things else delight indeed but such
As, used or not, works in the mind no change   525
Nor vehement desire: these delicacies
I mean of taste, sight, smell, herbs, fruits and flowers,
Walks, and the melody of birds. But here
Far otherwise: transported I behold,
Transported touch. Here passion first I felt,   530
Commotion strange. In all enjoyments else
Superior and unmoved, here only weak

508. *honor:* perhaps refers to Heb. 13:4: "Marriage is honourable in all, and the bed undefiled"; cf. 4.741–47.

509. *obsequious:* acquiescent (but not with its modern sense of fawning servility)

513. *Shed . . . influence:* Cf. the dance of the stars, "shedding sweet influence," as a portent of the happiness of the universe at its creation in 7.375.

518. *amorous bird of night:* the nightingale; cf. 5.39–41.

519. *the evening star:* Venus; its appearance was the traditional signal for lighting nuptial torches, as in Spenser: "Long though it be, at last I see it gloome / And the bright evening-star with golden crest / Appeare out of the east" ("Epithalamion," lines 285–87).

526. *vehement:* fervid, ardent (literally "deprived of mind"; Latin *vehe* = lacking + *mens* = mind)

529. *transported:* rapt, ecstatic, carried away by strong emotion

Against the charm° of beauty's powerful glance.   *magical spell*
Or° nature failed in me and left some part   *either*
Not proof enough such object to sustain,°   *withstand*
Or, from my side subducting,° took perhaps   *subtracting*
More than enough, at least on her bestowed
Too much of ornament, in outward show
Elaborate, of inward less exact.°   *perfect, complete*
For well I understand in the prime end   540
Of nature her the inferior in the mind
And inward faculties which most excel;
In outward also her resembling less
His image who made both and less expressing
The character of that dominion given   545
O'er other creatures; yet when I approach
Her loveliness so absolute she seems
And in herself complete, so well to know
Her own, that what she wills to do or say
Seems wisest, virtuousest, discreetest,° best;   *most discerning*
All higher knowledge in her presence falls
Degraded; wisdom in discourse with her
Loses discountenanced and like folly shows;
Authority and reason on her wait
As one intended first not after made   555
Occasionally; and, to consummate all,
Greatness of mind and nobleness their seat
Build in her loveliest and create an awe
About her as a guard angelic placed."
To whom the angel with contracted brow: 560
    "Accuse not nature; she hath done her part;
Do thou but thine and be not diffident°   *distrustful*
Of wisdom; she deserts thee not if thou
Dismiss not her when most thou need'st her nigh

535. *proof:* strong (both armored and experienced)

539. *Elaborate:* highly finished, carefully worked out

547–548. *so absolute . . . complete:* Adam's terms of praise are inappropriate, adopting terms appropriate only for God (see lines 415–26 above), perhaps evidence of his potentially dangerous infatuation; (*absolute* = perfect)

549. *own:* i.e., own mind

553. *Loses discountenanced:* is defeated

and put to shame; some editors prefer "Looses" here, meaning "goes to pieces," though that thought seems less exact than *Loses* and diminishes the parallel with "falls" in line 551.

556. *Occasionally:* for a specific need or occasion

557. *Greatness of mind:* not just intellectual excellence, but the classical virtue of magnanimity (see 7.511)

561–570. *Accuse . . . subjection:* Compare God's similar rebuke to Adam in 10.145–56.

By attributing overmuch to things   565
Less excellent, as thou thyself perceiv'st.
For what admir'st thou, what transports thee so?
An outside? Fair, no doubt, and worthy well
Thy cherishing, thy honoring, and thy love—
Not thy subjection. Weigh with her thyself,   570
Then value; oft times nothing profits more
Than self-esteem grounded on just and right
Well managed; of that skill the more thou know'st,
The more she will acknowledge thee her head
And to realities yield all her shows   575
Made so adorn for thy delight the more,
So awful° that with honor thou mayst love   *awe-inspiring*
Thy mate, who sees when thou art seen least wise.
But if the sense of touch whereby mankind
Is propagated seem such dear delight   580
Beyond all other, think the same vouchsafed
To cattle and each beast, which would not be
To them made common and divulged if aught
Therein enjoyed were worthy to subdue
The soul of man or passion in him move.   585
What higher in her society thou find'st
Attractive, human, rational, love still;
In loving thou dost well, in passion not,
Wherein true love consists not; love refines
The thoughts and heart enlarges, hath his seat   590
In reason and is judicious, is the scale

---

569. *cherishing . . . honoring . . . love:*
The marriage service in the Book of Common Prayer reads: "I take thee to my wedded wife . . . to love and to cherish."

573. *skill:* power or faculty, i.e., of managing well

574. *acknowledge thee her head:* following Paul's assertion that "the head of the woman is the man" (1 Cor. 11:3).

576. *adorn;* i.e., adorned

579–585. *But if . . . move:* In *Tetrachordon* (*Works* 4, 205), Milton holds that sexual pleasure enjoyed solely for its own sake is "farre beneath the soul of a rational and freeborne man."

588. *In loving . . . passion not:* The distinction is essentially between love and lust,

or the Neoplatonic distinction between sacred and profane love, which Spenser echoes in his "Hymne in Honour of Love": "Such is the power of that sweet passion. / That it all sordid basenesse doth expel, / And the refined mynd doth newly fashion / Unto a fairer forme, which now doth dwell / In his high thought, that would it selfe excel" (lines 190–94).

590. *enlarges:* makes more sensitive and capacious

591. *scale:* ladder; the Neoplatonic scale of love (see Plato, *Symposium* 211 C–D), but also Milton's "scale of nature," by which "we may ascend to God" (5.509–12); see 9.112. Love is the active principle of Milton's nature.

By which to heavenly love thou mayst ascend,
Not sunk in carnal pleasure, for which cause
Among the beasts no mate for thee was found."
        To whom thus, half-abashed, Adam replied: 595
"Neither her outside formed so fair nor aught
In procreation common to all kinds
(Though higher of the genial bed by far,
And with mysterious reverence I deem)
So much delights me as those graceful acts,   600
Those thousand decencies that daily flow
From all her words and actions mixed with love
And sweet compliance, which declare unfeigned
Union of mind or in us both one soul:
Harmony to behold in wedded pair   605
More grateful than harmonious sound to the ear.
Yet these subject not; I to thee disclose
What inward thence I feel, not therefore foiled
Who meet with various objects from the sense
Variously representing, yet, still free,   610
Approve the best and follow what I approve.
To love thou blam'st me not, for love thou say'st
Leads up to Heaven, is both the way and guide;
Bear with me, then, if lawful what I ask:
Love not the heavenly spirits, and how their love   615
Express they, by looks only or do they mix
Irradiance, virtual or immediate touch?"

592. *heavenly love:* the divine love of
Plato's *Symposium* as it had been Christian-
ized by poets from Dante to Spenser in pas-
sages like the latter's vision in "An Hymne of
Heavenly Love" of the divine passion inflam-
ing the spirit "With burning zeale, through
every part entire, / That in no earthly thing
thou shalt delight, / But in his sweet and
amiable sight" (lines 271–73)

598. *genial:* procreative, nuptial; cf.
4.712 and 7.282.

599. *mysterious:* sacred; cf. the two uses
of the word in Book 4: "the rites / Mysterious
of connubial love" in lines 742–43 and
"mysterious law" in line 750, both drawing
on the Pauline sense that marriage is "a great
mystery" (Eph. 5:32); i.e., to be revered.

601. *decencies:* examples of gracious or
decorous behavior

607. *subject not:* do not subject me to
her

608. *not therefore foiled:* not thereby
overcome (by the objects of sense); cf. Mark
7:18: "whatsoever thing from without en-
tereth into the man, it cannot defile him."

609–611. *Who meet . . . best:* i.e., who
encounter a variety of objects, which my
senses make variously appealing, but am al-
ways free to choose the best

616–617. *by looks . . . touch:* only by
looking, or do they touch in some way (*mix
Irradiance*), either by sharing emanations
(*virtual*) or in direct physical (*immediate*)
contact

    To whom the angel, with a smile that glowed
Celestial rosy red, love's proper hue,
Answered: "Let it suffice thee that thou know'st   620
Us happy, and without love no happiness.
Whatever pure thou in the body enjoy'st
(And pure thou wert created) we enjoy
In eminence and obstacle find none
Of membrane, joint, or limb, exclusive bars;   625
Easier than air with air, if spirits embrace,
Total they mix, union of pure with pure
Desiring, nor restrained conveyance need
As flesh to mix with flesh or soul with soul.
But I can now no more; the parting sun   630
Beyond the earth's Green Cape and Verdant Isles
Hesperean sets, my signal to depart.
Be strong, live happy, and love, but first of all
Him whom to love is to obey, and keep
His great command; take heed lest passion sway   635
Thy judgment to do aught which else free will
Would not admit;° thine and of all thy sons   *allow*
The weal or woe in thee is placed; beware.
I in thy persevering shall rejoice,

---

619. *Celestial rosy red . . . hue:* the angel blushes, as Eve does as she goes into the "nuptial bower" (line 510 above). Change of color is described as possible for the angels in the passage from Psellus on which 1.423–31 is based (see note at 1.428), but in blushing *Celestial rosy red* Raphael blushes, as does Eve, not in shame but in innocence and joy.

622–629. *Whatever . . . soul:* Physically, Milton conceived the angels much as Henry More in *The Immortality of the Soul* (Cambridge, 1659), as of "penetrable but indiscerptible [i.e., indestructible] body," and, like More, he imagined them "reaping the lawful pleasures of the very *Animal life,* in a far higher degree than we are capable of in this World. . . . Wherefore they cannot but enravish one another's Souls, while they are mutual Spectators of the perfect pulchritude of one another's persons, and comely carriage, of their graceful dancing, their melodious singing and playing" (pp. 420–1).

624. *In eminence:* to the highest degree

628. *restrained conveyance:* confining channels (i.e., sexual organs) or perhaps more generally, restricted forms of expression

631. *Green Cape and Verdant Isles:* i.e., Cape Verde in Senegal and the Cape Verde Islands, about 400 miles off the Senegalese coast

632. *Hesperean:* may modify *Isles,* for the Cape Verdes were sometimes identified with the Gardens of the Hesperides, the Islands of the Blessed that in classical myth were located at the western edge of the world and served as the home of the virtuous in the afterlife; but probably here merely means "westward," referring to the setting sun.

634–635. *Him . . . command:* Cf. 1 John 5:3: "For this is the love of God, that we keep his commandments."

639. *I . . . rejoice:* But in 3.213–15 it is clear that the angels know Adam and Eve will not persevere.

And all the blessed. Stand fast; to stand or fall   640
Free in thine own arbitrament° it lies.   *power to decide*
Perfect within, no outward aid require,°   *expect, request*
And all temptation to transgress repel."
   So saying, he arose, whom Adam thus
Followed with benediction: "Since° to part,   *since we have*
Go heavenly guest, ethereal messenger,
Sent from whose sovereign goodness I adore.
Gentle to me and affable hath been
Thy condescension, and shall be honored ever
With grateful memory. Thou to mankind   650
Be good and friendly still, and oft return."
   So parted they, the angel up to Heaven
From the thick shade and Adam to his bower.

The End of the Eighth Book.

---

640. *the blessed:* i.e., the blessed angels
stand fast: follows 1 Cor. 7:37: "he that
standeth stedfast in his heart . . . doeth well"
   645. *benediction:* Some early editions
objected that it is inappropriate for Adam to
offer a *benediction* to a superior being, but
see *PR* 3.127: "glory and benediction, that is
thanks."

647. *from:* i.e., from him
   649. *condescension:* courtesy, gracious-
ness, with the overtones discussed in note to
line 9 above
   653. *thick shade:* literal, but the tonal
darkening of the poem begins here

BOOK 9

The Argument

Satan, having compassed the earth, with meditated guile returns as a mist by night into Paradise, enters into the serpent sleeping. Adam and Eve in the morning go forth to their labors, which Eve proposes to divide in several places, each laboring apart: Adam consents not, alleging the danger lest that enemy, of whom they were forewarned, should attempt her found alone; Eve, loath to be thought not circumspect or firm enough, urges her going apart, the rather desirous to make trial of her strength; Adam at last yields. The serpent finds her alone: his subtle approach, first gazing then speaking, with much flattery extolling Eve above all other creatures. Eve, wondering to hear the serpent speak, asks how he attained to human speech and such understanding not till now; the serpent answers that by tasting of a certain tree in the garden he attained both to speech and reason, till then void of both; Eve requires him to bring her to that tree and finds it to be the Tree of Knowledge forbidden. The serpent, now grown bolder, with many wiles and arguments induces her at length to eat. She, pleased with the taste, deliberates awhile whether to impart thereof to Adam or not, at last brings him of the fruit, relates what persuaded her to eat thereof; Adam, at first amazed but perceiving her lost, resolves through vehemence of love to perish with her and, extenuating the trespass, eats also of the fruit. The effects thereof in them both; they seek to cover their nakedness, then fall to variance and accusation of one another.

No more of talk where God or angel guest°   *visit*
With man, as with his friend, familiar used
To sit indulgent and with him partake
Rural repast, permitting him the while
Venial° discourse unblamed; I now must change   *pardonable, permissible*

---

2. *familiar:* intimately (and also "as a family member")

3. *indulgent:* gracious, kind (an adjective modifying "God or angel" (line 1)

4. *Rural:* rustic, pastoral (referring to the setting, as at 4.247 and line 451 below); while there is at this time no urban alternative on earth, the fallen angels' Pandaemo-

nium is imagined as a "city," "their metropolis" (10.424 and 10.439).

5. *unblamed:* unblamable

5–9. *discourse . . . distaste:* Note the repeated syllable in *discourse, distrust, Disloyal, disobedience, distance, distaste,* the words themselves in order describing almost exactly the arc of Adam and Eve's relationship with God.

261

Those notes to tragic: foul distrust and breach
Disloyal on the part of man, revolt
And disobedience; on the part of Heaven,
Now alienated, distance and distaste,
Anger and just rebuke and judgment given,   10
That brought into this world a world of woe,
Sin and her shadow Death, and misery,
Death's harbinger. Sad task, yet argument
Not less but more heroic than the wrath
Of stern Achilles on his foe pursued   15
Thrice fugitive about Troy wall, or rage
Of Turnus for Lavinia disespoused,
Or Neptune's ire, or Juno's, that so long
Perplexed° the Greek and Cytherea's son,   *tormented*
If answerable° style I can obtain   *worthy, suitable, corresponding*
Of my celestial patroness who deigns
Her nightly visitation unimplored
And dictates to me slumbering or inspires
Easy my unpremeditated verse,

6. *tragic:* Milton announces a shift of tone (not of genre) here; but significantly his "notes" turn *tragic* not with Satan's fall but only with Adam and Eve's.

9. *distaste:* aversion, but with an emphasis upon the embedded word "taste," which, with its near homonym "test," functions as the crucial term of the temptation and fall; see "mortal taste" in 1.2.

12. *her shadow Death:* In 10.249–50, Sin calls Death "my shade / Inseparable."

13. *argument:* subject (as at lines 28 and 42)

14. *Not less but more heroic:* Milton insists that the story of Adam and Eve is even *more heroic* than the stories of the traditional epic even though it avoids the familiar epic subjects and themes.

14–16. *the wrath . . . wall:* In *Iliad* 22, Achilles pursues the fleeing (*fugitive*) Hector (*his foe*) around the walls of Troy, and Homer's poem begins by claiming *the wrath Of stern Achilles* as its subject.

16–17. *rage . . . disespoused:* In *Aeneid* 7, Turnus, who had been betrothed to Lavinia, became enraged after her father gave her to Aeneas, and he then led an army against the Trojans.

18–19. *Neptune's ire . . . Cytherea's son:* also invokes the classical epics: first, the *Odyssey,* where Neptune persecutes Ulysses for blinding his son, Polyphemus; and then the *Aeneid,* where Aeneas (*Cytherea's* [i.e., Venus'] *son*) is plagued by Juno, who is angry that his mother defeated her in a beauty contest. The anger of these gods, which drives the two classical epics, is implicitly contrasted with the justice of the God that motivates Milton's poem.

21. *celestial patroness:* i.e., Urania, named in 7.1

24. *unpremeditated:* The verse comes to him immediately from the inspiration of the muse; see 3.37–38, and also the *Apology to Smectymnuus* (1642) "whose mind so ever is fully possest with a fervent desire to know good things, and with the dearest charity to infuse the knowledge of them into others, when such a man would speak, his words (by what I can expresse), like so many nimble and airy servitors, trip about him at command, and in well-order'd files, as he would wish, fall aptly into their own places" (*Works* 3, part 1, 362).

Since first this subject for heroic song   25
Pleased me, long choosing and beginning late,
Not sedulous° by nature to indite   *eager, anxious*
Wars, hitherto the only argument
Heroic deemed, chief mastery to dissect
With long and tedious havoc° fabled knights   *fighting*
In battles feigned,° the better fortitude   *represented in fiction*
Of patience and heroic martyrdom
Unsung, or to describe races and games,
Or tilting furniture, emblazoned shields,
Impresas quaint, caparisons and steeds,   35
Bases and tinsel trappings, gorgeous knights
At joust and tournament, then marshalled feast
Served up in hall with sewers and seneschals:
The skill of artifice or office mean,
Not that which justly gives heroic name   40
To person or to poem. Me, of these
Nor skilled nor studious, higher argument
Remains sufficient of itself to raise
That name, unless an age too late, or cold

25–26. *Since first . . . and beginning late:* Milton had thought about writing an epic early in his life: as early as 1628 he had announced that one day his imagination would "soar / Above the wheeling poles"; about 1640 he had conceived various outlines for a tragedy on the theme of "Adam Unparadized"; sometime around 1646 he wrote some verses that eventually appeared in the poem (4.32–41); and by 1658 he seems to have been seriously at work on his epic, which Thomas Ellwood says that he saw in a completed form in 1665; see p. lii above.

27. *indite:* relate, write about

28–31. *Wars . . . feigned:* Milton declares his religious theme to be unlike that of any previous epic poem; cf. 1.16. Compare Samuel Pordage's *Mundorum Explicatio* (1661), where in the proem the poet professes: "I sing no Hero's douty gests and warrs, / Nor blazon forth some warlike Champion's Scarrs" (sig. [b]8ʳ).

34. *tilting furniture:* equipment for jousting

35. *Impresas quaint:* elaborate coats of arms (*quaint* = ingeniously designed) *caparisons:* richly ornamented trapping placed over the saddle and harness of a horse

36. *Bases . . . trappings:* decorated cloth housings (*Bases*) placed over the backs and sides of horses (*tinsel* = cloth made to glitter with threads of gold)

37. *marshalled:* with the guests seated in order of rank

38. *sewers and seneschals:* waiters and chief stewards

44. *That name:* i.e., the epic, which Milton's "higher argument" (line 42) has redeemed from the moral insignificance of its traditional focus on warfare.

44–45. *an age . . . Climate:* In the Preface to Book 2 of *Reason of Church Government* (*Works* 3, part 1, 237), Milton worried that "our climate or the fate of this age" might prove to be obstacles to his poetic ambition; since Aristotle, philosophers had claimed that people in northern climates lacked skill and intelligence (*Politics* 7.7.1),

Climate, or years, damp my intended wing   45
Depressed, and much they may if all be mine,
Not hers who brings it nightly to my ear.
      The sun was sunk, and after him the star
Of Hesperus, whose office is to bring
Twilight upon the earth, short arbiter   50
Twixt day and night; and now from end to end
Night's hemisphere had veiled the horizon round,
When Satan, who late fled before the threats
Of Gabriel out of Eden, now improved
In meditated fraud and malice, bent   55
On man's destruction, maugre° what might hap   *in spite of*
Of heavier° on himself, fearless returned.   *i.e., heavier punishment*
By night he fled and at midnight returned
From compassing the earth, cautious° of day   *wary*
Since Uriel, regent of the sun, descried   60
His entrance and forewarned the cherubim
That kept their watch; thence, full of anguish driven,
The space of seven continued nights he rode
With darkness, thrice the equinoctial line
He circled, four times crossed the car of Night   65
From pole to pole, traversing each colure;
On the eighth returned and on the coast averse
From entrance or cherubic watch by stealth
Found unsuspected way. There was a place,

and the theory that the world itself was de-
caying was common.

45. *years:* age; Milton was 58 in 1667,
when *PL* was first published.

45–46. *damp . . . Depressed:* extinguish
my faltering poetic ambition (*Depressed* in-
cludes its literal sense, "pressed down," fol-
lowing *damp,* as one might damp a fire or
musical string.)

46. *if all be mine:* if I alone am re-
sponsible

50. *arbiter:* mediator (refers to "Twi-
light")

53. *late:* recently (from the point of
view of the reader, in Book 4; in the chronol-
ogy of the poem, seven days earlier)

54. *improved:* Having learned from his
experience with Gabriel (4.874–1015),
Satan has refined his methods of deceit (or

possibly just "increased" or "intensified"
them).

59. *compassing the earth:* See Job 1:7:
"'Whence comest thou?' Then Satan an-
swered the Lord, and said, 'From going to
and fro in the earth . . .'"

60. *Uriel . . . sun:* See 3.648 and note.
descried: observed (see 4.567–68)

64. *equinoctial line:* in Ptolemaic as-
tronomy, the orbit of the sun around the
earth in the same plane as the earth's equator

65. *car:* chariot; cf. the "yron charet" of
Spenser's "grisly Night" in *Faerie Queene*
1.5.20.

66. *each colure:* Milton refers to the
supposition that the earth is banded by two
longitudinal circles that intersect at right
angles at the poles.

67. *coast averse:* the side opposite

Now not, though sin, not time, first wrought the change,   70
Where Tigris at the foot of Paradise
Into a gulf shot underground till part
Rose up a fountain by the Tree of Life;
In with the river sunk, and with it rose
Satan involved in rising mist, then sought   75
Where to lie hid. Sea he had searched and land
From Eden over Pontus and the pool
Maeotis up beyond the river Ob,
Downward as far Antarctic, and in length
West from Orontes to the ocean barred   80
At Darien, thence to the land where flows
Ganges and Indus. Thus the orb he roamed
With narrow° search, and with inspection deep   *close, meticulous*
Considered every creature, which of all
Most opportune might serve his wiles and found   85
The serpent subtlest beast of all the field.
Him, after long debate, irresolute
Of thoughts revolved, his final sentence chose
Fit vessel, fittest imp of fraud, in whom
To enter and his dark suggestions° hide   *temptations*

70. *Now not:* no longer existing

71. *Tigris . . . Paradise:* Gen. 2:10 speaks of a river that "went out of Eden to water the garden," which then divides into four: the Tigris is one of these, though in the King James Bible the river's name is Hiddekel, that "which goeth toward the east of Assyria" (Gen. 2:14).

75. *rising mist:* follows Gen. 2:6: "there went up a mist from the earth, and watered the whole face of the ground"

76–78. *sea . . . Ob:* Satan first flies north over *Pontus* (the Black Sea) and the *pool Maeotis* (Sea of Azov), *beyond the river Ob,* or the Obi, on the Arctic shore of Siberia.

80. *Orontes:* the chief river of Syria

80–81. *barred At Darien:* blocked at the Isthmus of Panama; Job 38:10 says that God "set bars and doors" to the ocean with the formation of the land masses.

81–82. *the land . . . Indus:* i.e., India, whose chief rivers are the Ganges and the Indus

86. *serpent . . . field:* Without mentioning Satan, Gen. 3:1, says that "the Serpent was more subtil than any beast of the field which the Lord had made."

87–88. *irresolute . . . revolved:* undecided among the thoughts he turned over in his mind

88. *sentence:* decision (but the phrase as it is initially encountered, "Him . . . his final sentence chose," makes it mean "condemnation" and exactly defines the poem's insistence that Satan chooses his own fate)

89. *imp of fraud:* Some editors see this as a horticultural image, with Satan's *fraud* grafted onto the serpent's body, but *imp* in this sense properly refers to the slip or shoot in the grafting rather than the stock, as this gloss supposes. More likely this means "child of the devil" (*OED* 4), as some editors have suggested, but this would make the serpent fallen before the fall, unless it is made clear that here *of* means "for" not "from"; *imp* is a figurative use of the word pointing to its instrumentality (note "fittest") for Satan's *fraud.*

From sharpest sight, for in the wily snake
Whatever sleights° none would suspicious mark,   *signs of cunning*
As from his wit and native subtlety
Proceeding which in other beasts observed
Doubt° might beget of diabolic power   *suspicion*
Active within beyond the sense of brute.
Thus he resolved, but first from inward grief
His bursting passion into plaints thus poured:
    "O earth, how like to Heaven, if not preferred
More justly, seat worthier of gods, as built   100
With second thoughts, reforming what was old!
For what God, after better, worse would build?
Terrestrial heaven, danced round by other heavens
That shine, yet bear their bright officious lamps,
Light above light, for thee alone, as seems,   105
In thee concentering all their precious beams
Of sacred influence: as God in Heaven
Is center yet extends to all, so thou
Centering receiv'st from all those orbs; in thee,
Not in themselves, all their known virtue appears   110
Productive in herb, plant, and nobler birth
Of creatures animate with gradual life
Of growth, sense, reason, all summed up in man.
With what delight could I have walked thee round,
If I could joy in aught, sweet interchange   115
Of hill and valley, rivers, woods, and plains,
Now land, now sea, and shores with forest crowned,
Rocks, dens, and caves; but I in none of these
Find place or refuge, and the more I see
Pleasures about me so much more I feel   120

92. *none . . . mark:* no one would think them suspicious

103–107. *Terrestrial . . . influence:* Satan echoes both Eve (4.657–58) and Adam (8.15–38) in wondering about the celestial economy.

103. *heaven . . . heavens:* Planet . . . heavenly bodies; the assumption here is that the heavens are geocentric.

104. *officious:* attentive, ministering (as in 8.99)

105. *for thee alone:* i.e., only for the earth; but cf. 8.100–106.

109. *Centering:* remaining in the center (as in the Ptolemaic system)

112. *gradual:* on a graduated scale of excellence

113. *growth, sense, reason:* the attributes of the three kinds of life: vegetable, animal, rational; *sense* = feeling

118. *Rocks, dens, and caves:* Satan's eye focuses delightedly on features familiar from hell; cf. the "Rocks, caves, lakes, fens, bogs, dens, and shades of death" in 2.621.

119. *place or refuge:* Bentley's edition of *PL* (1732) suggested that *or* should be

Torment within me, as from the hateful siege
Of contraries;° all good to me becomes   *conflicting emotions*
Bane, and in Heaven much worse would be my state.
But neither here seek I, no, nor in Heaven
To dwell, unless by mastering Heaven's supreme,°   *supreme ruler*
Nor hope to be myself less miserable
By what I seek but others to make such
As I, though thereby worse to me redound:
For only in destroying I find ease
To my relentless thoughts, and him destroyed   130
Or won to what may work his utter loss,
For whom all this was made, all this will soon
Follow, as to him linked in weal or woe—
In woe then, that destruction wide may range.
To me shall be the glory sole among   135
The infernal powers, in one day to have marred
What he, almighty styled,° six nights and days   *titled*
Continued making, and who knows how long
Before had been contriving, though perhaps
Not longer than since I in one night freed   140
From servitude inglorious well-nigh half
The angelic name and thinner left the throng
Of his adorers. He, to be avenged
And to repair his numbers thus impaired,
Whether such virtue° spent of old now failed   *power*
More angels to create (if they at least
Are his created) or to spite us more
Determined to advance into our room°   *place (in Heaven)*
A creature formed of earth and him endow,

emended to "of," but *place* = place to dwell
and *refuge* = refuge from God's anger.

121. *siege:* 1) attack; 2) seat

123. *Bane:* poison; cf. Satan's reflections
in 4.32–113 and lines 467–70 below; see
also 1.692.

128. *to me redound:* recoil upon me

133. *weal or woe:* a conventional for-
mula for "good fortune or bad"

141. *well-nigh half:* the same claim as in
1.632–33; but see 2.692 ("a third part") and
4.869 ("a third")

146–147. *if . . . his created:* The *if*
clause again voices Satan's unwillingness to
acknowledge that he was created (see also

5.853–63), but cf. his admission in 4.43 that
he is God's creature.

147. *to spite us more:* a typically Satanic
projection of motive onto God, but see
7.150–55, where God indeed does suggest a
negative motive for the creation, to prevent
Satan from taking pleasure "in the harm / Al-
ready done."

149–150. *creature . . . original:* Tasso in
Gerusalemme Liberata has Satan appeal to the
demons' contempt of "Vile man, begot of
clay, and born of dust," made worse since
"That sinful creature man elected is" and will
"possess" heaven "in our place" (trans. Fair-
fax, 1600, 4.10); *original* = origin

Exalted from so base original,   150
With heavenly spoils, *our* spoils. What he decreed
He effected; man he made and for him built
Magnificent this world and earth his seat,
Him lord pronounced and (O indignity!)
Subjected to his service angel wings   155
And flaming ministers to watch and tend
Their earthy charge. Of these the vigilance
I dread and, to elude, thus wrapped in mist
Of midnight vapor glide obscure and pry
In every bush and brake° where hap may find   *thicket*
The serpent sleeping in whose mazy folds
To hide me and the dark intent I bring.
O foul descent, that I who erst° contended   *formerly*
With gods to sit the highest, am now constrained°   *compressed, forced*
Into a beast and mixed with bestial slime,   165
This essence to incarnate and imbrute
That to the height of deity aspired.
But what will not ambition and revenge
Descend to? Who aspires must down as low
As high he soared, obnoxious first or last   170
To basest things. Revenge, at first though sweet,
Bitter ere long back on itself recoils.
Let it; I reck° not, so it light well-aimed,   *care*
Since higher° I fall short, on him who next   *aiming higher*
Provokes my envy, this new favorite   175
Of Heaven, this man of clay, son of despite,
Whom, us the more to spite, his maker raised
From dust; spite then with spite is best repaid."
     So saying, through each thicket dank or dry,

---

156. *flaming:* radiant; see the "flaming cherubim" 6.102 and Heb. 1:7: "Who maketh his angels spirits and his ministers a flame of fire."

166. *essence to incarnate:* i.e., this nature to embody in flesh; but cf. this *essence* with the "heavenly essences" of 1.138, and this act of incarnation with Christ's (see 3.315). *imbrute:* degrade, degenerate to the level of a beast; cf. *Comus,* lines 466–67: "The soul grows clotted by contagion, / Imbodies and imbrutes."

170. *obnoxious:* exposed, vulnerable (as at line 1094 below)

174. *next:* i.e., next to God

175. *envy:* Augustine in *City of God* (12.11) says that envy is the hatred of another's happiness; and in 14.11 accuses Satan of envying man's "constancy."

176. *despite:* i.e., God's spite, as Satan sees it, since in his view man is made only to spite the fallen angels

177. *the more to spite:* Cf. the charge against Beelzebub and Satan of doing all "to spite the great creator" (2.384–85).

Like a black mist low creeping, he held on   180
His midnight search where soonest he might find
The serpent. Him fast sleeping soon he found
In labyrinth of many a round self-rolled,
His head the midst, well-stored with subtle wiles;
Not yet in horrid shade or dismal den,   185
Nor nocent yet, but on the grassy herb
Fearless, unfeared, he slept. In at his mouth
The devil entered and his brutal° sense,   *animal, brutish*
In heart or head, possessing soon inspired
With act intelligential, but his sleep   190
Disturbed not, waiting close the approach of morn.
Now, when as sacred light began to dawn
In Eden on the humid flowers that breathed
Their morning incense, when all things that breathe
From the earth's great altar send up silent praise   195
To the creator and his nostrils fill
With grateful smell, forth came the human pair
And joined their vocal worship to the choir
Of creatures wanting voice; that done, partake
The season, prime for sweetest scents and airs,   200
Then commune how that day they best may ply°   *apply themselves to*
Their growing work, for much their work outgrew
The hands dispatch of two gardening so wide;
And Eve first to her husband thus began:
      "Adam, well may we labor still° to dress   *continually*

---

180. *black mist low creeping:* A reminis-
cence, perhaps, of Thetis rising "like a cloud"
from the sea to answer Achilles' prayer (*Iliad*
1.359), and an expression of a belief current
in Milton's time that "as in liquid clouds (ex-
haled thickly), / Water and Ayr (as moist) do
mingle quickly, / The evil Angells slide too
easily, / As subtle spirits into our fantasie"
(Du Bartas, *Divine Weeks,* trans. Sylvester,
1608, p. 251).

185. *horrid:* bristling (referring to the
shrubs that will provide *shade*)

186. *Nor nocent:* 1) not guilty, inno-
cent; 2) not harmful

190. *act intelligential:* the capacity for
rational action

191. *close:* hidden (but also "attentively")

197. *grateful smell:* So in Gen. 8:21,

where "the Lord smelled a sweet savour"
from the altars of sacrifice erected by Noah;
grateful = 1) pleasing; 2) full of gratitude

198–199. *choir . . . wanting voice:* i.e.,
"all things that breathe," who "send up silent
praise" (line 194–95); only the two humans
are considered to have *voice* (i.e., speech).

199–200. *partake The season:* partake of
(enjoy) the time of day (*OED* 12)   *prime:*
best (also the first hour of daylight; see 5.170)

204. *first to her husband . . . began:*
Some commentators have seen this *first* ex-
ample of Eve initiating the conversation as it-
self a violation of an ordained hierarchy, but
neither Adam nor the narrator seems at all
surprised or worried; in Eden she is his social
equal, for which Adam had asked God in
8.383–85.

This garden, still to tend plant, herb, and flower,
Our pleasant task enjoined,° but till more hands   *commanded*
Aid us, the work under our labor grows
Luxurious by restraint: what we by day
Lop overgrown, or prune or prop or bind,   210
One night or two with wanton growth derides,
Tending to wild. Thou, therefore, now advise
Or hear what to my mind first thoughts present:
Let us divide our labors, thou where choice
Leads thee or where most needs, whether to wind   215
The woodbine round this arbor or direct
The clasping ivy where to climb, while I
In yonder spring° of roses intermixed   *thicket, grove*
With myrtle find what to redress till noon.
For while so near each other thus all day   220
Our task we choose, what wonder if, so near,
Looks intervene and smiles, or object new
Casual discourse draw on, which intermits°   *interrupts*
Our day's work brought to little, though begun
Early, and the hour of supper comes unearned."   225
      To whom mild answer Adam thus returned:
"Sole Eve, associate sole, to me beyond
Compare above all living creatures dear,
Well hast thou motioned,° well thy thoughts employed   *suggested, proposed*

207. *till more hands:* at least momentarily *till* might be heard as a verb relating to their task; here and elsewhere, Milton exploits these ambiguities insisting that human experience, unlike the divine, unfolds in time. Properly understood as "until," it raises the question of how she imagines "more hands" to be created (see also lines 246–47 below).

208–212. *work . . . wild:* Unfallen nature still must be tended and pruned (presumably "lopped" branches do not die but somehow regenerate themselves); the warrant for this work is Gen. 1:28, with human "dominion" over created nature. Milton's emphasis upon the wildness of the garden recognizes the prolific growth of unfallen nature and differentiates Eden from the orderly, rationalized orchards and gardens of mid-17th-century England.

211. *wanton:* In the unfallen world, the word is morally neutral, referring, like "Luxurious" (i.e., "luxuriant") in line 209, to a natural tendency of things to grow profusely, demanding rational human control; but cf. its use at line 1015 below.

214. *divide:* The principle of efficiency invoked here also invokes the division (of Adam and Eve, of man and God; see lines 261–63 below) that will destroy the fundamental unity (note "entire," line 292; "unite," line 314; "integrity," line 329) of Eden.

219. *redress:* In a fallen world, this might mean "repair" or "restore"; here it must literally mean "re-dress," i.e., to do again what they were commanded to do each day, having been put in the Garden "to dress and to keep it" (Gen. 2:15).

227. *Sole . . . sole: Sole* oscillates in meaning between "only" and "unrivaled," and, with *associate,* suggests "soul"; the same word play appears at 4.411.

How we might best fulfill the work which here   230
God hath assigned us, nor of me shalt pass
Unpraised, for nothing lovelier can be found
In woman than to study household good
And good works in her husband to promote.
Yet not so strictly hath our Lord imposed   235
Labor as to debar us when we need
Refreshment, whether food or talk between,°   *in intervals of work*
Food of the mind or this sweet intercourse°   *exchange*
Of looks and smiles, for smiles from reason flow,
To brute denied, and are of love the food,   240
Love, not the lowest end of human life.
For not to irksome toil but to delight
I Ie made us, and delight to reason joined.
These paths and bowers doubt not but our joint hands
Will keep from wilderness° with ease as wide   *wildness*
As we need walk, till younger hands ere long
Assist us; but if much converse° perhaps   *conversation*
Thee satiate, to short absence I could yield,
For solitude sometimes is best society,
And short retirement urges sweet return.   250
But other doubt possesses me lest harm
Befall thee severed from me, for thou know'st
What hath been warned us: what malicious foe,
Envying our happiness and of his own
Despairing, seeks to work us woe and shame   255
By sly assault and somewhere nigh at hand
Watches, no doubt, with greedy hope to find
His wish and best advantage, us asunder,
Hopeless to circumvent us joined where each
To other speedy aid might lend at need,   260
Whether his first design be to withdraw
Our fealty from God or to disturb
Conjugal love, than which perhaps no bliss
Enjoyed by us excites his envy more—

232–234. *nothing lovelier . . . promote:*
Christian Doctrine II, xv rehearses the biblical
authority for understanding the "duties of
husband and wife," noting that they are ei-
ther "mutual or personal" (*Works* 17,
49–51); these are at least Adam's understand-
ing of Eve's "personal" duties.

249. *solitude . . . society:* See 8.427–28
and note.

262. *fealty:* loyalty (technically, the obe-
dience of, or loyalty from, feudal vassals to
their masters)

264. *envy:* Satan admits his *envy* at
4.503.

Or this, or worse; leave not the faithful side   265
That gave thee being, still shades thee and protects.
The wife, where danger or dishonor lurks,
Safest and seemliest by her husband stays,
Who guards her or with her the worst endures."
    To whom the virgin° majesty of Eve,   *chaste, maidenly*
As one who loves and some unkindness meets,
With sweet austere composure thus replied:
"Offspring of Heaven and earth, and all earth's lord,
That such an enemy we have who seeks
Our ruin, both by thee informed I learn   275
And from the parting angel overheard
As in a shady nook I stood behind,
Just then returned at shut of evening flowers.
But that thou shouldst my firmness therefore doubt
To God or thee because we have a foe   280
May° tempt it I expected not to hear.   *who may*
His violence thou fear'st not, being such
As we, not capable of death or pain,
Can either not receive° or can repel.   *be affected by*
His fraud is then thy fear, which plain infers   285
Thy equal fear that my firm faith and love
Can by his fraud be shaken or seduced,
Thoughts which, how found they harbor in thy breast,
Adam, misthought of her to thee so dear."
    To whom with healing words Adam replied: 290
"Daughter of God and man, immortal Eve,
For such thou art, from sin and blame entire;°   *untouched, unblemished*
Not diffident of thee do I dissuade
Thy absence from my sight but to avoid
The attempt itself intended by our foe.   295
For he who tempts, though in vain, at least asperses

265. *Or this, or worse:* i.e., whether his intent be this, or something worse

265–266. *the faithful side . . . being:* See 8.465–71.

272. *sweet austere:* an oxymoron (sweet/ sour), expressing her conflicted sense (as in line 271)

274–276. *That . . . overheard:* Eve's full, independent knowledge of the command not to eat the fruit of the Tree of Knowledge was often stressed by biblical commentators,

but there is some inconsistency between this account and what is said at 7.50.

278. *shut . . . flowers:* the hour the flowers close up, i.e., dusk

285. *plain infers:* clearly suggests

289. *misthought of:* misjudging

293. *diffident:* distrustful (Latin *dis* + *fidere* = to trust)

296. *asperses:* falsely charges (literally, "sprinkles")

The tempted with dishonor foul, supposed
Not incorruptible of faith,° not proof   *loyalty*
Against temptation. Thou thyself with scorn
And anger would'st resent the offered wrong,   300
Though ineffectual found; misdeem not, then,
If such affront I labor to avert
From thee alone which on us both at once
The enemy, though bold, will hardly dare,
Or daring, first on me the assault shall light.   305
Nor thou his malice and false guile contemn;°   *disdain, underestimate*
Subtle he needs must be who could seduce
Angels. Nor think superfluous others' aid.
I from the influence of thy looks receive
Access in every virtue, in thy sight   310
More wise, more watchful, stronger, if need were
Of outward strength, while shame, thou looking on,
Shame to be overcome or overreached,°   *deceived*
Would utmost vigor raise and, raised, unite.
Why shouldst not thou like sense within thee feel   315
When I am present, and thy trial choose
With me, best witness of thy virtue tried?"
        So spake domestic Adam in his care
And matrimonial love, but Eve, who thought
Less attributed to her faith sincere,°   *genuine, pure*
Thus her reply with accent sweet renewed:
"If this be our condition, thus to dwell
In narrow circuit straitened° by a foe   *confined, restricted*
Subtle or violent, we not endued
Single with like° defense wherever met,   *equivalent, matching*
How are we happy, still° in fear of harm?   *always*
But harm precedes not sin; only our foe
Tempting affronts us with his foul esteem°   *estimation*

---

301. *misdeem not:* do not misunder-
stand or take it amiss
310. *Access:* augmentation, enhance-
ment; Plato's insistence on the value of the
mutual stimulation of friends in lives of
virtue (*Symposium* 178–79) was prominent
in the thinking of the Renaissance about
friendship, though the astrological sense of
"influence" in line 309 makes the image as
much Petrarchan as Platonic.

314. *unite:* i.e., unite the "vigor" to
"every virtue" in line 310
315. *like sense:* the same sensation (of
strength)
318. *domestic:* The adjective is merited
precisely because of his "matrimonial love"
(line 319).
328. *Tempting:* i.e., the mere fact of try-
ing to tempt us

Of our integrity; his foul esteem
Sticks no dishonor on our front, but turns   330
Foul on himself; then wherefore shunned or feared
By us, who rather double honor gain
From his surmise proved false, find peace within,
Favor from heaven, our witness, from the event?
And what is faith, love, virtue unassayed,   335
Alone, without exterior help sustained?
Let us not then suspect our happy state
Left° so imperfect by the maker wise   *to have been left*
As not secure to single or combined.
Frail is our happiness if this be so,   340
And Eden were no Eden thus exposed."
    To whom thus Adam fervently replied:
"O woman, best are all things as the will
Of God ordained them; his creating hand
Nothing imperfect or deficient left   345
Of all that he created, much less man
Or aught that might his happy state secure,°   *protect*
Secure from outward force; within himself
The danger lies, yet lies within his power.
Against his will he can receive no harm.   350
But God left free the will, for what obeys
Reason is free, and reason he made right
But bid her well beware, and still erect,
Lest by some fair-appearing good surprised
She dictate false and misinform the will   355
To do what God expressly hath forbid.

---

330. *front:* brow or face, as in 2.302; her word picks up "affronts" in line 328.

334. *event:* outcome; cf. the similar use of *event* in 1.134, 2.82, etc.

339. *not . . . combined:* not to be safe for us, whether alone or together

342. *fervently:* passionately, excitedly (but not angrily; at line 1162 below, Adam is said to be "first incensed," so he cannot be angry; but note the shifting terms of address, from "immortal Eve" in Adam's previous speech (line 291) to "O woman" in line 343.

351–356. *God left . . . forbid:* Adam repeats the doctrine that he has learned from Raphael (5.520–40) and that has been dis-

tinctly stated by God in 3.96–128; In *Christian Doctrine* Milton said: "Reason has been implanted in all, by which they may of themselves resist bad desires" (I, iv; *Works* 14, 131).

352. *right:* perfectly, but also as in "right reason," i.e., *ratio recta,* the intuitive intelligence, or conscience, by which we know the laws of nature; see 6.42 and also Philip Sidney's "erected wit" in the *Defense of Poetry* (posthumously published in 1595); thus *right* here and "erect" in line 353 are related.

353. *still erect:* always alert (but see 7.508, where erect posture is the sign of reason; also see previous note)

Not then mistrust but tender love enjoins
That I should mind thee oft, and mind thou me.
Firm we subsist, yet possible to swerve,
Since reason not impossibly may meet   360
Some specious object by the foe suborned
And fall into deception unaware,
Not keeping strictest watch as she° was warned.   *i.e., reason*
Seek not temptation, then, which to avoid
Were better, and most likely if from me   365
Thou sever not; trial will come unsought.
Would'st thou approve° thy constancy, approve   *give proof of, demonstrate*
First thy obedience; the other who can know,
Not seeing thee attempted who attest?
But if thou think trial unsought may find   370
Us both securer than thus warned thou seem'st,
Go; for thy stay, not free, absents thee more;
Go in thy native innocence, rely
On what thou hast of virtue, summon all,
For God toward thee hath done his part; do thine."   375
    So spake the patriarch of mankind, but Eve
Persisted, yet submiss, though last, replied:
"With thy permission, then, and thus forewarned,
Chiefly by what thy own last reasoning words
Touched only, that our trial when least sought   380
May find us both perhaps far less prepared,
The willinger I go, nor much expect
A foe so proud will first the weaker seek;

357. *enjoins:* commands (and with the embedded "joins" participating in the set of words articulating the unity that is at risk; see line 214 and note).

358. *mind . . . mind:* remind . . . remind; also look after . . . look after (but the second *mind* can easily be heard as meaning "obey" or "pay heed to," unsettling the equality that the primary senses would establish).

361. *specious object . . . suborned:* Cf. Archimago's "suborned wyle" in the shape of speciously "falsed letters" in Spenser's *Faerie Queene* 2.1.1.3; (*suborned* = secretly enlisted to commit a crime)

368. *the other:* i.e., constancy

370–372. *But if . . . more:* Scholars debate whether Adam is at fault for allowing Eve to *Go*, or Eve for insisting that she

should. Adam's *Go* may be a bit of rhetorical manipulation, hoping that it may make her reconsider her decision, even as he realizes that he must recognize her free will in spite of his anxiety.

371. *securer:* less careful, less on guard; cf. "secure" in line 339 above and in 4.791.

376. *patriarch of mankind:* Is the epithet intended to reflect upon Adam's actions immediately before?

377. *yet submiss:* still submissive   *last:* She also spoke first in this exchange; see line 205.

378. *permission:* literally, the result of "*persisted*" and "*submiss*" in line 377

383. *the weaker:* Eve's phrase derives from 1 Peter 3:7: "the wife . . . the weaker vessel"; see also 6.908–9.

So bent, the more shall shame him his repulse."
Thus saying, from her husband's hand her hand   385
Soft she withdrew and, like a wood nymph light,°   *light-footed, quick*
Oread or dryad, or of Delia's train,
Betook her to the groves, but Delia's self
In gait surpassed and goddesslike deport,°   *deportment*
Though not as she with bow and quiver armed   390
But with such gardening tools as art yet rude,
Guiltless of fire, had formed or angels brought.
To Pales or Pomona, thus adorned,
Likest she seemed, Pomona when she fled
Vertumnus, or to Ceres in her prime,   395
Yet virgin of Proserpina from Jove.
Her long with ardent look his eye pursued
Delighted but desiring more her stay.
Oft he to her his charge of quick return
Repeated; she to him as oft engaged   400
To be returned by noon amid the bower,
And all things in best order to invite
Noontide repast or afternoon's repose.
O much deceived, much failing, hapless Eve,

384. *So bent:* if he does so intend

385–386. *from . . . withdrew:* a central panel in the reiterated focus on their hands throughout; e.g., 4.321, 4.488–89, and 4.739; this book lines 780 and 1037; and 12.648.

387. *Oread or dryad:* mountain or wood nymph   *Delia's train:* i.e., the nymphs attending Diana (Artemis), called *Delia* from her birthplace at Delos

389. *gait:* bearing

391–392. *tools . . . fire:* In the absence of *fire* (a result of the fall), tools cannot be forged and are therefore *yet rude, Guiltless of* = without experience of (and particularly apt, as fire became available to humans, according to classical myth, only after Prometheus stole it from the gods).

393. *Pales or Pomona, thus adorned:* *Pales* (two syllables) was a Roman goddess of flocks and herds; *Pomona*, the Roman goddess of fruit, was often shown with her symbolic pruning hook (see *Metamorphoses* 14.628).

394. *Likest:* most like; the 1674 text has "Likeliest," which many editors keep, although its thought, while possible, is more strained, and the additional syllable creates a hypermetrical line.

394–395. *Pomona . . . Vertumnus:* Milton recalls Ovid's story of Pomona's repeated and, finally, failed resistance to the pursuits of the shape-shifting wood god Vertumnus, a story not unlike Satan's temptation of Eve (*Metamorphoses* 14.642 ff.).

395–396. *Ceres . . . Jove:* Renaissance painters often represented Ceres, goddess of agriculture, with the symbolic plough that Ovid says she was the first to teach men to use (*Metamorphoses* 5.341); Milton's image is pointedly of the goddess before she was raped by Jove and the birth of their daughter, *Proserpina*, who was abducted by Pluto, god of the underworld.

395. *prime:* both prime of life and springtime; in classical mythology fall and winter are the result of Proserpina's abduction and rescue; see 4.269–72.

Of thy presumed return! Event perverse!   405
Thou never from that hour in Paradise
Found'st either sweet repast or sound repose,
Such ambush, hid among sweet flowers and shades,
Waited with hellish rancor imminent
To intercept thy way or send thee back   410
Despoiled of innocence, of faith, of bliss.
For now, and since first break of dawn, the fiend,
Mere serpent in appearance, forth was come,
And on his quest where likeliest he might find
The only two of mankind, but in them   415
The whole included race, his purposed prey.
In bower and field he sought, where any tuft
Of grove or garden plot more pleasant lay
Their tendance or plantation for delight;
By fountain or by shady rivulet   420
He sought them both but wished his hap° might find   *luck*
Eve separate; he wished, but not with hope
Of what so seldom chanced, when to his wish,
Beyond his hope, Eve separate he spies,
Veiled in a cloud of fragrance where she stood,   425
Half spied, so thick the roses bushing round
About her glowed, oft stooping to support
Each flower of slender stalk, whose head, though gay
Carnation, purple, azure, or specked with gold,
Hung drooping unsustained; them she upstays   430
Gently with myrtle band, mindless the while
Herself, though fairest unsupported flower
From her best prop so far and storm so nigh.
Nearer he drew and many a walk traversed
Of stateliest covert, cedar, pine, or palm,   435
Then voluble and bold, now hid, now seen

405. *Of:* about (goes with "deceived," line 404, common after intransitive verbs of knowing, thinking, etc.)

408. *shades:* i.e., trees

409. *imminent:* looming (a double syntax, both modifying *rancor* and applying "To intercept")

413. *Mere serpent:* entirely a serpent; i.e., the tempter was not the more or less humanized snake often seen with a woman's head in paintings of the temptation.

419. *Their tendance:* object of their care (cf. "nursery" in 8.46)

431. *mindless the while:* not noticing for the moment

435. *Of stateliest covert:* sheltered by stately trees

436. *voluble:* gliding, undulating (from its Latin meaning, "rolling upon itself," though the word anticipates the effect of his volubility (i.e., glibness, fluency) upon Eve (see lines 561 ff. below)

Among thick-woven arborets and flowers
Embroidered on each bank, the hand of Eve;
Spot more delicious than those gardens feigned°   *imagined*
Or of revived Adonis or renowned   440
Alcinous, host of old Laertes' son,
Or that, not mystic, where the sapient king
Held dalliance with his fair Egyptian spouse.
Much he the place admired, the person more.
As one who long in populous city pent,   445
Where houses thick and sewers annoy° the air,   *make unpleasant, pollute*
Forth issuing on a summer's morn to breathe
Among the pleasant villages and farms
Adjoined, from each thing met conceives delight—
The smell of grain, or tedded grass, or kine°   *cattle*
Or dairy, each rural sight, each rural sound—
If chance with nymphlike step fair virgin pass,
What pleasing seemed, for° her now pleases more,   *because of*
She most, and in her look sums all delight,
Such pleasure took the serpent to behold   455
This flowery plot, the sweet recess° of Eve   *seclusion*
Thus early, thus alone, her heavenly form
Angelic, but more soft and feminine
Her graceful innocence. Her every air
Of gesture or least action overawed   460
His malice and with rapine sweet bereaved°   *took from*
His fierceness of the fierce intent it brought.
That space the evil one abstracted stood

---

438. *hand:* handiwork; thus "Embroidered" seems the intended word at the beginning of the line, printed in 1674 as "Imborderd" (though "Embordered" is not impossible).

440. *Or . . . or:* either . . . or *revived Adonis:* Fatally wounded by a wild boar, Adonis was, in some versions of the myth, revived by his lover Venus (Aphrodite) and kept alive in a garden of delights, where, in Spenser's words, "he liueth in eternall blis, / Ioying his goddesse, and of her enioyd" (*Faerie Queene* 3.6.48); cf. Milton's use of the Garden of Adonis as a symbol of an earthly but mystical paradise in *Comus*, lines 976–1011.

440–441. *renowned Alcinous . . . son:* The luxurious gardens of Alcinous, who en-

tertained Odysseus (*old Laertes's son*) in *Odyssey* 7.112–35.

442–443. *that . . . spouse:* i.e., the gardens of King Solomon (*the sapient king*) in the Song of Solomon, where the King wooed the Queen of Sheba, *his fair Egyptian spouse;* these gardens were *not mystic* (i.e., not mythical) but, being reported in the bible, true.

450. *tedded:* spread out to dry (to make hay)

454. *sums:* gathers together and concentrates in herself

457–458. *her heavenly . . . feminine:* Adam seems to assume here that angels are masculine, but compare lines 423–31.

461. *rapine sweet:* delightful robbery

463. *abstracted:* drawn away from, removed from

From his own evil and for the time remained
Stupidly good, of enmity disarmed,   465
Of guile, of hate, of envy, of revenge;
But the hot hell that always in him burns,
Though in mid-Heaven, soon ended his delight
And tortures him now more the more he sees
Of pleasure not for him ordained; then soon   470
Fierce hate he recollects and, all his thoughts
Of mischief gratulating, thus excites:
    "Thoughts, whither have ye led me? With what sweet
Compulsion thus transported to forget
What hither brought us? Hate, not love, nor hope   475
Of Paradise for hell, hope here to taste
Of pleasure, but all pleasure to destroy
Save what is in destroying; other joy
To me is lost. Then let me not let pass
Occasion° which now smiles: behold alone   *opportunity*
The woman, opportune to all attempts,
Her husband, for I view far round, not nigh,
Whose higher intellectual more I shun,
And strength, of courage haughty° and of limb   *imposing*
Heroic built though of terrestrial mold: 485
Foe not informidable, exempt from wound,
I not, so much hath hell debased and pain
Enfeebled me to° what I was in Heaven.   *in comparison to*
She fair, divinely fair, fit love for gods,
Not terrible, though terror° be in love   *awe*
And beauty, not° approached by stronger hate,   *unless*
Hate stronger, under show of love well feigned,
The way which to her ruin now I tend."
    So spake the enemy of mankind, enclosed

---

465. *Stupidly:* in a stupor, stunned (but also *Stupidly* as "unintelligently," because this goodness does not serve his purposes; see lines 473–75).

467–468. *But the hot . . . delight:* Cf. 4.20 and 4.75, but note also how this belies his claim at 1.254–55 that "The mind is its own place and in itself / Can make a Heaven of hell, a hell of Heaven."

472. *gratulating:* welcoming, rejoicing in (the verb governing "his thoughts" in line 471)

479. *let pass:* ignore, let pass by

481. *opportune to:* favorably situated for, liable to

483. *higher intellectual:* superior intelligence

485. *terrestrial mold:* earthly substance, clay (see lines 149 and 176 above).

486. *exempt from wound:* See man's incapability of death or pain in line 283 above, and Satan's experience of *wound* in 6.327–329.

492. *under . . . feigned:* derives from Du Bartas, who also described Satan "as a false lover" (*Divine Weeks*, trans. Sylvester, 1608, p. 255)

In serpent, inmate bad, and toward Eve   495
Addressed his way, not with indented wave,
Prone on the ground, as since, but on his rear,
Circular base of rising folds that towered
Fold above fold a surging maze, his head
Crested aloft and carbuncle his eyes,   500
With burnished neck of verdant gold erect
Amidst his circling spires that on the grass
Floated redundant; pleasing was his shape
And lovely, never since of serpent kind
Lovelier, not those that in Illyria changed,   505
Hermione and Cadmus, or the god
In Epidaurus, nor to which transformed
Ammonian Jove or Capitoline was seen,
He with Olympias, this with her who bore
Scipio, the height of Rome. With tract oblique   510
At first, as one who sought access but feared
To interrupt, sidelong he works his way.
As when a ship by skillful steersman wrought

496. *indented:* zig-zagging, undulating; cf. *As You Like It* 4.3.112: "And with indented glides did slip away."

498–503. *Circular base . . . redundant:* The description of the serpent here is in part based on the "slippery" serpent of "seven huge coils" in *Aeneid* 5.84–89, and also the serpent in Tasso's *Gerusalemme Liberata*: "Armed with golden scales, his head and crest / He lifted high, his neck swell'd great with ire, / Flamed his eyes" (15.48, trans. Fairfax, 1600).

500. *carbuncle:* red, like carbuncle (a bright red gem stone); cf. *Hamlet* 2.2.459: "eyes like carbuncles."

502. *spires:* coils, spirals, though the coils rise up like *spires* in its more common architectural sense

503. *redundant:* abundantly (with the suggestion of excessively); its etymology (Latin *re + undare* = to surge, or rise in waves) relates the image to the "surging maze" in line 499).

505. *changed:* metamorphosed, took the form of (serpents)

506. *Hermione and Cadmus:* See Ovid's story of the metamorphosis of *Cadmus* and Harmonia (*Hermione*) into serpents in "Illyria," the modern Albania (*Metamorphoses* 4.563–603). George Sandys, in his translation of Ovid (1628), gives the names in the form Milton uses; see Sandys' commentary to Book 4.

506–507. *the god In Epidaurus:* i.e., Aesculapius, the deity of healing, whom Ovid described (*Metamorphoses* 15.760–74) as once appearing like a serpent, with head held as high as a man's breast and with flashing eyes, in his temple in Epidaurus, in the northeast Peloponnesus.

508. *Ammonian Jove:* In Edward Topsell's *Historie of Serpents* (1608), p. 5, four ancient authorities are skeptically cited for the story that Olympias, the mother of Alexander the Great, was loved by Jupiter Ammon (cf. 4.277) in the form of a serpent.

508–510. *Capitoline . . . Rome:* Topsell also gives authorities for the myth that the mother of Scipio Africanus, the greatest of Romans (*the height of Rome*), was loved by the *Capitoline* Jupiter in serpent form (p. 5).

510. *tract oblique:* indirect course

513. *wrought:* worked, in its nautical sense of "sailed" or "navigated"

Nigh river's mouth or foreland, where the wind
Veers oft, as oft so steers and shifts her sail,   515
So varied he, and of his tortuous train
Curled many a wanton wreath in sight of Eve
To lure her eye; she, busied, heard the sound
Of rustling leaves but minded not, as used
To such disport before her through the field   520
From every beast, more duteous at her call
Than at Circean call the herd disguised.
He, bolder now, uncalled before her stood
But as in gaze admiring. Oft he bowed
His turret crest and sleek enameled° neck,   *multicolored*
Fawning, and licked the ground whereon she trod.
His gentle dumb expression turned at length
The eye of Eve to mark his play; he, glad
Of her attention gained, with serpent tongue
Organic or impulse of vocal air,   530
His fraudulent temptation thus began:
    "Wonder not, sovereign mistress, if perhaps
Thou canst, who art sole wonder, much less arm
Thy looks, the heaven of mildness, with disdain,
Displeased that I approach thee thus and gaze   535
Insatiate, I thus single, nor have feared
Thy awful brow, more awful° thus retired.   *inspiring awe*
Fairest resemblance of thy maker fair,
Thee all things living gaze on, all things thine
By gift, and thy celestial beauty adore   540
With ravishment beheld, there best beheld
Where universally admired; but here
In this enclosure wild, these beasts among,
Beholders rude and shallow to discern
Half what in thee is fair, one man except,   545

516. *tortuous train:* twisting body
517. *wanton:* Here the unfallen mean-
ing, "gay" or "lively," gives way to "provoca-
tive"; see line 211 above.
522. *herd disguised:* men, who were
changed by Circe into swine, and who
greeted Odyssey's men, "like dogs fawning
on a returning master" (*Odyssey* 10.212–19;
see line 526 below). The implicit com-
parison of Eve with Circe is neutralized by
the fact that the beasts responding to Eve
are actually beasts instinctively responding
to her natural excellence rather than Circe's
magic.
530. *Organic . . . air:* Because the ser-
pent lacks the power to vocalize, Satan had
either to use its tongue as an instrument (*Or-
ganic* = serving as an organ or tool, instru-
mental), or else to produce vibrations in the
air in some manner, to produce speech.
532–548. *Wonder . . . train:* Cf. the
temptation in Eve's dream (5.38–93).
544. *shallow to discern:* too superficial
to recognize

Who sees thee (and what is one?), who shouldst be seen
A goddess among gods, adored and served
By angels numberless, thy daily train°?"   *attendants*
    So glozed the tempter, and his proem° tuned;   *prologue, preface*
Into the heart of Eve his words made way,   550
Though at the voice much marveling; at length
Not unamazed she thus in answer spake:
"What may this mean? Language of man pronounced
By tongue of brute and human sense expressed?
The first at least of these I thought denied   555
To beasts, whom God on their creation day
Created mute to all articulate sound;
The latter I demur,° for in their looks   *question, hesitate to affirm*
Much reason, and in their actions, oft appears.
Thee, serpent, subtlest beast of all the field   560
I knew, but not with human voice endued;
Redouble then this miracle, and say
How cam'st thou speakable of mute, and how
To me so friendly grown above the rest
Of brutal kind that daily are in sight.   565
Say, for such wonder claims attention due."
    To whom the guileful tempter thus replied:
"Empress of this fair world, resplendent Eve,
Easy to me it is to tell thee all
What thou command'st, and right thou shouldst be obeyed.   570
I was at first as other beasts that graze
The trodden herb: of abject° thoughts and low,   *mean-spirited, degraded*
As was my food, nor aught° but food discerned   *anything*
Or sex, and apprehended nothing high,
Till, on a day roving the field, I chanced   575
A goodly tree far distant to behold,
Loaden with fruit of fairest colors mixed,
Ruddy and gold. I nearer drew to gaze,

549. *glozed:* flattered, lied; recalls Comus' "glozing courtesy, / Baited with reasons not unplausible" (*Comus*, lines 161–62).

559. *Much reason:* God has said that the beasts "know, / And reason not contemptibly" (8.373–74).

560. *subtlest . . . field:* as at line 86, echoes Gen. 3:1; see also 2 Cor. 11:3: "as the serpent beguiled Eve through his subtilty."

563. *speakable of mute:* capable of speech after being mute

565. *brutal kind:* the animals; perhaps the paradox in the two words, unintended by Eve, is designed to expose the falseness of the situation.

571–574. *I . . . high:* Behind the lines is the Aristotelian distinction between the noble pleasures of which men are capable

When from the boughs a savory odor blown,
Grateful to appetite, more pleased my sense   580
Than smell of sweetest fennel, or the teats
Of ewe or goat dropping with milk at ev'n,
Unsucked of lamb or kid that tend° their play.   *are intent on*
To satisfy the sharp desire I had
Of tasting those fair apples I resolved   585
Not to defer; hunger and thirst at once,
Powerful persuaders, quickened at the scent
Of that alluring fruit, urged me so keen.
About the mossy trunk I wound me soon,
For high from ground the branches would require   590
Thy utmost reach or Adam's; round the tree
All other beasts that saw, with like desire
Longing and envying, stood but could not reach.
Amid the tree now got, where plenty hung
Tempting so nigh, to pluck and eat my fill   595
I spared not, for such pleasure till that hour
At feed or fountain never had I found.
Sated at length, ere long I might perceive
Strange alteration in me to degree
Of reason in my inward powers, and speech   600
Wanted not long, though to this shape retained.
Thenceforth to speculations high or deep
I turned my thoughts and with capacious mind
Considered all things visible in Heaven
Or earth or middle,° all things fair and good;   *the air between*
But all that fair and good in thy divine
Semblance and in thy beauty's heavenly ray

and the grosser experiences of the animals (*Nicomachean Ethics* 1.9.9).

579. *savory:* appetizing, appealing (but the word also meant "spiritually edifying")

581–582. *fennel . . . goat: fennel* was supposedly a favorite food of snakes; the belief seemingly derives from Pliny, who says fennel is "a herb wherein Snakes and such serpents take exceeding great delight" (*Natural History*, trans. P. Holland, 1601, vol. 2, p. 31). Another folk belief was that snakes sucked the teats of ewes, cows, and goats; see Francis Godolphin Waldron's *Continuation of Ben*

Jonson's Sad Shepherd (1783): "I spied an adder sucking o'kies [i.e., on a cow's] teat" (3.358).

585. *apples:* Genesis does not identify the fruit of the Tree of Knowledge as an apple, but by the late Middle Ages it was conventional to do so, no doubt because in Latin *malum* means both "apple" and (from *malus*) "evil." Satan alone in *PL* names the fruit an apple (see also 10.487).

586. *defer:* delay (but Satan has chosen *Not to defer* in other senses as well).

599–601. *to degree . . . retained:* to the extent (*degree*) of acquiring *reason,* to which

United I beheld, no fair to thine
Equivalent or second, which compelled
Me thus, though importune° perhaps, to come   *inopportunely*
And gaze, and worship thee of right declared
Sovereign of creatures, universal dame."
     So talked the spirited sly snake, and Eve
Yet more amazed unwary thus replied:
"Serpent, thy overpraising leaves in doubt   615
The virtue° of that fruit in thee first proved;   *power*
But say, where grows the tree, from hence how far?
For many are the trees of God that grow
In Paradise and various, yet° unknown   *still*
To us, in such abundance lies our choice   620
As leaves a greater store of fruit untouched,
Still hanging incorruptible, till men
Grow up to their provision, and more hands
Help to disburden nature of her birth."
     To whom the wily adder, blithe and glad: 625
"Empress, the way is ready° and not long: *nearby*
Beyond a row of myrtles, on a flat,
Fast by a fountain, one small thicket past
Of blowing myrrh and balm. If thou accept
My conduct, I can bring thee thither soon."   630
     "Lead then," said Eve. He, leading swiftly, rolled
In tangles and made intricate seem straight,
To mischief swift. Hope elevates, and joy
Brightens his crest. As when a wandering fire

---

speech was soon added (*Wanted not long*), al-
though there was no change in outward form
     608–609. *no . . . Equivalent or second:*
Cf. 7.406–7, where God says the same thing
of himself; the echo reveals the blasphemy of
the assertion here.
     612. *universal dame:* mistress of the
universe
     613. *spirited:* energetic, lively, but also
"spirit-possessed"
     616. *proved:* tested
     623. *to their provision:* to numbers pro-
portionate to what has been provided
     624. *birth:* yield, fruit; spelled "bearth"
in 1667 and 1674; here it combines the
meaning "offspring" with a sense of Norse

origin that the *OED* defines simply as a
"burden."
     629. *blowing:* blossoming (as at 5.22
and 7.319)
     634–642. *a wandering fire . . . far:* the
ignis fatuus, or will-o'-the-wisp; phosphores-
cent marsh gas. In John Swan's popular
Speculum Mundi (1643), he defines *ignis
fatuus* as "a fat and oily Exhalation, hot and
drie," which the "much terrified, ignorant
and superstitious people" have often mis-
taken for "walking spirits," and "those that
see them are amazed, and look so earnestly
after them that they forget their way: and
then . . . wander to and fro, . . . sometimes to
waters, pits, and other dangerous places" (pp.

Compact of unctuous° vapor which the night   *oily*
Condenses and the cold environs round,
Kindled through agitation to a flame,
Which oft, they say, some evil spirit attends,
Hovering and blazing with delusive light,
Misleads the amazed night-wanderer from his way   640
To bogs and mires and oft through pond or pool,
There swallowed up and lost, from succor far,
So glistered the dire snake and into fraud
Led Eve, our credulous mother, to the tree
Of prohibition, root of all our woe,   645
Which when she saw, thus to her guide she spake:
    "Serpent, we might have spared our coming hither,
Fruitless to me though fruit be here to excess,
The credit of whose virtue rest with thee,
Wondrous indeed if cause of such effects.   650
But of this tree we may not taste nor touch;
God so commanded and left that command
Sole daughter of his voice; the rest, we live
Law to ourselves; our reason is our law."
    To whom the tempter guilefully replied: 655
"Indeed? Hath God then said that of the fruit
Of all these garden trees ye shall not eat,
Yet lords declared of all in earth or air?"

88–89). See Kester Svendsen, *Milton and Science* (Cambridge: Harvard University Press, 1956), p. 109; see also *Comus*, lines 205–9 and 431–37.

635. *Compact:* composed, made; cf. *Titus Andronicus* 5.3.87: "My heart is not compact of flint nor steel."

636. *environs round:* envelops, encircles

642. *swallowed up and lost:* an exact echo of Belial at 2.149

643. *fraud:* a passive sense, i.e., the state of being defrauded

645. *root:* source, but obviously following from "tree" in line 644

648. *Fruitless . . . fruit:* The same pun is made by Spenser in *Faerie Queene* 2.7.4.1–3: "Here also sprong that goodly golden fruit, / With which Acontius got his lover trew, /

Whom he had long time sought with fruitless suit." See also this book, line 1188 below.

651. *touch:* Gen. 3:3, unlike Gen. 2:17, adds to the prohibition not to eat of the fruit, "neither shall ye touch it."

653. *Sole daughter of his voice:* At 7.8–12 it is made clear that God has two daughters, but here "that command" (line 652) is *Sole,* the single prohibition for Adam and Eve. In Hebrew, *Bath kol,* literally "daughter of a voice," means a "voice from Heaven."

654. *Law . . . law:* An echo of Paul's remark about the virtuous Gentiles who, though outside Hebrew law, were "a law unto themselves" (Rom. 2:14). Contrast the refusal of the devils to accept "Right reason for their law" in 6.42.

    To whom thus Eve yet sinless: "Of the fruit
Of each tree in the garden we may eat,   660
But of the fruit of this fair tree amidst
The garden, God hath said, 'Ye shall not eat
Thereof nor shall ye touch it, lest ye die.'"
    She scarce had said, though brief, when now more bold
The tempter, but, with show of zeal and love   665
To man and indignation at his wrong,
New part puts on and, as to passion moved,
Fluctuates° disturbed, yet comely, and in act   *undulates*
Raised as of some great matter to begin.
As when of old some orator renowned   670
In Athens or free Rome, where eloquence
Flourished, since mute, to some great cause addressed,
Stood in himself collected, while each part,
Motion, each act, won audience° ere the tongue   *attention, hearing*
Sometimes in height began, as no delay   675
Of preface brooking through his zeal of right,
So standing, moving, or to height upgrown,
The tempter all impassioned thus began:
    "O sacred, wise, and wisdom-giving plant,
Mother of science,° now I feel thy power   *knowledge*
Within me clear not only to discern
Things in their causes but to trace the ways
Of highest agents deemed however wise.
Queen of this universe, do not believe

659. *yet:* still; her sinful act occurs only in line 781.

666. *his wrong:* i.e., the wrong done to man

667. *New part puts on:* takes on a different role or style

669. *Raised:* elevated both stylistically and physically (as in "to height upgrown" in line 677 below)

671. *free Rome:* i.e., Rome when it was a republic (509–31 B.C.), before the emperors. No doubt Milton is thinking also of the failed commonwealth in England.

672. *since mute:* reflecting the belief that oratory had reached its height in classical Greece and republican Rome

673. *in himself collected:* in complete self-control; cf. 6.581.

675. *in height:* in the height of passion (rather than building up to it)

679–683. *O sacred . . . wise:* Satan asserts that eating the apple has conveyed both speech and knowledge, though in fact the apple only represents the relationship with God; see pp. xliv–xlvii above.

683. *highest agents:* both a euphemism (as Satan avoids naming God) and a kind of oxymoron, with the plural noun denying the superlative adjective; Satan regularly pluralizes "God" (e.g., lines 716–19 below) as part of the temptation to pride and disobedience.

684. *do not believe:* the very essence of the temptation

Those rigid threats of death; ye shall not die.   685
How should ye? By the fruit? It gives you life
To knowledge. By the threatener? Look on me,
Me who have touched and tasted, yet both live
And life more perfect have attained than fate
Meant me by venturing higher than my lot.   690
Shall that be shut to man which to the beast
Is open? Or will God incense his ire
For such a petty trespass, and not praise
Rather your dauntless virtue whom the pain
Of death denounced—whatever thing death be—   695
Deterred not from achieving what might lead
To happier life: knowledge of good and evil?
Of good, how just? Of evil, if what is evil
Be real, why not known, since easier shunned?
God, therefore, cannot hurt ye and be just;   700
Not just, not God; not feared then, nor obeyed.
Your fear itself of death removes the fear.
Why then was this forbid? Why but to awe,
Why but to keep ye low and ignorant,
His worshippers. He knows that in the day   705
Ye eat thereof your eyes, that seem so clear
Yet are but dim, shall perfectly be then

685. *ye shall not die:* Gen. 3:4: "And the
serpent said unto the woman, Ye shall not
surely die."

687. *To:* 1) leading to, eventuating in;
2) in addition to

689. *fate:* Cf. 7.123: "what I will is
Fate"; Satan, however, uses the term to sug-
gest agency other than that of God.

692. *incense his ire:* kindle his wrath

694. *pain:* used in its original Latin
sense, *poena* = punishment

695. *whatever thing death be:* hypocriti-
cal; Satan knows, since it has been explained
to him at 2.781–814. Adam sincerely won-
ders at 4.425–27, but instinctively under-
stands it is "Some dreadful thing."

698–699: *if . . . Be real:* The ontology
of evil posed a problem for theologians, who
could not make God responsible for evil (as
what he creates is "good"), but also could not
attribute evil to some other creative princi-
ple, since God is the creator of all things. The
alternative was to see evil as secondary and
parasitic, existing only as a turning away
from the good. Satan exploits this argument
to suggest that evil may not exist at all.

701. *Not just, not God:* though Satan
has not demonstrated that God has been un-
just; interestingly, this is the last time in *PL*
that Satan speaks of God in the singular.

702. *Your fear . . . fear:* Satan's thought
is obscure but seems to mean that the fear of
death implies that God is unjust, but an un-
just God is not God, and therefore is not ca-
pable of imposing death on mankind and so
is not to be feared.

703–709. *Why but . . . know:* As Henry
Lawrence (to whose son, Edward, Milton's
Sonnet 20 was addressed) explains in *Our
Communion and War with Angels* (1646), p.
98, when Satan tempted Eve he "accused
God" and "told her they should be as Gods,
knowing good and evil, this temptation
tooke, now hee intimated that God made

Opened and cleared, and ye shall be as gods,
Knowing both good and evil as they know.
That ye should be as gods since I as man,   710
Internal man, is but proportion meet:°   *exact*
I of brute, human; ye of human, gods.
So ye shall die perhaps, by putting off
Human, to put on gods: death to be wished,
Though threatened, which no worse than this can bring.   715
And what are gods that man may not become
As they, participating° godlike food?   *partaking of*
The gods are first and that advantage use
On our belief that all from them proceeds;
I question it, for this fair earth I see,   720
Warmed by the sun, producing every kind;
Them, nothing. If they all things, who enclosed
Knowledge of good and evil in this tree,
That whoso eats thereof forthwith attains
Wisdom without their leave? And wherein lies   725
The offence that man should thus attain to know?
What° can your knowledge hurt him, or this tree   *how*
Impart° against his will if all be his?   *give away*
Or is it envy, and can envy dwell
In heavenly breasts? These, these and many more   730
Causes import° your need of this fair fruit.   *indicate, demonstrate*
Goddess humane, reach, then, and freely taste."

that restraint out of envy, because hee would
have none so great and so happy as himself."
Interpreting the fall philosophically in *Con-
jectura Cabbalistica* (1653), Henry More has
the serpent say that "God indeed loves to keep
his creatures in awe, and to hold them in from
ranging too farre, and reaching too high; but
he knows very well that if you take your lib-
erty with us, and satiate your selves freely with
your own will, your eyes will be wonderfully
opened, . . . and like God know all things
whatsoever, whether good or evil" (p. 46).

710–712. *That ye . . . gods:* Satan argues
that as the serpent has (apparently) become
like a human by eating the apple, humans by
eating would, proportionately, improve to *be
as gods*; Adam argues much the same thing in
lines 932–37.

711. *Internal man:* refers to the ser-
pent's statement (line 600 above) that his

"inward powers" have become human
though his form is unchanged; he is *man* in
his mind, not in his body.

712. *of brute . . . gods:* from animal
(have become) human, you from human
(will become) gods

713–714. *putting off . . . put on:* Satan
here perverts the Pauline command to "put off
the old man" and "put on the new man, which
is renewed in knowledge after the image of
him that created him" (Col. 3:9–10).

716–717. *what . . . food:* Compare
Raphael's similar claim in 5.493–95.

719. *On our belief:* i.e., to make us be-
lieve

722. *If they all things:* i.e., if they (pro-
duced) all things

732. *Goddess humane:* the primary sense
of the adjective is "benevolent" or "compas-
sionate," but "human" and "humane" were

He ended, and his words replete with guile
Into her heart too easy entrance won.
Fixed on the fruit she gazed, which to behold   735
Might tempt alone, and in her ears the sound
Yet rung of his persuasive words impregned°   *impregnated*
With reason, to her seeming, and with truth.
Meanwhile the hour of noon drew on and waked
An eager appetite raised by the smell   740
So savory of that fruit, which with desire
Inclinable° now grown to touch or taste   *easily inclined, disposed*
Solicited her longing eye; yet first
Pausing awhile, thus to herself she mused:
   "Great are thy virtues, doubtless, best of fruits,   745
Though kept from man, and worthy to be admired,
Whose taste, too long forborne, at first assay°   *trial*
Gave elocution° to the mute and taught   *both speech and eloquence*
The tongue not made for speech to speak thy praise.
Thy praise he also who forbids thy use   750
Conceals not from us, naming thee the Tree
Of Knowledge, knowledge both of good and evil;
Forbids us then to taste, but his forbidding
Commends thee more while it infers° the good   *implies*
By thee communicated and our want: 755
For good unknown sure is not had, or had
And yet unknown is as not had at all.
In plain, then, what forbids he but to know,
Forbids us good, forbids us to be wise?
Such prohibitions bind not. But if death   760
Bind us with after-bands° what profits then   *subsequent restrictions*
Our inward freedom? In the day we eat
Of this fair fruit, our doom is we shall die.
How dies the serpent? He hath eaten and lives,

---

not yet distinguished in 17th-century
spelling, so the oxymoron of the phrase
"goddess human" is unavoidable, exposing
the fallacy of the serpent's claim.
  735–743. *Fixed . . . eye:* In Genesis, Eve
yields when she sees that the tree was "good
for food, and that it was pleasant to the eyes,
and a tree to be desired to make one wise"
(Gen. 3:6).

  741. *savory:* appetizing (but also edifying), as at line 579 above.
  744. *Pausing:* Milton emphasizes the
pause to make it clear that she eats as a matter of choice not reflex.
  755. *our want:* what we are missing
  758. *In plain:* in simple terms
  759. *forbids:* Eve uses some form of this
word six times between line 750 and here.

And knows, and speaks, and reasons, and discerns,   765
Irrational till then. For us alone
Was death invented? Or to us denied
This intellectual food for beasts reserved?
For beasts it seems, yet that one beast which first
Hath tasted envies° not but brings with joy   *begrudges*
The good befallen him, author unsuspect,
Friendly to man, far from deceit or guile.
What fear I then, rather, what know to fear
Under this ignorance of good and evil,
Of God or death, of law or penalty?   775
Here grows the cure of all, this fruit divine,
Fair to the eye, inviting to the taste,
Of virtue to make wise. What hinders then
To reach and feed at once both body and mind?"
    So saying, her rash hand in evil hour   780
Forth reaching to the fruit, she plucked, she ate:
Earth felt the wound, and nature, from her seat
Sighing, through all her works gave signs of woe
That all was lost. Back to the thicket slunk
The guilty serpent, and well might, for Eve,   785
Intent now wholly on her taste, naught else
Regarded, such delight till then as seemed
In fruit she never tasted, whether true
Or fancied so, through expectation high
Of knowledge, nor was godhead from her thought.   790
Greedily she engorged without restraint

---

771. *author unsuspect:* informant above
suspicion
  776. *cure of all:* remedy for everything
(but *cure,* from Latin *cura,* can also can mean
"care" or "trouble")
  778. *Of virtue to make wise:* i.e., having
the power (*virtue*) to make wise, but the
moral meaning of *virtue* in "fruit of . . .
virtue" inevitably is heard ironically.
  781. *ate:* This is spelled "eat" in the
early editions, creating an eye-rhyme with
"seat," probably pronounced "et," and cer-
tainly a past tense verb. On the poem's
rhymes, see pp. l–li above.
  782–784. *Earth felt . . . lost:* Cf. lines
1000–1004 below and 10.651–714. The

thought is dependent on Rom. 8:22: "the
whole creation groaneth and travaileth in
pain," and also on *Aeneid* 4.166–70. "Then
first the trembling earth the signal gave . . .
From this ill-omen'd hour in time arose / De-
bate and death, and all succeeding woes"
(trans. Dryden); it was widespread in English
poetry, from John Gower's *Mirrour de
l'Homme* (1380, lines 26 and 810–26) to
Joseph Beaumont's assertion that when Eve
touched the forbidden fruit, "she reach'd
away / All the Worlds Blisse whil'st she the
Apple took: / When low, the Earth did move,
the Heav'ns did stay, / Beasts and Birds
shiver'd, absent Adam shook" (*Psyche*, 1648,
6.254.1–4).

And knew not eating death. Satiate at length
And heightened as with wine, jocund and boon,
Thus to herself she pleasingly began:
   "O sovereign, virtuous, precious of all trees   795
In Paradise, of operation blessed
To sapience, hitherto obscured, infamed,°   *defamed*
And thy fair fruit let hang, as to no end
Created, but henceforth my early care,
Not without song each morning and due praise,   800
Shall tend thee and the fertile burden ease
Of thy full branches offered free to all,
Till dieted by thee I grow mature
In knowledge, as the gods who all things know,
Though others envy what they cannot give,   805
For had the gift been theirs it had not here
Thus grown. Experience, next to thee I owe,
Best guide; not following thee, I had remained
In ignorance; thou open'st wisdom's way
And giv'st access, though secret she retire.   810
And I perhaps am secret: Heaven is high,
High and remote to see from thence distinct
Each thing on earth, and other care perhaps
May have diverted from continual watch
Our great forbidder, safe with all his spies   815
About him. But to Adam in what sort
Shall I appear? Shall I to him make known
As yet my change and give him to partake

792. *knew not eating death:* various meanings arise from the knotty phrase, including: 1) understood not (that she was) eating death; 2) knew not, while eating, death; and 3) recognized not eating (i.e., devouring) death

793. *jocund and boon:* cheerful and convivial

795. *sovereign:* Eve uses for the tree the word that Satan uses in flattering her (line 532 above) and that is properly used for God (8.239).

796–797. *of operation blessed To sapience:* 1) with a blessed effect that produces wisdom; 2) that has an effect sacred to wisdom

804. *gods:* With the plural *gods,* Eve

perhaps echoes Satan's equivocal use of the word in line 712 above and shows that she has been deceived by his reasoning in lines 720–29, though "others" (i.e., God and Christ) in line 805 could suggest that she here means only "angels" (as at 5.60). The thought is no less flawed in either case.

810–811. *secret . . . secret:* concealed, uncommunicative . . . unseen (by God); in 10.32, God speaks "from his secret cloud."

815. *Our great forbidder:* The delay in revealing this as the object of the verb in line 814 emphasizes how outrageous is her epithet for God.

816–825. *to Adam . . . free:* Immediately she reveals the marks of her fallenness in her relationship with Adam, echoing

Full happiness with me? Or rather not,
But keep the odds° of knowledge in my power,   *advantage*
Without copartner, so to add what wants
In female sex, the more to draw his love
And render me more equal and, perhaps,
A thing not undesirable, sometime
Superior, for inferior who is free?   825
This may be well, but what if God have seen
And death ensue? Then I shall be no more,
And Adam, wedded to another Eve,
Shall live with her enjoying, I extinct:
A death to think. Confirmed then I resolve   830
Adam shall share with me in bliss or woe.
So dear I love him that with him all deaths
I could endure, without him live no life."
    So saying, from the tree her step she turned,
But first low reverence done as to the power   835
That dwelt within, whose presence had infused
Into the plant sciential sap derived
From nectar, drink of gods. Adam, the while
Waiting desirous her return, had wove°   *woven*
Of choicest flowers a garland to adorn   840
Her tresses and her rural labors crown,
As reapers oft are wont their harvest queen.
Great joy he promised to his thoughts and new
Solace in her return so long delayed;
Yet oft his heart, divine of something ill,   845
Misgave him; he the faltering measure felt
And forth to meet her went the way she took
That morn when first they parted; by the Tree
Of Knowledge he must pass; there he her met

Satan in her commitment to disguise (*in what sort Shall I appear*), desire for preeminence (*render me more equal . . . sometime Superior*), and misunderstanding the nature of true freedom (*inferior who is free?*).

821. *so . . . wants:* and by so doing add what is lacking

826–833. *what . . . life:* Eve understands *death* as extinction and jealously contemplates Adam with *another Eve*. Milton here seems to be consciously varying the terms of the well-known closing lines of

Horace's *Ode* (3.9): "yet I / Will live with thee, or else for thee will die" (Robert Herrick, "A Dialogue betwixt Horace and Lydia, Translated Anno 1627").

837. *sciential:* endowed with (and thus producing) knowledge

845. *divine of:* foreseeing, anticipating

846. *the faltering measure:* the irregular beat (of his heart), as well as the now-disordered rhythms of nature; both the 1667 and 1674 editions significantly spell the word "fault'ring."

Scarce from the tree returning, in her hand   850
A bough of fairest fruit that downy smiled
New gathered and ambrosial smell diffused.
To him she hasted; in her face excuse
Came prologue and apology to prompt,
Which with bland words at will she thus addressed: 855
  "Hast thou not wondered, Adam, at my stay?
Thee I have missed and thought it long, deprived
Thy presence, agony of love till now
Not felt, nor shall be twice, for never more
Mean I to try what rash untried I sought: 860
The pain of absence from thy sight. But strange
Hath been the cause and wonderful to hear:
This tree is not as we are told a tree
Of danger tasted° nor to evil unknown   *if tasted*
Opening the way, but of divine effect   865
To open eyes and make them gods who taste,
And hath been tasted° such. The serpent wise,   *proved by tasting*
Or° not restrained as we or not obeying,   *either*
Hath eaten of the fruit and is become
Not dead, as we are threatened, but thenceforth   870
Endued with human voice and human sense,
Reasoning to admiration, and with me
Persuasively hath so prevailed that I
Have also tasted and have also found
The effects to correspond: opener mine eyes,   875
Dim erst,° dilated spirits, ampler heart,   *before, formerly*
And growing up to godhead, which for thee
Chiefly I sought, without thee can despise.

851. *downy smiled:* attractively covered with down (the image probably derived from Virgil's second *Eclogue* [51], where he speaks of picking apples with tender down on them).

853–854. *excuse . . . prompt:* i.e., *excuse* came first, like the *prologue* to a play *to prompt* the *apology* (here, justification) of her conduct. The theatrical image recalls the one applied to Satan at line 667 above.

854. *to prompt:* Some editions (beginning with Elijah Fenton in his 1725 edition of *PL*) have emended to "too prompt" (i.e., too eagerly), but the theatrical meaning discussed in the previous note seems to be the intended sense.

855. *bland:* smooth (and with the suggestion of flattery, blandishment)   *at will:* at her command

860. *rash untried:* because I was rash and it was untried

864–865. *nor to . . . way:* Eve means that eating the fruit did not open *the way* to *evil,* which is still *unknown,* but the phrase, with its double negative, could admit the opposite meaning.

865. *of divine effect:* 1) of wondrous effect; 2) producing divinity

872. *to admiration:* so as to produce wonder

For bliss, as° thou hast part, to me is bliss;   *in so far as*
Tedious, unshared with thee, and odious soon.   880
Thou therefore also taste, that equal lot
May join us, equal joy as equal love,
Lest thou not tasting, different degree
Disjoin us, and I then too late renounce
Deity for thee when fate will not permit."   885
    Thus Eve with countenance blithe her story told,
But in her cheek distemper° flushing glowed.   *feverish excitement*
On the other side, Adam, soon as he heard
The fatal trespass done by Eve, amazed,
Astonied stood and blank, while horror chill   890
Ran through his veins and all his joints relaxed;
From his slack hand the garland wreathed for Eve
Down dropped, and all the faded roses shed.
Speechless he stood and pale, till thus at length
First to himself he inward silence broke: 895
    "O fairest of creation, last and best
Of all God's works, creature in whom excelled
Whatever can to sight or thought be formed,
Holy, divine, good, amiable, or sweet!
How art thou lost, how on a sudden lost,   900
Defaced, deflowered, and now to death devote?
Rather, how hast thou yielded to transgress
The strict forbiddance, how to violate
The sacred fruit forbidden? Some cursèd fraud

881. *equal lot:* shared fortune, fate; the language of Satan at lines 689–90 above; see also "consort" at 4.610 and elsewhere, which etymologically (Latin *con* = with + *sortis* = lot, fate) means virtually the same thing.

881–882. *equal . . . equal . . . equal:* The repetition reveals how alertly Satan recognizes the appeal of equality, even if he wishes superiority only for himself.

890–891. *Astonied . . . relaxed:* The language of Adam's dismay suggests both Job 17:8: "Upright men shall be astonied at this," and Virgil's description of Aeneas' horror: "Mute and amaz'd, my hair with terror stood, / Fear Shrunk my sinews, and congeal'd my blood" (*Aeneid* 3.29–30 trans. Dryden); *astonied* = stunned (literally, "made stone")

890. *blank:* blank of expression, dazed; but also deprived of speech (*OED* 5)

892–893. *From . . . shed:* Scholars have found many classical parallels for this passage, like Statius' *Thebaid* 7.148–50, where the frightened Bacchus drops his flowers and unspoiled grapes (unlike *the faded roses* here) fall from the vines that garlanded his head.

895. *to himself:* That there is a gap between his thoughts *to himself* and his speech to her is another sign of the division of unity brought on by the trespass.

901. *devote:* doomed (cf. 3.208); note also this as the last of the four alliterative words in the line, reinforcing the sense of loss in the reiterated "de."

904–905. *Some . . . unknown:* Oddly, in spite of having been warned by Raphael,

Of enemy hath beguiled thee, yet unknown,   905
And me with thee hath ruined, for with thee
Certain my resolution is to die.
How can I live without thee, how forgo
Thy sweet converse and love so dearly joined
To live again in these wild woods forlorn?   910
Should God create another Eve, and I
Another rib afford, yet loss of thee
Would never from my heart; no no, I feel
The link of nature draw me: flesh of flesh,
Bone of my bone thou art, and from thy state°   *condition, situation*
Mine never shall be parted, bliss or woe."
        So having said, as one from sad dismay
Recomforted, and after thoughts disturbed
Submitting to what seemed remediless,
Thus in calm mood his words to Eve he turned: 920
"Bold deed thou hast presumed, adventurous Eve,
And peril great provoked, who thus hath dared,
Had it been only coveting, to eye
That sacred fruit, sacred to abstinence,
Much more to taste it, under ban to touch.   925
But past who can recall, or done undo?

Adam does not seem to know here who has been behind the serpent's temptation of Eve. To escape this difficulty, some critics argue that what is *unknown* is the *fraud* rather than the *enemy,* which they often see as a reference to Satan (and often capitalize). But at lines 1068–69 below, Adam can still speak of the "false" serpent, "of whomsoever taught / To counterfeit man's voice"; and indeed, Adam does not identify Satan as the tempter until 10.1033–35.

906–907. *with thee. . . to die:* Critics debate the motives of his willingness to die with her, wondering if he is motivated more by his own anxiety about living without her than by his selfless love for her or whether he loves Eve more than he loves God. His response, however, strikes many readers as more appealing than would an immediate repudiation of her act and their relationship, even if it will also complete her sin. But at least here, before he has actually eaten of the apple, his exploration of his feelings is neither inappropriate nor unattractive.

909. *converse:* conversation (but also, intimacy)

910. *wild woods forlorn:* The wildness of the landscape is not a result of Eve's fall; Eden has from the first been described as "wild" (4.136); *forlorn* is not here an adjective modifying *woods* but an adverb modifying *To live.*

914–915. *flesh . . . art:* echoes 8.495

919. *Submitting to what seemed remediless:* Although Milton does not indicate precisely what remedies were available, *seemed* may suggest that Adam's decision was premature; among his unexplored options, he might have prayed, offered himself as sacrifice, or perhaps even divorced Eve (see Milton's *Tetrachordon*).

924. *sacred . . . sacred:* set apart . . . consecrated

925. *under . . . touch:* See line 651 and note.

Not God omnipotent nor fate, yet° so   *even*
Perhaps thou shalt not die; perhaps the fact
Is not so heinous now: foretasted° fruit,   *already tasted*
Profaned first by the serpent, by him first   930
Made common and unhallowed ere our taste,
Nor yet on him found deadly; he yet lives,
Lives, as thou said'st, and gains to live as man,
Higher degree of life, inducement strong
To us, as likely, tasting to attain   935
Proportional ascent, which cannot be
But to be gods or angels, demigods.
Nor can I think that God, creator wise
Though threatening, will in earnest so destroy
Us, his prime creatures, dignified so high,   940
Set over all his works, which in our fall,
For us created, needs with us must fail,
Dependent made; so God shall uncreate,
Be frustrate, do, undo, and labor lose,
Not well conceived of° God, who, though his power   *in the case of*
Creation could repeat, yet would be loath
Us to abolish lest the adversary
Triumph and say: 'Fickle their state whom God
Most favors. Who can please him long? Me first
He ruined, now mankind; whom will he next?'   950
Matter of scorn not to be given the foe.
However I with thee have fixed my lot,
Certain to undergo like doom; if death
Consort° with thee, death is to me as life,   *socialize, associate*
So forcible within my heart I feel   955
The bond of nature draw me to my own,

---

928. *Perhaps:* Compare Thomas Browne, *Pseudoxia Epidemica* (1646): "the commandment . . . positively said ye shall surely die, but [Eve] extenuating replied *ne forte moriamini,* lest perhaps ye die" (p. 2).

931. *our:* already assumes his taste, or at least his complicity in hers

936. *Proportional ascent:* exactly echoes Satan's argument at line 711 above

936–937. *which cannot . . . gods:* Note the way the first half of the thought at the end of line 936 seems like a denial, which line 937 then overwhelms.

940. *his prime creatures:* Has he forgotten the angels?

944. *frustrate:* frustrated (since seemingly he must "do, undo")

947. *the adversary:* i.e., Satan; see 6.282.

951. *Matter of:* subject for

953. *Certain:* resolved, translating Aeneas' phrase, *certus eundi,* expressing his determination to leave Carthage (*Aeneid* 4.554); see line 907 above.

956. *bond of nature:* At line 914, it was a "link of nature," perhaps a less coercive term.

My own in thee, for what thou art is mine;
Our state cannot be severed; we are one,
One flesh; to lose thee were to lose myself."
    So Adam, and thus Eve to him replied: 960
"O glorious trial of exceeding love,
Illustrious evidence, example high,
Engaging me to emulate, but short
Of thy perfection how shall I attain,
Adam, from whose dear side I boast me sprung,   965
And gladly of our union hear thee speak,
One heart, one soul in both, whereof good proof
This day affords, declaring thee resolved
Rather than death, or aught than death more dread,
Shall separate us, linked in love so dear,   970
To undergo with me one guilt, one crime,
If any be, of tasting this fair fruit,
Whose virtue (for of good still good proceeds,
Direct or by occasion) hath presented
This happy trial of thy love, which else   975
So eminently° never had been known.   *obviously*
Were it I thought death menaced would ensue
This my attempt, I would sustain alone
The worst and not persuade thee, rather die
Deserted than oblige thee with a fact   980
Pernicious to thy peace, chiefly assured
Remarkably so late of thy so true,
So faithful, love unequaled; but I feel
Far otherwise the event:° not death, but life   *outcome, consequence*
Augmented, opened eyes, new hopes, new joys,   985
Taste so divine, that what of sweet before
Hath touched my sense flat seems to° this and harsh.   *compared to*
On my experience, Adam, freely taste

---

958. *Our state . . . severed:* See *The Doc-trine and Discipline of Divorce* (1643) for Milton's earliest thinking about the legiti-macy of divorce. This and the four other "di-vorce" tracts argue that divorce should be permitted for fundamental spiritual discord between husband and wife.

961. *exceeding:* 1) exceptional; 2) ex-cessive

965. *boast me sprung:* proudly admit I am derived

967. *one soul in both:* Cf. 8.604, before their fall, "in us both one soul."

974. *Direct or by occasion:* directly or in-directly

980. *oblige thee with:* make you guilty of

982–983. *so . . . so . . . So:* The repeti-tion seems to reveal some deep anxiety.

And fear of death deliver to the winds."
    So saying, she embraced him, and for joy   990
Tenderly wept, much won that he his love
Had so ennobled as of choice to incur
Divine displeasure for her sake, or death.
In recompense (for such compliance bad
Such recompense best merits) from the bough   995
She gave him of that fair enticing fruit
With liberal hand. He scrupled not to eat
Against his better knowledge, not deceived
But fondly overcome with female charm.
Earth trembled from her entrails as again   1000
In pangs, and nature gave a second groan;
Sky loured° and, muttering thunder, some sad drops   *looked threatening*
Wept at completing of the mortal sin
Original, while Adam took no thought,
Eating his fill, nor Eve to iterate   1005
Her former trespass feared, the more to soothe
Him with her loved society that now,
As with new wine intoxicated both,
They swim in mirth and fancy that they feel
Divinity within them breeding wings   1010
Wherewith to scorn the earth. But that false fruit
Far other operation° first displayed,   *effect, influence*
Carnal desire enflaming; he on Eve
Began to cast lascivious eyes, she him

989. *deliver to the winds:* ignore, forget

994. *compliance bad:* inappropriate submission; cf. Gen. 3:17: "Because thou hast hearkened unto the voice of thy wife, and hast eaten of the tree."

998–999. *not deceived . . . charm:* Most familiar among the authorities for Milton's thought here was Augustine: "the first man did not yield to his wife in this transgression of God's precept, as if hee thought she said [truth]; but only being compelled to it by this social love to her . . . for it is not in vaine that the apostle says: 'Adam was not deceived, but the woman was deceived'" (*City of God* 14.11 trans. John Healy, 1610, p. 513). Augustine is quoting 1 Timothy 2:14.

999. *fondly:* foolishly (but the meaning "affectionately" must be heard as well)

1001. *second groan:* The first is heard at lines 782–83 above.

1003–1004. *sin Original:* The phrase "original sin" names the doctrine that all of humankind are infected with the sin of their first parents. See *Christian Doctrine* I, xi (*Works* 15, 180–82): "undoubtedly all sinned in Adam," insisting on the "principle uniformly acted upon in the divine proceedings, and recognized by all nations, . . . that the penalty incurred by the violation of things sacred (and such was the tree of the knowledge of good and evil) attaches not only to the criminal himself, but to the whole of his posterity." Rom. 5:12 holds that "by one man sin entered into the world."

As wantonly repaid; in lust they burn,   1015
Till Adam thus 'gan Eve to dalliance move:
    "Eve, now I see thou art exact of taste,
And elegant, of sapience no small part,
Since to each meaning savor we apply
And palate call judicious; I the praise   1020
Yield thee, so well this day thou hast purveyed.°   *provided food*
Much pleasure we have lost while we abstained
From this delightful fruit, nor known till now
True relish, tasting; if such pleasure be
In things to us forbidden, it might be wished   1025
For this one tree had been forbidden ten.
But come; so well refreshed now let us play
As meet° is after such delicious fare,   *appropriate*
For never did thy beauty since the day
I saw thee first and wedded thee, adorned   1030
With all perfections, so enflame my sense
With ardor to enjoy thee, fairer now
Than ever, bounty of this virtuous tree."
    So said he and forbore not glance or toy°   *caress*
Of amorous intent, well understood   1035
Of Eve, whose eye darted contagious fire.
Her hand he seized, and to a shady bank,
Thick overhead with verdant roof embowered,
He led her nothing loath; flowers were the couch,
Pansies, and violets, and asphodel,   1040
And hyacinth, earth's freshest, softest lap.

1017. *taste:* Milton plays on the literal and figurative meanings of *taste*, perhaps remembering Cicero's remark that "a man of discerning heart does not always lack a discerning palate" (*De finibus* 2.8).

1026. *forbidden ten:* anticipates the ten commandments

1027–1028. *now let us play . . . fare:* reflects 1 Cor. 10:7–8: "Neither be ye idolaters, as were some of them; as it is written, The people sat down to eat and drink, and rose up to play. Neither let us commit fornication, as some of them committed." Paul is quoting Exod. 32:6.

1029–1032. *For never . . . thee:* The language recalls Paris' to Helen in *Iliad*

3.441–42: "For never has love so enmeshed my senses since the day I seized you and took you from Sparta"; the most infamous classical example of illicit love provides the language for the fallen passion of Adam and Eve.

1037. *Her hand he seized:* in lines 385–86 above, Eve "withdrew" her hand from his, though they are now (forcibly) reunited; cf. the first (4.321) and last sight (12.648) of Adam and Eve "hand in hand" and the "gentle" seizing in 4.488–89.

1039–1041. *flowers . . . lap:* The scene is perhaps intended to recall *Iliad* 14.346–52, where earth prepares a bed of flowers for Hera and Zeus.

There they their fill of love and love's disport
Took largely, of their mutual guilt the seal,°   *confirmation, sign*
The solace of their sin, till dewy° sleep   *falling gently*
Oppressed them, wearied with their amorous play.   1045
Soon as the force of that fallacious° fruit,   *delusive, deceptive*
That with exhilarating vapor bland°   *pleasing*
About their spirits had played and inmost powers
Made err, was now exhaled, and grosser sleep,
Bred of unkindly° fumes, with conscious dreams   *unnatural*
Encumbered, now had left them, up they rose
As from unrest, and each the other viewing
Soon found their eyes how opened and their minds
How darkened; innocence, that as a veil
Had shadowed them from knowing ill, was gone,   1055
Just confidence and native righteousness
And honor from about° them, naked left   *around (like a garment)*
To guilty shame; he covered, but his robe
Uncovered more. So° rose the Danite, strong,   *just so, similarly*
Herculean Samson, from the harlot-lap   1060
Of Philistean Dalilah and waked
Shorn of his strength, they, destitute and bare
Of all their virtue. Silent and in face
Confounded long they sat as strucken mute,
Till Adam, though not less than Eve abashed,   1065
At length gave utterance to these words constrained:
      "O Eve, in evil hour thou didst give ear

1042–1044. *their . . . solace:* The line here echoes the words of the lewd woman in Prov. 8:18: "Come, let us take our fill of love until the morning; let us solace ourselves with loves"; cf. the true "solace" of their unfallen love as recently as line 844 above (see also 4.486).

1049. *grosser sleep:* contrasts with Adam's "airy light" sleep in 5.4

1050. *conscious:* guilty, with consciousness of wrongdoing

1053. *eyes how opened:* See Gen. 3:7: "And the eyes of them both were opened. And they knew that they were naked."

1058–1059. *he . . . more:* i.e., shame drove them to cover themselves, but *his* [i.e., shame's] *robe* ultimately leaves them even more exposed.

1059–1062. *the Danite . . . strength:* refers to the story of Samson, a member of the tribe of Dan, whose betrayal by his Philistine wife Dalilah (as Milton spells it, and usually expects an accent on the first syllable) is recorded in Judg. 16.

1062. *they:* Adam and Eve, both compared to Samson (not Eve as Dalilah); *they* = as they rose

1065. *abashed:* In 8.595, Adam is only "half-abashed" after Raphael warns him not to fall victim to excessive passion.

1067. *Eve, in evil hour:* The word play suggests a (false) etymological link between "Eve" and "evil"; "Eve," however, is indeed used as the name of the first woman only after the fall in Gen. 3:20.

To that false worm, of whomsoever taught
To counterfeit man's voice, true in° our fall,   *with respect to*
False in our promised rising, since our eyes   1070
Opened we find indeed and find we know
Both good and evil: good lost and evil got.
Bad fruit of knowledge if this be to know,
Which leaves us naked thus, of honor void,
Of innocence, of faith, of purity,   1075
Our wonted° ornaments now soiled and stained,   *accustomed*
And in our faces evident the signs
Of foul concupiscence, whence evil store,
Even shame, the last of evils; of the first
Be sure then. How shall I behold the face   1080
Henceforth of God or angel, erst with joy
And rapture so oft beheld? Those heavenly shapes
Will dazzle now this earthly with their blaze
Insufferably bright. O might I here
In solitude live savage in some glade   1085
Obscured where highest woods, impenetrable
To star or sunlight, spread their umbrage broad
And brown as evening. Cover me ye pines,
Ye cedars; with innumerable boughs

1068. *worm:* serpent; cf. *Antony and Cleopatra* 5.2.238–39: "the pretty worm / Of Nilus."

1072–1073. *Both . . . knowledge:* No new knowledge is achieved by their eating, except for their experiential understanding of the new reality brought about by their transgression. Like most commentators, Milton derived the name of the Tree of Knowledge "from the event; for since Adam tasted it, we not only know evil, but we know good only by means of evil" (*Christian Doctrine* I, x [*Works* 15, 115]).

1078. *whence evil store:* from which (came) evil in abundance (for *store* as "'in abundance," see Milton's youthful translation of Psalm 88: "cloy'd with woes and trouble store").

1079. *the first:* i.e., "concupiscence" (line 1078), not the first of all the evils, but their first sinful manifestation (as "shame" is the "last," following the act).

1080. *Be sure then:* i.e., be as certain that the effects of concupiscence are as obvious as the marks of our shame

1081. *erst:* formerly (as at line 163 above)

1083. *earthly:* earthly nature (as at 8.483)

1085. *In solitude:* Though in Book 8 it is precisely his desire to escape solitude that leads him to request a mate from God (lines 364–65).

1087. *umbrage:* shade; cf. "the shady roof / Of branching Elm Star-proof" in Milton's "Arcades," 89.

1088. *brown:* shadowy, dark; cf. "Embrowned" in 4.246.

1088–1090. *Cover me . . . more:* Their expression of shame echoes the language of Hosea anticipating the shame of a disobedient Israel: "They shall say to the mountains, Cover us; and to the hills, Fall on us" (10:8; and its echo in Rev. 6:16).

Hide me where I may never see them more.   1090
But let us now, as in bad plight, devise
What best may for the present serve to hide
The parts of each from other that seem most
To shame obnoxious and unseemliest seen,
Some tree whose broad smooth leaves, together sewed   1095
And girded on our loins, may cover round
Those middle parts that this newcomer, shame,
There sit not and reproach us as unclean."
    So counseled he, and both together went
Into the thickest wood; there soon they chose   1100
The fig tree, not that kind for fruit renowned,
But such as at this day to Indians known
In Malabar or Decan spreads her arms
Branching so broad and long that in the ground
The bended twigs take root and daughters grow   1105
About the mother tree, a pillared shade
High overarched, and echoing walks between;
There oft the Indian herdsman, shunning heat,
Shelters in cool and tends his pasturing herds
At loopholes cut through thickest shade. Those leaves   1110
They gathered, broad as Amazonian targe,
And with what skill they had, together sewed
To gird their waist, vain covering if to hide
Their guilt and dreaded shame. O how unlike
To that first naked glory! Such of late   1115

1090. *them:* i.e., the "heavenly shapes" at line 1082

1091–1098. *devise . . . unclean:* In *Christian Doctrine* I, xii (*Works* 15, 204) Milton interprets "They knew that they were naked" (Gen. 3:7) as signifying "a conscious degradation of mind, whence arises shame," as a result of which "they sewed fig-leaves together and made themselves aprons."

1094. *obnoxious:* exposed (as at line 170 above)

1101–1106. *The fig tree . . . tree:* The description here derives from the account of the banyan or "arched Indian Fig tree" in Gerard's *Herball* (1597), 1330–31, which declares that its branches touch the ground,

"where they take root and grow in such sort, that those twigs become great trees; . . . by meanes whereof it cometh to passe, that of one tree is made a great wood . . . which the Indians do use for coverture against the extreme heate of the sun. Some . . . cut loopholes or windows in some places, to the end to receiue thereby the fresh cool air, . . . as also for the light that they may see their cattell that feed thereby. From which vault doth rebound an admirable echo. . . . The first or mother of this wood is hard to be known from the children."

1103. *Malabar or Decan:* regions of southwestern and southern India

1111. *Amazonian targe:* shield of an Amazon

Columbus found the American so girt
With feathered cincture,° naked else and wild   *belt*
Among the trees on isles and woody shores.
Thus fenced, and, as they thought, their shame in part
Covered, but not at rest or ease of mind,   1120
They sat them down to weep; nor only tears
Rained at their eyes but high winds worse within
Began to rise, high passions, anger, hate,
Mistrust, suspicion, discord, and shook sore
Their inward state of mind, calm region once   1125
And full of peace, now tossed and turbulent;
For understanding ruled not, and the will
Heard not her lore, both in subjection now
To sensual appetite, who from beneath
Usurping over sovereign reason claimed   1130
Superior sway. From thus distempered breast,
Adam, estranged in look and altered style,
Speech intermitted thus to Eve renewed:
    "Would thou hadst hearkened to my words and stayed
With me as I besought thee when that strange   1135
Desire of wandering this unhappy morn
(I know not whence) possessed thee; we had then
Remained still happy, not as now despoiled
Of all our good, shamed, naked, miserable.
Let none henceforth seek needless cause to approve°   *give proof of*
The faith they owe; when earnestly they seek
Such proof, conclude they then begin to fail."
    To whom, soon moved with touch of blame, thus Eve:
"What words have passed thy lips, Adam severe?
Imput'st thou that to my default, or will   1145

1116–1118. *Columbus . . . shores:* Milton's reference to the new world discovery is interesting in that he, following the logic of his sense of original sin (and the new world descriptions by the English Colonists), does not assume the natives innocent.

1120–1131. *not . . . sway:* In *Christian Doctrine* I, xii (*Works* 15, 207) Adam's punishment "consists first in the loss, or at least in the darkening to a great extent of that right reason which enabled him to discern the chief good, and in which consisted the life of the understanding."

1121. *sat . . . weep:* Cf. Ps. 137:1: "by the rivers of Babylon, there we sat down, yea, we wept, when remembered Zion."

1132. *altered style:* changed manner (of speech)

1133. *intermitted:* interrupted, broken off (at line 1098)

1141. *owe:* both *owe* and "own," i.e., "under obligation to repay" and "possess"; Adam recalls Eve's words in lines 335–36 above.

1144. *What . . . lips:* The phrase echoes Odysseus' criticism of Agamemnon's rash speech in *Iliad* 14.83.

Of wandering, as thou call'st it, which who knows
But might as ill have happened thou being by
Or to thyself perhaps? Hadst thou been there,
Or here the attempt, thou couldst not have discerned
Fraud in the serpent, speaking as he spake,   1150
No ground of enmity between us known
Why he should mean me ill or seek to harm.
Was I to have never parted from thy side?
As good have grown there still a lifeless rib.
Being as I am, why didst not thou, the head,   1155
Command me absolutely not to go,
Going into such danger, as thou said'st?
Too facile then thou didst not much gainsay,
Nay, didst permit, approve, and fair dismiss.
Hadst thou been firm and fixed in thy dissent,   1160
Neither had I transgressed nor thou with me."
　　To whom, then first incensed, Adam replied:
　　"Is this the love, is this the recompense
Of mine to thee, ingrateful Eve, expressed
Immutable when thou wert lost, not I,   1165
Who might have lived and joyed immortal bliss
Yet willingly chose rather death with thee?
And am I now upbraided as the cause
Of thy transgressing, not enough severe
It seems in thy restraint? What could I more?   1170
I warned thee, I admonished thee, foretold
The danger and the lurking enemy
That lay in wait; beyond this had been force,
And force upon free will hath here no place.
But confidence then bore thee on, secure°   *overconfident*
Either to meet no danger or to find

1150–1152. *Fraud . . . harm:* Clearly Eve has no sense that the serpent's temptation was that about which Raphael had warned them.

1155. *the head:* In Cor. 11:3, Paul says: "the head of every man is Christ; and the head of the woman is the man; and the head of Christ is God"; cf. the different tone in Eve's use of "head" in 4.443.

1158. *facile:* It isn't obvious exactly what this charge implies; does *facile* mean "easy-going," or "easily led," or "lenient"? In *PR* Satan applies the adjective to Eve: "Adam and his facile consort Eve / Lost Paradise" (1.51–52).

1159. *fair dismiss:* dismiss me with your blessing; see lines 372–75.

1164–1165. *expressed Immutable:* shown to be unchanging by his actions (in lines 952–59 above, and praised by Eve there as "Illustrious evidence, example high" [line 962] of his love)

Matter of glorious trial; and perhaps
I also erred in overmuch admiring
What seemed in thee so perfect that I thought
No evil durst attempt thee; but I rue   1180
That error now, which is become my crime
And thou the accuser. Thus it shall befall
Him who, to worth in women overtrusting,
Lets her will rule; restraint she will not brook,
And, left to herself, if evil thence ensue,   1185
She first his weak indulgence will accuse."
        Thus they in mutual accusation spent
The fruitless hours, but neither self-condemning,
And of their vain contest appeared no end.

The End of the Ninth Book.

1177. *Matter of:* occasion for

1188. *fruitless:* picks up and makes poignant Eve's pun at line 648 *neither self-condemning:* In the early outline for *PL*, "Adam unparadiz'd," Milton wrote: "Adam then and Eve returne accuse one another but especially Adam layes the blame to his wife, is stubborn in his offence."

1189. *no end:* Book 9 begins "No more . . ."

BOOK 10

The Argument

Man's transgression known, the guardian angels forsake Paradise and return up to Heaven to approve their vigilance, and are approved, God declaring that the entrance of Satan could not be by them prevented. He sends his Son to judge the transgressors, who descends and gives sentence accordingly; then in pity clothes them both and reascends. Sin and Death, sitting till then at the gates of hell, by wondrous sympathy feeling the success of Satan in this new world, and the sin by man there committed, resolve to sit no longer confined in hell but to follow Satan, their sire, up to the place of man; to make the way easier from hell to this world to and fro, they pave a broad highway or bridge over chaos, according to the track that Satan first made; then, preparing for earth, they meet him, proud of his success, returning to hell; their mutual gratulation. Satan arrives at Pandaemonium, in full of assembly relates with boasting his success against man; instead of applause is entertained with a general hiss by all his audience, transformed with himself also suddenly into serpents, according to his doom given in Paradise; then, deluded with a show of the forbidden tree springing up before them, they, greedily reaching to take of the fruit, chew dust and bitter ashes. The proceedings of Sin and Death: God foretells the final victory of his Son over them and the renewing of all things, but for the present commands his angels to make several alterations in the heavens and elements. Adam, more and more perceiving his fallen condition, heavily bewails, rejects the condolement of Eve; she persists and at length appeases him; then, to evade the curse likely to fall on their offspring, proposes to Adam violent ways which he approves not, but conceiving better hope, puts her in mind of the late promise made them that her seed should be revenged on the serpent, and exhorts her with him to seek peace of the offended deity by repentance and supplication.

Meanwhile the heinous and despiteful act
Of Satan done in Paradise and how

---

1. *heinous:* In 9.928–31, Adam rationalizes that since the serpent anticipated Eve's eating of the fruit, perhaps her act "Is not so heinous now." *despiteful:* Milton has insisted that Satan's temptation of mankind was "a despite done against the most high" (6.906); as Satan himself says, seeing man, this "son of despite, / Whom us the more to spite his maker raised / From dust: spite then with spite is best repaid" (9.176–8).

306

He, in the serpent, had perverted° Eve,   *led astray*
Her husband she, to taste the fatal fruit
Was known in Heaven, for what can scape the eye   5
Of God all-seeing or deceive his heart
Omniscient, who, in all things wise and just,
Hindered not Satan to attempt the mind
Of man, with strength entire and free will armed,
Complete to have discovered and repulsed   10
Whatever wiles of foe or seeming friend.
For still° they knew and ought to have still remembered   *always*
The high injunction not to taste that fruit,
Whoever tempted, which they not obeying
Incurred (what could they less?) the penalty   15
And, manifold in sin, deserved to fall.
Up into Heaven from Paradise in haste
The angelic guards ascended, mute and sad
For man, for of his state by this they knew,
Much wondering how the subtle fiend had stolen   20
Entrance unseen. Soon as the unwelcome news
From earth arrived at Heaven gate, displeased
All were who heard; dim sadness did not spare
That time celestial visages, yet, mixed
With pity, violated not their bliss.   25
About the new-arrived, in multitudes
The ethereal people ran, to hear and know

5–7. *what . . . .Omniscient:* 3.534 and 3.578 similarly emphasize God's *eye*, whose ability to be *all-seeing* shows the folly of Eve's hope to be "secret" from his gaze in 9.811–15.

7–11. *who . . . friend:* These lines reiterate the claim of 3.95–99, and distil the thought in the chapter "Of the Divine Decrees" in *Christian Doctrine* I, iii, where Milton says that God "suffered both men and angels to stand or fall at their own uncontrolled choice, . . . not necessitating the evil consequences that ensued, but leaving them contingent" (*Works* 14, 81).

8. *attempt:* test, assault (though the embedded "tempt" is of course relevant)

10. *Complete:* fully able (modifies "mind" in line 8); cf. 9.292 and 9.351–56.

16. *manifold in sin:* with multiple sins (*manifold* = diverse, varied); in *Christian Doctrine* I, xi, Milton asks "what sin can be named which was not included in this one act?" (*Works* 15, 181)

18. *angelic guards:* i.e., Gabriel, Uzziel, Ithuriel, Zephon, and their troop; e.g., see 4.779–91.

19. *by this:* by this time

20–21. *how . . . Entrance unseen:* See 9.69–76 for the description of Satan's *entrance*, but following on lines 5–6 above, *unseen* can only mean by the angels' eyes.

24. *That time:* then

How all befell. They toward the throne supreme
Accountable made haste to make appear
With righteous plea their utmost vigilance,   30
And easily approved,° when the most high   *confirmed*
Eternal Father from his secret cloud
Amidst in thunder uttered thus his voice:
    "Assembled angels and ye powers returned
From unsuccessful charge, be not dismayed   35
Nor troubled at these tidings from the earth,
Which your sincerest care could not prevent,
Foretold so lately what would come to pass
When first this tempter crossed the gulf from hell.
I told ye then he should prevail and speed°   *succeed*
On his bad errand, man should be seduced
And flattered out of all, believing lies
Against his maker, no decree of mine
Concurring° to necessitate his fall   *intervening*
Or touch with lightest moment of impulse   45
His free will, to her own inclining left
In even scale. But fallen he is, and now
What rests but that the mortal sentence pass
On his transgression: death denounced that day,
Which he presumes already vain and void   50

28. *They:* i.e., the guards (not the rest of the angels, who stayed in Heaven)

29. *Accountable:* modifies "They" in line 28 (acknowledging their responsibility)

32–33. *from . . . thunder:* Cf. 2.263–68; the conception is colored by Exod. 33:9–10, where God descends in a "cloudy pillar," 1 Kings 8:10–11, where God also appears as a "cloud," and Rev. 4:5: "out of the throne proceeded lightnings and thunderings and voices."

35. *charge:* mission (see 9.157)

38. *Foretold so lately:* i.e., in 3.80–134

40. *I told ye then:* i.e., at 3.92–97

43–47. *no decree . . . scale:* God insists that his foreknowledge did not necessitate the *fall* or compromise man's *free will*, as in 3.111–25.

45. *moment of impulse:* degree of compulsion (*moment* = a small unit of weight able to affect the balance of a scale, as at 6.239)

48. *rests:* remains to be done; cf. *3 Henry VI* 5.7.42: "And now what rests but that we spend the time."

49. *denounced:* pronounced, formally proclaimed

49–53. *death . . . end:* Gen. 2:17 promised that "in the day that thou eatest thereof thou shalt surely die," but death is not immediate (Adam lived for 930 years), producing much commentary. "This death," Milton says in *Christian Doctrine* I, xii (*Works* 15, 206–8), "consists first, in the loss, or at least in the obscuration to a great extent of that right reason which enabled man to discern the chief good. . . . It consists, secondly, in . . . deprivation of righteousness and liberty to do good. . . . Lastly, sin is its own punishment, and produces . . . the death of the spiritual life"; cf. 9.1053–64.

50. *Which . . . void:* See 9.927–37.

Because not yet inflicted, as he feared,
By some immediate stroke, but soon shall find
Forbearance no acquittance ere day end.
Justice shall not return as bounty, scorned.
But whom send I to judge them? Whom but thee,   55
Vicegerent Son, to thee I have transferred
All judgment, whether in Heaven or earth or hell.
Easy it might be seen that I intend
Mercy colleague° with justice, sending thee,   *allied*
Man's friend, his mediator, his designed   60
Both ransom and redeemer voluntary,
And destined man himself to judge man fallen."
    So spake the Father, and, unfolding bright
Toward the right hand his glory, on the Son
Blazed forth unclouded deity; he full   65
Resplendent all his Father manifest
Expressed, and thus divinely answered mild:
    "Father eternal, thine is to decree;
Mine, both in Heaven and earth, to do thy will
Supreme, that thou in me, thy Son beloved,   70
Mayst ever rest well pleased. I go to judge
On earth these thy transgressors, but thou know'st,

53. *Forbearance no acquittance:* i.e., God's restraint (*Forbearance*) in not immediately ending Adam's life does not imply that Adam has been exonerated for his sin; cf. Spenser, *Faerie Queene* 4.3.11: "to forbeare doth not forgive the det."

54. *Justice . . . scorned:* i.e., God's justice, unlike his generosity (*bounty*), will not be ignored (*scorned*) by man

56. *Vicegerent:* deputy; cf. 5.609.

56–57. *to thee . . . judgment:* Cf. John 5:22: "For the Father judgeth no man, but hath committed all judgment unto the son."

60. *mediator:* i.e., between man and God; cf. 1 Tim. 2:5: "For there is one God, and one mediator between God and men, the man Christ Jesus"; see also *Christian Doctrine* I, xv: "The mediatorial office of Christ is that whereby . . . he voluntarily performed, and continues to perform, on behalf of man, whatever is requisite for obtaining reconciliation with God, and eternal salvation" (*Works* 15, 284).

61–62. *voluntary, And destined:* Christ voluntarily chooses to act as man's "ransom and redeemer," but in God's eternal plan he is *destined* to play these roles; both words are crucial to Milton's sense of how free will and providence coexist; either one without the other would rob the world of moral meaning.

63–65. *unfolding . . . deity:* Cf. the Son's participation in God's glory in 3.139 and 6.678–83. Cf. the description of Christ in Heb. 1:3: "Who being the brightness of his glory, and the express image of his person . . . sat down on the right hand of the Majesty on high."

71. *well pleased:* echoes Matt. 3:17, where John the Baptist anticipates God praising his "'beloved Son, in whom I am well pleased"

72. *thy transgressors:* i.e., transgressors against thee (but the ambiguity of the genitive allows this to be heard as a claim of God's responsibility for the transgression)

Whoever judged, the worst on me must light
When time shall be, for so I undertook
Before thee, and, not repenting, this obtain   75
Of right, that I may mitigate their doom
On me derived; yet I shall temper so
Justice with mercy as may illustrate° most   *show clearly*
Them fully satisfied and thee appease.
Attendance none shall need, nor train, where none   80
Are to behold the judgment but the judged,
Those two; the third, best absent, is condemned,
Convict by flight and rebel to all law;
Conviction to the serpent none belongs."
    Thus saying, from his radiant seat he rose   85
Of high collateral° glory. Him thrones and powers,   *side by side*
Princedoms and dominations ministrant
Accompanied to Heaven gate, from whence
Eden and all the coast in prospect lay.
Down he descended straight; the speed of gods   90
Time counts not though with swiftest minutes wingèd.
Now was the sun in western cadence low
From noon, and gentle airs, due at their hour
To fan the earth, now waked and usher in
The evening cool, when he, from wrath more cool,   95
Came the mild judge and intercessor both

74. *When time shall be:* Cf. the similar allusion in 3.284 to Gal. 4:4: "But when the fulness of the time was come, God sent forth his Son, made of a woman."

77. *derived:* keeps its Latin meaning (*derivare* = to draw off) of "diverted" or "turned aside"

79. *Them:* i.e., justice and mercy; it is their claims that must be satisfied (Christ's death will satisfy justice; man's redemption will satisfy mercy).

82. *the third:* i.e., Satan

83. *Convict by flight:* his guilt proven by his running away

84. *Conviction:* This would seem to mean "proof of guilt," which should not apply to the serpent because he was merely Satan's instrument, but see lines 165–68 below. Perhaps *Conviction* here means only "awareness of guilt," which the serpent as animal would not have.

87. *ministrant:* ministering (Heb. 1:14: "are they not all ministering spirits?")

89. *coast:* surrounding region; cf. 2.633 and 6.529.

90. *speed of gods:* Cf. Raphael's speed "almost spiritual" in 8.110; *gods* is used as it is of the heavenly beings in 2.352.

92. *cadence:* keeps its Latin meaning (from Latin *cadere* = to fall) of "descent" but also retains its musical sense with the play on "airs" in line 93

95–97. *The evening cool . . . man:* Milton transfigures Gen. 3:8: "And they heard the voice of the Lord God walking in the garden in the cool of the day: and Adam and his wife hid themselves from the presence of the Lord God amongst the trees of the garden." The following thirteen verses of Genesis are closely followed in lines 103–223 below.

96. *intercessor:* See 3.219 and 11.19.

To sentence man. The voice of God they heard
Now walking in the garden, by soft winds
Brought to their ears while day declined; they heard
And from his presence hid themselves among   100
The thickest trees, both man and wife, till God,
Approaching, thus to Adam called aloud:
    "Where art thou, Adam, wont with joy to meet
My coming seen far off? I miss thee here,
Not pleased thus entertained with solitude   105
Where obvious duty erewhile appeared unsought.
Or come I less conspicuous, or what change
Absents thee, or what chance detains? Come forth."
He came, and with him Eve, more loath though first
To offend, discountenanced both and discomposed.   110
Love was not in their looks, either to God
Or to each other, but apparent° guilt   *evident, conspicuous*
And shame, and perturbation, and despair,
Anger and obstinacy, and hate and guile.
Whence Adam faltering long, thus answered brief: 115
    "I heard thee in the garden and, of thy voice
Afraid, being naked, hid myself." To whom
The gracious judge without revile° replied: *reproach, abuse*
    "My voice thou oft hast heard and hast not feared
But still° rejoiced. How is it now become   *always*
So dreadful° to thee? That thou art naked, who   *frightening*
Hath told thee? Hast thou eaten of the tree
Whereof I gave thee charge thou shouldst not eat?"
    To whom thus Adam sore beset replied:
"O Heaven, in evil strait this day I stand   125
Before my judge, either to undergo
Myself the total crime or to accuse
My other self, the partner of my life,

101–102. *God, Approaching*: i.e., Christ, though in his role as God's "Vicegerent," line 56, in which he makes "all his Father manifest" (line 66)

102–103. *to Adam . . . Adam*: follows Gen. 3:9: "And the Lord God called unto Adam, and said unto him, where art thou?"

106. *obvious*: 1) plain, unmistakable; 2) coming forward to greet, welcoming

107–108. *what change . . . what chance*: Cf. 2.222: "what chance, what change"

110. *discountenanced . . . discomposed*: ashamed . . . agitated

115. *faltering long*: after much hesitation

116–117. *I heard . . . myself*: follows Gen. 3:10: "I heard thy voice in the garden, and I was afraid because I was naked; and I hid myself"

128. *other self*: God calls Eve Adam's *other self* in 8.450; but see also 4.488, 5.95, 8.495–96, and 9.959.

Whose failing, while her faith to me remains,
I should conceal and not expose to blame   130
By my complaint; but strict necessity
Subdues me and calamitous constraint,
Lest on my head both sin and punishment,
However insupportable, be all
Devolved, though, should I hold my peace yet thou   135
Wouldst easily detect what I conceal.
This woman whom thou mad'st to be my help
And gav'st me as thy perfect gift, so good,
So fit, so acceptable, so divine,
That from her hand I could suspect no ill,   140
And what she did, whatever in itself,
Her doing seemed to justify the deed—
She gave me of the tree, and I did eat."
    To whom the sovereign presence thus replied:
"Was she thy God that her thou didst obey   145
Before his voice? Or was she made thy guide,
Superior, or but° equal, that to her   *even, merely*
Thou didst resign thy manhood and the place
Wherein God set thee above her, made of thee,
And for thee, whose perfection far excelled   150
Hers in all real dignity? Adorned
She was indeed and lovely to attract
Thy love, not thy subjection, and her gifts
Were such as under government well seemed,
Unseemly to bear rule, which was thy part   155
And person hadst thou known thy self aright."
    So having said, he thus to Eve in few:
"Say, woman, what is this which thou hast done?"

131–132. *strict . . . me:* Cf. Satan's claim
of the necessity for his evil in 4.389–94.

134–135. *be all Devolved:* all descend

139. *so divine:* Remarkably, especially
given his interlocutor, Adam does not recog-
nize the impropriety of the adjective.

143. *She . . . eat:* an exact rendering of
the second half of Gen. 3:12

145–156. *Was . . . aright:* The rebuke
parallels Raphael's warning in 8.561–85, as
the preceding lines match Adam's preceding
speech in 8.540–59.

148–150. *the place . . . thee:* follows 1

Cor. 11:8–9: "For the man is not of the
woman; but the woman of the man. Neither
was the man created for the woman; but the
woman for the man."

151. *real:* 1) actual; 2) royal, regal

154–155. *Were . . . rule:* Cf. 1 Tim
2:12: "I suffer not a woman to teach, nor to
usurp authority over the man."

155–156. *part And person:* role and
character (both theatrical terms)

157. *few:* few words; cf. *2 Henry IV*
1.1.112: "In few, his death, whose spirit lent
a fire / Even to the dullest peasant."

To whom sad Eve, with shame nigh overwhelmed,
Confessing soon, yet not before her judge 160
Bold or loquacious, thus abashed replied:
   "The serpent me beguiled and I did eat."
   Which when the Lord God heard, without delay
To judgment he proceeded on the accused
Serpent, though brute, unable to transfer 165
The guilt on him who made him instrument
Of mischief and polluted from the end
Of his creation: justly then accursed
As vitiated in nature. More to know
Concerned not man (since he no further knew) 170
Nor altered his offence; yet God at last
To Satan first in sin his doom applied,
Though in mysterious° terms, judged as then best   *symbolic, allegorical*
And on the Serpent thus his curse let fall:
   "Because thou hast done this, thou art accursed 175
Above all cattle, each beast of the field;
Upon thy belly groveling thou shalt go
And dust shalt eat all the days of thy life.
Between thee and the woman I will put
Enmity, and between thine and her seed: 180
Her seed shall bruise thy head, thou bruise his heel."
   So spake this oracle, then verified
When Jesus, son of Mary, second Eve,
Saw Satan fall like lightning down from Heaven,

---

162. *The serpent . . . eat:* echoes Gen. 3:13: "The serpent beguiled me, and I did eat"; cf. Eve's single line of explanation with Adam's nineteen (lines 125–43).

165. *unable:* who was unable; i.e., the serpent is unable (though the syntax might initially suggest that the inability is God's).

166. *him . . . him:* Satan . . . the serpent

167–168. *end Of his creation:* purpose of the serpent's creation

168–169. *justly . . . nature:* The claim is that the serpent deserves his punishment since his nature has been corrupted (*vitiated*). The logic seems to follow Lev. 20:15–16, where it is said that if a man or woman "lie[s] with beast" not only should the human sinner "be put to death" but also

"ye shall slay the beast," punishing, in Andrew Willet's words, "the instrument with the principal" (*Hexapla* [1608], p. 52).

169–170. *More . . . knew:* i.e., Adam and Eve could not evaluate the justice of this act without *further* knowledge of the fulfillment of God's redemptive plan (not fully understood by them until 12.598–605 and 12.623).

171. *his:* i.e., man's

175–181. *Because . . . heel:* The oracle almost exactly echoes Gen. 3:14–15.

183. *Mary, second Eve:* See 5.386–87.

184. *Satan . . . Heaven:* In Luke 10:18, Jesus beholds "Satan as lightning fall from heaven," the fulfillment of the prophecy that the seed of the woman should bruise the serpent's head (line 181).

Prince of the air; then, rising from his grave,   185
Spoiled° principalities and powers, triumphed   *defeated*
In open show, and, with ascension bright,
Captivity led captive through the air,
The realm itself of Satan long usurped,
Whom he shall tread at last under our feet,   190
Even he who now foretold his° fatal bruise,   *Satan's*
And to the woman thus his sentence turned:
    "Thy sorrow I will greatly multiply
By thy conception; children thou shalt bring
In sorrow forth, and to thy husband's will   195
Thine shall submit: he over thee shall rule."
    On Adam last thus judgment he pronounced:
"Because thou hast hearkened to the voice of thy wife
And eaten of the tree concerning which
I charged thee, saying: 'Thou shalt not eat thereof,'   200
Cursèd is the ground for thy sake; thou in sorrow
Shalt eat thereof all the days of thy life;
Thorns also and thistles it shall bring thee forth
Unbid, and thou shalt eat the herb of the field.
In the sweat of thy face shalt thou eat bread   205
Till thou return unto the ground, for thou
Out of the ground wast taken: know thy birth,
For dust thou art and shalt to dust return."
    So judged he man, both judge and savior sent,
And the instant stroke of death, denounced that day,   210
Removed far off; then pitying how they stood
Before him naked to the air that now

185. *Prince of the air:* See 1.516, where the demons "ruled the middle air." In Eph. 2:2, Satan is called the "prince of the power of the air."   *his:* Christ's (though after "fall" in line 184 easily misread as Satan *rising*)

186–188. *Spoiled . . . air:* The terms of victory blend Ps. 68:18: "Thou hast ascended on high, thou hast led captivity captive," with Paul's prophecy of Christ's "having spoiled principalities and powers" and "triumphing over them" (Col. 2:15).

190. *he . . . feet:* Echoes Paul in Rom. 16:20: "And the god of peace shall bruise Satan under your feet shortly" and in 1 Cor. 15:25: "For he must reign, till he hath put all enemies under his feet."

196. *over thee shall rule:* In terms of the poem's much debated gender politics, one must ask, is this a reassertion of their unfallen condition in Eden or a further effect of the fall? In *Christian Doctrine* I, x, Milton writes: "The power of the husband was even increased after the fall" (*Works* 15, 121).

198–208. *Because . . . return:* Milton here almost exactly follows Gen. 3:17–19.

210. *denounced:* pronounced (as a sentence)

Must suffer change, disdained not to begin
Thenceforth the form of servant to assume,
As when he washed his servants' feet, so now,   215
As father of his family, he clad
Their nakedness with skins of beasts, or slain
Or, as the snake, with youthful coat repaid,
And thought not much to clothe his enemies.
Nor he their outward only with the skins   220
Of beasts but inward nakedness, much more
Opprobrious, with his robe of righteousness
Arraying, covered from his Father's sight.
To him with swift ascent he up returned,
Into his blissful bosom reassumed   225
In glory as of old. To him, appeased,
All, though all-knowing, what had passed with man
Recounted, mixing intercession sweet.
Meanwhile, ere thus was sinned and judged on earth,
Within the gates of hell sat Sin and Death,   230
In counterview within the gates that now
Stood open wide, belching outrageous flame
Far into chaos since the fiend passed through,
Sin opening, who thus now to Death began:
    "O Son, why sit we here each other viewing   235
Idly, while Satan, our great author, thrives

213. *change:* refers both to Adam and Eve, standing "before him [i.e., Christ] naked," who now *Must suffer change,* and, more immediately to the "air"; see lines 692–706: the description of the "changes in the heavens . . . [that] produced / Like changes on sea and land."

213–215. *disdained . . . feet:* Gen. 3:21, says that "Unto Adam and also to his wife did the Lord God make coats of skins and clothed them," but Milton thought also of Christ's taking "upon him the form of a servant" (Phil. 2:7) and washing the feet of the disciples (John 13:5).

217–218. *or slain . . . repaid:* i.e., either (*or*) beasts were slain for their pelts or survived the natural loss (like a molting *snake*), and were *repaid* with a new skin

219. *thought not much:* was not concerned   *enemies:* i.e., Adam and Eve (*enemies* because their sin demands his sacrifice)

220. *outward:* i.e., outward nakedness

222. *robe of righteousness:* quoting Isa. 61:10; cf. 9.1058: the "robe" of "shame."

226. *appeased:* God is *appeased,* syntactically before the events are "Recounted" (line 228), but of course, as God is "all-knowing" (line 227), not before he knows "what had passed" (line 227).

227. *All:* everything that took place, the direct object of "Recounted" (line 228)

231. *In counterview:* facing each other (as Sin and Death sit "Before the gates" in 2.648–49)

232. *open wide:* In 2.871–84, Sin opens the gates but "to shut / Excelled her power."

234. *opening:* i.e.,"the gates" (line 231)

In other worlds and happier seat° provides   *home*
For us, his offspring dear? It cannot be
But that success attends him; if mishap,
Ere this he had returned with fury driven   240
By his avengers, since no place like° this   *as well as*
Can fit his punishment or their revenge.
Methinks I feel new strength within me rise,
Wings growing, and dominion given me large
Beyond this deep; whatever draws me on,   245
Or sympathy or some connatural force
Powerful at greatest distance to unite
With secret amity things of like kind
By secretest conveyance. Thou, my shade
Inseparable, must° with me along,   *must go*
For Death from Sin no power can separate.
But lest the difficulty of passing back
Stay° his return perhaps over this gulf   *delay*
Impassable, impervious,° let us try   *impenetrable*
Adventurous work, yet to thy power and mine   255
Not unagreeable, to found° a path   *build*
Over this main from hell to that new world
Where Satan now prevails, a monument
Of merit high to all the infernal host,
Easing their passage hence, for intercourse   260
Or transmigration as their lot shall lead.
Nor can I miss the way, so strongly drawn
By this new felt attraction and instinct."
     Whom thus the meager shadow answered soon:
"Go whither fate and inclination strong   265
Leads thee; I shall not lag behind nor err°   *wander from*
The way, thou leading, such a scent I draw°   *smell, inhale*
Of carnage, prey innumerable, and taste
The savor of death from all things there that live.

---

239. *mishap:* i.e., he had failed

246. *Or . . . force:* i.e., either an intense affinity (see the "wondrous sympathy" in the Argument) or some innate (*connatural*) attractive force (like magnetism)

249. *conveyance:* communication, transmission

257. *main:* the sea of chaos over which Satan voyages in 2.919   *new world:*

See also line 377 below, and 2.403 and 2.867; the references to earth as the *new world* make Satan history's earliest colonial adventurer (see also 9.1116–118).

260–261. *intercourse Or transmigration:* back and forth traffic (as at 2.1031) or one-way emigration

264. *meager:* emaciated (since, before the fall, there was nothing for Death to feed upon)

Nor shall I to the work thou enterprisest°　　　　　　　*undertake*
Be wanting but afford thee equal aid."
　　So saying, with delight he snuffed the smell
Of mortal change on earth. As when a flock
Of ravenous fowl, though many a league remote,
Against° the day of battle to a field　　　　　　　　　*awaiting*
Where armies lie encamped come flying, lured
With scent of living carcasses designed°　　　　　　　*marked out*
For death the following day in bloody fight,
So scented the grim feature° and upturned　　　　　*shape, creature*
His nostril wide into the murky air,　　　　　　　　　　280
Sagacious of his quarry from so far.
Then both from out hell gates into the waste
Wide anarchy of chaos damp and dark
Flew diverse° and with power (their power was great)　　*in different directions*
Hovering upon the waters; what they met　　　　　　　285
Solid or slimy, as in raging sea
Tossed up and down, together crowded drove
From each side shoaling toward the mouth of hell,
As when two polar winds blowing adverse°　　　　*from opposite directions*
Upon the Cronian Sea together drive　　　　　　　　　290
Mountains of ice that stop the imagined way
Beyond Pechora eastward to the rich
Cathayan coast. The aggregated soil
Death with his mace petrific, cold and dry,
As with a trident smote and fixed as firm　　　　　　295
As Delos floating once; the rest his look

274. *ravenous fowl:* birds of prey
281. *Sagacious of:* sensing, smelling
282–305. *Then both . . . hell:* a grim
travesty of God's creative powers in the sev-
enth book, here undertaken by birds of prey
"Hovering upon the waters," parodying the
creation, which began when "on the watery
calm / His brooding wings the spirit of God
outspread" (7.234–35).
288. *shoaling:* forming into a solid mass
290. *the Cronian Sea:* the Arctic Ocean
291. *the imagined way:* the long-sought
northeast sea passage to China for which
Henry Hudson vainly searched in 1608
292. *Pechora:* an important river in
Russia rising in the northern Urals and emp-
tying into the Barents Sea

293. *Cathayan coast:* The coast of
Cathay, in what is now northeastern China,
but which was in Milton's time distinguished
as a separate country; see "Cathayan Khan"
in 11.388.
294. *mace petrific:* Death's scepter that
turns things to stone; cf. Marlowe's *Tragedy
of Dido* (1594): "pale death's stony mace
(2.1.114); but *petrific* inevitably suggests
Peter, "this rock" (Matt. 16:18) upon which
the Catholic Church is built, the basis of
papal authority; the *mace* also stands as a
recognizable symbol of royal power.
cold and dry modify "soil" in line 293, not
mace
296. *Delos floating once:* To provide a
safe place where his lover Latona could give

Bound with Gorgonian rigor not to move
And with asphaltic slime. Broad as the gate,
Deep to the roots of hell the gathered beach
They fastened, and the mole° immense wrought on   *causeway, pier*
Over the foaming deep high-arched, a bridge
Of length prodigious joining to the wall
Immovable of this now fenceless° world   *defenseless (against death)*
Forfeit to Death; from hence a passage broad,
Smooth, easy, inoffensive, down to hell.   305
So, if great things to small may be compared,
Xerxes, the liberty of Greece to yoke,
From Susa, his Memnonian palace high,
Came to the sea and, over Hellespont
Bridging his way, Europe with Asia joined   310
And scourged with many a stroke the indignant waves.
Now had they brought the work by wondrous art
Pontifical, a ridge of pendent rock
Over the vexed abyss, following the track
Of Satan to the selfsame place where he   315
First lighted from his wing and landed safe
From out of chaos to the outside bare

birth to his children (Apollo and Artemis), Jupiter anchored ("fixed," line 295) the island of *Delos,* which had formerly *floated* freely in the Aegean (see Callimachus, *Hymns* 4.31); a type of Eden, which also gets used in various Restoration idealizations of England (for Milton no more true than the Greek myth). *the rest:* i.e., the rest of the elemental humors, hot and moist (see "cold and dry" in line 294).

297. *Gorgonian rigor:* the stone to which people were turned at the look of one of the snaky-haired Gorgons

298. *asphaltic slime:* pitch, tar

299. *gathered beach:* accumulated sand ("The aggregated soil" of line 293) used for the foundation of the bridge

302. *the wall:* the boundary of the created universe (see 2.1023–30)

305. *inoffensive:* unobstructed (but also "not giving offense")

306. *if great . . . compared:* a familiar

classical *topos;* see also *PL* 2.258, 2.921–22, and 6.310–11.

307–311. *Xerxes . . . waves:* Xerxes, the King of Persia, had the waves whipped after they broke the bridge of ships he had set up in the Hellespont, the strait between the European and Asiatic shores of the Dardanelles; see Lucan, *Pharsalia* 2.672–77.

308. *Susa:* The biblical Shushan, winter capital of the Persian kings, was putatively founded by Tithonus, the mythical lover of Aurora, with whom he had a son, Memnon, after whom the palace was named.

313. *Pontifical:* literally, bridge-building, but its ecclesiastical meaning, "papal," is unavoidable. (The pope is *pontifical* because his office is to build a bridge between this world and Heaven; Milton's view of this is obvious.)

314. *vexed:* tossed about, harried by storms

315. *selfsame place:* Satan lights on "the firm opacous globe" in 3.418–22.

Of this round world. With pins of adamant
And chains they made all fast,° too fast they made   *secure, firmly fastened*
And durable; and now in little space   320
The confines met of empyrean Heaven
And of this world, and on the left hand hell
With long reach interposed: three several ways
In sight to each of these three places led.
And now their way to earth they had descried,   325
To Paradise first tending, when behold
Satan, in likeness of an angel bright,
Betwixt the Centaur and the Scorpion steering
His zenith, while the Sun in Aries rose.
Disguised he came, but those his children dear   330
Their parent soon discerned though in disguise.
He, after Eve seduced, unminded° slunk   *unnoticed*
Into the wood fast by and, changing shape
To observe the sequel,° saw his guileful act   *consequence*
By Eve, though all unweeting,° seconded   *unaware, unsuspecting*
Upon her husband, saw their shame that sought
Vain covertures; but when he saw descend
The Son of God to judge them, terrified
He fled, not hoping to escape but shun
The present, fearing, guilty, what his° wrath   *i.e., Christ's*
Might suddenly inflict; that past, returned
By night and, listening where the hapless pair
Sat in their sad discourse and various plaint,
Thence gathered his own doom, which understood

320–324. *now . . . led:* Now there are *three* passage ways: the *confines* (shared boundaries) that previously existed at the bottom end of the stairway that unite the empyrean Heaven to the universe in 3.510 and the passage inside the universe, down to the earth (3.526–28), joined now by the causeway that Sin and Death have built (*on the left hand,* because of the Latin *sinister,* which dominated the iconography of evil; see Matt. 25:33 and 41).

328–329. *Betwixt . . . rose:* Satan flies between Sagittarius and Scorpio (having entered in Libra at 3.558), probably, as Fowler suggests, because that area of the sky is dom-

inated by the constellation Ophiuchus, the Serpent Bearer (see 2.708–11), or merely because it is far from the rising sun.

332. *after Eve seduced:* after the seduction of Eve; cf. 1.573 for the same Latinate construction.

335. *seconded:* repeated

337. *covertures:* coverings; the garments made of leaves in 9.1110–113, but also pointing to the excuses and evasions of lines 116–42 above.

344–345. *which . . . time:* i.e., when he (i.e., Satan) understood that his punishment would not occur immediately but in the future; see lines 1030–37 below.

Not instant but of future time. With joy   345
And tidings fraught to hell he now returned
And at the brink of chaos, near the foot
Of this new wondrous pontifice, unhoped ·
Met who to meet him came, his offspring dear.
Great joy was at their meeting, and at sight   350
Of that stupendous bridge his joy increased.
Long he admiring stood, till Sin, his fair
Enchanting daughter, thus the silence broke:
    "O parent, these are thy magnific deeds,
Thy trophies, which thou view'st as not thine own;   355
Thou art their author and prime architect,
For I no sooner in my heart divined—
My heart, which by a secret harmony
Still° moves with thine, joined in connection sweet—   *always*
That thou on earth hadst prospered, which thy looks   360
Now also evidence, but straight I felt,
Though distant from thee worlds between, yet felt
That I must after thee with this thy son,
Such fatal consequence unites us three.
Hell could no longer hold us in her bounds,   365
Nor this unvoyageable gulf obscure
Detain from following thy illustrious track.
Thou hast achieved our liberty, confined
Within hell gates till now, thou us empowered
To fortify thus far and overlay   370
With this portentous bridge the dark abyss.
Thine now is all this world; thy virtue° hath won   *ability*
What thy hands builded not; thy wisdom gained
With odds° what war hath lost and fully avenged   *additional benefit*
Our foil° in Heaven. Here thou shalt monarch reign,   *defeat*
There, didst not; there let him still victor sway
As battle hath adjudged, from this new world
Retiring, by his own doom° alienated,   *judgment*
And henceforth monarchy with thee divide

345–346. *joy . . . fraught:* joyful tidings
laden
    347. *foot:* bottom of the slope of the
bridge ("pontifice," but see line 313 and
note) leading to the universe from hell
    358. *secret harmony:* i.e., the "sympa-
thy" of line 246 above

364. *fatal consequence:* deadly connection
    370. *fortify:* construct (what amounts
to a military road)
    371. *portentous:* immense (but also
ominous)
    379. *monarchy with thee divide:* by defi-
nition *monarchy* (literally, rule by one) can-

Of all things, parted by the empyreal bounds,   380
His quadrature from thy orbicular° world,   *round*
Or try° thee now more dangerous to his throne."   *find through experience*
      Whom thus the prince of darkness answered glad:
"Fair daughter and thou, son and grandchild both,
High proof ye now have given to be the race   385
Of Satan (for I glory in the name,
Antagonist of Heaven's almighty king)
Amply have merited of me, of all
The infernal empire, that so near Heaven's door
Triumphal with triumphal act have met,   390
Mine with this glorious work, and made one realm
Hell and this world, one realm, one continent°   *continuous tract of land*
Of easy thoroughfare. Therefore while I
Descend through darkness on your road with ease
To my associate powers, them to acquaint   395
With these successes and with them rejoice,
You two this way, among these numerous orbs
All yours, right down to Paradise descend;
There dwell and reign in bliss, thence on the earth
Dominion exercise and in the air,   400
Chiefly on man, sole lord of all declared:
Him first make sure your thrall and lastly kill.
My substitutes I send ye and create
Plenipotent on earth, of matchless might
Issuing from me. On your joint vigor now   405
My hold of this new kingdom all depends,
Through Sin to Death exposed by my exploit.

not be divided; see 4.111: "Divided empire
with Heaven's king I hold."

381. *quadrature:* Heaven is "foursquare,"
as in Rev. 21:16.

383. *prince of darkness:* Ephesians 6:12
speaks of the "rulers of the darkness of this
world" ("princes" in the Geneva translation);
see also *All's Well That Ends Well* 4.5.42–43:
"the prince of darkness, alias the devil."

384. *son and grandchild:* Death is Satan's
son, but since his mother is Satan's daughter,
he is also Satan's *grandchild.*

386–387. *Of Satan . . . king: Satan* in
Hebrew means "adversary" or "*Antagonist.*"
This is the only time he uses his name. There is

irony at Satan's expense in having him claim
to be the antagonist of the "almighty king."

390. *Triumphal . . . met:* Satan's tri-
umph in Eden is matched by the triumphal
work of Sin and Death, their bridge imag-
ined as a triumphal arch like those erected
for royal entries (as for that of the restored
Charles II).

400. *Dominion exercise:* a Satanic par-
ody of God's gift to mankind of *Dominion*
over the earth; see 7.531–34.

402. *make sure your thrall:* keep your
victims firmly enslaved (by their sin)

404. *Plenipotent:* with full power and
authority (see lines 56–57 above)

If your joint power prevails, the affairs of hell
No detriment need fear; go and be strong."
    So saying he dismissed them; they with speed   410
Their course through thickest constellations held,
Spreading their bane; the blasted stars looked wan,
And planets, planet-struck, real eclipse
Then suffered. The other way Satan went down
The causey to hell gate; on either side   415
Disparted Chaos over-built° exclaimed   *built over*
And with rebounding surge the bars assailed
That scorned his indignation. Through the gate,
Wide open and unguarded, Satan passed
And all about found desolate, for those   420
Appointed to sit there had left their charge,
Flown to the upper world; the rest were all
Far to the inland retired about the walls
Of Pandaemonium, city and proud seat
Of Lucifer, so by allusion° called   *metaphor*
Of that bright star to Satan paragoned.
There kept their watch the legions, while the grand
In council sat, solicitous° what chance   *anxious about*
Might intercept their emperor sent, so he
Departing gave command and they observed.°   *obeyed*
As when the Tartar from his Russian foe
By Astrakhan over the snowy plains

409. *detriment:* harm; Milton is thinking of a formula used in giving Roman consuls supreme power in crises to protect Rome against all *detriment* (*detrimentum*) or injury.

412. *bane:* poison (which, breathed upon the *stars*, leaves them "blasted" ([i.e., diminished, weakened]; hence "wan")

413. *planet-struck:* adversely affected by the influence of a planet; the withering effects of adverse planets are now applied to the planets themselves.   *real eclipse:* actually effaced instead of merely seeming to be effaced from the vantage of the earth

415. *causey:* causeway; i.e., the "mole immense," or bridge, in line 300 above.

416. *Disparted:* divided (by the bridge)

420. *those:* i.e., Sin and Death

424. *Pandaemonium:* literally, home of all the demons; the city built in hell in 1.670 ff.

426. *bright star . . . paragoned:* The *bright star* is Lucifer (or Venus), the light-bringing morning star (cf. 7.132–33); *paragoned* = compared

427. *the grand:* the "great consulting peers" at line 456 below; the same as the "seraphic lords and cherubim" who sat in "secret conclave" in the "infernal court" at 1.791–97.

431–433. *the Tartar . . . Retires:* Milton is probably recalling accounts of the army of the Tartars as it retreated (*Retires*) through *Astrakhan,* near the mouth of the Volga, after it was defeated by Ivan the Terrible in 1556.

Retires, or Bactrian Sophy, from the horns
Of Turkish crescent, leaves all waste beyond
The realm of Aladule in his retreat   435
To Tauris or Casbeen, so these, the late
Heaven-banished host, left desert° utmost hell   *empty*
Many a dark league, reduced in careful watch
Round their metropolis and now expecting
Each hour their great adventurer from the search   440
Of foreign worlds. He through the midst unmarked,
In show plebeian° angel militant   *ordinary*
Of lowest order, passed and, from the door
Of that Plutonian hall, invisible
Ascended his high throne, which, under state   445
Of richest texture spread, at the upper end
Was placed in regal luster. Down awhile
He sat and round about him saw, unseen.°   *himself out of sight*
At last, as from a cloud, his fulgent head
And shape star-bright appeared, or brighter, clad   450
With what permissive glory since his fall
Was left him, or false glitter. All amazed
At that so-sudden blaze, the Stygian throng
Bent their aspect, and whom they wished, beheld:
Their mighty chief returned. Loud was the acclaim.   455
Forth rushed in haste the great consulting peers,
Raised from their dark divan, and with like joy

433–436. *Bactrian Sophy . . . Casbeen:* Milton's example here is of the Persian Shah (*Bactrian Sophy;* Bactria was a principality of Persia in what is modern Afghanistan), probably Uzun Hasan, who in 1474 was defeated by the Turks (whose symbol was the *crescent*) and fled east into what is now Northern Iran, to the cities of *Casbeen* (the modern Kazvin) and *Tauris* (the modern Tabriz), along the way plundering the lands of *Aladule* (Armenia, taking the name from Aladule, or Aladulus, the last King of Armenia before it was conquered by the Turks under Selimus I in 1514).

438. *reduced:* drawn together (the subject is "these" in line 436)

444. *Plutonian:* hellish (literally, of Pluto, ruler of the classical Roman underworld)

445. *state:* a canopy over a throne or chair of state, like Satan's in 2.1–4, where he is compared with a Turkish sultan, as he is again in lines 456–57 below

449. *fulgent:* resplendent (but seemingly an aphetic diminution of the true "effulgence" of Christ in 6.680); perhaps, then, here merely glittering

451. *permissive:* permitted (i.e., by God); cf. 1.211–13.

453. *Stygian throng:* i.e., the fallen angels (Styx is the river of hell); see the "Stygian council" in 2.506.

454. *Bent . . . beheld:* turned their gaze and saw (*beheld*) him (i.e., Satan), whom they hoped to see

457. *dark divan:* secret council; *divan,* the term used for the council of state in early Turkey, has given its name to the cushioned

Congratulant° approached him, who with hand,   *enthusiastically welcoming*
Silence, and with these words attention won:
    "Thrones, dominations, princedoms, virtues, powers,   460
For in possession such, not only of right,
I call ye and declare ye now, returned,
Successful beyond hope, to lead ye forth
Triumphant out of this infernal pit
Abominable, accursed, the house of woe,   465
And dungeon of our tyrant. Now possess
As lords a spacious world, to our native Heaven
Little inferior, by my adventure hard
With peril great achieved. Long were to tell
What I have done, what suffered, with what pain   470
Voyaged the unreal, vast, unbounded deep
Of horrible confusion, over which
By Sin and Death a broad way now is paved
To expedite your glorious march; but I
Toiled out my uncouth passage, forced to ride   475
The untractable abyss, plunged in the womb
Of unoriginal Night and Chaos wild,
That jealous of their secrets fiercely opposed
My journey strange with clamorous uproar
Protesting° fate supreme; thence how I found   *appealing to*
The new created world, which fame in Heaven
Long had foretold, a fabric° wonderful   *structure*

seats on which the councilors sat; both
meanings are present here.

    459. *won:* What is won is both "silence"
and "attention," the first by his hand gesture,
the latter with "words."

    461–462. *For . . . ye:* Satan calls them
by their old angelic titles (line 460), which
he had earlier seen as degraded because of
Christ's exaltation (5.772–76) and after their
revolt, were truly rendered "merely titular";
but now, he says, their titles again have
meaning, not only by their historical *right* to
them but also, with his success, by actual
possession (of the earth).

    463. *Successful beyond hope:* Satan means
that he was even more successful than it was
possible to hope for, but *beyond hope* is the
very definition of the theological despair that
damns the fallen angels.

    465. *house of woe:* echoes 6.877

    471. *the unreal . . . deep:* Cf. "the unap-
parent deep" in 7.103; its formlessness makes
it *unreal,* even as it is *vast* and *unbounded.*

    473. *a broad way:* derives from Matt.
7:13: "broad is the way, that leadeth to de-
struction."

    475. *uncouth passage:* voyage into the
unknown

    476. *untractable:* intractable, unman-
ageable, difficult to negotiate

    476–480. *plunged . . . supreme:* Satan's
account here is, unsurprisingly, false: Night
does not oppose him, and Chaos helps him
on his way in 2.999–1009.

    477. *unoriginal:* without beginning or
origin; Night, which in 2.962 is "eldest of
things," is *unoriginal* because nothing existed
before it to originate it.

    481. *fame:* rumor (see 1.651–54)

Of absolute perfection, therein man
Placed in a Paradise, by our exile
Made happy. Him by fraud I have seduced   485
From his creator and, the more to increase
Your wonder, with an apple! He thereat
Offended, worth your laughter, hath given up
Both his beloved man and all his world
To Sin and Death a prey, and so to us,   490
Without our hazard, labor, or alarm,°   *call to battle*
To range in, and to dwell, and over man
To rule, as over all he should have ruled.
True is, me also he hath judged, or rather
Me not, but the brute serpent in whose shape   495
Man I deceived; that which to me belongs
Is enmity which he will put between
Me and mankind: I am to bruise his heel;
His seed (when is not set) shall bruise my head.
A world who would not purchase with a bruise   500
Or much more grievous pain? Ye have the account
Of my performance. What remains, ye gods,
But up and enter now into full bliss?"
     So having said, awhile he stood, expecting
Their universal shout and high applause   505
To fill his ear, when contrary he hears
On all sides, from innumerable tongues,
A dismal universal hiss, the sound
Of public scorn; he wondered, but not long
Had leisure, wondering at himself now more;   510
His visage drawn° he felt to sharp and spare,   *contracted*

487. *apple:* Only Satan names the fruit (unidentified in Genesis) an *apple;* see 9.585 and note.

488. *Offended:* thwarted (stronger than its modern sense)

496. *that . . . belongs:* i.e., that which pertains to me

500. *A . . . bruise:* Satan is a literalist and misunderstands what *bruise* will mean; the formulation here is interestingly similar to the reports of Henri IV's abjuration of Protestantism in 1593: "Paris is well worth a mass" (*Paris vaut bien une messe*).

503. *bliss:* Ironically, the last word that Satan speaks in the poem, its promise imme-
diately undercut by the anticipation of the "dismal universal hiss" in line 508 below.

508–509. *dismal . . . scorn:* As many critics have noted the alliterative *s*'s here create a hissing sound.

511–520. *His visage . . . serpents:* The episode is indebted to Ovid's account of the metamorphosis of Cadmus into a serpent in *Metamorphoses* 4.575–80: "His belly lengthned, . . . Tough scales upon his hardned outside grew; . . . / Then, falling on his breast, his thighs unite; / And in a spiny progresse stretch out-right" (trans. Sandys).

511. *sharp and spare:* pointed and thin

His arms clung to his ribs, his legs entwining
Each other, till supplanted° down he fell,   *tripped up, overthrown*
A monstrous serpent on his belly prone,
Reluctant, but in vain; a greater power   515
Now ruled him, punished in the shape he sinned,
According to his doom.° He would have spoke,   *judgment, punishment*
But hiss for hiss returned with forkèd tongue
To forkèd tongue, for now were all transformed
Alike to serpents, all as accessories   520
To his bold riot.° Dreadful was the din   *revolt*
Of hissing through the hall, thick swarming now
With complicated monsters head and tail,
Scorpion and asp and amphisbaena dire,
Cerastes horned, hydrus, and ellops drear,   525
And dipsas (not so thick swarmed once the soil
Bedropped with blood of Gorgon, or the Isle
Ophiusa). But still greatest he the midst,
Now dragon grown, larger than whom the sun
Engendered in the Pythian vale on slime,   530
Huge python, and his power no less he seemed

515. *Reluctant:* stronger than its usual sense, emphasizing its Latin root *reluctans* = struggling, resisting (see also 2.337)

523. *complicated:* intertwined, tangled (and also writhing); that is, the serpents as a group are *complicated,* and also each individual is.

524–532. *Scorpion . . . retain:* Milton's catalogue of serpents echoes Lucan's digression in Book 9 of the *Pharsalia,* where he tells of the serpents that spring from the blood dripping from the severed head of Medusa (lines 698–733); also see lines 526–27 below; most of these are also mentioned by Pliny, *History of the World* (1601, trans. Philemon Holland, p. 434).

524. *amphisbaena:* a mythical serpent with a head at each end (the name means "moving both ways")

525. *Cerastes . . . drear: Cerastes* was supposedly a four-horned snake; *hydrus,* an aggressive water snake capable of killing crocodiles; the *ellops,* a dreadful (*drear*) ser-

pent, like most of these, named by Pliny (see 524–532n) as a "venomous beast."

526. *dipsas:* Often known as the "thirst snake," its bite produced unquenchable thirst.

528. *Ophiusa:* The name means "full of snakes" and was a name given by the Greeks to various snake-filled islands, including modern Formentera, in the Balearic Islands off the coast of Spain, as well as several islands, including Rhodes, in the Aegean.

529. *Now dragon grown:* See Rev. 12:9: "the great dragon was cast out, that old serpent, called the Devil, and Satan." In *The Purple Island* (1633), Phineas Fletcher describes the rebel angels being "turn'd to serpents" and "their Prince" falling as "a Dragon" (7.11).

530–531. *Engendered . . . python:* Ovid tells the story of the engendering of the giant serpent *python* out of *slime* left from the flood, and its eventual destruction by the thousand arrows shot by Apollo, the sun god (*Metamorphoses* 1.438–44), anticipating Christ's victory over Satan.

Above the rest still to retain; they all
Him followed, issuing forth to the open field,
Where all yet left of that revolted rout,
Heaven-fallen, in station stood or just array   535
Sublime with expectation when to see
In triumph issuing forth their glorious chief.
They saw, but other sight instead: a crowd
Of ugly serpents. Horror on them fell
And horrid sympathy, for what they saw,   540
They felt themselves now changing:° down their arms,   *changing into, becoming*
Down fell both spear and shield, down they as fast,
And the dire hiss renewed; and the dire form
Catched° by contagion, like in punishment,   *caught*
As in their crime. Thus was the applause they meant   545
Turned to exploding hiss, triumph to shame
Cast on themselves from their own mouths. There stood
A grove hard° by, sprung up with this their change,   *near*
(His will who reigns above, to aggravate
Their penance°) laden with fair fruit like that   *punishment*
Which grew in Paradise, the bait of Eve
Used by the tempter. On that prospect° strange   *sight*
Their earnest eyes they fixed, imagining
For° one forbidden tree a multitude   *in place of*
Now risen to work them further woe or shame;   555
Yet parched with scalding thirst and hunger fierce,
Though to delude them sent, could not abstain,
But on they rolled in heaps and, up the trees
Climbing, sat thicker than the snaky locks
That curled Megaera. Greedily they plucked   560
The fruitage fair to sight, like that which grew
Near that bituminous lake where Sodom flamed;

---

535. *in station . . . just array:* stood at
their posts or arrayed in orderly ranks
536. *Sublime:* upraised (in both body
and spirit)
544. *like:* alike
546. *exploding:* not just "bursting
forth," but specifically a theatrical word
meaning "jeering" or "hissing" (from a nega-
tion of the Latin *plaudere* = to clap; see "ap-
plause" in line 545).   *triumph to
shame:* See Hosea 4:7: "they sinned against

me: therefore will I change their glory into
shame."
551. *bait of:* enticement for
560. *Megaera:* one of the furies, the
snake-haired goddesses of Greek mythology
who avenge crime; cf. 2.596 and line 620
and notes below.
562. *bituminous lake . . . flamed:* i.e.,
the Dead Sea near the city of Sodom, which, as
Josephus writes, "for the impiety of its inhabi-
tants, was burnt by lightning" (*Wars* 4.8.4)

This, more delusive, not the touch but taste
Deceived; they fondly° thinking to allay   *foolishly*
Their appetite with gust,° instead of fruit   *keen relish, gusto*
Chewed bitter ashes, which the offended taste
With spattering noise rejected; oft they assayed,
Hunger and thirst constraining; drugged° as oft,   *nauseated*
With hatefullest disrelish writhed their jaws
With soot and cinders filled; so oft they fell   .   570
Into the same illusion, not as man,
Whom they triumphed once lapsed. Thus were they plagued
And worn, with famine long and ceaseless hiss,
Till their lost shape, permitted, they resumed,
Yearly enjoined, some say, to undergo   575
This annual humbling certain numbered days
To dash their pride and joy for man seduced.
However some tradition they dispersed
Among the heathen of their purchase got,
And fabled how the serpent, whom they called   580
Ophion, with Eurynome (the wide-
Encroaching Eve, perhaps) had first the rule
Of high Olympus, thence by Saturn driven

565–566. *instead . . . ashes:* See *Eiko-noklastes:* "These pious flourishes . . . are like the Apples of *Asphaetis*, appearing goodly to the sudden eye, but look well upon them, or at least touch them, and they turne into Cinders" (*Works* 5, 263).

566–570. *Chewed . . . filled:* reflects Gen. 3:14: "And the Lord God said unto the serpent . . . dust shalt thou eat all the days of thy life"; and Isa. 65:25: "dust shall be the serpent's meat." Naturalists, like Edward Topsell, in his *History of Serpents* (1608), however, knew that serpents "are *Omniuori*, deuorers of flesh, fish, herbs, or any other thinges" (p. 16).

572. *triumphed:* triumphed over, vanquished   *once lapsed:* 1) sinned only once; 2) at the moment he sinned

574. *permitted:* by God; see line 451 above.

576. *annual humbling:* their yearly return to serpent shape

577. *man seduced:* having seduced man

578–579. *some tradition . . . got:* ac-cording to some traditions that the devils (*they*) spread among the *heathen* people about their success (*purchase got* = acquisition gained)

580–583. *fabled . . . Olympus:* told stories about how Satan and Eve were the first rulers of Heaven, though the Greeks called them Ophion and Eurynome

580. *they:* "the heathen" people (line 579; i.e., the Greeks)

581. *Ophion, with Eurynome:* In the *Argonautica* 1.503–6, Apollonius recounts how Olympus was ruled by *Ophion* ("the serpent") and his wife *Eurynome* (literally "wide-ruling" or "wide-Encroaching") until the Titans were overthrown by Saturn and his wife Rhea, whom Milton calls "Ops" (line 584).

581–582. *the wide-Encroaching Eve, perhaps:* i.e., Eve, who is *perhaps* herself *wide-Encroaching* (as her transgression affected the totality of the human race, which descends from her); *wide-Encroaching*, spread over two lines, enacts a visual pun.

And Ops ere yet Dictaean Jove was born.
Meanwhile in Paradise the hellish pair   585
Too soon arrived: Sin there in power before,
Once actual, now in body and to dwell
Habitual habitant; behind her Death
Close following pace for pace, not mounted yet
On his pale horse, to whom Sin thus began: 590
    "Second of Satan sprung, all-conquering Death,
What think'st thou of our empire now, though earned
With travail difficult? Not better far
Than still at hell's dark threshold to have sat watch,
Unnamed, undreaded, and thyself half starved?"   595
    Whom thus the Sin-born monster answered soon:
"To me, who with eternal famine pine,
Alike is hell or Paradise or Heaven,
There best where most with ravin° I may meet,   *prey*
Which here, though plenteous, all too little seems   600
To stuff this maw, this vast unhidebound corpse."
    To whom the incestuous mother thus replied:
"Thou, therefore, on these herbs and fruits and flowers
Feed first, on each beast next, and fish and fowl,
No homely morsels, and whatever thing   605
The scythe of Time mows down devour unspared,
Till I, in man residing through the race,
His thoughts, his looks, words, actions, all infect
And season him thy last and sweetest prey."
    This said, they both betook them several° ways,   *separate*

584. *Dictaean Jove:* Jove, who was from Dicte, the mountain in Crete (see 1.515) on which he grew up

586–588. *Sin . . . habitant:* Sin was in Eden and *in power* from the moment Adam and Eve transgressed (*once actual;* see *Christian Doctrine* I, xi, which defines "actual sin" as "the crime itself, or the act of sinning" (*Works* 15, 199), but now is physically present on earth (*in body*) and will remain potent (*Habitual habitant*).

590. *his pale horse:* follows Rev. 6:8: "And I looked, and behold a pale horse; and his name that sat on him was Death, and Hell followed with him."

593. *travail:* both hard work (*travail*) and travel

595. *Unnamed:* Death is named in 2.787–89, but the name is not known until God "pronounced it" in 4.427 *undreaded:* because till now unknown

601. *unhidebound:* loose-skinned (because in need of food, which, with the fall, will now be in abundance)

605. *No homely:* i.e., choice, appealing (not available in hell)

606. *scythe of Time:* familiar emblem of devouring time (see Shakespeare, Sonnet 12: "nothing 'gainst time's scythe can make defence"); but the idea that time destroys

Both to destroy or unimmortal make
All kinds,° and for destruction to mature   *species*
Sooner or later, which, the almighty seeing,
From his transcendent seat the saints among,
To those bright orders uttered thus his voice: 615
    "See with what heat these dogs of hell advance
To waste and havoc yonder world, which I
So fair and good created, and had still
Kept in that state had not the folly of man
Let in these wasteful furies who impute   620
Folly to me (so doth the prince of hell
And his adherents), that° with so much ease   *because*
I suffer them to enter and possess
A place so heavenly, and, conniving, seem
To gratify my scornful enemies,   625
That laugh as if, transported with some fit
Of passion, I to them had quitted° all,   *surrendered, handed over*
At random yielded up to their misrule—
And know not that I called and drew them thither,
My hellhounds, to lick up the draff° and filth   *dregs, swill*
Which man's polluting sin with taint hath shed
On what was pure, till, crammed and gorged, nigh burst
With sucked and glutted offal, at one sling
Of thy victorious arm, well-pleasing Son,
Both Sin and Death and yawning grave, at last   635
Through chaos hurled, obstruct the mouth of hell
Forever and seal up his ravenous jaws.
Then heaven and earth renewed shall be made pure

---

contrasts with Raphael's optimistic view in
5.493–500.
    611. *unimmortal make:* make mortal,
though the double negative in *unimmortal* is
a reminder of the original condition (and
one of a series of negative compounds begin-
ning in line 595 that reveal the essential neg-
ativity of Sin and Death, as opposed to the
fundamental creativity of God)
    615. *orders:* i.e., orders (ranks) of angels
    617. *havoc:* ravage, devastate; often it was
used as a battle cry (see *Julius Caesar* 3.1.273:
"Cry 'havoc' and let slip the dogs of war").
    620. *furies:* avenging spirits, the name
derived from the classical furies, or Eu-

menides, as in Aeschylus' play of that name.
Du Bartas' *Divine Weeks and Works* (1608,
trans. Sylvester), includes "The Furies" (2.1),
on the results of the fall.
    624. *conniving:* overlooking, pretend-
ing ignorance
    626–627. *transported . . . passion:* modi-
fies "I" (not "enemies")
    633. *sling:* Cf. 1 Sam. 25:29: "The
souls of thine enemies, them shall he sling
out, as out of the middle of a sling."
    638–639. *heaven . . . stain:* Milton's po-
etic version of the apocalyptic purification in
Revelation 21.1: "And I saw a new heaven
and a new earth: for the first heaven and the

To sanctity that shall receive no stain;
Till then the curse pronounced on both precedes."   640
    He ended, and the heavenly audience loud
Sung "Hallelujah," as the sound of seas,
Through multitude that sung: "Just are thy ways,
Righteous are thy decrees on all thy works;
Who can extenuate° thee? Next, to the Son,   *disparage, belittle*
Destined restorer of mankind, by whom
New heaven and earth shall to the ages rise
Or down from Heaven descend." Such was their song,
While the creator calling forth by name
His mighty angels gave them several charge   650
As sorted° best with present things. The sun   *corresponded*
Had first his precept° so to move, so shine,   *order*
As might affect the earth with cold and heat
Scarce tolerable, and from the north to call
Decrepit winter, from the south to bring   655
Solstitial summer's heat. To the blank° moon   *pale*
Her office they prescribed, to the other five
Their planetary motions and aspects,
In sextile, square, and trine, and opposite,
Of noxious efficacy, and when to join   660
In synod° unbenign, and taught the fixed   *conjunction*

first earth had passed away; and there was no
more sea." In *Christian Doctrine* I, xxxiii
(*Works* 16, 368), Milton stated his faith in "a
new heaven and a new earth . . . coming
down from God out of heaven" and in the
"destruction of the present unclean and pol-
luted world."
    640. *both:* heaven and earth (see line
638); i.e., this universe now cursed with
mortality as a result of the fall, as in Henry
Vaughan's "Corruption": "He drew the curse
upon the world and cracked / The whole
frame with his fall" (lines 14–15).
precedes: takes precedence, remains in effect
    641–642. *heavenly . . . Sung:* Cf. "And I
heard as it were the voice of a great multi-
tude, and as the voice of many waters, . . .
saying 'Alleluia'" (Rev. 19:6); *loud* is both an
adjective (modifying *audience*) and an adverb
(modifying *Sung*).

    643–644. *Just . . . decrees:* See Revela-
tion 16:7: "true and righteous are thy judg-
ments."
    650. *several charge:* different duties
    657. *the other five:* the other five plan-
ets; see 5.177.
    659. *sextile . . . . opposite:* astrological
names for certain "aspects" (line 658) or an-
gles of any two planets in relation to the
earth: sextile = a 60° angle formed by two
imaginary lines drawn from each planet to
the earth; square = 90°; trine = 120°; oppo-
site = 180°.
    660. *Of noxious efficacy:* i.e., responsible
for various malign influences (though it isn't
clear if the phrase is intended to qualify only
"opposite" or all four of the "aspects" men-
tioned).
    661. *fixed:* i.e., fixed stars

Their influence malignant when to shower,
Which of them, rising with the sun or falling,
Should prove tempestuous. To the winds they set
Their corners, when with bluster to confound   665
Sea, air, and shore; the thunder when to roll
With terror through the dark aerial hall.
Some say he bid his angels turn askance
The poles of earth twice ten degrees and more
From the sun's axle; they with labor pushed   670
Oblique the centric globe. Some say the sun
Was bid turn reins from the equinoctial road
Like distant breadth to Taurus with the seven
Atlantic Sisters and the Spartan Twins
Up to the tropic Crab, thence down amain°   *quickly*
By Leo and the Virgin and the Scales,
As deep as Capricorn, to bring in change
Of seasons to each clime;° else had the spring   *region*
Perpetual smiled on earth with vernant flowers,
Equal in days and nights, except to those   680
Beyond the polar circles; to them day
Had unbenighted° shone, while the low sun,   *without night*
To recompense his distance, in their sight
Had rounded still the horizon and not known

662. *influence malignant:* contrast with the "selectest influence" of the constellations in 8.513

664–665. *winds . . . corners:* refers to the belief, often indicated on early maps, that the winds blow from the four *corners* of the earth (*set* = established); cf. Donne, "Holy Sonnet" 4: "At the round earth's imagined corners."

668–678. *Some say . . . clime:* Assuming here that before the fall the sun traveled in an orbit parallel to the equator (*the equinoctial road*), thus creating perpetual spring ("except to those / Beyond the polar circles," lines 680–81), Milton offers alternative explanations for the obliquity of the sun in the fallen heavens in relation to the earth, which produces the change of seasons (cf. "the penalty of Adam / The seasons' difference," in *As You Like It* 2.1.5–6): either the angels tilted the earth's axis or the sun was ordered to change its course. Either way, now the sun travels at

an angle to the equator, and Milton traces its course, beginning as it ascends north toward the constellation *Taurus,* which includes the *Atlantic Sisters* (the Pleiades, cf. 7.374), and then climbing through the *Spartan Twins* (Gemini) to the *Crab* (in the Tropic of Cancer). In July, August, and September it then descends through *Leo,* the *Virgin* (Virgo), and the *Scales* (Libra) to cross the equator southward to the Tropic of *Capricorn.*

669. *twice ten degrees and more:* The sun is in fact at an angle of 23½ degrees from the line of the equator.

671. *centric globe:* i.e., the earth

678–680. *else . . . nights:* otherwise (*else*) there would be perpetual spring and no daily change in the proportion of day and night

679. *vernant flowers:* flowers that bloom only in spring

684–685. *not known . . . or west:* had not risen or set

Or east or west, which had forbid the snow   685
From cold Estotiland, and south as far
Beneath Magellan. At that tasted fruit,
The sun, as from Thyestean banquet, turned
His course intended; else how had the world
Inhabited, though sinless, more than now   690
Avoided pinching cold and scorching heat?
These changes in the heavens, though slow, produced
Like° change on sea and land, sideral blast,   *similar*
Vapor and mist and exhalation hot,
Corrupt and pestilent. Now from the north   695
Of Norumbega and the Samoed shore,
Bursting their brazen dungeon armed with ice,
And snow and hail, and stormy gust and flaw,°   *squall*
Boreas and Caecias and Argestes loud
And Thrascias rend the woods and seas upturn;   700
With adverse blast upturns them from the south
Notus and Afer black with thunderous clouds
From Serraliona; thwart of these, as fierce,
Forth rush the levant and the ponent winds,
Eurus and Zephyr, with their lateral noise,   705
Sirocco and Libecchio. Thus began
Outrage° from lifeless things; but Discord, first   *violence*
Daughter of Sin, among the irrational°   *i.e., the animals*
Death introduced through fierce antipathy:
Beast now with beast 'gan war, and fowl with fowl,   710

---

686. *Estotiland:* On early maps *Estoti-land* appears on the northeastern coast of what is now Labrador.

687. *Magellan:* either the Strait of Magellan, on the southern tip of South America or more likely Argentina, often named "Magellonoca" on early maps; e.g. Peter Heylyn's *Cosmographie in Four Books* (London, 1652), 4.2.

688. *Thyestean banquet, turned:* In Seneca's *Thyestes,* Atreus, to revenge his cuckolding, served his brother Thyestes with a meal made from the flesh of Thyestes' sons; the sun turned so as not to witness the horror (lines 776ff).

693. *sideral blast:* malign influence from the stars

694. *exhalation hot:* meteor

696. *Norumbega . . . Samoed shore:* two northern coastal regions: *Norumbega,* what is now northeast Canada and the United States; *Samoed shore,* the coast of Siberia (Samoedia, on some early maps)

699–706. *Boreas . . . Libecchio:* various winds that had been identified by early cosmographers, as on Peter Apian's chart in his *Cosmographia* (1580) or those in Jan Jansson's *Orbis Maritimus* (1650).

703. *Serraliona:* the modern Sierra Leone, on the West African coast   *thwart of:* blowing across

704. *levant . . . ponent:* eastern and the western

707–708. *first Daughter:* Various classical texts name Discordia as Death's sister, hence, in Milton's genealogy, the *first Daughter of Sin.*

And fish with fish; to graze the herb all leaving
Devoured each other, nor stood much in awe
Of man, but fled him or with countenance grim
Glared on him passing. These were from without
The growing miseries which Adam saw   715
Already in part though hid in gloomiest shade,
To sorrow abandoned, but worse felt within,
And, in a troubled sea of passion tossed,
Thus to disburden sought with sad complaint:
    "O miserable of° happy! Is this the end   *from, after being*
Of this new glorious world and me, so late°   *recently*
The glory of that glory, who now become
Accursed of blessèd, hide me from the face
Of God, whom to behold was then my height
Of happiness? Yet well if here would end   725
The misery. I deserved it and would bear
My own deservings; but this will not serve.
All that I eat or drink or shall beget
Is propagated curse. O voice once heard
Delightfully, 'Increase and multiply,'   730
Now death to hear! For what can I increase
Or multiply but curses on my head?
Who of all ages to succeed but, feeling
The evil on him brought by me, will curse
My head: 'ill fare our ancestor impure;   735
For this we may thank Adam.' But his thanks
Shall be the execration.° So besides   *curse, condemnation*
Mine own that bide upon me, all from me
Shall with a fierce reflux on me redound,
On me as on their natural center light   740
Heavy, though in their place. O fleeting joys
Of Paradise, dear bought with lasting woes!

---

711. *graze . . . leaving:* Meat-eating
comes with the fall; the prelapsarian diet was
herbaceous (Gen. 1:30: "I have given every
green herb for meat"). Even fish, as Milton
says in 7.404, "Graze the seaweed their
pasture."
    718. *troubled . . . passion:* The
metaphor, now a cliché, goes back to Isa.
57:20: "The wicked are like the troubled sea,
when it cannot rest."
    729. *Is propagated curse:* extends the curse
    730. *Increase and multiply:* Cf. God's

blessing in Gen. 1:28: "Be fruitful, and
multiply."
    738. *Mine own:* refers to "curses" in line
732   *bide upon:* live with, attach
themselves to
    739. *redound:* recoil, flow back (like a
returning wave)
    740. *natural center:* appropriate target
(*center* = "a point towards which things move
or are attracted," *OED* 6b)
    740–741. *light Heavy:* land heavily (but
the oxymoron must be heard)

Did I request thee, maker, from my clay
To mold me man? Did I solicit thee
From darkness to promote me or here place   745
In this delicious garden? As my will
Concurred not to my being, it were but right
And equal° to reduce me to my dust,   *just, fair*
Desirous to resign and render back
All I received, unable to perform   750
Thy terms too hard by which I was to hold
The good I sought not. To the loss of that,
Sufficient penalty, why hast thou added
The sense of endless woes? Inexplicable
Thy justice seems; yet, to say truth, too late   755
I thus contest; then should have been refused
Those terms whatever when they were proposed.
Thou didst accept them. Wilt thou enjoy the good,
Then cavil° the conditions? And, though God   *object to, quibble about*
Made thee without thy leave, what if thy son   760
Prove disobedient, and, reproved, retort:
'Wherefore didst thou beget me? I sought it not.'
Wouldst thou admit for his contempt of thee
That proud excuse? Yet him not thy election°   *choice*
But natural necessity begot.   765
God made thee of choice his own and of his own
To serve him; thy reward was of his grace;
Thy punishment, then, justly is at his will.
Be it so, for I submit; his doom° is fair   *judgment*
That dust I am and shall to dust return—   770
O welcome hour whenever! Why delays
His hand to execute what his decree
Fixed on this day? Why do I overlive?
Why am I mocked with death and lengthened out
To deathless pain? How gladly would I meet   775
Mortality, my sentence, and be earth
Insensible; how glad would lay me down
As in my mother's lap! There I should rest

743–744. *Did . . . man:* Cf. Isa. 45:9:
"Woe unto him that striveth with his Maker
. . . Shall the clay say to him that fashioneth
it, 'What makest thou?'"

762. *Wherefore . . . not:* Cf. Isa. 45:10:
"Woe unto him that saith unto his father,
'What begettest thou?'"

766. *of choice:* 1) by (his) choice; 2)
with the ability to choose

770. *dust . . . return:* echoes Gen. 3:19:
"Dust thou art, and unto dust shalt thou re-
turn"

778. *mother's lap:* activates the cliché
of Mother Earth; Michael refers to "thy

And sleep secure; his dreadful voice no more
Would thunder in my ears, no fear of worse   780
To me and to my offspring would torment me
With cruel expectation. Yet one doubt
Pursues me still: lest all I cannot die,
Lest that pure breath of life, the spirit of man
Which God inspired, cannot together perish   785
With this corporeal clod, then, in the grave
Or in some other dismal place, who knows
But I shall die a living death. O thought
Horrid if true! Yet why? It was but breath
Of life that sinned. What dies but what had life   790
And sin? The body properly hath neither.
All of me then shall die. Let this appease
The doubt since human reach° no further knows.   comprehension
For though the Lord of all be infinite,
Is his wrath also? Be it, man is not so,   795
But mortal doomed. How can he exercise
Wrath without end on man, whom death must end?
Can he make deathless death? That were to make
Strange contradiction, which to God himself

mother's lap" in 11.536. See also Spenser's
Faerie Queene 5.7.9: "on their mother Earth's
deare lap."
    782–789. *one doubt . . . true:* Adam's
doubt is whether *the spirit* (line 784) might
live after the body dies. To Adam that possi-
bility of *a living death* (line 788) seems *Hor-
rid* (line 789). This *doubt* was confidently
answered in *Christian Doctrine* I, xiii: "What
could be more absurd than that the mind,
which is the part principally offending,
should escape the threatened death; and that
the body alone . . . should pay the penalty of
sin by undergoing death" (*Works* 15, 219), a
heterodox position known as "mortalism,"
which flourished in response to the Protes-
tant rejection of Purgatory, where the souls
of the dead were thought to reside until the
day of Judgment.
    785. *inspired:* breathed into me; see
Gen. 2:7: "The Lord God . . . breathed into
his nostrils the breath of life."
    783. *all I:* all of me
    789. *Yet why?:* But why should it be true?

    789–792. *It was . . . die:* Adam reasons
that since the spirit is responsible for sinning,
it must be held responsible and so must die;
therefore body and soul will die together.
    792. *All of me then shall die:* Cf. Christ's
"All that of me can die" (3.246)
appease: satisfy, put to rest
    795. *Be it:* even if it is
    796–800: *How . . . held:* Adam's strength-
ening conviction that the soul will die with
the body now leads him to become confident
that God's wrath must therefore be finite,
but he has not considered that body and soul
might be resurrected and so still be subject to
Wrath without end (line 797). He has seem-
ingly forgotten that Raphael had forewarned
him about the possibility of "eternal misery"
(6.904).
    799. *Strange contradiction:* Although
Adam's conviction is still fragile enough to be
expressed only in the form of rhetorical ques-
tions, he takes confidence from the fact that
a "deathless death" is a contradiction and
that contradictions are impossible for God;

Impossible is held, as argument°   *evidence*
Of weakness not of power. Will he draw out,
For anger's sake, finite to infinite
In punished man to satisfy his rigor,
Satisfied never? That were to extend
His sentence beyond dust and nature's law,   805
By which all causes else, according still
To the reception of their matter, act,
Not to the extent of their own sphere. But say
That death be not one stroke, as I supposed,
Bereaving sense, but endless misery   810
From this day onward, which I feel begun
Both in me and without° me, and so last   *outside*
To perpetuity. Ay me, that fear
Comes thundering back with dreadful revolution°   *recurrence*
On my defenseless head; both death and I   815
Am found eternal and incorporate both,
Nor I on my part single: in me all
Posterity stands cursed. Fair patrimony
That I must leave ye, sons. O were I able
To waste it all myself and leave ye none!   820
So disinherited, how would ye bless
Me, now° your curse! Ah, why should all mankind   *who is now*
For one man's fault thus guiltless be condemned
If guiltless? But from me what can proceed
But all corrupt, both mind and will depraved,   825
Not to do only, but to will the same

---

cf. 2 Tim. 2:13: "He cannot deny himself"; see also *Christian Doctrine* I, ii: "it must be remembered that the power of God is not exerted in things which imply a contradiction" (*Works* 14, 49).

800. *held:* i.e., is to be held

805–808. *nature's law . . . sphere:* Adam argues that it is a fundamental principle in nature that an agent's ability to act is limited by the capacity of the recipient (*reception of their matter*) to be acted upon rather than its own innate capacity (*extent*). Newton (1749) quoted the axiom: "Every efficient [i.e., everything which acts] acts according to the powers of what receives its action, not ac-

cording to its own powers." Man's finitude, therefore, must limit God's *infinite* wrath.

810. *Bereaving sense:* extinguishing feeling

815–816. *death . . . both:* The singular verb *am* expresses his recognition that mortality is now coextensive with his being (*incorporate* = united in one body).

817. *single:* confined to myself (i.e., his mortality, which is communicated to all his posterity; cf. 2 Esd. 7:48: "thou art not fallen alone but, we all that come of thee."

820. *waste it:* use it up

825. *all:* both "everyone" and "completely"

With me? How can they then acquitted stand
In sight of God? Him, after all disputes,
Forced° I absolve; all my evasions vain   *necessarily*
And reasonings, though through mazes, lead me still   830
But to my own conviction: first and last
On me, me only, as the source and spring
Of all corruption, all the blame lights due;
So might the wrath. Fond wish! Could'st thou support
That burden heavier than the earth to bear,   835
Than all the world much heavier, though divided
With that bad woman? Thus what thou desir'st
And what thou fear'st alike destroys all hope
Of refuge and concludes thee miserable
Beyond all past example and future,   840
To Satan only like both crime and doom.
O conscience, into what abyss of fears
And horrors hast thou driven me, out of which
I find no way, from deep to deeper plunged!"
    Thus Adam to himself lamented loud   845
Through the still night, not now, as ere man fell,
Wholesome and cool and mild, but with black air
Accompanied, with damps° and dreadful gloom,   *noxious vapors*
Which to his evil conscience represented
All things with double terror. On the ground   850
Outstretched he lay, on the cold ground, and oft
Cursed his creation, death as oft accused
Of tardy execution since denounced°   *it had been proclaimed*
The day of his offence. "Why comes not death,"
Said he, "with one thrice-acceptable stroke   855
To end me? Shall Truth fail to keep her word,
Justice divine not hasten to be just?

---

831. *conviction:* 1) recognition of my own sin; 2) being found guilty (as in a court of law)

834. *So might the wrath:* i.e., I wish God's wrath were also (limited to me)

836. *world:* universe (intensifying "heavier than the earth" in line 835)

839. *concludes thee:* proves conclusively that you are

841. *like both:* alike in both

842–844. *O conscience . . . plunged:* For Satan, too, "conscience wakes despair"

(4.23), expressed in terms similar to Adam's (4.73–78).

846. *still night:* The *night* is *still* because after the fall, human ears no longer are able to hear the "Celestial voices" that "Both day and night" praise "their great creator" (4.677–84).

856–857. *Shall Truth . . . just:* From Ps. 85, theologians developed the idea of the four daughters of God: Truth, Justice, Mercy, and Peace; Adam intuitively invokes only the two who judge man, not the two who might reconcile him with God.

But death comes not at call; Justice divine
Mends° not her slowest pace for prayers or cries.   *adjusts (quickens)*
O woods, O fountains, hillocks, dales and bowers,   860
With other echo late° I taught your shades   *recently*
To answer and resound far other song."
Whom thus afflicted when sad Eve beheld,
Desolate where she sat, approaching nigh,
Soft words to his fierce passion she assayed,°   *applied*
But her with stern regard he thus repelled:
    "Out of my sight, thou serpent; that name best
Befits thee with him leagued, thyself as false
And hateful; nothing wants but that thy shape,
Like his, and color serpentine may show   870
Thy inward fraud to warn all creatures from thee
Henceforth, lest that too-heavenly form, pretended
To hellish falsehood, snare them. But for thee
I had persisted happy, had not thy pride
And wandering vanity, when least was safe,   875
Rejected my forewarning and disdained
Not to be trusted, longing to be seen,
Though by the devil himself, him overweening
To overreach, but with the serpent meeting
Fooled and beguiled: by him, thou; I, by thee,   880
To trust thee from my side, imagined wise,
Constant, mature, proof against all assaults,
And understood not all was but a show
Rather than solid virtue, all but a rib
Crooked by nature, bent, as now appears,   885
More to the part sinister from me drawn,

867. *thou serpent:* The term, as many scholars have noted, registers a potential pun in Hebrew on Eve and Heve (serpent).

872–873. *pretended To:* has its Latin force (*prae* = before + *tendere* = to extend) of "held up in front of" (as a screen or disguise).

875. *wandering:* erring (unlike its earlier innocent uses, see 7.50 and 7.302)

878–879. *him . . . overreach:* presumptuously thinking to outsmart him

880. *I, by thee:* But the completion of this thought shows that Adam as yet has not accepted his full role in the fall itself; here he is thinking only of his willingness to let her part from him.

885. *Crooked . . . bent:* A misogynistic medieval tradition insisted that since the rib from which Eve was formed was *Crooked* or *bent*, it predisposed her supposed moral limitations. Ester Sowernam ironically answered the tradition by asking "If Woman received her crookednesse from the rib and consequently from the Man, how doth man excell in crookednesse, who hath more of those crooked ribs?" (*Ester Hath Hang'd Haman*, 1617, p. 3).

886. *the part sinister:* Before their fall, *sinister* could have only its Latin meaning of "left," and indeed it was often argued that the rib was drawn from the left side (though Gen.

Well if thrown out as supernumerary
To my just number found. O why did God,
Creator wise, that peopled highest Heaven
With spirits masculine, create at last   890
This novelty on earth, this fair defect
Of nature, and not fill the world at once
With men as angels, without feminine,
Or find some other way to generate
Mankind? This mischief had not then befallen   895
And more that shall befall: innumerable
Disturbances on earth through female snares
And straight conjunction with this sex; for either
He never shall find out fit mate but such
As some misfortune brings him, or mistake,   900
Or whom he wishes most shall seldom gain
Through her perverseness, but shall see her gained
By a far worse, or, if she love, withheld
By parents, or his happiest choice too late
Shall meet, already linked and wedlock-bound   905
To a fell° adversary, his hate or shame,   *cruel*
Which infinite calamity shall cause
To human life and household peace confound."
       He added not and from her turned, but Eve,
Not so repulsed, with tears that ceased not flowing   910

2:21–22 does not specify the side) because it
was closer to Adam's heart (see 8.465 and
note); now the negative figurative meanings
("corrupt," "dangerous," etc.) are inescapable;
Sin is born from "the left side" of Satan's head
in 2.755, and in the bible the left is deni-
grated: e.g., Eccl. 10:2: "A wise man's heart is
at his right hand; but a fool's heart at his left."
       887. *supernumerary:* an addition; refer-
ring to an extra-biblical tradition that Adam
was created with an extra rib designed for the
creation of Eve. The line itself has an extra
syllable, perhaps a metrical echo of the idea it
expresses.
       888–895. *why did . . . Mankind:* Cf.
Euripides' invective against women in *Hip-
polytus* 616–18, and Milton's reflection on
them in *SA* 1053–60; but note also that
Adam's question about why God created
Eve ignores the fact that her creation was

directly in response to Adam's own request
(8.364–433).
       890. *With spirits masculine:* Recall that
at 1.424, it is said that angels can "either sex
assume, or both."
       894–895. *find . . . Mankind:* Cf.
Posthumous' similarly misogynistic thought
in Shakespeare, *Cymbeline* 2.5.1–2: "Is there
no way for men to be, but women / Must be
half-workers?"
       898. *strait conjunction:* close relations
       899–908. *He never . . . confound:* a pre-
posterous catalogue of the emotional grief
that comes from "conjunction with this sex"
(line 898), not least as there are as yet no
other people on the earth; cf. Lysander's sim-
ilar complaint in *A Midsummer Night's
Dream* 1.1.134–42.
       909. *from her turned:* Cf. 4.741–43.
       910. *so repulsed:* thereby discouraged

And tresses all disordered, at his feet
Fell humble, and, embracing them, besought
His peace, and thus proceeded in her plaint:
      "Forsake me not thus, Adam; witness Heaven
What love sincere and reverence in my heart   915
I bear thee, and unweeting° have offended,   *unknowingly*
Unhappily deceived; thy suppliant
I beg and clasp thy knees. Bereave me not
Whereon I live, thy gentle looks, thy aid,
Thy counsel in this uttermost distress,   920
My only strength and stay. Forlorn of thee,
Whither shall I betake me, where subsist?
While yet we live, scarce one short hour perhaps,
Between us two let there be peace, both joining,
As joined in injuries, one enmity   925
Against a foe by doom express assigned us,
That cruel serpent. On me exercise not
Thy hatred for this misery befallen,
On me already lost, me than thyself
More miserable; both have sinned, but thou   930
Against God only, I against God and thee,
And to the place of judgment will return,
There with my cries importune Heaven that all
The sentence from thy head removed may light
On me, sole cause to thee of all this woe,   935
Me, me only, just object of his ire."
      She ended weeping, and her lowly plight,
Immovable till peace obtained from fault
Acknowledged and deplored, in Adam wrought
Commiseration; soon his heart relented   940
Toward her, his life so late° and sole delight   *recently*
Now at his feet submissive in distress,
Creature so fair his reconcilement seeking,

---

918. *Bereave me not:* do not deprive
me of

921. *Forlorn of:* abandoned by

923. *one short hour:* Eve forgets that
Christ has told them that "the instant stroke
of death" has been "Removed far off" (lines
210–11 above).

926. *doom express:* explicit judgment;
see lines 175–81 above.

927–929. *On me . . . On me . . . me:* Cf.
line 832 above, and 3.236–38 and note.

931. *Against God only . . . God:* See Ps.
51:4: "Against thee, thee only have I sinned."

938. *Immovable:* 1) unchangeable (re-
ferring to her "plight," until her sin, "Ac-
knowledged and deplored," line 939, changes
Adam's attitude toward her; 2) implacable
(referring to Adam) until her acknowledge-
ment of her fault moves his compassion

His counsel whom she had displeased, his aid;
As one disarmed, his anger all he lost,   945
And thus with peaceful words upraised her soon:
    "Unwary and too desirous, as before,
So now of what thou know'st not, who desir'st
The punishment all on thyself; alas,
Bear thine own first, ill able to sustain   950
His full wrath whose° thou feel'st as yet least part,   *which*
And my displeasure bear'st so ill. If prayers
Could alter high decrees, I to that place
Would speed before thee and be louder heard
That on my head all might be visited,   955
Thy frailty and infirmer sex forgiven,
To me committed and by me exposed.
But rise; let us no more contend, nor blame
Each other, blamed enough elsewhere, but strive
In offices° of love how we may lighten   *required acts*
Each other's burden in our share of woe,
Since this day's death denounced, if ought I see,
Will prove no sudden but a slow-paced evil,
A long day's dying to augment our pain
And to our seed (O hapless seed!) derived."°   *transmitted, passed down*
    To whom thus Eve, recovering heart, replied:
"Adam, by sad experiment° I know   *experience*
How little weight my words with thee can find,
Found so erroneous, thence by just event°   *outcome*
Found so unfortunate; nevertheless,   970
Restored by thee, vile as I am, to place
Of new acceptance, hopeful to regain
Thy love, the sole contentment of my heart,
Living or dying, from thee I will not hide
What thoughts in my unquiet breast are risen,   975
Tending to some relief of our extremes,°   *difficulties*
Or end, though sharp and sad, yet tolerable,
As in our evils and of easier choice.
If care of our descent° perplex us most,   *descendants*
Which must be born to certain woe, devoured   980

953. *that place:* i.e., "the place of judg-
ment" (line 932) where they spoke with Christ
near the "thickest trees" (line 101 above)
    957. *by me:* Although he admits his re-
sponsibility, it is still only for exposing Eve to
the temptation.

959. *elsewhere:* i.e., in Heaven
    960–961. *lighten Each other's burden:*
echoes Gal. 6:2: "Bear ye one another's
burdens."
    978. *As in:* since it is included among
    979. *perplex:* torment

By death at last (and miserable it is
To be to others cause of misery),
Our own begotten, and of our loins to bring
Into this cursèd world a woeful race,
That after wretched life must be at last   985
Food for so foul a monster, in thy power
It lies, yet ere conception, to prevent
The race unblessed, to being yet unbegot.
Childless thou art, childless remain: so Death
Shall be deceived his glut and with us two   990
Be forced to satisfy his ravenous maw.
But if thou judge it hard and difficult,
Conversing, looking, loving, to abstain
From love's due rites, nuptial embraces sweet,
And with desire to languish without hope   995
Before the present object languishing
With like desire, which would be misery
And torment less than none of what we dread,
Then, both ourselves and seed at once to free
From what we fear for both, let us make short;   1000
Let us seek death or, he not found, supply
With our own hands his office on ourselves;
Why stand we longer shivering under fears
That show no end but death and have the power,
Of many ways to die the shortest choosing,   1005
Destruction with destruction to destroy."
    She ended here, or vehement despair
Broke off the rest; so much of death her thoughts

987. *prevent:* forestall, cut off in advance; cf. 4.996.

989. *so death:* In 1667 and 1674, these two words are at the beginning of line 990, forming two metrically anomalous lines. Some editors argue that the metrical defect in 989 is appropriate for a line discussing childlessness, just as the excess of 990 is appropriate for one mentioning "glut," and thus rationalize the preservation of the lineation of the early editions. The mimetic argument weakens, however, when it is noted that line 990 is in fact about the absence of glut and, while there are a (very) few examples of hypermetrical lines in the poem (almost all an extra unstressed syllable at the end of a line), there are no other example of consecutive lines that vary so dramatically from the poem's pentameter norm, so it seems probable that this is simply a mislineation in 1667 that the second edition perpetuated.

994. *rites:* as at 4.742–43; something of their prelapsarian love has returned

996. *the present object:* i.e., Eve herself, standing in Adam's presence; perhaps the odd periphrasis betrays her self-loathing.

1001–1002. *supply . . . office:* perform ourselves his duty (as executioner)

1004. *Of . . . choosing:* selecting the quickest from among the many possible ways to die

1007. *vehement:* passionate (as in 9.431)

Had entertained as dyed her cheeks with pale.
But Adam, with such counsel nothing° swayed,   *not at all*
To better hopes his more attentive mind
Laboring had raised and thus to Eve replied:
    "Eve, thy contempt of life and pleasure seems
To argue in thee something more sublime
And excellent than what thy mind contemns;   1015
But self-destruction therefore sought refutes
That excellence thought in thee and implies
Not thy contempt but anguish and regret
For loss of life and pleasure overloved.
Or if thou covet death as utmost end   1020
Of misery, so thinking to evade
The penalty pronounced, doubt not but God
Hath wiselier armed his vengeful ire than so
To be forestalled; much more I fear lest death
So snatched will not exempt us from the pain   1025
We are by doom to pay; rather such acts
Of contumacy° will provoke the highest   .   *disobedience*
To make death in us live. Then let us seek
Some safer resolution, which methinks
I have in view, calling to mind with heed   1030
Part of our sentence: that thy seed shall bruise
The serpent's head; piteous amends, unless
Be meant, whom I conjecture, our grand foe
Satan, who in the serpent hath contrived
Against us this deceit. To crush his head   1035
Would be revenge indeed, which will be lost
By death brought on ourselves or childless days
Resolved as thou proposest; so our foe
Shall scape his punishment ordained, and we
Instead shall double ours upon our heads.   1040
No more be mentioned, then, of violence
Against ourselves and willful barrenness
That cuts us off from hope and savors only
Rancor and pride, impatience and despite,

1009. *dyed . . . pale:* turned her cheeks pale; but *dyed* is an obvious pun, confirming how much her thoughts have been "entertained" (occupied) by death.

1016–1024. *self-destruction . . . forestalled:* Although it is possible to find various sources for Adam's reasoning here,

basically the thought is as general as Hamlet's wish that "th' Everlasting had not fixed / His canon 'gainst self-slaughter" (*Hamlet* 1.2.131–32).

1031–1035. *our sentence . . . head:* Cf. lines 168–84 above.

1032. *piteous amends:* small consolation

Reluctance against God and his just yoke   1045
Laid on our necks. Remember with what mild
And gracious temper he both heard and judged,
Without wrath or reviling. We expected
Immediate dissolution, which we thought
Was meant by death that day, when, lo, to thee   1050
Pains only in childbearing were foretold
And bringing forth, soon recompensed with joy,
Fruit of thy womb. On me the curse aslope
Glanced on the ground: with labor I must earn
My bread. What harm? Idleness had been worse;   1055
My labor will sustain me, and, lest cold
Or heat should injure us, his timely care
Hath unbesought provided, and his hands
Clothed us unworthy, pitying while he judged.
How much more, if we pray him, will his ear   1060
Be open and his heart to pity incline,
And teach us further by what means to shun
The inclement seasons, rain, ice, hail, and snow,
Which now the sky with various face begins
To show us in this mountain while the winds   1065
Blow moist and keen, shattering the graceful locks
Of these fair spreading trees, which bids us seek
Some better shroud,° some better warmth to cherish   *shelter*
Our limbs benumbed, ere this diurnal star
Leave cold the night, how° we, his gathered beams   *seek how*
Reflected, may with matter sere foment,
Or by collision of two bodies grind
The air attrite to fire, as late the clouds
Jostling or pushed with winds rude in their shock
Tine° the slant lightning, whose thwart flame driven down   *kindle, ignite*
Kindles the gummy bark of fir or pine

1045. *Reluctance:* struggling, resistance (see line 515 and note above)

1050. *that day:* i.e., the preceding day

1053–1054. *aslope . . . ground:* The curse has struck only a glancing blow and fallen to the ground, like an arrow that has grazed its mark (*aslope* = indirectly); cf. line 201 above.

1065. *this mountain:* In 4.132–72, Paradise has been described as a mountain.

1066. *shattering . . . locks:* scattering the leaves; Spenser speaks in *The Shepheardes*

Calendar ("November," line 125) of "faded lockes" that "fall from the loftie oke." See also "Lycidas" (line 5): "Shatter your leaves before the mellowing year."

1069. *this diurnal star:* the sun (*diurnal* = daily; cf. "the day-star" in "Lycidas," line 168)

1071. *with matter sere foment:* start a fire with dry kindling

1073. *attrite to:* rubbed to produce

1075. *thwart:* diagonal, slanting

1075–1078. *lightning . . . far:* The *locus classicus* for theory that fire originated from

And sends a comfortable heat from far,
Which might supply° the sun. Such fire to use   *replace*
And what may else be remedy or cure
To evils which our own misdeeds have wrought,   1080
He will instruct us praying° and of grace   *if we pray*
Beseeching him, so as we need not fear
To pass commodiously° this life, sustained   *comfortably*
By him with many comforts till we end
In dust, our final rest and native home.   1085
What better can we do than, to the place
Repairing where he judged us, prostrate fall
Before him reverent, and there confess
Humbly our faults and pardon beg, with tears
Watering the ground and with our sighs the air   1090
Frequenting, sent from hearts contrite, in sign
Of sorrow unfeigned and humiliation meek?
Undoubtedly he will relent and turn
From his displeasure, in whose look serene,
When angry most he seemed and most severe,   1095
What else but favor, grace, and mercy shone?"
        So spake our father penitent, nor Eve
Felt less remorse. They, forthwith to the place
Repairing where he judged them, prostrate fell
Before him reverent, and both confessed   1100
Humbly their faults and pardon begged, with tears
Watering the ground, and with their sighs the air
Frequenting, sent from hearts contrite, in sign
Of sorrow unfeigned and humiliation meek.

The End of the Tenth Book.

the kindling of the forests by lightning is Lucretius' *De rerum natura* 5.1091–95.

1081. *of:* for

1087. *Repairing:* returning to, but also they are re-pairing (reuniting) and are healing (repairing) in spirit. In various senses their contrition repairs what has been damaged by their transgression.

1091. *Frequenting:* retains its Latin meaning of "filling" or "crowding" (*frequens* = crowded)

1098–1104. *They forthwith . . . meek:* essentially repeats lines 1086–92 above, only with the tenses and modes of the verbs changed; the repetition is odd, but it works as an almost ritualistic confirmation of Adam's instincts about God's grace; what, however, is not repeated here (and hence not confirmed) is Adam's hope that God "will relent and turn / From his displeasure" (lines 1093–94).

BOOK 11

The Argument

The Son of God presents to his Father the prayers of our first parents now repenting and intercedes for them; God accepts them, but declares that they must no longer abide in Paradise; sends Michael with a band of cherubim to dispossess them, but first to reveal to Adam future things. Michael's coming down. Adam shows to Eve certain ominous signs; he discerns Michael's approach, goes out to meet him; the angel denounces their departure. Eve's lamentation. Adam pleads, but submits. The angel leads him up to a high hill, sets before him in vision what shall happen till the flood.

Thus they in lowliest plight repentant stood
Praying, for from the mercy-seat above
Prevenient grace descending had removed
The stony from their hearts and made new flesh
Regenerate grow instead, that sighs now breathed   5
Unutterable which the spirit of prayer
Inspired, and wingèd for Heaven with speedier flight
Than loudest oratory; yet their port°   *bearing, posture*
Not of mean suitors, nor important less
Seemed their petition than when the ancient pair   10
In fables old, less ancient yet than these,

---

1. *stood:* seems inconsistent with "prostrate" in 10.1099, but in 4.720, Adam stands to pray. Nonetheless, *stood* could as easily mean "remained" (where "prostrate fell") and not refer to their posture at all. Milton says that, "No particular posture of the body in prayer was enjoined, even under the law" (*Christian Doctrine* II, iv; [*Works* 17, 90]). See line 14 below: "stood devout."

2. *mercy-seat:* i.e., God's throne; the image is the "mercy-seat" in Aaron's tabernacle with its "two cherubims of gold, of beaten work, . . . in the two ends" (Exod. 25:17–18), which Christian exegetes used as a type of the intercession of angels, or of Christ, in Heaven.

3. *Prevenient grace:* grace that anticipates repentance (see Ps. 59:10: "The God of my mercy shall prevent me"). *Prevenient* (like "prevent" in the quote from Ps. 59) is from the Latin *praevenire* = to come before.

3–4. *removed . . . flesh:* See Ezek. 11:19: "I will take the stony heart out of their flesh, and will give them an heart of flesh."

5–6. *sighs . . . Unutterable:* Cf. Rom. 8:26: "the Spirit itself maketh intercession for us with groanings which cannot be uttered."

10. *the ancient pair:* i.e., Deucalion and Pyrrha, whom Ovid describes (*Metamorphoses* 1.321–80) as praying effectually to Themis, the goddess of justice, after they

Deucalion and chaste Pyrrha, to restore
The race of mankind drowned, before the shrine
Of Themis stood devout. To Heaven their prayers
Flew up, nor missed the way by envious° winds   *malicious*
Blown vagabond or frustrate. In they passed
Dimensionless through heavenly doors, then, clad
With incense where the golden altar fumed
By their great intercessor, came in sight
Before the Father's throne; them the glad Son   20
Presenting, thus to intercede began:
      "See, Father, what first fruits on earth are sprung
From thy implanted grace in man, these sighs
And prayers, which in this golden censer mixed
With incense I, thy priest, before thee bring,   25
Fruits of more pleasing savor from thy seed
Sown with contrition in his heart than those
Which, his own hand manuring, all the trees
Of Paradise could have produced ere fallen
From innocence. Now therefore bend thine ear   30
To supplication; hear his sighs though mute,
Unskillful with what words to pray; let me
Interpret for him, me, his advocate
And propitiation; all his works on me,
Good or not good, engraft; my merit those   35
Shall perfect, and for these my death shall pay.

survived a great flood (but the Ovidian pair is
"less ancient," line 11, than Adam and Eve).

   14–16. *prayers . . . frustrate:* These
prayers, not *vagabond or frustrate* (lost or
thwarted), are contrasted with the "fruits /
Of painful superstition and blind zeal" in
3.451–52, which "a violent cross wind . . .
blows . . . transverse" (3.487–88) in the
limbo of vanity.

   17. *Dimensionless:* without physical ex-
tension, implying the immateriality of prayer

   17–18. *clad . . . fumed:* The prayers are
accompanied by burning incense, not in im-
itation of Catholic worship, but like those
that are presented by the angel in Rev. 8:3,
who "stood at the altar, having a golden
censer; and there was given unto him much
incense, that he should offer it with the
prayers of all saints."

   19. *intercessor:* i.e., Christ, who makes
intercession by "appearing in the presence of
God for us" and by "rendering our prayers
agreeable to God" (*Christian Doctrine* I, xv
[*Works* 15, 294]; see also Heb. 9:24).

   20. *the glad Son:* Cf. "the sun more
glad" at 4.150; *glad* = pleased, but also bright,
shining, beautiful (*OED* 1).

   24. *censer:* vessel in which incense is
burned (and see lines 17–18 and note)

   28. *manuring:* tending, cultivating; cf.
4.628.

   33–34. *advocate And propitiation:* Cf.
"We have an advocate with the Father, Jesus
Christ the righteous: And he is the propitia-
tion for our sins" (1 John 2:1–2).

   35. *engraft:* part of a series of horticul-
tural images, starting with "fruits" in line 22;
for the image of grafting, see 3.293–94,

Accept me, and in me from these receive
The smell of peace toward mankind; let him live
Before thee reconciled at least his days
Numbered,° though sad, till death his doom (which I   *finite*
To mitigate thus plead, not to reverse)
To better life shall yield him, where with me
All my redeemed may dwell in joy and bliss,
Made one with me, as I with thee am one."

    To whom the Father, without cloud, serene: 45
"All thy request for man, accepted° Son,   *approved, well-received*
Obtain; all thy request was my decree.
But longer in that Paradise to dwell
The law I gave to nature him forbids:
Those pure immortal elements that know   50
No gross, no unharmonious mixture foul,
Eject him tainted now and purge him off
As a distemper gross, to air as gross
And mortal food as may dispose him best
For dissolution wrought by sin, that first   55
Distempered all things, and of incorrupt
Corrupted. I at first with two fair gifts
Created him endowed: with happiness

where God says to Christ that man will "live in thee transplanted, and from thee / Receive new life." The imagery emphasizes the necessity of grace for salvation, qualifying Milton's Arminianism.

37. *these:* i.e., the prayers

40–41. *which . . . reverse:* Christ pleads not to *reverse* God's judgment (which cannot be cancelled) but to *mitigate* (see 10.76) man's "doom" through his sacrifice.

44. *Made one . . . one:* echoes John 17:22–23: " that they may be one, even as we are one: I in them, and thou in me, that they may be perfect in one."

45. *without cloud:* i.e., God is pure light; see 3.378–79 (but also without frown, with no expression of displeasure at the transgression; cf. line 880 below).

48–49. *longer . . . forbids:* It is "nature's law," as Adam names it in 10.805, that insists upon their expulsion from Eden, not

solely as punishment but as an inevitable effect of the changes that occur with their fall.

50–57. *Those . . . Corrupted:* The *pure . . . elements* of Eden are what expel fallen man, just as, in Belial's words, "the ethereal mold" of Heaven, "incapable of stain," would automatically "expel" or "purge off the baser fire" of the rebel angels if they were to attack God (2.139–41).

51. *gross:* polluted; see 6.661: "Purest at first, now gross by sinning grown."

53. *distemper gross:* foul disease   *to air as gross:* into air as gross as he is; i.e., the air of the fallen world instead of the "pure now purer air" of Paradise (4.153).

54. *mortal food:* i.e., the food that he will eat in his now gross, *mortal* condition

55. *dissolution:* death (but with the secondary sense of "dissolute living")

56. *Distempered:* unbalanced, destroyed the proper harmony in

And immortality; that fondly lost,
This other served but to eternize woe   60
Till I provided death; so death becomes
His final remedy, and after life
Tried in sharp tribulation and refined
By faith and faithful works, to second life,
Waked in the renovation of the just,   65
Resigns him up with Heaven and earth renewed.
But let us call to synod° all the blessed   *assembly*
Through Heaven's wide bounds; from them I will not hide
My judgments: how with mankind I proceed
As how with peccant° angels late they saw   *sinful*
And in their state, though firm, stood more confirmed."
        He ended, and the Son gave signal high
To the bright minister that watched; he blew
His trumpet, heard in Oreb since perhaps
When God descended and perhaps once more   75
To sound at general doom. The angelic blast
Filled all the regions. From their blissful bowers
Of amaranthine shade, fountain or spring,
By the waters of life, where'er they sat
In fellowships of joy, the sons of light   80
Hasted, resorting° to the summons high,   *returning*
And took their seats, till from his throne supreme
The almighty thus pronounced his sovereign will:
        "O sons, like one of us man is become
To know both good and evil since his taste   85
Of that defended fruit; but let him boast

---

59. *that fondly:* i.e., happiness foolishly
60. *This other:* i.e., immortality
64. *By faith and faithful works:* Here and in 12.427 ("faith not void of works"), Milton indicates qualified assent to the Lutheran doctrine of justification by faith; cf. *Christian Doctrine* I, xxii; *Works* 16, 39): "we are justified by faith without the works of the law, but not without the works of faith."
65. *renovation:* renewal (specifically the resurrection of the body at the final judgment); see Luke 14.14: "Thou shalt be recompensed at the resurrection of the just."
71. *their:* i.e., the faithful angels
74–76. *trumpet . . . doom:* The *trumpet,* which summoned Michael's forces in Heaven (6.60), Milton says may have been heard on earth immediately before God gave the Ten Commandments to Moses on Mount Sinai, or Oreb (1.6–7 and Exod. 19:16), and may be heard again when God "shall send his angels with a great sound of a trumpet" (Matt. 24:31) for the last judgment (*general doom*).
78. *amaranthine:* Amaranth was a mythical flower that never faded (see 3.352–56).
79. *the waters of life:* "the fount of life" of 3.357
84–85. *like one . . . evil:* See Gen. 3:22: "And the Lord God said, 'Behold, the man is become as one of us, to know good and evil.'"
86. *defended:* forbidden; cf. 12.207.

His knowledge of good lost and evil got;
Happier had it sufficed him to have known
Good by itself and evil not at all.
He sorrows now, repents, and prays contrite,   90
My motions in him, longer than they move,
His heart I know, how variable and vain
Self-left.° Lest, therefore, his now bolder hand   *if left to itself*
Reach also of the Tree of Life and eat
And live forever—dream at least to live   95
Forever—to remove him I decree
And send him from the garden forth to till
The ground whence he was taken, fitter soil.
    Michael, this my behest have thou in charge:
Take to thee from among the cherubim   100
Thy choice of flaming warriors, lest the fiend,
Or in behalf of man or to invade
Vacant possession some new trouble raise.
Haste thee, and from the Paradise of God
Without remorse drive out the sinful pair,   105
From hallowed ground the unholy, and denounce°   *announce, proclaim*
To them and to their progeny from thence
Perpetual banishment. Yet lest they faint°   *lose courage*
At the sad sentence rigorously urged
(For I behold them softened and with tears   110
Bewailing their excess°) all terror hide.   *transgression*
If patiently thy bidding they obey,
Dismiss them not disconsolate; reveal
To Adam what shall come in future days
As I shall thee enlighten; intermix   115
My covenant in the woman's seed renewed;
So send them forth, though sorrowing, yet in peace;

88–89. *Happier . . . all:* The claim contradicts the idea of the "fortunate fall."

90. *sorrows . . . repents . . . prays:* The triptych marks stages in Adam and Eve's regeneration.

91. *motions:* influence, stirrings (i.e., the "Prevenient grace" of line 3 above) *longer than:* i.e., because the sorrow, prayer, and contrition (line 90) are motivated by God's impulses (*motions*), they will affect ("move") his "heart" "longer" than if they

were solely dependent on man's own instincts

98. *fitter soil:* i.e., fitter now for him, since less pure; see line 262 below.

99. *Michael:* See 6.44.

102. *Or in behalf of:* Either claiming to act for (or possibly "Either in regard to," but not "Either for man's benefit"); *Or . . . or =* Either . . . or

103. *Vacant possession:* abandoned property

And on the east side of the garden place,
Where entrance up from Eden easiest climbs,
Cherubic watch,° and of a sword, the flame   *sentinels*
Wide waving, all approach far off to fright
And guard all passage to the Tree of Life,
Lest Paradise a receptacle prove
To spirits foul and all my trees their prey,
With whose stolen fruit man once more to delude."   125
   He ceased, and the archangelic power prepared
For swift descent, with him the cohort° bright   *squadron, unit*
Of watchful cherubim. Four faces each
Had, like a double Janus; all their shape
Spangled with eyes more numerous than those   130
Of Argus and more wakeful than to drowse,
Charmed with Arcadian pipe, the pastoral reed
Of Hermes, or his opiate rod. Meanwhile,
To resalute the world with sacred light,
Leucothea waked and with fresh dews embalmed   135
The earth, when Adam and first matron, Eve,
Had ended now their orisons and found,
Strength added from above, new hope to spring
Out of despair, joy but with fear yet linked,
Which thus to Eve his welcome words renewed: 140
   "Eve, easily may faith admit that all
The good which we enjoy from Heaven descends,

118–122. *on . . . Life:* follows Gen. 3:24: "So he drove out the man; and he placed at the east of the garden of Eden cherubims, and a flaming sword which turned every way, to keep the way of the tree of life"

129. *a double Janus:* The cherubs are compared to the Roman god of gates, *Janus,* who was usually sculpted with two, but often with four faces (the *Janus Quadrifrons*) and often associated with the angels of Ezekiel's vision (Ezek. 1:6); cf. 6.750–59.

130–133. *with eyes . . . rod:* The allusions span the description of the cherubs as "full of eyes" in Ezek. 1:18, and Ovid's description (*Metamorphoses* 1.625–26) of Juno's commission of Argus, whose head was "starr'd" with "a hundred eyes," to watch her rival Io, though later Hermes is able to "subdue each wakeful eye" with his medi-

cated rod and his pipes (ibid., lines 684–719).

135. *Leucothea:* the "shining goddess," identified by Ovid (*Fasti* 479 and 545) with the Roman goddess of the dawn, Matuta

135–136. *embalmed The earth:* anointed the ground (but *embalmed* as "prepared a corpse to prevent decay" is unmistakable, reflecting the mortality that has come into the world).

139. *fear:* a mark of the limits of their "joy," but also potentially useful; cf. Prov. 1:7: "The fear of the Lord is the beginning of knowledge."

140. *renewed:* not just "resumed" but also with the sense of spiritually "regenerated," which his speech will demonstrate

141. *faith:* This is the first time either Adam or Eve speaks the word, evidence of their renewal; see line 140 above.

But that from us aught° should ascend to Heaven   *anything*
So prevalent° as to concern the mind   *powerful, efficacious*
Of God high-blessed or to incline his will,   145
Hard to believe may seem; yet this will prayer,
Or one short sigh of human breath, upborne
Even to the seat of God. For since I sought
By prayer the offended deity to appease,
Kneeled and before him humbled all my heart,   150
Methought I saw him, placable° and mild,   *forgiving*
Bending his ear; persuasion in me grew
That I was heard with favor; peace returned
Home to my breast, and to my memory
His promise that thy seed shall bruise our foe,   155
Which, then not minded° in dismay, yet now   *attended to*
Assures me that the bitterness of death
Is past and we shall live. Whence hail to thee,
Eve rightly called, mother of all mankind,
Mother of all things living, since by thee   160
Man is to live and all things live for man."
       To whom thus Eve with sad demeanor meek:
"Ill worthy I such title should belong
To me transgressor, who for thee ordained
A help became thy snare; to me reproach   165
Rather belongs, distrust and all dispraise;
But infinite in pardon was my judge,
That I, who first brought death on all, am graced
The source of life; next favorable thou,
Who highly thus to entitle me vouchsaf'st,   170
Far other name deserving. But the field
To labor calls us now with sweat imposed,
Though after sleepless night; for see the morn,
All unconcerned with our unrest, begins

146. *this will prayer:* i.e., this prayer will accomplish

148. *seat of God:* the "mercy-seat" in line 2 above

155. *promise:* See 10.179–81.

158. *hail:* In 5.385–87, Eve is identified as she "on whom the angel 'hail' / bestowed, the holy salutation used / . . . to blessed Mary, a second Eve," recalling the Annunciation (Luke 1:28). Here Adam's "hail" invokes the typology that neither can yet understand.

159. *Eve rightly called:* See Gen. 3:20: "And Adam called his wife's name Eve; because she was the mother of all living." "Eve" is derived from the Hebrew *havah* = live.

162. *sad:* serious, grave (cf. Satan's "sad resolution" in 6.541).

164–165. *for thee . . help:* See Gen. 2:18: "I will make him an help meet for him" (and 8.450).

172. *with sweat imposed:* as a result of the fall, *sweat* is *imposed:* "In the sweat of thy face shalt thou eat bread" (Gen. 3:19).

Her rosy progress smiling. Let us forth,   175
I never from thy side henceforth to stray,
Where'er our day's work lies, though now enjoined°   *required*
Laborious, till day droop. While here we dwell,
What can be toilsome in these pleasant walks?
Here let us live, though in fallen state, content."   180
    So spake, so wished, much-humbled Eve, but fate
Subscribed° not; nature first gave signs, impressed   *assented*
On bird, beast, air, air suddenly eclipsed
After short blush of morn; nigh in her sight
The bird of Jove, stooped from his airy tower,   185
Two birds of gayest plume before him drove;
Down from a hill the beast that reigns in woods,
First hunter then, pursued a gentle brace,°   *pair*
Goodliest of all the forest, hart and hind;
Direct to the eastern gate was bent their flight.   190
Adam observed and, with his eye the chase
Pursuing, not unmoved to Eve thus spake:
    "O Eve, some further change awaits us nigh,
Which Heaven by these mute signs in nature shows
Forerunners of his purpose or to warn   195
Us haply too secure of our discharge
From penalty, because from death released
Some days. How long and what till then our life,
Who knows, or more than this: that we are dust
And thither must return and be no more.   200
Why else this double object in our sight
Of flight pursued in the air and o'er the ground

182–190. *nature . . . flight:* These are not the *first* symptoms of a now degenerate nature (already seen at 10.710–11) but the first symbolic events (symbolism itself being a product of the fall). These are *signs* of Adam and Eve's (themselves a *brace,* line 188) new relation to God: the sun in eclipse signifies the hidden God (the Deus absconditus of Isa. 45:15) who is all that fallen humanity will know (see lines 315–17 below); the eagle attacking two other birds marks the sharp distinction that now exists between God and mankind, before the fall a mere difference of degree; and the lion hunting the deer driven *to the eastern gate* portends their

expulsion and the inescapable mortality that is their fallen condition. These are the "mute signs" (line 194) that warn them against feeling "too secure" (line 196) in their "fallen state" (line 180).

185. *bird of Jove:* i.e., eagle (see *Cymbeline* 5.4.113: "I saw Jove's bird, the Roman eagle"). *stooped:* having swooped down (to strike) *airy tower:* the apex of his flight

196. *haply too secure:* perhaps overconfident

199–200. *we . . . return:* echoes Gen. 3:19: "for dust thou art, and unto dust shalt thou return"

One way the selfsame hour? Why in the east
Darkness ere day's mid-course and morning light
More orient in yon western cloud that draws   205
O'er the blue firmament a radiant white
And slow descends, with something heavenly fraught?"
    He erred not, for by this° the heavenly bands,   *this time*
Down from a sky of jasper, lighted now
In Paradise and on a hill made halt,   210
A glorious apparition, had not doubt
And carnal fear that day dimmed Adam's eye.
Not that more glorious when the angels met
Jacob in Mahanaim, where he saw
The field pavilioned with his guardians bright,   215
Nor that which on the flaming mount appeared
In Dothan covered with a camp of fire
Against the Syrian king, who to surprise
One man, assassin-like had levied war,
War unproclaimed. The princely hierarch   220
In their bright stand there left his powers to seize
Possession of the garden; he alone,
To find where Adam sheltered, took his way
Not unperceived of Adam, who to Eve,
While the great visitant approached, thus spake: 225
    "Eve, now expect great tidings, which perhaps
Of us will soon determine,° or impose   *put an end*
New laws to be observed, for I descry

205. *orient:* bright (though the meaning "eastern" is what suggests the word to Adam as he enjoys the paradox)

209. *lighted:* alighted, landed (but following "sky," this might momentarily be read as "lit up," but the "and" in line 210 demands a prior verb).

210. *made halt:* came to a halt (a military term, like "stand" in line 221)

212. *carnal fear:* fear of death; cf. George Wither's "A Composure" (1661): "Now live or die, my dear, God's will be done; / He fills my heart, and my distemper's gone. / Since God hath freed me from this carnal fear, / Let world and devil henceforth do what they dare. / The greater weights they shall upon me lay, / The sooner I from them shall scape away."

214. *Mahanaim:* Jacob's name for the place where "the angels of God met him" (Gen. 32:1–2).

215: *pavilioned:* covered with tents; cf. *Henry V* 1.2.129: "And lie pavilioned in the fields of France."

216–219. *that which . . . war:* cf. the vision of a mountain "full of horses and chariots of fire round about Elisha" that his servant saw protecting the prophet (the "One man" of line 219) from the Syrians in Dothan, after he had warned the king of Israel about their impending attack (2 Kings 6:17).

220. *princely hierarch:* i.e., Michael

221. *bright stand:* radiant formation ("their" refers to the band of angels in lines 208–9).

From yonder blazing cloud that veils the hill
One of the heavenly host and, by his gait,   230
None of the meanest—some great potentate
Or of the thrones above—such majesty
Invests° him coming; yet not terrible,   *surrounds, clothes*
That I should fear, nor sociably mild,
As Raphael, that I should much confide,   235
But solemn and sublime, whom, not to offend,
With reverence I must meet, and thou retire."
He ended, and the archangel soon drew nigh,
Not in his shape celestial but as man
Clad to meet man; over his lucid arms   240
A military vest of purple flowed
Livelier than Meliboean or the grain
Of Sarra worn by kings and heroes old
In time of truce; Iris had dipped the woof.
His starry helm° unbuckled showed him prime   *helmet*
In manhood where youth ended; by his side,
As in a glistering zodiac, hung the sword,
Satan's dire dread, and in his hand the spear.
Adam bowed low; he, kingly, from his state
Inclined° not, but his coming thus declared: *bowed*
    "Adam, Heaven's high behest no preface needs:
Sufficient that thy prayers are heard, and Death,
Then due by sentence when thou didst transgress,
Defeated of his seizure many days
Given thee of grace, wherein thou mayst repent,   255
And one bad act with many deeds well done

230–231. *by . . . meanest:* Cf. *King Lear*
5.3.176–77: "Methought thy very gait did
prophesy / A royal nobleness."
    234–235. *sociably . . . Raphael:* See the
reference to Raphael as "the sociable spirit"
in 5.221.
    240–241. *over . . . vest:* i.e., instead of
wings covering his arms (which are *lucid* =
bright)
    242–243. *Meliboean . . . Sarra:* the dyes
(*grain*) from the Thessalian town of Meliboea,
famous as Virgil suggests in the *Aeneid* 5.251,
or from *Sarra,* the ancient name of Tyre,
which was itself renowned for its dyes as early

as its king's dispatch of "a man skilful to work
. . . in purple, in blue, and in fine linen" to
help build Solomon's temple (2 Chron. 2:14).
    244. *Iris . . . woof:* the goddess Iris had
dyed the fabric; cf.: "sky-robes spun out of
Iris' woof" in *Comus,* line 83, as a description
of the rainbow.
    247. *glistering zodiac:* The belt holding
Michael's sword is compared to the belt of
zodiacal constellations in the sky.
    249. *he:* i.e., Michael   *state:* state-
liness, dignity of demeanor (*OED* 18)
    254. *Defeated of his seizure:* deprived of
his possession, kept from what by law is his

Mayst cover. Well may then thy Lord appeased
Redeem thee quite from Death's rapacious claim;
But longer in this Paradise to dwell
Permits not; to remove thee I am come   260
And send thee from the garden forth to till
The ground whence thou wast taken, fitter soil."
    He added not, for Adam at the news
Heart-struck with chilling grip of sorrow stood
That all his senses bound;° Eve, who unseen   *seized up*
Yet all had heard, with audible lament
Discovered soon the place of her retire:°   *withdrawal, retreat*
    "O unexpected stroke, worse than of death!
Must I thus leave thee, Paradise? Thus leave
Thee, native soil, these happy walks and shades,   270
Fit haunt of gods, where I had hope to spend,
Quiet though sad, the respite of that day
That must be mortal to us both? O flowers,
That never will in other climate grow,
My early visitation and my last   275
At ev'n, which I bred up with tender hand
From the first opening bud and gave ye names,
Who now shall rear ye to the sun, or rank°   *arrange*
Your tribes, and water from the ambrosial fount?
Thee, lastly, nuptial bower, by me adorned   280
With what to sight or smell was sweet, from thee
How shall I part, and whither wander down
Into a lower world, to° this obscure   *in comparison to*
And wild? How shall we breathe in other air
Less pure, accustomed to immortal fruits?"   285
    Whom thus the angel interrupted mild:
"Lament not, Eve, but patiently resign
What justly thou hast lost; nor set thy heart,

267. *Discovered:* divulged, revealed

268. *O . . . death:* Eve again speaks before Adam.

270. *native soil:* Only Eve is *native* to Eden; Adam was created elsewhere (see 7.536–38, but also see line 292 below).

272. *respite:* delay; the remainder of the time granted by God's postponement of the sentence of physical death

275–276. *early . . . ev'n:* morning . . . evening

277. *gave ye names:* parallel to Adam's naming of "beast, fish, and fowl" in 8.340–52, but no mention is made there or in Gen. 2:19 about the naming of plants. The Genesis account, however, is immediately bracketed with sentences about Adam's need for a "partner," so Milton's addition is logical, though without biblical warrant.

279. *ambrosial fount:* See 4.237–40, the description of the "fount" in Eden, which "Ran nectar."

Thus overfond, on that which is not thine.
Thy going is not lonely; with thee goes   290
Thy husband; him to follow thou art bound;
Where he abides think there thy native soil."
    Adam, by this° from the cold sudden damp   *this time*
Recovering and his scattered spirits returned,
To Michael thus his humble words addressed: 295
    "Celestial, whether among the thrones or named
Of them the highest, for such of shape may seem
Prince above princes, gently hast thou told
Thy message, which might else in telling wound,
And in performing end us; what besides   300
Of sorrow and dejection and despair
Our frailty can sustain, thy tidings bring:
Departure from this happy place, our sweet
Recess° and only consolation left   *refuge*
Familiar to our eyes; all places else   305
Inhospitable appear and desolate,
Nor knowing us, nor known. And if by prayer
Incessant I could hope to change the will
Of him who all things can, I would not cease
To weary him with my assiduous cries;   310
But prayer against his absolute decree
No more avails than breath against the wind,
Blown stifling back on him that breathes it forth;
Therefore to his great bidding I submit.
This most afflicts me, that departing hence   315
As from his face I shall be hid, deprived
His blessèd countenance; here I could frequent,
With worship, place by place where he vouchsafed°   *established*
Presence divine, and to my sons relate:

291. *bound:* Cf. the usage above at line
265.
    293. *damp:* stupor; cf. Eve's "damp hor-
ror" in 5.65.
    296–297. *whether . . . highest:* Only
after he is fallen does Adam consider angelic
rank.
    309. *can:* 1) can do; 2) knows (*OED*
1.1b)
    310. *weary:* importune (*OED* 2.5.b)
but also its conventional meaning, "tire out";

Milton contrasts God with the unjust judge
of Luke 18:5–7, who would yield only to
wearisome importunity.
    316. *from . . . hid:* Adam's words are
similar to Cain's after he is cursed for the
murder of Abel: "Behold, thou hast driven
me out this day from the face of the earth;
and from thy face shall I be hid" (Gen. 4:14).
    319. *to my sons relate:* Adam imagines
the conversations he would have had with his
sons had he not transgressed.

'On this mount he appeared, under this tree   320
Stood visible, among these pines his voice
I heard, here with him at this fountain talked.'
So many grateful altars I would rear
Of grassy turf and pile up every stone
Of luster from the brook, in memory   325
Or monument to ages, and thereon
Offer sweet smelling gums and fruits and flowers.
In yonder nether world where shall I seek
His bright appearances or footstep trace?
For though I fled him angry, yet° recalled   *since*
To life prolonged and promised race, I now
Gladly behold though but his utmost skirts
Of glory, and far off his steps adore."
    To whom thus Michael with regard benign:
"Adam, thou know'st Heaven his and all the earth,   335
Not this rock only; his omnipresence fills
Land, sea, and air, and every kind that lives,
Fomented by his virtual power and warmed.
All the earth he gave thee to possess and rule,
No despicable gift; surmise not then   340
His presence to these narrow bounds confined
Of Paradise or Eden. This had been
Perhaps thy capital seat from whence had spread
All generations and had hither come
From all the ends of the earth to celebrate   345
And reverence thee their great progenitor.
But this preeminence thou hast lost, brought down

---

323. *grateful:* 1) showing gratitude; 2) pleasing

331. *promised race:* the human race; Adam prays in 4.732–33: "thou hast promised from us two a race / To fill the earth."

332. *utmost skirts:* distant robe; for God's *skirts,* see 3.380.

335–338. *thou . . . warmed:* The thought of God's *omnipresence* fuses Christ's warning to the woman of Samaria against worshipping God only "in this mountain" (John 4:21) with Jeremiah's questions: "Can any hide himself in secret places that I shall not see him? Saith the Lord: do not I fill heaven and earth?" (Jer. 23:24).

336. *Not this rock only:* i.e., "not only this place," but *rock* specifically suggests the Catholic Church (in Matt. 16:18, Jesus says of Peter, "upon this rock I will build my church," punning on Peter's name and the Latin word for "rock," *petrus;* Catholicism traces the authority of its hierarchy to this assertion). Milton here denies the claim that individuals have access to God only through the mediation of the Church; for the forward Protestant the individual conscience is the true church of God.

338. *Fomented:* nurtured; cf. 4.669. *virtual:* effective, capable of influencing

To dwell on even ground now with thy sons.
Yet doubt not but in valley and in plain
God is as here and will be found alike   350
Present, and of his presence many a sign
Still following thee, still compassing thee round
With goodness and paternal love, his face
Express, and of his steps the track divine.
Which that thou mayst believe and be confirmed   355
Ere thou from hence depart, know I am sent
To show thee what shall come in future days
To thee and to thy offspring. Good with bad
Expect to hear, supernal° grace contending   *heavenly*
With sinfulness of men, thereby to learn   360
True patience and to temper joy with fear
And pious sorrow, equally inured
By moderation either state to bear,
Prosperous or adverse. So shalt thou lead
Safest thy life and best prepared endure   365
Thy mortal passage when it comes. Ascend
This hill; let Eve (for I have drenched° her eyes)   *applied a potion to*
Here sleep below while thou to foresight wak'st,
As once thou slept'st while she to life was formed."
     To whom thus Adam gratefully replied: 370
"Ascend; I follow thee, safe guide, the path
Thou lead'st me, and to the hand of Heaven submit,
However chastening, to the evil turn
My obvious° breast, arming to overcome   *exposed, vulnerable*
By suffering, and earn rest from labor won   375
If so I may attain." So both ascend

352. *compassing . . . round:* surround-
ing; cf. Ps. 5:12: "with favor wilt thou com-
pass him as with a shield."
    357–360. *To show . . . men:* Adam's vi-
sion of the future of mankind rests on epic
precedent like the vision of Rome's future
that Aeneas sees in the Elysian Fields (*Aeneid*
6.754–854) and Britomart's vision of her
progeny in the *Faerie Queene* 3.3.29–49; but
cf. Dan. 10:14: "Now I am come to make
thee understand what shall befall thy people
in the latter days."
    361. *True patience:* in contrast to the
"stubborn patience" of 2.569

362. *pious sorrow:* sorrow that leads to
neither self-hatred nor loss of faith; cf. "sor-
rowing, yet in peace" (line 117 above).
    363–364. *By moderation . . . adverse:*
The phrasing suggests the title of Petrarch's
treatise *de Remediis Utriusque Fortunae*,
(which Thomas Twine translated in 1579 as
*Phisicke Against Fortune, as well Prosperous as
Aduerse*).
    374–375. *to overcome . . . suffering:* Cf.
the Latin proverb: *vincit qui patitur* (who en-
dures conquers).
    376–378. *ascend . . . highest:* Milton is
echoing Ezek. 40:2: "In the visions of God

In the visions of God. It was a hill
Of Paradise the highest, from whose top
The hemisphere of earth in clearest ken°   *view*
Stretched out to amplest reach of prospect° lay.   *sight*
Not higher that hill nor wider looking round,
Whereon for different cause the tempter set
Our second Adam in the wilderness
To show him all earth's kingdoms and their glory.
His eye might there command wherever stood   385
City of old or modern fame, the seat
Of mightiest empire, from the destined walls
Of Cambalu, seat of Cathayan Khan,
And Samarkand by Oxus, Temir's throne,
To Paquin of Sinaean° kings, and thence   *Chinese*
To Agra and Lahore of great Mogul,
Down to the golden Chersonese, or where
The Persian in Ecbatan sat or since
In Hispahan, or where the Russian czar
In Moscow, or the sultan in Bizance,   395
Turkestan born; nor could his eye not ken
The empire of negus to his utmost port,
Ercoco, and the less maritime kings,°   *kingdoms*
Mombasa and Quiloa and Melind,

brought he me into the land of Israel, and set me upon a very high mountain."

381–384. *Not higher . . . glory:* The scene is similar to that in Matt. 4:8, where Satan tempts Jesus by taking "him up into an exceeding high mountain and sheweth him all the kingdoms of the world." See also *PR* 3.251–344.

383. *second Adam:* Jesus Christ

388. *Cambalu . . . . Khan:* called "Cambaluc" (or "Khanbalic") by Marco Polo, built on the site of what is modern Beijing by Kubla Khan in the 13th century

389. *Samarkand . . . throne:* Samarkand, on the river *Oxus* in modern Uzbekistan, the capital of the Asian land ruled by *Temir* (i.e., Timur, or Tamburlaine)

390. *Paquin:* Peking (modern Beijing)

391. *Agra and Lahore:* major Mogul cities in what today is northwest India and Pakistan

392. *golden Chersonese:* the Malay peninsula (often indicated on maps as "Chersonesus Aurea" (the Golden Peninsula); see *PR* 4.74.

393. *Ecbatan:* Ecbatana (now Hamadan in Iran) was the summer residence of the ancient Persian rulers.

394. *Hispahan:* Hispahan (or Isfahan) replaced Kazvin as the Persian capital about 1600 under Shah Abbas the Great.

395. *Bizance:* Byzantium, the modern Constantinople, in 1453 conquered by the Turks (hence "the sultan . . . Turkestan-born" in lines 395–96)

397–398. *negus . . . Ercoco:* The *negus* (ruler) of Abyssinia (northern Ethiopia) controlled the port of *Ercoco,* the modern Arkiko, on the Red Sea.

399. *Mombasa . . . Quiloa . . . Melind:* Mombasa, like Melind, is a coastal city in Kenya, and *Quiloa* (Kilwa-Kisiwani) is an island port off the coast of Tanzania.

And Sofala, thought Ophir, to the realm   400
Of Congo and Angola farthest south;
Or thence from Niger flood to Atlas mount
The Kingdoms of Almansor: Fez and Sus,
Morocco and Algiers, and Tremisen;
On Europe thence and where Rome was to sway   405
The world. In spirit perhaps he also saw
Rich Mexico, the seat of Montezume,
And Cuzco in Peru, the richer seat
Of Atabalipa, and yet unspoiled
Guyana, whose great city Geryon's sons   410
Call El Dorado. But to nobler sights
Michael from Adam's eyes the film removed,
Which that false fruit that promised clearer sight
Had bred, then purged with euphrasy and rue
The visual nerve, for he had much to see,   415
And from the Well of Life three drops instilled.
So deep the power of these ingredients pierced,
Even to the inmost seat of mental sight,
That Adam, now enforced to close his eyes,

400. *Sofala, thought Ophir: Sofala* is a wealthy port city in modern Mozambique, sometimes thought to be identical with the biblical *Ophir,* famous for its gold (see 1 Kings 10:11 and Isa. 13:12).

402. *from Niger . . . Atlas mount:* from the *Niger* River (the principal river of western Africa, running in a crescent from modern Guinea to Nigeria) to Mount *Atlas* in Mauritania

403–404. *Kingdoms . . . Tremisen: Almansor* ("al-mansur," the victorious one, the name assumed by various Muslim rulers) controlled "Fez" and "Sus" (Tunis) in Morocco, Tremisen (modern Tlemcen) in Algeria, and parts of Spain.

407. *Montezume:* the Aztec ruler, Montezuma, whom Cortez conquered in 1520

408–409. *Cuzco . . . Atabalipa: Cuzco* was the capital of the Peruvian emperor *Atabalipa* (or Atahualpa), whom Pizarro conquered in 1533.

410–411. *Guyana . . . El Dorado:* In 1595 Sir Walter Raleigh set out to find *Guyana* and its reported golden city of *El*

Dorado. He sailed down the Orinoco in search of the "abundance of gold" reputed to be there but found nothing of value (which was why it was "yet unspoiled"), except for the evidence that the Spanish had been there before him. *Geryon's sons* refer to the Spanish conquistadors, named after the three-bodied, winged monster that Hercules slays (and for Spenser, in *Faerie Queene* 5.10.8, the symbol of the "huge power and great oppression" of Spain).

414. *euphrasy and rue:* herbs renowned for promoting good eyesight; *euphrasy,* or "Eiebright," says Gerard's *Herball,* p. 537, "is very much commended for the eies . . . It preserveth the sight, increaseth it, and being feeble and lost it restoreth the same." Of *rue,* Gerard writes: "when a little is boyled or scalded, and kept in pickle . . . and eaten," it "quickeneth the sight" (p. 1074), and Shakespeare, in *Hamlet* 4.5.181, calls it the "herb of grace."

416. *Well of Life:* See line 279 above; cf. Ps. 36:9: "With thee is the fountain of life: in thy light shall we see light."

Sunk down, and all his spirits became entranced;   420
But him the gentle angel by the hand
Soon raised and his attention thus recalled:
  "Adam, now ope thine eyes and first behold
The effects which thy original crime hath wrought
In some to spring from thee, who never touched   425
The excepted tree, nor with the snake conspired
Nor sinned thy sin, yet from that sin derive
Corruption to bring forth more violent deeds."
  His eyes he opened and beheld a field,
Part arable and tilth whereon were sheaves   430
New reaped, the other part, sheep walks and folds;
I' the midst an altar as the landmark° stood   *boundary marker*
Rustic of grassy sward; thither anon
A sweaty reaper from his tillage brought
First fruits, the green ear and the yellow sheaf   435
Unculled as came to hand; a shepherd next,
More meek, came with the firstlings of his flock
Choicest and best, then sacrificing laid
The innards and their fat with incense strewed
On the cleft wood and all due rites performed.   440
His offering soon propitious fire from Heaven
Consumed with nimble glance and grateful steam;
The other's not, for his was not sincere,
Whereat° he inly raged, and, as they talked,   *at which*

420. *entranced:* Daniel (Dan. 10:8–14) sinks into trance in the vision to which line 357 above refers.

425. *who:* refers not to Adam but to the race that springs from him

425–428. *who never . . . Corruption:* The actions of both Eve and Adam make up *that sin* from which they *derive Corruption.*

426. *excepted:* excluded (the one exception to their dominion over nature)

427. *sinned thy sin:* The jingle is biblical: Exod. 32:30: "Ye have sinned a great sin."

430. *Part arable and tilth:* part (was set aside for) cultivated (*arable* = fit for planting; *tilth* = cultivated land)

431. *the other . . . folds:* the other part (was set aside for) pastures and pens for sheep

432–433. *an altar . . . of grassy sward:* Cf. lines 323–24 above, where Adam imagines the "graceful altars [he] would rear on grassy turf."

434–437: *A sweaty reaper . . . flock:* See Gen. 4:2–4: "Abel was a keeper of sheep, but Cain was a tiller of the ground."

435. *First fruits:* See line 22 above.

436. *Unculled:* not distinguished, picked at random (in contrast with "Choicest and best" in line 438)

441. *propitious:* favorably disposed (modifies "fire")

441–442. *fire . . . Consumed:* The consumption of the sacrifice by the fire is the sign of God's acceptance (see, for example, Lev. 9:4 and 1 Chron. 21:26).

442. *nimble glance:* quick flash   *grateful steam:* smoke found pleasing or acceptable

Smote him into the midriff with a stone   445
That beat out life; he fell, and deadly pale
Groaned out his soul with gushing blood effused.
Much at that sight was Adam in his heart
Dismayed, and thus in haste to the angel cried:
    "O teacher, some great mischief hath befallen   450
To that meek man who well had sacrificed.
Is piety thus and pure devotion paid?"
    To whom Michael thus, he also moved, replied:
"These two are brethren, Adam, and to come
Out of thy loins; the unjust the just hath slain   455
For° envy that his brother's offering found   *because of*
From Heaven acceptance; but the bloody fact
Will be avenged, and the other's faith, approved,
Lose° no reward, though here thou see him die,   *will lose*
Rolling in dust and gore." To which our sire: 460
    "Alas, both for the deed and for the cause!
But have I now seen death? Is this the way
I must return to native dust? O sight
Of terror, foul and ugly to behold,
Horrid to think, how horrible to feel!"   465
    To whom thus Michael: "Death thou hast seen
In his first shape on man, but many shapes
Of death and many are the ways that lead
To his grim cave, all dismal, yet to sense
More terrible at the entrance than within.   470
Some, as thou saw'st, by violent stroke shall die,
By fire, flood, famine; by intemperance more
In meats and drinks, which on the earth shall bring
Diseases dire, of which a monstrous crew
Before thee shall appear that thou mayst know   475
What misery the inabstinence of Eve
Shall bring on men." Immediately a place
Before his eyes appeared, sad, noisome,° dark;   *unpleasant, foul-smelling*

---

445. *him:* i.e., Abel (not the "he," Cain, who "inly raged" in line 444)

445–446. *stone . . . life:* Gen. 4:8 does not specify the weapon that Cain used to kill his brother. Abraham Crowley, in his *Davideis* (1656), says that "neither is it declared in what manner [Cain] slew his *Brother:* and therefore I had the liberty to chuse that which I thought most probable; which is, that he knockt him on the head with some great stone" (Book 1, note 16).

450. *mischief:* harm, injury; stronger than its modern meaning.

457. *fact:* deed, crime (as at 9.928)

469. *all dismal:* presumably refers back to "shapes" in line 467, but could refer to

A lazar-house it seemed wherein were laid
Numbers of all diseased, all maladies   480
Of ghastly spasm or racking torture, qualms°   *fits*
Of heartsick agony, all feverous kinds,
Convulsions, epilepsies, fierce catarrhs,
Intestine stone and ulcer, colic pangs,
Demoniac frenzy, moping melancholy   485
And moonstruck madness, pining atrophy,
Marasmus and wide-wasting pestilence,
Dropsies and asthmas and joint-racking rheums.
Dire was the tossing, deep the groans; despair
Tended the sick busiest from couch to couch;   490
And over them triumphant Death his dart
Shook, but delayed to strike though oft invoked
With vows, as their chief good and final hope.
Sight so deform what heart of rock could long
Dry-eyed behold? Adam could not, but wept   495
Though not of woman born; compassion quelled
His best of man and gave him up to tears
A space, till firmer thoughts restrained excess,
And scarce recovering words his plaint renewed:
        "O miserable mankind, to what fall   500
Degraded, to what wretched state reserved!
Better end here unborn. Why is life given
To be thus wrested from us? Rather why
Obtruded° on us thus? Who, if we knew   *forced*

"cave," *all dismal* in the sense of being "com-
pletely dismal" (*all* functioning as it does in
"all-powerful")

479. *lazar-house:* hospital (mainly for
lepers, but here, as the catalogue of infirmi-
ties makes clear, for all diseases)

485–487. *Demoniac...pestilence:* These
lines were added by Milton in 1674.

486. *moonstruck madness:* an almost lit-
eral 17th-century definition of lunacy, a
mental derangement thought to be caused by
the phases of the moon

487. *Marasmus:* any wasting away or
consumption of the body

492. *though oft invoked:* not, as some
editors assume, a vague allusion to literary
precedents, but the persistent cries of the sick
calling on Death to end their suffering

494. *Sight so deform:* the object of the
verb "behold" in line 495; *deform* = hideous

496. *not of woman born:* refers to the
unique circumstances of Adam's creation
(which supposedly might make him less
likely to weep than other men), but the
recollection of *Macbeth,* where the witches
say that "none of woman born / Shall harm
Macbeth" (4.1.80–81), is striking.

497. *His best of man:* courage; again the
reminiscence is of *Macbeth:* "it hath cowed
my better part of man" (5.8.18), though
Shakespeare's play finally rejects these as-
sumptions of the value of unfeeling male sto-
icism (4.3.221–24).

504–506. *Who ... down:* In making
Adam guilty of what Sir Thomas Browne
called the "underweening of this life,"

What we receive, would either not accept   505
Life offered or soon beg to lay it down,
Glad to be so dismissed in peace? Can thus
The image of God in man, created once
So goodly and erect, though faulty since,
To such unsightly sufferings be debased   510
Under inhuman pains? Why should not man,
Retaining still divine similitude
In part, from such deformities be free
And, for his maker's image sake, exempt?"
    "Their maker's image," answered Michael, "then   515
Forsook them when themselves they vilified
To serve ungoverned appetite and took
His image whom they served, a brutish vice,
Inductive mainly to the sin of Eve.
Therefore so abject is their punishment,   520
Disfiguring not God's likeness but their own,
Or, if his likeness, by themselves defaced,
While they pervert pure nature's healthful rules
To loathsome sickness, worthily, since they
God's image did not reverence in themselves."   525
    "I yield it just," said Adam, "and submit.
But is there yet no other way besides
These painful passages how we may come
To death and mix with our connatural dust?"
    "There is," said Michael, "if thou well observe   530
The rule of not too much, by temperance taught,

Milton was probably thinking, in Browne's
words, of the saying of "the Stoick [Seneca]
. . . that life would not be accepted, if it were
offered unto such as knew it" (*Christian
Morals*, published posthumously in 1716,
3.25); though Milton thought of suicide as
"a perverse hatred of self, . . . presumptuous
sin" (*Christian Doctrine* II, viii [*Works*
17, 201]).
    512–514. *Retaining . . . exempt:* Adam
assumes that the fall obscures but does not
extinguish the *divine similitude,* though he
wonders if humanity should not even thus be
exempt from such disfiguring diseases *for his
maker's image sake.* Though theologians
sometimes did distinguish between the

imago dei and the *similitudo dei* (likeness of
God), Milton uses them as synonyms here.
    516. *vilified:* literally, made vile, de-
graded
    518. *His image:* not now God's *image,*
but the image of Gluttony ("ungoverned ap-
petite")
    519. *Inductive:* 1) traceable; 2) con-
ducive
    528. *passages:* deaths (passages out of
life); see line 366 above.
    529. *connatural:* of shared nature (since
man comes of dust and will return to it; see
Gen. 3:19).
    531. *rule of not too much:* a translation
of an adage reportedly carved on the temple

In what thou eat'st and drink'st, seeking from thence
Due nourishment, not gluttonous delight,
Till many years over thy head return.
So mayst thou live, till like ripe fruit thou drop   535
Into thy mother's lap or be with ease
Gathered, not harshly plucked, for death mature.
This is old age, but then thou must outlive
Thy youth, thy strength, thy beauty, which will change
To withered, weak, and gray; thy senses then   540
Obtuse,° all taste of pleasure must forgo   *dull*
To° what thou hast, and for the air of youth,   *in comparison to*
Hopeful and cheerful, in thy blood will reign
A melancholy damp of cold and dry
To weigh thy spirits down and last consume   545
The balm of life." To whom our ancestor:
    "Henceforth I fly not death, nor would prolong
Life much, bent rather how I may be quit°   *released*
Fairest and easiest of this cumbrous charge
Which I must keep till my appointed day   550
Of rendering up, and patiently attend
My dissolution." Michael replied:
    "Nor love thy life nor hate, but what thou liv'st
Live well—how long or short permit to Heaven.

at Delphi (Plato, *Protagoras* 343b), convey-
ing the idea that "health is destroyed by too
much and too little food and drink" as Aris-
totle puts it in the *Nicomachean Ethics* 2.2.6.
Milton's usual term is "temperance" (*Christ-
ian Doctrine* II, ix [*Works* 17, 213 ff.]).
    535–536. *like ripe . . . lap:* The ano-
dyne simile of death as *ripe fruit* dropping
was familiar from Job 5:26: "Thou shalt
come to thy grave in a full age, like as a shock
of corn cometh in his season," but also from
non-biblical sources ranging from Cicero's
Of Old Age (19) through Dante's *Convito* (4)
and Spenser's image of being "made ripe for
death by eld" (*Faerie Queene* 2.10.32).
    543–544. *in . . . dry:* In the Galenic
physiology based on a theory of "humors,"
old age was marked by the predominance of
phlegm and black bile, which produced
melancholy; cf. Robert Burton on old age as
the most frequent cause of melancholy, since
it is "cold and dry, and of the same quality as

melancholy is, . . . needs must cause it, by
diminution of spirits and substance"
(*Anatomy of Melancholy*, 1621, 1.2.1 and
1.2.5); *damp* = depression (or what causes it,
a noxious vapor)
    546. *balm of life:* life-giving spirit
    549. *cumbrous charge:* wearisome re-
sponsibility (i.e., the body)
    551–552. *and patiently . . . dissolution:*
Milton's insertion in the second edition. The
reader in 1667 was perhaps expected to com-
plete the thought from Job 14:14: "All the
days of my appointed time will I wait, till my
change come"; *attend* = await.
    553. *Nor love . . . hate:* The maxim re-
peats Martial's tenth epigram: "Neither
dread nor desire thy last hour" and similar
advice in Horace's "Soracte" Ode (1.9.9) and
in Seneca's *Epistles* 24.24 and 65.18.
    554. *permit:* give up, leave; cf. Horace,
Odes 1.9.9: "Leave (*permitte*) to the Gods."

And now prepare thee for another sight."   555
   He looked and saw a spacious plain whereon
Were tents of various hue: by some were herds
Of cattle grazing; others, whence the sound
Of instruments that made melodious chime
Was heard, of harp and organ, and who moved   560
Their stops and chords was seen: his volant° touch   *nimble, "flying"*
Instinct through all proportions low and high
Fled and pursued transverse the resonant fugue.
In other part stood one who, at the forge
Laboring, two massy° clods of iron and brass   *massive*
Had melted (whether found where casual fire
Had wasted woods on mountain or in vale
Down to the veins of earth, thence gliding hot
To some cave's mouth, or whether washed by stream
From underground). The liquid ore he drained   570
Into fit molds prepared, from which he formed
First his own tools, then what might else be wrought
Fusile or graven in metal. After these,
But on the hither side, a different sort
From the high neighboring hills which was their seat   575

556–573. *spacious plain . . . metal:* The basis for the scenes in the *spacious plain* is the account in Gen. 4:20–22 of the sons of Lamech: Jabal, "the father of such as dwell in tents," Jubal, "the father of all such as handle the harp and organ," and Tubal-cain, "an instructor of every artificer in brass and iron."

560. *who:* one who (i.e., Jubal)

562. *Instinct:* various constructions are possible, but probably means "instinctively," an adverb attached to "Fled" (line 563); i.e., his nimble "touch" moved instinctively (as he was not trained) "through all proportions low and high" ("proportions" = musical harmonies).

563. *Fled and pursued transverse:* The verbs are both used as musical terms for playing the contrapuntal "fugue" (derived from Latin *fugare = to flee*), the image of flight and pursuit exactly indicating the musical form's particular texture and momentum—and here especially appropriate for the sons of

Cain, who is told in Gen. 4:12 that he shall be "a fugitive."

564–573. *at the forge . . . metal:* The lines reflect Lucretius' account of the discovery of metals when they were first laid bare by lightning-kindled forest fires and accidentally fused in natural pits (*De rerum natura* 5.1241–68).

564. *one:* i.e., Tubal-cain (Gen. 4:22)

566. *casual:* accidental (i.e., accidentally ignited by lightning)

573. *Fusile or graven:* molded or sculpted

573–627. *After these . . . weep:* The scene shifts to *the hither side,* the west of Eden (since Cain "went out from the presence of the Lord, and dwelt . . . on the east of Eden" [Gen. 4:16]). A tradition stemming from Gen. 6:2–4 represents the sons of Seth as deservedly called the "sons of God" until they were lured from their mountain homes to marry and beget a giant race with the daughters of Cain.

574. *a different sort:* the sons of Seth

Down to the plain descended. By their guise
Just men they seemed, and all their study bent
To worship God aright and know his works
Not hid, nor those things last which might preserve
Freedom and peace to men. They on the plain   580
Long had not walked, when from the tents behold
A bevy of fair women, richly gay°   *ornamented*
In gems and wanton dress; to the harp they sung
Soft amorous ditties and in dance came on.
The men, though grave, eyed them and let their eyes   585
Rove without rein till, in the amorous net
Fast caught, they liked, and each his liking chose;
And now of love they treat° till the evening star,   *talk*
Love's harbinger, appeared; then all in heat
They light the nuptial torch and bid invoke   590
Hymen, then first to marriage rites invoked;
With feast and music all the tents resound.
Such happy interview and fair event
Of love and youth not lost, songs, garlands, flowers,
And charming symphonies attached the heart   595
Of Adam, soon inclined to admit delight,
The bent° of nature, which he thus expressed: *natural inclination*
    "True opener of mine eyes, prime angel blessed,
Much better seems this vision, and more hope
Of peaceful days portends than those two past: 600
Those were of hate and death, or pain much worse;
Here nature seems fulfilled in all her ends."
    To whom thus Michael: "Judge not what is best
By pleasure, though to nature seeming meet,°   *proper*
Created as thou art to nobler end   605

---

577. *study bent:* effort directed (though *bent* suggests also "deformed")

578–579. *know his works Not hid:* the study of visible nature; see 8.167; see also Deut. 29:29: "The secret things belong unto the Lord our God: but those things which are revealed belong unto us and to our children for ever."

579–580. *those . . . men:* i.e., did they leave to the end the study of good government

582. *bevy:* group; cf. *Faerie Queene* 2.9.34: "A lovely bevy of faire Ladies."

588. *the evening star:* Venus, as in 8.519

589. *in heat:* emphasizes the animal nature of desire in the fallen world

591. *Hymen:* Renaissance writers often invoked Hymen, the god of marriage, such as Spenser's cry of the groomsmen in *Epithalamion* 140: "Hymen, Iö Hymen, Hymen, they do shout" (see also "L'Allegro," 125–29), though possibly here the classicism is no less a mark of the fall than "in heat" above.

595. *symphonies attached:* harmonious music took hold of

Holy and pure, conformity divine.
Those tents thou saw'st so pleasant were the tents
Of wickedness, wherein shall dwell his race
Who slew his brother; studious they appear
Of arts that polish life, inventors rare,   610
Unmindful of their maker, though his spirit
Taught them, but they his gifts acknowledged none.
Yet they a beauteous offspring shall beget:
For that fair female troop thou saw'st that seemed
Of goddesses, so blithe, so smooth, so gay,   615
Yet empty of all good wherein consists
Woman's domestic honor and chief praise,
Bred only and completed to the taste
Of lustful appetence°—to sing, to dance,   *appetite, craving*
To dress and troll the tongue and roll the eye—   620
To these that sober race of men, whose lives
Religious titled them the sons of God,
Shall yield up all their virtue, all their fame
Ignobly, to the trains° and to the smiles   *lures, wiles*
Of these fair atheists, and now swim in joy,   625
(Erelong to swim at large) and laugh, for which
The world erelong a world of tears must weep."
    To whom thus Adam of short joy bereft:
"O pity and shame that they who to live well
Entered so fair should turn aside to tread   630

606. *conformity divine:* i.e., like God in being holy and pure (though the phrase suggests a distinction between *conformity divine* and that mandated by the 1662 Act of Conformity, which required all ministers in England and Wales to be ordained by a bishop and to assent to everything in the Book of Common Prayer)

607–608. *tents Of wickedness:* derives from Ps. 84:10: "I had rather be a doorkeeper in the house of my God, than to dwell in the tents of wickedness."

611. *spirit:* not the Holy Spirit, the third person of the Trinity, but the animating power of God, as in 12.487–88

613. *a beauteous offspring:* not a specific child, but the "fair female troop" in line 614

618. *completed:* equipped (*OED,* "complete," 3)

620. *troll the tongue:* lick one's lips (as a sign of desire)

621–623. *sober race . . . virtue:* refers to Gen. 6:1–2: "it came to pass, when men began to multiply on the face of the earth, and daughters were born unto them, That the sons of God saw the daughters of men that they were fair; and they took them wives of all which they chose." There was an exegetical tradition that identified these "sons of God" as angels that lay with the daughters of men; cf. 3.461–63, but here they are clearly human.

625–626. *swim . . . swim:* The ironic repetition literalizing the initial metaphoric use of *swim* anticipates the flood in lines 818–73 below (but, of course, Adam does not get the point).

Paths indirect or in the mid-way faint!
But still I see the tenor of man's woe
Holds on the same: from woman to begin."
   "From man's effeminate slackness it begins,"
Said the angel, "who should better hold his place   635
By wisdom and superior gifts received.
But now prepare thee for another scene."
   He looked and saw wide territory spread
Before him, towns, and rural works between,
Cities of men with lofty gates and towers,   640
Concourse° in arms, fierce faces threatening war,   *hostile encounter*
Giants of mighty bone and bold emprise;
Part wield their arms, part curb the foaming steed,
Single or in array of battle ranged
Both horse and foot, nor idly mustering stood.   645
One way a band select from forage drives
A herd of beeves, fair oxen and fair kine
From a fat° meadow ground, or fleecy flock,   *fertile*
Ewes and their bleating lambs, over the plain,
Their booty; scarce with life the shepherds fly,   650
But call in aid which makes a bloody fray;
With cruel tournament the squadrons join;
Where cattle pastured late, now scattered lies
With carcasses and arms the ensanguined° field   *blood-stained*
Deserted. Others to a city strong   655
Lay siege, encamped, by battery, scale, and mine
Assaulting; others from the wall defend
With dart and javelin, stones and sulfurous fire;
On each hand slaughter and gigantic° deeds.   *giant-like*
In other part the sceptered heralds call   660
To council in the city gates. Anon

632. *man's woe:* To illustrate the false etymology, *OED* quotes John Heywood's *Proverbs* 2.7: "A woman! As who saith, woe to the man!"

634. *effeminate slackness:* weakness, not that supposedly characteristic of women, but weakness that comes from loving immoderately; the distinction is part of Michael's correction of Adam's misogyny in lines 632–33.

638–673. *wide . . . found:* The panorama has many obvious Homeric echoes, particularly of the description of the shield of Achilles (*Iliad* 18.478–616). The scenes here elaborate Genesis 6:4.

642. *emprise:* enterprise, adventure; cf. *Comus,* line 609: "bold emprise."

644. *array of battle ranged:* arrayed in military formations

646. *band select:* a band of picked men

656. *battery, scale, and mine:* battering rams, ladders, and tunnels

660–663. *call . . . Assemble:* The council of elders called together by heralds while a city is besieged is similar to that in *Iliad*

Grey-headed men and grave, with warriors mixed,
Assemble, and harangues are heard, but soon
In factious opposition, till at last
Of middle age one rising, eminent   665
In wise deport, spake much of right and wrong,
Of justice, of religion, truth and peace,
And judgment from above. Him old and young
Exploded and had seized with violent hands
Had not a cloud descending snatched him thence   670
Unseen amid the throng. So violence
Proceeded, and oppression, and sword-law
Through all the plain, and refuge none was found.
Adam was all in tears and to his guide,
Lamenting, turned full sad: "O what are these?   675
Death's ministers, not men, who thus deal death
Inhumanly to men and multiply
Ten thousandfold the sin of him who slew
His brother. For of whom such massacre
Make they but of their brethren, men of men?   680
But who was that just man, whom had not Heaven
Rescued, had in his righteousness been lost?"
    To whom thus Michael: "These are the product
Of those ill-mated marriages thou saw'st,
Where good with bad were matched, who of themselves   685
Abhor to join and, by imprudence mixed,
Produce prodigious° births of body or mind.   *monstrous*
Such were these giants, men of high renown;
For in those days might only shall be admired,
And valor and heroic virtue called;   690

18.503–10; assemblies at the city gates have various biblical precedent including Gen. 34:20: "Hamor and Shechem his son came unto the gate of their city, and communed with the men of their city."

665. *Of middle age one rising:* Enoch, who "walked with God" (Gen. 5:22) and was translated to Heaven at 365 years of age, the *middle age* in comparison with that of many of the patriarchs (e.g., Adam's 930 years, or Seth's 912, Gen. 5:4, 5:8, 5:23).

669. *Exploded:* hooted at, scorned (as with "exploding" in 10.546)

672. *sword-law:* rule by force; cf.

Richard III 5.3.311: "Our strong arms be our conscience, swords our law."

685–686. *of themselves . . . join:* refuse to marry their own kind

688. *giants . . . renown:* Cf. Gen. 6:4: "There were giants in the earth . . . when the sons of God came in unto the daughters of men, and the bare children to them, the same became mighty men which were of old, men of renown."

689–699. *might only . . . hid:* the traditional values celebrated by epic, which Milton rejects for "the better fortitude / Of patience and heroic martyrdom" (9.31–32)

To overcome in battle and subdue
Nations and bring home spoils with infinite
Manslaughter shall be held the highest pitch
Of human glory, and, for glory done,
Of triumph to be styled great conquerors,   695
Patrons of mankind, gods, and sons of gods,
Destroyers rightlier called and plagues of men.
Thus fame shall be achieved, renown on earth,
And what most merits fame in silence hid.
But he, the seventh from thee, whom thou beheld'st   700
The only righteous in a world perverse
And therefore hated, therefore so beset
With foes for daring single to be just
And utter odious truth that God would come
To judge them with his saints, him the most high   705
Rapt in a balmy cloud with wingèd steeds
Did, as thou saw'st, receive to walk with God
High in salvation and the climes of bliss,
Exempt from death, to show thee what reward
Awaits the good, the rest what punishment,   710
Which° now direct thine eyes and soon behold."   *to which*
     He looked and saw the face of things quite changed:
The brazen throat of war had ceased to roar;
All now was turned to jollity and game,
To luxury and riot, feast and dance,   715
Marrying or prostituting, as befell,
Rape or adultery, where passing fair
Allured them; thence from cups to civil broils.

695. *Of triumph:* by public ceremony

700. *he, the seventh from thee:* i.e., Enoch, seventh in descent from Adam; Jude 1:14 refers to Enoch as "the seventh from Adam."

703. *daring single to be just:* like Abdiel, "who single hast maintained / Against revolted multitudes the cause / Of truth" (6.30–32).

707. *walk with God:* See Gen. 5:24: "And Enoch walked with God: and he was not; for God took him." "God tooke him away," says the Geneva gloss, "To shew that there was a better life prepared, and to be a

testimonie of the immortalitie of soules and bodies."

713. *brazen throat of war:* Cf. Richard Crashaw's "Music's Duel" (1646): "the brasen voyce of warr's hoarce bird" (line 101).

714–753. *All now . . . embarked:* This next vision, describing the depravity of mankind and the flood, is an elaboration of Gen. 6:9–9:17.

715. *luxury and riot:* lust and debauchery; cf. 1.496–99.

717. *passing fair:* surpassing beauty (but also "women passing by")

At length a reverend sire among them came
And of their doings great dislike declared,   720
And testified against their ways; he oft
Frequented their assemblies whereso met,
Triumphs° or festivals, and to them preached   *triumphal processions*
Conversion and repentance as to souls
In prison under judgments imminent.   725
But all in vain, which when he saw he ceased
Contending and removed his tents far off;
Then, from the mountain hewing timber tall,
Began to build a vessel of huge bulk,
Measured by cubit, length and breadth, and height,   730
Smeared round with pitch, and in the side a door
Contrived, and of provisions laid in large
For man and beast, when, lo, a wonder strange!
Of every beast and bird and insect small
Came sevens and pairs, and entered in as taught   735
Their order, last the sire and his three sons
With their four wives, and God made fast the door.
Meanwhile the south wind rose, and, with black wings
Wide hovering, all the clouds together drove
From under heaven; the hills to their supply°   *assistance*
Vapor, and exhalation dusk and moist,
Sent up amain;° and now the thickened sky   *violently*
Like a dark ceiling stood. Down rushed the rain
Impetuous and continued till the earth
No more was seen. The floating vessel swum   745

719. *reverend sire:* i.e., Noah, who was
"six hundred years old when the flood of
waters was upon the earth" (Gen. 7: 6).

724–725. *to souls In prison:* In 1 Pet.
3:19–20, Jesus "preached unto the spirits in
prison," whom Peter typologically identifies
with the unregenerate "in the days of Noah,
while the ark was a preparing."

730. *cubit:* ancient unit of linear meas-
urement, from the elbow to the fingertip; the
ark was 300 by 50 by 30 cubits (Gen. 6:15).

734. *insect small:* although Genesis
makes no mention of insects on the ark

735. *sevens and pairs:* follows Gen. 7:2:
"Of every clean beast thou shalt take to thee
by sevens, the male and his female: and of
beasts that are not clean by two"

738–753. *Meanwhile . . . embarked:*
Milton turns here to Ovid (*Metamorphoses*
1.262–347) for details of the flood. The
Ovidian account of the flood of Deucalion
and Pyrrha serves as a corroboration of the
truthfulness of the biblical story.

738–745. *the south wind . . . seen:* Cf.:
"Out flyes the South, with dropping wings;
who shrouds / His terrible aspect in pitchie
clouds. / His white haire streams, his Beard
big-swoln with showres; / Mists bind his
brows; Raine from his bosome poures, / As
with his hands the hanging clouds he crusht:
/ They roar'd, and downe in showres together
rusht" (*Metamorphoses* 1.264–69; trans.
Sandys).

741. *exhalation dusk:* dark mist

Uplifted and, secure with beakèd prow,
Rode tilting o'er the waves; all dwellings else
Flood overwhelmed, and them with all their pomp
Deep under water rolled. Sea covered sea,
Sea without shore, and in their palaces,   750
Where luxury late reigned, sea-monsters whelped
And stabled. Of mankind, so numerous late,
All left in one small bottom swum embarked.
How didst thou grieve then, Adam, to behold
The end of all thy offspring, end so sad,   755
Depopulation. Thee another flood,
Of tears and sorrow a flood thee also drowned
And sunk thee as thy sons, till gently reared
By the angel, on thy feet thou stood'st at last,
Though comfortless, as when a father mourns   760
His children all in view destroyed at once,
And scarce° to the angel uttered'st thus thy plaint: *barely, hardly able*
    "O visions ill foreseen! Better had I
Lived ignorant of future, so had borne
My part of evil only, each day's lot   765
Enough to bear; those now that were dispensed,
The burden of many ages, on me light
At once, by my foreknowledge gaining birth
Abortive to torment me ere their being
With thought that they must be. Let no man seek   770
Henceforth to be foretold what shall befall
Him or his children: evil, he may be sure,
Which neither his foreknowing can prevent,
And he the future evil shall no less
In apprehension than in substance feel   775

749–750. *Sea . . . without shore:* Cf.:
"For all was Sea, nor had the Sea a shore"
(*Metamorphoses* 1.292 [trans. Sandys]).

753. *in . . . embarked:* in one small boat
sailed, having embarked (*bottom* = boat, as in
Twelfth Night 5.1.57: "the most noble bot-
tom of our fleet")

765–766. *each day's . . . bear:* Adam says
that he can just about bear the daily evidence
of his own evil, echoing Matt. 6:34: "Suffi-
cient unto the day is the evil thereof."

766. *dispensed:* given (refers to the "vi-
sions ill foreseen," line 763)

767. *light:* alight; one might be tempted
momentarily to read this as an adjective
meaning "not heavy" following "burden,"
but the point is that this burden that he must
bear—the knowledge of all who will die for
sins deriving from his own—is anything but
light in that sense, the rejected pun empha-
sizing Adam's anguish.

768–769. *birth Abortive:* 1) monstrous
birth; 2) aborted birth. Adam's tortured
metaphor is that the knowledge he has been
given of the "Depopulation" (line 756 above)
of the earth works to bring to life those who

Grievous to bear. But that care now is past;
Man is not whom to warn. Those few escaped
Famine and anguish will at last consume,
Wandering that watery desert. I had hope
When violence was ceased and war on earth   780
All would have then gone well; peace would have crowned
With length of happy days the race of man.
But I was far deceived, for now I see
Peace to corrupt no less than war to waste.
How comes it thus? Unfold, celestial guide,   785
And whether here the race of man will end?"
   To whom thus Michael: "Those whom last thou saw'st
In triumph and luxurious wealth are they
First seen in acts of prowess eminent
And great exploits but of true virtue void,   790
Who, having spilt much blood and done much waste
Subduing nations and achieved thereby
Fame in the world, high titles, and rich prey,
Shall change their course to pleasure, ease, and sloth,
Surfeit and lust, till wantonness and pride   795
Raise out of friendship hostile deeds in peace.
The conquered, also, and enslaved by war
Shall, with their freedom lost, all virtue lose
And fear of God, from whom their piety feigned
In sharp contest of battle found no aid   800
Against invaders; therefore, cooled in zeal
Thenceforth shall practice how to live secure,
Worldly or dissolute, on what their lords
Shall leave them to enjoy, for the earth shall bear

have not yet lived, but since what he knows
is that they will be destroyed, their lives
(both in his imagination and eventually in
fact) are monstrous (*Abortive*) to him and cut
short (*Abortive*) for them.
   777. *Man is not whom:* there is no man
left
   778. *consume:* kill; cf. *Metamorphoses*
1.311–12: "The waves the greater part de-
voure: the rest, / Death, with long-wanted
sustenance, opprest" (trans. Sandys).
   787. *To:* Neither 1667 nor 1674 in-
dents here, though new speeches are nor-
mally marked by new verse paragraphs.

Perhaps as the speech begins a new page in
the early editions, the compositor missed the
instruction. Most editions emend.
   801–804. *cooled . . . enjoy:* This seems
to be Milton's bitter response to an England
that has backslid and abandoned its revolu-
tionary fervor; the *zeal* of the revolution and
the interregnum has given way to a desire
merely for security and comfort. The confi-
dence of *Areopagitica* (1644), which saw
England as "a noble and puissant Nation, . . .
entering the glorious ways of truth and pros-
perous virtue, destined to become great and
honorable in these latter ages" (*Works* 4,

More than enough that temperance may be tried.°   *tested*
So all shall turn degenerate, all depraved,
Justice and temperance, truth and faith forgot,
One man except, the only son of light
In a dark age against example good,
Against allurement, custom, and a world   810
Offended,° fearless of reproach and scorn   *sinned against*
Or violence. He of their wicked ways
Shall them admonish and before them set
The paths of righteousness, how much more safe
And full of peace, denouncing° wrath to come   *proclaiming*
On their impenitence, and shall return
Of° them derided, but of God observed   *by*
The one just man alive. By his command
Shall build a wondrous ark, as thou beheld'st,
To save himself and household from amidst   820
A world devote to universal wrack.
No sooner he, with them of man and beast
Select° for life, shall in the ark be lodged   *chosen*
And sheltered round, but all the cataracts
Of heaven set open on the earth shall pour   825
Rain day and night, all fountains of the deep,
Broke up, shall heave the ocean to usurp
Beyond all bounds till inundation rise
Above the highest hills. Then shall this mount
Of Paradise by might of waves be moved   830
Out of his place, pushed by the hornèd flood,
With all his verdure spoiled and trees adrift,
Down the great river to the opening gulf,

---

344), here gives way to a disillusionment about a nation where people *shall practice how to live secure . . . on what their lords / Shall give them to enjoy.*

808. *One man except:* i.e., Noah

821. *devote to universal wrack:* doomed to complete destruction; cf. 3.207–8.

824. *cataracts:* floodgates; in the 1638 volume of elegies for Edward King in which "Lycidas" appears, Samson Briggs, in his "When Common Sounds Break from their Courser Clay" writes: "God opened all / Heavens cataracts."

831. *hornèd:* most likely "divided"; Virgil describes the Po as dividing its stream into horns: "Po first issues from his dark abodes, . . . / Two golden horns on his large front he wears, / And his grim face a bull's resemblance bears" (*Georgics* 4.370–73 [trans. Dryden]); but possibly meaning "bull-like," referring to the power of the waters that can move even "this mount Of Paradise" (lines 829–30).

833. *the great river:* "the great river, the river Euphrates" (Gen. 15:18), which empties into the Persian "[G]ulf"

And there take root, an island salt and bare,
The haunt of seals and orcs° and sea-mews' clang,   *whales*
To teach thee that God attributes to place
No sanctity if none be thither brought
By men who there frequent or therein dwell.
And now what further shall ensue, behold."
    He looked and saw the ark hull° on the flood,   *drift, float*
Which now abated, for the clouds were fled,
Driven by a keen north wind that, blowing dry,
Wrinkled the face of deluge, as decayed;
And the clear sun on his wide watery glass
Gazed hot and of the fresh wave largely drew,   845
As after thirst, which made their flowing shrink
From standing lake to tripping ebb, that stole
With soft foot toward the deep, who now had stopped
His sluices, as the heaven his windows shut.
The ark no more now floats but seems on ground   850
Fast on the top of some high mountain fixed.
And now the tops of hills as rocks appear.
With clamor thence the rapid currents drive
Toward the retreating sea their furious tide.
Forthwith from out the ark a raven flies   855
And after him, the surer messenger:
A dove sent forth once and again to spy°   *espy, see*
Green tree or ground whereon his foot may light;
The second time returning, in his bill
An olive leaf he brings, pacific sign.   860
Anon dry ground appears, and from his ark
The ancient sire descends with all his train;

834. *an island . . . bare:* the fate of Para-
dise after the flood
    835. *sea-mews' clang:* harsh cry of gulls
(as at 7.422)
    840–843. *the flood . . . decayed:* Milton's
account of the abating of the flood waters has
multiple literary debts—Gen. 8:1: "God
made a wind to pass over the earth, and the
waters asswaged"; Ovid makes a north wind
drive away the clouds after Deucalion's flood
(*Metamorphoses* 1.328); and Sidney opens
the *Arcadia* (1590) with the scene of "a ship
. . . hulling there, part broken, part burned,
part drowned. . . . A number of dead bodies

(as it were) filled the wrinkles of the sea
visage."
    844. *watery glass:* The sea, now calm, is
like a mirror, into which the "clear sun"
gazes.
    847. *tripping ebb:* running stream
    851. *some high mountain:* Gen. 8:4
names it as "the mountains of Ararat."
    857. *once and again:* Noah released the
dove twice—the first time it returned having
failed to find land; the second time, seven
days later, it returned with the olive branch
(Gen. 8:8–12).
    860. *pacific sign:* sign of peace

Then, with uplifted hands and eyes devout,
Grateful to Heaven, over his head beholds
A dewy cloud and in the cloud a bow   865
Conspicuous with three listed° colors gay,   *banded, striped*
Betokening peace from God and covenant new.
Whereat the heart of Adam, erst° so sad,   *formerly*
Greatly rejoiced, and thus his joy broke forth:
    "O thou who future things canst represent   870
As present, heavenly instructor, I revive
At this last sight, assured that man shall live,
With all the creatures and their seed preserve.
Far less I now lament for one whole world
Of wicked sons destroyed than I rejoice   875
For one man found so perfect and so just
That God vouchsafes to raise another world
From him and all his anger to forget.
But say what mean those colored streaks in heaven,
Distended as the brow of God appeased,   880
Or serve they as a flowery verge° to bind   *border*
The fluid skirts of that same watery cloud,
Lest it again dissolve and shower the earth?"
    To whom the Archangel: "Dexterously thou aim'st;
So willingly doth God remit his ire,   885
Though late repenting him of man depraved,
Grieved at his heart when looking down he saw
The whole earth filled with violence, and all flesh
Corrupting each their way; yet, those removed,
Such grace shall one just man find in his sight   890
That he relents, not to blot out mankind,
And makes a covenant never to destroy
The earth again by flood, nor° let the sea   *neither*
Surpass his bounds nor rain to drown the world
With man therein or beast; but when he brings   895

864. *Grateful:* 1) showing gratitude; 2) pleasing (the same punning usage as at line 323 above)

866. *gay:* bright

867. *covenant:* the promise of God, of which the rainbow was the pledge, never again to flood the world (Gen. 9:11–17)

880. *Distended:* spread (rather than contracted, as is God's angry brow)

886–887. *repenting . . . heart:* Milton picks up the verbs of Gen. 6:6: "it repented the Lord that he had made man on the earth, and it grieved him at his heart."

888–889. *violence . . . Corrupting:* Cf.: "The earth also was corrupt before God, and the earth was filled with violence" (Gen. 6:11).

Over the earth a cloud will therein set
His triple-colored bow whereon to look
And call to mind his covenant: day and night,
Seed time and harvest, heat and hoary frost
Shall hold their course, till fire purge all things new,   900
Both heaven and earth, wherein the just shall dwell."

The End of the Eleventh Book.

898–900. *day . . . course:* The terms of
God's sustaining promise in Gen. 8:21–22:
"neither will I again smite any more every
thing living, as I have done. While the earth
remaineth, seedtime and harvest, and cold
and heat, and summer and winter, and day
and night shall not cease."

900–901. *till fire purge . . . dwell:* 2 Pet.
3:6–13 recalls the flood, "whereby the world

that then was . . . perished," as well as God's
promise now to preserve "the heavens and
the earth," which are "reserved unto fire
against the day of judgment and the perdi-
tion of ungodly men"; and he then invokes
the apocalypse, when "the heavens shall pass
away with a great noise, the earth also," but
there shall be formed "new heavens and a
new earth, wherein dwelleth righteousness."

BOOK 12

The Argument

The angel Michael continues from the flood to relate what shall succeed; then, in the mention of Abraham, comes by degrees to explain who that seed of the woman shall be which was promised Adam and Eve in the fall: his incarnation, death, resurrection, and ascension; the state of the church till his second coming. Adam, greatly satisfied and recomforted by these relations and promises, descends the hill with Michael; wakens Eve, who all this while had slept, but with gentle dreams composed to quietness of mind and submission. Michael in either hand leads them out of paradise, the fiery sword waving behind them, and the cherubim taking their stations to guard the place.

As one who in his journey baits at noon,
Though bent on speed, so here the archangel paused
Betwixt the world destroyed and world restored,
If Adam aught° perhaps might interpose,   *anything*
Then with transition sweet new speech resumes: 5
    "Thus thou hast seen one world begin and end
And man as from a second stock proceed.
Much thou hast yet to see, but I perceive
Thy mortal sight to fail: objects divine
Must needs impair and weary human sense.   10
Henceforth what is to come I will relate;
Thou, therefore, give due audience and attend.

1–5. *As . . . resumes:* These lines were added in 1674 when the tenth book of 1667 was divided to form the last two books of the second edition, and thus, likely the last poem Milton wrote.

1. *baits:* stops for rest and refreshment (though possibly "bates," i.e., "abates," meaning reduces speed or pauses)

7. *second stock:* After the flood, "the race of men" must now develop from Noah, a new branch from the original root; *stock,*

however, also looks to the Pauline metaphor of the grafting of mankind to Christ; see 3.287–89, where God says to Christ that "in thee, / As from a second root, shall be restored / As many as are restored."

11. *I will relate:* In this book of *PL,* the visions are narrated, not shown: words, not images, bring Adam to understanding, following Romans 10:17: "So then faith cometh by hearing, and hearing by the word of God."

This second source of men, while yet but few,
And while the dread of judgment past remains
Fresh in their minds, fearing the deity   15
With some regard to what is just and right
Shall lead their lives and multiply apace,
Laboring° the soil and reaping plenteous crop,   *tilling*
Corn, wine, and oil; and from the herd or flock
Oft sacrificing bullock, lamb, or kid,   20
With large wine-offerings poured and sacred feast,
Shall spend their days in joy unblamed and dwell
Long time in peace, by families and tribes
Under paternal rule, till one shall rise
Of proud ambitious heart, who, not content   25
With fair equality, fraternal state,
Will arrogate dominion undeserved
Over his brethren and quite dispossess
Concord and law of nature from the earth,
Hunting (and men not beasts shall be his game)   30
With war and hostile snare such as refuse
Subjection to his empire tyrannous.
A mighty hunter thence he shall be styled
Before the Lord, as in despite of Heaven
Or from Heaven claiming second sovereignty,   35

19. *Corn, wine, and oil:* follows Deut. 14:23: "And thou shalt eat before thy God . . . the tithe of thy corn, of thy wine, of thine oil"; perhaps unsurprisingly Book 12 is the book with the greatest density of biblical reference.

24. *paternal rule:* patriarchal authority, but not at odds with its chiming "fraternal state" in line 26

24–62. *one shall rise . . . named:* Nimrod, unnamed here, is "a mighty hunter before the Lord," whose "kingdom was Babel" (Gen. 10:9–10), but he is not mentioned in the biblical account of building of the tower and the confusion of tongues at Babel (Gen. 11:1–9). His character as the foiled empire builder is found first in Josephus' *Antiquities* 1.4.2, and developed in Gregory's commentary on Genesis in *On the Trinity and Its Works* and in Dante's *Purgatory* (12.34; cf. *Inferno* 31.77). Sir Thomas Browne (*Pseu-*

doxia Epidemica, 1646) discusses Nimrod's "secret design to settle unto himselfe a place of dominion, and rule over the rest of his brethren" (p. 349); and Milton calls him "the first that founded Monarchy" (*Eikonoklastes* [*Works* 5, 185]).

29. *law of nature:* not a Hobbesian law of nature based on will and power, but a natural law grounded in reason and piety

33–34. *styled . . . Lord:* said to be *Before the Lord,* the ambiguous phrase of Gen. 10:9 (see note on lines 24–62 above), whose meanings are explored in lines 34–35 below.

34–35. *as in despite . . . sovereignty:* Milton unravels the two possible interpretations of "Before the Lord": 1) in contempt (*despite*) of God ("Before" = "more important than"); and 2) accountable only to ("Before" = "in front of") God (like Charles I, as he was tried for treason, claiming that no earthly court had authority over him). Thus

And from rebellion shall derive his name
Though of rebellion others he accuse.
He with a crew, whom like ambition joins
With him or under him to tyrannize,
Marching from Eden toward the west, shall find   40
The plain wherein a black bituminous gurge
Boils out from underground, the mouth of hell.
Of brick, and of that stuff, they cast to build
A city and tower whose top may reach to Heaven,
And get themselves a name, lest, far dispersed   45
In foreign lands, their memory be lost,
Regardless whether good or evil fame.
But God, who oft descends to visit men
Unseen and through their habitations walks
To mark their doings, them beholding soon,   50
Comes down to see their city, ere the tower
Obstruct Heaven's towers, and in derision sets
Upon their tongues a various° spirit to raze   *quarrelsome, divisive*
Quite out their native language and instead
To sow a jangling noise of words unknown.   55
Forthwith a hideous gabble rises loud
Among the builders; each to other calls
Not understood, till, hoarse and all in rage,
As mocked they storm; great laughter was in Heaven,
And looking down to see the hubbub strange   60
And hear the din; thus was the building left

atheism and absolutism alike are derived
from Nimrod.

36. *from rebellion shall derive his name:*
A false etymology held that Nimrod meant
"rebel."

41. *plain:* The plain of Shinar (Sen-
naar) in ancient Babylon, mentioned in
3.467 and note.

41–42. *gurge Boils out:* viscous liquid
bubbles up (*gurge* means "whirlpool," but the
usage here is inexact, almost onomatopoeic).

43. *cast:* 1) plan; 2) mold

45–46. *lest . . . their memory be lost:* a
critique of the epic value of fame; the rheto-
ric here reflects Gen. 11:4: "Let us make us a
name, lest we be scattered abroad upon the
face of the whole earth."

52–58. *sets . . . understood:* "Lan-
guages," said Milton in the *Logic* I,
xxiv (*Works* 11, 220), "both that first one
which Adam spoke in Eden, and those
varied ones also possibly derived from the
first, which the builders of the tower of
Babel suddenly received, are without doubt
divinely given."

55. *a jangling noise:* Sylvester's Du Bar-
tas (*Divine Weeks*, 1608) also has "a jangling
noyse" (p. 336).

56. *gabble:* unintelligible talk (the "jan-
gling noise of words unknown" in line 55)

59. *great laughter . . . Heaven:* See Ps.
2:4: "he that sitteth in the Heavens shall
laugh: the Lord shall have them in derision";
also see "in derision" in line 52 above.

Ridiculous and the work 'Confusion' named."
Whereto thus Adam, fatherly displeased:
"O execrable son so to aspire
Above his brethren, to himself assuming   65
Authority usurped from God, not given:
He gave us only over beast, fish, fowl
Dominion absolute; that right we hold
By his donation; but man over men
He made not lord, such title to himself   70
Reserving, human left from human free.
But this usurper his encroachment proud
Stays not on man; to God his tower intends°   *threatens*
Siege and defiance. Wretched man! What food
Will he convey up thither to sustain   75
Himself and his rash army, where thin air
Above the clouds will pine° his entrails gross   *distress, waste away*
And famish him of breath, if not of bread?"
To whom thus Michael: "Justly thou abhorr'st
That son who on the quiet state of men   80
Such trouble brought, affecting° to subdue   *aspiring*
Rational liberty; yet know withal,
Since thy original lapse, true liberty

62. *'Confusion' named:* Gen. 11:9 ex-
plains: "Therefore is the name of it called
Babel; because the Lord did there confound
the language of all the earth." The name
"Babel" seems to mean in Hebrew "gate of
the Gods," but Josephus erroneously de-
clared that "the tower is now called Babylon
because of the confusion of that language
which they readily understood before, for the
Hebrews mean by the word Babel, Confu-
sion" (*Antiquities* 1.4.3). In fact, Hebrew
"balal" = confusion, though the tower's name
may be a conscious pun.
64–65. *to aspire . . . brethren:* the defini-
tion of tyrannical ambition: the desire to es-
tablish rule over one's equals (Satan's very
claim against God, vitiated by the fact they
are not equals; see 5.794–97).
68. *Dominion absolute:* unlimited, com-
plete
69–70. *man over men . . . lord:* In claim-
ing that "Dominion" (line 68) is proper only
over lesser creatures, and that any claim to

the contrary is a usurpation of divine author-
ity, Milton's antimonarchical position is un-
mistakable; cf. Augustine, *City of God* (1610,
trans. Healy): "Hee made him reasonable,
and LORD, only over the unreasonable, not
over man, but over beasts" (p. 772).
73. *Stays not on:* stops not with
82. *Rational liberty:* i.e., the liberty that
reason demands; Milton's experience of Eng-
lish history saw this liberty always at risk,
though even as the restoration of the monar-
chy became inevitable in 1660, he still hoped
that through God the English people could
again "become children of a reviving libertie"
(*The Readie and Easie Way* [*Works* 6, 463]).
83–101. *Since . . . lost:* Milton explains
tyranny as an effect of the fall and the loss
therein of "that right reason which enabled
man to discern the chief good" (*Christian
Doctrine* I, xii [*Works* 15, 206]).
83. *thy original lapse:* though spoken
only to Adam, must also include Eve's role in
the fall

Is lost, which always with right reason dwells
Twinned, and from her hath no dividual° being.   *separate*
Reason in man obscured, or not obeyed,
Immediately inordinate desires
And upstart passions catch the government
From reason, and to servitude reduce
Man, till then free. Therefore, since he permits   90
Within himself unworthy powers to reign
Over free reason, God, in judgment just,
Subjects him from without to violent lords,
Who oft as undeservedly enthrall
His outward freedom. Tyranny must be,   95
Though to the tyrant thereby no excuse.
Yet sometimes nations will decline so low
From virtue, which is reason, that no wrong,
But justice and some fatal curse annexed
Deprives them of their outward liberty,   100
Their inward lost: witness the irreverent son
Of him who built the ark, who, for the shame
Done to his father, heard this heavy curse,
'Servant of servants,' on his vicious° race.   *depraved, full of vice*
Thus will this latter, as the former, world   105
Still tend from bad to worse, till God, at last
Wearied with their iniquities, withdraw
His presence from among them and avert
His holy eyes, resolving from thenceforth
To leave them to their own polluted ways,   110
And one peculiar nation to select
From all the rest of whom to be invoked,

84. *right reason:* conscience; the instinctive ability to distinguish between right and wrong

88. *catch:* seize and keep apart, remove

95–96. *Tyranny . . . excuse:* i.e., because of the fall, tyranny is inevitable, but that doesn't excuse the tyrant's actions

101–104. *the irreverent son . . . race:* i.e., Ham, son of Noah, *irreverent* because he saw his drunken father naked, though his brothers looked away; for his indiscretion a curse was placed on his son, Canaan: "And [Noah] said, 'Cursed be Canaan; a servant of servants shall he be unto his brethren'" (Gen. 9:25); *race* = descendants, not an ethnic classification.

107. *Wearied . . . iniquities:* Cf. Isa. 43:24: "thou hast wearied me with thine iniquities."

111. *one peculiar nation:* i.e., Israel, God's chosen people; *peculiar* = special, as in Deut. 14:2: "The Lord hath chosen thee to be a peculiar people unto himself." In *Christian Doctrine* I, iv (*Works* 14, 99), Milton recognizes "that general, or national election by which God chose the whole nation of Israel for his own people."

A nation from one faithful man to spring:
Him on this side Euphrates yet residing,
Bred up in idol-worship. O that men   115
(Canst thou believe?) should be so stupid grown
While yet the patriarch lived who scaped the flood
As to forsake the living God and fall
To worship their own work in wood and stone
For gods! Yet him° God the most high vouchsafes   *i.e., Abraham*
To call by vision from his father's house,
His kindred, and false gods, into a land
Which he will show him, and from him will raise
A mighty nation and upon him shower
His benediction so,° that in his seed   *so gracious*
All nations shall be blessed. He straight obeys
Not knowing to what land, yet firm believes.
I see him, but thou canst not, with what faith
He leaves his gods, his friends, and native soil,
Ur of Chaldea, passing now the ford   130
To Haran, after him a cumbrous train
Of herds and flocks and numerous servitude,
Not wandering poor, but trusting all his wealth
With God who called him in a land unknown.
Canaan he now attains. I see his tents   135

113. *one faithful man:* i.e., Abraham (not named until line 152), to whom God says: "I will make of thee a great nation" (Gen. 12:2)

114. *on this side Euphrates:* follows Josh. 24:2: "Your fathers dwelt on the other side of the flood in old time, even Terah, the father of Abraham"

115. *Bred up in idol-worship:* Terah, Abraham's father, "served other gods" (Josh. 24:2); God called Abraham "from his father's house," said Milton (*Christian Doctrine* I, xvii [*Works* 15, 351]), although he "was even an idolater at the time."

117. *the patriarch:* i.e., Noah, who lived, according to Gen. 9:28, 350 years "after the flood"

118. *fall:* The word, in its emphatic position, articulates the source and shared nature of all sin.

125–126. *seed . . . blessed:* echoes Gen.

12:3: "In thee shall all families of the earth be blessed"

126. *straight obeys:* immediately obeys; cf. Heb. 11:8: "By faith, Abraham, when he was called to go out into a place which he should after receive for an inheritance, obeyed."

130. *Ur of Chaldea:* a city on the west bank of the Euphrates, where Abraham was born (see Gen. 11:28–31)

131. *Haran:* a province in Canaan (and also the name of Abraham's brother) about 400 miles northwest of Ur; cf. 4.210–11 (Haran = Auran).

131–132. *train . . . servitude:* The story of the migration as told in Gen. 12:5–6 is traced on one of Ortelius' large maps in a diagram called *Abrahami Patriarchae Perigrinatio et Vita,* on which the place names of lines 131–46 are marked; *servitude* = slaves and servants.

Pitched about Sichem and the neighboring plain
Of Moreh; there, by promise, he receives
Gift to his progeny of all that land:
From Hamath northward to the desert south
(Things by their names I call, though yet unnamed),   140
From Hermon east to the great western sea.
Mount Hermon, yonder sea, each place behold
In prospect as I point them: on the shore,
Mount Carmel; here, the double-founted stream,
Jordan, true limit eastward; but his sons   145
Shall dwell to Senir, that long ridge of hills.
This ponder: that all nations of the earth
Shall in his seed be blessèd. (By that seed
Is meant thy great deliverer, who shall bruise
The serpent's head, whereof to thee anon   150
Plainlier shall be revealed.) This patriarch blessed,
Whom 'faithful Abraham' due time shall call,
A son, and of his son a grandchild, leaves
Like him in faith, in wisdom, and renown.
The grandchild, with twelve sons increased, departs   155
From Canaan to a land hereafter called

136–137. *Sichem . . . Moreh:* follows Gen. 12:6: "And Abram passed through the land unto the place of Sichem, unto the plain of Moreh," both sites in central Canaan, near Mount Gerizem

137. *by promise:* Gen. 12:7: "the Lord appeared unto Abram, and said, 'Unto thy seed I will give this land.'"

139. *Hamath . . . south: Hamath* was a city on the Orontes river in what is now Syria, some 100 miles north of Damascus, that served to mark the northern border of Canaan; *the desert south* refers to "the wilderness of Zin," Canaan's southern border (see Numb. 34:3–8).

141. *Hermon . . . great western sea:* Mount *Hermon,* a landmark on Canaan's eastern border (Josh. 13:5), while *the great western sea* is the Mediterranean.

143–144. *on the shore, Mount Carmel:* mountain on the Mediterranean coast, near modern Haifa in Israel; even for God, a

proverbial mark of certainty: "as Carmel by the sea, so shall he come" (Jer. 46:18).

144–145. *double-founted stream, Jordan:* The notion that the Jordan was formed by the confluence of two nonexistent streams, the Jor and the Dan, seems ultimately to have stemmed from Jerome's commentary on Genesis 14:14 but survives well into the 17th century (e.g., in *Sandy's Travels,* 1615, p. 141).

146. *Senir:* According to Deut. 3:9, the Amorite name of Mount Hermon, but in 1 Chron. 5:23 it is, as here, identified as the ridge leading up to the mountain.

147–151. *all nations . . . revealed:* The prophecy of 10.179–81 is here partially explained, the rest made *Plainlier* only at lines 427–31 below.

152. *faithful Abraham:* Gal. 3:9 calls him "faithful Abraham"; in Gen. 17:5, Abram's name is changed to Abraham to confirm he will be "a father of many nations."

153. *A son . . . a grandchild:* i.e., Isaac and Jacob

Egypt, divided by the river Nile—
See where it flows, disgorging at seven mouths
Into the sea. To sojourn in that land
He comes, invited by a younger son°   *i.e., Joseph*
In time of dearth,° a son whose worthy deeds   *famine*
Raise him to be the second in that realm
Of Pharaoh; there he dies and leaves his race
Growing into a nation and, now grown,
Suspected to a sequent king, who seeks   165
To stop their overgrowth as inmate° guests   *foreign*
Too numerous; whence of guests he makes them slaves
Inhospitably and kills their infant males,
Till by two brethren (those two brethren call
Moses and Aaron) sent from God to claim   170
His people from enthrallment, they return
With glory and spoil back to their promised land.
But first the lawless tyrant, who denies°   *refuses*
To know their God or message to regard,
Must be compelled by signs and judgments dire: 175
To blood unshed the rivers must be turned;
Frogs, lice, and flies must all his palace fill
With loathed intrusion and fill all the land;
His cattle must of rot and murrain die;
Botches and blains must all his flesh emboss   180
And all his people; thunder mixed with hail,
Hail mixed with fire, must rend the Egyptian sky
And wheel on the earth, devouring where it rolls;
What it devours not, herb or fruit or grain,
A darksome cloud of locusts swarming down   185
Must eat and on the ground leave nothing green;
Darkness must overshadow all his bounds,
Palpable darkness, and blot out three days;
Last, with one midnight stroke, all the first-born

164. *now grown:* i.e., having become a nation

165. *Suspected to a sequent king:* mistrusted by a succeeding king (i.e., Busiris, see 1.307)

172. *spoil:* i.e., the "jewels of silver, and jewels of gold, and raiment" that were "borrowed of the Egyptians" as the Israelites were leaving (Exod. 12:35)

175. *signs and judgments:* i.e., the plagues of Exod. 7–12

179. *rot and murrain:* two virulent and highly infectious diseases affecting livestock

180. *Botches . . . emboss:* Boils and blisters will swell up on his skin.

188. *Palpable darkness:* the plague of "thick darkness" (Exod. 10:21–22); cf. 2.406.

Of Egypt must lie dead. Thus with ten wounds   190
The river dragon, tamed at length, submits
To let his sojourners depart and oft
Humbles his stubborn heart, but still as ice
More hardened after thaw, till in his rage,
Pursuing whom he late dismissed, the sea°   *i.e., the Red Sea*
Swallows him with his host, but them lets pass
As on dry land between two crystal walls,
Awed by the rod of Moses so to stand
Divided, till his rescued gain their shore.
Such wondrous power God to his saint will lend,   200
Though present in his angel, who shall go
Before them in a cloud and pillar of fire,
By day a cloud, by night a pillar of fire,
To guide them in their journey and remove
Behind them while the obdurate king pursues.   205
All night he will pursue, but his approach
Darkness defends between till morning watch;
Then, through the fiery pillar and the cloud,
God looking forth will trouble all his host
And craze° their chariot wheels, when, by command,   *shatter*
Moses once more his potent rod extends
Over the sea; the sea his rod obeys;
On their embattled ranks the waves return
And overwhelm their war.° The race elect   *army*

190. *ten wounds:* the ten plagues of
Exod. 7–12

191. *river dragon:* i.e., the pharaoh; see
Ezek. 29:3: "Behold, I am against thee,
Pharaoh king of Egypt, the great dragon that
lieth in the midst of his rivers"; but also a
type or figure of Satan, see 4.3 and 10.529.

194. *More . . . thaw:* refers to the belief
that refrozen ice was harder than ice that had
not ever melted

197. *two crystal walls:* The image of the
divided Red Sea derives from Sylvester's
translation of Du Bartas' description of the
same event: "And on each side is flanked all
along / With walls of crystal, beautiful and
strong" (*Divine Weeks*, 1608, p. 476). Cf.
Milton's boyish paraphrase of Ps. 136, which
includes the line: "The floods stood still like
walls of glass."

201–204. *his angel . . . journey:* echoes
Exod. 13:21: "The Lord went before them
by day in a pillar of a cloud . . . and by night
in a pillar of fire, to give them light."

205–214. *obdurate king . . . war:* fol-
lows Exodus 14

207. *defends between:* prevents, holds
off (by coming *between* Pharaoh and the
Israelites)

211. *Moses . . . extends:* Cf. 1.338–39:
"As when the potent rod / Of Amram's son."

214. *race elect:* chosen people; Protes-
tants in England had since the late 1500s ar-
gued that England was similarly an "elect
nation," Milton himself writing in
Aeropagitica: "Why else was this Nation
chos'n before any other, that out of her as out
of *Sion* should be proclaim'd and sounded
forth the first tidings and trumpet of Refor-
mation to all of *Europe*" (*Works* 4, 340).

Safe toward Canaan from the shore advance   215
Through the wild desert, not the readiest way,
Lest, entering on the Canaanite alarmed,
War terrify them inexpert,° and fear   *inexperienced and unskilled*
Return them back to Egypt, choosing rather
Inglorious life with servitude, for life   220
To noble and ignoble is more sweet
Untrained in arms, where rashness leads not on.
This also shall they gain by their delay
In the wide wilderness: there they shall found
Their government, and their great senate choose   225
Through the twelve tribes, to rule by laws ordained.
God, from the mount of Sinai, whose gray top
Shall tremble, he descending, will himself,
In thunder, lightning, and loud trumpets sound,
Ordain them laws, part such as appertain   230
To civil justice, part religious rites
Of sacrifice, informing them by types
And shadows of that destined seed to bruise
The serpent, by what means he shall achieve
Mankind's deliverance. But the voice of God   235
To mortal ear is dreadful; they beseech
That Moses might report to them his will,
And terror cease; he grants what they besought,

216. *not the readiest way:* The meandering route of Israel during its years in the wilderness on the way to Canaan was clearly traced on 17th-century maps. Milton's explanation in lines 217–18 for Israel's route comes from Exod. 13:17–18. His phrasing here recalls the title of his prose tract, *The Readie and Easie Way* (1660), which condemns the nation's abandonment of its revolutionary commitments.

217. *alarmed:* aroused, ready to fight (modifies "Canaanite")

225. *government . . . great senate:* Milton's republican politics find precedent in the example of the seventy elders in Numb. 11:16–30, whom Moses gathers at God's command. For many republicans, this is the divinely constituted form of government, founded, as James Harrington said, "in the fabrick of the *Commonwealth* of *Israel*," which, with the support of the "Magistracy and People," provides for later times the perfect pattern of government by law rather than by royal power (*The Commonwealth of Oceana*, 1656, p. 1).

232–233. *types And shadows:* persons or events in the Hebrew bible that are held to prefigure or foreshadow persons and events in the New Testament (e.g., Abraham's willing "sacrifice" of his son Isaac as a type of God's willing sacrifice of his Son on the Cross, or Noah's ark as a "type" of baptism); cf. Heb. 8:5: "Who serve unto the example and shadow of heavenly things."

236. *To mortal ear is dreadful:* In Exod. 20:19, the Israelites say "unto Moses, Speak thou with us, and we will hear: but let not God speak with us, lest we die."

Instructed that to God is no access
Without mediator, whose high office now   240
Moses in figure bears to introduce
One greater, of whose day he shall foretell,
And all the prophets in their age the times
Of great Messiah shall sing. Thus laws and rites
Established, such delight hath God in men   245
Obedient to his will that he vouchsafes
Among them to set up his tabernacle,
The holy one with mortal men to dwell.
By his prescript a sanctuary is framed
Of cedar overlaid with gold, therein   250
An ark, and in the ark his testimony,
The records of his covenant; over these
A mercy-seat of gold between the wings
Of two bright cherubim; before him burn
Seven lamps as in a zodiac representing   255
The heavenly fires; over the tent a cloud
Shall rest by day, a fiery gleam by night,
Save when they journey; and at length they come,
Conducted by his angel, to the land
Promised to Abraham and his seed. The rest   260
Were long to tell: how many battles fought,
How many kings destroyed and kingdoms won,
Or how the sun shall in mid-heaven stand still
A day entire and night's due course adjourn,
Man's voice commanding, 'sun in Gibeon stand,   265

239–242. *to God . . . foretell:* Christian commentators treated Moses as the first of the types of Christ as *mediator* (cf. 10.60) mainly because Deut. 18:15 is quoted in Acts 3:22: "For Moses truly said unto the fathers, 'A Prophet shall the Lord your God raise up unto you of your brethren, like unto me.'" In *Christian Doctrine* I, xv, Milton writes: "The name and office of mediator is in a certain sense ascribed to Moses, as a type of Christ" (*Works* 15, 287).

241. *in figure:* as a type (see line 232 above and note)

247–256. *tabernacle . . . fires:* The description of the *tabernacle* (a portable sanctuary, the ark of the covenant) is based upon Exodus 25.

253. *mercy-seat:* not God's actual "mercy-seat" of Book 11, but the tabernacle, conceived metaphorically as the seat of God

255. *lamps as in a zodiac:* Josephus describes the golden candlestick of the tabernacle as having "seven lamps . . . in imitation of the number of planets" (*Antiquities* 3.6.7).

259–260. *land . . . seed:* The allusion is to the promise to Abraham in Gen. 17:8: "And I will give unto thee, and to thy seed after thee, the land wherein thou art a stranger, all the land of Canaan, for an everlasting possession."

263–267. *how . . . overcome:* See Josh. 10:12–13, where Joshua "said in the sight of Israel, Sun, stand thou still upon Gibeon; and thou, Moon, in the valley of Ajelon . . .

And thou, moon, in the vale of Ajalon,
Till Israel overcome'—so call the third
From Abraham, son of Isaac, and from him
His whole descent, who thus shall Canaan win."

    Here Adam interposed: "O sent from Heaven,   270
Enlightener of my darkness, gracious things
Thou hast revealed, those chiefly which concern
Just Abraham and his seed; now first I find
Mine eyes true opening and my heart much eased,
Erewhile perplexed with thoughts what would become   275
Of me and all mankind; but now I see
His day in whom all nations shall be blessed,
Favor unmerited by me who sought
Forbidden knowledge by forbidden means.
This yet I apprehend not: why to those   280
Among whom God will deign to dwell on earth
So many and so various laws are given?
So many laws argue so many sins
Among them. How can God with such reside?"

    To whom thus Michael: "Doubt not but that sin   285
Will reign among them, as of thee begot;
And therefore was law given them to evince
Their natural pravity by stirring up
Sin against law to fight, that when they see
Law can discover sin but not remove,   290
Save by those shadowy expiations weak,

until the people had avenged themselves upon their enemies." Sylvester's Du Bartas similarly paraphrased Joshua's command: "Stay, stand thou still, stand still in Gabaon; / And thou, O Moone, i'th'vale of Aialon" (*Divine Weeks,* 1608, p. 516).

    267–269. *so call . . . win:* The name "Israel" (i.e., "he that striveth with God") was given to Jacob (Gen. 32:28) and later to all his descendants, who would be known as "the children of Israel."

    274. *true opening:* Compare this with 9.707–09, 9.985, and 9.1053.

    277. *His day:* i.e., the age of Abraham, which Adam mistakenly takes as the fulfillment of God's promise of redemption instead of only a type; see John 8:56: "Your father Abraham rejoiced to see my day."

    283. *argue:* indicate (*OED* 3)

    287. *evince:* 1) make manifest; 2) subdue

    288. *natural pravity:* basic sinfulness, but also "original sin," in its theological sense (*pravity* = depravity)

    290. *Law . . . remove:* The line fuses several Pauline passages that teach "by the law is the knowledge of sin" (Rom. 3:20) but also that "a man is justified by faith without the deeds of the law" (Rom. 3:28).

    291. *shadowy expiations:* Milton describes the sacrifices "of bulls and goats" (line 292) as shadows or types of Christ's expiation of sin through his greater sacrifice ("blood more precious," line 293), as the law is said to have "a shadow of good things to come" in Heb. 10:1, though the "sacrifices which they offered year by year continually" could never "make the comers thereunto perfect."

The blood of bulls and goats, they may conclude
Some blood more precious must be paid for man,
Just for unjust, that in such righteousness,
To them by faith imputed, they may find   295
Justification toward God and peace
Of conscience, which the law by ceremonies
Cannot appease, nor man the moral part
Perform and, not performing, cannot live.
So law appears imperfect, and but° given   *only*
With purpose to resign° them in full time   *bring, consign*
Up to a better covenant, disciplined
From shadowy types to truth, from flesh to spirit,
From imposition of strict laws to free
Acceptance of large grace, from servile fear   305
To filial, works of law to works of faith.
And therefore shall not Moses, though of God
Highly beloved, being but the minister
Of law, his people into Canaan lead,
But Joshua, whom the gentiles 'Jesus' call,   310
His name and office bearing who shall quell
The adversary serpent and bring back
Through the world's wilderness long-wandered man
Safe to eternal Paradise of rest.
Meanwhile they, in their earthly Canaan placed,   315

292. *they:* refers back to "those / Among whom God will deign to dwell on earth" (lines 280–81 above)

294. *Just for unjust:* See 1 Pet. 3:18: "For Christ also hath once suffered for sins, the just for the unjust."

295. *imputed:* attributed vicariously (a theological term referring to the action by which Christ's righteousness becomes available to the faithful and also by which Adam's sin was initially *imputed* to his descendents)

302. *better covenant:* See Heb. 8:6–13, where Christ is called "the mediator of a better covenant," not the one "made with their fathers in the day when [God] took them by the hand to lead them out of the land of Egypt," but "a new covenant" in which God "will put [his] laws into their minds, and write them in their hearts."

303–306. *shadowy types . . . faith:* expressing the supercessional view that Judaism is not a separate religion but both an earlier stage and a prefiguration of Christianity, the two faiths at once joined and differentiated in the binary of the old law of justice and the new law of mercy; see line 232 and note above.

307–310. *not Moses . . . Joshua:* a typological understanding of the events of Joshua 1, where Joshua, not Moses, leads the Israelites into Canaan, as in *Christian Doctrine* I, xxvi (*Works* 16, 110): "the imperfection of the law was manifested in . . . Moses himself; for Moses, who was a type of the law, could not bring the children of Israel into the land of Canaan, that is, into eternal rest; but an entrance was given to them under Joshua, or Jesus"

315. *earthly Canaan:* i.e., the literal Canaan rather than its typological sense as a prefiguration of the "eternal Paradise" Jesus will win for all mankind (line 314).

Long time shall dwell and prosper, but° when sins   °*except*
National interrupt their public peace,
Provoking God to raise them enemies,
From whom as oft he saves them penitent
By judges first, then under kings, of whom   320
The second, both for piety renowned
And puissant deeds, a promise shall receive
Irrevocable: that his regal throne
Forever shall endure. The like shall sing
All prophecy: that of the royal stock   325
Of David (so I name this King) shall rise
A son—the woman's seed to thee foretold,
Foretold to Abraham, as in whom shall trust
All nations, and to kings foretold, of kings
The last, for of his reign shall be no end.   330
But first a long succession must ensue;
And his next son, for wealth and wisdom famed,
The clouded ark of God, till then in tents
Wandering, shall in a glorious temple enshrine.
Such follow him as shall be registered   335
Part good, part bad, of bad the longer scroll,
Whose foul idolatries and other faults
Heaped to the popular sum will so incense
God as to leave them and expose their land,
Their city, his temple, and his holy ark   340

316–317. *sins National:* sins commit-
ted by the whole nation (e.g., worshipping
the local false gods)
   320. *judges:* generals (who ruled before
the advent of kings in Israel); see Judg. 2:16:
"the Lord raised up judges, which delivered
them out of the hand of those that spoiled
them." *then under kings:* See 1 Sam.
11:15: "And all the people went to Gilgal;
and there they made Saul king before the
Lord in Gilgal."
   321. *The second:* i.e., David, the second
king of Israel (after Saul)
   322. *a promise:* refers to Nathan's prom-
ise to David: "thy throne shall be established
for ever" (2 Sam. 7:16).
   325. *stock:* i.e., line of descent; the ge-
nealogies of Jesus emphasized his descent

from David (e.g., Luke 1:32: "The Lord God
shall give unto him the throne of his father
David"); see line 7 above.
   327. *to thee foretold:* See 10.179–81.
   328. *Foretold to Abraham:* in Exod.
22:18
   332. *his next son:* i.e., David's son,
Solomon
   333. *clouded ark:* follows Exod. 40:34:
"a cloud covered the tent of the congregation"
   334. *glorious temple:* the temple of
Solomon in Jerusalem, described in 1 Kings
6–7 and 2 Chron. 3–4.
   337. *foul idolatries:* See 1 Kings 11:1–7,
which tells of Solomon's wives leading him
into idolatry; see 1.399–403.
   338. *Heaped . . . sum:* added to the sins
of his people

With all his sacred things, a scorn and prey
To that proud city whose high walls thou saw'st
Left in confusion, Babylon thence called.
There in captivity he lets them dwell
The space of seventy years, then brings them back,   345
Remembering mercy and his covenant sworn
To David, 'stablished as the days of Heaven.
Returned from Babylon by leave of kings,
Their lords, whom God disposed, the house of God
They first re-edify° and for awhile   *rebuild*
In mean estate live moderate, till, grown
In wealth and multitude, factious they grow;
But first among the priests dissension springs,
Men who attend the altar and should most
Endeavor peace; their strife pollution brings   355
Upon the temple itself. At last they seize
The scepter and regard not David's sons,
Then lose it to a stranger, that the true
Anointed king, Messiah, might be born
Barred of his right; yet at his birth a star,   360
Unseen before in Heaven, proclaims him come
And guides the eastern sages, who inquire
His place, to offer incense, myrrh, and gold.
His place of birth a solemn angel tells

343–345. *Babylon . . . seventy years*: the
Babylonian *captivity* of the Israelites, seen as
God's punishment for their sins (586–516
B.C., when the new Temple was com-
pleted); see Jer. 39:2, Kings 17:24–26, and
2 Chron. 36.

345–347. *brings . . . David*: The return
of the Hebrew exiles from Babylon to
Jerusalem in 536 B.C. is seen as a fulfillment
of God's *covenant* with David to make "his
throne as the days of heaven" (Psalm 89:29).
The change to *covenant* from the "promise"
in line 322 establishes this episode as another
type of Christ's triumph (see line 302 above).

348. *by leave of kings*: The Jews were
permitted to rebuild Jerusalem under Cyrus
the Great, Darius, and Artaxerxes (see the
book of Ezra).

349. *disposed*: i.e., made favorably dis-
posed

352–358. *factious . . . stranger*: In sum-
marizing the struggle for the high priest-

hood in the second century B.C., Milton fol-
lows 2 Macc. 3–4, and Josephus' *Antiquities*
12.4–5.

356–357. *seize . . . sons*: one of David's
descendants, Aristobulus I, was deposed by
the priests (see Josephus, *Antiquities* 13.40)

356. *they*: the Asmonean family, which
held the priesthood from 153 to 35 B.C.

358. *stranger*: Antipater, the Idumaean
(hence *stranger* = foreigner) who was ap-
pointed by the Romans' governor of Jeru-
salem in 61 B.C.

358–359. *that . . . born*: Jesus was born
under the reign of Herod the Great, Antipa-
ter's son; *that* (i.e., so that) reflects the provi-
dential direction of this history.

360–369. *at his birth . . . high*: the fa-
miliar story of the birth of Jesus, following
the first two chapters of Matthew and Luke

364. *solemn*: holy (but also "awe inspir-
ing" [*OED* 7])

To simple shepherds keeping watch by night;   365
They gladly thither haste and by a choir
Of squadroned angels hear his carol sung.
A virgin is his mother, but his sire
The power of the most high; he shall ascend
The throne hereditary and bound his reign   370
With earth's wide bounds, his glory with the Heavens.'"°   *i.e., Heaven's glory*
    He ceased, discerning Adam with such joy
Surcharged° as had, like grief, been dewed in tears   *overwhelmed*
Without the vent of words, which these he breathed:
    "O prophet of glad tidings, finisher   375
Of utmost hope! Now clear I understand
What oft my steadiest thoughts have searched in vain,
Why our great expectation should be called
The seed of woman: virgin mother, hail,
High in the love of Heaven; yet from my loins   380
Thou shalt proceed and from thy womb the Son
Of God most high, so God with man unites.
Needs must the serpent now his capital bruise
Expect with mortal pain. Say where and when
Their fight, what stroke shall bruise the victor's heel."   385
    To whom thus Michael: "Dream not of their fight
As of a duel, or the local wounds
Of head or heel. Not therefore joins the Son
Manhood to godhead, with more strength to foil
Thy enemy, nor so is overcome   390
Satan, whose fall from Heaven, a deadlier bruise,

366. *thither:* i.e., to Bethlehem, Christ's "place of birth" (line 364)

368–369. *his sire . . . high: Christian Doctrine* I, xiv (*Works* 15, 280) declares the "efficient cause" of the conception of Christ to be the "Holy Spirit," which Milton says he is inclined to regard as "the power and spirit of the Father," interpreting Luke 1:35.

369–371. *he shall . . . Heavens':* The lines blends the promise in Ps. 2:8 ("Ask of me, and I shall give thee . . . the uttermost parts of the earth for thy possession") with Virgil's prophecy that the fame of Augustus should be bounded by the stars (*Aeneid* 1.287).

375. *finisher:* But the revelation is not yet finished, because Adam still does not understand the full nature of what is being revealed; see also Heb. 12:2 : Christ as "finisher of our faith."

379. *hail:* the Angel's greeting to Mary at the Annunciation (Luke 1:28); see also 5.385–87 and 11.158.

383. *capital:* deadly (but plays on the literal Latin meaning, "pertaining to the head," where the serpent is to be bruised)

386–388. *Dream not . . . heel:* Michael warns against overliteral interpretation of the prophecy, but also adds to the poem's rejection of the terms of the traditional epic in insisting that this *fight* not be conceived *As of a duel.*

Disabled not to give thee thy death's wound,
Which he, who comes thy Savior, shall recure,°   *heal, restore*
Not by destroying Satan but his works
In thee and in thy seed. Nor can this be   395
But by fulfilling that which thou didst want:°   *lack*
Obedience to the law of God imposed
On penalty of death, and suffering death,
The penalty to thy transgression due,
And due to theirs which out of thine will grow: 400
So only can high justice rest apaid.
The law of God exact he shall fulfill
Both by obedience and by love, though love
Alone fulfill the law; thy punishment
He shall endure by coming in the flesh   405
To a reproachful life and cursèd death,
Proclaiming life to all who shall believe
In his redemption, and that his obedience
Imputed becomes theirs by faith, his merits
To save them, not their own, though legal, works.   410
For this he shall live hated, be blasphemed,
Seized on by force, judged, and to death condemned,
A shameful and accursed, nailed to the cross
By his own nation, slain for bringing life;
But to the cross he nails thy enemies: 415
The law that is against thee and the sins
Of all mankind with him there crucified,
Never to hurt them more who rightly trust

---

394. *Not . . . works:* follows 1 John 3:8: "For this purpose of the Son of God was manifested, that he might destroy the works of the devil"

396–397. *by fulfilling . . . God:* Cf. Rom. 5:19: "For as by one man's disobedience many were made sinners, so by the obedience of one shall many be made righteous."

401. *apaid:* satisfied; cf. 3.210–11.

401–458. *So only . . . Heaven:* The doctrinal elements of this passage are expressly affirmed in Milton's detailed assertion of Christ's "voluntary submission of himself to the divine justice both in life and in death

. . . for man's redemption," and his resurrection and ascension "to a state of immortality and highest glory" in *Christian Doctrine* I, xvi (*Works* 15, 302).

402. *exact:* precisely, an adverb modifying "fulfill"; see 3.212.   *fulfill:* See Matt. 5:17: "Think not that I am come to destroy the law . . . I am not come to destroy but to fulfill."

403–404. *love Alone . . . law:* follows Rom. 13:10: "love is the fulfilling of the law"

409. *Imputed:* See line 295 and note.

413–415. *nailed . . . slain . . . nails:* The three words, in the center of consecutive lines, define Christ's victory; see Col. 2:14,

In this his satisfaction; so he dies,
But soon revives; death over him no power   420
Shall long usurp; ere the third dawning light
Return, the stars of morn shall see him rise
Out of his grave, fresh as the dawning light,
Thy ransom paid, which man from death redeems,
His death for man, as many as offered life   425
Neglect not and the benefit embrace
By faith not devoid of works. This godlike act
Annuls thy doom, the death thou shouldst have died,
In sin forever lost from life; this act
Shall bruise the head of Satan, crush his strength   430
Defeating Sin and Death, his two main arms,
And fix far deeper in his head their stings
Than temporal death shall bruise the victor's heel,
Or theirs whom he redeems, a death like sleep,
A gentle wafting° to immortal life.   *passage, transporting*
Nor after resurrection shall he stay
Longer on earth than certain times to appear
To his disciples, men who in his life
Still followed him; to them shall leave in charge
To teach all nations what of him they learned   440
And his salvation, them who shall believe
Baptizing in the profluent stream, the sign
Of washing them from guilt of sin to life
Pure, and in mind prepared, if so befall,
For death like that which the redeemer died.   445
All nations they shall teach, for from that day

which sees Jesus' victory as the "blotting out
of the handwriting of ordinances that was
against us . . . nailing it to his cross."

419. *satisfaction:* i.e., satisfaction of the
claims of justice

420–421. *death . . . usurp:* Cf. Rom.
6:9: "Death hath no more dominion over
him."

422. *stars of morn:* literally the stars still
visible in the early morning sky, but see Job
38.7: "the morning stars sang together, and
all the sons of God shouted for joy"

426. *Neglect not:* i.e., accept (the offer
of "life," line 425); *Neglect* = disregard (Latin
nec = not + *legere* = to pick up)

427. *faith not devoid of works:* See 11.64

and note; see also Jam. 2:26: "faith without
works is dead also."

430–431. *Satan . . . arms:* the last men-
tion of the unholy trinity: Satan, Sin, and
Death.

432. *stings:* deadly effects (from Cor.
15:55: "O death, where is thy sting?")

433. *temporal death:* the death of the
body

442. *profluent:* flowing; derived from
the Latin word used in Milton's discussion of
baptism, which some held should be per-
formed in running water ([in *profluentum
aquam*] *Christian Doctrine* I, xxviii [*Works*
16, 168]), different from the "aspersion"
(sprinkling) of water that became the sacra-
mental norm.

Not only to the sons of Abraham's loins
Salvation shall be preached, but to the sons
Of Abraham's faith wherever through the world;
So in his seed all nations shall be blessed.   450
Then to the Heaven of Heavens he shall ascend
With victory, triumphing through the air
Over his foes and thine; there shall surprise
The serpent, prince of air, and drag in chains
Through all his realm, and there confounded leave;   455
Then enter into glory and resume
His seat at God's right hand, exalted high
Above all names in Heaven; and thence shall come,
When this world's dissolution shall be ripe,
With glory and power to judge both quick and dead—   460
To judge the unfaithful dead but to reward
His faithful and receive them into bliss,
Whether in Heaven or earth, for then the earth
Shall all be Paradise, far happier place
Than this of Eden, and far happier days."   465
    So spake the archangel Michael, then paused,
As at the world's great period; ¡ and our sire,   *conclusion, termination*
Replete with joy and wonder, thus replied:
    "O goodness infinite, goodness immense! ¡   *immeasurable*
That all this good of evil shall produce   470
And evil turn to good, more wonderful
Than that which by creation first brought forth
Light out of darkness! Full of doubt I stand,
Whether I should repent me now of sin
By me done and occasioned, or rejoice   475
Much more that much more good thereof shall spring—

447–450. *Not only . . . blessed:* follows
Gal. 3:8: "And the scripture, foreseeing that
God would justify the heathen through faith,
preached before the gospel unto Abraham,
saying, 'In thee shall all nations be blessed.'"

454. *prince of air:* derives from Eph.
2:2: "the prince of the power of the air"

458. *Above . . . Heaven:* Cf. Phil. 2:9:
"Wherefore God also hath highly exalted
him, and given him a name which is above
every name."

460. *quick and dead:* living and dead;
the phrase is from the Apostles' Creed, sup-

posedly written the tenth day after Christ's
ascension; the earliest written form dates
from about 215 A.D.

466. *paused:* Notice that Michael also
paused in line 2 above.

469–478. *O goodness . . . abound:*
Adam, perhaps too eagerly, assumes that his
was a fortunate fall, an idea popular from the
middle ages, as in *O felix culpa* (O happy sin)
from the Holy Week hymn *Exsultet*, "happy"
because it allowed God to show his love for
mankind. *Christian Doctrine* asserts that
mankind, "through Jesus Christ, is raised to a

To God more glory, more good will to men
From God—and over wrath grace shall abound.
But say, if our deliverer up to Heaven
Must reascend, what will betide the few   480
His faithful, left among the unfaithful herd,
The enemies of truth? Who then shall guide
His people, who defend? Will they not deal
Worse with his followers than with him they dealt?"
    "Be sure they will," said the angel; "but from Heaven   485
He to his own a comforter will send,
The promise of the Father, who shall dwell
His spirit within them, and the law of faith,
Working through love, upon their hearts shall write
To guide them in all truth, and also arm   490
With spiritual armor, able to resist
Satan's assaults and quench his fiery darts,
What man can do against them, not afraid,
Though to the death, against such cruelties
With inward consolations recompensed   495
And oft supported so as shall amaze
Their proudest persecutors: for the spirit,
Poured first on his apostles whom he sends
To evangelize the nations, then on all
Baptized, shall them with wondrous gifts endue   500
To speak all tongues and do all miracles,
As did their Lord before them. Thus they win

far more excellent state of grace and glory
than that from which he had fallen" (I, xiv
[*Works* 15, 251]).

478. *wrath . . . abound:* echoes Rom.
5:20: "Where sin abounded, grace did much
more abound."

486. *comforter:* as in John 25:26: "when
the Comforter is come, whom I will send
unto you from the Father, even the Spirit of
truth . . . he shall testify of me" (often under-
stood as the Holy Spirit)

487. *shall dwell:* i.e., shall cause to dwell

489. *upon their hearts shall write:* Heb.
8:10, echoing Jer. 31:33: "this is the covenant
that I will make with the house of Israel . . . I
will put my laws into their mind, and write
them in their hearts"

490. *To guide . . . truth:* Cf. John 16:13:
"when he, the Spirit of truth is come, he will
guide you into all truth."

491. *spiritual armor:* derives from Eph.
6:11–17: "Put on the whole armour of
God," including "the shield of faith, where-
with ye shall be able to quench all the fiery
darts of the wicked."

493. *What . . . afraid:* echoes Ps. 56:11:
"I will not be afraid what man can do unto
me"

496. *so:* i.e., so greatly (adverbial use, as
in line 125 above)

499. *evangelize:* convert to Christianity

501. *speak all tongues:* as in Acts 2:4–7,
where the apostles, "filled with the Holy
Ghost . . . began to speak with other

Great numbers of each nation to receive
With joy the tidings brought from Heaven. At length,
Their ministry performed and race well run,   505
Their doctrine and their story written left,
They die, but in their room, as they forewarn,
Wolves shall succeed for teachers, grievous wolves,
Who all the sacred mysteries of Heaven
To their own vile advantages shall turn   510
Of lucre and ambition, and the truth
With superstitions and traditions taint,
Left only in those written records pure,
Though not but° by the spirit understood.   *except*
Then shall they seek to avail themselves of names,°   *honors*
Places,° and titles, and with these to join   *ranks, offices*
Secular power, though feigning still to act
By spiritual, to themselves appropriating
The spirit of God, promised alike and given
To all believers, and, from that pretense,   520
Spiritual laws by carnal° power shall force   *secular*
On every conscience, laws which none shall find
Left them enrolled, or what the spirit within
Shall on the heart engrave. What will they then
But force the spirit of grace itself, and bind   525
His consort liberty? What but unbuild

tongues"; cf. the "jangling noise of words un-
known" that followed the tower at Babel in
lines 24–63 above.

505. *race well run:* The metaphor
comes from 1 Cor. 9:24: "Know ye not that
they which run in a race run all, but one re-
ceiveth the prize? So run, that ye may ob-
tain." See also Heb. 12:1.

508. *grievous wolves:* i.e., the clergy; the
term of contempt is Paul's in Acts 20:29,
which Milton previously echoed in the "grim
wolf" in his attack on the corrupt clergy in
"Lycidas," line 128, and again in his sonnet
to Cromwell: "hireling wolves whose gospel
is their maw" (line 14).

511–514. *the truth . . . understood:* Mil-
ton advances the familiar *sola scriptura* theme
of Protestantism (*written records pure*), as he
condemns the claimed authority of the
Catholic Church as an unnecessary and dis-
torting medium placed between the individ-

ual and revealed *truth,* though he admits that
the bible must be *by the spirit understood;* i.e.,
1) with the help of God's spirit; and 2) un-
derstood in terms of the spirit rather than the
letter of what is written.

520–528. *from . . . another's:* Christian
Doctrine I, xxx (*Works* 16, 280) denounced
all efforts to impose "human authority in
matters of religion" as attempts "to impose a
yoke, not on man, but on the Holy Spirit it-
self."

523. *Left them enrolled:* left for them in
written form (i.e., in scripture)

525–526. *force . . . liberty:* The lan-
guage derives from 2 Cor. 3.17: "Now the
Lord is that Spirit; and where the Spirit of
the Lord is, there is Liberty." In *Christian
Doctrine,* Milton writes that "liberty must be
considered as belonging especially to the
gospel, and as consorting therewith" (I, xxvii;
Works 16, 153).

His living temples built by faith to stand,
Their own faith, not another's—for on earth
Who against faith and conscience can be heard
Infallible? Yet many will presume,   530
Whence heavy persecution shall arise
On all who in the worship persevere
Of spirit and truth; the rest, far greater part,
Will deem in outward rites and specious forms
Religion satisfied; truth shall retire   535
Bestuck with slanderous darts, and works of faith
Rarely be found. So shall the world go on,
To good malignant, to bad men benign,
Under her own weight groaning, till the day
Appear of respiration to the just   540
And vengeance to the wicked at return
Of him so lately promised to thy aid,
The woman's seed, obscurely then foretold,
Now amplier known thy savior and thy Lord,
Last in the clouds from Heaven to be revealed   545
In glory of the Father, to dissolve
Satan with his perverted world, then raise
From the conflagrant mass, purged and refined,
New heavens, new earth, ages of endless date
Founded in righteousness and peace and love   550

527. *living temples:* i.e., the Christian faithful; in 1 Cor. Paul says "The temple of God is holy, which temple ye are" (3:17), and calls the body "the temple of the Holy Ghost" (6:19).

529–530. *Who . . . Infallible:* contests the papal claim to infallibility, which, although formalized by the Catholic Church only in 1870, was a familiar assertion and object of attack; hence Milton says that "all true protestants account the pope antichrist, for that he assumes to himself this infallibilitie over both the conscience and the scripture" (*Of Civil Power* [*Works* 6, 8]).

532–533. *all . . . truth:* derives from John 4:23: "True worshippers shall worship the Father in spirit and in truth"

536. *works of faith:* See line 306 above.

539–551. *till the day . . . bliss:* Milton interprets Peter's "times of refreshing . . . from the presence of the Lord" (Acts 3:19) as the day of Christ's coming "with clouds" (Rev. 1:7) at the last judgment, when, as *Christian Doctrine* says (I, xxxiii [*Works* 16, 355]), "Christ shall judge the evil angels and the whole race of mankind." Also see 3.334–38 and 11.900–901.

540. *respiration:* i.e., comfort, respite (as in the metaphor "breathing space")

546. *dissolve:* echoes 2 Pet. 3:11–12: "all these things shall be dissolved . . . the heavens being on fire shall be dissolved"; the Greek word translated as "dissolved" also means "destroyed." This usage also picks up an alchemical sense (*OED* 3) meaning "reduce to its original elements by destroying its binding power."

547. *perverted:* depraved; but literally, "turned away" (from God)

549. *New heavens, new earth:* See 2 Pet. 3:13: "we, according to his promise, look for new heavens and a new earth" (see also Rev. 21:1).   *endless date:* eternity; see *Of Reformation:* "the dateless and

To bring forth fruits, joy, and eternal bliss."

He ended; and thus Adam last replied:
"How soon hath thy prediction, seer blessed,
Measured this transient world, the race of time,
Till time stand fixed. Beyond is all abyss,   555
Eternity, whose end no eye can reach.
Greatly instructed I shall hence depart.
Greatly in peace of thought, and have my fill
Of knowledge, what this vessel can contain,
Beyond which was my folly to aspire.   560
Henceforth I learn that to obey is best,
And love with fear the only God, to walk
As in his presence, ever to observe
His providence, and on him sole depend,
Merciful over all his works, with good   565
Still° overcoming evil and by small   *continually, always*
Accomplishing great things, by things deemed weak
Subverting worldly strong, and worldly wise
By simply meek, that suffering for truth's sake
Is fortitude to highest victory,   570
And, to the faithful, death the gate of life:
Taught this by his example whom I now
Acknowledge my redeemer ever blessed."

To whom thus also the angel last replied:
"This having learned, thou hast attained the sum   575
Of wisdom; hope no higher, though all the stars
Thou knew'st by name and all the ethereal powers,
All secrets of the deep, all nature's works,
Or works of God in Heaven, air, earth, or sea,
And all the riches of this world enjoy'dst,   580
And all the rule, one empire. Only add

---

irrevoluble Circle of Eternity" (*Works* 3, part 1, 9).

559. *what . . . contain: Christian Doctrine* warns that humans are able to understand God only "in such manner as may be within the scope of our comprehension" (*Works* 14, 61); cf. 8.167–73.

561. *to obey is best:* Cf. 1 Sam. 15:22: "to obey is better than sacrifice."

565. *Merciful . . . works:* echoes Ps. 145:9: "His tender mercies are over all his works"

567–568. *weak . . . strong:* the familiar radical promise of Christianity: "God hath

chosen the weak things of the world to confound the things which are mighty" (1 Cor. 1:27).

569–570. *suffering . . . victory:* Cf. 9.31–32 and *SA*, line 654: "Extolling patience as the truest fortitude."

576–577. *all . . name:* alludes to Ps. 147:4: "He telleth the number of the stars; he calleth them all by their names"

581–585. *Only add . . . rest:* Milton's transformation of 2 Pet. 1:5–7: "Add to your faith virtue; and to virtue knowledge; And to knowledge temperance; and to temperance

Deeds to thy knowledge answerable; add faith,
Add virtue, patience, temperance; add love,
By name to come called 'charity,' the soul
Of all the rest: then wilt thou not be loath   585
To leave this Paradise but shalt possess
A paradise within thee, happier far.
Let us descend now, therefore, from this top
Of speculation, for the hour precise
Exacts° our parting hence; and see, the guards,   *demands*
By me encamped on yonder hill, expect
Their motion, at whose front a flaming sword,
In signal of remove,° waves fiercely round;   *departure*
We may no longer stay. Go, waken Eve;
Her also I with gentle dreams have calmed,   595
Portending good, and all her spirits composed
To meek submission. Thou at season fit
Let her with thee partake what thou hast heard,
Chiefly what may concern her faith to know:
The great deliverance by her seed to come   600
(For by the woman's seed) on all mankind,
That ye may live, which will be many days,
Both in one faith unanimous, though sad
With cause for° evils past, yet much more cheered   *in consequence of*
With meditation on the happy end."   605
        He ended, and they both descend the hill;
Descended, Adam to the bower where Eve
Lay sleeping ran before, but found her waked,

patience; and to patience godliness; and to
godliness brotherly kindness; and to broth-
erly kindness charity."
    587. *paradise within thee:* The promise
is in sharp contrast to the "hell within" that
Satan suffers (see 4.20); scholars have noted
the echo of Robert Croft's *A Paradise within
Us or the Happie Mind* (1640).   *hap-*
pier far: Can this inner paradise really be
"happier far" than what they knew in Para-
dise, or is the unanchored comparative an in-
vitation to qualify the claim (i.e., *happier far*
than what?)?
    588–589. *top Of speculation:* the "top"
of the "hill / of Paradise" that Michael and
Adam "ascend" in 11.376–80 to see the

"visions of God" (but *speculation* is easily
heard in a cognitive sense, so also, the
"height of theological inquiry," especially as
the vision of the future in Book 12 is nar-
rated to Adam, rather than shown).
    591–592. *expect Their motion:* await
their orders
    602. *many days:* Gen. 5:5 says that "the
days that Adam lived were nine hundred and
thirty years"; there is no biblical mention of
the length of Eve's life.
    608. *found her waked:* The Argument
to Book 12, however, says Adam "wakens
Eve," and Michael, in line 594, tells Adam:
"Go, waken Eve."

And thus with words not sad° she him received: *disconsolate*
    "Whence thou return'st and whither went'st I know,   610
For God is also in sleep, and dreams advise,
Which he hath sent propitious, some great good
Presaging, since with sorrow and heart's distress
Wearied I fell asleep. But now lead on;
In me is no delay; with thee to go   615
Is to stay here; without thee here to stay
Is to go hence unwilling. Thou to me
Art all things under Heaven, all places thou,
Who for my willful crime art banished hence.
This further consolation yet secure   620
I carry hence: though all by me is lost,
Such favor I unworthy am vouchsafed,
By me the promised seed shall all restore."
    So spake our mother Eve, and Adam heard
Well pleased, but answered not, for now too nigh   625
The archangel stood, and from the other hill
To their fixed station, all in bright array,
The cherubim descended, on the ground
Gliding meteorous° as evening mist   *in mid air*
Risen from a river o'er the marish° glides   *marsh*
And gathers ground fast at the laborer's heel
Homeward returning. High in front advanced,
The brandished sword of God before them blazed
Fierce as a comet, which with torrid heat
And vapor, as the Libyan air adust,°   *burnt*
Began to parch that temperate clime; whereat
In either hand the hastening angel caught
Our lingering parents and to the eastern gate
Led them direct and down the cliff as fast
To the subjected° plain, then disappeared.   *lying beneath*

---

611. *God . . . sleep:* Perhaps there is a trace of Achilles' insistence to Agamemnon that dreams come from Zeus (*Iliad* 1.63), but the notion that God communicates through dreams is familiar, as in Num. 12:6, where God says of his "prophet" that he "will speak unto him in a dream."

615–618. *with thee . . . thou:* Eve's commitment to Adam echoes Ruth 1:16: "Intreat me not to leave thee, or to return from following after thee: for whither thou goest, I will go, and where thou lodgest, I will lodge."

631. *heel:* a place of vulnerability; as in the prophecy to Adam that Satan is "to bruise his heel" (10.498), but also the place of Achilles' weakness (Statius, *Achilleid* 1.133–34).

632. *High in front advanced:* i.e., carried high in front of them (by Michael)

They, looking back, all the eastern side beheld
Of Paradise, so late their happy seat,
Waved over by that flaming brand, the gate
With dreadful° faces thronged and fiery arms.   *fearsome*
Some natural tears they dropped, but wiped them soon: 645
The world was all before them, where to choose
Their place of rest, and providence their guide;
They hand in hand, with wandering steps and slow,
Through Eden took their solitary way.

THE END

641–649. *They . . . solitary way:* The
final nine lines are perfectly balanced: four
lines of Adam and Eve *looking back;* a pivot
line with a sharp caesura (line 645), which
registers first their sadness, and then the shift
of mode; and four lines of their acceptance of
the world stretching out *all before them.* The
equilibrium perfectly reflects Michael's com-
mission to "send them forth, though sorrow-
ing, yet in peace," and with a "new hope"
born "of despair" (11.117 and 11.138–39).

643. *brand:* the "flaming sword" of
Gen. 3:24.

646. *choose:* Even fallen, choice is still at
the center of their being.

648. *hand in hand:* Like the first vision
of Adam and Eve (4.321), the two are again
hand in hand (but see 9.384–85 and
9.1037).

648–649. *with wandering . . . way*
echoes Ps. 107:4: "They wandered in the
wilderness in a solitary way." Cf. Bentley's
notorious emendation in 1732 of these lines:
"Then hand in hand with social steps their
way / Through Eden took, with heav'nly
comfort cheer'd."

649. *Eden:* It is not merely Paradise
from which they are banished but all of
Eden; see 4.208–10. On illustrations of the
expulsion, see Merritt Y. Hughes in *JEGP* 60
(1961): 670–79.

THE LIFE OF MILTON

(1694)
By Edward Phillips*

Of all the several parts of history, that which sets forth the lives, and commemorates the most remarkable actions, sayings, or writings of famous and illustrious persons, whether in war or peace, whether many together, or any one in particular, as it is not the least useful in itself, so it is in highest vogue and esteem among the studious and reading part of mankind.

The most eminent in this way of history were, among the ancients, Plutarch and Diogenes Laertius, of the Greeks; the first wrote the lives, for the most part, of the most renowned heroes and warriors of the Greeks and Romans; the other, the lives of the ancient Greek philosophers. And Cornelius Nepos (or as some will have it Æmilius Probus) of the Latins, who wrote the lives of the most illustrious Greek and Roman generals.

Among the moderns, Machiavelli, a noble Florentine, who elegantly wrote the life of Castruccio Castracani, Lord of Lucca. And of our nation, Sir Fulke Greville, who wrote the life of his most intimate friend, Sir Philip Sidney; Mr. Thomas Stanley of Cumberlo-Green, who made a most elaborate improvement to the foresaid Laertius, by adding to what he found in him, what by diligent search and enquiry he collected from other authors of best authority; [and] Isaac Walton, who wrote the lives of Sir Henry Wotton, Dr. Donne, and for his divine poems, the admired Mr. George Herbert. Lastly, not to mention several other biographers of considerable note, the great Gassendus of France, the worthy celebrator of two no less worthy subjects of his impartial pen; *viz.* the noble philosopher Epicurus, and the most politely learned virtuoso of his age, his countryman, Monsieur Peiresk.

And pity it is the person whose memory we have here undertaken to perpetuate by recounting the most memorable transactions of his life (though his works sufficiently recommend him to the world), finds not a well-informed pen able to set him forth, equal with the best of those here mentioned; for doubtless, had his fame been as much spread through Europe in Thuanus's time, as now it is and hath been for several years, he had justly merited from that great historian, an eulogy not inferior to the highest by

---

* Edward Phillips left the fullest and least unreliable of the early biographies of his uncle. He was the son of Anne Milton Phillips (the poet's sister) and Edward Phillips, senior, and was born in the autumn of 1630. He and his brother John were both pupils of Milton and must have lived with him for several years, but in the end both of them seem to have become sympathizers with the position of the Royalists. Edward, however, remained personally loyal to Milton and translated his *Letters of State* into English after his death.

him given to all the learned and ingenious that lived within the compass of his history. For we may safely and justly affirm, that take him in all respects, for acumen of wit, quickness of apprehension, sagacity of judgment, depth of argument, and elegancy of style, as well in Latin as English, as well in verse as prose, he is scarce to be paralleled by any the best of writers our nation hath in any age brought forth.

He was born in London, in a house in Bread Street, the lease whereof, as I take it, but for certain it was a house in Bread Street, became in time part of his estate, in the year of our Lord 1606.[1] His father John Milton, an honest, worthy, and substantial citizen of London, by profession a scrivener; to which he voluntarily betook himself by the advice and assistance of an intimate friend of his eminent in that calling, upon his being cast out by his father, a bigoted Roman Catholic, for embracing, when young, the protestant faith, and abjuring the popish tenets. For he is said to have been descended of an ancient family of the Miltons, of Milton near Abingdon in Oxfordshire; where they had been a long time seated, as appears by the monuments still to be seen in Milton church; till one of the family having taken the wrong side, in the contest between the Houses of York and Lancaster, was sequestered of all his estate, but what he held by his wife. However, certain it is that this vocation he followed for many years, at his said house in Bread Street, with success suitable to his industry and prudent conduct of his affairs. Yet he did not so far quit his own generous and ingenious inclinations as to make himself wholly a slave to the world; for he sometimes found vacant hours to the study (which he made his recreation) of the noble science of music, in which he advanced to that perfection that as I have been told, and as I take it by our author himself, he composed an *In Nomine* of forty parts; for which he was rewarded with a gold medal and chain by a Polish prince, to whom he presented it. However, this is a truth not to be denied, that for several songs of his composition after the way of these times (three or four of which are still to be seen in Old Wilby's set of Airs, besides some compositions of his in Ravenscroft's Psalms) he gained the reputation of a considerable master in this most charming of all the liberal sciences. Yet all this while he managed his grand affair of this world with such prudence and diligence that by the assistance of divine Providence favoring his honest endeavors, he gained a competent estate, whereby he was enabled to make a handsome provision both for the education and maintenance of his children; for three he had, and no more, all by one wife Sarah, of the family of the Castons, derived originally from Wales, a woman of incomparable virtue and goodness: John the eldest, the subject of our present work, Christopher, and an only daughter Ann.

---

[1] The correct date of Milton's birth is Dec. 9, 1608.

Christopher, being principally designed for the study of the common law of England, was entered young a student of the Inner Temple, of which house he lived to be an ancient bencher, and keeping close to that study and profession all his life-time, except in the time of the civil wars of England; when being a great favorer and asserter of the King's cause, and obnoxious to the Parliament's side, by acting to his utmost power against them, so long as he kept his station at Reading; and after that town was taken by the Parliament forces, being forced to quit his house there, he steered his course according to the motion of the King's army. But when the war was ended with victory and success to the Parliament party by the valor of General Fairfax and the craft and conduct of Cromwell, and his composition made by the help of his brother's interest with the then prevailing power, he betook himself again to his former study and profession, following chamber-practice every term; yet came to no advancement in the world in a long time, except some small employ in the town of Ipswich, where (and near it) he lived all the latter time of his life; for he was a person of a modest, quiet temper, preferring justice and virtue before all worldly pleasure or grandeur. But in the beginning of the reign of King James the II, for his known integrity and ability in the law, he was by some persons of quality recommended to the King, and at a call of sergeants received the coif, and the same day was sworn one of the barons of the Exchequer, and soon after made one of the judges of the Common Pleas. But his years and indisposition not well brooking the fatigue of public employment, he continued not long in either of these stations; but having his *quietus est*, retired to a country life, his study and devotion.

Ann, the only daughter of the said John Milton, the elder, had a considerable dowry given her by her father in marriage with Edward Philips, the son of Edward Philips of Shrewsbury, who, coming up young to town, was bred up in the crown-office in Chancery, and at length came to be secondary of the office under old Mr. Bembo. By him she had, besides other children that died infants, two sons yet surviving, of whom more hereafter; and by a second husband, Mr. Thomas Agar (who, upon the death of his intimate friend Mr. Philips, worthily succeeded in the place, which, except some time of exclusion before and during the Interregnum, he held for many years, and left it to Mr. Thomas Milton, the son of the aforementioned Sir Christopher, who at this day executes it with great reputation and ability), two daughters, Mary who died very young, and Ann yet surviving.

But to hasten back to our matter in hand. John, our author, who was destined to be the ornament and glory of his country, was sent, together with his brother, to Paul's school, whereof Dr. Gill the elder was then chief master; where he was entered into the first rudiments of learning, and advanced therein with that admirable success, not more by the discipline of the school and good instructions of his masters (for that he had another master, possibly at his father's house, appears by the *Fourth Elegy* of his Latin poems written in his 18th year, to Thomas Young, pastor of the English Company of Merchants at Hamburg, wherein he owns and styles him his master), than by his own happy genius, prompt wit and apprehension, and insuperable industry: for he generally sat up half the night, as well in voluntary improvements of his own choice, as the exact perfecting of his school exercises. So that at the age of 15 he was full ripe for academic learning, and accordingly was sent to the University of Cambridge; where in Christ's College under the tuition of a very eminent learned man, whose name I cannot call to mind, he studied seven years and took his degree of Master of Arts; and for the extraordinary wit and reading he had shown in his performances to attain his degree (some whereof, spoken at a *Vacation Exercise* in his 19th year of age, are to be yet seen in his *Miscellaneous Poems*), he was loved and admired by the whole university, particularly by the fellows and most ingenious persons of his house. Among the rest there was a young gentleman, one Mr. King, with whom, for his great learning and parts, he had contracted a particular friendship and intimacy; whose death (for he was drowned on the Irish seas in his passage from Chester to Ireland) he bewails in that most excellent monody in his forementioned poems, entitled *Lycidas*. Never was the loss of friend so elegantly lamented; and among the rest of his *Juvenile Poems,* some he wrote at the age of 15, which contain a poetical genius scarce to be paralleled by any English writer.

Soon after he had taken his Master's degree, he thought fit to leave the university: not upon any disgust or discontent for want of preferment, as some ill-willers have reported; nor upon any cause whatsoever forced to fly, as his detractors maliciously feign; but from which aspersion he sufficiently clears himself in his *Second Answer to Alexander Morus,* the author of a book called *Clamor Regii Sanguinis ad Coelum,* the chief of his calumniators; in which he plainly makes it out that after his leaving the university, to the no small trouble of his fellow-collegiates, who in general regretted his absence, he for the space of five years lived for the most part with his father and mother at their house at Horton near Colebrook in Berkshire; whither his father, having got an estate to his content and left off all business, was retired from the cares and fatigues of the world.

After the said term of five years, his mother then dying, he was willing to add to his acquired learning the observation of foreign customs, manners, and institutions; and thereupon took a resolution to travel, more especially designing for Italy; and accordingly, with his father's consent and assistance, he put himself into an equipage suitable to such a design; and so, intending to go by the way of France, he set out for Paris, accompanied only with one man, who attended him through all his travels; for his prudence was his guide, and his learning his introduction and presentation to persons of most eminent quality. However, he had also a most civil and obliging letter of direction and advice from Sir Henry Wotton, then Provost of Eton, and formerly resident Ambassador from King James the First to the state of Venice; which letter is to be seen in the first edition of his *Miscellaneous Poems*.

At Paris, being recommended by the said Sir Henry and other persons of quality, he went first to wait upon my Lord Scudamore, then Ambassador in France from King Charles the First. My Lord received him with wonderful civility; and understanding he had a desire to make a visit to the great Hugo Grotius, he sent several of his attendants to wait upon him and to present him in his name to that renowned doctor and statesman, who was at that time Ambassador from Christina, Queen of Sweden, to the French king. Grotius took the visit kindly, and gave him entertainment suitable to his worth and the high commendations he had heard of him. After a few days, not intending to make the usual tour of France, he took his leave of my Lord, who at his departure from Paris, gave him letters to the English merchants residing in any part through which he was to travel, in which they were requested to show him all the kindness and do him all the good offices that lay in their power.

From Paris he hastened on his journey to Nice, where he took shipping, and in a short space arrived at Genoa; from whence he went to Leghorn, thence to Pisa, and so to Florence. In this city he met with many charming objects, which invited him to stay a longer time than he intended; the pleasant situation of the place, the nobleness of the structures, the exact humanity and civility of the inhabitants, the more polite and refined sort of language there than elsewhere. During the time of his stay here, which was about two months, he visited all the private academies of the city, which are places established for the improvement of wit and learning, and maintained a correspondence and perpetual friendship among gentlemen fitly qualified for such an institution; and such sort of academies there are in all or most of the most noted cities in Italy. Visiting these places he was soon taken notice of by the most learned and ingenious of the nobility and the grand wits of Florence, who caressed him with all the honors and civilities imaginable; particularly Jacobo Gaddi, Carlo Dati, Antonio Francini, Frescobaldo, Cultellino, Bonmatthei and Clementillo: whereof Gaddi hath a large, elegant Italian canzonet in his praise, [and] Dati, a Latin epistle, both printed before his Latin poems, together with a Latin distich of the Marquis of Villa, and another of Selvaggi, and a Latin tetrastich of Giovanni Salsilli, a Roman.

From Florence he took his journey to Siena, from thence to Rome, where he was detained much about the same time he had been at Florence; as well by his desire of seeing all the rarities and antiquities of that most glorious and renowned city, as by the conversation of Lucas Holstenius and other learned and ingenious men, who highly valued his acquaintance and treated him with all possible respect.

From Rome he travelled to Naples, where he was introduced by a certain hermit who accompanied him in his journey from Rome thither, into the knowledge of Giovanni Baptista Manso, Marquis of Villa, a Neapolitan by birth, a person of high nobility, virtue, and honor, to whom the famous Italian poet, Torquato Tasso, wrote his treatise *De Amicitia;* and moreover mentions him with great honor in that illustrious poem of his, entitled *Gierusalemme Liberata.* This noble marquis received him with extraordinary respect and civility, and went with him himself to give him a sight of all that was of note and remark in the city, particularly the viceroy's palace, and was often in person to visit him at his lodging. Moreover, this noble marquis honored him so far, as to make a Latin distich in his praise, as hath been already mentioned; which being no less pithy than short, though already in print, it will not be unworth the while here to repeat.

> *Ut mens, forma, decor, facies, [mos,] si pietas sic*
> *Non Anglus, verum hercle Angelus ipse foret.*

In return of this honor, and in gratitude for the many favors and civilities received of him, he presented him at his departure with a large Latin eclogue, entitled *Mansus,* afterwards published among his *Latin Poems.* The marquis at his taking leave of him, gave him this compliment: that he would have done him many more offices of kindness and civility, but was therefore rendered incapable, in regard he had been over-liberal in his speech against the religion of the country.

He had entertained some thoughts of passing over into Sicily and Greece, but was diverted by the news he received from England that affairs there were tending toward a civil war; thinking it a thing unworthy in him to be taking his pleasure in foreign parts while his countrymen at home were fighting for their liberty: but first resolved to see Rome once more; and though the merchants gave him a caution that the Jesuits were hatching designs against him in case he should return thither, by reason of the freedom he took in all his discourses of religion; nevertheless he ventured to prosecute his resolution, and to Rome the second time he went; determining with himself not industriously to begin to fall into any discourse about religion, but, being asked, not to deny or endeavor to conceal his own sentiments. Two months he stayed at Rome, and in all that time never flinched, but was ready to defend the orthodox faith against all opposers; and so well he succeeded therein, that, good Providence guarding him, he went safe from Rome back to Florence, where his return to his friends of that city was welcomed with as much joy and affection as had it been to his friends and relations in his own country, he could not have come a more joyful and welcome guest.

Here, having stayed as long as at his first coming, excepting an excursion of a few days to Lucca, crossing the Apennine and passing through Bononia and Ferrara, he arrived at Venice; where when he had spent a month's time in viewing of that stately city and shipped up a parcel of curious and rare books which he had picked up in his travels (particularly a chest or two of choice music-books of the best masters flourishing about that time in Italy, namely, Luca Marenzo, Monte Verde, Horatio Vecchi, Cifa, the Prince of Venosa, and several others), he took his course through Verona, Milan, and the Poenine Alps, and so by the lake Leman to Geneva, where he stayed for some time, and had daily converse with the most learned Giovanni Deodati, theology professor in that city; and so returning through France, by the same way he had passed it going to Italy, he, after a peregrination of one complete year and about three months, arrived safe in England about the time of the King's making his second expedition against the Scots.

Soon after his return and visits paid to his father and other friends, he took him a lodging in St. Bride's Churchyard, at the house of one Russel, a tailor, where he first undertook the education and instruction of his sister's two sons, the younger whereof had been wholly committed to his charge and care.

And here by the way, I judge it not impertinent to mention the many authors both of the Latin and Greek, which through his excellent judgment and way of teaching, far above the pedantry of common public schools (where such authors are scarce ever heard of), were run over within no greater compass of time, than from ten to fifteen or sixteen years of age. Of the Latin, the four grand authors *De Re Rustica*, Cato, Varro, Columella and Palladius; Cornelius Celsus, an ancient physician of the Romans; a great part of Pliny's *Natural History;* Vitruvius his *Architecture;* Frontinus his *Stratagems;* with the two egregious poets, Lucretius and Manilius. Of the Greek, Hesiod, a poet equal with Homer; Aratus his *Phaenomena,* and *Diosemeia;* Dionysius Afer *De Situ Orbis;* Oppian's *Cynegetics* and *Halieutics;* Quintus Calaber his *Poem of the Trojan War* continued from Homer; Apollonius Rhodius his *Argonautics:* and in prose, Plutarch's *Placita Philosophorum,* and Περι Παιδων 'Αγογιας [*sic*]; Geminus's *Astronomy;* Xenophon's *Cyri Institutio,* and *Anabasis;* Ælian's *Tactics;* and Polyænus his *Warlike Stratagems.* Thus by teaching he in some measure increased his own knowledge, having the reading of all these authors as it were by proxy; and all this might possibly have conduced to the preserving of his eyesight, had he not moreover been perpetually busied in his own laborious undertakings of the book and pen.

Nor did the time thus studiously employed in conquering the Greek and Latin tongues, hinder the attaining to the chief oriental languages, *viz.,* the Hebrew, Chaldee, and Syriac, so far as to go through the *Pentateuch,* or Five Books of Moses in Hebrew, to make a good entrance into the *Targum,* or Chaldee Paraphrase, and to understand several chapters of St. Matthew in the

Syriac Testament: besides an introduction into several arts and sciences, by reading Urstisius his *Arithmetic,* Riff's *Geometry,* Petiscus his *Trigonometry,* Johannes de Sacro Bosco *De Sphæra;* and into the Italian and French tongues, by reading in Italian Giovan Villani's *History of the Transactions between several petty States of Italy;* and in French a great part of Pierre Davity, the famous geographer of France in his time.

The Sunday's work was, for the most part, the reading each day a chapter of the Greek Testament, and hearing his learned exposition upon the same (and how this savored of atheism in him, I leave to the courteous backbiter to judge). The next work after this was the writing from his own dictation, some part, from time to time, of a tractate which he thought fit to collect from the ablest of divines who had written of that subject: Amesius, Wollebius, &c., *viz. A perfect System of Divinity,* of which more hereafter.

Now persons so far manuducted into the highest paths of literature both divine and human, had they received his documents with the same acuteness of wit and apprehension, the same industry, alacrity, and thirst after knowledge, as the instructor was indued with, what prodigies of wit and learning might they have proved! The scholars might in some degree have come near to the equalling of the master, or at least have in some sort made good what he seems to predict in the close of an elegy he made in the seventeenth year of his age, upon the death of one of his sister's children (a daughter), who died in her infancy:

> Then thou, the mother of so sweet a child,
> Her false, imagin'd loss cease to lament,
> And wisely learn to curb thy sorrows wild:
> This if thou do, he will an offspring give,
> That till the world's last end shall make thy name to live.

But to return to the thread of our discourse. He made no long stay in his lodgings in St. Bride's Church-yard; necessity of having a place to dispose his books in, and other goods fit for the furnishing of a good, handsome house, hastening him to take one; and, accordingly, a pretty garden-house he took in Aldersgate-street, at the end of an entry and therefore the fitter for his turn by the reason of the privacy; besides that there are few streets in London more free from noise than that. Here first it was that his academic erudition was put in practice, and vigorously proceeded, he himself giving an example to those under him (for it was not long after his taking this house, ere his elder nephew was put to board with him also) of hard study and spare diet; only this advantage he had, that once in three weeks or a month, he would drop into the society of some young sparks of his acquaintance, the chief whereof were Mr. Alphry and Mr. Miller, two gentlemen of Gray's Inn, the beaux of those times, but nothing near so bad as those now-a-days; with these gentlemen he would so far make bold with his body as now and then to keep a gawdyday.

In this house he continued several years, in the one or two first whereof he set out several treatises, *viz.*, that *Of Reformation*; that *Against Prelatical Episcopacy; The Reason of Church-Government; The Defence of Smectymnuus,* at least the greatest part of them, but as I take it, all; and some time after, one sheet *Of Education* which he dedicated to Mr. Samuel Hartlib, he that wrote so much of husbandry (this sheet is printed at the end of the second edition of his *Poems*), and lastly *Areopagitica*.

During the time also of his continuance in this house, there fell out several occasions of the increasing of his family. His father, who till the taking of Reading by the Earl of Essex his forces, had lived with his other son at his house there, was upon that son's dissettlement necessitated to betake himself to this his eldest son, with whom he lived for some years, even to his dying day. In the next place he had an addition of some scholars; to which may be added, his entering into matrimony; but he had his wife's company so small a time, that he may well be said to have become a single man again soon after.

About Whitsuntide it was, or a little after, that he took a journey into the country; no body about him certainly knowing the reason, or that it was any more than a journey of recreation; after a month's stay, home he returns a married man, that went out a bachelor; his wife being Mary, the eldest daughter of Mr. Richard Powell, then a justice of peace, of Forresthill, near Shotover in Oxfordshire; some few of her nearest relations accompanying the bride to her new habitation; which by reason the father nor any body else were yet come, was able to receive them; where the feasting held for some days in celebration of the nuptials and for entertainment of the bride's friends. At length they took their leave and returning to Forresthill left the sister behind, probably not much to her satisfaction as appeared by the sequel. By that time she had for a month or thereabout led a philosophical life (after having been used to a great house, and much company and joviality), her friends, possibly incited by her own desire, made earnest suit by letter, to have her company the remaining part of the summer, which was granted, on condition of her return at the time appointed, Michaelmas, or thereabout. In the meantime came his father, and some of the forementioned disciples.

And now the studies went on with so much the more vigor, as there were more hands and heads employed; the old gentleman living wholly retired to his rest and devotion, without the least trouble imaginable. Our author, now as it were a single man again, made it his chief diversion now and then in an evening, to visit the Lady Margaret Lee, daughter to the ———— Lee, Earl of Marlborough, Lord High Treasurer of England, and President of the

Privy Council to King James the First. This lady being a woman of great wit and ingenuity, had a particular honor for him and took much delight in his company, as likewise her husband Captain Hobson, a very accomplished gentleman; and what esteem he at the same time had for her, appears by a sonnet he made in praise of her, to be seen among his other *Sonnets* in his extant *Poems*.

Michaelmas being come, and no news of his wife's return, he sent for her by letter; and receiving no answer, sent several other letters, which were also unanswered; so that at last he dispatched down a foot messenger with a letter, desiring her return. But the messenger came back not only without an answer, at least a satisfactory one, but to the best of my remembrance, reported that he was dismissed with some sort of contempt. This proceeding in all probability was grounded upon no other cause but this, namely, that the family being generally addicted to the cavalier party, as they called it, and some of them possibly engaged in the King's service, who by this time had his headquarters at Oxford, and was in some prospect of success, they began to repent them of having matched the eldest daughter of the family to a person so contrary to them in opinion; and thought it would be a blot in their escutcheon, whenever that court should come to flourish again.

However, it so incensed our author that he thought it would be dishonorable ever to receive her again, after such a repulse; so that he forthwith prepared to fortify himself with arguments for such a resolution, and accordingly wrote two treatises, by which he undertook to maintain, that it was against reason, and the enjoinment of it not provable by Scripture, for any married couple disagreeable in humor and temper, or having an aversion to each other, to be forced to live yoked together all their days. The first was his *Doctrine and Discipline of Divorce,* of which there was printed a second edition with some additions. The other in prosecution of the first, was styled *Tetrachordon.* Then the better to confirm his own opinion by the attestation of others, he set out a piece called *The Judgment of Martin Bucer,* a protestant minister, being a translation out of that reverend divine, of some part of his works exactly agreeing with him in sentiment. Lastly, he wrote in answer to a pragmatical clerk, who would needs give himself the honor of writing against so great a man, his *Colasterion,* or *Rod of Correction for a Saucy Impertinent.*

Not very long after the setting forth of these treatises, having application made to him by several gentlemen of his acquaintance for the education of their sons, as understanding haply the progress he had infixed by his first undertakings of that nature, he laid out for a larger house, and soon found it out.

But in the interim before he removed, there fell out a passage, which though it altered not the whole course he was going to steer, yet it put a stop or rather an end to a grand affair, which was more than probably thought to be then in agitation; it was indeed a design of marrying one of Dr. Davis's daughters, a very handsome and witty gentlewoman, but averse, as it is said, to this motion. However, the intelligence hereof, and the then declining state of the King's cause, and consequently of the circumstances of Justice Powell's family, caused them to set all engines on work to restore the late married woman to the station wherein they a little before had planted her. At last this device was pitched upon. There dwelt in the lane of St. Martin's le Grand, which was hard by, a relation of our author's, one Blackborough, whom it was known he often visited, and upon this occasion the visits were the more narrowly observed, and possibly there might be a combination between both parties; the friends on both sides concentring in the same action, though on different behalfs. One time above the rest, he making his usual visit, the wife was ready in another room, and on a sudden he was surprised to see one whom he thought to have never seen more, making submission and begging pardon on her knees before him. He might probably at first make some show of aversion and rejection; but partly his own generous nature more inclinable to reconciliation than to perseverance in anger and revenge and partly the strong intercession of friends on both sides, soon brought him to an act of oblivion and a firm league of peace for the future; and it was at length concluded that she should remain at a friend's house till such time as he was settled in his new house at Barbican, and all things for her reception in order; the place agreed on for her present abode was the widow Webber's house in St. Clement's Church-yard, whose second daughter had been married to the other brother many years before. The first fruits of her return to her husband was a brave girl, born within a year after; though, whether by ill constitution or want of care, she grew more and more decrepit.

But it was not only by children that she increased the number of the family; for in no very long time after her coming, she had a great resort of her kindred with her in the house, *viz.* her father and mother, and several of her brothers and sisters, which were in all pretty numerous; who upon his father's sickening and dying soon after, went away.

And now the house looked again like a house of the Muses only, though the accession of scholars was not great. Possibly his proceeding thus far in the education of youth may have been the occasion of some of his adversaries calling him pedagogue and schoolmaster; whereas it is well known he never set up for a public school to teach all the young fry of the parish, but only was willing to impart his learning and knowledge to relations, and the sons of some gentlemen that were his intimate friends; besides, that neither his converse, nor his writings, nor his manner of teaching ever savored in the least anything of pedantry; and probably he might have some prospect of putting in practice his academical institution, according to the model laid down in his sheet *Of Education.* The progress of which design was afterwards diverted by a series of alteration in the affairs of state; for I am much mistaken if there were not about this time a design in agitation of making him adjutant-general in Sir William Waller's army. But the new modeling of the army soon following proved an obstruction to that design; and Sir William, his commission being laid down, began, as the common saying is, to turn *cat in pan.*

It was not long after the march of Fairfax and Cromwell through the city of London with the whole army, to quell the insurrections Brown and Massey, now malcontents also, were endeavoring to raise in the city against the army's proceedings, ere he left his great house in Barbican, and betook himself to a smaller in High Holburn, among those that open backward into Lincoln's Inn Fields. Here he lived a private and quiet life, still prosecuting his studies and curious search into knowledge, the grand affair perpetually of his life; till such time as, the war being now at an end, with complete victory to the Parliament's side, as the Parliament then stood purged of all its dissenting members, and the King after some treaties with the army *re infecta,* brought to his trial; the form of government being now changed into a free state, he was hereupon obliged to write a treatise, called *The Tenure of Kings and Magistrates.*

After which his thoughts were bent upon retiring again to his own private studies, and falling upon such subjects as his proper genius prompted him to write of, among which was the history of our own nation from the beginning till the Norman Conquest, wherein he had made some progress. When (for this his last treatise, reviving the fame of other things he had formerly published) being more and more taken notice of for his excellency of style, and depth of judgment, he was courted into the service of this new commonwealth and at last prevailed with (for he never hunted after preferment, nor affected the tintamar and hurry of public business) to take upon him the office of Latin secretary to the Council of State, for all their letters to foreign princes and states; for they stuck to this noble and generous resolution, not to write to any, or to receive answers from them, but in a language most proper to maintain a correspondence among the learned of all nations in this part of the world; scorning to carry on their affairs in the wheedling, lisping jargon of the cringing French, especially having a minister of state able to cope with the ablest any prince or state could employ, for the Latin tongue. And so well he acquitted himself in this station that he gained from abroad both reputation to himself and credit to the state that employed him.

And it was well the business of his office came not very fast upon him, for he was scarce well warm in his secretaryship before other work flowed in upon him, which took him up for some considerable time. In the first place there came out a book said to have been written by the king, and finished a little before his death, entitled Εἰκὼν βασιλική, that is, *The Royal Image;* a book highly cried up for its smooth style, and pathetical composure; wherefore to obviate the impression it was like to make among the many, he was obliged to write an answer, which he entitled Εἰκονοκλάστης or *Image-Breaker.*

And upon the heels of that, out comes in public the great kill-cow of Christendom, with his *Defensio Regis contra Populum Anglicanum;* a man so famous and cried up for his Plinian Exercitations and other pieces of reputed learning, that there could no where have been found a champion that durst lift up the pen against so formidable an adversary, had not our little English David had the courage to undertake this great French Goliath, to whom he gave such a hit in the forehead, that he presently staggered, and soon after fell. For immediately upon the coming out of the answer, entitled, *Defensio Populi Anglicani contra Claudium Anonymum,* &c. he that till then had been chief minister and superintendent in the court of the learned Christina, Queen of Sweden, dwindled in esteem to that degree that he at last vouchsafed to speak to the meanest servant. In short, he was dismissed with so cold and slighting an adieu, that after a faint dying reply, he was glad to have recourse to death, the remedy of evils and ender of controversies.

And now I presume our author had some breathing space, but it was not long. For though Salmasius was departed, he left some stings behind; new enemies started up barkers, though no great biters. Who the first asserter of Salmasius his cause was, is not certainly known but variously conjectured at, some supposing it to be one Janus, a lawyer of Gray's Inn, some Dr. Bramhal, made by King Charles the Second, after his restoration, Archbishop of Armagh in Ireland; but whoever the author was, the book was thought fit to be taken into correction; and our author not thinking it worth his own undertaking, to the disturbing the progress of whatever more chosen work he had then in hands, committed this task to the youngest of his nephews; but with such exact emendations before it went to the press that it might have very well passed for his, but that he was willing the person that took the pains to prepare it for his examination and polishment should have the name and credit of being the author; so that it came forth under this title, *Joannis Philippi Angli Defensio pro Populo Anglicano contra,* &c.

During the writing and publishing of this book, he lodged at one Thomson's next door to the Bull-head tavern at Charing-Cross, opening into the Spring-Garden; which seems to have been only a lodging taken till his designed apartment in Scotland-Yard was prepared for him. For hither he soon removed from the aforesaid place; and here his third child, a son, was born, which through the ill usage, or bad constitution, of an ill chosen nurse, died an infant.

From this apartment, whether he thought it not healthy, or otherwise convenient for his use, or whatever else was the reason, he soon after took a pretty garden-house in Petty-France in Westminster, next door to the Lord Scudamore's, and opening into St. James's Park. Here he remained no less than eight years, namely, from the year 1652, till within a few weeks of King Charles the Second's restoration.

In this house his first wife dying in childbed, he married a second, who after a year's time died in childbed also. This his second marriage was about two or three years after his being wholly deprived of sight, which was just going about the time of his answering Salmasius; whereupon his adversaries gladly take occasion of imputing his blindness as a judgment upon him for his answering the King's book, &c. whereas it is most certainly known that his sight, what with his continual study, his being subject to the headache, and his perpetual tampering with physic to preserve it, had been decaying for above a dozen years before, and the sight of one for a long time clearly lost. Here he wrote, by his amanuensis, his two *Answers to Alexander More,* who upon the last answer quitted the field.

So that being now quiet from state adversaries and public contests, he had leisure again for his own studies and private designs; which were his aforesaid *History of England,* and a new *Thesaurus Linguæ Latinæ,* according to the manner of Stephanus, a work he had been long since collecting from his own reading, and still went on with it at times, even very near to his dying day; but the papers after his death were so discomposed and deficient that it could not be made fit for the press; however, what there was of it was made use of for another dictionary.

But the height of his noble fancy and invention began now to be seriously and mainly employed in a subject worthy of such a Muse, *viz.* a heroic poem, entitled *Paradise Lost;* the noblest in the general esteem of learned and judicious persons of any yet written by any either ancient or modern. This subject was first designed a tragedy, and in the fourth book of the poem there are six verses, which several years before the poem was begun, were shown to me and some others, as designed for the very beginning of the said tragedy. The verses are these: —

> O thou that with surpassing glory crown'd!
> Look'st from thy sole dominion, like the god
> Of this new world; at whose sight all the stars
> Hide their diminish'd heads; to thee I call,
> But with no friendly voice; and add thy name,
> O Sun! to tell thee how I hate thy beams
> That bring to my remembrance, from what state
> I fell, how glorious once above thy sphere;

Till pride and worse ambition threw me down,
Warring in Heaven, against Heaven's glorious King.

There is another very remarkable passage in the composure of this poem, which I have a particular occasion to remember; for whereas I had the perusal of it from the very beginning, for some years, as I went from time to time to visit him, in a parcel of ten, twenty, or thirty verses at a time, which being written by whatever hand came next, might possibly want correction as to the orthography and pointing; having as the summer came on, not having been showed any for a considerable while, and, desiring the reason thereof, was answered: That his vein never happily flowed but from the autumnal equinoctial to the vernal,[2] and that whatever he attempted [otherwise] was never to his satisfaction, though he courted his fancy never so much, so that in all the years he was about this poem, he may be said to have spent but half his time therein.

It was but a little before the King's restoration that he wrote and published his book *In Defence of a Commonwealth,* so undaunted he was in declaring his true sentiments to the world; and not long before, his *Power of the Civil Magistrate in Ecclesiastical Affairs,* and his *Treatise against Hirelings,* just upon the King's coming over; having a little before been sequestered from his office of Latin secretary and the salary thereunto belonging.

He was forced to leave his house also in Petty-France, where all the time of his abode there, which was eight years as above-mentioned, he was frequently visited by persons of quality, particularly my Lady Ranalagh, whose son for some time he instructed; all learned foreigners of note, who could not part out of this city, without giving a visit to a person so eminent; and lastly, by particular friends that had a high esteem for him, *viz.* Mr. Andrew Marvel, young Lawrence (the son of him that was president of Oliver's council), to whom there is a sonnet among the rest, in his printed *Poems;* Mr. Marchamont Needham, the writer of *Politicus;* but above all, Mr. Cyriac Skinner whom he honored with two sonnets, one long since public among his *Poems,* the other but newly printed.

His next removal was, by the advice of those that wished him well and had a concern for his preservation, into a place of retirement and abscondance, till such time as the current of affairs for the future should instruct him what farther course to take. It was a friend's house in Bartholomew Close, where he lived till the act of oblivion came forth; which it pleased

---

[2] See T. B. Stroup, "Climatic Influence on Milton," *MLQ* 4 (1943): 185–89, who quotes John Toland, another of Milton's early biographers, saying that Milton "composed best in warm weather."

God, proved as favorable to him as could be hoped or expected, through the intercession of some that stood his friends both in Council and Parliament; particularly in the House of Commons, Mr. Andrew Marvel, a member for Hull, acted vigorously in his behalf and made a considerable party for him; so that, together with John Goodwin of Coleman Street, he was only so far excepted as not to bear any office in the Commonwealth.

Soon after appearing again in public, he took a house in Holborn near Red Lyon Fields; where he stayed not long, before his pardon having passed the seal, he removed to Jewin Street. There he lived when he married his 3rd wife, recommended to him by his old friend Dr. Paget in Coleman Street. But he stayed not long after his new marriage, ere he removed to a house in the Artillery-walk leading to Bunhill Fields. And this was his last stage in this world, but it was of many years continuance, more perhaps than he had had in any other place besides.

Here he finished his noble poem, and published it in the year 1666. The first edition was printed in quarto by one Simons, a printer in Aldersgate Street; the other in a large octavo, by Starky near Temple-Bar, amended, enlarged, and differently disposed as to the number of books by his own hand, that is by his own appointment; the last set forth, many years since his death, in a large folio, with cuts added, by Jacob Tonson.

Here it was also that he finished and published his history of our nation till the Conquest, all complete so far as he went, some passages only excepted; which, being thought too sharp against the clergy, could not pass the hand of the licenser, were in the hands of the late Earl of Anglesey while he lived; where at present is uncertain.

It cannot certainly be concluded when he wrote his excellent tragedy entitled *Samson Agonistes,* but sure enough it is that it came forth after his publication of *Paradise Lost,* together with his other poem called *Paradise Regained,* which doubtless was begun and finished and printed after the other was published, and that in a wonderful short space considering the sublimeness of it; however, it is generally censured to be much inferior to the other, though he could not hear with patience any such thing when related to him. Possibly the subject may not afford such variety of invention, but it is thought by the most judicious to be little or nothing inferior to the other for style and decorum.

The said Earl of Anglesey, whom he presented with a copy of the unlicensed papers of his history, came often here to visit him, as very much coveting his society and converse; as likewise others of the nobility and many persons of eminent quality; nor were the visits of foreigners ever more frequent than in this place, almost to his dying day.

His treatise *Of True Religion, Heresy, Schism and Toleration,* &c. was doubtless the last thing of his writing that was published before his death.

He had, as I remember, prepared for the press an answer to some little scribing quack in London, who had written a scurrilous libel against him; but whether by the dissuasion of friends, as thinking him a fellow not worth his notice, or for what other cause I know not, this answer was never published.

He died in the year 1673[3] towards the latter end of the summer and had a very decent interment according to his quality, in the church of St. Giles, Cripplegate, being attended from his house to the church by several gentlemen then in town, his principal well-wishers and admirers.

He had three daughters who survived him many years (and a son) all by his first wife (of whom sufficient mention hath been made): Anne his eldest as above said, and Mary his second, who were both born at his house in Barbican; and Deborah the youngest, who is yet living, born at his house in Petty-France, between whom and his second daughter, the son, named John, was born as above-mentioned, at his apartment in Scotland Yard. By his second wife, Catharine, the daughter of captain Woodcock of Hackney, he had only one daughter, of which the mother, the first year after her marriage, died in childbed, and the child also within a month after. By his third wife Elizabeth, the daughter of one Mr. Minshal of Cheshire, (and kinswoman to Dr. Paget), who survived him, and is said to be yet living, he never had any child.

And those he had by the first he made serviceable to him in that very particular in which he most wanted their service, and supplied his want of eyesight by their eyes and tongue. For though he had daily about him one or other to read to him; some persons of man's estate, who of their own accord greedily catched at the opportunity of being his readers, that they might as well reap the benefit of what they read to him as oblige him by the benefit of their reading; others of younger years sent by their parents to the same end; yet, excusing only the eldest daughter by reason of her bodily infirmity and difficult utterance of speech (which to say truth I doubt was the principal cause of excusing her), the other two were condemned to the performance of reading and exactly pronouncing of all the languages of whatever book he should at one time or other think fit to peruse; *viz.* the Hebrew (and I think the Syriac), the Greek, the Latin, the Italian, Spanish, and French. All which sorts of books to be confined to read, without understanding one word, must needs be a trial of patience almost beyond endurance; yet it was endured by both for a long time. Yet the irksomeness of this employment could not always be concealed, but broke out more and more into expressions of uneasiness; so that at length they were all (even the eldest also) sent out to learn some curious and ingenious sorts of manufacture

---

[3] Milton died November 8 [?], 1674.

that are proper for women to learn, particularly embroideries in gold or silver. It had been happy indeed if the daughters of such a person had been made in some measure inheritrixes of their father's learning; but since fate otherwise decreed, the greatest honor that can be ascribed to this now living (and so would have been to the others had they lived) is to be daughter to a man of his extraordinary character.

He is said to have died worth 1500£ in money (a considerable estate, all things considered) besides household goods; for he sustained such losses as might well have broke any person less frugal and temperate than himself; no less than 2000£ which he had put for security and improvement into the excise office, but neglecting to recall it in time could never after get it out, with all the power and interest he had in the great ones of those times; besides another great sum by mismanagement and for want of good advice.

Thus I have reduced into form and order whatever I have been able to rally up, either from the recollection of my own memory of things trans-acted while I was with him, or the information of others equally conversant afterwards, or from his own mouth by frequent visits to the last.

I shall conclude with two material passages which though they relate not immediately to our author, or his own particular concerns, yet in regard they happened during his public employ and consequently fell especially most under his cognizance, it will not be amiss here to subjoin them. The first was this:

Before the war broke forth between the States of England and the Dutch, the Hollanders sent over three ambassadors in order to an accom-modation; but they returning *re infecta,* the Dutch sent away a plenipoten-tiary, to offer peace upon much milder terms, or at least to gain more time. But this plenipotentiary could not make such haste but that the Parliament had procured a copy of their instructions in Holland, which were delivered by our author to his kinsman that was then with him, to translate for the Council to view before the said plenipotentiary had taken shipping for England; an answer to all he had in charge lay ready for him, before he made his public entry into London.

In the next place there came a person with a very sumptuous train, pre-tending himself an agent from the prince of Condé, then in arms against Cardinal Mazarin: the Parliament mistrusting him, set their instrument so busily at work, that in four or five days they had procured intelligence from Paris that he was a spy from King Charles; whereupon the very next morn-ing our author's kinsman was sent to him with an order of Council com-manding him to depart the kingdom within three days, or expect the punishment of a spy.

By these two remarkable passages, we may clearly discover the industry and good intelligence of those times.

A CHRONOLOGY OF THE MAIN EVENTS IN MILTON'S LIFE

1608, Dec. 9: Birth in Bread Street, Cheapside, London to John and Sara Milton

1615, Nov.: Brother Christopher born

1620 (?): Attendance at St. Paul's School begun

1625, Feb. 12: Admission to Christ's College, Cambridge. **March 27:** Charles I becomes King

1629, March: Receives B.A. degree. **December:** Writes "On the Morning of Christ's Nativity"

1632, July 3: Admission to the degree of M.A. "On Shakespeare" published in the second Shakespeare folio

1632–1635: Residence at Hammersmith

1633: William Laud becomes Archbishop

1634, Sept. 29: First performance of *A Masque* (*Comus*)

1635–1638: Residence at Horton

1637: *A Masque* (*Comus*) published. **April 3:** Mother dies

1638: "Lycidas" published in volume of elegies for Edward King. **May:** Leaves for France and begins Continental tour

1639, March: War with Scotland. **July:** Returns to England and begins tutoring in London

1640: Impeachment of Laud and Stafford. **Nov. 3:** Long Parliament convened

1641: *Of Reformation in England*, Milton's first anti-episcopal tract, published; also *Of Prelatical Episcopacy, Animadversions upon the Remonstrant's Defense*

1642: *The Reason of Church Government* and *An Apology for Smectymnuus* published   **June** (?): Marriage to Mary Powell.   **Aug.** (?): Return of Mary to her father's home in Buckinghamshire.   **Aug. 22:** "Beginning" of the Civil War

1643, Aug. 1: *The Doctrine and Discipline of Divorce* published

1644, June 5: *Of Education* published.   **Aug. 6:** *The Judgment of Martin Bucer Concerning Divorce* published.   **Nov. 23:** *Areopagitica* published

1645, March 4: *Tetrachordon* and *Colasterion* published.   **Summer** (?): Return of Mary Powell Milton to her husband in London

1646, Jan.: *Poems of Mr. John Milton* published (dated 1645).   **July 29:** Birth of Milton's daughter Anne

1647, March 13: Father dies

1648, Oct. 25: Birth of Milton's daughter Mary

1649, Jan. 30: Charles I executed.   **Feb. 13:** *The Tenure of Kings and Magistrates* published.   **March 15:** Milton appointed Secretary of Foreign Tongues to the Council of State.   **Oct. 6:** *Eikonoklastes* published

1651, Feb. 24: *Defensio pro Populo Anglicano* (*A Defense of the English People*) published.   **March 16:** Birth of Milton's son John

1652, Feb. (?): Milton's blindness becomes almost total.   **May 2:** Birth of Milton's daughter Deborah.   **May 5** (?): Death of Mary Powell Milton.   **June 16** (?): Death of Milton's son John

1653, April 20: Cromwell dissolves Rump Parliament.   **Dec. 16:** Cromwell becomes Lord Protector

1654, May 30: *Defensio Secunda* (*A Second Defense of the English People*) published

1655, Aug.: *Pro Se Defensio* published

1656, Nov. 12: Marriage to Katherine Woodcock

1657, Oct. 19: Birth of Milton's daughter Katherine

1658, Feb. 3: Death of Katherine Woodcock Milton.   **March 17:** Daughter Katherine dies.   **Sept. 3:** Oliver Cromwell dies

1659, Feb. (?): *A Treatise of Civil Power in Ecclesiastical Causes* published

1660, Feb.: *The Ready and Easy Way to Establish a Free Commonwealth* first published (second edition in April).   **May:** Charles II enters London;

Milton goes into hiding. **Aug.:** Milton's books burned. **Oct.:** Milton imprisoned (until December)

1663, Feb. 24: Marriage to Elizabeth Minshull

1666, Sept. 2–6: Great Fire of London

1667, Aug. (?): *Paradise Lost. A Poem Written in Ten Books* published

1670: *The History of Britain* published

1671: *Paradise Regained* and *Samson Agonistes* published

1673: *Of True Religion, Heresy, Schism, and Toleration* published; Revised edition of *Poems* (1645) published

1674: *Paradise Lost. A Poem in Twelve Books* published. **Nov. 8(?):** Death. **Nov. 12:** Milton buried in St. Giles, Cripplegate